New Mexico Art Through Time

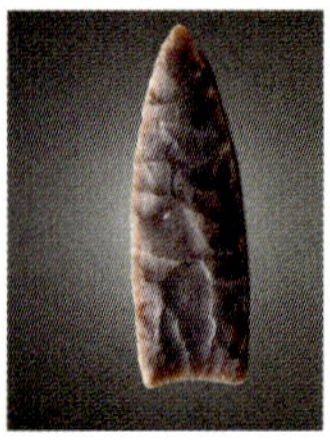
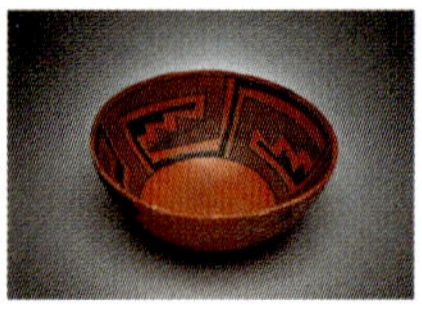
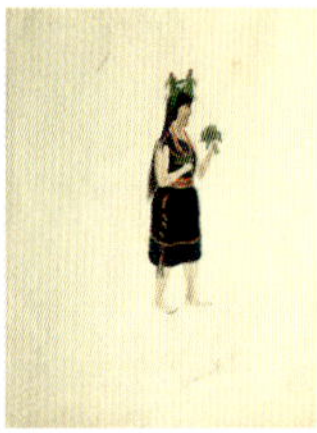
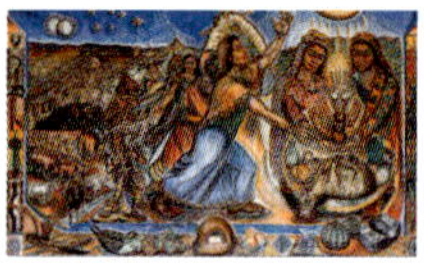
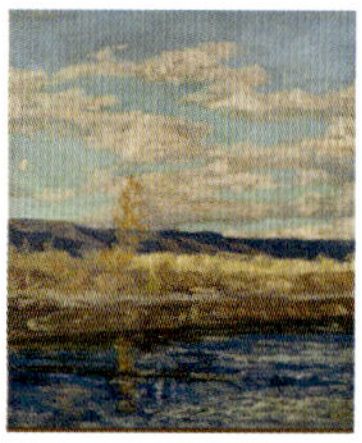
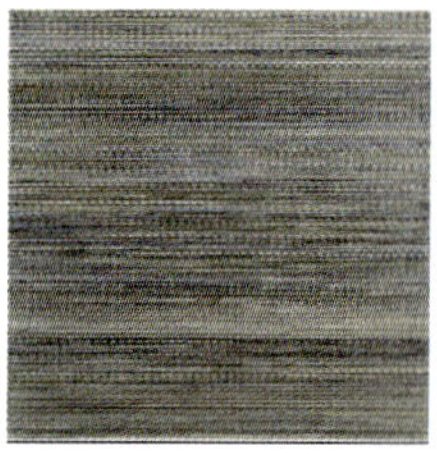

New Mexico Art Through Time

PREHISTORY TO THE PRESENT

By Joseph Traugott

MUSEUM OF NEW MEXICO PRESS
SANTA FE

IN ASSOCIATION WITH
NEW MEXICO MUSEUM OF ART

Generous funding provided by New Mexico Humanities Council, Newman's Own Foundation, and Museum of New Mexico Foundation.

Project editor: Mary Wachs
Production and design: David Skolkin
Composition: Set in Stempel Garamond
Manufactured in China
10 9 8 7 6 5 4 3 2 1

ISBN 978-089013-545-7

Library of Congress Cataloging-in-Publication Data
available from the publisher upon request.

Museum of New Mexico Press
Post Office Box 2087
Santa Fe, New Mexico 87504
www.mnmpress.org

Contents

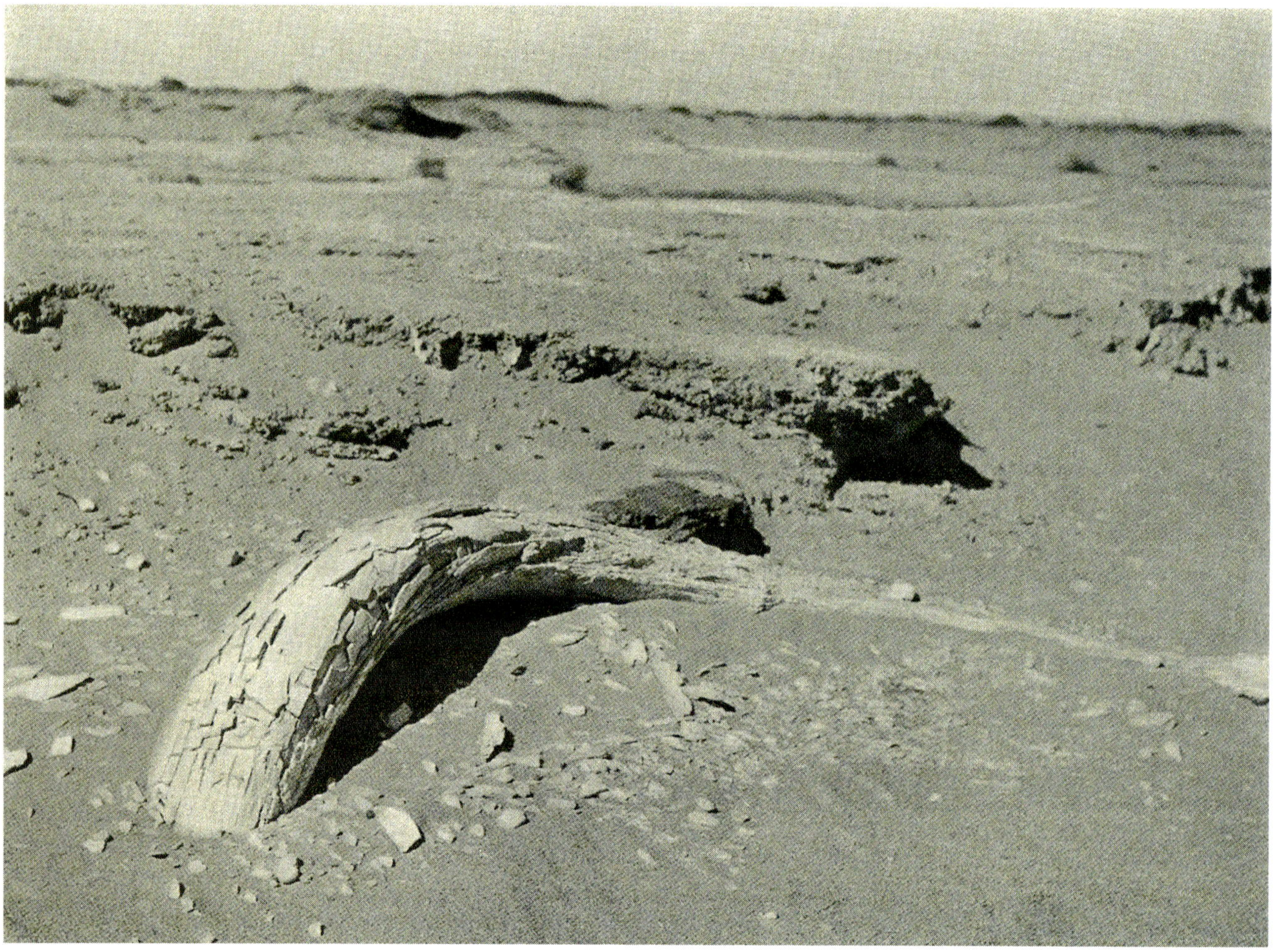

PREFACE

It's about Art and Time

The High Plains in eastern New Mexico became an art center 14,000 years ago and remain so today. Artesian springs near Portales, New Mexico, located at the Llano Estacado on the edge of the Great Plains, fed ponds and streams at the end of the last Ice Age. These springs attracted a variety of giant mammoths, sloths, and bison, as well as the Paleo-Indian hunters and gatherers who stalked them. Now called the Blackwater Draw, the landscape in the area had been dotted with mammoth tusks and bones from Ice Age animals eroding out of the earth (fig. 1).

Paleo-Indians expertly knapped flint into Clovis points that they used to hunt mammoths (fig. 2). Knappers made these objects from high-quality cherts and agates often acquired hundreds of miles from the Draw. The unique chipping patterns and unusual thinning flakes found on these tools transcended any functional requirements. These aestheticized actions signify aspects of their makers' worldview and values important to them that may be difficult to understand today.

Later Paleo-Indian hunters stalked bison larger and more robust than their modern counterparts, often driving them off the edges of arroyos to send them crashing to the ground. Hunters then used their specialized stone tools to strip the animals of massive amounts of meat.

At the end of the Pleistocene era, eight thousand years ago, the climate in New Mexico and the Blackwater Draw became drier, and Native peoples adapted to the warmer environment. Nomadic populations decreased over a long period, but the springs at Blackwater Draw continued to attract archaic gatherers and hunters. Ancestral Pueblo hunting parties stalked antelope and buffalo in the area, and in 1541 the Coronado Expedition passed through. By the nineteenth century, Hispanic shepherds raised flocks of sheep on the Llano Estacado, and Texas ranchers also ran herds of longhorn there.

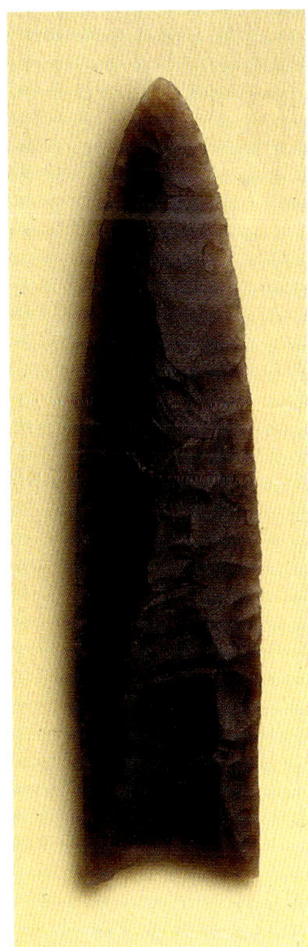

OPPOSITE

1
EDGAR B. HOWARD (DATES UNKNOWN)
TYPICAL BASIN SITE NEAR CLOVIS, NEW MEXICO, 1935
GELATIN SILVER PRINT, 8 x 10 IN. (20.3 x 25.4 CM)

2
MAKER UNKNOWN
CLOVIS POINT, CIRCA 13,650–12,800 BP
CHALCEDONY, 4¼ IN. (10.8 CM)

Cowboy Jack Thorpe passed through Portales on horseback while riding from Chimney Lake, New Mexico, to Higgins, Texas. On the way he composed "Little Joe, the Wrangler," a classic ballad about a young cowpoke who tried to stop a stampeding herd at night and fell to his death, just like bison that Paleo-Indian hunters had driven into the Draw:

> Next morning just at sunup we found where Rocket fell
> Down in a washout twenty feet below
> Beneath his horse mashed to a pulp his spurs had rung the knell
> For our little Texas stray—poor wrangler Joe.

In the early twentieth century, the Portales area grew as an important connection for shipping cattle to Midwestern markets, and as a center for the production and processing of Valencia peanuts (fig. 3). During the Great Depression, a community college opened in Portales to serve the needs of the thriving community. The college eventually evolved into Eastern New Mexico University, which acquired the commissioned pair of canvases *Art* and *Science*, by Raymond Jonson, *Abstract* by Stuart Walker, and *Acoma* by Gene Kloss, all created under the auspices of federal art projects.

Photographers hired by the Farm Security Administration traversed New Mexico recording images of Americans at work, particularly of women with jobs once held by men who had joined the military. In 1943, as part of this project, Jack Delano photographed the declining American railroad system between Chicago and Los Angeles. In Clovis, New Mexico, he photographed Beatrice Davis proudly standing in front of boxcars carrying potash on the Atchison, Topeka and Santa Fe Railway (fig. 4).

3
BLAIR CLARK (B. 1954)
PEANUT PROCESSING PLANT, 2011
DIGITAL PHOTOGRAPH, 8 x 10 IN.
(20.3 x 25.4 CM)

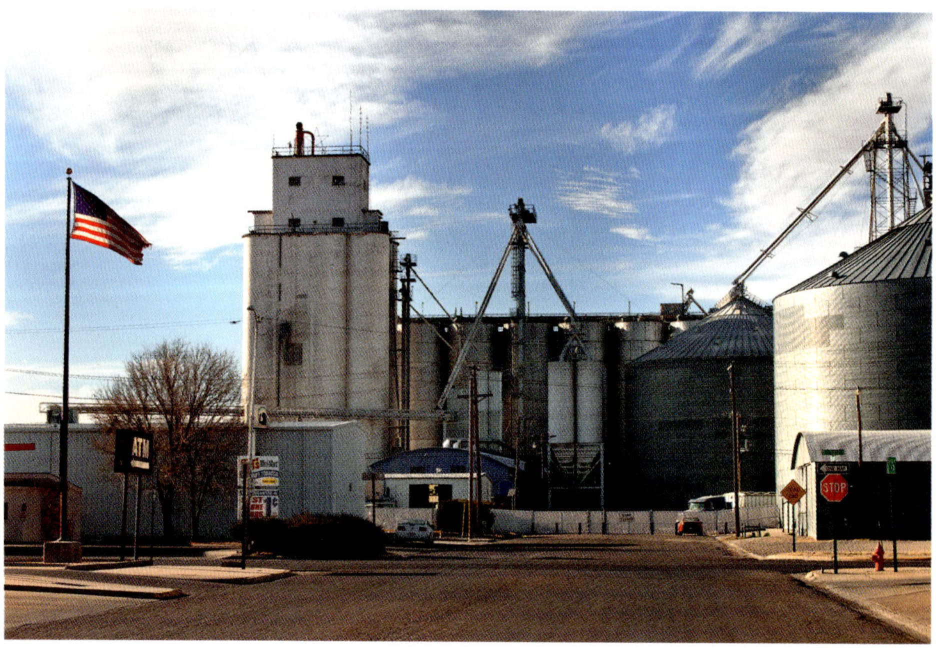

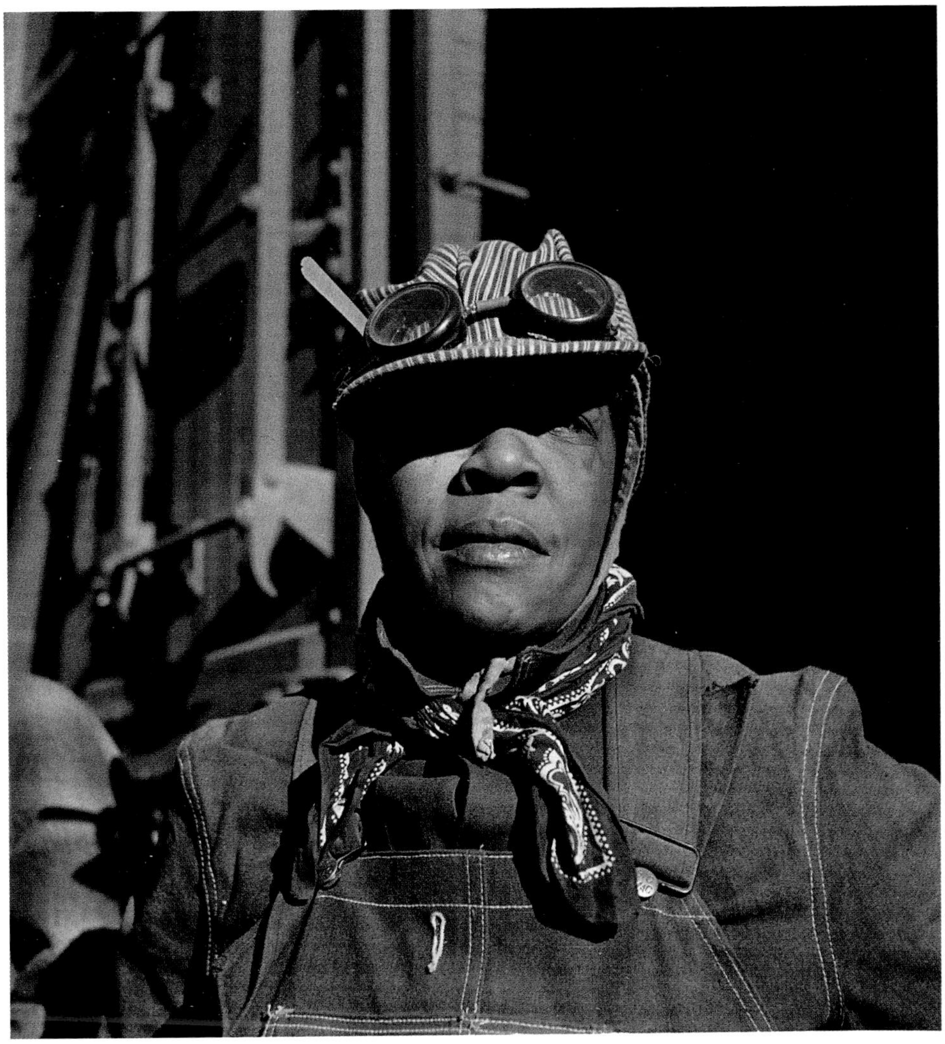

4
JACK DELANO (1914–1997)
BEATRICE DAVIS, CLOVIS, N.M., 1943
(PRINTED 1990)
GELATIN SILVER PRINT, 11 X 10⅜ IN.
(27.9 X 26.4 CM)

Pop culture ruled the Plains after World War II. Buddy Holly, the Crickets, the Fireballs, and Roy Orbison recorded rockabilly and rock 'n' roll tunes at the Norman Petty Studios in Clovis.

By the end of the twentieth century, it was common to see low flying jets from nearby Cannon Air Force Base. Patrick Nagatani photographed a youngster at Cannon with a photograph of an overweight man just as a formation of jets flew overhead (fig. 5). The photo, part of Nagatani's *Nuclear Enchantment* series, is titled *"Fat Man and Little Boy," F-111Ds, 27th Tactical Fighter Wing* and alludes to the two nuclear weapons dropped on Japan at the end of World War II, a powerful reminder of how blasé modern society has become about nuclear weapons.

Throughout eastern New Mexico, contemporary artists working on the edge of the Great Plains are well known for their creations, for example Terry Bumpass and his *Ridge Chalice* (fig 6). Portales continues to be a hub of art on the Great Plains. Eastern New Mexico University's Department of Art offers a comprehensive program of art

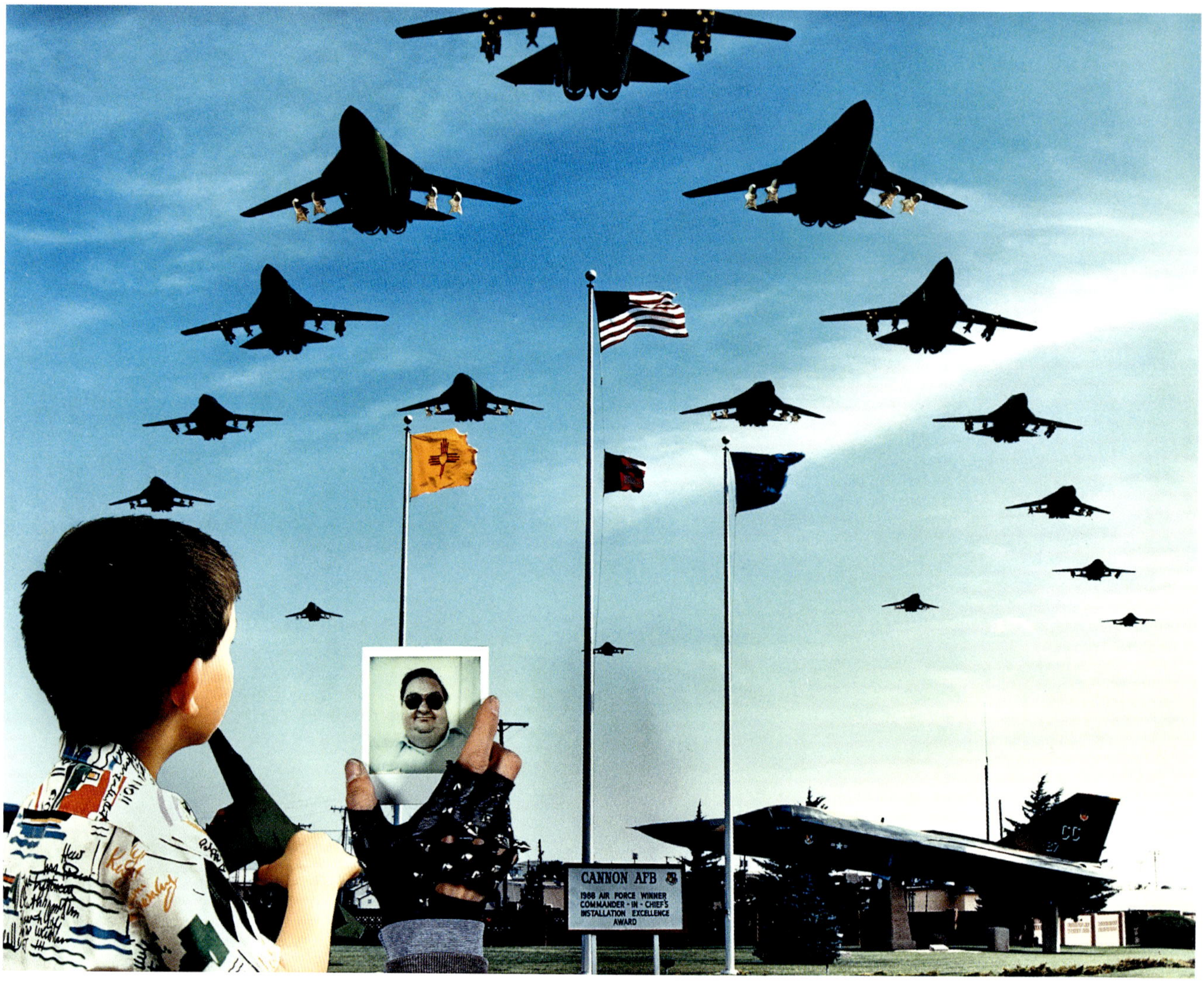

5
PATRICK NAGATANI (B. 1945)
"FAT MAN AND LITTLE BOY," F-111DS, 27TH TACTICAL FIGHTER WING, CANNON AIR FORCE BASE, NEAR CLOVIS, NEW MEXICO, 1990
DYE BLEACH PRINT, 20 x 24 IN. (50.8 x 61 CM)

studio and art history courses coordinated with exhibitions in the school's Runnels Gallery, where faculty, student, and regional art attracts viewers from throughout the community. Simultaneously, the works of art made by Paleo-Indian hunters can be seen at the Miles Anthropological Museum on campus, the regional Blackwater Draw Museum, and the Blackwater Draw Site that is on the National Register of Historic Places.

Time now seems compressed at Blackwater Draw. Each fall, the Draw hosts a spear-throwing competition whose participants use atlatls—the tools used by Paleo-Indians to give their spears more power and speed (fig. 7). Throwing a spear with an atlatl is not easy, and contemporary observers may comment that they would probably starve if spears, atlatls, and stone knives were their only tools.

Despite their long history, Portales and the area around the Draw offer a condensed version of the 14,000 years of New Mexico art.

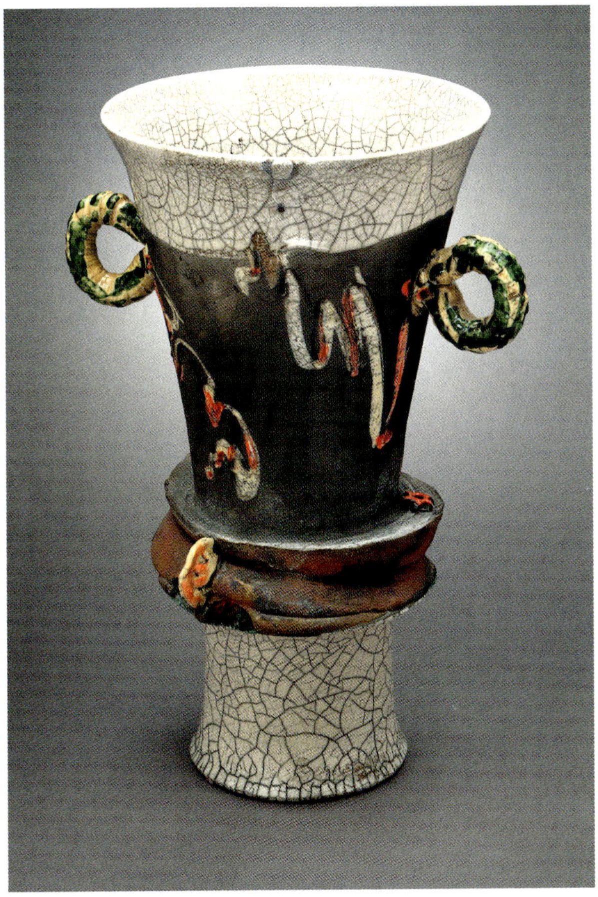

6
TERRY BUMPASS (B. 1948)
RIDGE CHALICE, 2010
RAKU, 14 X 10 IN. (35.6 X 25.4 CM)

7
JAMES OLSON (B. 1948)
MODERN HUNTER WITH ATLATL, 2010
DIGITAL PHOTOGRAPH, 8 X 10 IN.
(20.3 X 25.4 CM)

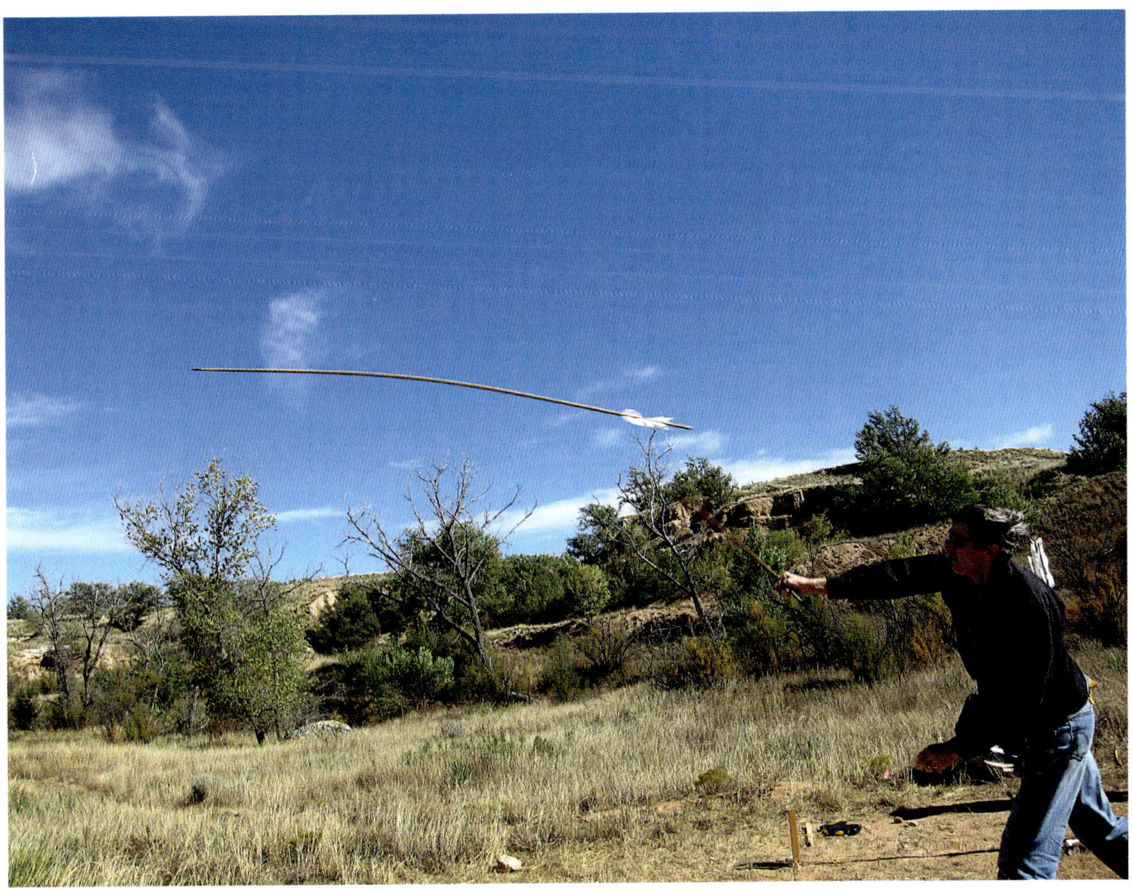

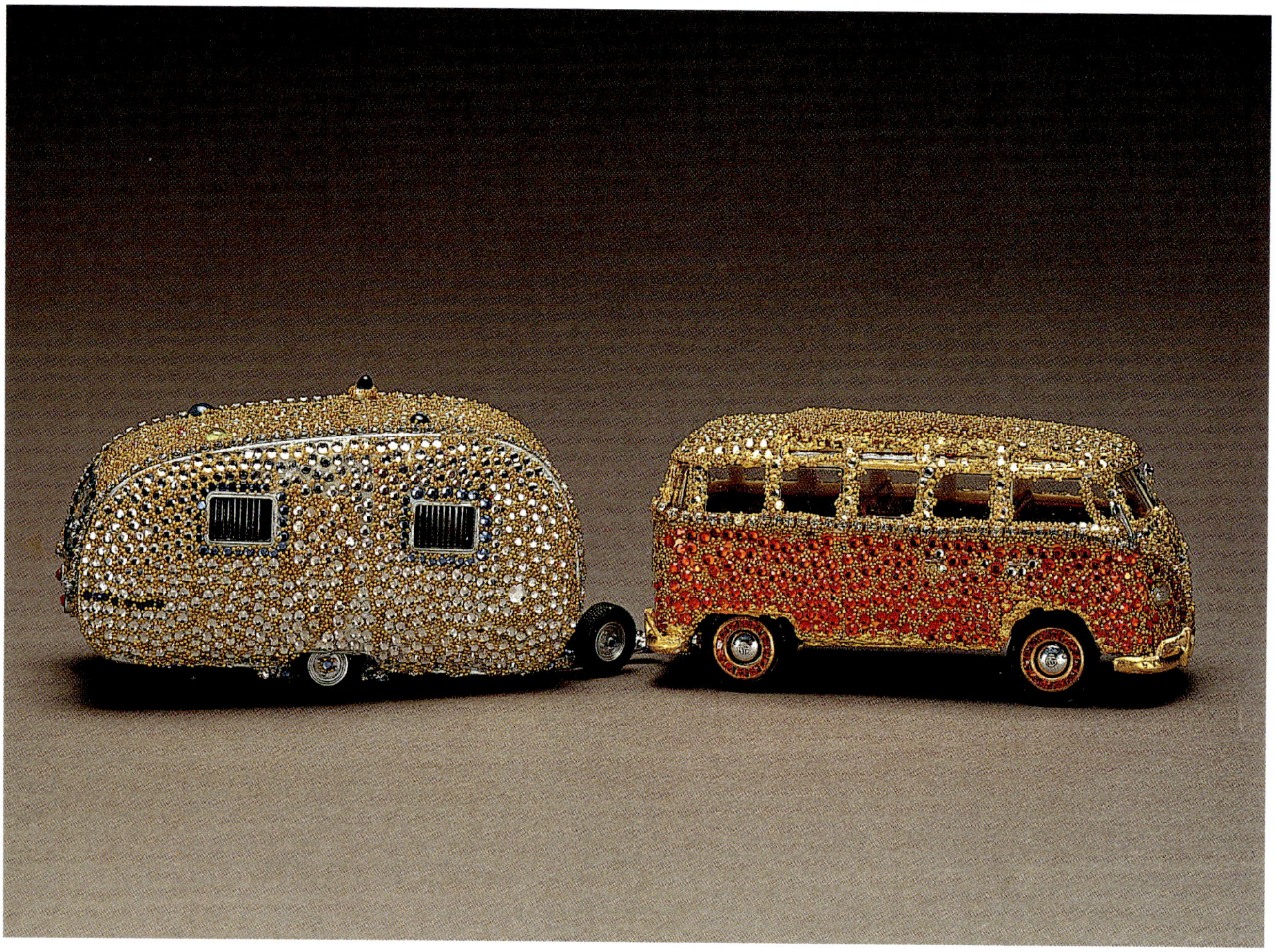

It's about Art and Culture

New Mexicans—people living in the region we today call "New Mexico"—have always made aestheticized objects that reflect the makers' worldviews. In short, we have always made art. From beautifully made Paleo-Indian tools to contemporary art, New Mexico art has evolved to reflect changing economic, ethnic, ideological, religious, and cultural perspectives. The region has attracted multiple ethnic groups who have exchanged aesthetic ideas and fused them into new expressions. And New Mexico art has always balanced individual responses with powerful cultural contexts. It's about time we investigate New Mexico art in a new manner that focuses on objects that best reflect these ever-changing aesthetic and cultural perspectives.

By considering objects across a vast time horizon and presenting individual ethnic perspectives within a single, extended chronology, *New Mexico Art Through Time* celebrates the diverse art forms, the aesthetic complexity, and cultural breadth that developed in New Mexico and the greater Southwest.

This approach is in concert with Jacques Maquet's definition of art as "a socially constructed reality" (Maquet 1979, 5) in which multiple definitions of art coexist and represent different artistic paradigms. As individuals consider objects across cultural divides, the points of view of the makers and the observers, though equally valid, can present conflicting conclusions. Maquet addresses this paradox in his *Introduction to Aesthetic Anthropology* by distinguishing between works "destined" to be art and those that don't begin as art but undergo a "metamorphosis" to become works of art in new cultural contexts (Maquet 1979, 9). This perspective validates the makers' original intent as well as the concepts brought to the works over time by viewers who may have radically different cultural values. This concept is particularly useful for the study of New Mexico art, whose makers range from long-vanished bands of hunter-gatherers to postindustrial artists. While this discussion takes place at the beginning of the twenty-first century, it is possible for modern viewers to use contemporary knowledge to understand prehistoric objects in terms of both their function and aesthetic qualities, and to comprehend that ancient peoples viewed these objects from multiple perspectives as well.

Viewers can alter the original meaning of an artwork by superimposing their own ethnocentric aesthetic perspectives on it. Although contemporary American attitudes don't always jibe with the art of the past, one goal of this study is to encourage people to think about art in broader conceptual terms that transcend the idea that modern aesthetic traditions are the most valid and sophisticated.

8
CAROL SARKISIAN (B. 1936)
DELUXE SAMBA PULLING BAMBI, 2005
FOUND OBJECTS, GLASS BEADS, GOLD LEAF, SILVER LEAF, AND RHINESTONES, 2 X 8½ X 2 IN. (5.1 X 21.6 X 5.1 CM)

What is so profound about art in New Mexico is its ability to empower concurrent but contradictory points of view, ones that can be transformed over time. The makers' insider and the viewers' outsider perspectives can change as objects pass from one cultural context to another and become part of the larger, evolving meaning of art in New Mexico. Members of indigenous Native cultures often note that their languages did not have a term for art until contact with European Americans. However, today it is easy to recognize that objects made by Native cultures were created with both functionality and beauty in mind, enabling modern viewers to now see them as works of art.

The dynamic between works destined to be art and those that become art through metamorphosis is not limited to ethnic arts. This concept is also an essential aspect of contemporary art, where the artists' intentions may be well known and documented. Makers lose control of the personal meaning of works of art as soon as they leave the studio and assume a new context in a gallery, private residence, museum, or other public setting. In these new contexts, viewers are free to transform the works according to their own values and interpretations.

IT'S ABOUT TERM LIMITS

Art terminology can empower mainstream views but also denigrate alternative aesthetic paradigms. Conventional mainstream views usually make hierarchical distinctions between art and craft, decorative arts and fine art, high art and folk art, popular arts and material culture. These terms reflect the conventional wisdom that there is a dichotomy between functional objects—including craft objects that have decorative elements but lack conceptual depth—and nonfunctional artworks whose only "use" is to be seen, contemplated, and appreciated. Conventional views ascribe less cultural importance to functional objects and assign nonfunctional works with a special, elevated meaning.

Hierarchies also exist within conventional views of fine art, for example, that paintings and sculptures are more important than drawings, photographs, and prints. Carol Sarkisian's *Deluxe Samba Pulling Bambi* exemplifies this confusion that can result from such hierarchies and valuations (fig. 8). Is the work sculpture? jewelry? craft? pop culture? or kitsch? Ultimately, such distinctions really don't matter because most people would like to own Sarkisian's artwork and would treat it reverentially in any context.

Changing ethnic identities, fueled by political change at the end of the twentieth century, add to the confusion surrounding terminology. Many Native groups in New Mexico are still known by the descriptive names first used by Spanish colonists. To enforce their power over Native populations, Catholic priests often designated Pueblo Indian villages with the names of saints—such as Santo Domingo Pueblo, Santa Clara Pueblo, San Ildefonso Pueblo, and San Juan Pueblo. Recently, however, many Pueblo groups have rejected this remnant of colonial domination and resumed using their tribal names. Consequently, San Juan Pueblo is now Ohkay Owingeh, and Santo Domingo Pueblo is now referred to as Kewa. This text reflects these and other tribal name variations, such as Diné for Navajo and Ancestral Pueblo for Anasazi (a derivation of the Diné word for "enemy"). Past word usage makes these changes seem awkward, but this is an important change and soon will seem traditional.

Popular terms used to designate Hispanic identity within Hispanic communities will also be used in this text in appropriate contexts, including Spanish, Mexican, Spanish American, and Latina/Latino. As author Michael L.Trujillo points out in *Land of Disenchantment: Latina/o Identities and Transformations in Northern New Mexico:* "Often a person will state a different term of self-identification depending on the context and will prefer the term Spanish in ethnically/racially mixed group settings but call themselves Mexican in in-group settings"(Trujillo 2009, 42).

Another confusing term is "Anglo," short for Anglo Saxon and then Anglo American, to refer to people with European and American backgrounds living in the Southwest, as immigrants coming to the region were not exclusively from England. Nonetheless, these and other evolving distinctions in identity terminology help clarify the nature of art and culture in New Mexico.

IT'S ABOUT PRIME OBJECTS AND PARADIGM SHIFTS

It is difficult to grasp that humans have been living in the American Southwest for such a vast expanse of time and that art was made in New Mexico so long ago. The timeline of New Mexico art and culture (pp. 16–17) helps clarify the relationship between the art and lifeways of peoples living in New Mexico. What the timeline makes most clear is the slow rate of change during most of this history, in contrast to the fast changes that began with the arrival of Spanish colonists. In fact, the entire period of European influence represents less than 5 percent of the time that people have lived in New Mexico but the time when most of the artistic change occurred.

Further, the timeline shows how short periods of artistic invention are followed by long periods of artistic stasis. George Kubler, in *The Shape of Time,* focuses on the concept of "prime objects" of change as well as "replications." Prime objects of change incorporate new underlying assumptions. When prime objects are so well known that they become conventional, or traditional, they become replications and lose their sense of innovation. Kubler's concept is related to Thomas S. Kuhn's concept of paradigms—the underlying assumptions and conclusions that underpin human constructs, discussed in his book *The Structure of Scientific Revolutions.*

Kubler's prime objects of change are also examples of Kuhn's changing paradigms. As cultural paradigms gain acceptance, their principles become the conventional wisdom that remains unchallenged until superceded by a new paradigm. The idea of changing paradigms can thus be related to the difference between the paradigm that an artist intends in creating a work and that which a viewer superimposes on the piece. These different paradigms show how a viewer's interpretation of a work of art can be fundamentally different from the artist's intent.

By necessity, *New Mexico Art Through Time* focuses on the prime objects of cultural change and not replications that have become conventionalized. For example, in the early twentieth century realist artists such as Henry C. Balink (fig. 9) came to New Mexico and made successful careers painting portraits of individuals from then little-known cultures. While some artists today still paint these types of portraits and do so with great skill, the genre is now so well known that it has lost much of its affective power. The meaning of

NATIVE AMERICAN

PALEOINDIAN

14,000 BP 13,000 BP 12,000 BP 11,000 BP 10,000 BP 9000 BP 8000 BP 700

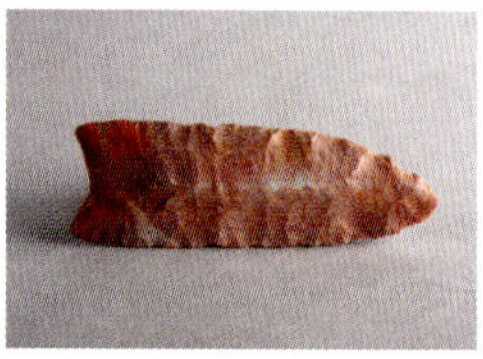

1.

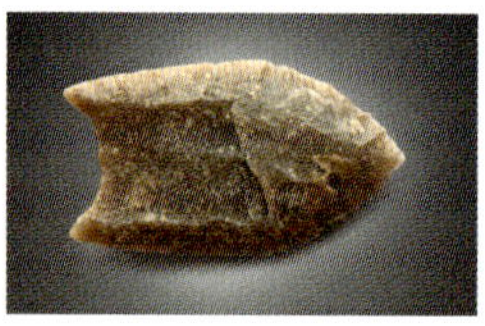

2.

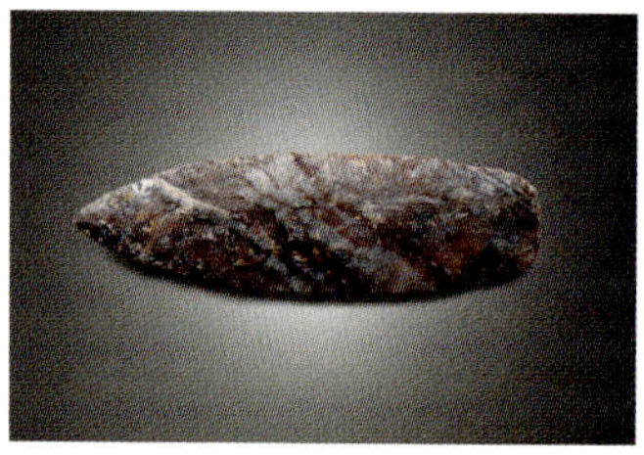

3.

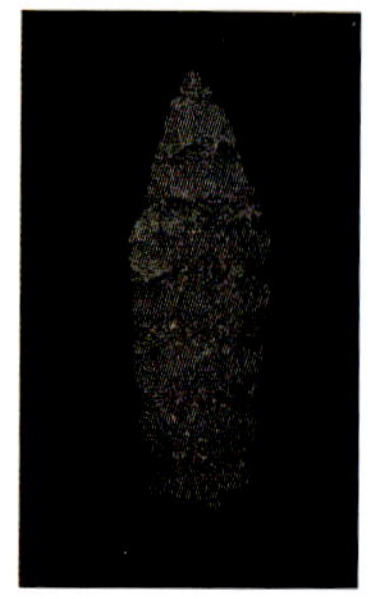

4.

TIMELINE OF NEW MEXICO ART AND CULTURE

1. **CLOVIS POINT**, CIRCA 13,650–12,800 BP
2. **FOLSOM POINT**, CIRCA 12,900–11,950 BP
3. **AGATE BASIN POINT**, CIRCA 12,000–11,400 BP
4. **EARLY ARCHAIC, JAY PHASE SPEAR POINT OR PROJECTILE**, CIRCA 6800–7800 BP
5. **SAN JOSÉ-LIKE PROJECTILE POINT**, CIRCA 6300–4500 BP
6. **ANCESTRAL PUEBLO BI-LOBED BURDEN BASKET**, CIRCA 1200 CE
7. **PUEBLO BONITO CYLINDER JAR**, CIRCA 1100 CE
8. **TULAROSA FILLET RIM BOWL**, CIRCA 1100–1300 CE
9. A. J. SANTERO (ACTIVE 1820–1840), **NUESTRA SEÑORA DE GUADALUPE / OUR LADY OF GUADALUPE**, CIRCA 1825
10. **POWHOGE POLYCHROME JAR**, CIRCA 1830
11. GERALD CASSIDY, **CUI BONO?**, CIRCA 1911
12. GEORGIA O'KEEFFE, **PEDERNAL WITH RED HILLS**, 1936
13. BERLYN B. BRIXNER, **FIRST ATOMIC EXPLOSION AT A DISTANCE OF ABOUT FIVE MILES, TRINITY SITE, NEW MEXICO**, JULY 16, 1945
14. PATROCINIO BARELA, **THE GARDEN OF EDEN**, CIRCA 1948
15. T. C. CANNON, **WASHINGTON LANDSCAPE WITH PEACE MEDAL INDIAN**, 1976
16. DIEGO ROMERO, **SIEGE OF SANTA FE**, 2009

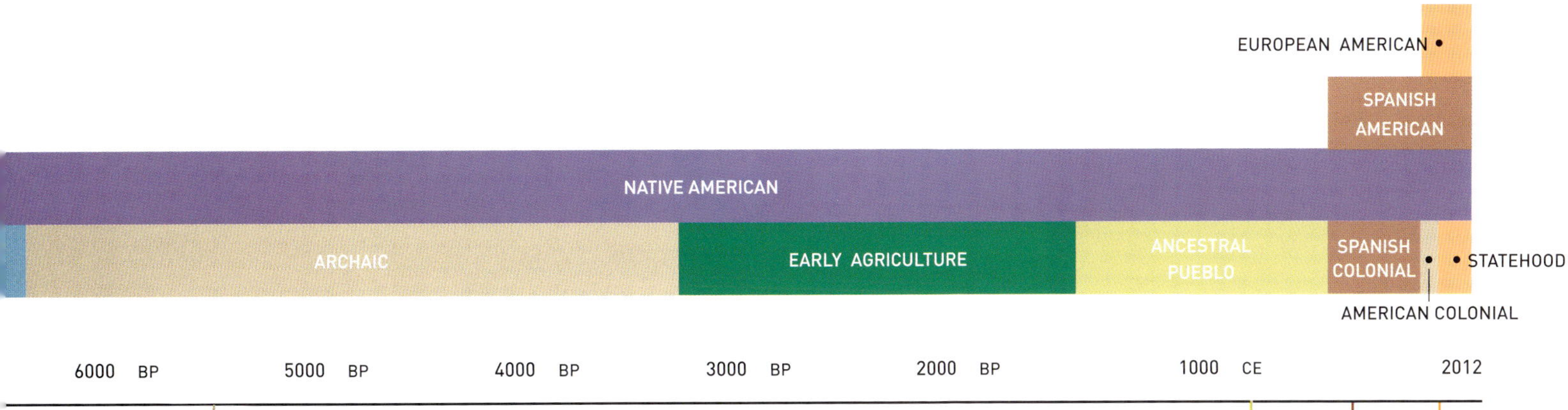

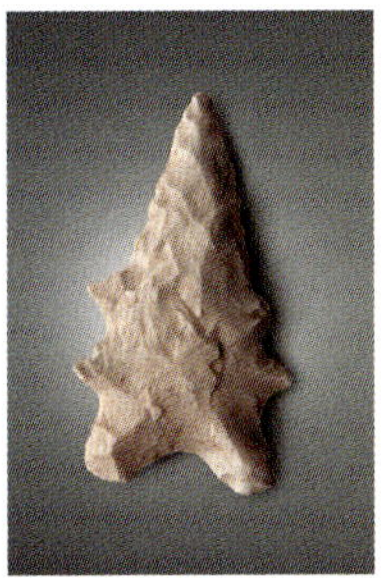

5.

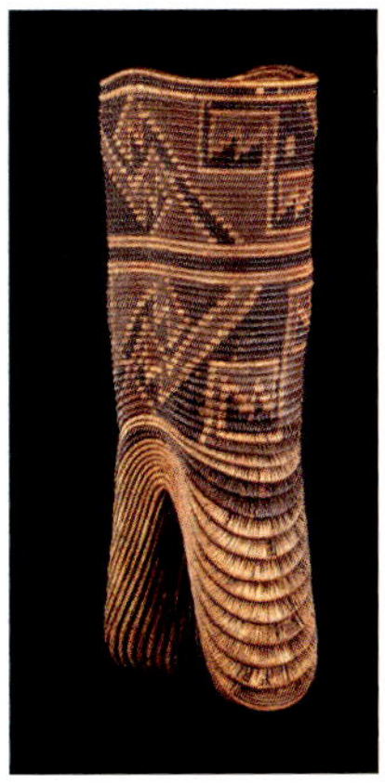

6.

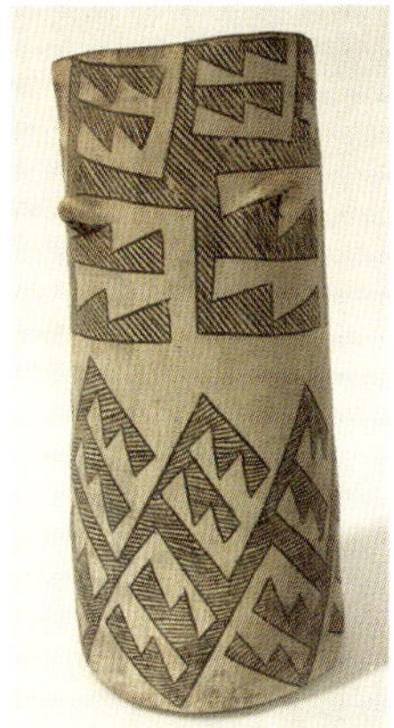

7.

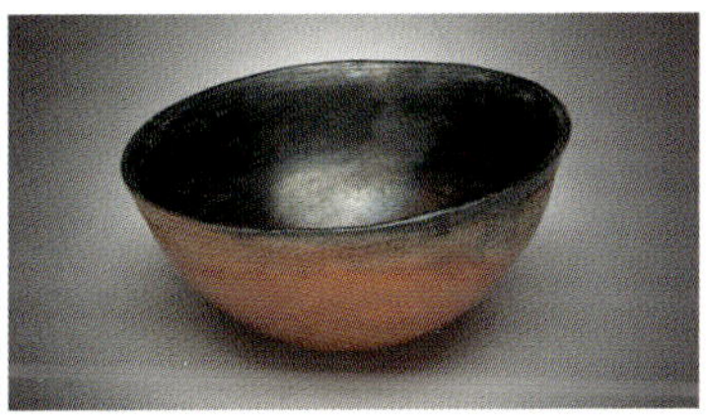

8.

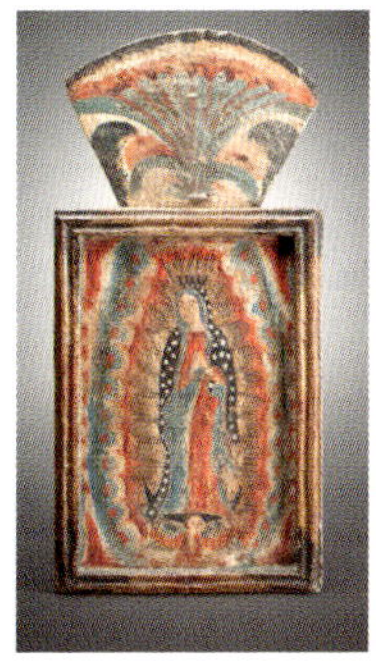

9.

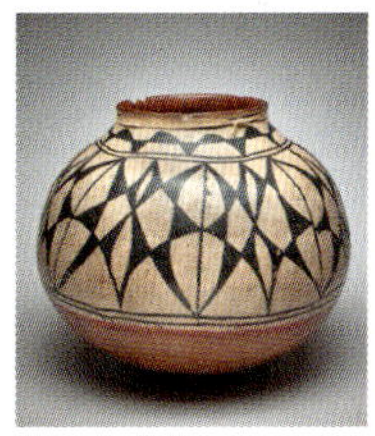

10.

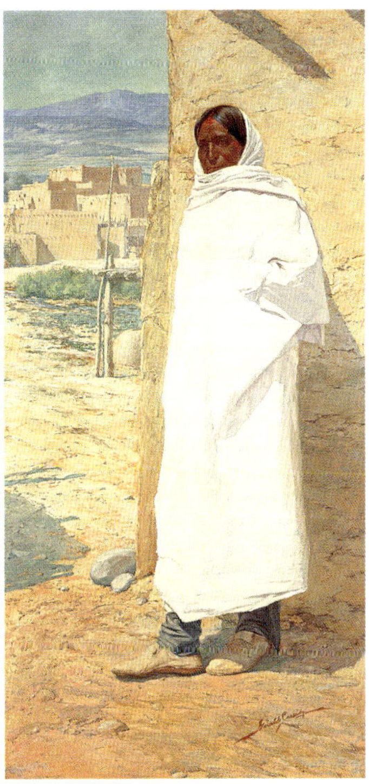

11.

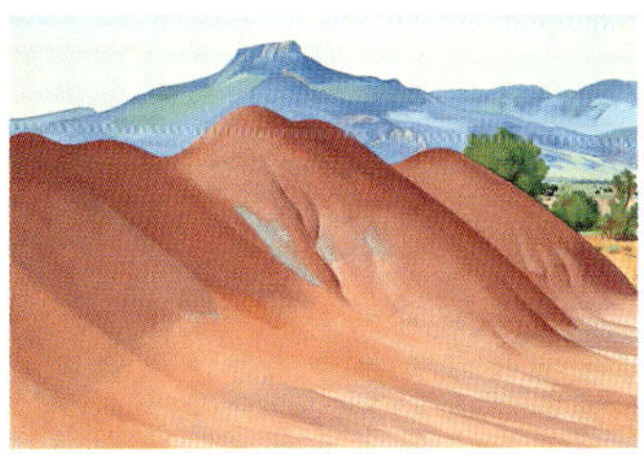

12.

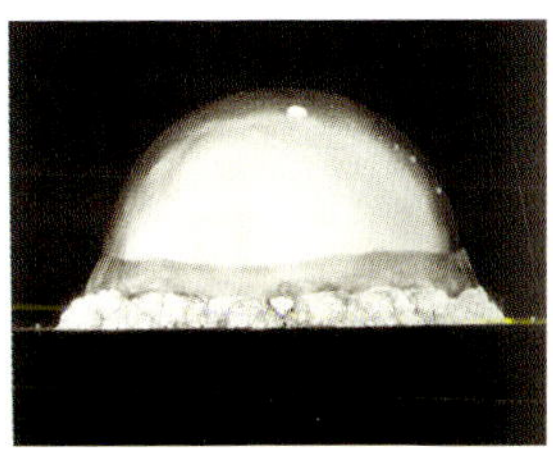

13.

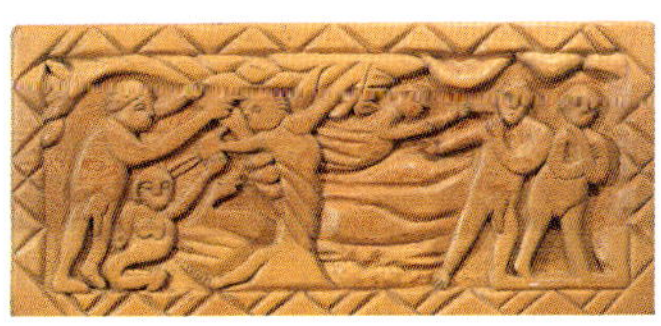

14.

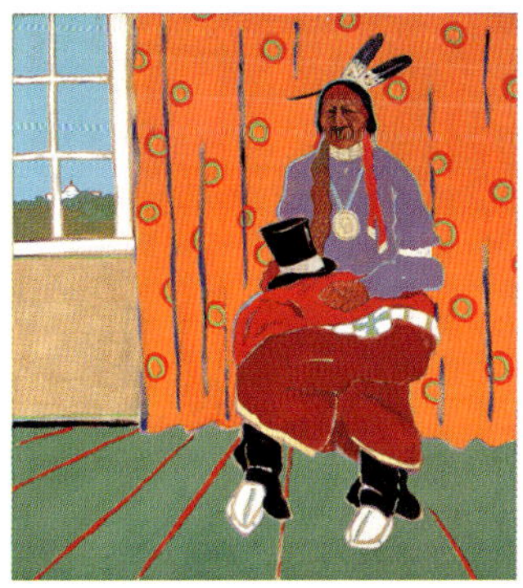

15.

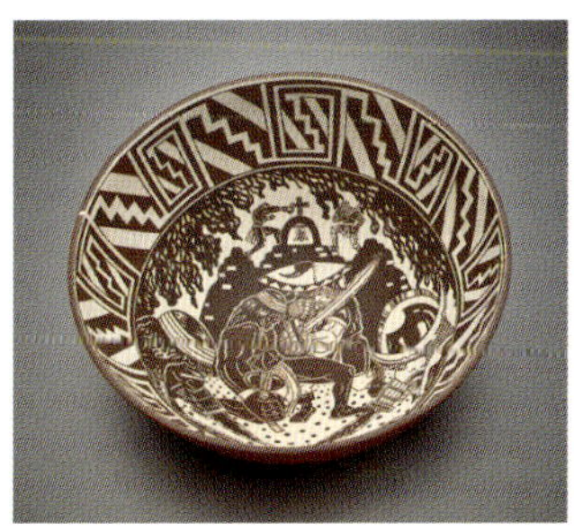

16.

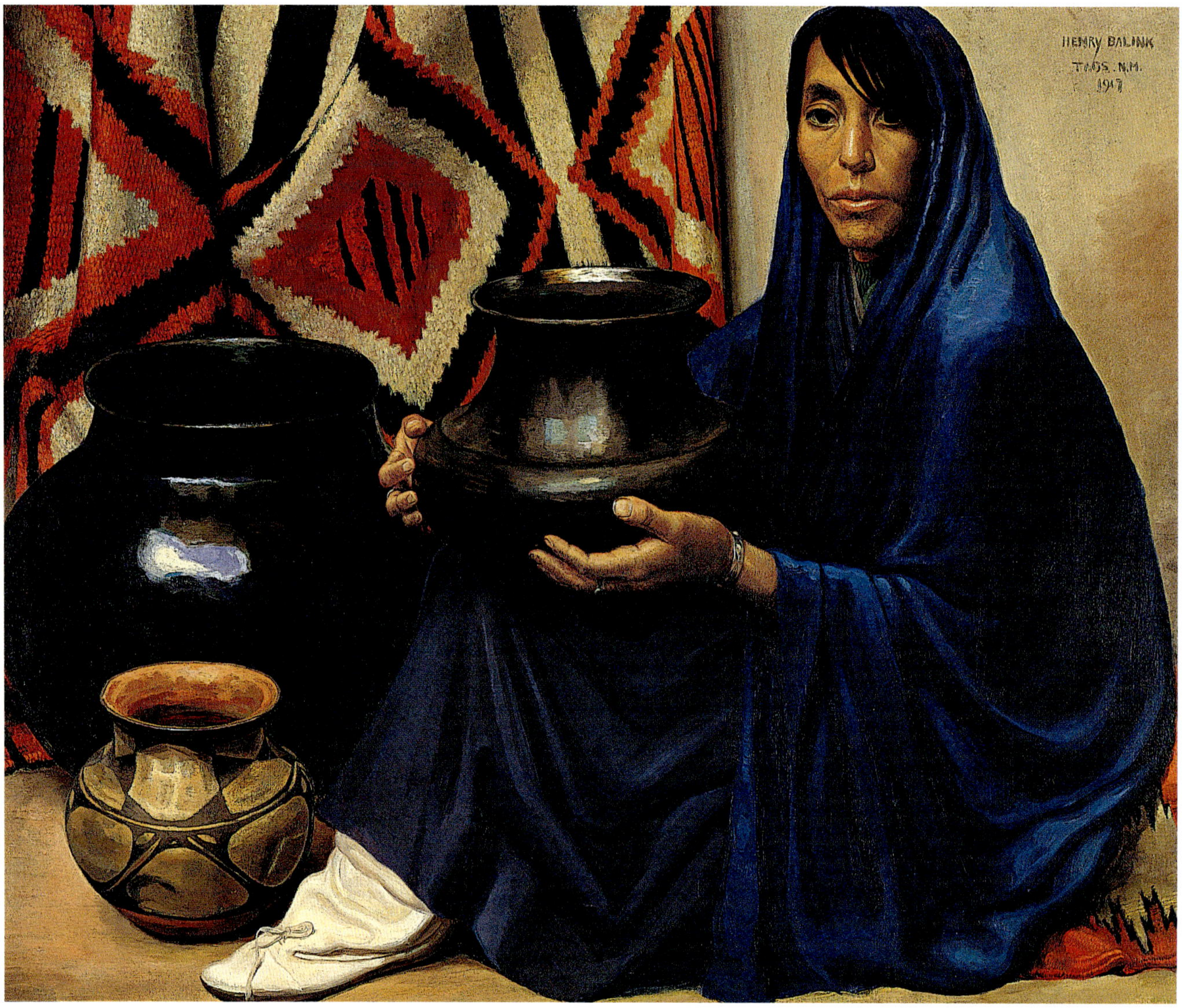

9
HENRY C. BALINK (1882–1963)
PUEBLO POTTERY, 1917
OIL ON CANVAS, 27 x 33 IN.
(68.6 x 83.8 CM)

these replications is therefore quite different from the prime objects that Balink and others painted a century ago.

IT'S ABOUT THREE CULTURES, ISN'T IT?

Depictions of the Southwest as a region of tricultural harmony were an important component in the drive for statehood. Museum of New Mexico founder Edgar Lee Hewett incorporated this idea into the programs he developed in Santa Fe during the 1910s and 1920s. Hewett and other early twentieth-century popularizers of New Mexico were masters at simplifying the cultural landscape of the region by using broad ethnic categories, however inadequate this approach was to accounting for the cultural diversity of New Mexico and the greater Southwest.

Today it is no longer appropriate to simplify New Mexico by viewing it as a tricultural region composed of Native Americans, Hispanos, and European Americans.

Each of these broad categories can be subdivided into multiple ethnicities, and further divided by class, caste, gender, status, and geography. Nonetheless, the simplistic view of three cultures is so ingrained that sweeping generalizations about the region continue to be made, undermining understanding of the complexity of New Mexico art and culture. Yet it seems all but impossible to transcend the lumping of artistic and cultural traditions into broad categories without resorting to long-winded qualifiers that confuse the issues. Consequently, this study emphasizes the prime objects of aesthetic change—those works of art that have been catalysts for transformations in the cultures and lifeways in New Mexico over the last 14,000 years.

Fascination by non-Native peoples and tourists with southwestern rituals has created a thriving market for objects and images related to religious events. Over time, this has led to sensationalist stories and depictions of private rituals that have offended local communities. Charles F. Lummis's 1892 tales in *Some Strange Corners of Our Country* (fig. 10) is one example of an ethnocentric view that is demeaning to many ethnic groups living in the Southwest.

Today, many Native and Hispanic groups strenuously object to the reproduction of ritual images and religious objects by non-Natives. This publication does not include representations of Pueblo katsinas, kiva paintings, Penitente ceremonies, depictions of masks, or materials associated with mortuary practices, including paintings of prehistoric Mimbres art from southwest New Mexico (fig. 11). The major points of this study remain intact without reproducing works that may offend individuals who are part of indigenous traditions in the Southwest.

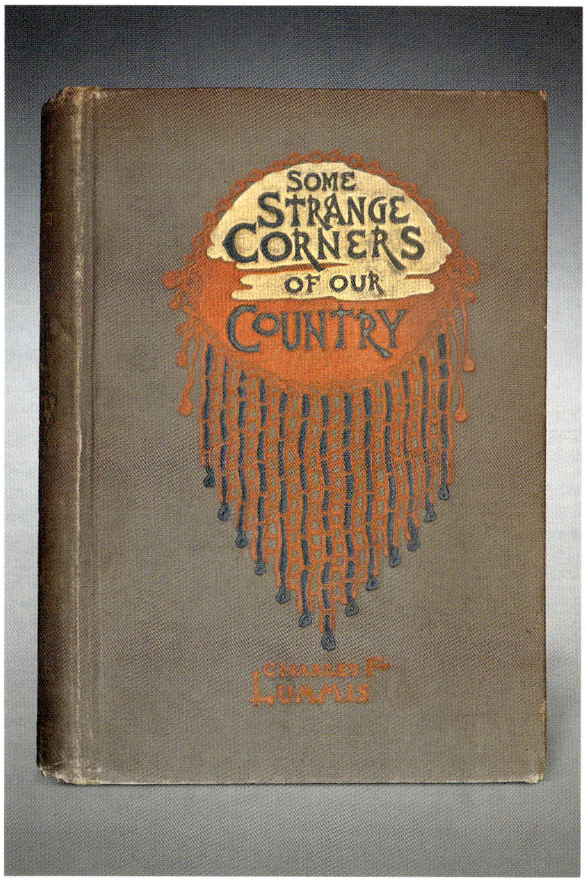

10
CHARLES F. LUMMIS (1859–1928)
SOME STRANGE CORNERS OF OUR COUNTRY: THE WONDERLAND OF THE SOUTHWEST, 1892
7¾ x 5¾ IN. (19.7 x 14.6 CM)

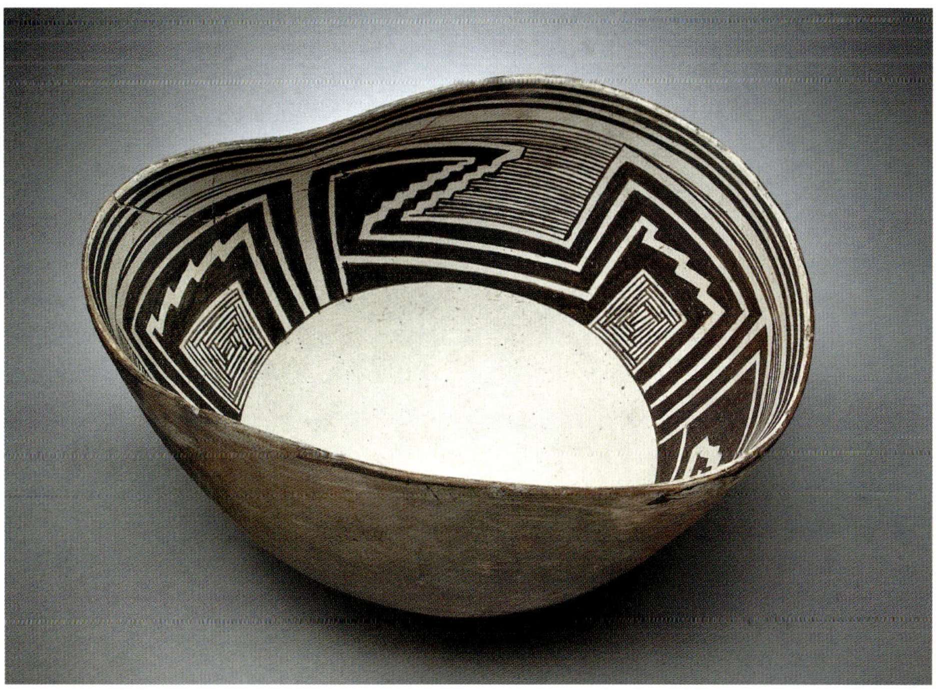

11
MAKER UNKNOWN
MIMBRES BLACK-ON-WHITE BOWL, CIRCA 1060–1110 CE
CLAY AND PIGMENTS, 12 x 8⅞ IN. (30.5 x 22.6 CM)

IT'S ABOUT TIME TO THINK ABOUT TIME

Archaeologists rely heavily on carbon-14 dating, a technique based on the breakdown of carbon isotopes over time. Carbon dates are presented as a single date with a range of years, such as 11,657 plus or minus 300 years. However, the amount of carbon dioxide in the atmosphere is not constant and alters the results of carbon-14 testing. Thus carbon-14 dates can differ from one calendar year to another as the age of a specimen increases. Scientists have corrected this problem by devising tables that translate carbon-14 dates into calendar years.

This study translates carbon-14 dates to calendar years using graphs by P. J. Reimer. For example, remains from the Clovis culture have carbon dates ranging from 11,650 to 10,700 before the present. But the modern calendar equivalent for this period is off by approximately 2,000 years. A more understandable age for nonarchaeologist readers is therefore 13,650 to 12,700 calendar years before the present (CYBP). This study assumes that archaeologists have neither found nor dated the charcoal from the first human campfire in New Mexico, so the starting point for this project is 14,000 calendar years before the present, or a few hundred years before the first radiocarbon date for Clovis culture.

To keep time frames consistent throughout this project, all carbon-14 dates are corrected to calendar years. Dates between the beginning of the Common Era (the nonreligious version of AD) and before the sixteenth-century Spanish *entrada* will be designated CE. Events after European contact will be given a date, such as 1598, with the understanding that it refers to the Common Era.

One of the most interesting results from this study is seeing the shape of artistic time in New Mexico. For most of the 14,000 years that humans have inhabited the state, the lifeways and resulting works of art reflect hunting and gathering economies. This successful strategy lasted for almost 11,000 years before Native peoples began to adopt agricultural practices. Another two millennia passed before agriculture provided the food resources that facilitated the development of Ancestral Pueblo villages. Hispanic colonization of the Pueblo world began four centuries ago, increasing the pace of change. With statehood in 1912, the art of New Mexico changed even more rapidly with a proliferation of prime objects of artistic change.

New Mexico Art Through Time includes works that were intended to be art by their makers, as well as objects that ultimately became art through metamorphosis. Many of the works in this investigation look at other cultures and the southwestern landscape with an aestheticized eye, such as William Brooks Clift's black-and-white photograph *White House Ruin, Canyon de Chelly, Arizona* (fig. 12), in which the lighting has been manipulated to create a dynamic view of the cultural landscape that transcends the physical experience of place.

To modern viewers, the prehistoric and historic works of art illustrated in this volume will have multiple meanings, serving as complex symbols of history, progress, salvage, humanity, cultural roots, and ancestral lifeways. Unfortunately, the need to compress such a multifaceted history into a short text and 241 images means that many categories of art and ethnic traditions, as well as hundreds of artists, could not be included in this book. Instead, *New Mexico Art Through Time* offers a way to rethink the art of New Mexico in a less ethnocentric manner along the vast continuum of time.

As markers of the past and present, the works of art in *New Mexico Art Through Time* may spur aesthetic responses and a deeper understanding of the region's diverse cultures. As a humanities project, this study encourages readers to rethink the meaning of art and aesthetics in an intercultural manner. By doing so, we can transcend our personal perspectives on art and understand and appreciate alternative visions and traditions.

12
WILLIAM BROOKS CLIFT III (B. 1944)
WHITE HOUSE RUIN, CANYON DE CHELLY, ARIZONA, 1975
GELATIN SILVER PRINT, 6⅝ X 9⅝ IN. (16.8 X 24.4 CM)

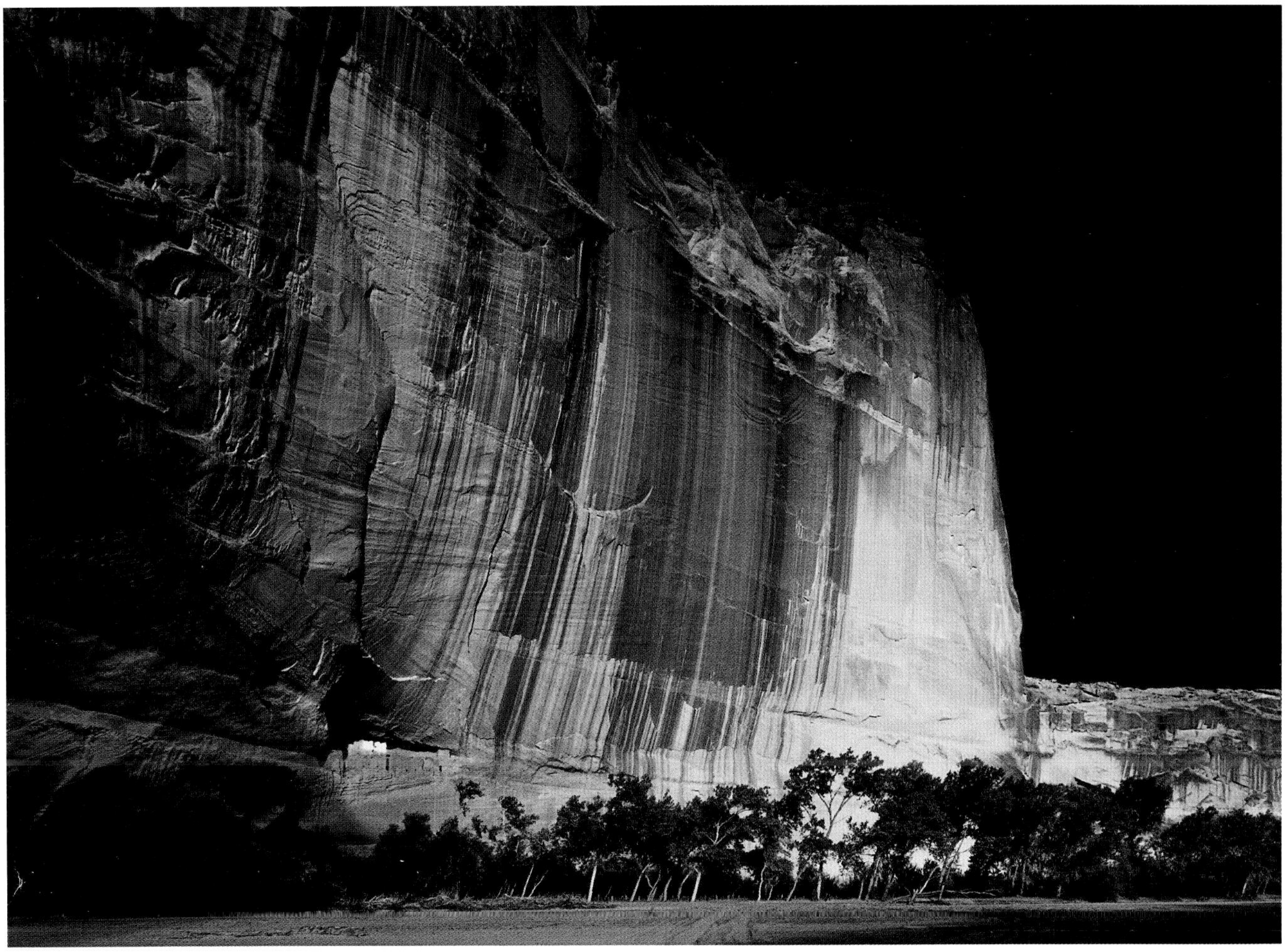

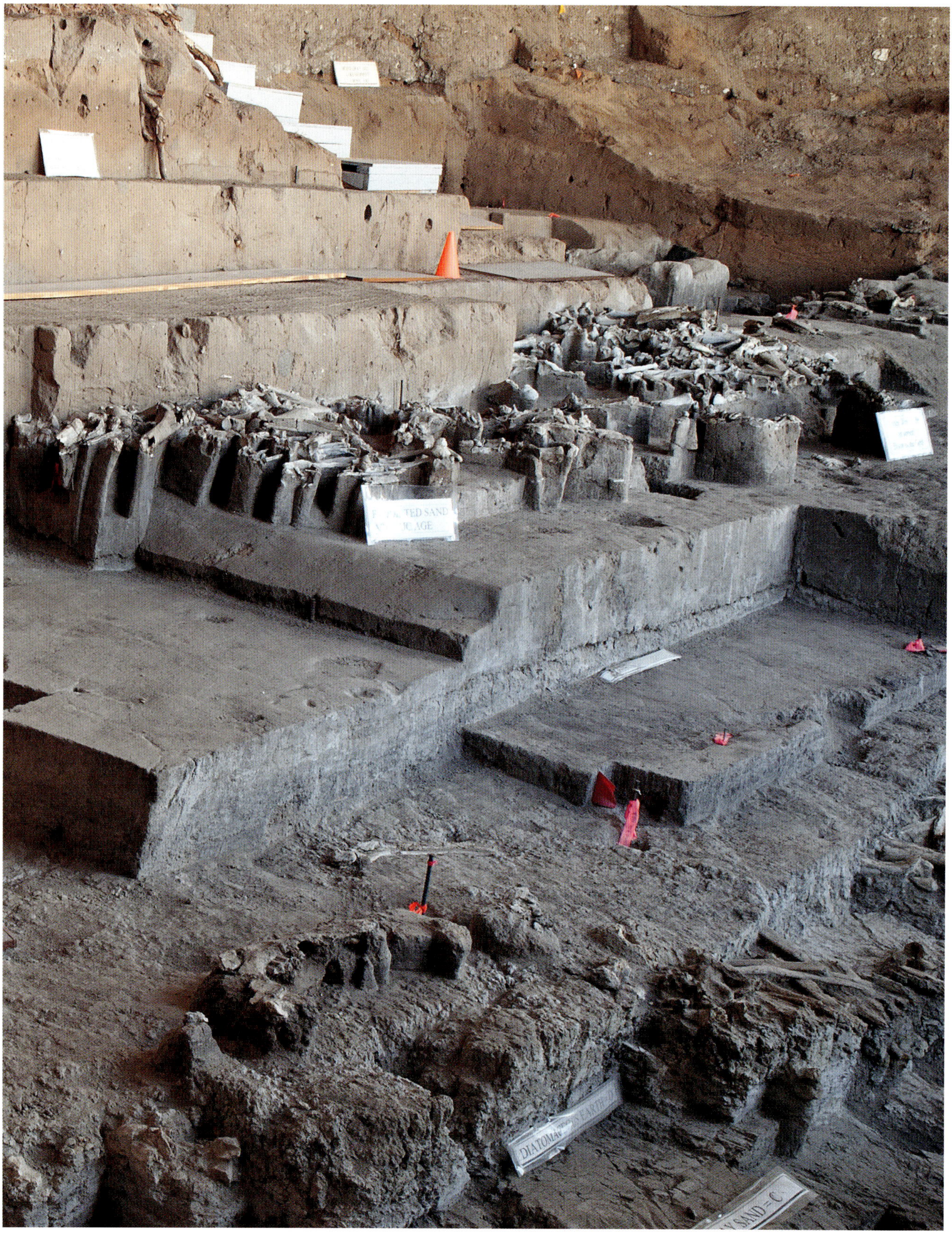

CHAPTER 1

The Art of Hunters, Gatherers, and Early Agriculturalists

The climate at the end of the last Ice Age was much colder and moister than today, with less fluctuation between winter and summer temperatures. A series of spring-fed streams and shallow ponds at what is now called Blackwater Draw near Portales, New Mexico, created conditions that promoted vegetation and provided food for a variety of mammoths, camels, horses, and bison. These animals, in turn, provided food for Paleo-Indians, New Mexico's first hunter-gatherers, who stalked, ambushed, and slaughtered their prey at the Draw, leaving behind layers of discarded bones.

At the beginning of the Great Depression, road crews working on the Llano Estacado in southeastern New Mexico prompted the commercial development of gravel pits at the dry ponds of Blackwater Draw on the outskirts of Portales. Horse-drawn scoops stripped the soil to reach gravel that had once filled artesian ponds. The earthwork also revealed stone tools and bones from extinct mammoths and other prehistoric fauna.

At the same time, archaeologists Edgar B. Howard and John L. Cotter had been searching New Mexico for evidence of the earliest Americans (Boldurian and Cotter 1999). In 1934, they began a series of excavations at the gravel pit, but it took two years before they discovered a large spear point associated with mammoth bones (fig. 13).

These hunter-gatherers and the artifacts they created were named by Howard and Cotter for the nearby town of Clovis. Subsequent studies dated Clovis culture to more than 13,650 calendar years before the present. (All dates are translated from carbon-14 dating in Cordell 1997.) Because most remains from Clovis culture have disintegrated, little is known about the social organization of these nomadic hunters. However, tracking mammoths, bison, and other large animals undoubtedly required the collective skills of a hunting party rather than a lone individual.

Clovis points are rare but have occasionally been found in places other than mammoth kill sites, for instance at a site south of the Santa Fe Airport on land owned by the Bureau of Land Management (fig. 14), supporting the belief that Clovis culture bands traveled widely through New Mexico. While Clovis points can be up to five inches long and over an inch wide, they also can be quite small, for example, the two-inch-long Clovis point knapped from Alibates agate that was found at Blackwater Draw (fig. 15).

Bows and arrows were a late technology in New Mexico, so Clovis hunters were limited to spears. It is assumed that Clovis hunters launched their spears with the assistance of atlatls—wood or bone throwing sticks with grooves that cradled the ends of

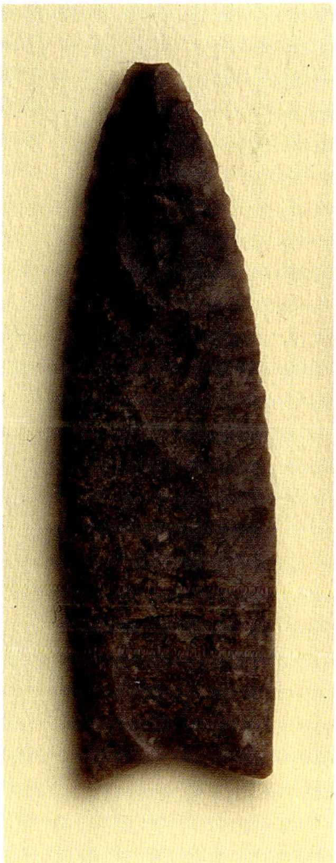

13
MAKER UNKNOWN
CLOVIS POINT, CIRCA 13,650–12,800 BP
CHALCEDONY, 3¼ IN. (8.3 CM)

14
MAKER UNKNOWN
CLOVIS POINT, CIRCA 13,650–12,800 BP
PETRIFIED WOOD, 3⅗ IN. (9.2 CM)

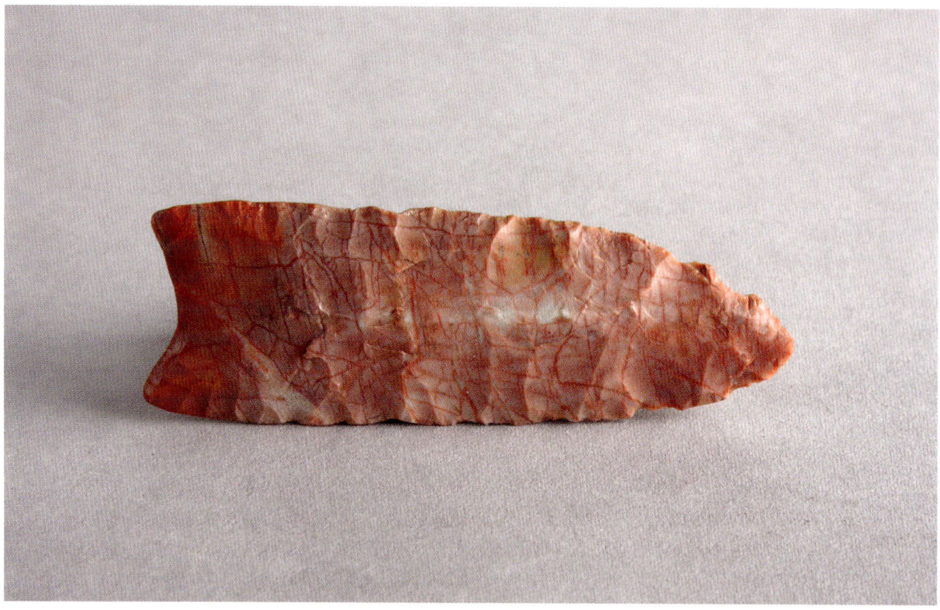

15
MAKER UNKNOWN
CLOVIS POINT, CIRCA 13,650–12,800 BP
ALIBATES AGATE, 2¼ IN. (5.7 CM)

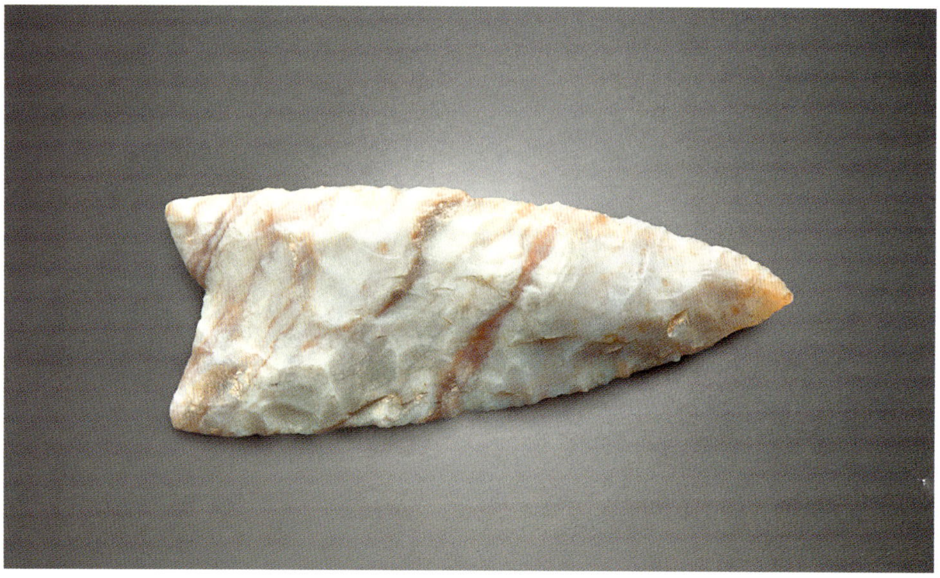

spears, serving as extensions of the throwers' arms and significantly increasing the spears' power.

The Clovis hunters and gatherers who roamed New Mexico between 13,650 and 12,800 years before the present were not the only Paleo-Indians. They were followed by hunters and gatherers of the Folsom culture, who hunted now-extinct bison between 12,900 and 12,000 years before the present. The discovery of artifacts associated with the bison hunts of the Folsom culture can be traced to African American cowboy George McJunkin, who was tracking lost steers after a massive flood hit northeast New Mexico in 1908 (Boldurian and Cotter 1999) and noticed large bones larger than those of modern cows and bison protruding from an arroyo . But McJunkin had trouble interesting others in his find, and knowledge of the unusual bones did not reach paleontologists at the Denver Museum of Natural History until after his death.

In 1927, museum paleontologists excavated bison skeletons in the area of McJunkin's find and discovered a small spear point between one's ribs (fig. 16), conclusively demonstrating the relationship between Paleo-Indian hunters and the large extinct bison, as well as affirming the long span of human habitation in New Mexico. This type of spear point became known as a Folsom point in honor of the town nearest its discovery.

In terms of the knapper's skill, it might appear that Folsom points (fig. 17) were relatively simple to make because they are smaller in length, width, and thickness than Clovis

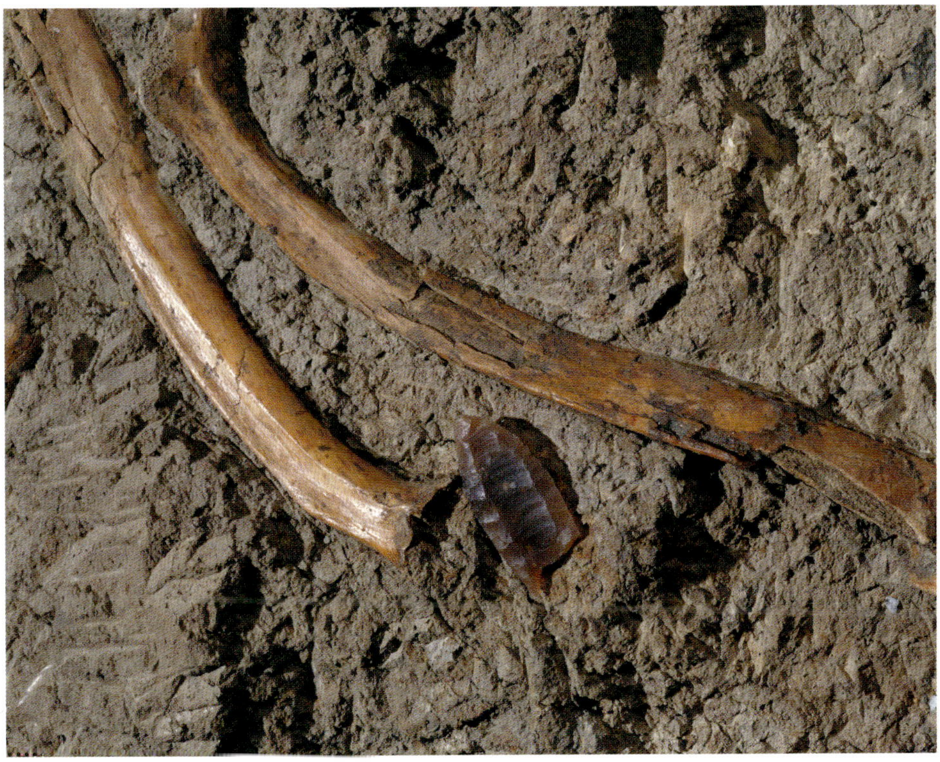

16
MAKER UNKNOWN
FOLSOM POINT IN SITU,
CIRCA 12,900–11,950 BP
CHALCEDONY (POINT), $1\frac{7}{8}$ X $\frac{13}{16}$ X $\frac{13}{16}$ IN.
(4.7 X 2.1 X .4 CM)

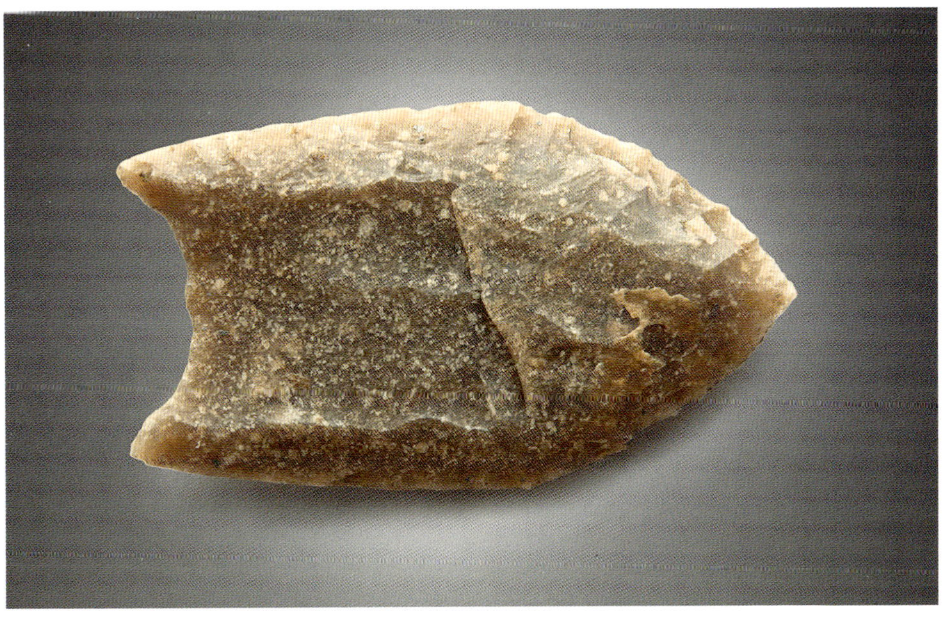

17
MAKER UNKNOWN
FOLSOM POINT, CIRCA 12,900–11,950 BP
STONE, $1\frac{5}{16}$ IN. (3.4 CM)

18
MAKER UNKNOWN
AGATE BASIN POINT,
CIRCA 12,000–11,400 BP
ALIBATES AGATE, 3 IN. (7.6 CM)

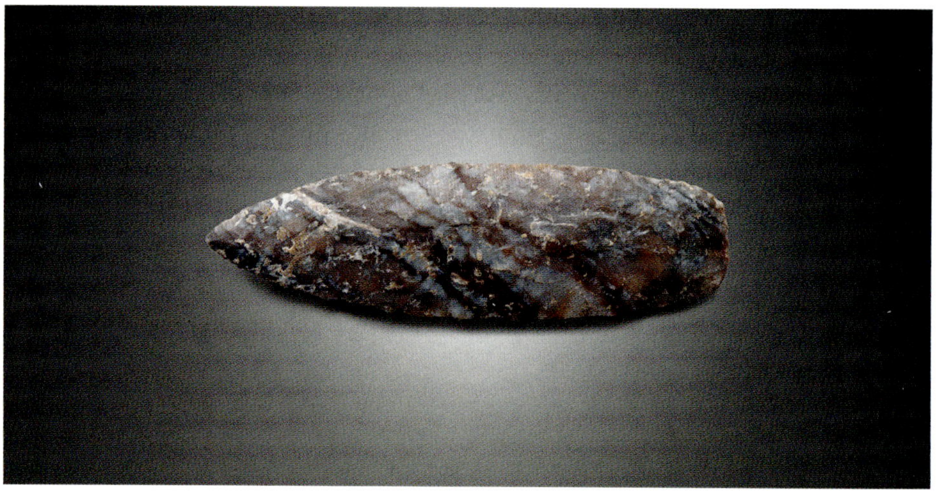

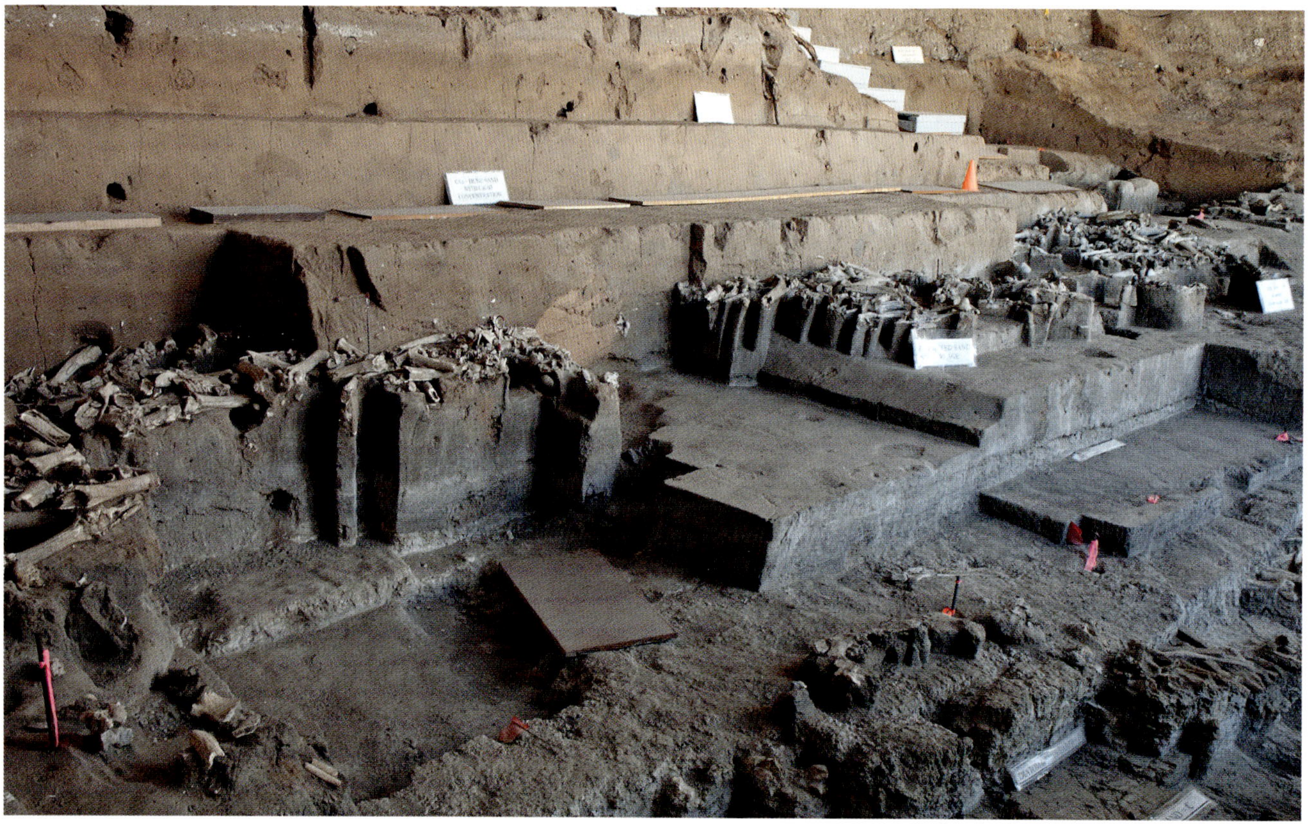

19
BLAIR CLARK (B. 1954)
EXCAVATION OF THE PALEO-INDIAN AND ARCHAIC-AGE BISON KILLS IN THE OUTFLOW CHANNEL, BLACKWATER DRAW SITE, 2011
DIGITAL PHOTOGRAPH, 8 X 10 IN. (20.3 X 25.4 CM)

points. But in reality the opposite is true. The flutes on Folsom points cover approximately 80 percent of them, and the striking of each flute threatens to shatter the object.

Later Paleo-Indians created spear points with long thin blades but no flutes. Such tools changed very little between 12,000 and 8,350 years before the present, implying that these hunters and their prey also changed little over 5,000 years. Some specialists consider some varieties of these spear points—Eden, Cody, Plain View, or Agate Basin styles—to simply be large, unfluted versions of Folsom points. However, Agate Basin points (fig. 18) have much longer and thinner forms than Folsom points. In this case, the makers' ability to produce such slender, thin tools without shattering them was a remarkable feat.

As archaeological investigations continued through the decades (fig. 19), they revealed a complex history, beginning with Clovis culture, continuing through Folsom culture and late Paleo-Indian traditions, followed by a long period of Archaic habitations. A portion of these excavations is now preserved under a permanent building, the Blackwater Draw, between Portales and Clovis, which displays layers of cultural material and animal bones.

PALEO-INDIAN ART

So what makes stone tools art? There are two ways to answer this question. One is from the perspective of the Paleo-Indian toolmakers, and the other is from a twenty-first-century point of view where, to use Jacques Maquet's argument, these well-crafted objects became transformed by contemporary culture into works of art that represent the extreme antiquity of the first New Mexicans and symbolize their hunting and gathering lifeways.

The first answer may be difficult to comprehend because these hunters are long gone and left no written records. However, their stone objects reveal their exceptional skill as flint knappers who used exotic thinning flakes that left flutes in the bases of the tools and utilized high-quality raw materials that often were colorful, transluscent, and procured over great distances. Because these qualities of toolmaking go far beyond what was necessary to create effective spear points, the exceptional efforts of these knappers can be interpreted as a form of aesthetic activity, making their tools art. Clovis and Folsom points are excellent examples of objects that are both functional and art; complex but surprisingly simple; sophisticated yet basic.

The best materials used by Paleo-Indians were not always found locally. Their sources were often hundreds of miles away, indicating the importance placed on the choice of specific materials. For example, the red-and-cream-colored Alibates agate found at Blackwater Draw came from north of Amarillo, Texas, a distance of 90 miles. And the most common material found at the Draw, opaque gray Edwards Plateau chert, came from central Texas, more than 150 miles away.

Clovis points made from exotic materials provide a visual contrast between the knapping patterns and the visual aspects of the stone. Clovis bands in Colorado often used flints from the Green River formation in the northwest corner of the state, a material that features light and dark bands of color that run through the matrix. When worked, these bands of striated color run lengthwise across the flat of the blank, creating ovals of changing colors that mirror the object's overall shape.

Paleo-Indian knappers did not lug boulders of fine flint and agate around the plains, but they knapped large nodules into bifaces (fig. 20). Such double-faced objects flaked on both sides could be used like a large unhafted knife, or later, as a core for producing points or large cutting blades. The large biface seen in figure 20 is a good example of overshot flaking—the creation of wide, flat, thinning flakes that skim from one side of a tool to

20
MAKER UNKNOWN
LARGE CLOVIS BIFACE,
CIRCA 13,650–12,800 BP
EDWARDS PLATEAU CHERT, 10 5/16 IN.
(26.2 CM)

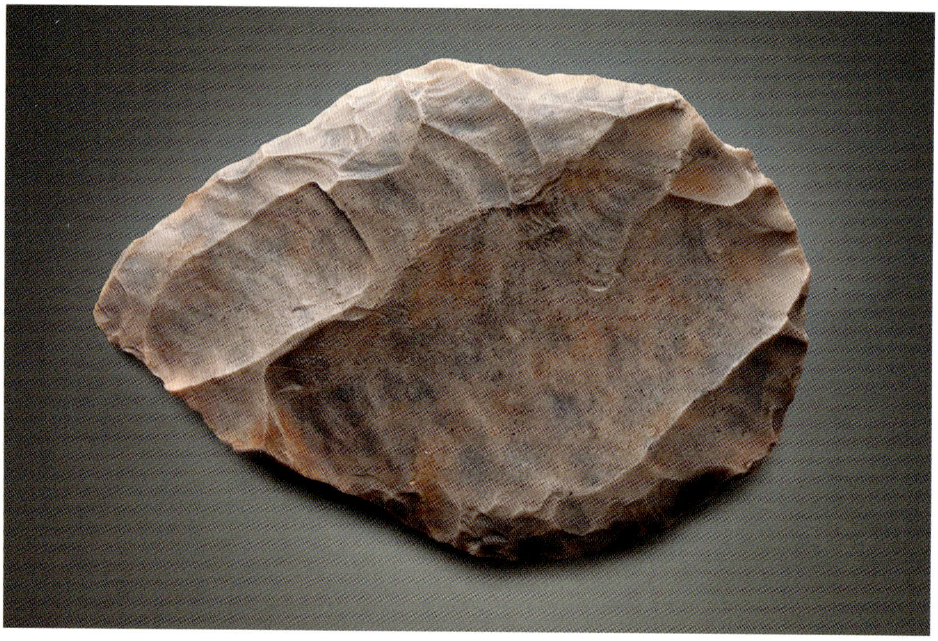

21
MAKER UNKNOWN
CLOVIS UNIFACIAL KNIFE,
CIRCA 13,650–12,800 BP
EDWARDS PLATEAU CHERT, 7 IN.
(17.9 CM)

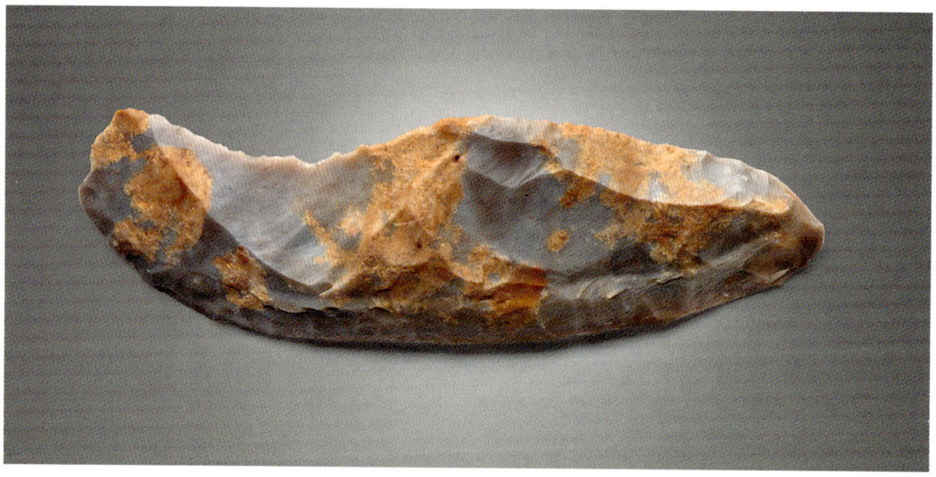

the other. Produced with a single strike from a leg bone of a large animal, such flakes are extremely difficult to make and are only found on Paleo-Indian objects.

Clovis knappers also produced exceptionally sharp blades struck from long cores. These knives were used for multiple tasks and could be resharpened on the cutting edge, as seen in the blade in figure 21. A close look reveals that the blade was razor sharp when struck from a core, but there are now small chips on the cutting edge caused by use.

An obvious characteristic of both Clovis and Folsom points was the removal of large thinning flakes at the end of the manufacturing process, leaving scars, or flutes, in both Clovis points (fig. 22) and Folsom points (fig. 23). A great deal of perfectly directed force was required to remove the channel flake to produce such flutes. It was a delicate task that left the blank exceptionally thin and prone to shattering when the second flute

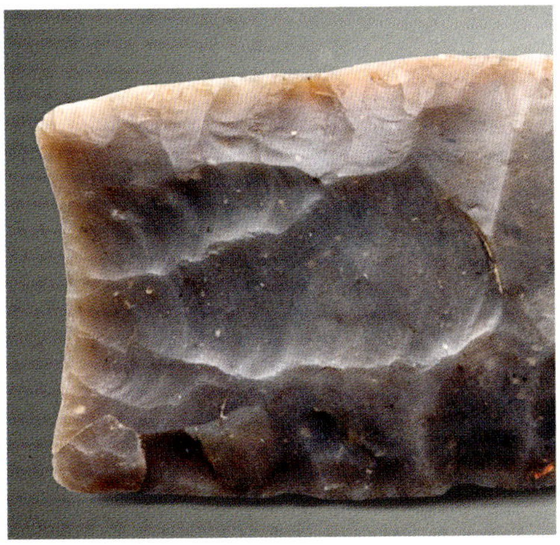

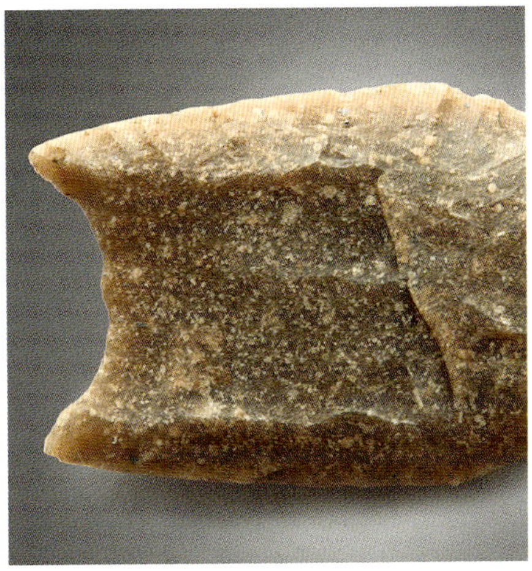

22
MAKER UNKNOWN
CLOVIS POINT (DETAIL),
CIRCA 13,650–12,800 BP
EDWARDS PLATEAU CHERT,
4⅜ IN. (11.1 CM)

23
MAKER UNKNOWN
FOLSOM POINT (DETAIL),
CIRCA 12,900–11,950 BP
STONE, 1⁵⁄₁₆ IN. (3.4 CM)

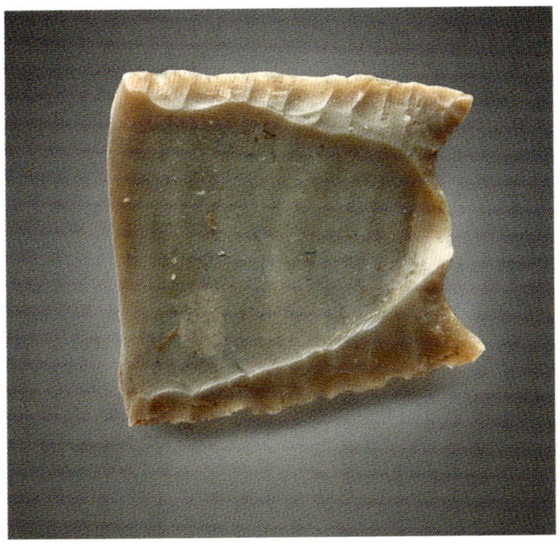

24
MAKER UNKNOWN
FOLSOM POINT, CIRCA 12,900–11,950 BP
EDWARDS PLATEAU CHERT,
1⅜ IN. (3.5 CM)

was struck. An instructive example of the difficulty of this type of fluting can be seen in a Folsom point that broke when a second channel flake was struck at the wrong angle and split the blank (fig. 24).

After the fluting process, both Clovis and Folsom points were refined along the outline and sharpened along the edges. Both types of points, however, often broke after continuous use and were resharpened if enough of the tool remained. It is interesting to compare the shape of an original "textbook" Clovis point (fig. 25) with a resharpened point (fig. 26). The latter is considerably narrower than the point that has not been reworked.

Later Paleo-Indian spear points were not fluted. Instead, they incorporated chipping patterns from the edge to the middle of the long, slender points, a process that also occurred at the end of the manufacturing process. Details of the chipping on an Eden point (fig. 27) from Blackwater Draw clearly reveal fine patterns of chipping cuts across the point that create a diamond-shaped cross section and contrast with the grain and color of the petrified wood from which it was made.

The stone tools left by Paleo-Indian hunters represent more than just functional objects used to kill and butcher huge animals. From a conceptual perspective, these tools reflect the cultural knowledge and engineering technology that allowed these nomadic

25
MAKER UNKNOWN
CLOVIS POINT, CIRCA 13,650–12,800 BP
EDWARDS PLATEAU CHERT,
4⅜ IN. (11.1 CM)

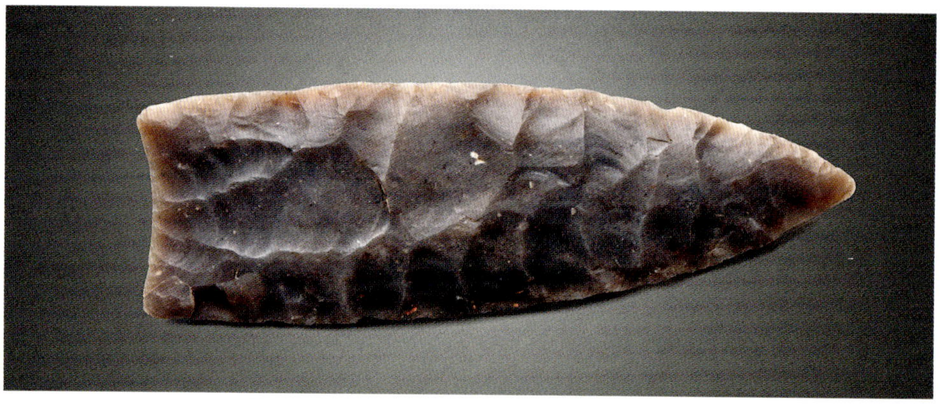

26
MAKER UNKNOWN
CLOVIS POINT, CIRCA 13,650–12,800 BP
EDWARDS PLATEAU CHERT,
4⅛ IN. (10.5 CM)

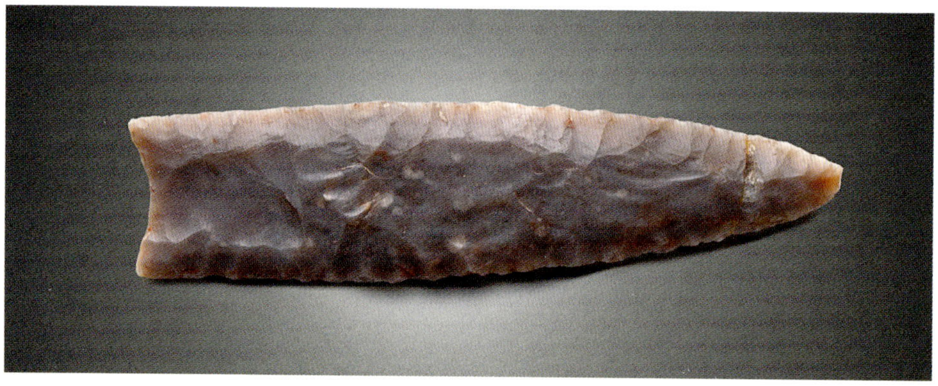

27
MAKER UNKNOWN
MIDSECTION OF AN EDEN (LATE PALEO-INDIAN) POINT (DETAIL),
CIRCA 10,700–7000 BP
SILICIFIED WOOD, 2 7/16 IN. (6.2 CM)

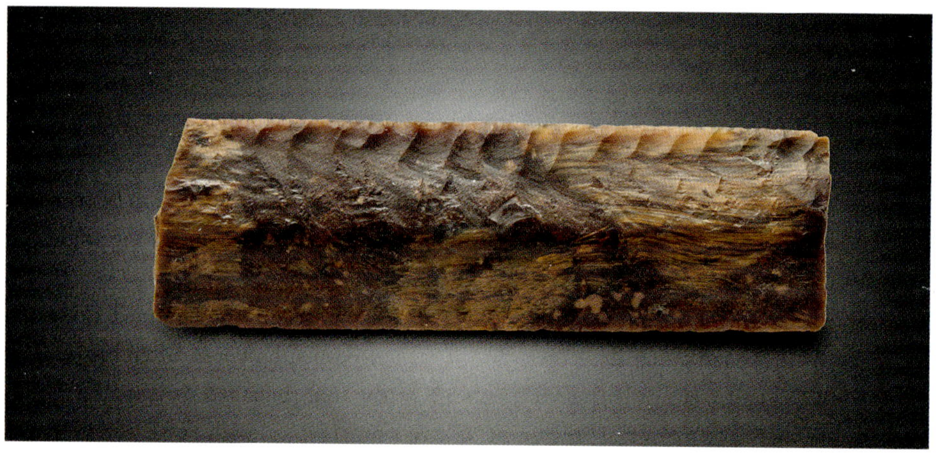

tribes to survive. The skill required to make Paleo-Indian flaked tools took years of practice, a practical knowledge and understanding of regional geology and ecology, and the awareness to select high-quality raw materials that facilitated the production of fluted points.

Taken together, these characteristics of Paleo-Indian tools demonstrate their makers' supreme skill as toolmakers, skills that had not only functional but also aesthetic elements. Thus these tools appear to express aestheticized activities from a Paleo-Indian perspective.

Today, Paleo-Indian stone objects have been incorporated into modern life as icons of the long history of human habitation in New Mexico and the Southwest. Viewers can interpret Paleo-Indian chipped stone tools as symbolizing the sophistication of Paleo-Indian culture and its adaptation to changing environments and food sources at the end of the Pleistocene era. Modern viewers can also interpret these tools as works of art that reflect Paleo-Indian worldviews and symbolize the lifeways of the earliest New Mexicans.

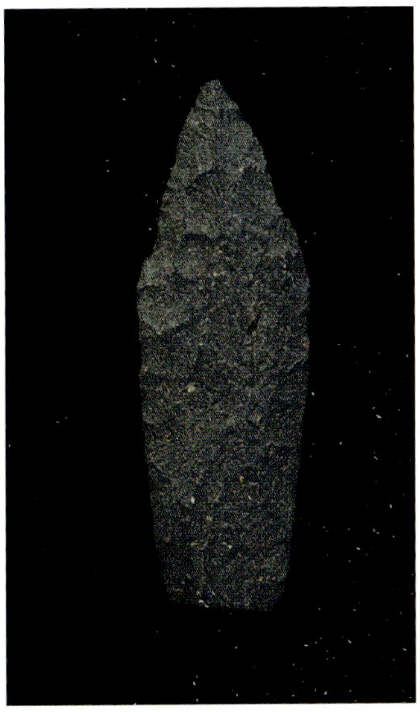

28
MAKER UNKNOWN
EARLY ARCHAIC, JAY PHASE SPEAR POINT OR PROJECTILE,
CIRCA 7800–6800 BP
FINE-GRAINED BASALT, 2 3/16 IN. (5.6 CM)

THE ARCHAIC PERIOD

Eight thousand years ago the climate changed radically as temperatures warmed, creating dryer conditions similar to the present climate in the Southwest. The massive bison associated with Paleo-Indian hunters and gatherers had become extinct, and Native peoples adapted to the new environment by emphasizing the gathering of plant resources. Archaeologists call this the Archaic period, which lasted approximately 6,500 years, from 8,500 years before the present to the beginning of the Common Era.

Archaic campsites are found in the Rio Grande basin, on the Great Plains, and in other areas with permanent water resources. Archaic bands were less mobile than Paleo-Indians and camped in close proximity to food and other resources. Little remains of the organic materials and brush shelters associated with early Archaic people's lifeways, but their stone tools reveal their hunting and knapping practices. Archaic hunters adapted projectile points so they could hunt smaller game, including deer, elk, and antelope. These points were smaller than Paleo-Indian ones and surprisingly thick and heavy for their size, indicating that they were probably dart points to spear shafts and thrown with atlatls.

The transition to the Archaic period is associated with the leaf-shaped Jay points found on the Eastern Plains and in the central Rio Grande Valley (fig. 28). These points average three inches long, were knapped with uneven thinning and shaping flakes, and feature a straight base that was hafted to a spear shaft. Their irregularity may be directly related to lesser-quality raw materials, such as basalt or local cherts, that existed within the more limited ranges of the Archaic hunter-gatherer tribes.

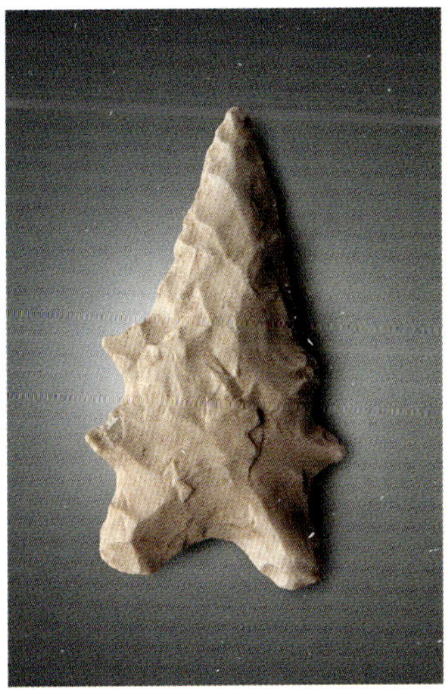

29
MAKER UNKNOWN
SAN JOSÉ-LIKE POINT,
CIRCA 6300–4500 BP
STONE, 1 1/4 IN. (3.2 CM)

Later Archaic period spear points are smaller in size with a thicker cross section. For example, San José points, which date between 6,300 and 4,500 years before the present (fig. 29). They are characterized by the removal of heavy, conchoidal flakes that were spaced apart to produce a serrated edge.

While there are subtle differences among Archaic points, they all have similar shapes and are relatively heavy for their small size. Compared to Paleo-Indian points, however, Archaic chipped stone points are simpler and more crudely made, indicating that Archaic hunters could accomplish their goals without resorting to earlier levels of craftsmanship. Unlike the severe overshot thinning that had been a characteristic of Paleo-Indian technology, the disjointed chipping on Jay points indicates that precision knapping was not a valued attribute of Archaic lifeways, and that gathering had assumed a more important role than hunting. And while spear points were still a significant part of the culture, they must have been well adapted for local game because they demonstrate remarkable uniformity over thousands of years.

30
MAKER UNKNOWN
ALMA PLAIN SEED JAR,
CIRCA 400–600 CE
CLAY, 10 x 11¼ IN. (25.4 x 28.6 CM)

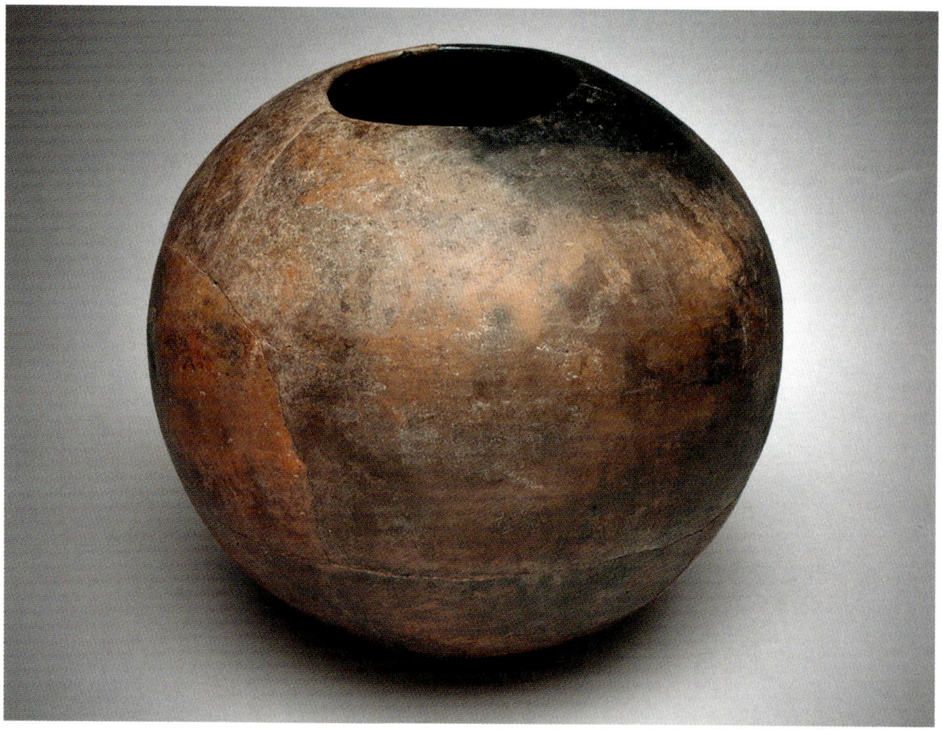

Beginning 3,000 to 4,000 years ago, Archaic gatherers began experimenting with agriculture in the mountainous highlands of southern New Mexico. These areas received more moisture, which supported the cultivation of corn, squash, and other agriculture that added to the basic economy. Embryonic corn from the period produced small cobs with only a few kernels, but as agriculture became more widespread, more productive strains of corn, beans, and, eventually, squash were planted and adapted to a variety of New Mexico environments.

While the period from 2,500 years before the present to 200 CE often is called the Late Archaic or Early Basketmaker period, archaeologist Bruce Huckell has named it Early Agriculture, emphasizing its changing economy due to the rise of agriculture, which fundamentally altered the nomadic lifeways of gatherers in New Mexico. Farmers were now required to tend and continuously watch crops to protect these resources from foraging deer and rabbits.

During this period, communities constructed pit houses, which were built into the ground with a superstructure of wooden posts, lintels, and small wood poles then sealed in adobe. As communities expanded, pit houses were built larger with more complexity, and agricultural surpluses were kept in storage rooms and storage pits, the importance of which reflected the success of agricultural lifeways.

In the uplands of southwestern New Mexico surrounding the town of Reserve, rectangular pit houses were more permanently constructed with vertical posts that supported a roof and lean-to sides that were covered with brush and sealed with adobe. Aggregations of families into communities of pit houses offered a more stable solution to the needs of Archaic farmers. Rather than the earlier practice of continuously moving the entire community to locate food and resources, pit house villages served as a home base for farming, gathering, and hunting. This more sedentary period also gave rise to the introduction of pottery, circa 200 CE.

AGRICULTURAL COMMUNITIES AND THE ORIGINS OF POTTERY

Pottery making after 200 CE marks the transition from nomadic lifeways to permanent communities. Early ceramics were not well fired and tended to fragment into small, silver dollar–sized shards. Archaeologists expressed their displeasure at having to process the tiny unpainted shards, alternately disparaging the objects as "clubby brown ware" or "grungy grey ware."

The iron-rich clay sources in the Mogollon highlands of southern New Mexico produced pottery that was predominantly dark red to brown in color. Potters polished the surfaces of Alma Plain pottery to produce a lightly polished surface that reflected light (fig. 30). These containers often mimic the shape of gourds and small baskets used by Archaic pit house peoples. While Alma Plain pottery was unpainted, it was occasionally decorated by scratching or poking the damp clay after the vessels were formed.

As works of art, pottery vessels are prime objects of social, economic, and aesthetic change in pit house village communities, reflecting the worldview of early Native agriculturalists. Pottery is as much a symbol of the importance of agriculture to Native populations in New Mexico as Clovis points were a symbol of hunting and gathering during Paleo-Indian periods. To more modern viewers, however, the visual interest in early pottery is in its emphasis on form.

In summary, over more than a 12,000-year period, from 14,000 to 1,500 years before the present, Native peoples living in New Mexico made art. However, little remains from the Paleo-Indian, Archaic periods in New Mexico. Most of the organic materials used by these New Mexicans disintegrated centuries ago, except stone tools and pottery. Hunters, gatherers, and early agriculturists aestheticized these objects in unique ways that reflected deeply held ideals associated with their cultures. From a modern perspective, these works broaden our understanding of art, culture, and time.

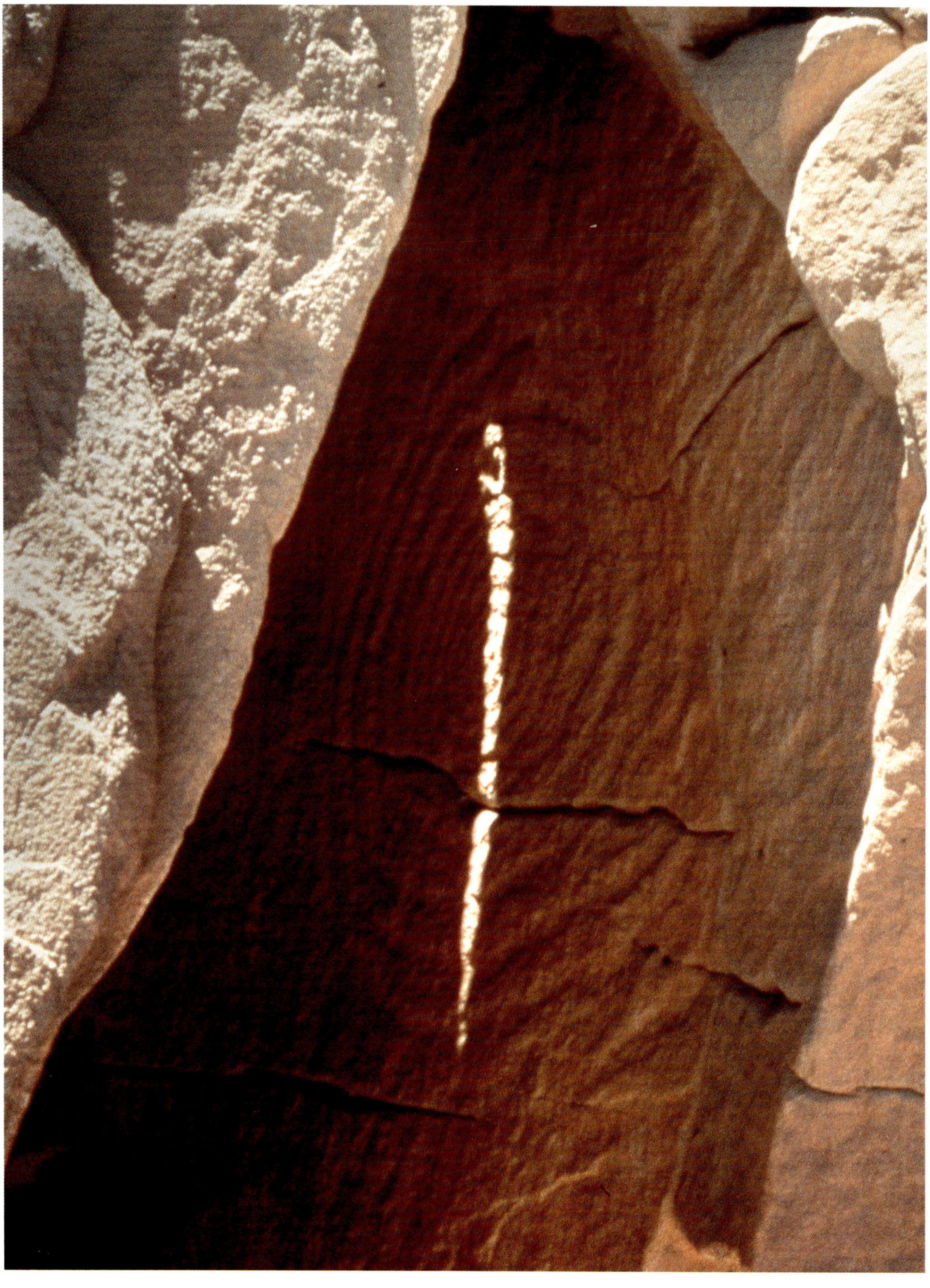

CHAPTER 2

The Art of Ancestral Pueblo Villages

Agriculture in the ancient Southwest required an intimate knowledge of seasonal cycles, precipitation patterns, and local microclimates. It was understood that the sun rose and set at different spots along the horizon in a cyclical procession throughout the year. The summer solstice, when the sun rises and sets farthest to the north, occurs on June 21, while the winter solstice, when the sun rises and sets farthest to the south, is on December 21. During the spring and fall equinoxes on March 21 and September 21, respectively, the days and nights are equally long. This basic understanding of seasonal cycles allowed ancestral populations to coordinate their activities with the environment.

THE UNITY OF THE ENVIRONMENT AND THE PUEBLO WORLD

With their thorough understanding of the environment around their villages, agricultural peoples shaped their landscapes in correspondence with astronomical events (Sofaer 2008 and Williamson 1984). The timing of rituals and planting cycles was determined by counting forward from a cardinal solar event. Knowledge of astronomy was also reflected in petroglyphs, whose locations sometimes marked places for observation of astronomical events.

The best-known solar marker in the Southwest is Sun Dagger, located on the side of Fajada Butte in Chaco Canyon National Monument, which identifies calendrical events. This was discovered when archaeo-astronomer Anna Sofaer was recording petroglyphs in 1977 and noticed that three sandstone slabs were perfectly arranged to project a dagger-shaped shaft of light onto two petroglyphs carved into the face of the butte. Karl Kernberger's photograph *Summer Solstice Solar Dagger, Fajada Butte, Chaco Canyon* (fig. 31) records this event.

Later studies determined that the movement of the light coincides with the winter solstice, spring equinox, summer solstice, and fall equinox, as well as with lunar cycles. Sun Dagger affirmed the importance of astronomical calculations in the agricultural and religious lifeways of Ancestral Pueblo people. Unfortunately, in 1989 the soft soils under the sandstone slabs caused them to shift, destroying the ancient rock art calendar.

A similar astronomical marker can be found along an arroyo leading to Chaco Wash, where a south-facing ledge casts a shadow on a large rock with two petroglyphs of concentric circles. The two petroglyphs mark the shadow's position at high noon during the

31
KARL KERNBERGER (B. 1939)
SUMMER SOLSTICE SOLAR DAGGER, FAJADA BUTTE, CHACO CANYON, N.D.
DIGITAL PHOTOGRAPH, 2.6 X 3.59 IN.
(6.6 X 9.13 CM)

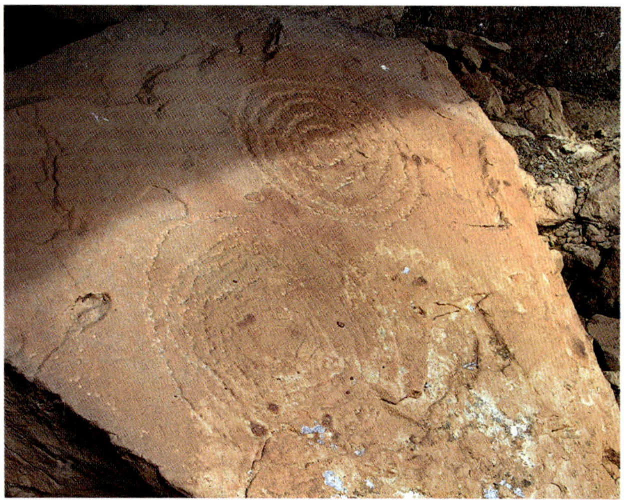

fall and spring equinoxes. When the sun rises on those two days, the shadow slowly moves forward until at high noon it hits the center of the easternmost petroglyph (fig. 32) and aligns with the top of the other petroglyph.

Such solar markers reflect conscious acts that demonstrate Ancestral Puebloans' understanding of astronomy. Rock art exists throughout New Mexico, but those marking celestial motions underscore the importance of environmental cycles to agricultural peoples. From a modern perspective, contemporary viewers of rock art may understand the recording of celestial motion as an aesthetic act expressing the inseparability of the Pueblo world and the natural environment.

32
MAKER UNKNOWN
EQUINOX MARKER, CIRCA 1000–1200 CE
STONE, 72 x 48 IN. (182.9 x 121.9 CM)

ANCESTRAL PUEBLOS

By 600 CE, pit houses had outlived their usefulness as long-term residences in agricultural communities. As agriculture became more successful and communities occupied areas for longer periods of time, the need for more permanent structures increased. At first, families added one or two aboveground rooms to their pit houses, but eventually Puebloans replaced pit houses altogether with aboveground buildings constructed of stone and adobe. Their flat roofs had large wooden beams crossed with smaller sticks and brush then sealed in a thick coat of adobe. Residents entered these structures through a smoke hole in the roof rather than through doors, a design that kept rodents and insects out of the buildings and away from stored food supplies. The flat roofs also provided alternative workspaces for a variety of activities that included the drying of locally grown foodstuffs.

After 850 CE, populations grew dramatically in areas with proven agricultural success and abundant water, firewood, game, building materials, and plant life. As Pueblo communities expanded, extended families grew into small, multifamily communities called unit pueblos. These aboveground stone pueblos included underground ceremonial rooms, called kivas, which served the religious needs of the communities. The growing populations of agriculturalists living in small pueblos also increased the need for pottery.

CERAMIC ARTS AND PUEBLO COMMUNITIES

Pueblo communities created ceramic vessels for use as cooking pots, water jars, and crop storage. Pueblo potters produced plain wares during the first few centuries of pottery development. But around 600 CE, potters from the Mogollon highlands and throughout the Colorado Plateau began adding painted decorations to their wares.

At the same time that they worked to perfect the process of painted pottery design, Pueblo potters also experimented with textured surfaces that would not be effaced by cooking fires. A banded Kana-a Gray pitcher from the Cibola region in west-central New Mexico (fig. 33) exemplifies such textural design. Created between 760 and 900 CE, the

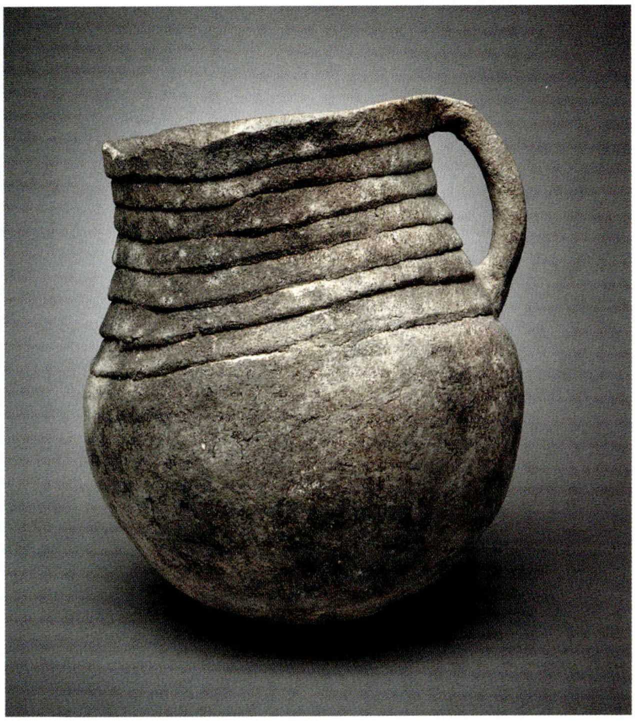

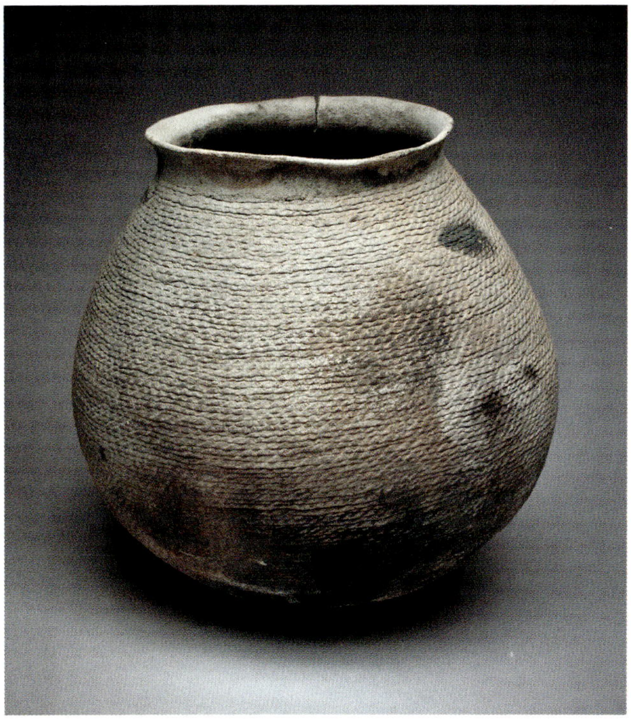

33
MAKER UNKNOWN
KANA-A NECKBAND PITCHER,
CIRCA 760–900 CE
CLAY, 7½ X 6½ IN. (19.1 X 16.5)

34
MAKER UNKNOWN
CHACO CORRUGATED JAR,
CIRCA 1050–1110 CE
CLAY, 14¼ X 14¾ IN. (36.2 X 37.5 CM)

pitcher was shaped with coiled rolls of clay that were then smoothed both inside and outside without obliterating the coils from the shoulder to the rim. The carbonization on the outside of the pitcher shows that it was used to heat liquids or foodstuffs. However, the decorative bands remained on the pitcher's surface in spite of the carbon cook-fire stains.

An integration of form, function, and decoration occurred as a potter created a corrugated surface by deftly pinching and twisting coils of wet clay together while simultaneously smoothing the vessel inside to lock the coils in place. The potter repeated this motion thousands of times for a large cooking pot or storage vessel. Sometimes a potter altered the style of corrugation or changed the hand motion to create exterior patterns. For example, as the circumference changes from the bottom to the rim on a corrugated jar, the corrugations cast shadows that create a swirling spiral pattern that accentuates the jar's form.

A Chaco storage jar from 1050–1110 CE (fig. 34) shows how corrugations were slightly smoothed as a vessel was constructed. An interesting aspect of the jar is the fire cloud pattern along the rim—accidental carbonization caused during the firing that contrasts with the regularity of the corrugated surface. It is unclear how Pueblo potters felt about fire clouds, but many modern viewers consider their appearance on unpainted and corrugated vessels to be intentional aestheticized marks of the artist's process.

Another style of corrugated vessel, the Tularosa Fillet Rim bowl (fig. 35), which was made in the Mogollon highlands between 1100 and1300 CE, presents an astounding combination of color, texture, and form. The bowl features two rows of exterior corrugations just below the rim that contrast with its finely polished black interior. The potter added a rich orange-red exterior of the bowl by oxidizing the iron-rich clay. Before the

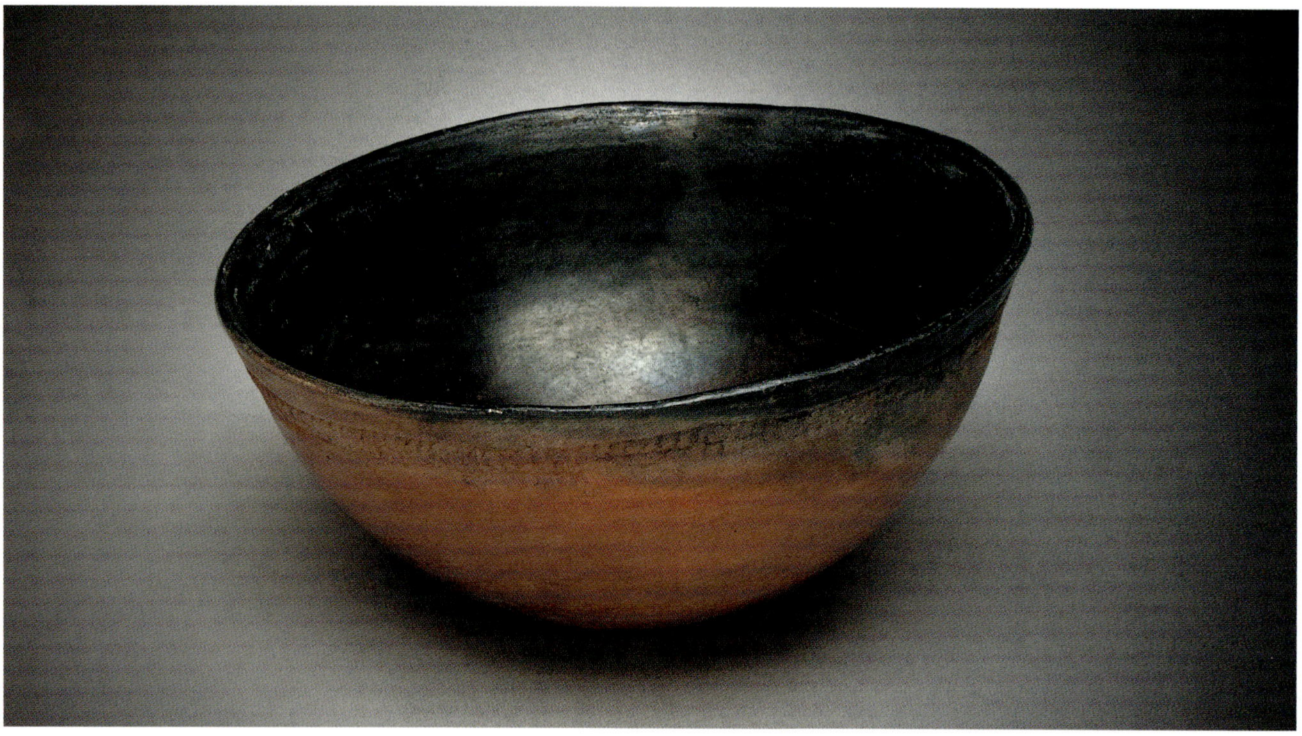

35
MAKER UNKNOWN
TULAROSA FILLET RIM BOWL,
CIRCA 1100–1300 CE
CLAY, 3½ x 7½ IN. (8.9 x 19.1 CM)

bowl cooled, the potter also placed an organic material, probably pine needles full of pitch, inside the vessel to smolder and create the glossy black interior.

The simple elegance of corrugated wares appeals to modern viewers accustomed to flowing, reductive forms. As aesthetic reflections of Ancestral Pueblo life, these works of art are just as important as painted pottery.

Adding painted designs to pottery required experimentation with diverse clay sources, pigments, and firing techniques, and created observable differences in Pueblo pottery. Potters in southern New Mexico painted iron-rich mineral pigments onto their pottery, while potters on the Colorado Plateau used organic pigments extracted from plant juices as well as mineral pigments.

A La Plata/White Mound Black-on-white seed jar from 625–875 CE (fig. 36) exemplifies the simple patterns, such as zigzag lines, that were common on early painted wares. These motifs were painted with brushes made from plant fibers such as yucca leaf. Painters pulled the brushes in straight lines across the vessel surface, much like a modern pinstriping brush, rather than using the back and forth stroking motions of a modern watercolor brush. The pulling motion created long, straight lines, or long smooth curves, with even widths.

Painted pottery designs evolved quickly, and by 850 CE, potters were conscious of the aesthetic difference between painted and unpainted surfaces. A Red Mesa Black-on-white pitcher (fig. 37) from the Puerco River area of west-central New Mexico demonstrates the evolution of painted designs from 900–1050 CE. Here bands of painted motifs are bordered by thin framing lines, with the design elements connected to either the top or bottom framing line within each band.

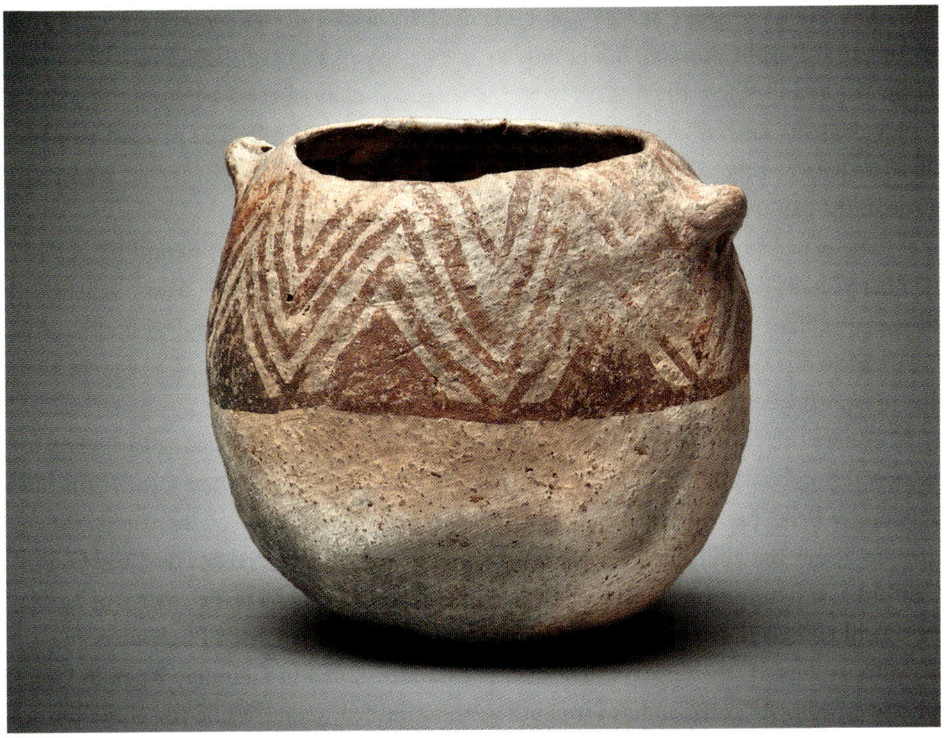

36
MAKER UNKNOWN
LA PLATA / WHITE MOUND BLACK-ON-WHITE SEED JAR, CIRCA 625–875 CE
CLAY AND PIGMENTS, 3⅛ X 3¼ IN.
(7.9 X 8.3 CM)

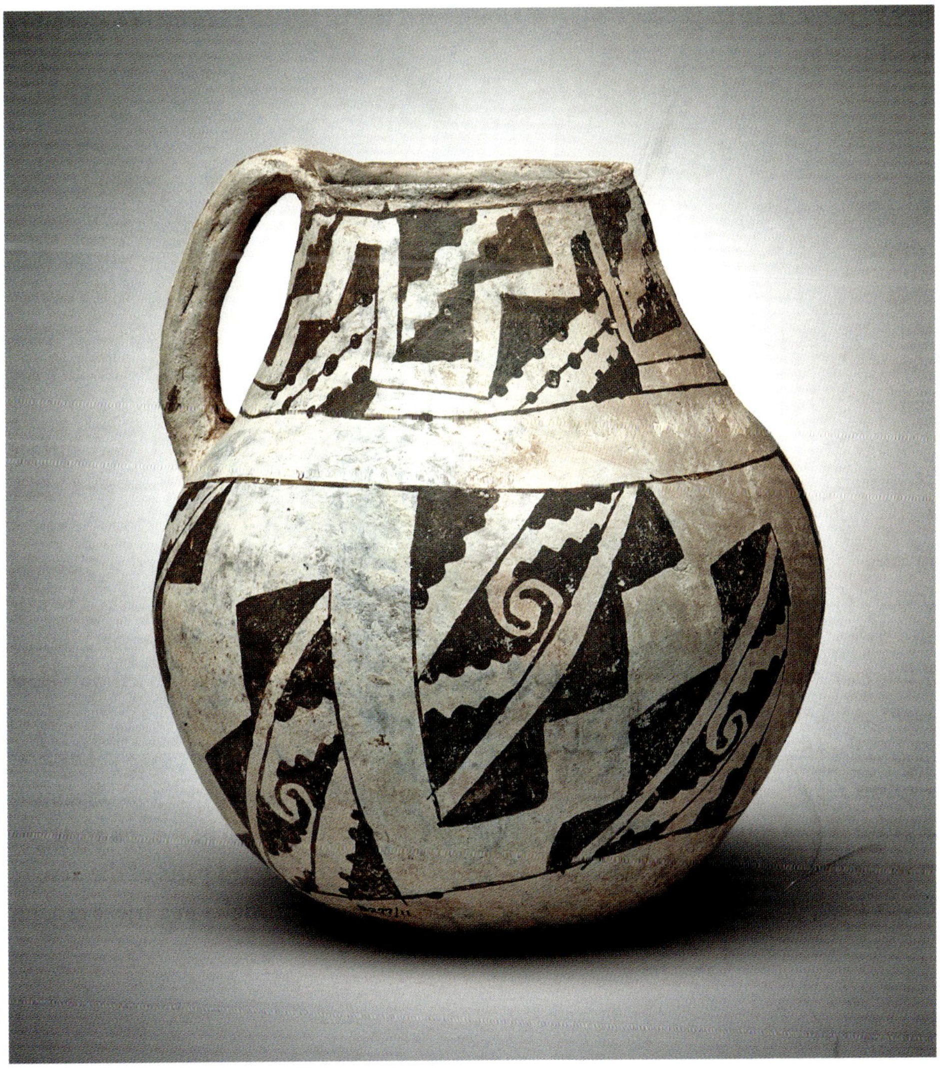

37
MAKER UNKNOWN
RED MESA BLACK-ON-WHITE PITCHER,
CIRCA 900–1050 CE
CLAY AND PIGMENTS, 6½ X 6 IN.
(16.5 X 15.2 CM)

The use of negative space—the unpainted areas of a design—plays a critical role in Ancestral Pueblo pottery. While modern viewers may be predisposed to concentrate on the painted forms of the pitcher in figure 39, the unpainted areas between the painted design elements seem to dominate both the vessel's neck and body. The painted elements alternate between the two friezes, emphasizing the unpainted white areas that are woven through the painted elements.

The expansion of small, unit pueblos into larger, aggregated communities accelerated between 850 and 1000 CE in areas such as Chaco Canyon. After 1000 CE, aggregated villages at Chaco Canyon developed in a planned manner that resulted in multistoried towns known as Great Houses with central plazas, large numbers of kivas, and great kivas that presumably served more than local residents.

A network of cleared roadways connected Great Houses in Chaco with aggregated villages throughout the region. The discovery of high-status materials at Chaco—including copper bells, parrots, shell, and turquoise, as well as evidence of the use of chocolate—indicates the village's extensive trade connections with central Mexico, the Gulf of California, and turquoise mines around Santa Fe. Taken together, these elements of Ancestral Pueblo lifeways on the Colorado Plateau are known as the Chaco Phenomenon.

In its heyday, the Chaco Phenomenon extended north to Chimney Rock in Colorado, west into Arizona, and as far south as the Zuni Salt Lake. While the communities in the Cibola region, just south of Chaco, also developed into aggregated communities, they were not as large as Chaco's Great Houses and lacked Chaco's extensive cooperative social systems.

ISOMERIC DESIGNS

The growing social complexity of Ancestral Pueblo communities is reflected in evolving pottery designs, such as a Gallup Black-on-white bowl from the Chetro Ketl ruin, a Great House in Chaco Canyon (fig. 38). At first glance, this painted, positive design looks like a series of four hatched elements surrounding the bowl's unpainted, rectangular center. But on closer inspection it's clear that the unpainted negative shapes are exactly the same as the painted forms, the two fitting together like lock and key (fig. 39).

What initially appears to be a simple design painted on a white slipped surface becomes a visually ambiguous optical phenomenon. Was the artist's intent to create a black design on a white background, a white design on a black background, or a duality of visual equals? My term for designs created from positive and negative shapes equal in size and graphic power is isomeric compositions. The term "isomer" combines the Greek words *isos,* meaning "equal," and *méros,* meaning "part." In the Pueblo world, isomeric design is utilizing pairs of positive and negative shapes to create arrangements based on visual dualities.

Three basic isomeric design strategies are used on Ancestral Pueblo pottery. The first involves repeating a series of motifs composed of painted positive shapes and unpainted negative shapes equal in size. An excellent example of this strategy can be seen on a tall cylinder jar from Pueblo Bonito at Chaco Canyon (fig. 40). The painted parts of the design, which are tipped at an angle, create an interconnected web of triangles in a frieze around

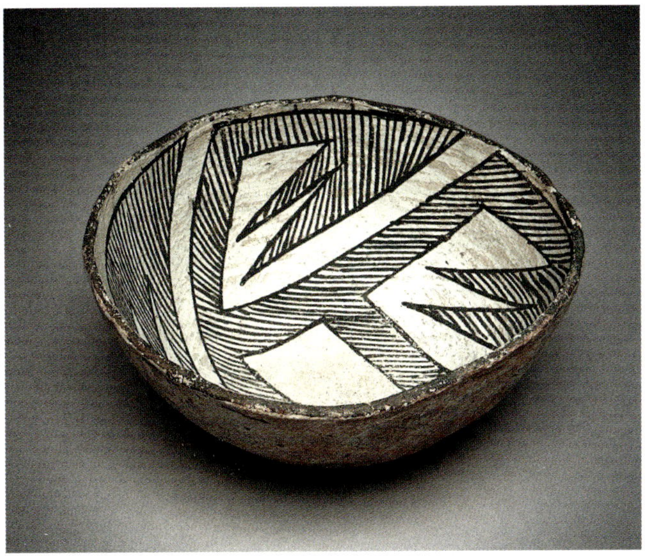

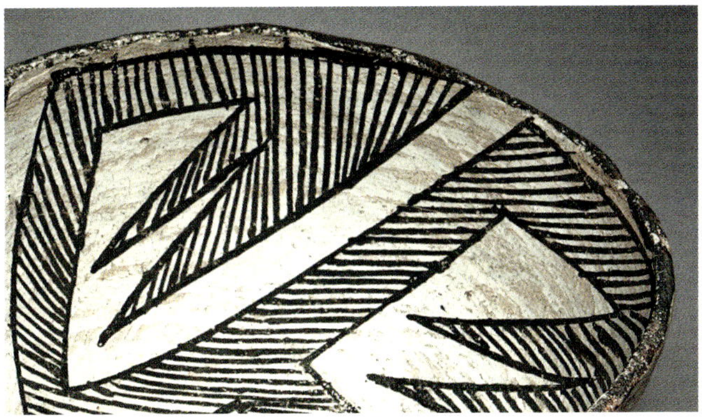

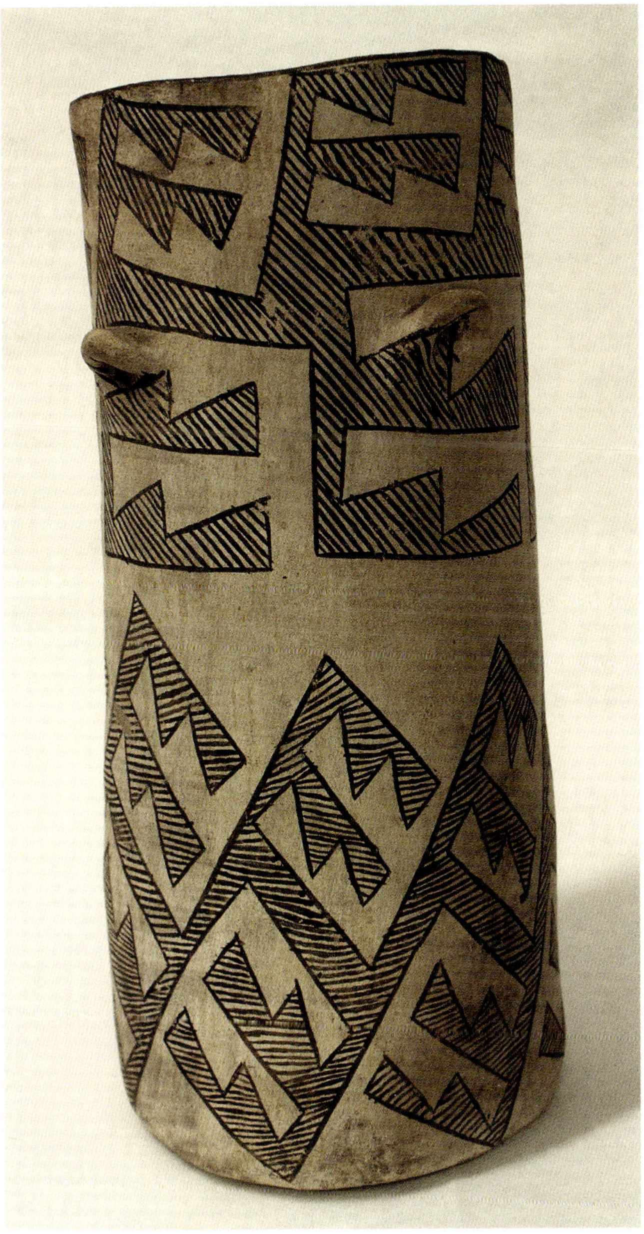

CLOCKWISE TOP LEFT

38
MAKER UNKNOWN
GALLUP BLACK-ON-WHITE BOWL FROM CHETRO KETL,
CIRCA 1000–1125 CE
CLAY AND PIGMENTS, 2¾ X 6 IN. (7 X 15.2 CM)

39
MAKER UNKNOWN
GALLUP BLACK-ON-WHITE BOWL FROM CHETRO KETL (DETAIL),
CIRCA 1000–1125 CE
CLAY AND PIGMENTS, 2¾ X 6 IN. (7 X 15.2 CM)

40
MAKER UNKNOWN
PUEBLO BONITO CYLINDER JAR, N.D.
CLAY AND PIGMENTS, 9½ X 4½ IN. (24.2 X 11.5 CM)

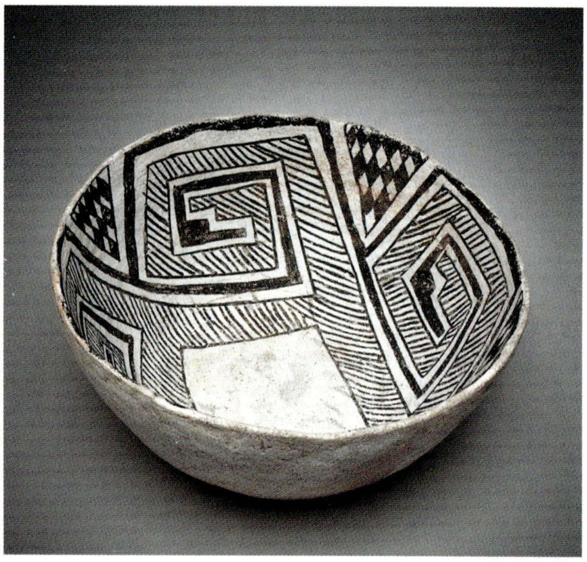

41
MAKER UNKNOWN
GALLUP BLACK-ON-WHITE BOWL,
CIRCA 1000–1150 CE
CLAY AND PIGMENTS, 3⅛ X 6⁹⁄₁₆ X 6¾ IN.
(7.9 X 16.7 X 17.1 CM)

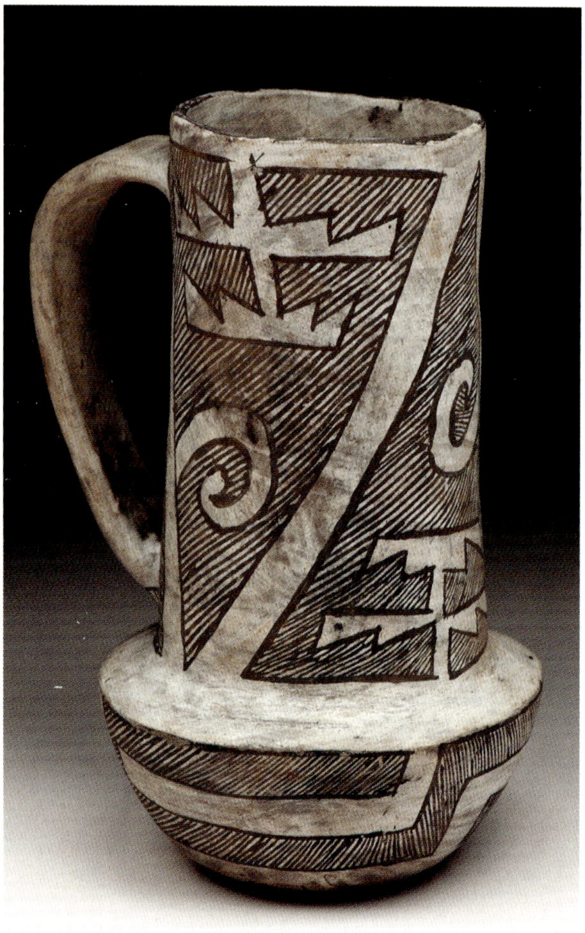

42
MAKER UNKNOWN
PUEBLO BONITO PITCHER, N.D.
CLAY AND PIGMENTS

the vessel, while the unpainted areas are a reversal of the painted forms. The optical ambiguity—is this a gray design on a white form or white on gray—is called a figure-ground relationship composed of equal-sized positive and negative shapes. Invariably, when modern viewers first see isomeric pairs they interpret them as dark forms on a light background. Is this simply a result of modern eyes familiar with reading black letters on white paper, or did the artist intend for the viewer to concentrate on the unpainted shapes?

A second isomeric design strategy used in Ancestral Pueblo pottery involves painting both elements of an isomeric pair but leaving a negative space between the elements. A Gallup Black-on-white bowl from the San José River valley incorporates this strategy with hatched and solid elements (fig. 41). In this approach, the two elements must be separated so that the unpainted negative spaces reverse visually to become positive images.

A third isomeric design strategy involves flipping design elements, as seen in a pitcher from Pueblo Bonito (fig. 42). The pitcher features two friezes, with the painting on the upper portion composed of two forms of hatched triangles with isomeric elements. The triangles are flipped so that they appear dominant within the unpainted areas of the upper body. This optical reversal is also reflected in a painted area of the lower body. In this case, the painted element on the pitcher's base leads the viewer to focus on the unpainted spaces on the upper portion of the pitcher.

The painting on a seed jar (fig. 43) provides insight into the process of creating visual isomers on Ancestral Pueblo pottery. The surface of this globular vessel is divided into a grid of squares set at a forty-five-degree angle. The grid slightly expands or contracts to adjust for the changes in circumference on the spherical surface. The potter created equally shaped forms at the center of each motif by filling in some squares, while leaving others marked only with simple dots. The potter then worked back from each isomeric pair to create a larger design based on interlocking spirals.

The spiral design above the jar's equator is flipped on the jar's lower half, repeating the design. The jar's design is so well conceived that the two friezes fuse together to form a single, unbroken decoration on the jar. This example demonstrates how dualities that are formed by black-and-white central elements, pairs of spirals, and friezes can be merged into a holistic design based on isomeric elements.

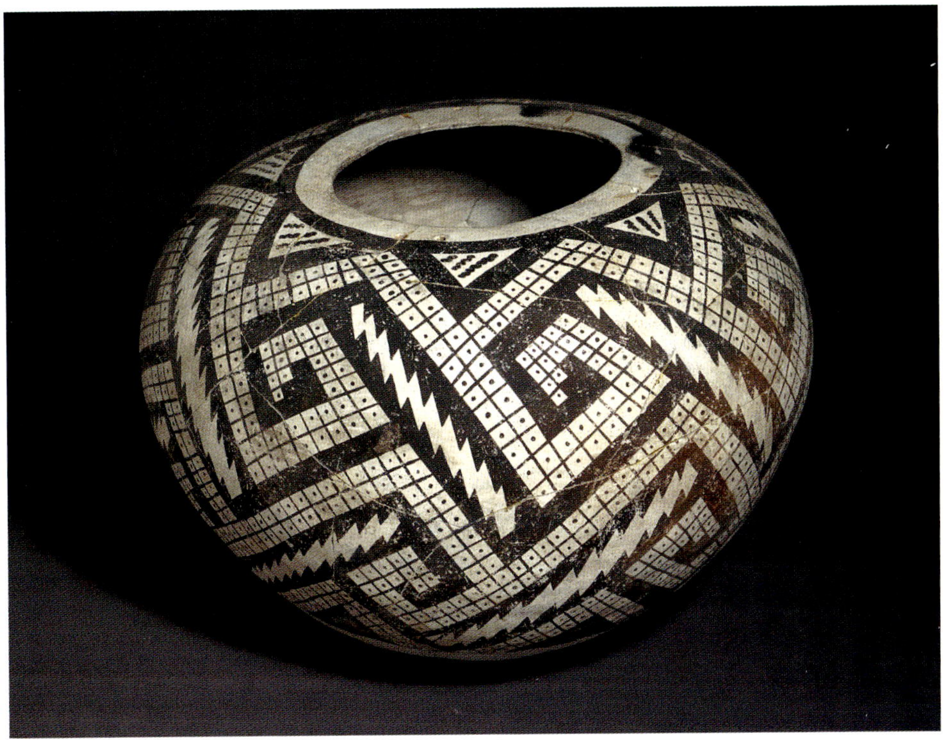

43
MAKER UNKNOWN
GALLUP SEED JAR, CIRCA 1050–1250 CE
CLAY AND PIGMENTS, 12 X 13½ IN. (30.5 X 34.3 CM)

Not all Ancestral Pueblo potters painted isomeric designs, even after these principles were well known. While it seems easy to create isomeric designs on gridded paper, it is difficult to envision painting such motifs on the curved surface of a vessel, making the design fit perfectly. A large Gallup Black-on-white water jar from the Chaco region (fig. 44) demonstrates the challenge of successfully creating isomeric designs. The jar is well crafted with two handholds molded into the lower side. But the hatched isomeric design is wavy and not painted with much control.

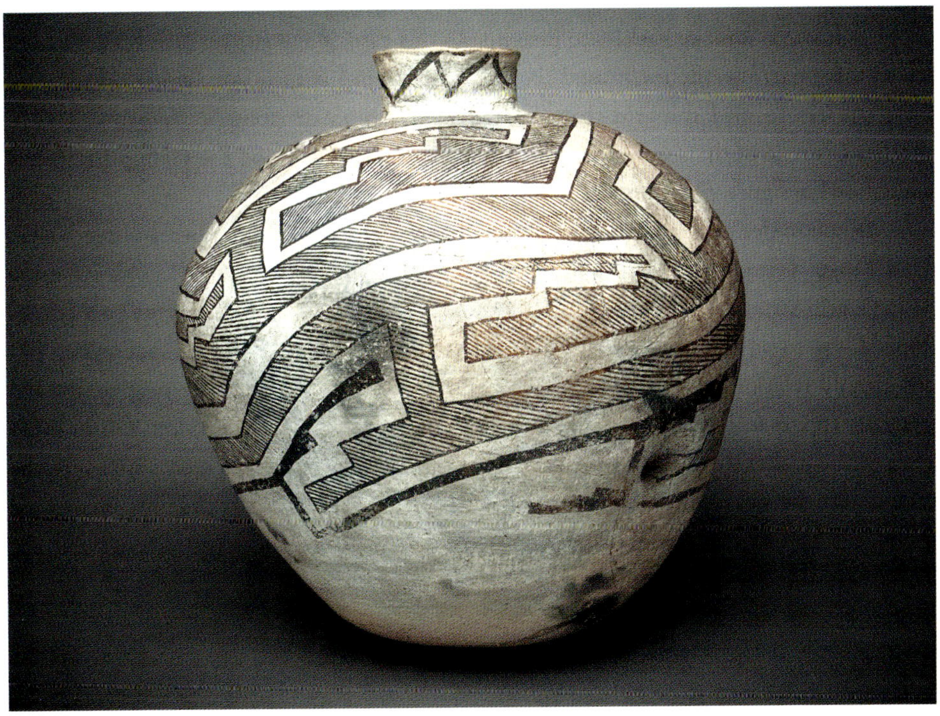

44
MAKER UNKNOWN
GALLUP BLACK-ON-WHITE JAR, CIRCA 1000–1150 CE
CLAY AND PIGMENTS, 14½ X 14½ IN. (36.8 X 36.8 CM)

45
MAKER UNKNOWN
PUEBLO BONITO SANDAL, N.D.
PLANT FIBER

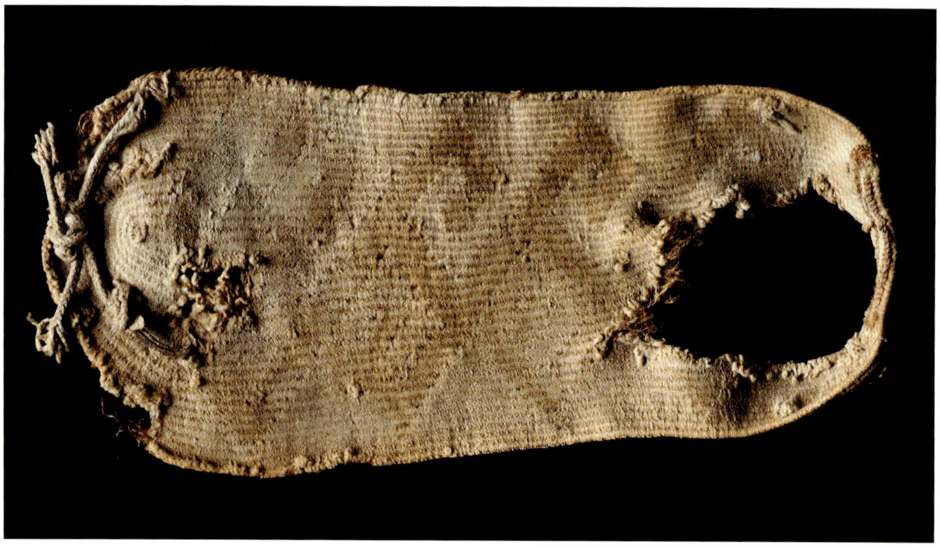

The artistic logic behind isomeric design most likely developed from the warp and weft structure of woven goods. In weaving, visual isomers can be created using different colors of fiber. While this may seem like a simple idea, Pueblo artists pushed the concept to create complex designs on weavings, including on hand-woven sandals. A sandal from Pueblo Bonito (fig. 45) is an excellent study in the development of isomeric designs. The weaver created the design by using dyed fibers in multiple hues, and the resulting interlocking elements are similar to the painting on the Pueblo Bonito cylinder jar in figure 40.

Another example of a woven isomeric design can be seen on an Ancestral Pueblo basket from the Grants, New Mexico, region, southeast of Chaco Canyon (fig. 46). This design features isomeric elements from fibers dyed red and black. Rather than focusing on the colors, however, the viewer is more likely to concentrate on the complex negative patterns between the dyed elements.

The skill required to conceive and execute such a complex design is difficult for people who do not make baskets to imagine. In this case, it appears that the basket maker sewed three narrow stitches around the structural elements to make a square shape, and these squares formed the grid that allowed the creation of isomeric elements. This is another example of the second strategy of isomeric design seen on the Gallup Black-on-white bowl in figure 41.

Isomeric design is also found in a nine-hundred-year-old bi-lobed burden basket from Mogui Canyon in Utah (fig. 47). Here the weaver expanded and contracted the basket's grid structure to construct the bottom lobes. The design highlights two friezes flopped, top to bottom, and within each frieze are multiple pairs of isomers, creating figure-ground relationships that frequently change visually. From one perspective, the red elements appear to be the figure while the black elements form the ground. But in other areas of the basket the black elements pop forward so that the red elements appear as the ground. At the same time the undyed stitches also appear as figures against pigmented grounds. These ambiguous visual relationships were probably more prominent when the basket was new, yet the ambiguity remains.

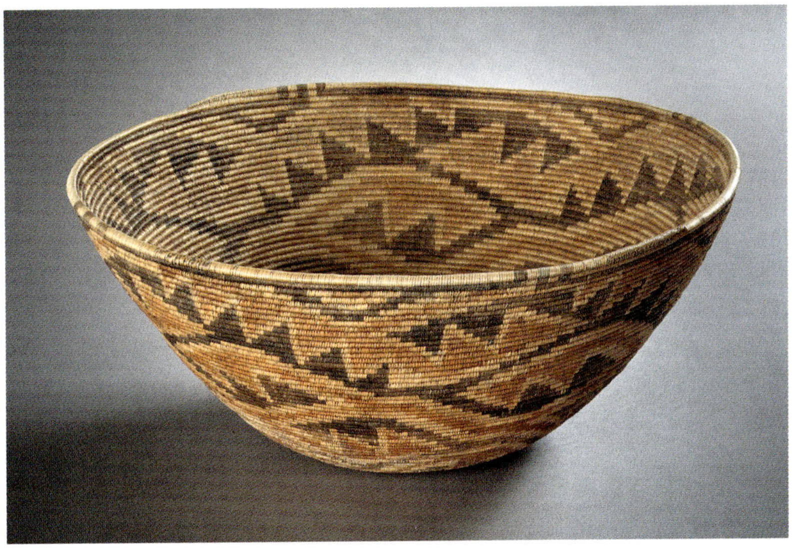

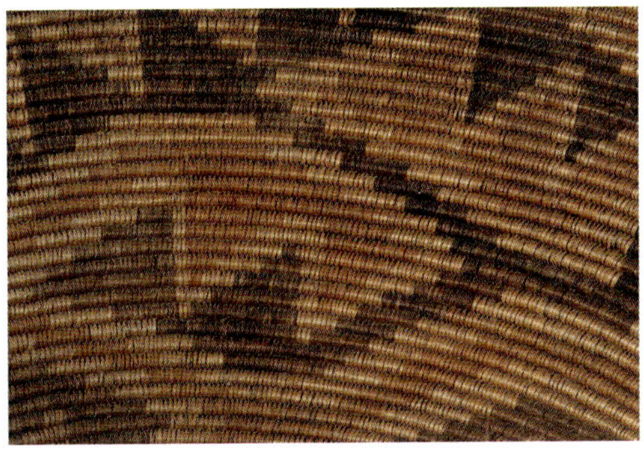

46
MAKER UNKNOWN
COILED PUEBLO BASKET, CIRCA 1200 CE
PLANT FIBER

An Escavada Black-on-white water jar with a small neck from the Cibola region south of Chaco (fig. 48) demonstrates the evolution of isomeric designs into an all-over pattern. The design centers around positive and negative isomeric elements created from painted and unpainted motifs within rectangular forms. While the concept may seem simple, the potter's ability to achieve such a complex design on a spherical form is extraordinary.

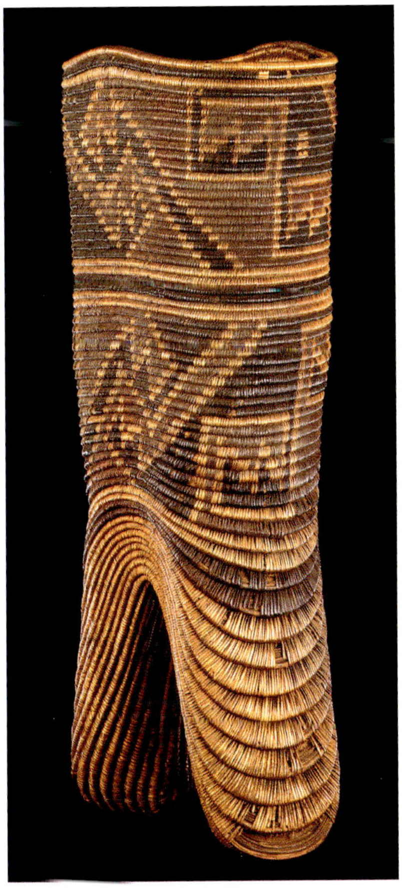

47
MAKER UNKNOWN
ANCESTRAL PUEBLO BI-LOBED BURDEN BASKET, CIRCA 1200 CE
PLANT FIBER, 19 11/16 x 5 7/8 IN. (50 x 15 CM)

48
MAKER UNKNOWN
ESCAVADA BLACK-ON-WHITE JAR, CIRCA 925–1125 CE
CLAY AND PIGMENTS, 11 15/16 x 12 5/16 IN (30.4 x 31.2 CM)

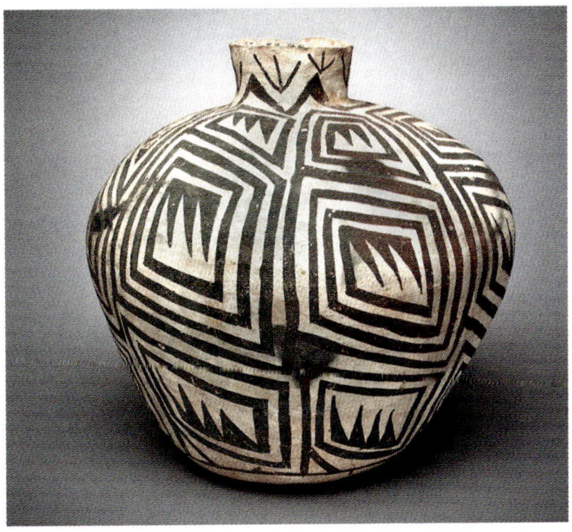

49
MAKER UNKNOWN
PUERCO BLACK-ON-RED BOWL,
CIRCA 1050–1175 CE
CLAY AND PIGMENTS, 4⅛ X 9¼ IN.
(10.4 X 23.5 CM)

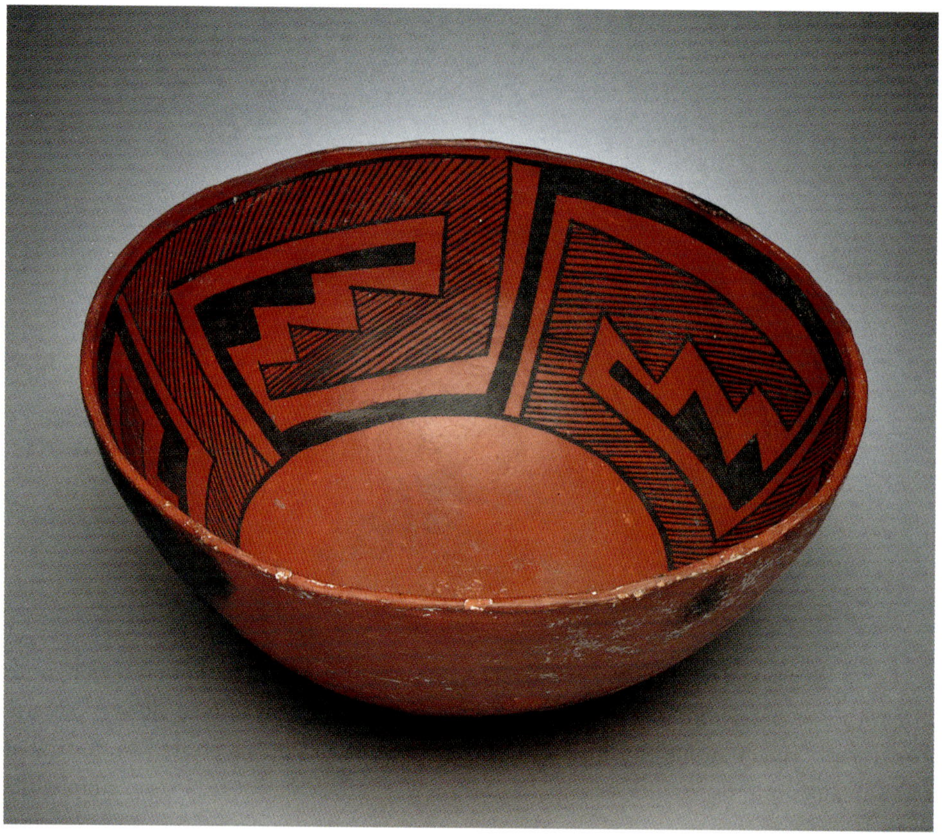

In west-central New Mexico after 1000 CE, potters began experimenting with "Socorro" designs, such as on a Wingate, or Puerco, Black-on-red bowl (fig. 49). The four isomeric pairs in the design are placed in a frieze between two framing lines. Each segment of the design has a three-step motif connected to both a framing line and the adjoining segment of the design. One element of each isomeric motif is hatched with diagonal lines, while the other element is solid.

The Socorro painting style evolved into more complex Tularosa designs based on dualities formed by combinations of unpainted, hatched, and solid forms. Isomeric designs in Tularosa Black-on-white vessels (fig. 50) combine interlocking painted and unpainted spirals within imaginative friezes. Tularosa designs are well suited to the small, globular jars with high, straight necks popular between 1100 and 1200 CE. As exemplified by the jar illustrated in figure 50, small handles are often molded as anthropomorphic forms.

Tularosa-style painting also occurred as a Black-on-red version called St. John's Black-on-red and St. John's Polychrome, a version that added white geometric designs painted with pure kaolin clay on the exterior. Isomeric elements on St. John's Polychrome bowls are found on both the black painted interior and the white exterior designs (fig. 51).

As the technology required to fire iron-based clays to a bright red color became well known, potters experimented with designs painted with copper and lead pigments that caused the paint to sinter and create glaze designs. Although designs painted with such pigments did not make the vessels watertight, they nevertheless became popular at the end of the Great House period. St. John's Black-on-red and St. John's Polychrome

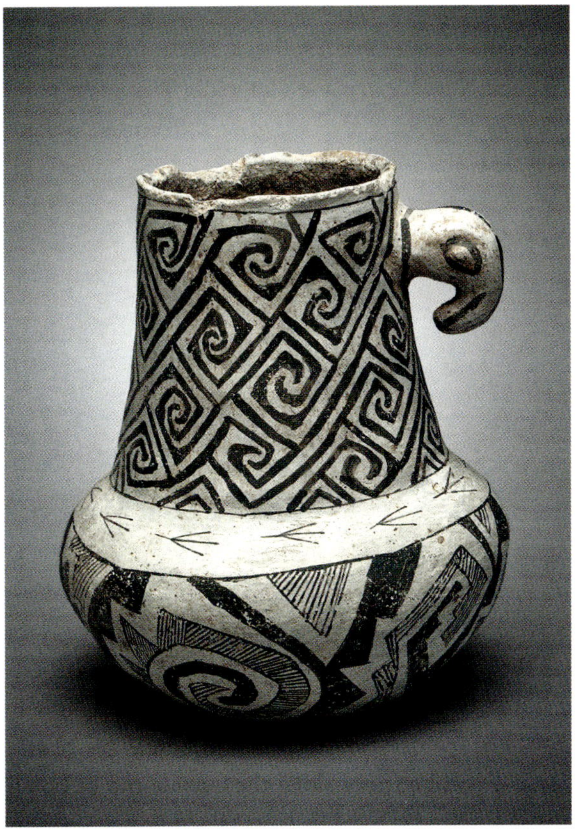

50
MAKER UNKNOWN
TULAROSA BLACK-ON-WHITE JAR,
CIRCA 1100–1200 CE
CLAY AND PIGMENTS, 6⅛ X 4¹⁵⁄₁₆ IN.
(15.5 X 12.5 CM)

51
MAKER UNKNOWN
ST. JOHN'S POLYCHROME BOWL,
CIRCA 1175–1300 CE
CLAY AND PIGMENTS, 5¹³⁄₁₆ X 11¹³⁄₁₆ IN.
(14.8 X 30 CM)

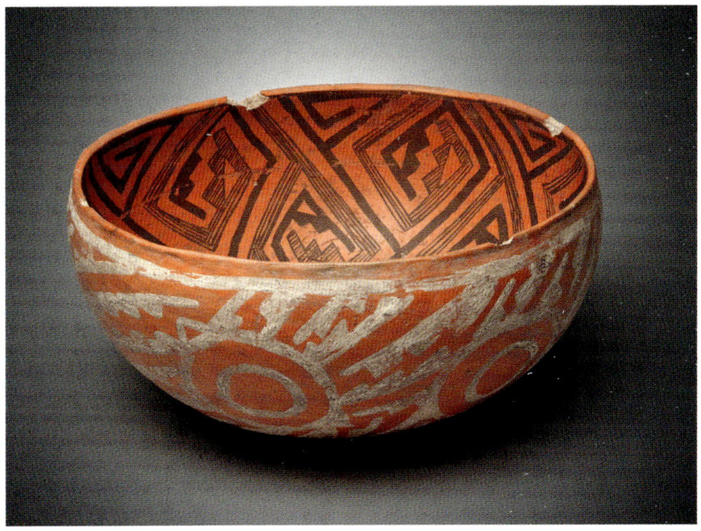

styles, for example, occurred throughout central New Mexico from the Rio Grande west to eastern Arizona. These ceramics formed the basis for the glaze-painted White Mountain Red Wares in Arizona, which were made into the 1400s. Isomeric elements continued to be incorporated within these red ware designs, even though the designs often focused on a single, asymmetric figure painted in the Tularosa style—such as a spiral motif or a mask.

Isomeric designs were also created in the Mimbres area in southwestern New Mexico, although the Ancestral Pueblo pottery from this region is better known for abstract designs of plants, animals, and humans. The borders surrounding these representational depictions and narrative scenes often incorporated isomeric motifs. However, the vessels painted with purely geometric designs have a complexity and visual energy that is astounding (fig. 52). Many examples of this design strategy were painted on mortuary bowls, works that over decades have been illustrated in many other publications, though not in this study. The presence of these designs on Mimbres pottery, however, indicates that this was more than a Chaco phenomenon.

BELOW
52
MAKER UNKNOWN
MIMBRES BLACK-ON-WHITE BOWL,
CIRCA 1060–1110 CE
CLAY AND PIGMENTS, 12 X 8⅞ IN.
(30.5 X 22.6 CM)

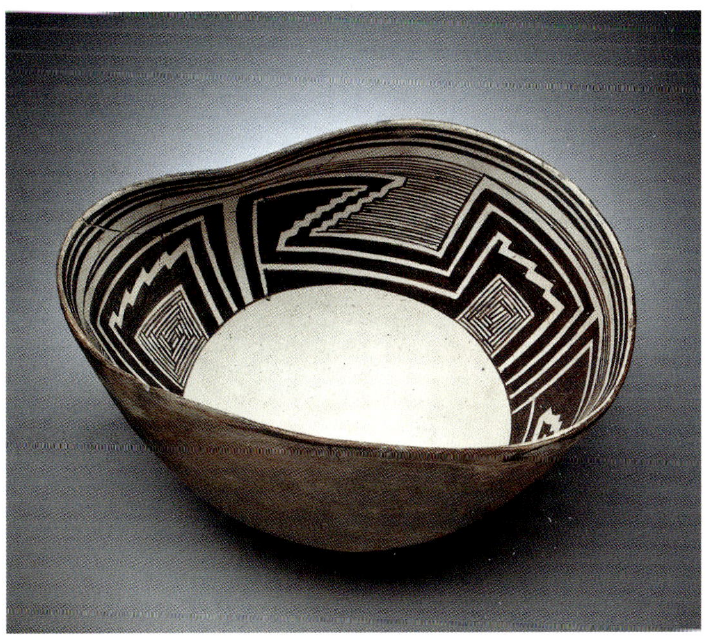

ABANDONMENT AND CONSOLIDATION

During the 1100s, the population in the greater Chaco region moved north to the San Juan River drainage on the border between New Mexico and Colorado. These new communities lasted for another century before they were also abandoned. Isomeric designs continued to be used on the ceramic art from this period. However, potters no longer utilized fine-line hatched elements and emphasized bolder painting of repeated isomeric pairs within friezes. Mesa Verde Black-on-white pottery was painted with vegetal pigments that were absorbed into the polished white slip of the vessel. Organic pigments create lines that appear softer on the edges and do not have the dimensionality of mineral pigments.

By 1325, Ancestral Pueblo populations completely abandoned northern New Mexico and migrated throughout the Southwest. Many moved to the Cibola and Zuni areas, while others congregated along the Rio Grande. These communities established large aggregated villages that did not last long as populations continued to move within the region.

Population shifts in Arizona after the abandonment of the Colorado Plateau resulted in the production of polychrome vessels called Salado wares. These quickly spread from the Hohokam areas around Phoenix, Arizona, into western New Mexico and northern Mexico between 1275 and the early 1400s. Salado vessels were painted with organic black pigments on white backgrounds, and then red slips were applied around the black-on-white motifs to emphasize the images.The black-and-white design blocks were usually angled on the vessel rather than being aligned with its vertical and horizontal axes. Early Salado pottery includes a separate black-on-white frieze along the outside rim of bowls with the majority of the exterior covered with red slip, while later Salado pottery is characterized by increasing complexity and visual dynamism.

Archaeologist Patricia L. Crown analyzed Salado wares and concluded that the people who made them represented a southwestern cult that organized diverse populations into new communities. Curiously, Salado wares, including Escondida Polychromes from northern Mexico (fig. 53), incorporate a variety of isomeric motifs, underscoring the continuation of this design strategy after the abandonment of northwestern New Mexico.

Large populations congregated throughout the Rio Grande and other river valleys from present-day Taos in the north past Socorro in the south. Many of these pueblos were the beginnings of settlements and towns that would still be prosperous during the mid-sixteenth century, when the first Europeans ventured into New Mexico.

The pottery produced by the Ancestral Pueblo populations along the Rio Grande incorporated new design strategies that rarely included isomeric elements. Bowls among these consolidated communities often featured a series of geometric designs that hug the rims of the vessels and flare into their centers. A parrot or other bird form may be painted at the apex of such long, triangular designs. This design style was painted on glazed vessels, such as a Cieneguilla Glaze-on-yellow bowl (fig. 54), as well as on black-on-white pottery. A Jemez Black-on-white bowl (fig. 55) creates a dynamic visual effect as the designs flip back and forth.

Bandelier Black-on-gray pottery produced in the 1400s and 1500s also incorporated triangular motifs. A Bandelier jar with this design strategy (fig. 56) had a soft paste, a characteristic that resulted in such pottery becoming called biscuit ware since it was known to

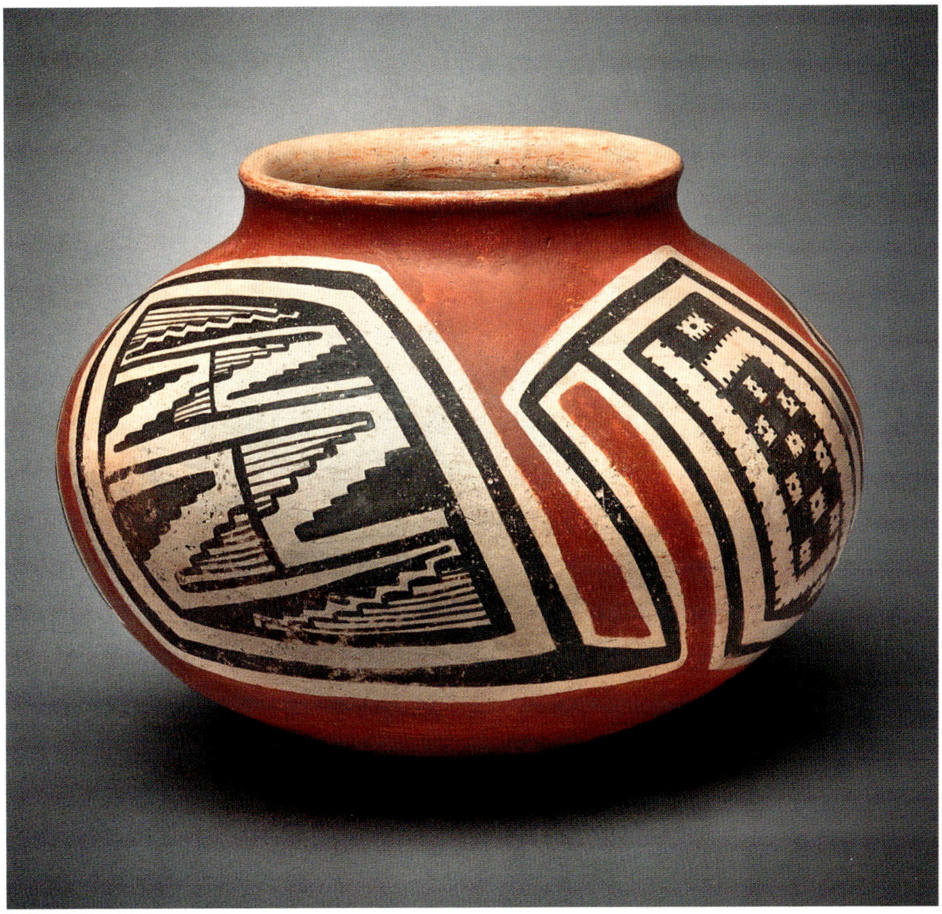

53
MAKER UNKNOWN
ESCONDIDA POLYCHROME JAR,
CIRCA 1275–1400 CE
CLAY AND PIGMENTS, 7 13/16 X 8 3/4 IN.
(19.9 X 22.3 CM)

54
MAKER UNKNOWN
CIENEGUILLA GLAZE-ON-YELLOW BOWL, CIRCA 1325–1425 CE
CLAY AND PIGMENTS, 5 1/8 X 12 3/4 IN.
(13 X 32.4 CM)

55
MAKER UNKNOWN
JEMEZ BLACK-ON-WHITE BOWL,
CIRCA 1300–1750 CE
CLAY AND PIGMENTS, 5 3/16 X 12 3/16 IN.
(13.2 X 31 CM)

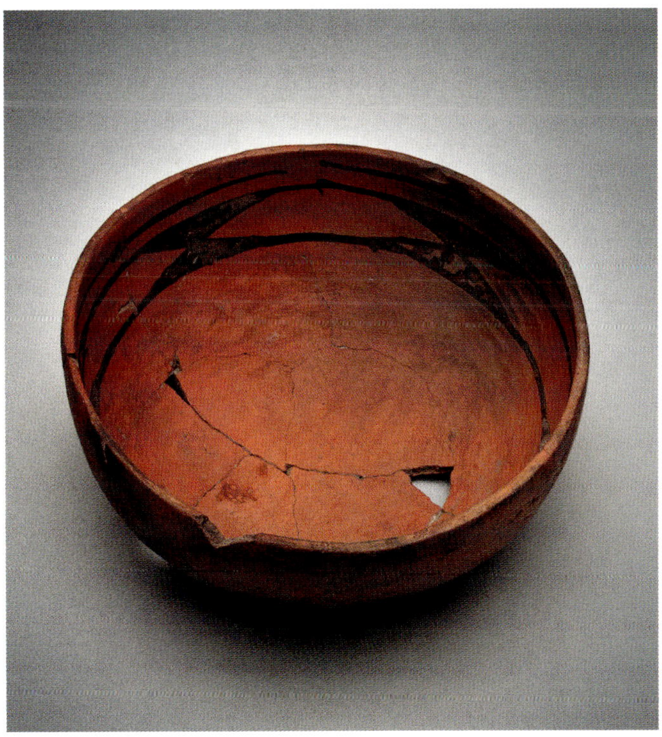

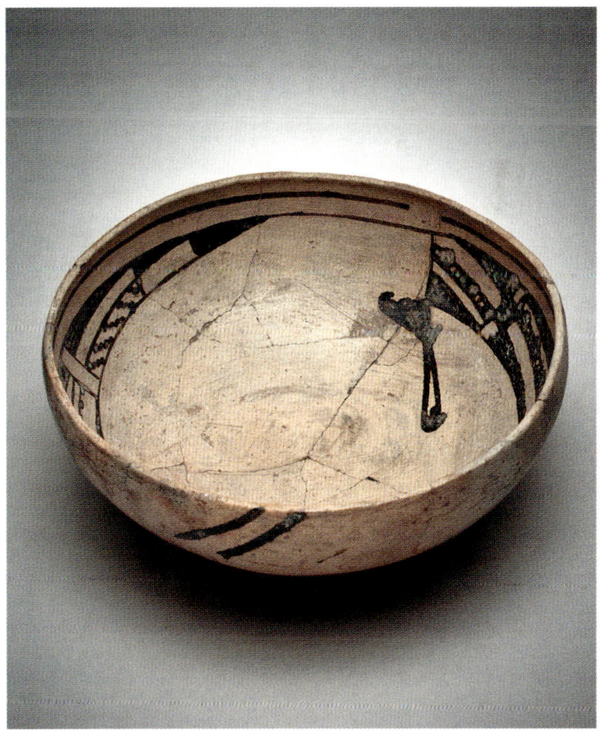

56
MAKER UNKNOWN
BANDELIER BLACK-ON-GRAY JAR,
CIRCA 1400–1550 CE
CLAY AND PIGMENTS, 9 15/16 X 15 3/8 IN.
(25.3 X 39.1 CM)

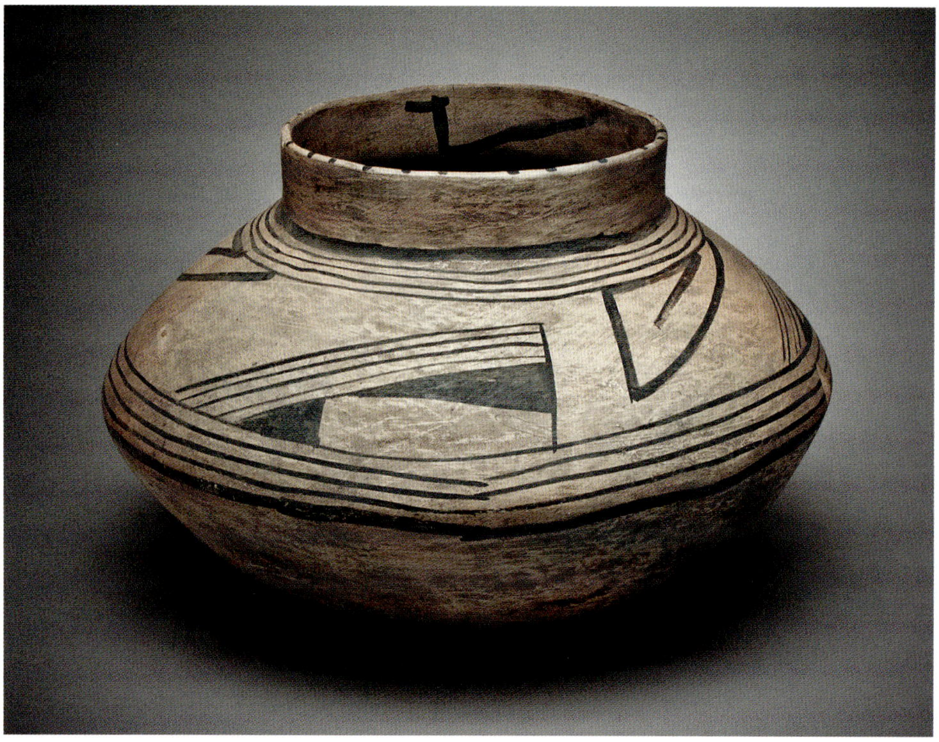

57
MAKER UNKNOWN
PUARAY GLAZE POLYCHROME JAR,
CIRCA 1515–1650 CE
CLAY AND PIGMENTS, 10 5/8 X 14 11/16 IN.
(27 X 37.3 CM)

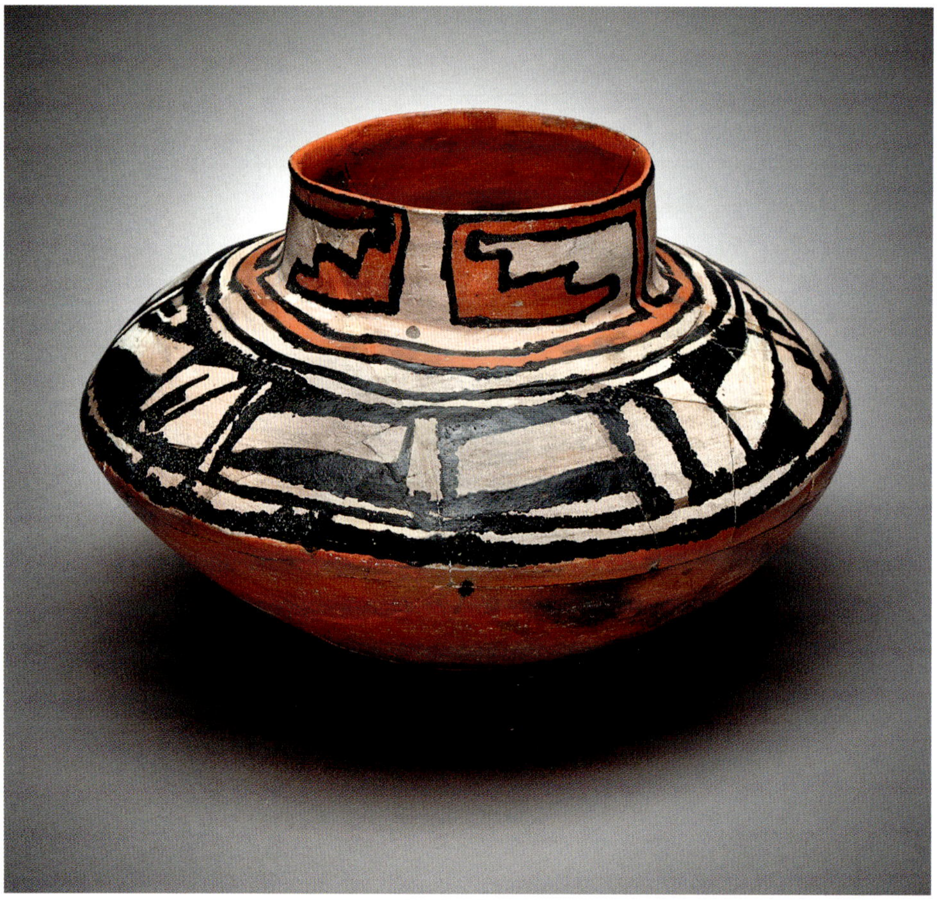

crumble. Squat jars with high collars were popular throughout the Rio Grande pueblos after the consolidations of the fourteenth century.

At the end of the ancestral period, when the first Hispanic explorers ventured north from Mexico City, Pueblo potters still painted designs associated with the consolidated Rio Grande communities. Sometimes these works incorporated isomeric pairs as well. For example, a Puaray Glaze Polychrome jar produced between 1515 and 1650 incorporates a frieze of them around its high neck (fig. 57). This work is particularly interesting because the glaze pigments flowed loosely as they vitrified during the firing. Most isomeric designs were associated with precision painting, but this work celebrates the imprecise motifs that occurred by accident.

Art historian J. J. Brody notes that archaeologists who categorize Pueblo pottery are either "lumpers" or "splitters." Indeed, archaeologists have divided the styles of Ancestral Pueblo pottery into hundreds of categories based primarily on minute differences in the qualities of materials. However, the use of isomeric elements appears in a wide variety of archaeologist-defined ceramic styles.

The use of isomeric motifs was first associated with the consolidation of agricultural communities into villages and Great House economic systems. After the 1200s, as large communities coalesced from migrating groups, they continued to be used, along with new design strategies. These designs appear to represent important aspects of Ancestral Pueblo society. A contemporary view of Pueblo pottery from this period interprets the use of isomeric motifs as reflections of the Pueblo world, as metonyms of the successful agricultural communities that triumphed over a challenging environment.

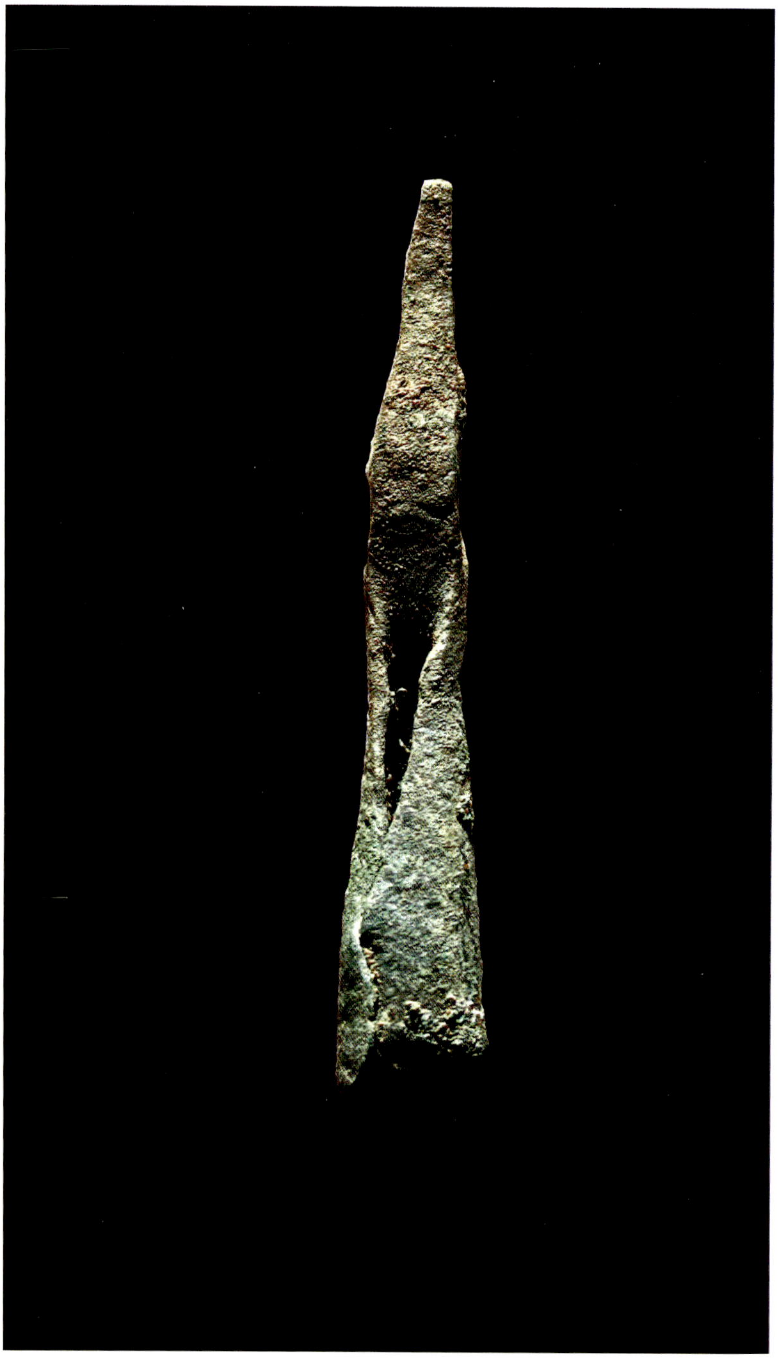

CHAPTER 3

From the Spanish Entrada to the Mexican Republic

In recent archaeological surveys, Charles Haecker and Clay Mathers discovered unusual arrowheads at Piedras Marcadas, a campsite north of Albuquerque on the banks of the Rio Grande (Wilcox 2009). These weren't ordinary flint projectile points but copper points crafted for crossbows in a style that hasn't been made since the mid-sixteenth century (fig. 58). The discovery affirmed that Francisco Vásquez de Coronado's New Mexico expedition had camped at the site between 1540 and 1542.

Coronado led the first major *entrada* (entry) into northern New Spain—now New Mexico—in the winter of 1540. Coronado's search for riches led him to the Zuni pueblo of Hawikuh in the Cibola region, a town reputed to be larger than Mexico City. The slow-moving expedition proceeded with foot soldiers, armored horsemen, and more than a thousand Indian servants and slaves, plus livestock, horses, mules, and supply carts.

Coronado led an advance party of more than one hundred soldiers to Hawikuh, where they quickly realized that Hawikuh was not as big as Mexico City, nor were its residents adorned with gold or silver. In fact, Hawikuh was nearly abandoned, as women and children had fled, leaving only warriors to defend the village. On July 7, 1540, Coronado declared the Cibola region a province of New Spain, an order that put the Zunis under the civil rule of King Charles V and the religious authority of the Catholic Church.

When the Zunis did not immediately comply with the Spaniards' demands for food and supplies, war ensued. But the Zuni warriors' hide shields were no match for their opponents' shotgun-like harquebuses and powerful crossbows. And when the battle was over, Coronado's troops sacked the town in frustration at finding no gold, no luxury goods, and little food.

Next, Coronado moved his forces to the Tiguex pueblos on the banks of the Rio Grande north of present-day Albuquerque. From a base camp at Tiguex, he sent contingents west to the Hopi mesas in Arizona, north to Taos Pueblo, east to the Great Plains near Blackwater Draw, and to Quivira and Salinas pueblos. Each of these groups also returned without riches. After the expedition's dreams of instant wealth were dashed, once more soldiers again unleashed their anger against the Pueblo peoples, causing Spanish-Pueblo relations to further deteriorate. When Spanish sieges at the pueblos of Moho and Arenal destroyed the villages, Pueblo resistance mounted in the middle Rio Grande. Coronado responded by burning ten Tiwa villages in northern New Mexico in the spring of 1542.

58
MAKER UNKNOWN
CROSSBOW ARROW POINT OR "BOLT HEAD," CIRCA 1540
COPPER, 2 1/16 IN. (5.3 CM)

But Coronado's actions had violated Spanish law. He and his officers were convicted in absentia in Mexico City of crimes against the Pueblos. Upon hearing of the conviction, Coronado returned to Mexico City and successfully appealed the verdict. Nonetheless, the expedition left the Pueblo world with animosity toward Spaniards.

Don Juan de Oñate finally organized the first permanent Spanish colony in New Mexico in 1598, after a half-century of other failed explorations. Like others before him, Oñate sought to save Native souls, develop mining interests, and expand the Crown's landholdings. The expedition included ten Franciscan priests, more than one hundred soldiers with nearly fifty oxcarts, and six thousand head of livestock—a huge caravan to be moving through areas with few water resources. Recalling their earlier experiences with Coronado, some southern Tiwa communities abandoned their villages in fear of the advancing expedition.

Oñate camped at Ohkay Owingeh, changing its name to San Juan Pueblo and demanding food and shelter for the colonists, who turned part of the pueblo into a Spanish compound. Now the official governor of New Mexico, Oñate designated five pueblos provinces—Acoma, Hopi, Santo Domingo (now called Kewa), San Juan, and Zuni—and assigned a priest to each.

However, Oñate's search for mineral wealth was proving no more successful than that of others before him. As part of this search, small parties were sent outside of the Rio Grande Valley. While on a march to the Pacific Ocean in the fall of 1598, Juan de Zaldívar stopped at Acoma Pueblo and offered tools in exchange for provisions. When residents did not respond, Zaldívar and some of his men climbed the high pueblo mesa to demand supplies. The Acomas attacked, and Zaldívar and thirteen others were killed.

Oñate sent a force of seventy soldiers to avenge the deaths, and between January 21 and 25, 1599, more than eight hundred Acoma warriors were killed. Nearly six hundred prisoners were then marched to colony headquarters. After presiding over their trial, Oñate sentenced the detainees. As punishment, two Hopi men had a hand amputated, while Acoma men over twenty-five years of age had a foot severed. Boys and women over twelve were sentenced to twenty years of servitude, and girls were sent to convents in Mexico. The extreme punishments were intended to demonstrate that challenges to Spanish authority would not be tolerated.

In 1605, Oñate led an expedition of thirty soldiers to the Gulf of California and returned by way of Inscription Rock, now known as El Morro National Monument. Oñate left an inscription that journalist Charles F. Lummis later translated and published in *Some Strange Corners of Our Country*:

> Passed by here the officer Don Juan de Oñate to the discovery of the sea of the South on the 16th of April, year 1605. (Lummis 1892,170)

A photograph of Oñate's inscription shows that it was written over a Pueblo petroglyph of a katsina figure, an act that can only be interpreted as an expression of Spanish domination over the Pueblos (fig. 59). Lummis also published a sketchy wood engraving produced from his photograph of the inscription, but his published image omitted the petroglyph.

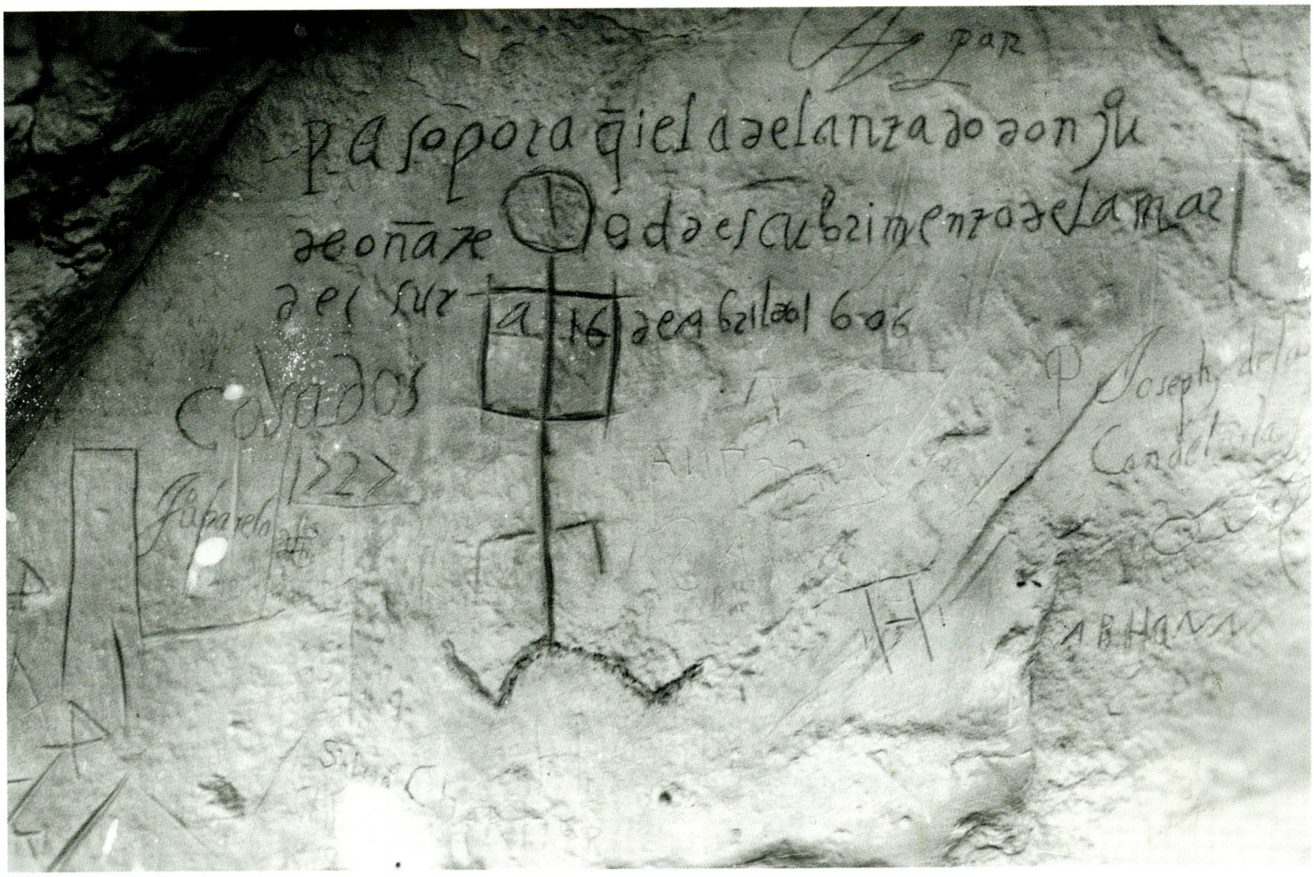

59

DOROTHY STEWART (1891–1955)

PASSED BY HERE THE ADELANTADO (GOVERNOR) JUAN DE OÑATE TO THE DISCOVERY OF THE SEA OF THE SOUTH ON THE 16 APRIL THE YEAR 1605,

CIRCA 1930–1940

GELATIN SILVER PRINT, 5 x 7 IN. (12.7 x 17.8 CM)

SUMMARY OF *ENCOMIENDA* RELATIONSHIPS

The Spanish colonists brought to New Mexico an economy based on the *encomienda*, a system of rights granted to individuals by the Spanish Crown in exchange for tribute and other obligations to the colony. In reality, the *encomienda* system established feudal relationships between the king of Spain, his representatives in New Mexico, and the pueblos. European feudalism defined relationships between kings and nobles, and between landowners and the landless serfs who worked the farms. However, in New Mexico, the Native communities were not landless but held their lands in common, the Spanish concept of private land ownership being foreign to the Pueblo people.

The complex rules of the *encomienda* system also involved mutual obligations between Hispanic colonists, Franciscan missionaries, and Pueblo communities. The colonists and missionaries were required to teach Native peoples about Christ and provide military protection. The system also allowed civil authorities and Franciscans to conscript Indian labor for governmental projects, to build churches, for domestic servitude, and to provide food and other local resources. While slavery was illegal, it was legal to capture individuals and indenture them for twenty years or sell them into servitude for a fixed period so that, technically, they were not considered slaves. Captured individuals from nomadic Apache, Comanche, Navajo, and Ute tribes provided a long-term source of labor that was an important component of the colony's economy.

60
MAKER UNKNOWN
TEWA POLYCHROME SOUP BOWL,
CIRCA 1650–1725
CLAY AND PIGMENTS

61
MAKER UNKNOWN
KOTYITI GLAZE POLYCHROME JAR,
CIRCA 1650–1700
CLAY AND PIGMENTS, 8⅞ X 9 13/16 IN. (22.5 x 25 CM)

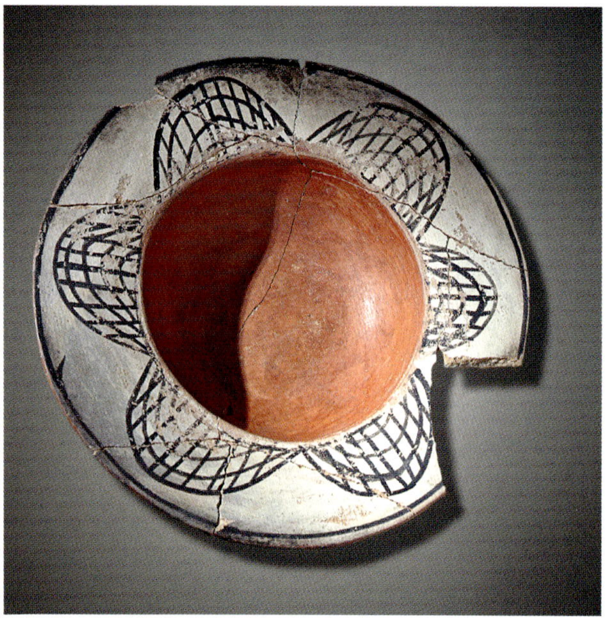

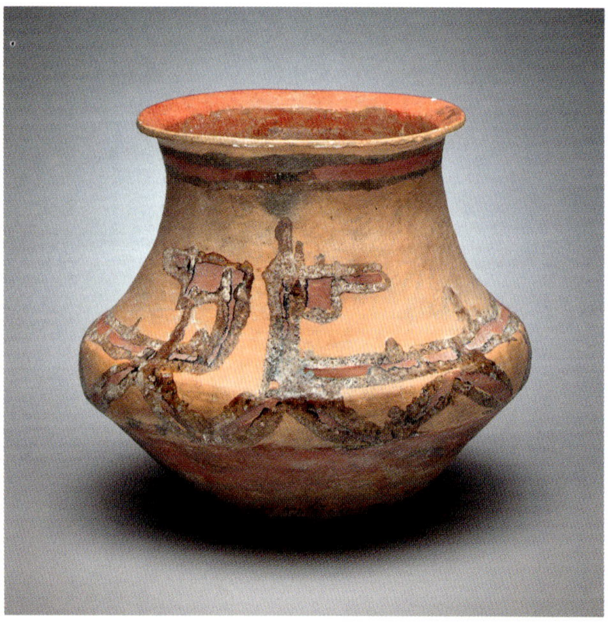

ART DURING THE COLONIZATION

Franciscan missionaries maintained tight control over the religious art of the region during the first eighty years of Spanish colonization. Virtually all Catholic imagery in New Mexico was imported via Mexico, including the religious paintings, sculptures, and altar screens used to adorn Hispanic churches and for religious instruction in the Pueblo missions. The local friars exercised strict control over Pueblo religious activities, forbidding them to practice their religions or speak disparagingly about the friars or Catholicism. While the friars did not require the Pueblos to attend church, they destroyed the religious paraphernalia necessary for them to maintain their ritual activities.

As relationships developed between the Pueblos and Hispanic colonists, Pueblo artists produced pottery that reflected their fast-changing world. A Tewa Polychrome soup bowl from Cuyamungue, north of Santa Fe, is an example of the cultural fusions that occurred during the 1600s (fig. 60). This European-style soup bowl represents a form that was not made until after the arrival of Hispanic colonists. The painting on the bowl, however, incorporates traditional Tewa designs and a red-slipped bottom.

In addition to matte-paint pottery, glaze wares were still produced at pueblos at the Galisteo Basin, Pecos, and Zia during the early colonial period. Kotyiti Glaze Polychrome is an example of the late glaze pottery produced at this time (fig. 61). Pottery expert Francis H. Harlow complained that Kotyiti Glaze Polychrome pottery is often "slightly asymmetric" with "bumpy surfaces." He further noted that its decoration and soft slips "do not wear well" (Harlow 1973, 44). Perhaps Harlow's problem with seventeenth-century Pueblo glaze wares is that they offer an alternative aesthetic paradigm to the precise linear painting associated with earlier styles. Indeed, the flowing glazes on Kotyiti vessels emphasize the visual accidents associated with glaze pigments.

Ironically, Pueblo pottery was not heavily influenced by the Spaniards' domination in economic and social affairs. Colonists were forbidden to live on Pueblo lands, and this kept the two communities separated. In addition, the number of colonists during the seventeenth century was quite small compared to the number of Native peoples in New Mexico. In 1630, for example, 250 Spaniards lived in Santa Fe with 750 Indian and mixed race servants (Gutiérrez 1991, 104). The entire Pueblo population was estimated at 60,000, though this was probably an exaggeration. These conditions accounted for the different aesthetic perspectives among communities.

The Franciscans also played a role in the maintenance of cultural distance between the colonists and the Pueblos.

Rather than engaging with the communities they served, friars generally did not learn Pueblo languages, relying on indigenous translators instead. And their ongoing disagreements with the Spanish government over who had ultimate authority over the Pueblos—God or government—further widened the cultural divide. Ultimately, all of these factors limited the interactions between Indians and Hispanic colonists, between Pueblo and Spanish culture, and between the multiple aesthetic traditions of the time.

THE PUEBLO REVOLT

Religious, cultural, and economic tensions between the Spaniards and the Pueblos were exacerbated by a series of droughts beginning in the 1650s. The demands for tribute in corn, cotton, hides, and other goods by holders of *encomienda* rights placed an increased burden on the Pueblos during years of drought. Pueblo religious leaders blamed the drought on the Spaniards and friars, who had forbidden them to perform ritual rain dances and had destroyed their religious objects. As harvests failed in the 1660s and 1670s, Pueblo revivalists gained political power. By the 1660s, Spanish authorities discovered a plot against the kingdom and hanged six Piro Indian men.

A second plot was soon organized by Esteban Clemente, a Piro Indian who had learned to read and was a favorite of the friars. Navajo and Apache raids were on the rise as they searched for stored grain and corn, and the efforts of the friars failed to ameliorate conditions. In an effort to encourage rains, Clemente collected ritual sculptures and hid them in his room. When the governor learned of his plan, Clemente, too, was hanged.

A third and more ambitious plot to expel the Spanish was now envisioned by Po'Pay (also spelled Popé), a religious leader from Ohkay Owingeh. Po'Pay argued that the agricultural failures were a sign that the katsinas were angered by Pueblo allegiance to Spanish ways and the Catholic Church. After months of careful planning, the Pueblos began a revolt at dawn on August 10, 1680. By the time it was over, the Pueblos had destroyed all vestiges of Catholicism and Spanish culture: churches were sacked, bells destroyed, religious images burned, and homes ravaged. Nineteen priests, two lay brothers, and 380 colonists were killed, compared to forty-seven Pueblo rebels. The Pueblos' victory was clear as Governor Otermín led 1,946 men, women, children, servants, and slaves south on foot to safety in El Paso del Norte.

Virtually nothing remains from the Spanish artistic record of the first eighty-two years of Spanish occupation. With the exception of iron, guns, horses, agricultural products, and other useful materials introduced by the Spaniards, the Pueblos cleansed themselves of all things Spanish.

RECONQUEST

While it might seem that Pueblo unity would be invigorated by the Pueblo Revolt, the opposite occurred. The Pueblos quarreled among themselves, and discontent grew between Tewa and Keres groups. Po'Pay's organizational skills could not overcome the dissention, and despite his role in the revolt he disappeared from the political scene.

Meanwhile, Governor Otermín in El Paso del Norte would not accept defeat and began planning a return to Santa Fe. Beginning in 1681 his and other attempts at reconquest would fail. The appointment of Don Diego de Vargas in 1690, however, led to the successful reconquest of New Mexico. By September 13, 1692, Vargas and a force of Spanish soldiers and Indian allies, including Keres warriors, were standing in front of the Palace of the Governors, which now was occupied by Pueblo people. The next day Vargas and three friars marched into the palace and took possession of New Mexico for the second time.

At the time, it appeared that the reconquest had been accomplished without bloodshed. But when a caravan of one thousand new colonists arrived in Santa Fe in December 1693, unprepared for the harsh New Mexico winter, tensions mounted. Cold and short of food and supplies, the colonists demanded that the Pueblo people vacate the palace to make room for them. A daylong battle began in which Vargas captured and shot seventy Tewa and Tano warriors, initiating a war that would last three more years. As violence raged, Vargas supplemented his troops with Pueblo allies who fought with the Spaniards against Pueblos who opposed the colonists.

The Pueblo Revolt had sparked massive population movements throughout New Mexico. Pueblos who feared retribution if the Spanish returned to the area moved to defensive, mountainous locations or to other Pueblo communities. Tewa groups from San Lazaro and San Cristobal, south of Santa Fe, moved to Hopi, in Arizona, where they constructed a Tewa village on First Mesa. Residents from San Marcos and San Felipe moved to Cochiti, and refugees from Zia and Santa Ana founded La Alameda. Other families from multiple pueblos relocated on impregnable Black Mesa, while Jemez people reoccupied abandoned mountain sites and created new pueblos.

In 1694, major battles were fought between the Spaniards and refugee communities occupying inaccessible mesas at Cochiti, Jemez, and San Ildefonso. A skirmish at San Ildefonso's Black Mesa finally drove the refugees back to their villages. And after a two-year battle, Vargas forced the abandonment of a refugee community composed of residents from Alameda, Jemez, Puaray, Sandia, Santa Ana, and Zia, then burned the village so it could not be reused.

A fragile truce was maintained between forces until another revolt was launched in June 1696, during which five Franciscans were killed and Spanish missions burned. Vargas and troops defeated the rebels after six months of fighting. Pueblo populations again moved to escape retribution. Residents from Jemez fled to the rough terrain and inaccessible buttes of the Gobernador region of northwest New Mexico, where consolidated communities of Navajo and Pueblo peoples lived until 1750.

Pottery produced after the Pueblo Revolt naturally reflected the tribal unrest and shifting populations. Some pottery styles, such as Kotyiti Glaze Polychrome (fig. 61), came to an end, while new styles emerged as consolidated communities merged aesthetic ideas and materials. These artistic fusions are evident in the pottery known as Pueblo Gobernador Polychrome, whose design reflects the political uncertainty after the reconquest. In the example shown in figure 62, friezes are subdivided into smaller panels, each containing a design element from a different pottery tradition.

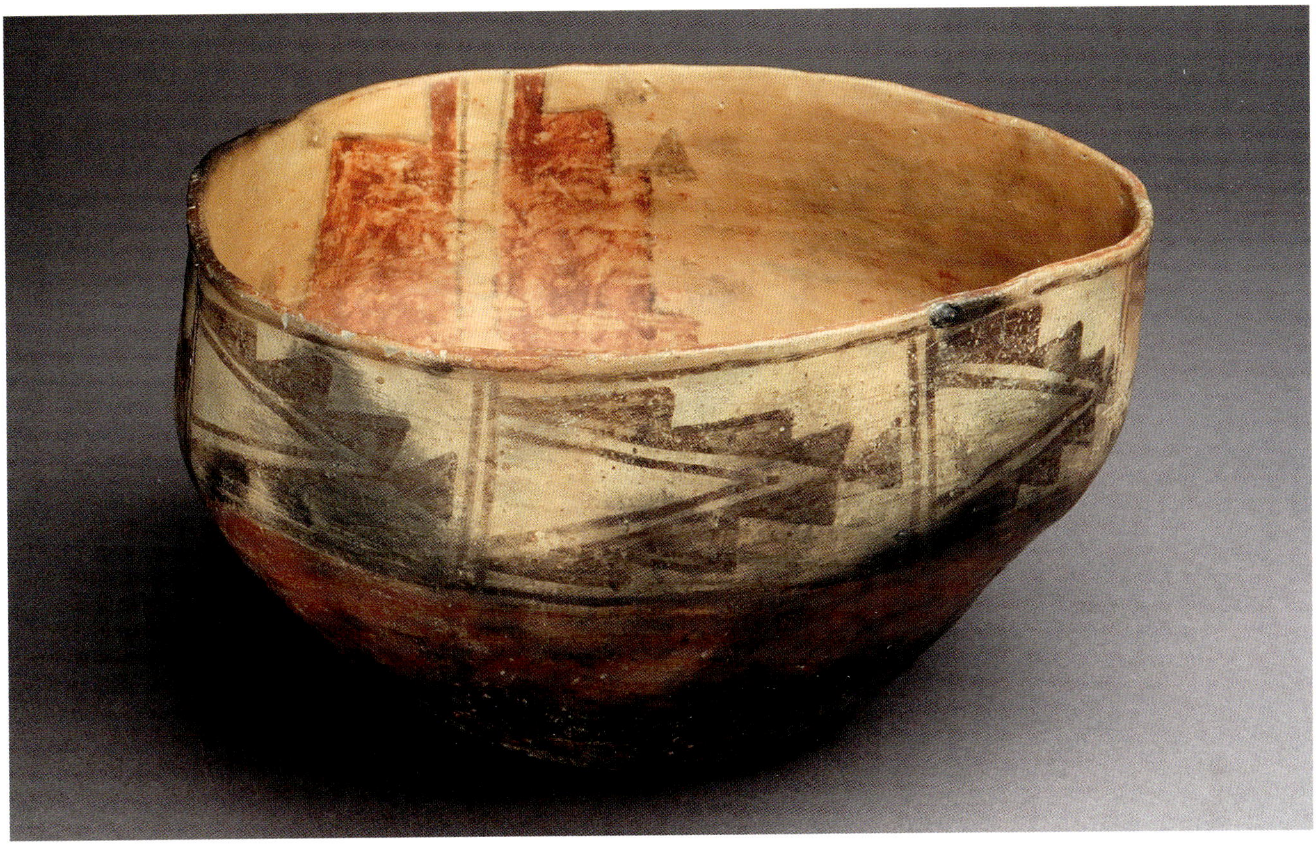

62
MAKER UNKNOWN
PUEBLO GOBERNADOR POLYCHROME BOWL, CIRCA 1700–1750
CLAY AND PIGMENTS, 4¾ X 8¾ IN.
(12.1 X 22.2 CM)

A NEW FORM OF COLONIALISM

After the reconquest, the *encomienda* system was abolished. The friars were more flexible in their attitudes toward Pueblo lifeways; Pueblo activities formerly considered to be satanic were now often ignored. Better relationships between Spanish and Pueblo communities developed in part because of mutual understanding that a combined defense against nomadic Indian raids was important to the survival of both cultures.

With the arrival of more colonists by the early 1700s, the full social complexity of Spanish society took root. Class distinctions were based on wealth and land, political distinctions were based on political practices in Mexico and Spain, racial distinctions were determined by family background, and caste distinctions were created within communities. These civil relationships were further complicated by the hierarchy of the Catholic Church and the rules of the Inquisition in Mexico City. Disputes raged throughout the colonial period between the Church and the Crown over who was mightier, God or king.

Trade flourished. While the Spanish king continued to control commerce, Mexico held a monopoly on goods imported into New Mexico. The need for religious objects increased rapidly as the Hispanic population grew and new churches and Pueblo missions were built to replace those destroyed in the Pueblo Revolt. In addition to imported religious objects from Mexico, Spain, and elsewhere in Europe, local paintings on animal skins became an important source of Catholic imagery. Franciscan friars painted saints

63
MAKER UNKNOWN ("FRANCISCAN F" STYLE, NEW MEXICO)
SAN FRANCISCO DE ASÍS / ST. FRANCIS OF ASSISI, EARLY 1700S
WATER-SOLUBLE PAINT ON HIDE,
68 7/8 X 41 5/16 IN. (175 X 105 CM)

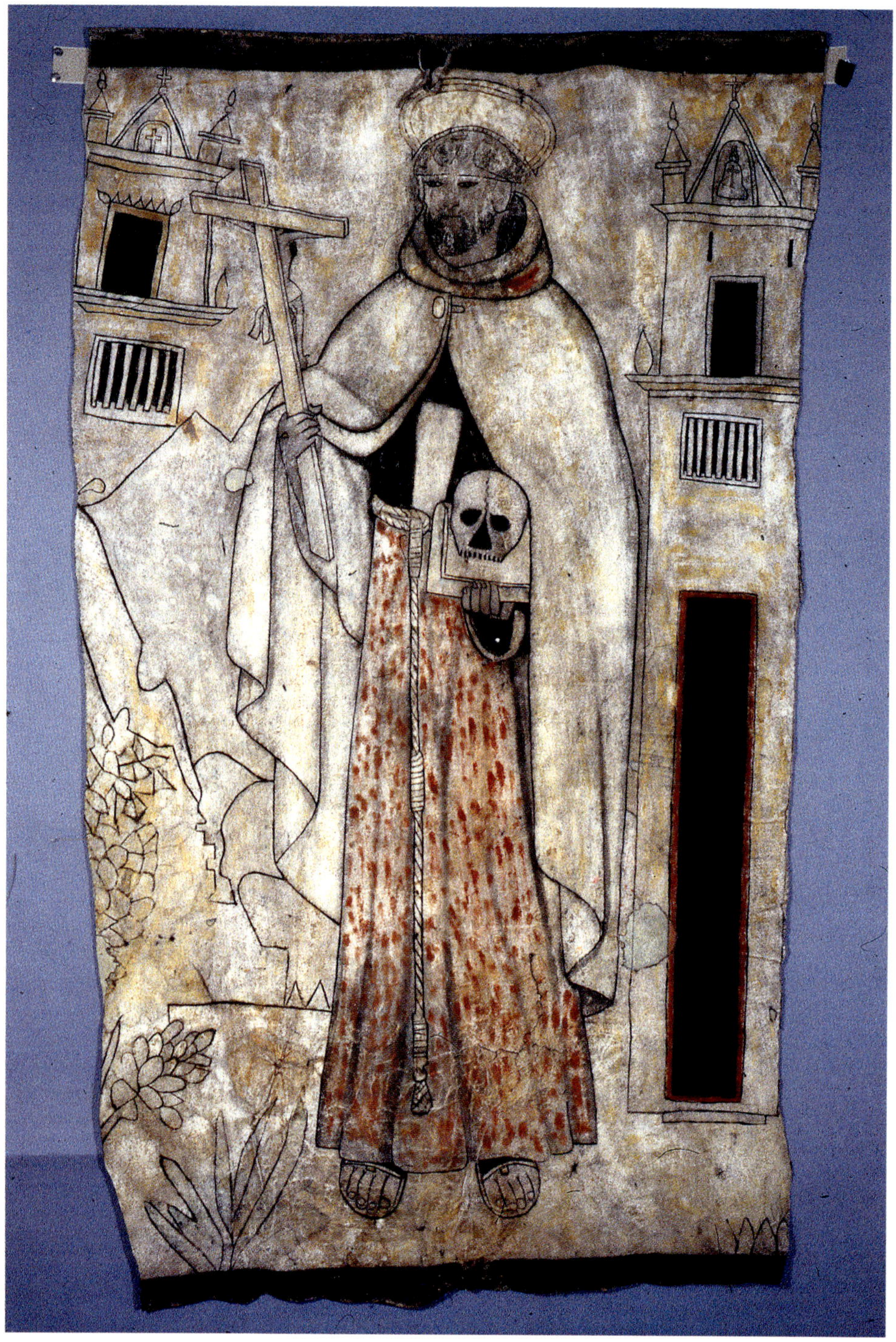

on the tanned hides, a material they had adopted from Pueblo artists as early as the seventeenth century. It is believed that some Pueblo artists may have even been employed to create religious hide paintings.

An example of a religious hide painting from the early 1700s is *San Francisco de Asís (St. Francis of Assisi)* (fig. 63.). Painted with water-based pigments, the nearly six-foot-long image of St. Francis appears like a greatly enlarged engraving in-painted with local pigments. The figure is well proportioned despite being almost life size, a difficult feat even for a well-trained artist.

As New Mexico prospered and supplies of grain, sheep, and other livestock grew, the province became a more frequent target of nomadic Indian tribes. The Spanish militia enlisted Pueblo support to defend the province and to capture raiders and their children to sell as slaves. The sale of Navajo, Apache, and Comanche captives into servitude or slavery during the eighteenth century was a profitable business. Young Indians were stripped of their tribal affiliations, baptized, given Christian names, and assimilated into Hispanic families as servants. These detribalized individuals were called *genízaros:*

> [They] were not Spaniards because they were designated as an Indian pueblo, but neither were they typical Pueblo Indians because the wellspring of their Indian identity—their ceremonies, their religious beliefs, and their religious shrines—were from different cultures and were thoroughly repressed and destroyed by Spanish officials and priests. (Ebright and Hendricks 2006, 4)

Another method for defending Spanish and Pueblo communities against attacks by tribes was the creation of border communities. Group land rights, or land grants, were granted by New Mexico governors to citizens in northern, eastern, and southern areas bordering major established communities, and land grants soon stretched from Belen to Taos.

In 1754, Governor Vélez Cachupín granted sixty *genízaro* families the Abiquiu Pueblo land grant, the first permanent settlement on the northern frontier of Hispanic New Mexico. The grant was challenged by squatters and land speculators, but the *genízaro* residents of the pueblo defended their status. Curiously, in 1900 Abiquiu changed its identity to a Hispanic community.

Meanwhile, Spain felt its colony was threatened by other European traders who were exploring west of the Mississippi River in the 1700s. In 1720, Lieutenant Governor and Commander-in-chief Pedro de Villasur led a New Mexico force of one hundred soldiers and Pueblo auxilaries into Kansas to investigate the presence of French trappers and traders working among the Pawnees. Spanish troops were attacked at daybreak on August 13, 1720, and Villasur was killed along with almost half of his force. A detail of the battle is recorded as part of a series of painted hides known as the Segesser hides. A close-up of the main skirmish is seen in figure 64.

Pueblo women continued to produce pottery for local trade, which expanded with the rising population of newly arrived colonists. Since the *encomienda* system had been abolished and the Pueblos no longer had to make payments of food and products to the Spanish, some rented unused fields to landless Hispanic farmers for the production of corn, wheat, and vegetables. Pueblo women traded bowls, cooking pots, and storage jars for the grain and vegetables grown by the Hispanic farmers.

Pueblo pottery changed little from the preconquest period until the mid-1600s, when red slips were added to monochrome pottery, such as on a Tewa Polychrome jar

64
MAKER UNKNOWN
SEGESSER II, CIRCA 1720–1729
WATER-SOLUBLE PAINT ON HIDE, 204 X 54 IN. (518.2 X 137.2 CM)

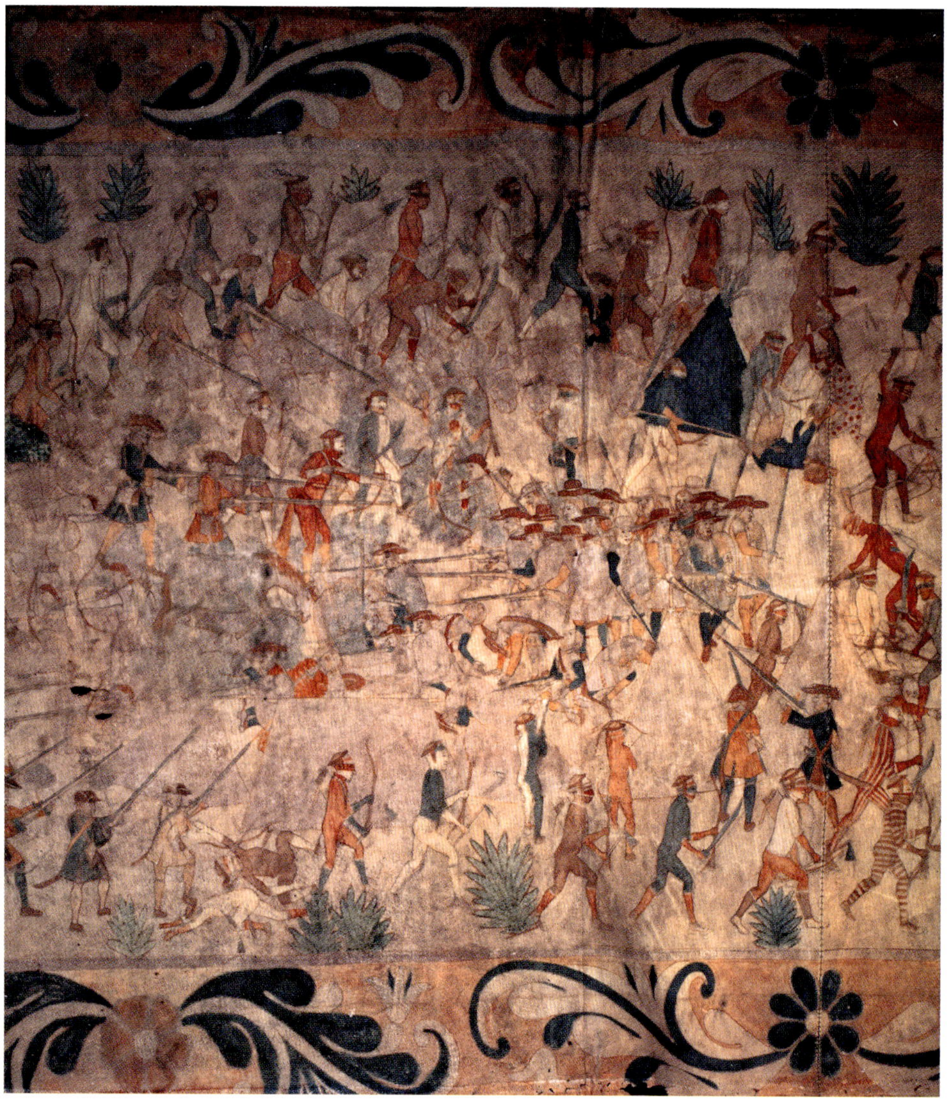

from about 1690 (fig. 65). Historic pottery expert Francis H. Harlow notes that in matte-paint pottery after 1600 "the use of red has been ascribed to Spanish influence" but argues that this is "doubtful," citing "little or no effect of Spanish suggestions as to form or design" in seventeenth-century matte-paint polychrome pottery (Harlow 1973, 28). In the eighteenth century, however, Pueblo pottery changed as more solid trade relationships developed between the Pueblos and the colonists. For example, in the 1760s high-neck jars popular in the Tewa and northern Keres pueblos quickly evolved into spherical vessels.

The western pueblos produced variants of a pottery style known as Ako Polychrome during the early 1700s (fig. 66). The underbodies of Ako vessels were painted with solid red slips that accentuated the globular upper bodies, which were painted with feather motifs tailored to the curved form. Similar changes occurred in the western pueblos at Zuni, Acoma, and Laguna. The Ako-style jars that had dominated the region—vessels with

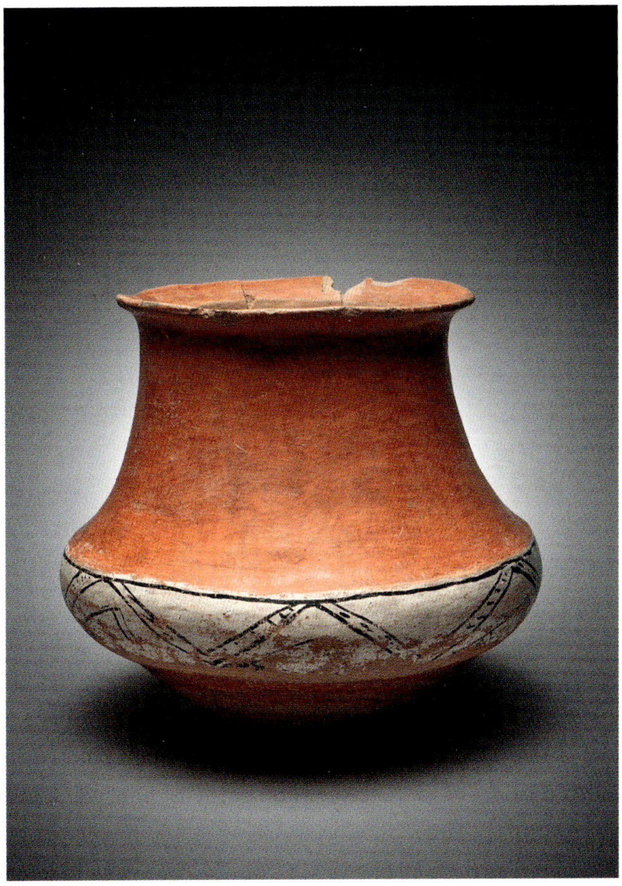

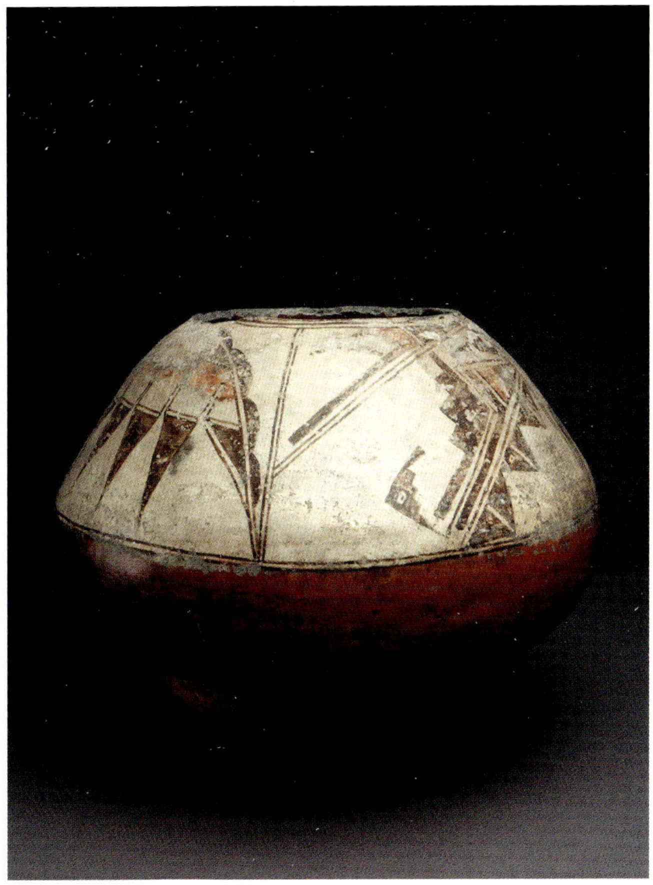

constricted bases, expanding shoulders, constricted upper bodies, and knotted necks—also evolved into spherical forms but still had constricted bases into the nineteenth century.

While New Mexico's Hispanic population expanded rapidly after the 1760s, Pueblo populations did not. By now the Franciscans had become frustrated with the slow pace of Pueblo acceptance of Christianity, yet they felt obligated to serve the religious needs of Spanish colonists who lived near Pueblo communities. Thus, when Governor Juan Bautista de Anza reduced the number of Franciscans serving the colony from twenty-three to seventeen, the friars shifted their focus from missionary work in the pueblos to serving the interests of Hispanic colonists.

The need for religious items increased further as Hispanic communities prospered through trade with the Pueblos and northern Mexico. Ritual objects from Mexico could not meet the rising demand, particularly from newly created communities. Consequently, in addition to hide paintings other types of religious objects were made locally. These objects characterized what became known as the New Mexico *santero* tradition, a local style of Catholic religious art. The *santero* tradition began in the late eighteenth century at the end of the Spanish Colonial period and lasted through the Mexican Republic from 1821 to 1846 and into the American Territorial period. However, the period of greatest activity was between 1810 and 1850.

65
MAKER UNKNOWN
TEWA POLYCHROME JAR, CIRCA 1690
CLAY AND PIGMENTS, 10⅝ X 12 IN.
(27 X 30.5 CM)

66
MAKER UNKNOWN
ACOMA PUEBLO AKO POLYCHROME JAR, CIRCA 1730
CLAY AND PIGMENTS, 12 X 15 IN.
(30.5 X 38.1 CM)

Santeros, or saint makers, produced flat painted wooden *retablos* and polychromed *bultos*, or sculptures, mostly painted with water-based pigments. The *santeros* emphasized the iconographic details associated with each saint, which served as references to a saint's life story and encouraged educational discussions at church and home. These artists developed a style that incorporated the linear qualities of engravings that were imported into New Mexico from Spain or Mexico. As the painters became more skilled, they added shadows cast by draped fabric and modeling of facial features. Backgrounds usually were rendered as deep space so that the viewer would concentrate on the saints rather than on the pictures as a whole. Only a few *santeros* are known by name, with most identified by the location in which they worked or by some aspect of their art.

Military officer Bernardo Miera y Pacheco, a well-known Spanish explorer and cartographer born and educated in Mexico, is the earliest identified *santero* in New Mexico. Miera y Pacheco used his skills as a painter and sculptor to produce works in the baroque style popular in eighteenth-century Mexican, Spanish, and New Mexican churches. In 1761, he carved a massive stone altar screen dedicated to Our Lady of Light, now in the Cristo Rey Church in Santa Fe.

Miera y Pacheco's 1780 oil-on-pine painting of San Rafael (fig. 67) is a stellar example of a work created in New Mexico that reflects the artist's effort to reproduce the religious art of Spain and Mexico. The painting portrays the saint against a background of angel wings and desert plants and is set inside a frame of carved columns. Though painted to create the illusion of dimensionality, the images are not as well modeled as those produced in Mexico.

An unidentified local artist known as the Eighteenth Century Novice, who painted *Nuestra Señora y el Niño / Our Lady and the Infant Jesus* (fig. 68), worked in oils and copied the style of religious painting then popular in Mexico. This artist was not as accomplished as Miera y Pacheco, yet his work exudes an honesty and sincerity understood by Hispanos of the period. A close look at the Virgin's face reveals significant paint loss, the result of generations of highly religious New Mexicans touching the painting with reverence.

Late in the eighteenth century, New Mexican Hispanics began to develop a sense of separateness from Spain and Mexico. Generations of their families had now been born in New Mexico, and they had proven that they could prosper through hard work and trade relationships with the pueblos. This sense of independence further encouraged local artists to produce religious imagery for homes, private chapels, and churches.

As the movement progressed, individual craftsmen expanded their operations to include other workers who cut boards out of logs, planed wood, prepared surfaces with gesso, and mixed water-based pigments. It is believed that some *santeros* were itinerant artists who traveled from village to village, providing images to those who could afford them.

The Truchas Master, thought to be Pedro Antonio Fresquís, who worked between 1780 and the 1820s, created linear works strongly reminiscent of printed engravings. In *Santa Coleta/St. Colette* (fig. 69), Fresquís painted red and black lines to outline the figure. The background includes decorative plant forms organized without regard to naturalistic space or scale.

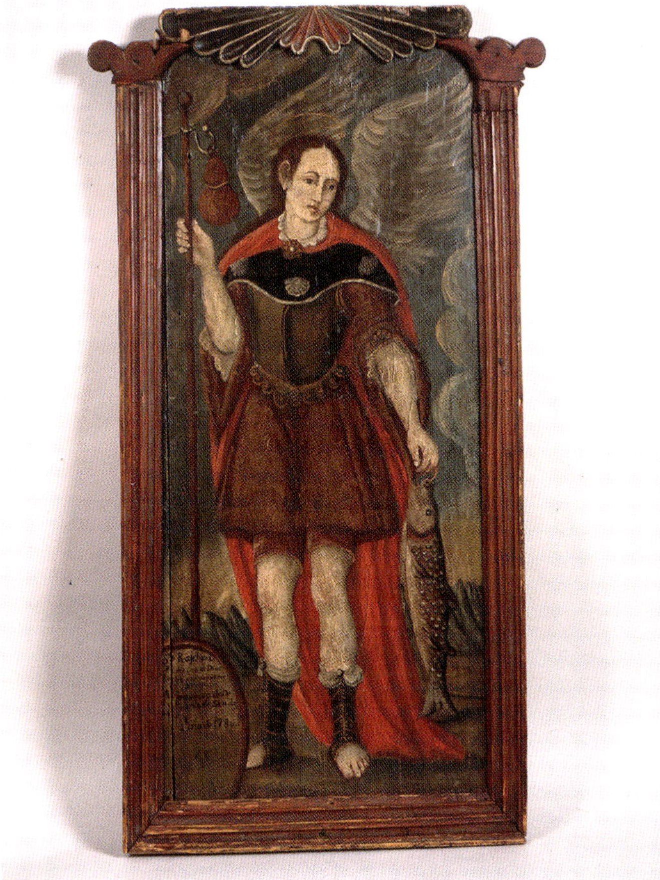

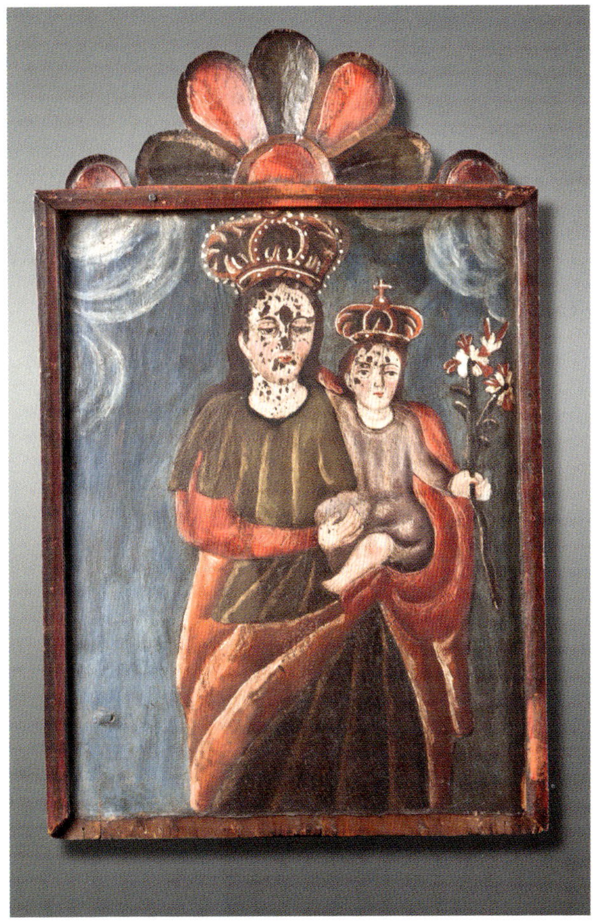

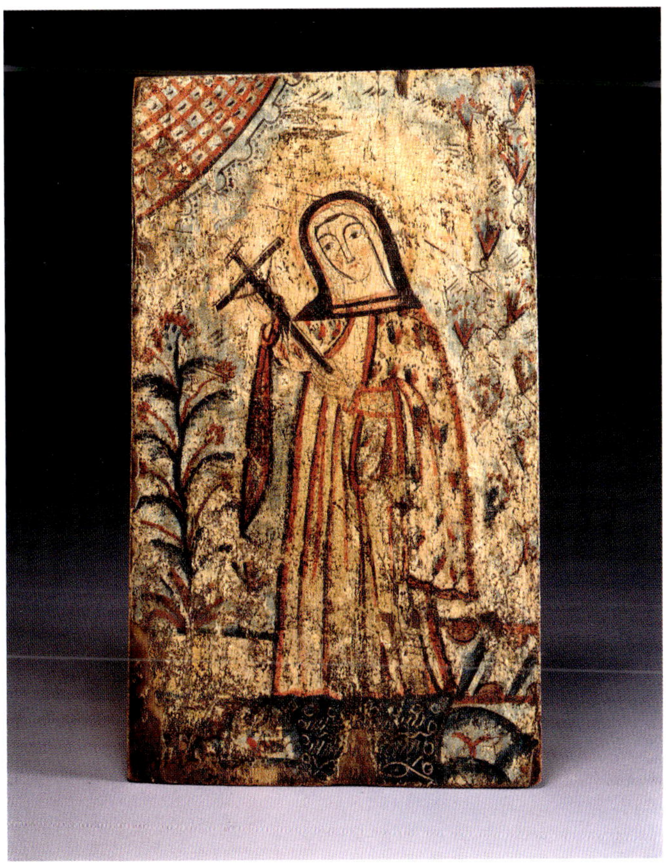

CLOCKWISE TOP LEFT

67

BERNARDO MIERA Y PACHECO

(1714–1785)

SAN RAFAEL / ST. RAPHAEL, 1780

GESSO AND OIL PAINT ON PINE,

49 X 24 IN. (124.5 X 61 CM)

68

THE 18TH CENTURY NOVICE

(DATES UNKNOWN)

NUESTRA SEÑORA Y EL NIÑO /

OUR LADY AND THE INFANT JESUS,

1780–1800

GESSO AND PAINT ON WOOD,

25½ X 16¼ IN. (64.8 X 41.3 CM)

69

TRUCHAS MASTER, ATTRIBUTED TO

PEDRO ANTONIO FRESQUÍS (1749–1831)

SANTA COLETA / ST. COLETTE,

1780–1820S

GESSO AND WATER-SOLUBLE PAINT ON

WOOD, $17\frac{15}{16}$ X $10\frac{7}{16}$ IN. (45.5 X 26.5 CM)

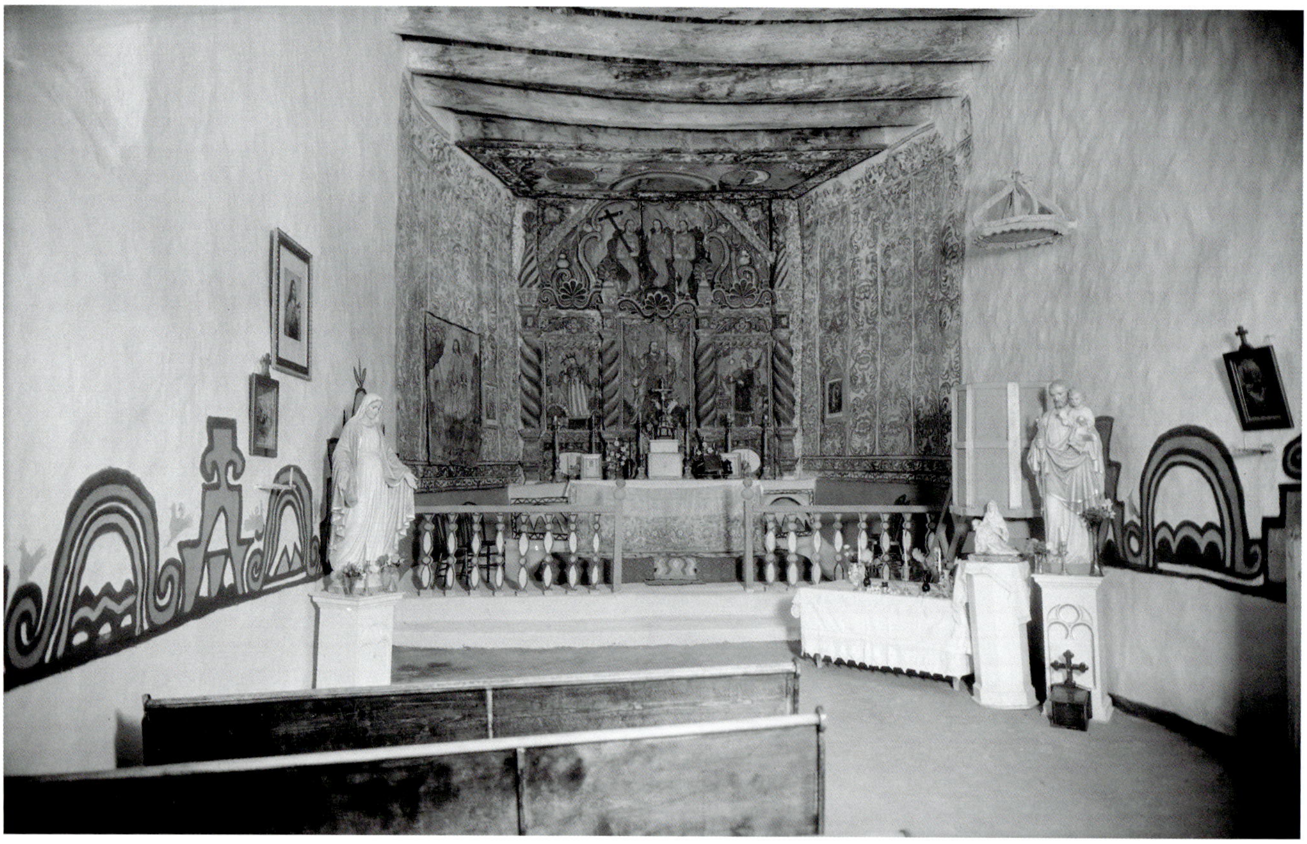

70
T. HARMON PARKHURST (1883–1952)
MISSION CHURCH INTERIOR, LAGUNA PUEBLO, NEW MEXICO, CIRCA 1935
FILM NEGATIVE, 7 X 11 IN. (17.8 X 27.9 CM)

71
MAKER UNKNOWN
LAGUNA POLYCHROME JAR,
CIRCA 1875–1885
CLAY AND PIGMENTS, 9¼ X 11¾ IN. (23.5 X 29.8 CM)

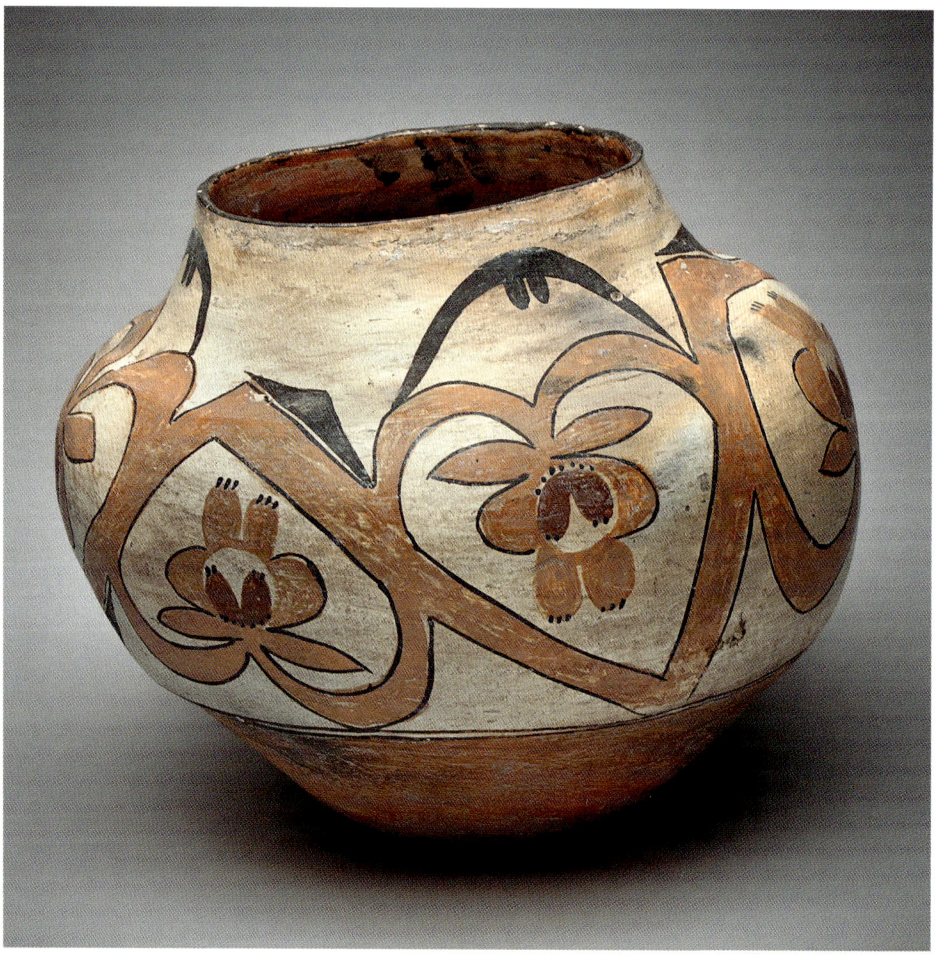

The Laguna Santero was an anonymous artist believed to be from Mexico who worked in New Mexico between the late 1790s and 1808. He is best known for painting the altar screen at the Laguna Pueblo Mission Church, which is an example of the early nineteenth-century integration of Catholic and Pueblo iconography (fig. 70). The mission provides an interesting context for the *santero*'s work, since its side walls are painted with rainbows and other design elements that reference Native American imagery. A fascinating comparison can be made between these designs and those painted on a Laguna Polychrome vessel from the same period (fig. 71). The similarity affirms the synthesis of Native and Hispanic designs and reflects the cultural interplay at the end of the Spanish Colonial period.

The Laguna Santero also produced major mission altar screens at the pueblos of Pojoaque (ca. 1796–1800), Santa Ana (ca. 1798), Zia (1798), Acoma (1802), and Laguna (1800–1808), as well as at the San José chapel (ca. 1796) and San Miguel chapel (ca. 1798), both in Santa Fe. Stylistically, his works set the tone for other *santeros*, depicting saints as rather flattened figures in the foregrounds with plain backgrounds. Although his works largely rely on flattened imagery with references to symbols related to an individual saint's life, the artist's efforts at three-dimensionality imply formal training in Mexico. The Laguna Santero's *San Juan Nepomuceno/St. John Nepomuk* (fig. 72) presents a combination of elements that characterizes the *santero* style during the last decades of Spanish rule.

Works by Molleno, who was active from 1815 to 1845, bear strong similarities to *retablos* by the Laguna Santero. Molleno was a prolific painter who produced images such as *Santiago Matamoros/St. James the Moor Slayer* (fig. 73) that emphasize figures with flattened faces and hands against rather plain backgrounds. While he attempted to produce flowing robes in the round, his efforts were more decorative than naturalistic.

Molleno also created vignette images such as *San Antonio/St. Anthony* (fig. 74), which features a decorative painted border around the saint. Though the background includes a broken horizon line, the landscape is painted as a flat, decorative space. Molleno's style of *retablos* would dominate the *santero* tradition during the period of the Mexican Republic between 1821 and 1846.

In the middle of the New Mexican *santero* period, Mexico declared its independence from Spain. After a rocky start in the eighteenth century, Pueblo and Hispanic communities had learned to work together for common

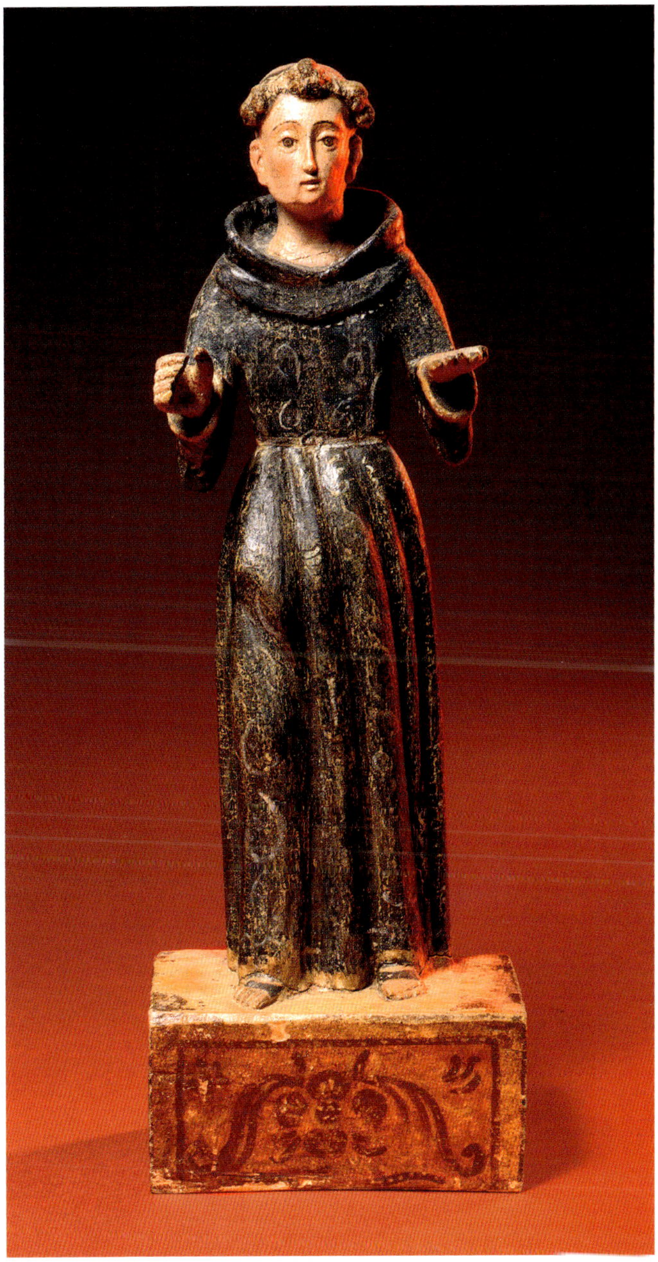

72
SCHOOL OF THE LAGUNA SANTERO
(ACTIVE LATE 1790s–1808)
SAN JUAN NEPOMUCENO / ST. JOHN NEPOMUK, EARLY 19TH CENTURY
GESSO AND WATER-SOLUBLE PAINT ON WOOD, 13⅜ X 9⅝ X 9/16 IN. (34 X 24.5 X 1.5 CM)

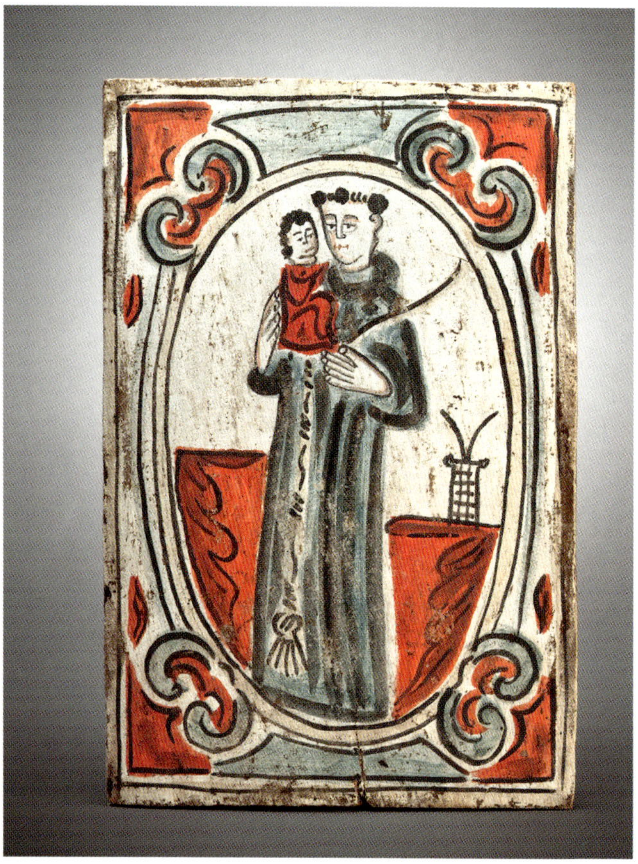

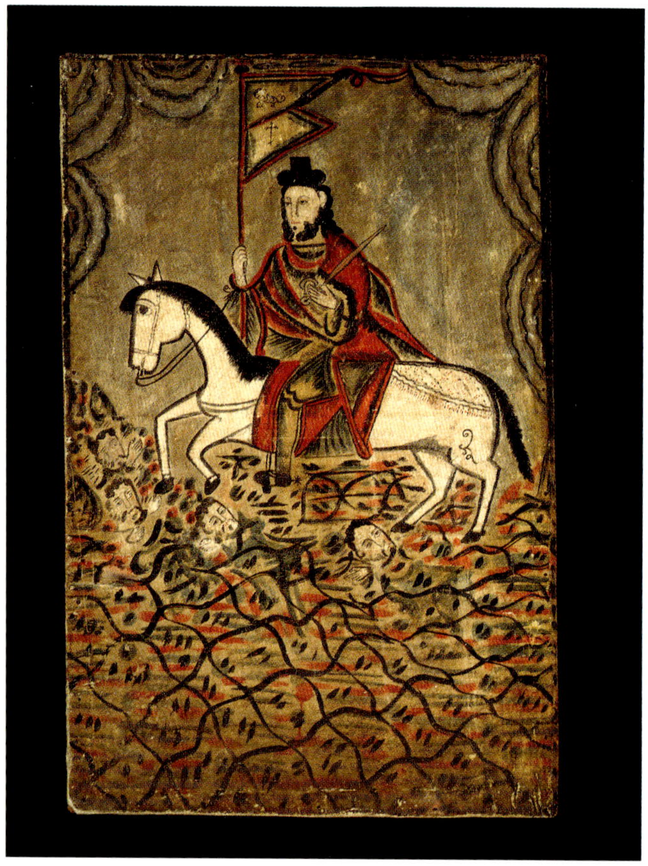

73
MOLLENO (ACTIVE 1815–1845)
SANTIAGO MATAMOROS / ST. JAMES THE MOOR SLAYER,
1815–1854
WATER-SOLUBLE PAINT ON HIDE, 59 1/16 X 38 9/16 IN. (150 X 98 CM)

74
MOLLENO (ACTIVE 1815–1845)
SAN ANTONIO / ST. ANTHONY,
CIRCA 1835
GESSO AND WATER-SOLUBLE PAINT ON WOOD, 10 7/8 X 7 7/16 IN. (27.6 X 18.9 CM)

ends. Members of communities had intermarried, the feudal *encomienda* system had proved unworkable, and the worst aspects of the Spanish caste systems had dissolved. By the end of the eighteenth century, the stage had been set for independence as Spain found itself financially unable to maintain its colony at the far end of the northern frontier of New Spain. With Mexican independence came open trade with the United States. The opening of the Santa Fe Trail in 1822 formalized the exchange of goods between the two republics and brought new influences to local artists.

The A. J. Santero worked during the first decade after Mexican independence. In strong contrast to the somber tone of many images produced by *santeros* during Spanish rule, this artist's works exhibit the bolder colors and joyous expressions associated with this period of cultural and political change. *Nuestra Señora de Guadalupe/Our Lady of Guadalupe* illustrates the electric qualities of the A. J. Santero's imagery (fig. 75). The combination of radiating black lines and a black shawl with white dots accentuates the visual power of the painting and the spiritual power of the saint.

José Aragón, who was probably born in Spain, produced *retablos* between 1820 and 1835. His compositions utilize the full frame of the *retablo*, incorporating the figure into the space rather than simply isolating it within a frame. His *Crucifixion with Mourning Figures* (fig. 76) includes representations of St. John and the Virgin Mary with a curious juxtaposition of scale, implying a saintly hierarchy.

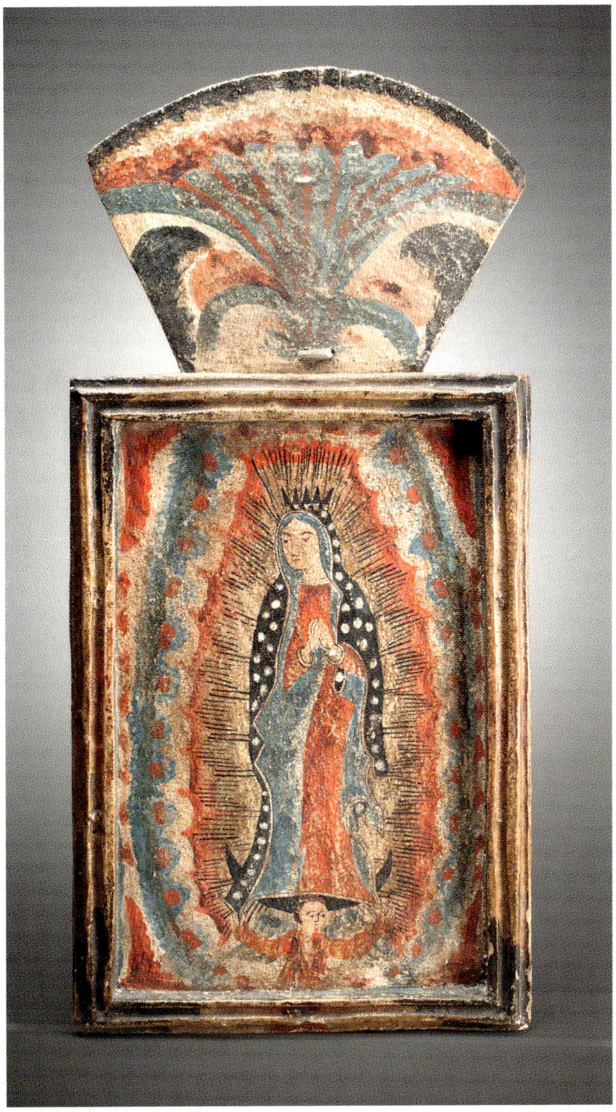

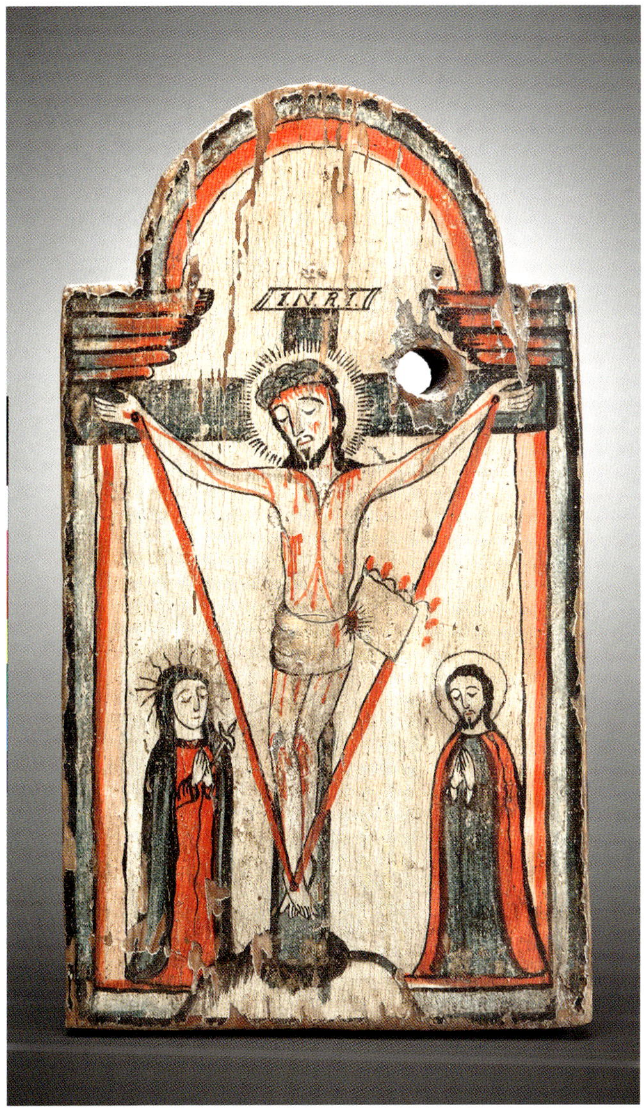

Though Aragón produced one of the altar pieces at the Santuario de Chimayó, he is also known for smaller works. Among these is *Santa Dulubina* (fig. 77), a small *retablo* that underscores the popularity of his images among working New Mexicans. This painting was stored in a leather pouch with a straight razor and probably used by a shepherd in the field while tending a flock.

José Rafael Aragón—best known as simply Rafael Aragón—created religious art in Santa Fe and later in the village of Córdova. Aragón lived near Antonio and Lorenzo Lucero, two carpenters who probably taught him woodworking techniques and who may have been his brothers-in-law. Aragón's *retablos* exhibit a visual confidence that is often lacking in the work of other *santeros* of this period, while his sculptures represent the pinnacle of early nineteenth-century *santero* art.

Aragón's sculpture *San Acacio/St. Achatius* (fig. 78) combines diverse aspects of the *santero* tradition in New Mexico. The symmetrical composition of bold carved forms is

75
A. J. SANTERO (ACTIVE 1820–1840)
NUESTRA SEÑORA DE GUADALUPE / OUR LADY OF GUADALUPE, CIRCA 1825
GESSO AND WATER-SOLUBLE PAINT ON WOOD, 26 x 12⅝ x 1⅜ IN. (66 x 32 x 3.5 CM)

76
JOSÉ ARAGÓN (CIRCA 1785–POST-1850)
CRUCIFIXION WITH MOURNING FIGURES, 1820–1835
GESSO AND WATER-SOLUBLE PAINT ON WOOD, 11½ x 6½ IN. (29.2 x 16.5 CM)

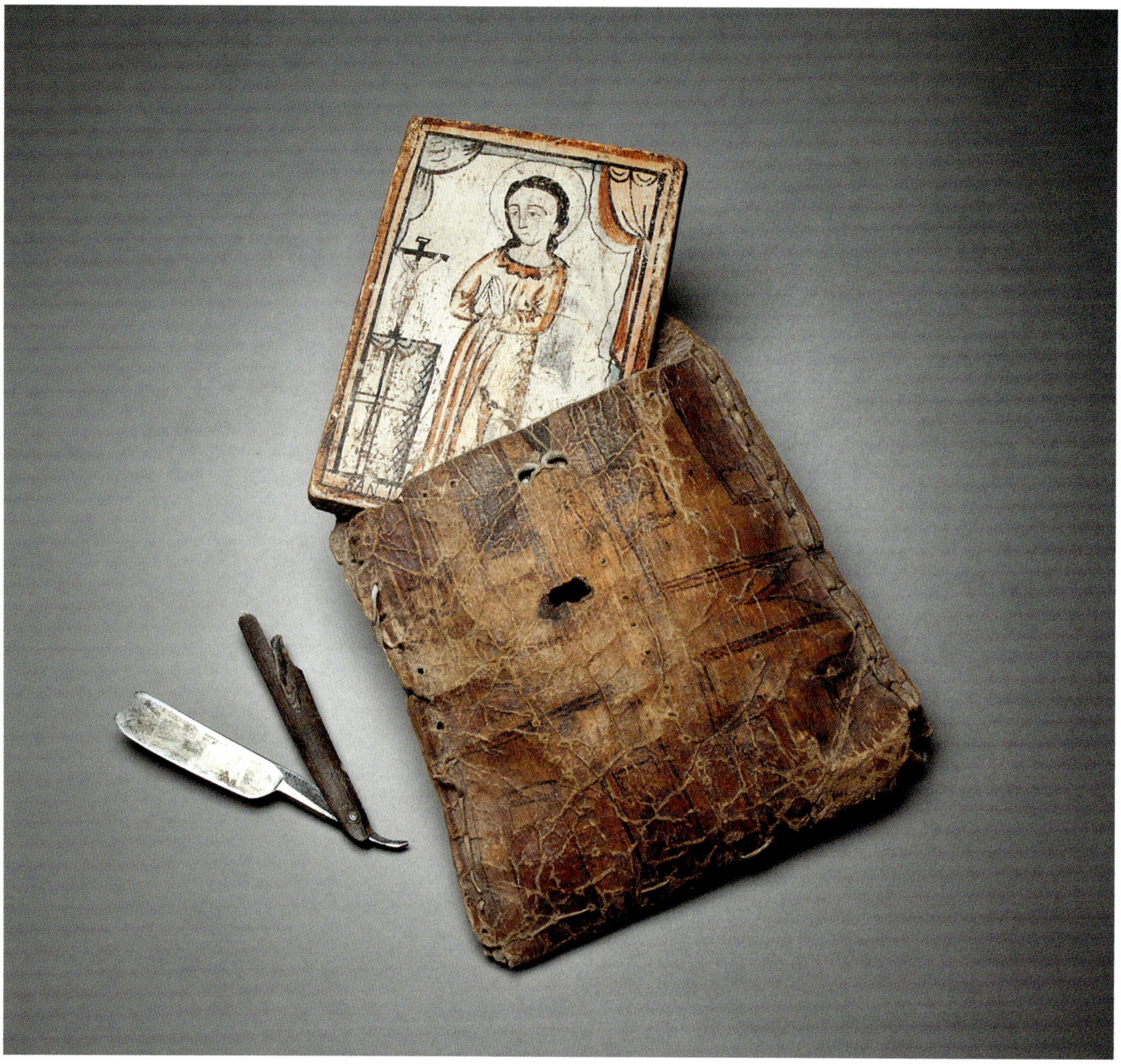

77
JOSÉ ARAGÓN (CIRCA 1785–POST-1850)
SANTA DULUBINA, CIRCA 1825–1835
TEMPERA ON GESSO ON HAND-ADZED PLANED WOOD PANEL, 7½ X 4¹⁵⁄₁₆ IN.
(19 X 12.6 CM)

78
JOSÉ RAFAEL ARAGÓN
(CIRCA 1796–1862)
SAN ACACIO / ST. ACHATIUS, 1820–1862
GESSO AND WATER-SOLUBLE PAINT ON WOOD, 23¼ X 15⅜ X 2³⁄₁₆ IN.
(59.1 X 39.1 X 5.6 CM)

enhanced by delicate painting. The quality of the carving and the painting of the figures are exceptional. These aesthetic qualities are also found in his sculpture *Nuestra Señora de Guadalupe* (fig. 79), which appears as a three-dimensional cutout of a painted *retablo*. The cut and polychromed rays that emanate from the figure energize the sculpture and act as a foil for the decorative elements around the painting's perimeter. The cutout within the framing line, and outside the figure, creates a void that mimics the plain backdrops of many *retablos* of the time.

The anonymous artist known as the Santo Niño Santero, who worked at the end of the Mexican period, is noted for images of the Christ Child and other subjects rendered in a distinctive style. These works present flattened figures with large in-painted areas of color. *Retablos* such as *Santo Niño de Atocha/The Holy Child of Atocha,* created between 1830 and1860, depict iconic images as flattened figures with relatively large, open compositions

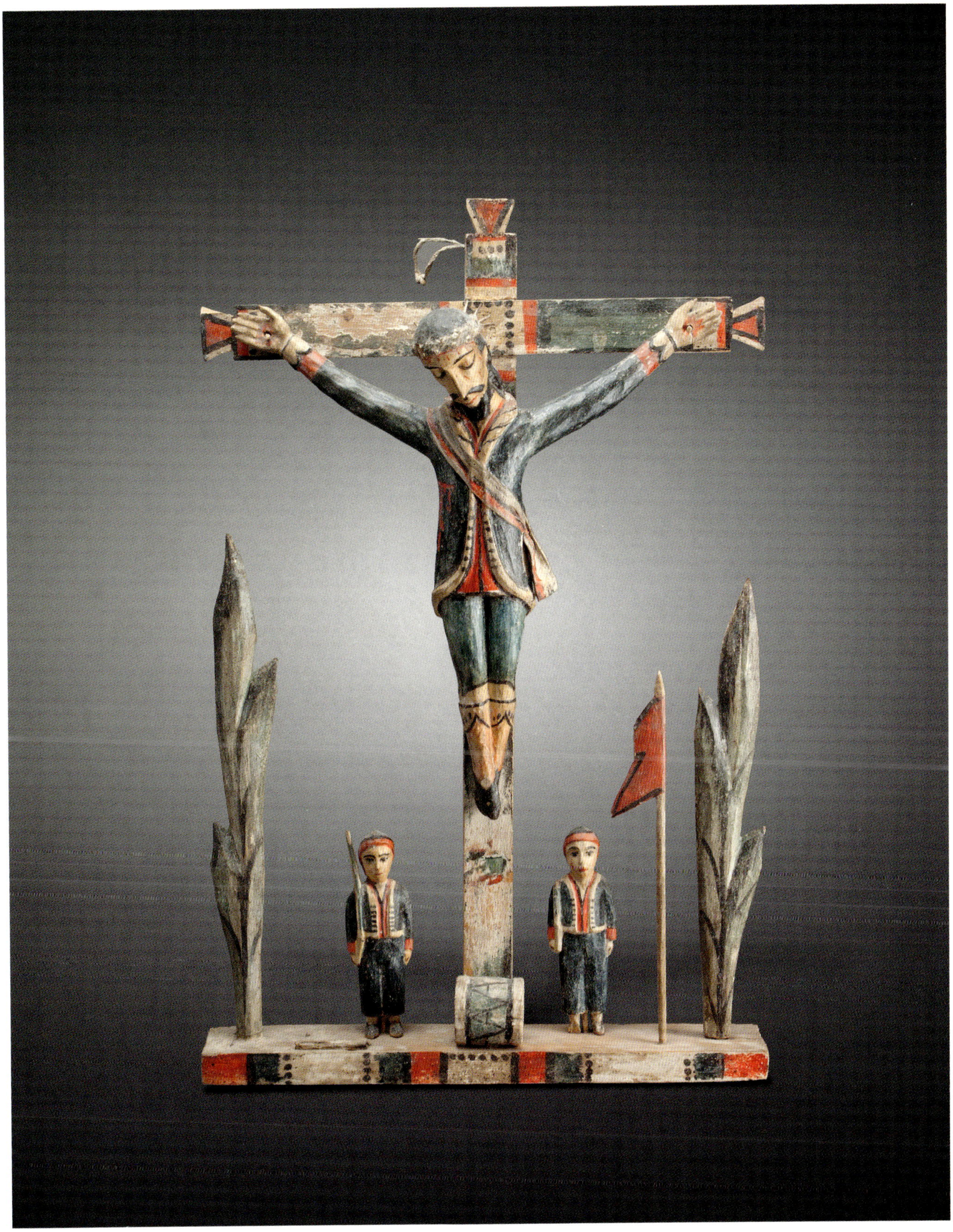

79
JOSÉ RAFAEL ARAGÓN
(CIRCA 1796–1862)
NUESTRA SEÑORA DE GUADALUPE / OUR LADY OF GUADALUPE, 1820–1862
GESSO AND WATER-SOLUBLE PAINT ON WOOD, 24 7/16 X 11 1/4 X 5 1/4 IN.
(62.9 X 28.6 X 13.3 CM)

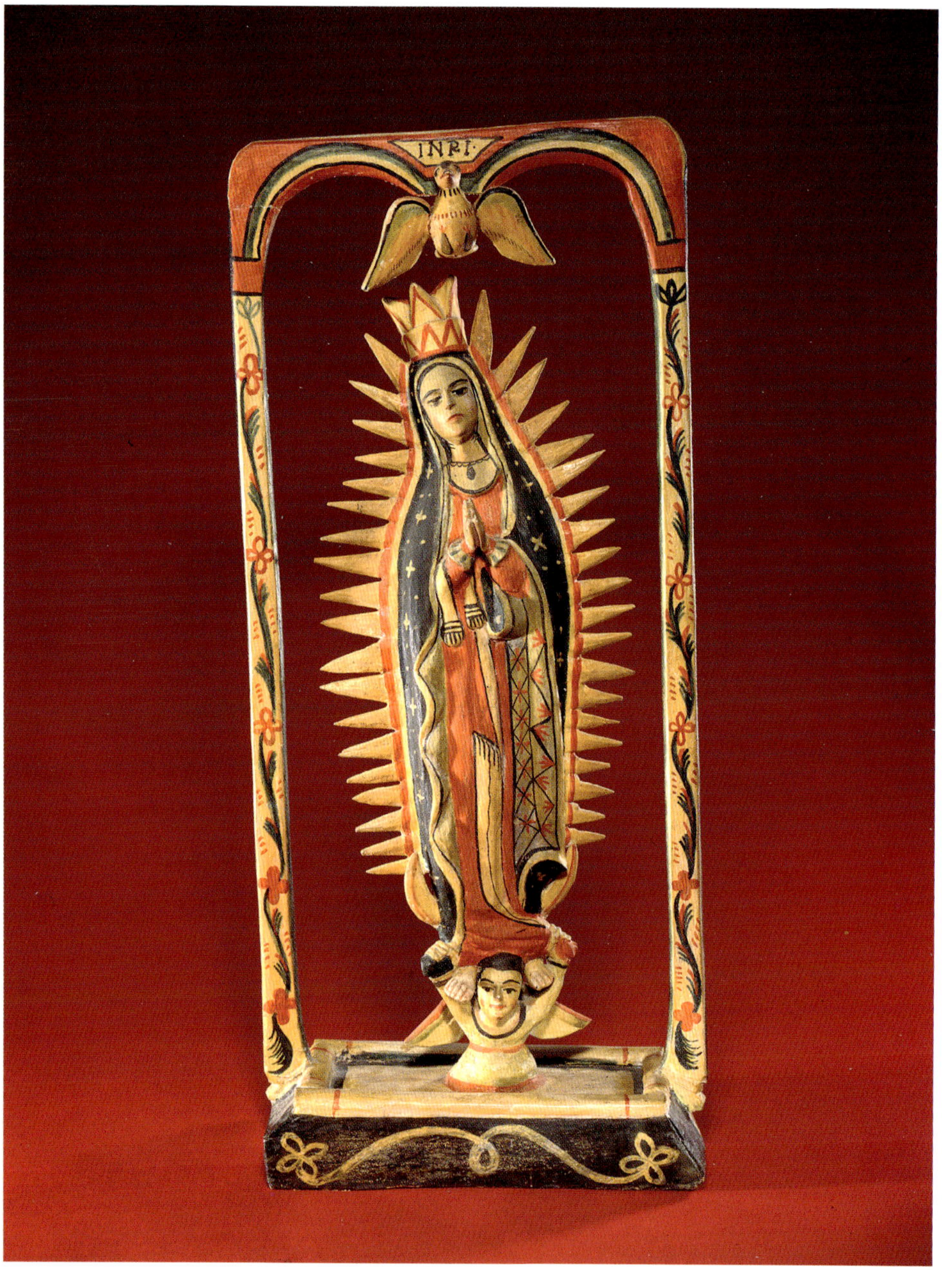

(fig. 80). Border details are often rendered with plant or flower forms without any attempt at three-dimensional illusions.

Pueblo pottery changed again with the rise of the *santero* tradition in the new era of the Mexico Republic. The popularity of globular forms continued, though their painted designs moved away from recognizable feather and plant forms to geometric motifs painted in friezes across the upper body and neck. This visual shift to geometric designs appears to reference Pueblo lifeways less specifically, as seen in a Powhoge Polychrome jar from the first half of the nineteenth century (fig. 81). Because it was culturally more

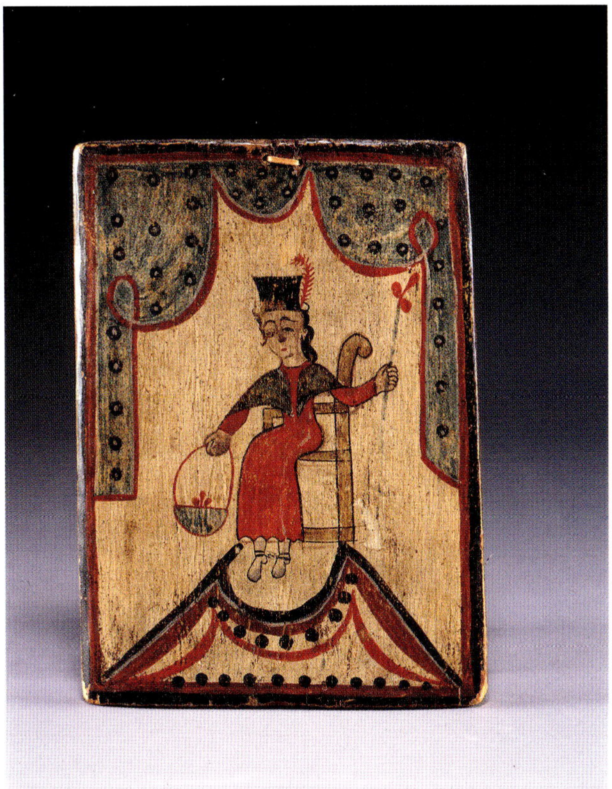

80
SANTO NIÑO SANTERO
(ACTIVE 1830–CIRCA 1860)
SANTO NIÑO DE ATOCHA / THE HOLY CHILD OF ATOCHA, 1830–1860
GESSO AND WATER-SOLUBLE PAINT ON WOOD, 9 X 6 IN. (22.8 X 15.3 CM)

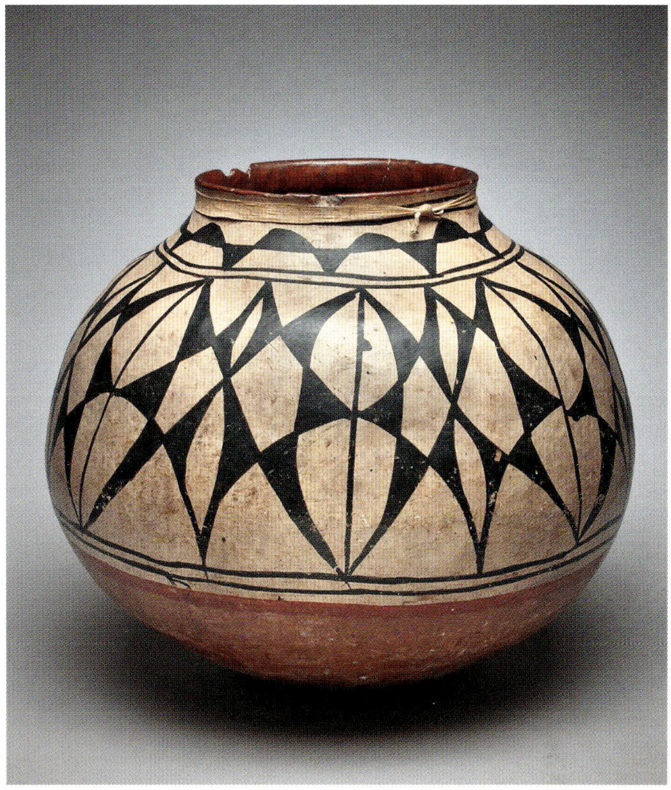

81
MAKER UNKNOWN
POWHOGE POLYCHROME JAR, CIRCA 1830
CLAY AND PIGMENTS, 13¾ X 15¾ IN (35 X 40 CM)

neutral than earlier wares, this style of Pueblo vessel was probably more easily traded to local Hispanic communities and in New Mexico's expanding trade markets in Chihuahua and along the Santa Fe Trail.

In summary, the Spanish *entrada* brought new social relationships to New Mexico: an economy based on trade, tribute, indentured servitude, and private property, along with Christianity and the subordination of Native religions. Tensions caused by these relationships led to the Pueblo Revolt of 1680 and the expulsion of Hispanics from New Mexico. The Spanish Crown instituted reforms after the reconquest at the end of the seventeenth century, and relationships between Native and Hispanic communities improved. At the end of the 1700s, the *santeros* in New Mexico flourished and created religious paintings and sculpture for missions, churches, private chapels, and homes. While the creation of locally made *retablos* and *bultos* may dominate the period, Pueblo art forms continued to be produced. The art of the Spanish Colonial period represents a combination of Native and Hispanic aesthetic traditions.

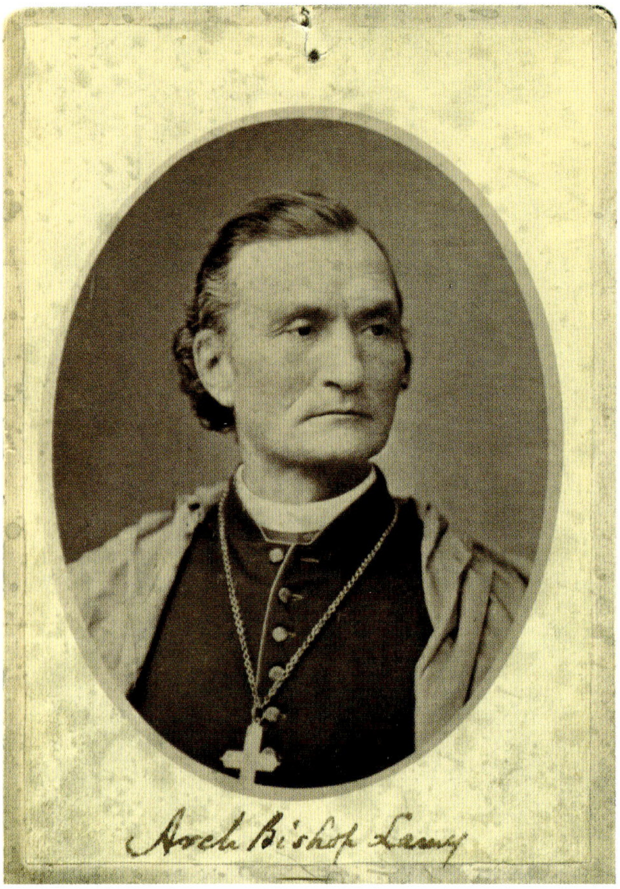
Arch Bishop Lamy

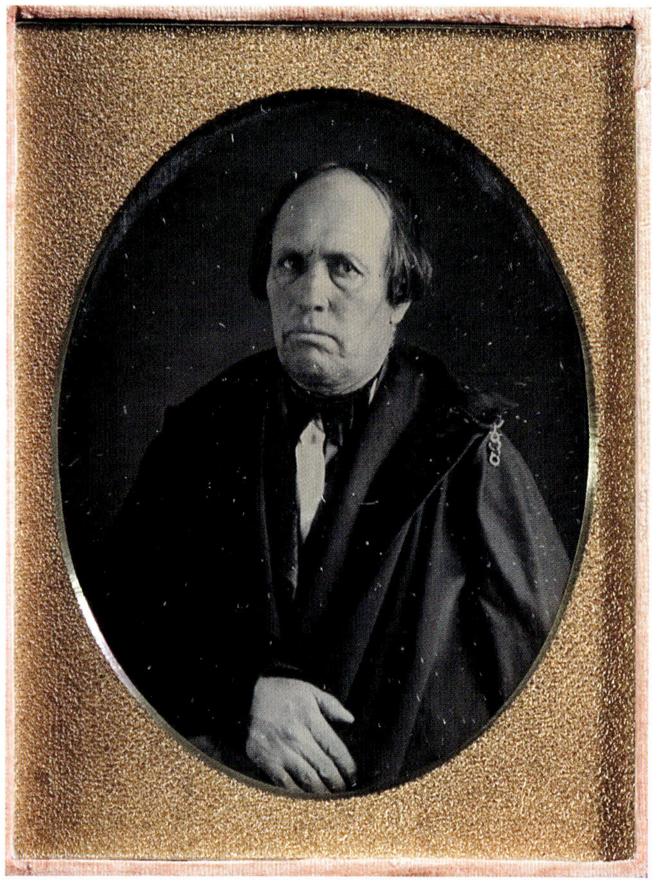

CHAPTER 4

American Colonialism in New Mexico

WEALTHY FAMILIES BOLTED THEIR DOORS as word reached Santa Fe that U.S. troops from the Army of the West were approaching from the east. Governor Manuel Armijo vowed to defend New Mexico against the American invasion and sent defenders of the Mexican Republic to construct barricades outside Santa Fe. But at the last minute Armijo dismissed the defenders and fled to El Paso, becoming the last governor of New Mexico under the rule of the Mexican Republic.

On August 18, 1846, General Stephen Watts Kearny marched unopposed into Santa Fe and claimed New Mexico as United States territory. While the American Army imposed U.S. law, the general established the "Kearny Code" of basic laws for the new territory. A new colonial government was installed, and an influx of traders and citizens from the East flowed to the territory.

The United States consolidated its control over New Mexico with the signing of the Treaty of Guadalupe-Hidalgo on February 2, 1848. The American Catholic Church also exerted its control in 1851 by sending Bishop Jean Baptiste Lamy (fig. 82) to direct New Mexico Catholics. Soon to be archbishop, Lamy opposed the traditional Hispanic religious arts that filled New Mexico's missions, churches, private chapels, and homes. He built churches in rural areas and furnished them with paintings and sculptures imported from Europe and the East Coast. While some *santeros* continued to create *retablos* and *bultos*, production of locally made traditional Hispanic religious art decreased markedly as a consequence of Lamy's dictates.

With the decline in the number of friars serving New Mexico between the end of the eighteenth century and early nineteenth century, many rural Catholics had taken charge of their own religious rituals. The Penitentes, a lay male brotherhood that conducted regular ceremonies, were opposed by Archbishop Lamy as he superimposed his brand of Catholicism on the region. His strict, puritanical views and opposition to local customs created strife with well-established Hispanic clerics and their devoted followers, including Padre Antonio José Martinez of Taos (fig. 83).

The Mexican-American War and U.S. colonial policy in New Mexico were part of a greater plan to connect the East and West coasts. Trade between New Mexico and the United States had boomed after Mexican independence from Spain in 1821 and the opening of the Santa Fe Trail the following year. Goods moved freely along the Santa Fe Trail between Missouri and New Mexico and as far as Mexico City via El Camino Real, or the

82
WILLIAM HENRY BROWN (1844–1886)
ARCHBISHOP JEAN BAPTISTE LAMY,
CIRCA 1870–1880
GELATIN SILVER PRINT, 8 x 10 IN.
(20.3 x 25.4 CM)

83
MAKER UNKNOWN
PADRE ANTONIO JOSÉ MARTINEZ,
1847–1848
DAGUERREOTYPE, 4 1/8 x 3 1/4 IN.
(10.5 x 8.3 CM)

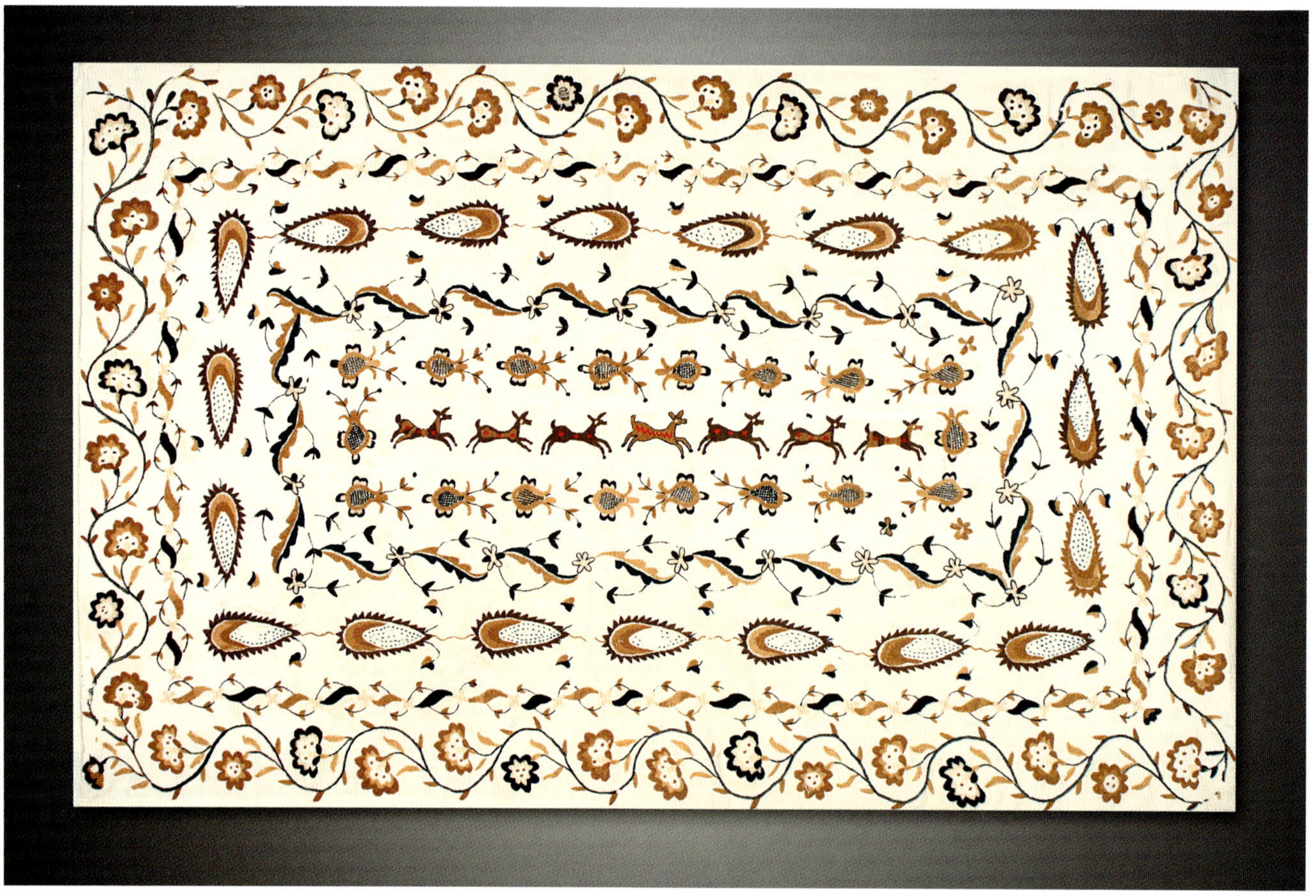

84
MAKER UNKNOWN
COLCHA EMBROIDERY, CIRCA 1840–1865
COTTON AND WOOL, 55 1/8 X 83 7/16 IN.
(140 X 212 CM)

Royal Road. The expanded trade had made clear to U.S. business interests and the federal government that control of the Southwest was essential to America's future progress.

John L. O'Sullivan, a journalist supporting democratic initiatives in 1845, called the expansion our "great experiment in liberty," writing that "our manifest destiny is to overspread and possess the whole continent which providence has given us" (Simmons 1988, 121). Known as manifest destiny, the ideology justified America's westward expansion to the Pacific Ocean. Many Americans believed that God had endowed the United States with abundant resources to be utilized, and thus it was incumbent on Americans to create a unified country and trade routes from the Atlantic to the Pacific.

But manifest destiny deadlocked at the border of the Texas Republic, a state that declared its independence from the Mexican Republic in 1836. After a decade of negotiations, the United States annexed Texas as the twenty-eighth state in 1845, setting the Mexican-American War in motion. Acquisition of New Mexico was next in the plan, but negotiations ended with Armijo's flight from Kearny's troops.

The United States brought its laws and a free-wheeling form of capitalism to New Mexico. Hispano, Pueblo, and Diné fears that they would suffer under American colonialism caused these communities to band together and led to a rebellion in Taos in 1847, during which Governor Charles Bent, a Taos merchant, was murdered by an angry mob. U.S. forces quickly quelled this and other efforts against the American occupation.

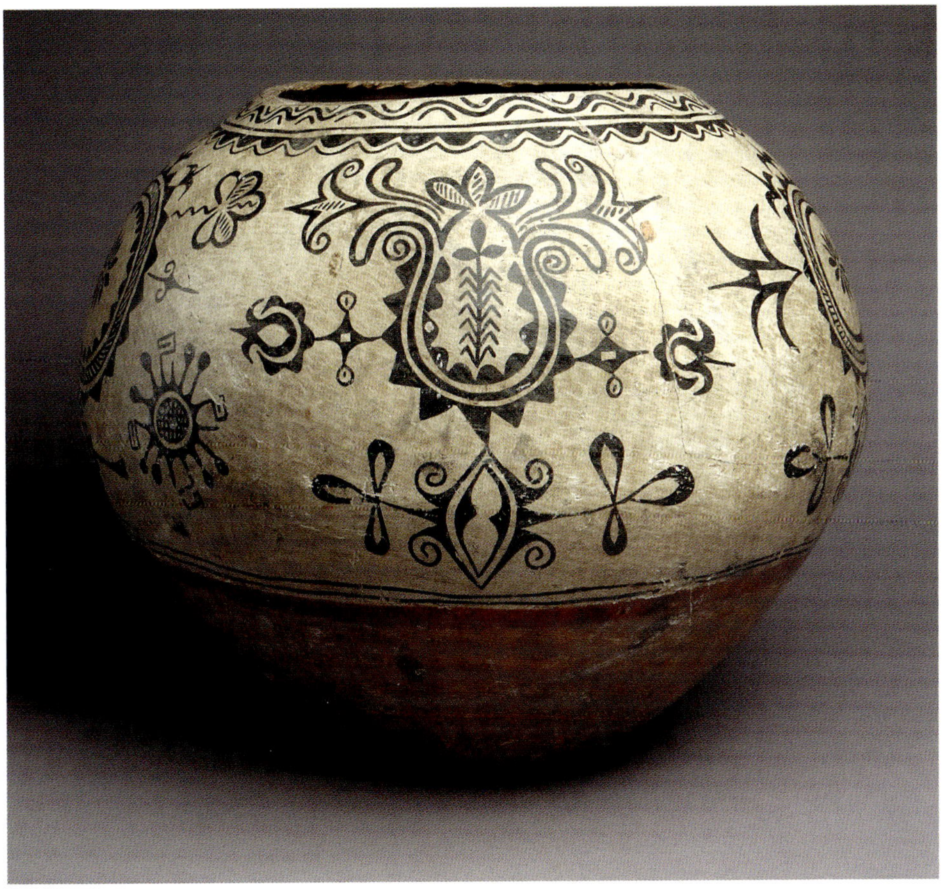

85
MAKER UNKNOWN
TESUQUE PUEBLO POLYCHROME JAR,
CIRCA 1870–1880
CLAY AND PIGMENTS, 17½ x 21 IN.
(44.4 x 53.3 CM)

Meanwhile, communities continued to borrow aesthetic ideas from one another, producing cultural fusions that simultaneously demonstrated their closeness and their separateness. One popular Hispanic art form was *colcha*, hand-embroidered fabrics that served primarily as bed coverings. Colcha yarns were made from hand-dyed wool and sewn onto either cotton or woolen base fabrics. A colcha coverlet made between 1840 and 1865 incorporates interlocking flower motifs and deer-like animals with abstract designs that resemble filigree jewelry (fig. 84).

Similar filigree-like design elements can be seen on a Tesuque Pueblo Polychrome jar, also from the mid-nineteenth century (fig. 85). These elements alternate with painted emblems reminiscent of the silver medallions on Diné concha belts. The jar does not look like earlier Tewa Polychrome pottery from the seventeenth and eighteenth centuries; its globular shape has no neck, and none of its painted design elements resemble the feather motifs associated with the earlier period.

The juxtaposition of Native and Hispanic design elements can be seen in small crosses produced in Hispanic and Pueblo communities during the nineteenth century. Often the crosses are painted with water-based pigments and incorporate decorations that allude to their cultural origins. A well-used nineteenth-century cross believed to be of Pueblo origin has the remains of what appear to be Pueblo motifs painted in black and red pigments (fig. 86). Hence this work combines Christian and Pueblo forms into an

86
MAKER UNKNOWN
CRUZ / CROSS, EARLY 1800S
PAINTED WOOD, 25 9/16 X 2 3/4 IN.
(65 X 7 CM)

87
MAKER UNKNOWN
CRUZ / CROSS, LATE 1700s–EARLY 1800s
WOOD AND STRAW, 15 3/4 X 9 1/4 IN.
(40 X 23.5 CM)

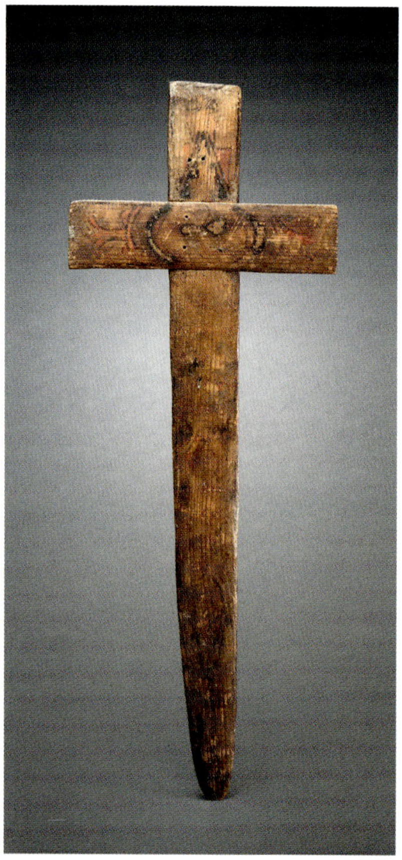

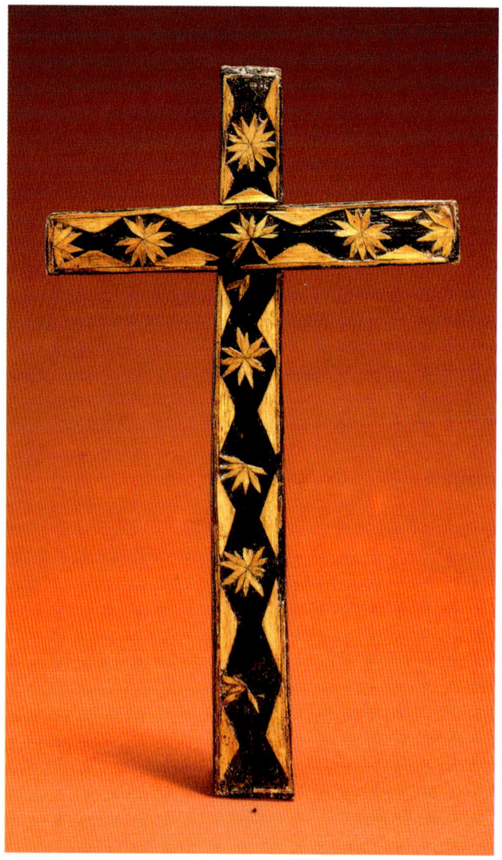

object that was used for decades. A similar Hispanic cross is decorated with straw inlays (fig. 87).

New Mexico entered the Civil War in the summer of 1861 when Confederate troops of the Texas Mounted Volunteers took control of southern New Mexico and then occupied Albuquerque. New Mexico militia, Colorado Volunteers, and federal troops congregated in Las Vegas and at Fort Union. However, the decisive battle of the Civil War in New Mexico was fought on March 27 and 28, 1862, at Glorieta Pass, east of Santa Fe. Major John M. Chivington of the Colorado Volunteers discovered the Confederate supply caravan at the rear of their column and routed the defenders, burning 64 wagons and killing 1,100 burros. The Confederates retreated, but it took a second battle near Peralta, south of Albuquerque, to ensure their defeat.

The U.S. Army now sent Colonel Kit Carson with a force of 750 soldiers to stop repeated Diné attacks on the European-American settlers of western New Mexico and Arizona. Carson forcibly marched 8,500 Diné from their traditional homelands to Fort Sumner at Bosque Redondo, in east-central New Mexico. The harsh conditions and loss of life along the four-hundred-mile "Long Walk" permanently tainted relations between the Diné and the federal government.

During four years of captivity at Bosque Redondo, the Diné expanded their use of iron and silver through contact with army blacksmiths and Hispanic silversmiths. After the government provided Hispanic-made Rio Grande blankets to the detainees at Bosque Redondo, Diné weavers also began to incorporate designs whose origins can be traced to Hispanic Saltillo blankets, which had been imported to New Mexico from northern Mexico throughout the Spanish Colonial period.

The Diné Treaty of June 1, 1868, returned the Diné to their traditional lands and granted them land, horses, sheep, seed corn, and other supplies. The Diné continued weaving with wool from their new flocks, while also acquiring commercial dyes and commercially spun yarns through contact with the army, registered Indian traders, and traders along the Santa Fe railroad. Diné women also now adopted blouses and skirts for apparel instead of woven woolen dresses.

Other weavings from the end of the nineteenth century reflect an interesting mix of aesthetic interaction and cultural independence among Hispanic, Diné, and Pueblo communities. According to conventional wisdom, when the Diné moved into the Southwest during the fifteenth or sixteenth centuries they traded with the Pueblos, who taught them to weave. Spanish explorers and colonists brought sheep to the Southwest, and by the early seventeenth century woolens were being woven in Hispanic households on treadle looms.

Traditionally, in Pueblo communities, men were the weavers. They wove cotton fabrics, but after the arrival of the Spanish they also worked with wool. Among the Diné, women were the weavers, while men tended flocks of sheep. In Hispanic communities, men both tended sheep and wove part-time (fig. 88.). Each of the three cultures used a different kind of loom, creating different structural relationships.

Garment forms, designs, and uses differed as well. Pueblo weavers, mostly at the Hopi villages in Arizona, were known for their ceremonial kilts and mantas worn by women, draped over one shoulder and pinned along the side to make a dress. By the mid-nineteenth century, the Rio Grande Pueblos had abandoned weaving altogether, instead acquiring woven goods through trade with the Hopis. Hispanic weavers were known for their wearing blankets that resembled Saltillo weavings, as well as for *jergas*, generally black-and-white twill plaids used as blankets or floor coverings. Diné weavings, prized by tribes outside the Southwest and traded as "chief's blankets" (fig. 89), incorporated striped or banded designs reminiscent of Hopi mantas or Hispanic Rio Grande weavings.

It seems all but impossible to determine with any accuracy which weavers started the styles popular during the American Colonial period. The complexities of social relationships between Hispanic, Pueblo, and Diné communities, and within Hispanic communities, suggest there was a great deal of interaction among weavers. One of the most interesting works reproduced in this study is a late-nineteenth-century blanket woven by Manuelita Sisneros, a Navajo captive raised in the *genízaro* community of Abiquiu (fig. 90). The cultural roots of this woman and her weaving are known because the blanket had remained in the family for more than a century.

The political situation in New Mexico deteriorated after the Civil War as an influx of corrupt politicians, lawyers, land speculators, squatters, and other wheeler-dealers moved to the Southwest in an effort to gain control of Native, Hispanic, and federally owned lands (Simmons 1988). New American laws did not recognize land grants or group land rights as had earlier Spanish and Mexican laws. Crooked deals that cheated Hispanos and

88
MAKER UNKNOWN
RIO GRANDE BLANKET (NEW MEXICO),
CIRCA 1870
HANDSPUN NATURAL WOOL, UNDYED AND SYNTHETIC DYES, 88 X 53 IN. (223.5 X 134.6 CM)

89
MAKER UNKNOWN
NAVAJO (DINÉ) CHIEF'S BLANKET, VARIANT OF THIRD PHASE DESIGN,
CIRCA 1875–1880
HANDSPUN RAVELED WOOL YARN WITH COCHINEAL, INDIGO, VEGETAL, AND POSSIBLY ANILINE DYES, 42½ X 57 11/16 IN. (108 X 146.5 CM)

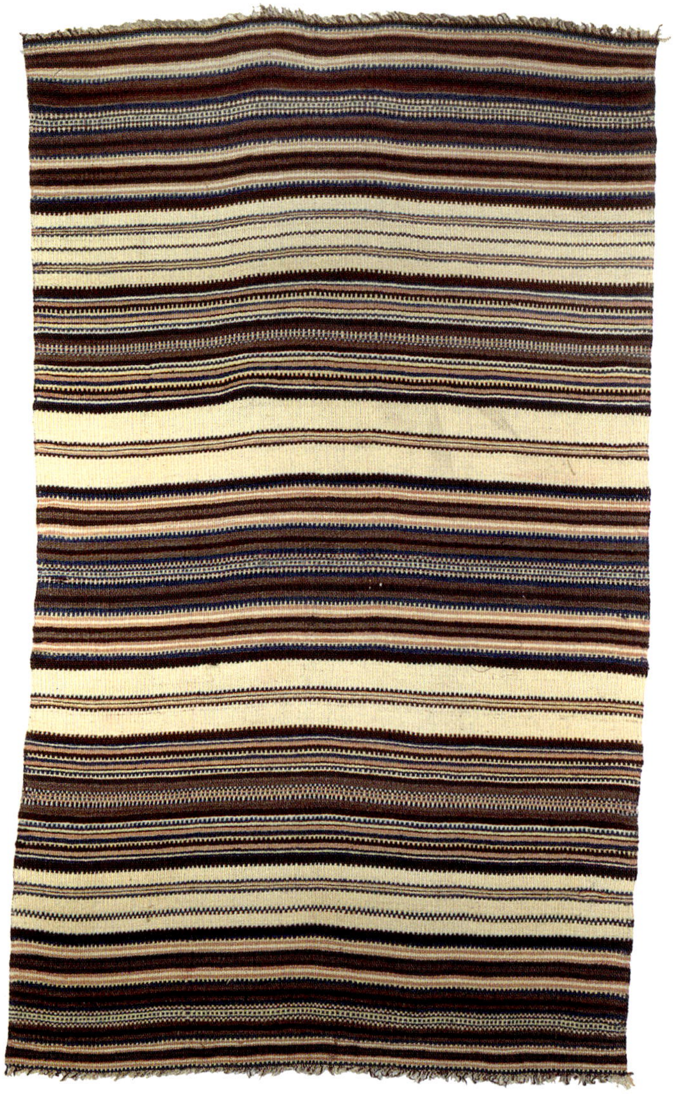

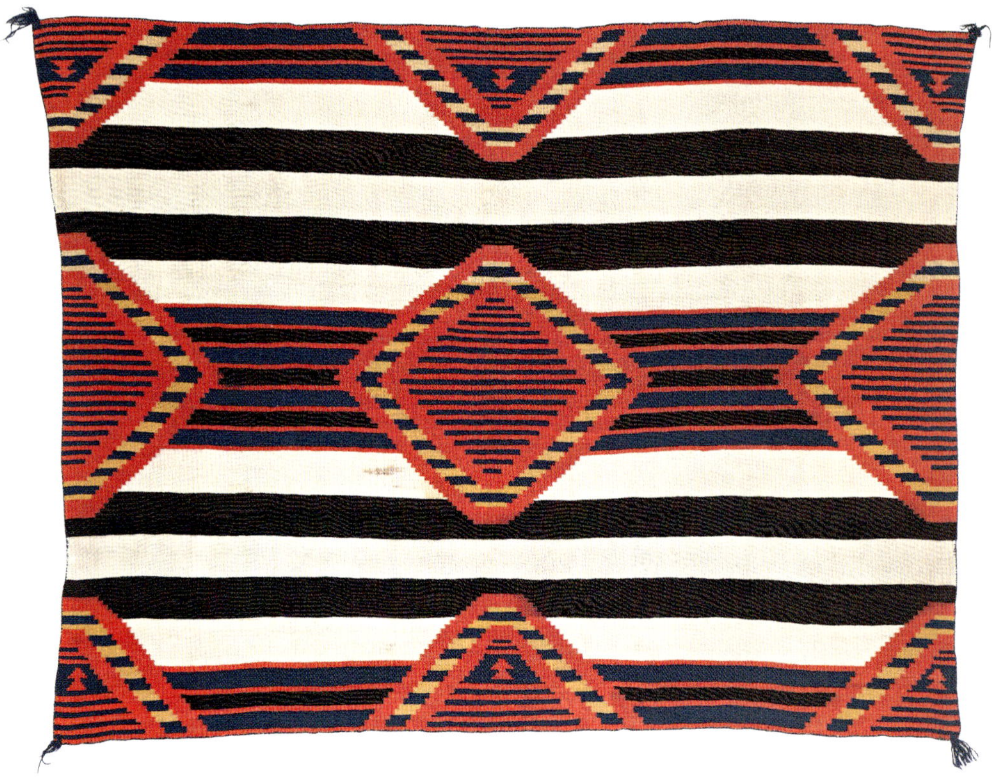

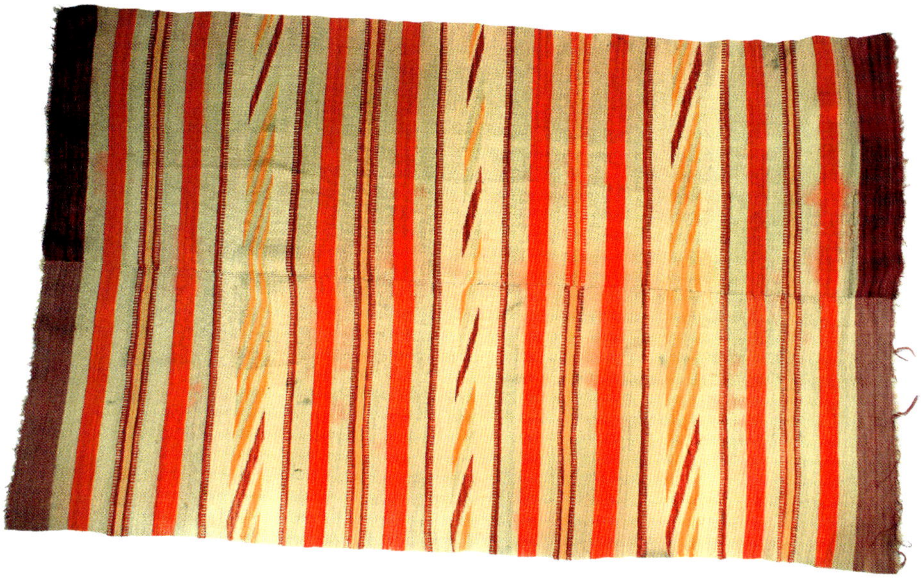

90
MANUELITA SISNEROS
(DATES UNKNOWN)
BLANKET (ABIQUIU, NEW MEXICO),
CIRCA 1880s
WOOL, NATURAL AND SYNTHETIC DYES

Pueblos out of their previously legal land rights were complicated by self-serving, government-appointed officials and judges who were driven by their own efforts to gain wealth. Many get-rich-quick schemes went bust, leading to lawsuits over bankruptcies that further complicated legal title to lands. Claims against squatters from heirs to land grants and Pueblo peoples would continue well into the twentieth century.

Beginning in the 1870s the "Santa Fe Ring," a cabal of Republican politicians, land speculators, and court officials, conspired to gain lands and transform them into cash-paying mines, ranches, and real estate deals. The most notorious of these deals involved the Maxwell Grant in northeastern New Mexico and southeastern Colorado. Settlers were brought in to populate the area to prove that it was inhabited and not vacant federal land. The Colfax County War erupted when the owners acquired the patent for the grant and expelled the homesteaders so they could exercise complete control over their lands.

Other deals involved attempts by the Santa Fe Ring to control government supply contracts and acquire vast ranch lands in southeastern New Mexico, unscrupulous efforts that led to the Lincoln County War when locals, including William "Billy the Kid" Bonney, opposed the Ring's activities and fought to maintain control of the area.

The opportunists in New Mexico gained political control at the same time that the federal government conducted the great surveys, four major expeditions that examined the local mineral deposits and geography of the West and Southwest to determine possible railway passages to the West Coast. Photographers on these expeditions included Alexander Gardner and William Henry Jackson on the Francis Hayden Survey; John K. Hillers on the John Wesley Powell Survey through the Grand Canyon and Utah; and Timothy H. O'Sullivan on both the George Wheeler Survey west of the Hundredth Meridian and the Clarence King Survey of the Fortieth Parallel. Their photographs, and the lithographs drawn from them, were incorporated into the published survey reports.

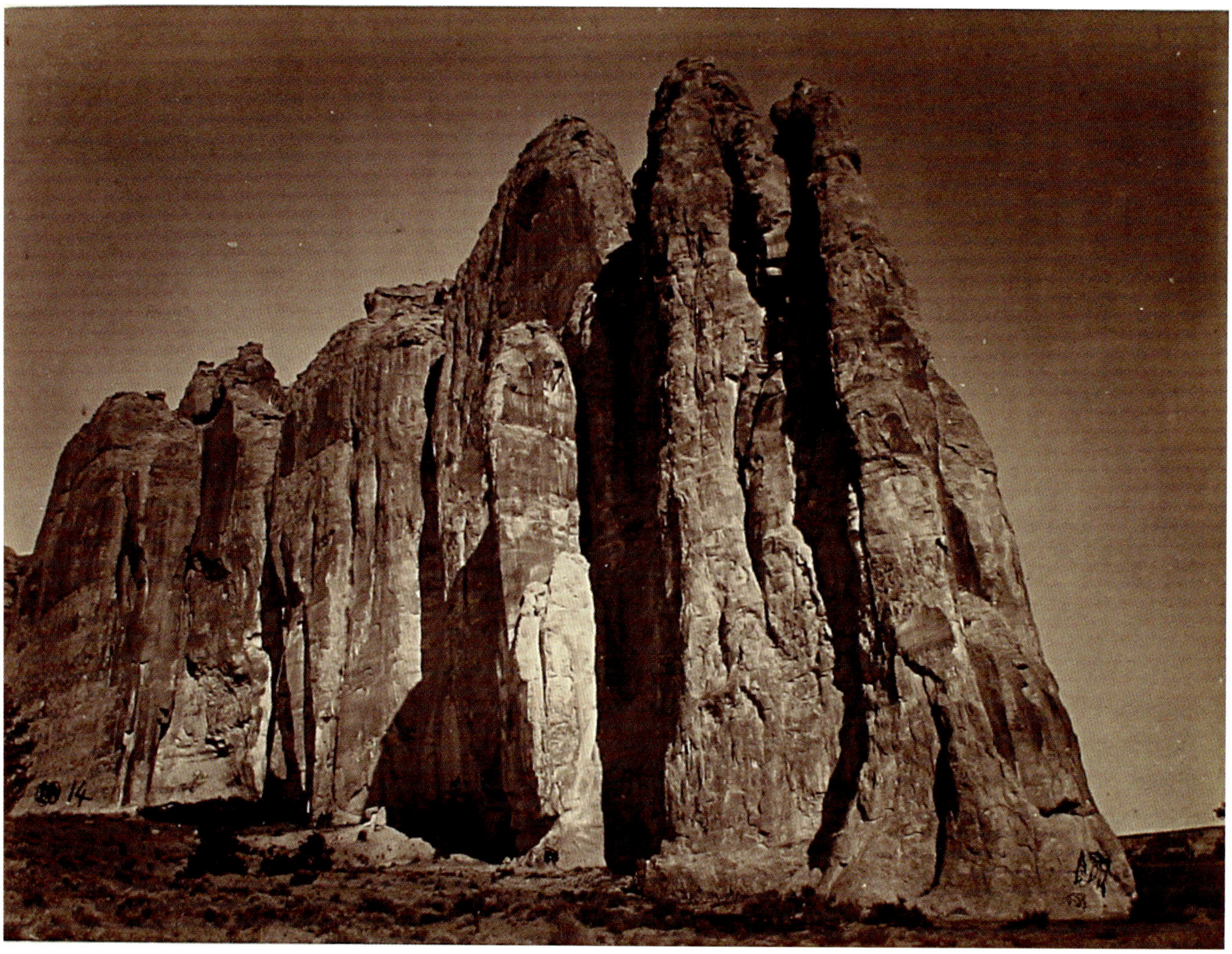

91
TIMOTHY H. O'SULLIVAN
(CIRCA 1840–1882)
SOUTH SIDE OF INSCRIPTION ROCK, 1873
ALBUMEN SILVER PRINT, 11 x 13 IN.
(27.9 x 33 CM)

Perhaps most memorable are O'Sullivan's photographs, which capture aestheticized, romantic views of western landscapes that transcend their intended scientific purpose. For example, O'Sullivan's 1873 photograph *South Side of Inscription Rock* (fig. 91) offers a spellbinding view of the rock walls where, nearly three centuries earlier, Juan de Oñate and other Spanish explorers inscribed messages into the soft sandstone and where Pueblo Indians had etched petroglyphs even earlier. His large-format contact print was tipped onto a printed sheet featuring an engraved description of the scene. These types of photographs were the most modern images available to elite Victorians, who found their warm tones truly affective.

THE RUSH TO DOCUMENT LIFE IN THE SOUTHWEST

The transformation of New Mexico from a Spanish colony to an American colony accelerated in 1879, when the Santa Fe Railway crossed from Colorado into New Mexico at Raton Pass. Connecting the Southwest first to the Midwest and then to Los Angeles,

California, the railway expanded the trade in tools, canned goods, and other American materials imported to New Mexico.

Shipping crates, tin cans, and packing materials were reused and reconfigured by locals. Sheet metal from used cans was flattened, punched with designs, and soldered into frames for photographs and other utilitarian objects. The best-known tin artist of the period, the Isleta Tinsmith, created rather baroque punched and cut designs that often incorporated panels of reverse painting on glass and sometimes printed information from his source materials, such as a label from a can of lard (fig. 92). Labels would be hidden as engravings of saints or photographs of family members were slipped into the frames. While glazing protected heirloom photographs and images (fig. 93), other items were often slid, unprotected, between the glass and the edge of the tin frame.

Tin buckets and cast-iron Dutch ovens imported by rail quickly replaced ceramic water jars and cooking pots in New Mexico kitchens, and inexpensive printed cloth, such as calico, was adopted by Native and Hispanic families. With such changes, handmade utilitarian items fell into disuse and were discarded, traded, or sold for supplies.

Yarns imported from the Germantown section of Philadelphia, Pennsylvania, proved to be particularly popular with Diné weavers during the period from 1880 to 1890. Germantown weavings could be made from pre-dyed yarn, or the weaver could dye wool carded and spun from local sheep. Both yarns were colored with aniline dyes made from coal tar and were noted for their intense hues, primary colors, and uniform size. Unlike dyes made from local plants, aniline dyes did not fade.

The resulting Germantown "eye dazzlers"—brightly colored weavings featuring strong contrasts of hue and tone—found a ready market with many European-American

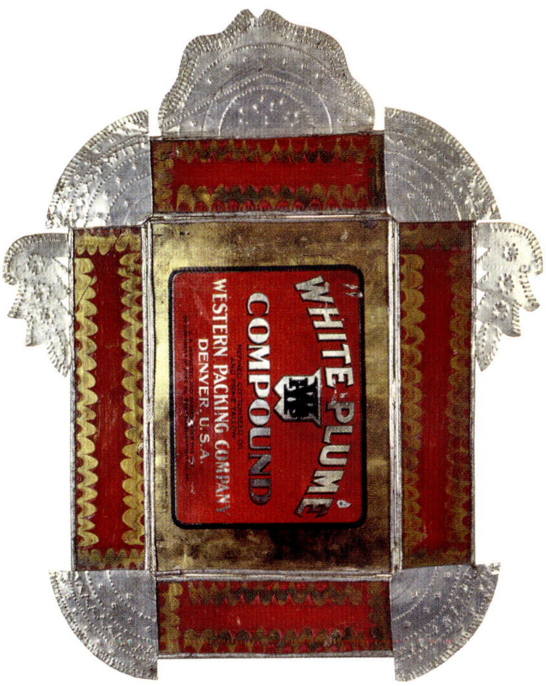

92
ISLETA (NEW MEXICO) TINSMITH
(DATES UNKNOWN)
TIN FRAME, CIRCA 1910
TINPLATE, GLASS, AND WATER-BASED PAINT, 31 X 21½ IN. (78.7 X 54.6 CM)

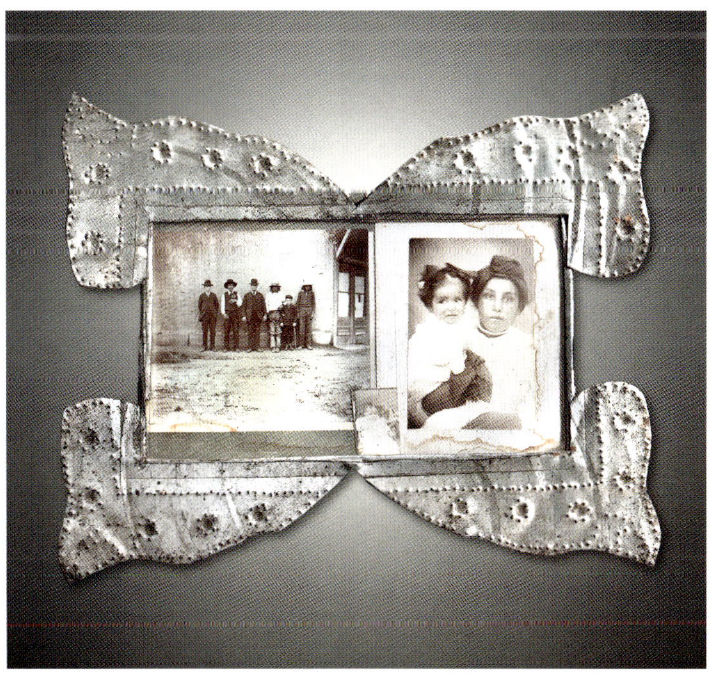

93
ISLETA (NEW MEXICO) TINSMITH
(DATES UNKNOWN)
TIN FRAME, EARLY 1900s
TIN, GLASS, PAPER, SOLDER, AND PHOTOGRAPHS, $9\frac{13}{16}$ X $12\frac{5}{8}$ IN. (25 X 32 CM)

buyers. Nonetheless, the weavings ultimately struck most buyers as gaudy and cheap, in contrast to the more restrained designs and subdued colors found in earlier wearing blankets (fig. 94). Consequently, the style only lasted for little more than a decade.

Around 1880, potters at Cochiti Pueblo began making and selling figurines to travelers, often depicting barnyard animals and other creatures from the Southwest or circus performers who traveled through on the train or performed in Santa Fe. An untitled 1890s Cochiti sculpture (fig. 95) demonstrates the mixing of sources that informed such work.

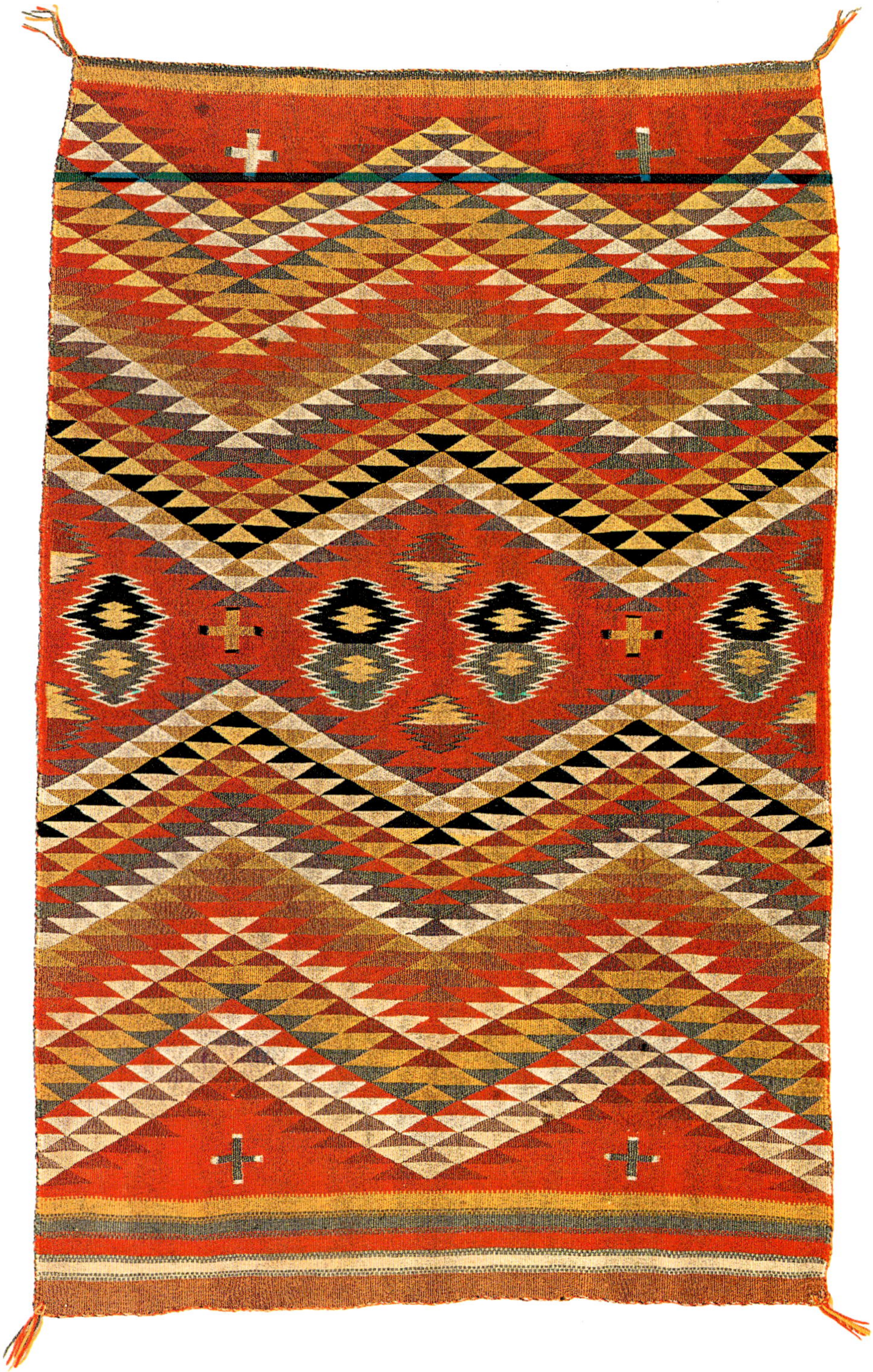

94
MAKER UNKNOWN
NAVAJO (DINÉ) GERMANTOWN DOUBLE SADDLE BLANKET, CIRCA 1880–1890
COTTON STRING, GERMANTOWN WOOL YARN, AND ANILINE DYES, 47 X 31 IN. (119.4 X 78.7 CM)

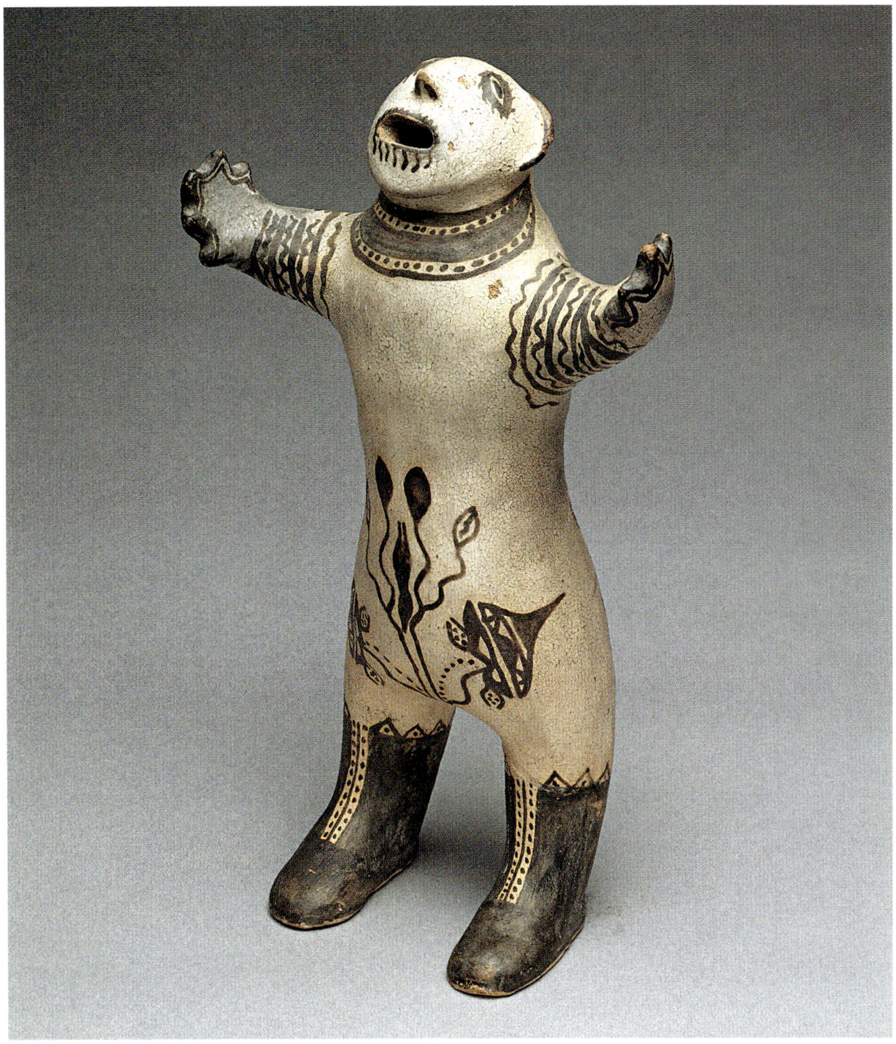

95
MAKER UNKNOWN
COCHITI FIGURINE, 1890s
CLAY AND PIGMENTS, 11¼ X 6½ X 3 IN.
(28.6 X 16.5 X 7.6 CM)

The figure is simplified in form, with painted designs taken from late nineteenth-century pottery, except for its tall lace shoes.

As Native artists experimented with new art forms, such as secular sculptures, the Hispanic *santero* tradition came to a temporary end. José Benito Ortega, who was the last commercial *santero*, worked at the end of the nineteenth century, creating his last religious art in 1906. Ortega's works, such as *Nuestra Señora del Carmen / Our Lady of Mt. Carmel* (fig. 96), continued the sacred tradition that was over a hundred years old. But with the availability of manufactured religious images the Hispanic community largely lost interest in works made by hand in a vernacular style.

Many Americans thought the completion of the transcontinental railroad fulfilled America's manifest destiny and would result in the demise of indigenous cultures, hoping, as had the Franciscan missionaries before them, that aspects of New Mexico culture they considered pagan would give way to Christianity and other mainstream lifeways. But the belief that Southwest cultures were rapidly disappearing also brought an influx of anthropologists and artists to New Mexico.

96
JOSÉ BENITO ORTEGA (1858–1941)
NUESTRA SEÑORA DEL CARMEN / OUR LADY OF MT. CARMEL, LATE 1800s
GESSO AND WATER-SOLUBLE PAINT ON WOOD, 18½ x 11½ IN. (47 x 29.2 CM)

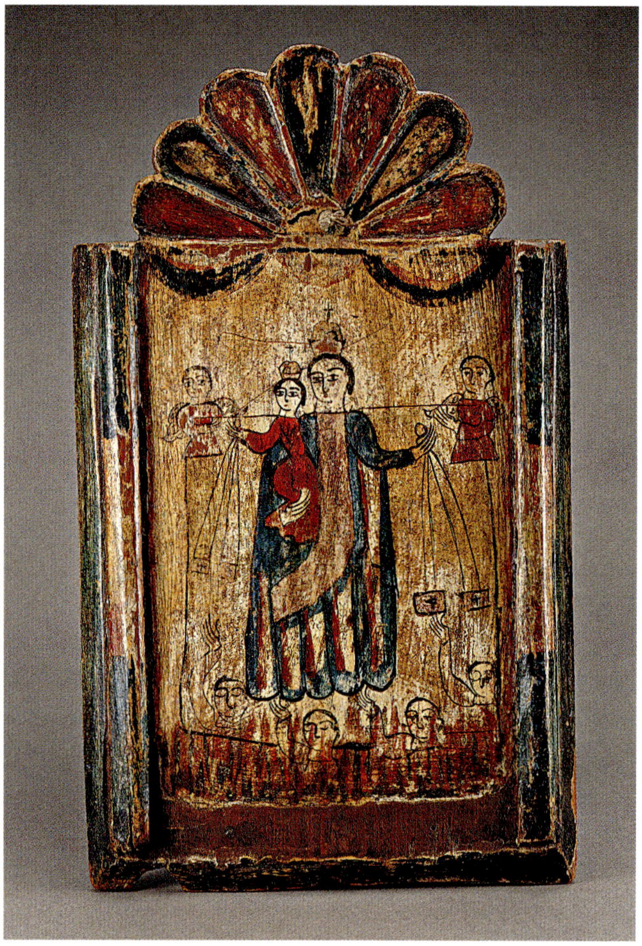

Serious ethnographic research in the Southwest began in 1879 when James Stevenson led an expedition to document lifeways, collect artifacts, and photograph daily activities at Zuni Pueblo. Self-styled anthropologist Frank Hamilton Cushing was a member of the Stevenson Expedition and wrote "My Adventures in Zuñi," an illustrated, three-part tale that appeared in *Century Magazine* in 1882–83. Cushing's sympathetic view of Pueblo life was published at the same time as racist articles depicting Plains Indians unfavorably during the High Plains Wars. His report demonstrated the basic humanity of the Zunis to readers accustomed only to negative stereotypes and inflammatory depictions of Indian warriors.

The most powerful image in the Cushing series was *Dance of the Great Knife*, a wood engraving produced from a gouache painting by Willard Leroy Metcalf (fig. 97) that was created from several photographs taken by expedition photographer John K. Hillers. The engraving illustrates a tense confrontation in Cushing's tale when a Zuni "warrior," probably a Pueblo sacred clown, staged a mock attack on the gullible anthropologist, probably in an effort to make him stop documenting Zuni religious events. The frail Cushing defended himself and believed that his bravery had foiled the attack. In all likelihood, the attack was a practical joke that Cushing did not fully understand, but it caused him to be more respectful of the tribe's wishes.

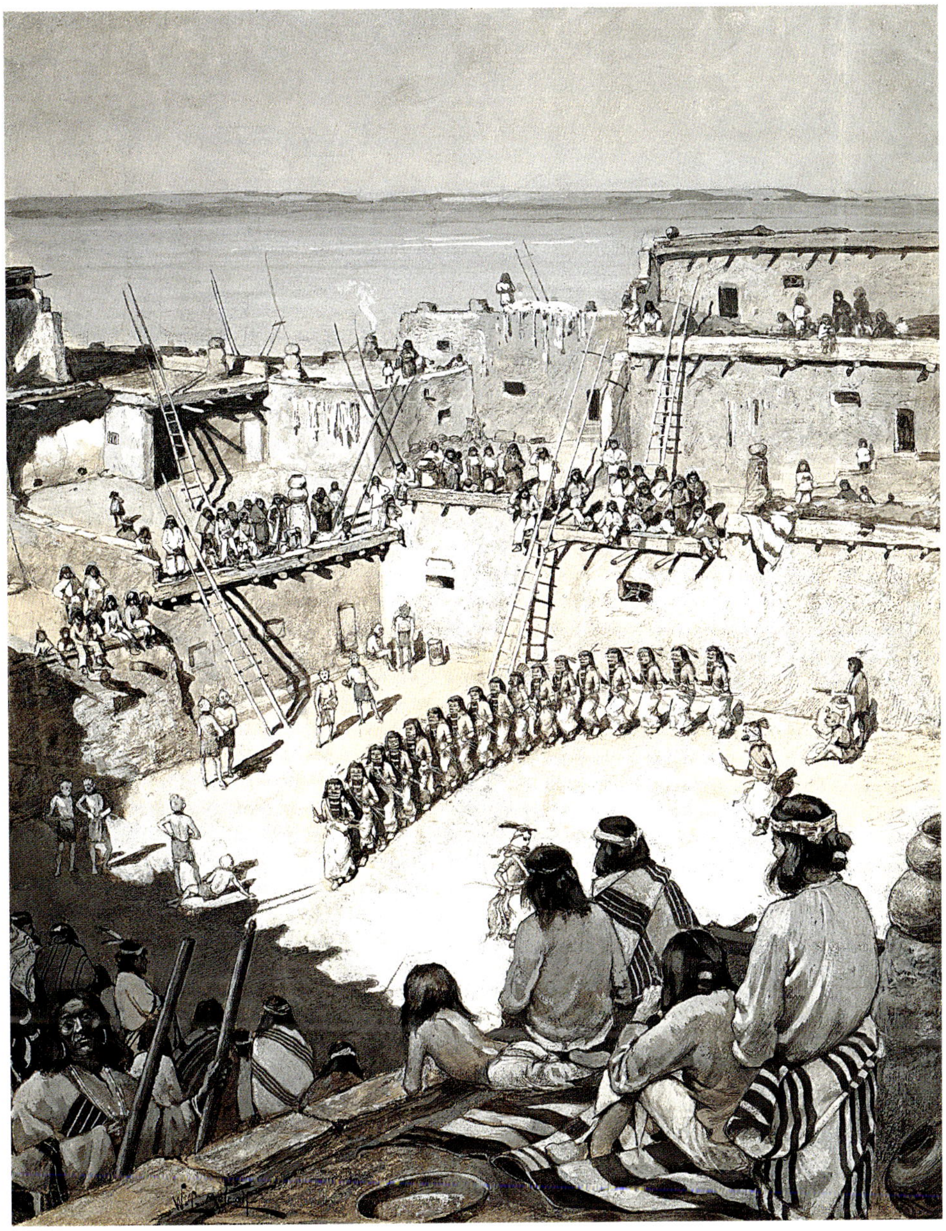

97
WILLARD LEROY METCALF (1858–1925)
DANCE OF THE GREAT KNIFE, 1882
GOUACHE ON PAPER, 19¾ X 15¾ IN.
(50.2 X 40 CM)

Century readers responded enthusiastically to the narrative and illustrations, the combination of New Mexico landscape, Pueblo architecture, and unfamiliar rituals exotic and provocative. Because the Zunis were well removed from Hispanic settlements, ethnologists and painters considered them to be more authentically Puebloan than the Rio Grande Pueblos, who by then had closely interacted with Hispanic colonists for three hundred years.

Cushing's essay brought the last vestiges of the western frontier into the cozy parlors of staid Victorian readers. Its acceptance reflected changing attitudes in society that refuted negative stereotypes about Native Americans in mainstream culture. The article's words and illustrations were so persuasive that it became a model for presenting a liberal interpretation of Native peoples at the end of the nineteenth century. Helen Hunt Jackson's novel *Ramona,* and her political protest *A Century of Dishonor,* also reflected this changing view of Native Americans and the history of European-American conflict with Indians.

Charles Craig was one artist who raced to the Southwest to find scenes of Native lifeways unaltered by contact with the modern world. His circa 1883 *Interior Courtyard of Pueblo, Santa Clara, New Mexico* records the mood and foreign qualities of Pueblo architecture, which was then unknown to non-southwestern audiences (fig. 98). Craig's depiction of a block of residential rooms at Santa Clara Pueblo presents a warm, homey view of Pueblo life and another sympathetic portrayal of Native Americans.

Although *Interior Courtyard* illustrates the endurance of Native architecture and lifeways that were expected to disappear with manifest destiny, this and other paintings of the genre should not be interpreted as ethnographically realistic. Instead, they reflect the artist's control of composition, color, and tone in presenting an idealized view of the Pueblo villages intended to distinguish the "good" agrarian Indians from the "bad" Plains warriors. Ironically, after Plains tribes adapted to the constraints of reservation life and governmental domination, Craig painted equally nostalgic pictures of the nomadic lifeways of Plains Indians of the past.

Craig's quaint view of Santa Clara Pueblo is at odds with Charles F. Lummis's 1889 cyanotype *Dance, Pueblo of Santa Clara, N.M.* (fig. 99). Initially, the photograph, which depicts tourists in black dresses and suits observing a Pueblo dance, seems like any other dance image from the late nineteenth century. However, the key to understanding the photograph is the series of dark, horizontal forms in the near background, which reveal a slightly out-of-focus Denver and Rio Grande train stopped on the tracks behind the pueblo.

Dance, Pueblo of Santa Clara is one of the earliest southwestern photographs to document the complex interrelationship between the railways, tourists, and Indian tribes in the Southwest. Whether the train happened to stop at the dance or coaches were specially chartered to bring tourists to the religious event is an intriguing question that the photograph does not answer, although the dearth of Pueblo participants implies that this was a staged tourist encounter.

Lummis also introduced New Mexico Hispanic culture to national literary circles in 1889 when *The Cosmopolitan Magazine* published his essay "The Penitent Brothers." This sensationalist narrative detailed the rites of the brotherhood in rural areas of northern New Mexico and southern Colorado. Lummis photographed the rituals against the group's wishes, even threatening them with a pistol in order to photograph a mock Penitente crucifixion (fig.100). Lummis's descriptions and photo-based drawings created false, negative stereotypes about Hispanic lifeways. The popularity of his Southwest narratives and photographs, however, underscored the public's interest in exotic scenes from New Mexico.

Paintings of Penitente rituals as well as the Hopi Snake Dance of Arizona remained popular subjects throughout the first half of the twentieth century—despite objections raised by the groups depicted that the images were insensitive and inaccurate portrayals of their communities.

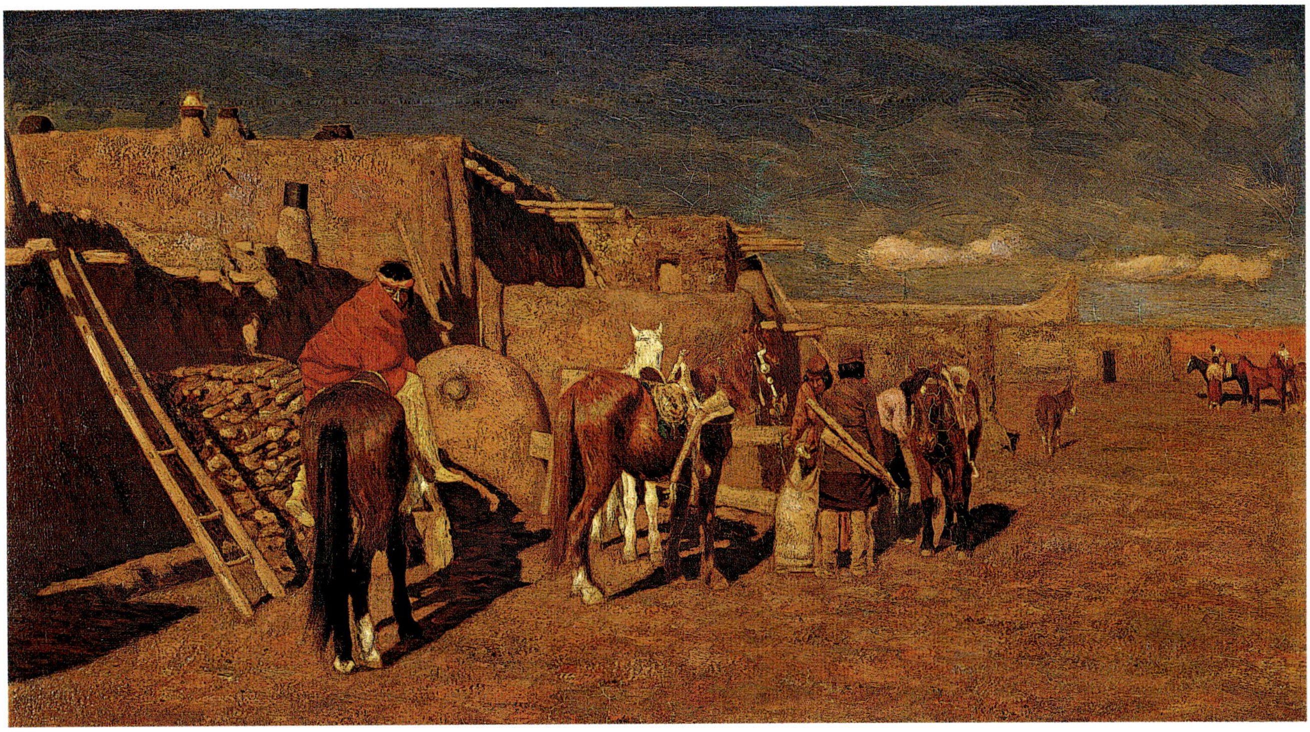

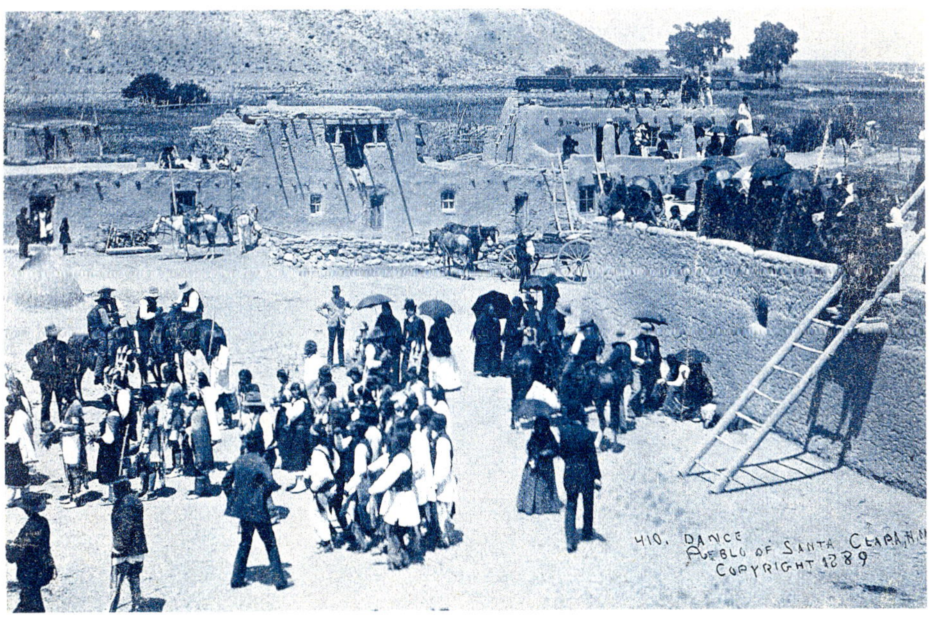

98
CHARLES CRAIG (1846–1931)
INTERIOR COURTYARD OF PUEBLO, SANTA CLARA, NEW MEXICO, CIRCA 1883
OIL ON CANVAS, 21½ X 39½ IN.
(54.6 X 100.3 CM)

99
CHARLES F. LUMMIS (1859–1928)
DANCE, PUEBLO OF SANTA CLARA, N.M., 1889
CYANOTYPE, 4½ X 6¾ IN. (11.4 X 17.1 CM)

100
W. MARTIN JOHNSON (DATES UNKNOWN)
THE CRUCIFIXION, 1889
PHOTOENGRAVING OF A PEN-AND-INK DRAWING AFTER A PHOTOGRAPH BY CHARLES F. LUMMIS, 3¼ X 5 IN. (8.3 X 12.7 CM)

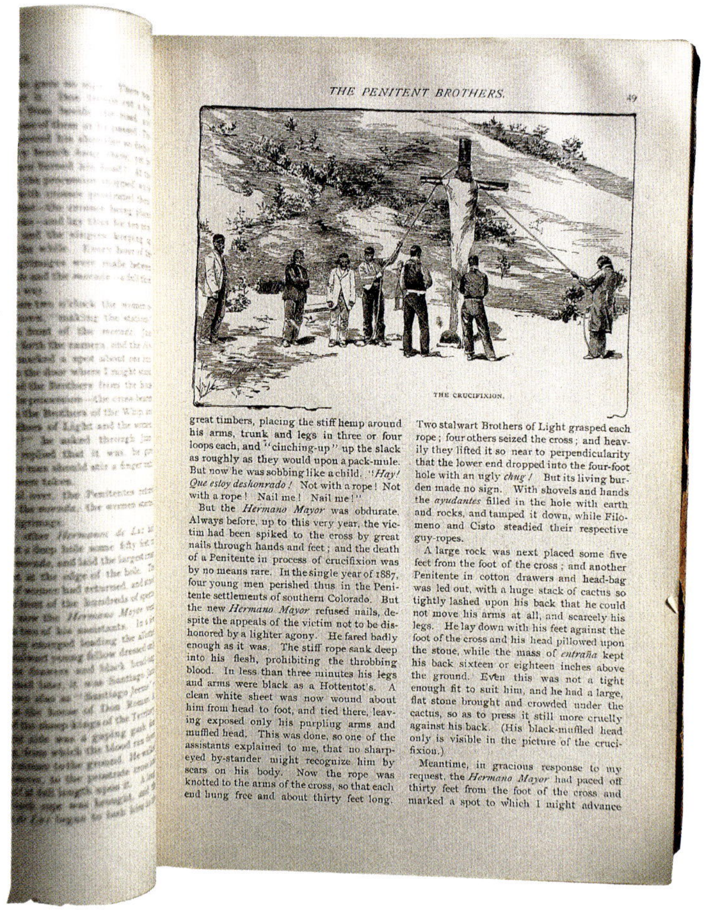

THE PENITENT BROTHERS. 49

THE CRUCIFIXION.

great timbers, placing the stiff hemp around his arms, trunk and legs in three or four loops each, and "cinching-up" up the slack as roughly as they would upon a pack-mule. But now he was sobbing like a child. "¡*Hay! Que estoy deshonrado!* Not with a rope! Not with a rope! Nail me! Nail me!"

But the *Hermano Mayor* was obdurate. Always before, up to this very year, the victim had been spiked to the cross by great nails through hands and feet; and the death of a Penitente in process of crucifixion was by no means rare. In the single year of 1887, four young men perished thus in the Penitente settlements of southern Colorado. But the new *Hermano Mayor* refused nails, despite the appeals of the victim not to be dishonored by a lighter agony. He fared badly enough as it was. The stiff rope sank deep into his flesh, prohibiting the throbbing blood. In less than three minutes his legs and arms were black as a Hottentot's. A clean white sheet was now wound about him from head to foot, and tied there, leaving exposed only his purpling arms and muffled head. This was done, so one of the assistants explained to me, that no sharp-eyed by-stander might recognize him by scars on his body. Now the rope was knotted to the arms of the cross, so that each end hung free and about thirty feet long. Two stalwart Brothers of Light grasped each rope; four others seized the cross; and heavily they lifted it so near to perpendicularity that the lower end dropped into the four-foot hole with an ugly *chug!* But its living burden made no sign. With shovels and hands the *ayudantes* filled in the hole with earth and rocks, and tamped it down, while Filomeno and Cisto steadied their respective guy-ropes.

A large rock was next placed some five feet from the foot of the cross; and another Penitente in cotton drawers and head-bag was led out, with a huge stack of cactus so tightly lashed upon his back that he could not move his arms at all, and scarcely his legs. He lay down with his feet against the foot of the cross and his head pillowed upon the stone, while the mass of *entraña* kept his back sixteen or eighteen inches above the ground. Even this was not a tight enough fit to suit him, and he had a large, flat stone brought and crowded under the cactus, so as to press it still more cruelly against his back. (His black-muffled head only is visible in the picture of the crucifixion.)

Meantime, in gracious response to my request, the *Hermano Mayor* had paced off thirty feet from the foot of the cross and marked a spot to which I might advance

Lummis repeatedly utilized the picturesque as a synonym for his interpretations of the Southwest. Just as the travel literature of the 1880s and 1890s created an exotic, mythic view of North Africa and the Middle East now known as "Orientalism," Lummis created an exotic, mythic "southwesternist" vision of New Mexico, by focusing on provocative sights and by comparing the region to the Near East. Lummis utilized his photographs to assert the veracity of his articles, which express an eclectic mix of euphoric praise and condescending criticism.

While picturesque depictions emphasized the positive aspects of the Southwest, Lummis's derogatory comments about aspects of Native and Hispanic peoples and their customs underscored his intellectual dominance. Lummis blended reverence and bigotry into a southwesternist literary genre that stereotyped indigenous peoples as exotic players in a cultural theater.

Such contradictory attitudes dominated New Mexico art at the end of the nineteenth century. Josephine Foard was a supporter of the 1890s arts and crafts movement who was interested in alleviating poverty in the pueblos. Foard thought that Pueblo jars would be more salable as beautiful vases for summer flowers. But there was just one problem: Pueblo jars were not watertight and ruined wooden tables as the ceramic wept. To solve the problem, Foard moved to Laguna Pueblo, a stop on the Santa Fe Railway line, to teach potters how to glaze their pottery and make it watertight. But it made no sense to them to seal a water jar as they believed evaporation was needed to cool the water in the vessels.

To make her case, Foard simply purchased vessels from Pueblo potters, lined their interiors with a glaze, and refired them in a wood-burning kiln that she built at Laguna. A vessel molded and painted by Queaustea from Acoma Pueblo is an example of a Pueblo jar that Foard altered (fig. 101). The interior reveals a thick clear glaze, but on the outside the refiring slightly smudged the pearly white slip so important in Acoma ceramics.

Ironically, Foard's reworked Pueblo vessels did not sell well when she took them to arts and crafts sales on the East Coast. Her efforts are another example of the inherent belief in the superiority of European Americans' cultural knowledge. Foard's modifications of Pueblo art summarized the aesthetic and cultural clash that occurred during the American colonial experience in New Mexico.

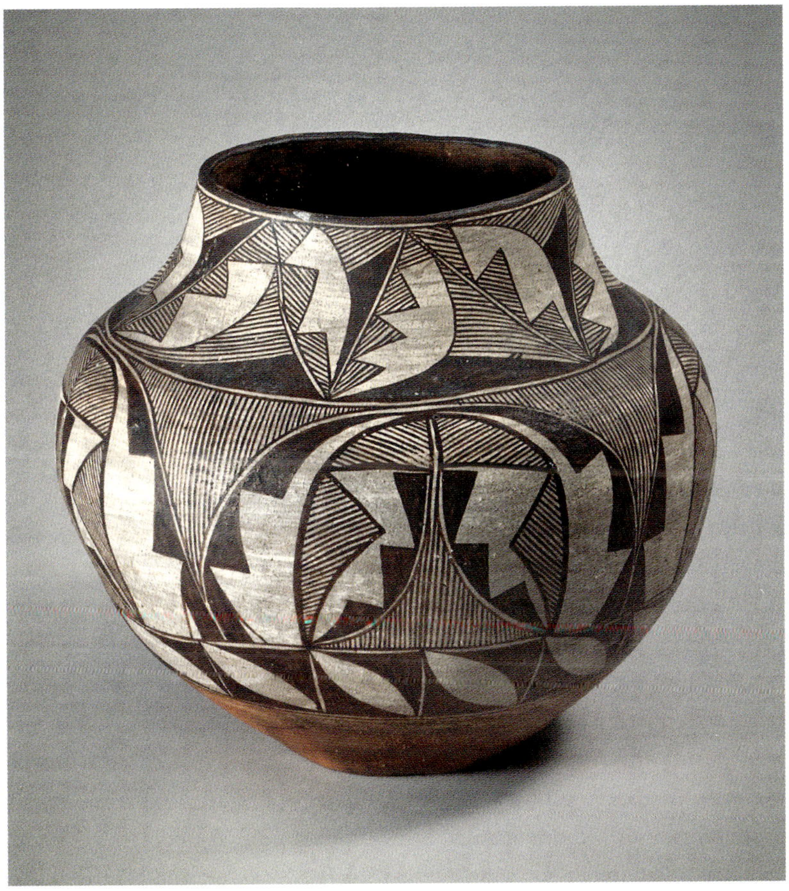

101
QUEAUSTEA AND JOSEPHINE FOARD
(DATES UNKNOWN)
UNTITLED (WATERPROOFED ACOMA JAR), 1900–1905
CLAY, PIGMENTS, AND GLAZE,
10¼ x 12 IN. (26 x 30.5 CM)

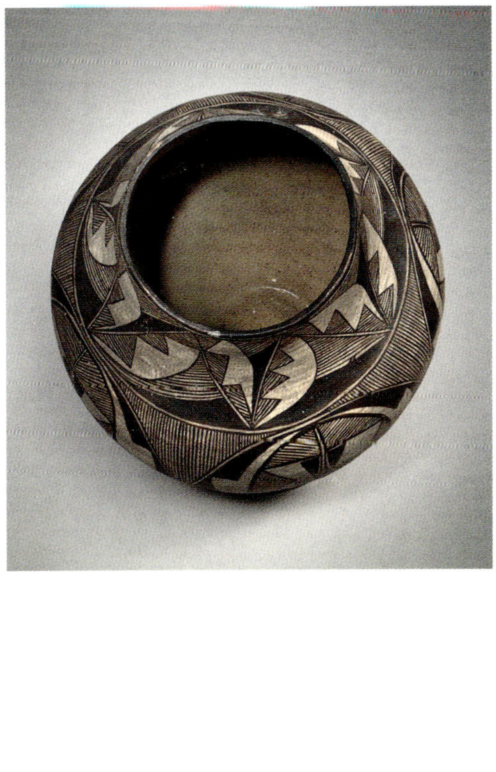

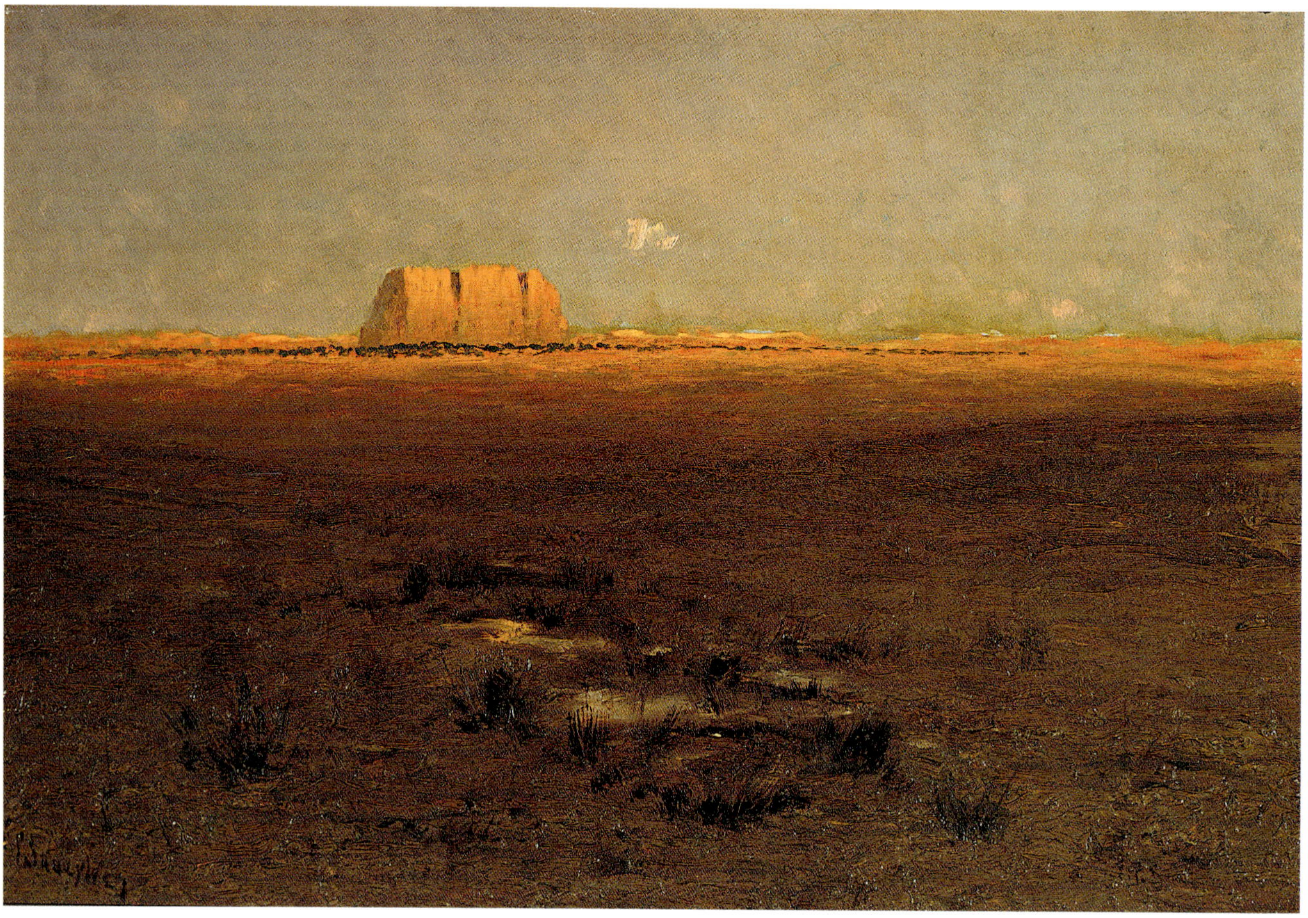

102
FRANK SAUERWEIN (1871–1910)
ENCHANTED MESA, 1902
OIL ON CANVAS, 11⅝ X 17¾ IN. (29.5 X 45.1 CM)

Frank Sauerwein produced a romantic depiction of an ancestral home of Acoma Pueblo, *Enchanted Mesa* (fig. 102). One day, according to legend, while pueblo residents worked in their fields, a massive rock fell and trapped three elderly women on the mesa top. The women perished when rescuers could not build ladders tall enough to connect the broken trail with the top of the mesa. While Sauerwein's image is one of beauty to easterners just discovering New Mexico, its underlying story is one of tragedy in the Pueblo world. Such images and their accompanying tales made New Mexico more exotic and visually intriguing to eastern audiences.

In summary, during the American Colonial period European-American painters superimposed their aesthetic views on New Mexico. Despite some efforts to present accurate descriptions of indigenous peoples in the Southwest, European-American artists and writers most often promoted the region's indigenous cultures as exotic and bizarre. Like Lummis, many photographers took photographs of indigenous peoples against their will. A snapshot of the train station and Alvarado Hotel in Albuquerque, for example, shows Pueblo pottery sellers covering up so they could not be photographed (fig. 103).

The colonial period in New Mexico ended with a downturn in the production of Native American and Hispanic arts. By the first decade of the twentieth century, Pueblo potters were abandoning the production of fine wares and substituting inexpensive items for sale to tourists. The *santero* tradition temporarily declined due to use of official Catholic imagery. Manufactured goods from the East were rapidly replacing indigenous objects made for internal use.

Images in popular publications presented misconceptions about life in New Mexico that reinforced colonial attitudes and racist stereotypes. These misconceptions became profitable as traders encouraged tourists to visit the Southwest and view unusual people and their strange practices. Ironically, the promotion of southwesternist stereotypes of indigenous lifeways would help encourage the arrival of European-American artists seeking new subjects after New Mexico achieved statehood.

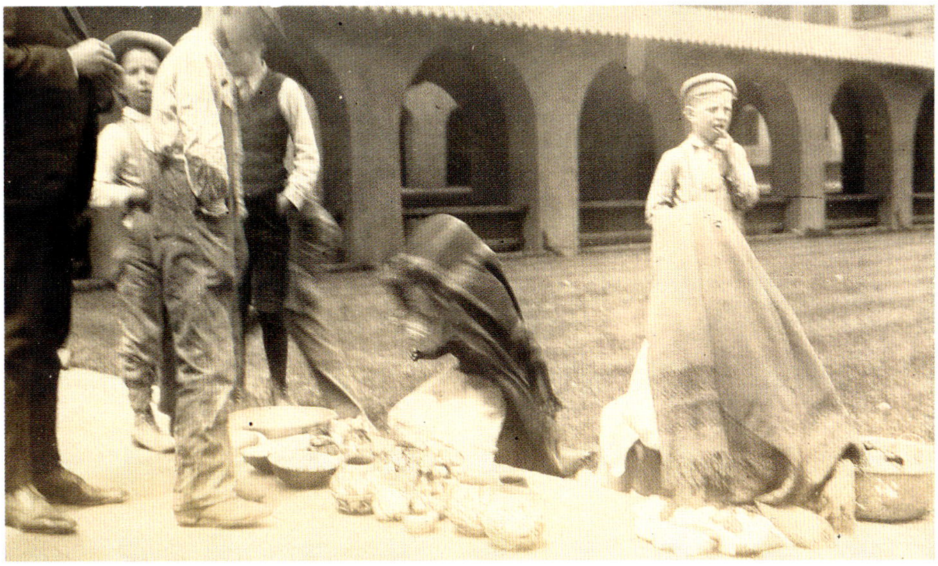

103
MAKER UNKNOWN
OUTSIDE THE ALVARADO, 1905–1910
GELATIN SILVER PRINT, 3½ x 5½ IN. (8.9 x 14 CM)

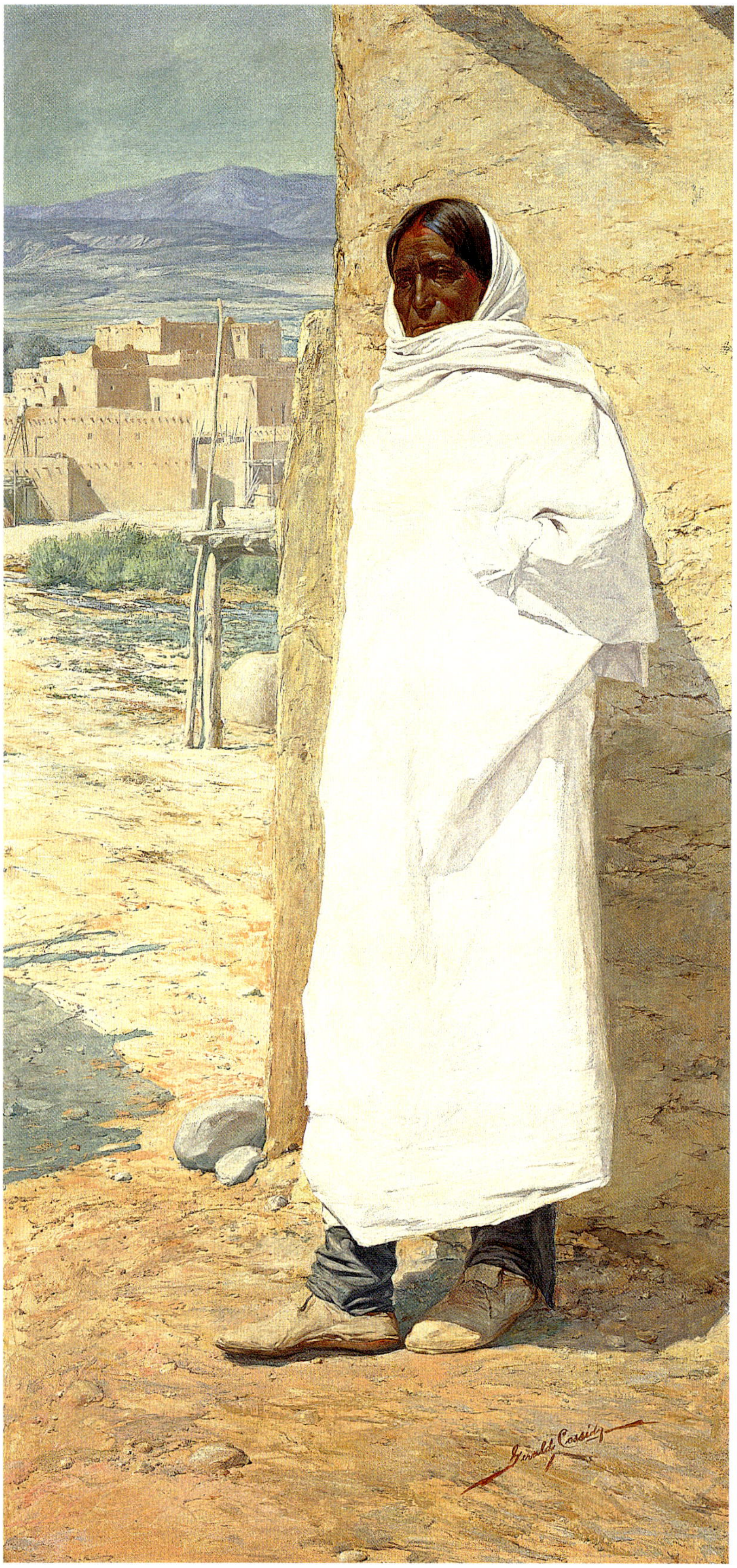
Gerald Cassidy

CHAPTER 5

Artist Fraternities after New Mexico Statehood

Gerald Cassidy's painting *Cui Bono?* (fig. 104) captured the uncertainty that New Mexicans felt on the cusp of statehood. *Cui Bono?*—Latin for "Who Benefits?"—asked New Mexicans to consider who would benefit from the impending changes in government. Proponents of economic development hoped that statehood would break the economic stagnation that gripped the Southwest. Just as entrepreneurs flocked to New Mexico after the Mexican-American War with get-rich-quick schemes, businessmen congregated in Santa Fe and wondered how they could make statehood financially rewarding.

In *Cui Bono?*, an anonymous man from Taos Pueblo wears a commercially woven, white cotton blanket that was Pueblo summer wear circa 1910 but is also a sign that commercial goods would soon replace handmade items. In a broader sense, the painting questions the benefits of statehood for the majority of New Mexico residents, who at the time were either Hispanos or Native Americans. This perspective resonated throughout New Mexico during the first decades after statehood.

A small band of European-American academic artists found their way to New Mexico before World War I, regarding themselves pioneers blazing a painterly trail into an aesthetic wilderness without artists. Although fascinated by Pueblo pottery, Navajo weavings, and Hispanic *retablos* and *bultos*, these outsiders collected these objects not as indigenous works of art but as studio props that lent an air of ethnographic authenticity to their paintings. This first wave of artists also did not consider the region's indigenous artists to be artists. Paul A. F. Walter expressed the ethnocentric, condescending attitude of the time when he noted that the academic artists had a "fondness for primitive color and patterns" and the "naive crudities of aboriginal art" (Walter 1916, 238).

SEE NEW MEXICO FIRST

The achievement of New Mexico statehood on January 6, 1912, initiated efforts to promote economic development through cultural tourism. The state's interest in economic development meshed seamlessly with the national "City Beautiful" and "See America First" movements, and with the promotional efforts of the Santa Fe Railway. These movements sought to improve quality of life through the modernization of public services and to encourage Americans to travel at home rather than abroad.

104
GERALD CASSIDY (1869–1934)
CUI BONO?, CIRCA 1911
OIL ON CANVAS, 93½ X 48 IN.
(237.5 X 121.9 CM)

Santa Fe's economic development efforts evolved into a "See New Mexico First" campaign promoted by the political coalition that had achieved statehood. Small exhibitions, such as the 1912–13 "New-Old Santa Fe" in the Palace of the Governors, offered possible promotional ideas that concentrated on the region's unique architectural style, artists, and landscape views. The exhibition synthesized cultural documentation, nostalgia, and preservation into an invented architectural style, Pueblo–Spanish Revival, that promoters hoped would set Santa Fe apart as a tourist destination. It was decided that building an art museum in the Spanish–Pueblo Revival style could attract artists and visitors while establishing an architectural image for the city.

The central players in the partnership involved in building the museum included four prominent Santa Feans: lawyer and rancher Frank Springer, who was president of the Maxwell Land Grant and did legal work for the Santa Fe Railway; journalist turned banker Paul A. F. Walter; archaeologist and culture promoter Edgar Lee Hewett; and Hewett's able assistant, commercial artist Kenneth Chapman. Their alliance brought together financial, legislative, cultural, and artistic interests.

Hewett's first attempt to promote New Mexico art and tourism had occurred at the 1915 Panama–California Exposition in San Diego, where he served as curator of exhibitions and used his position to feature New Mexico art and culture. The New Mexico pavilion, designed by the Colorado architectural firm of Rapp, Rapp, and Hendrickson, which based it on the San Estevan Mission at Acoma Pueblo, functioned like a theater set, where San Ildefonso potters Maria and Julian Martinez and others from the pueblo demonstrated Pueblo arts.

As part of the pavilion, Hewett and Springer commissioned Donald Beauregard to design a series of murals to narrate the life of St. Francis, the patron saint of Santa Fe, but Beauregard died before finishing the project. Kenneth Chapman and artist Carlos Vierra completed the murals (fig. 105), though not in time for the Panama–California displays.

Early in the summer of 1915, Hewett organized exhibitions in the Palace of the Governors of works by Santa Fe artists who supported making the city an artist's destination, including Cassidy, Chapman, Vierra, Sheldon Parsons, and Charles Rawles. A second display presented works by a group of painters who had just formed the Taos Society of Artists: Oscar E. Berninghaus, Ernest L. Blumenschein, E. Irving Couse, W. Herbert Dunton, Bert Geer Phillips, and Joseph Henry Sharp. The dark exhibition rooms of the Palace underscored the need for a new art museum as part of a long-range plan for economic development.

While working on the Panama–California Exposition, Hewett met Robert Henri, the New York artist, educator, and anarchist who was painting Indian portraits in southern California. Henri was well known as a member of the Ash Can School, a group of independent artists who painted social commentaries and street scenes in an anti-academic manner. Hewett invited Henri to paint in Santa Fe, and he accepted the offer of a studio in the Palace during the summers of 1916 and 1917.

Henri painted a portrait of Dieguito Roybal (fig. 106), a well-known drummer from San Ildefonso Pueblo who accompanied Pueblo dancers who performed in downtown Santa Fe. Henri then donated the painting to the new art museum for its opening exhibi-

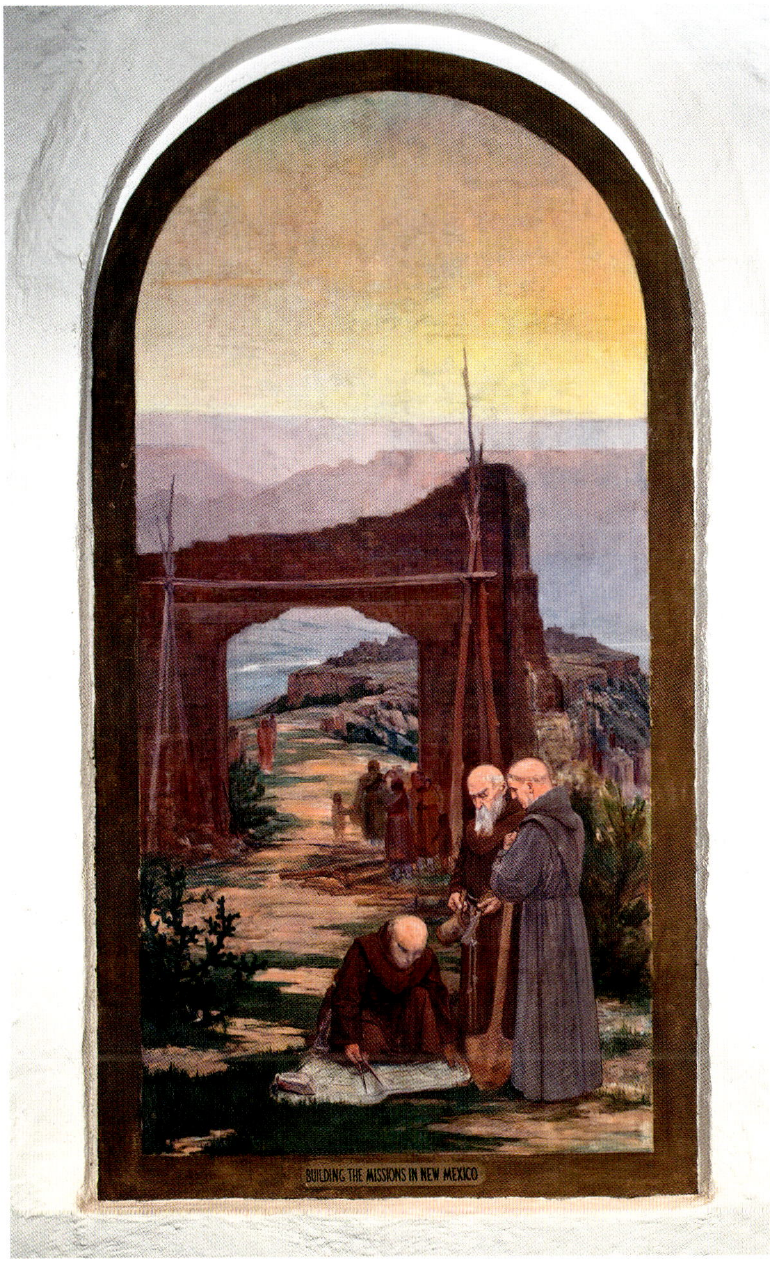

105
DESIGNED BY DONALD BEAUREGARD (1884–1914), PAINTED BY CARLOS VIERRA (1876–1937)
BUILDING OF THE MISSIONS IN NEW MEXICO, 1917
OIL ON CANVAS, 129½ x 65¾ IN. (328.9 x 167 CM)

tion. But perhaps a larger gift from Henri was convincing Hewett that the museum should not have curators. In his democratic spirit, Henri believed that any artist working in New Mexico should be allowed to exhibit their art in the museum without the approval of juries, administrators, or patrons, a radical perspective that would set the Museum of New Mexico Art Gallery (today's New Mexico Museum of Art) apart from virtually every other art museum in the country. This open-door policy appealed to other modernist and academic artists in New York and Chicago who had been systematically excluded from established institutions.

106
ROBERT HENRI (1865–1929)
PORTRAIT OF DIEGUITO ROYBAL, SAN ILDEFONSO PUEBLO, 1916
OIL ON CANVAS, 67 X 40 IN.
(170.2 X 101.6 CM)

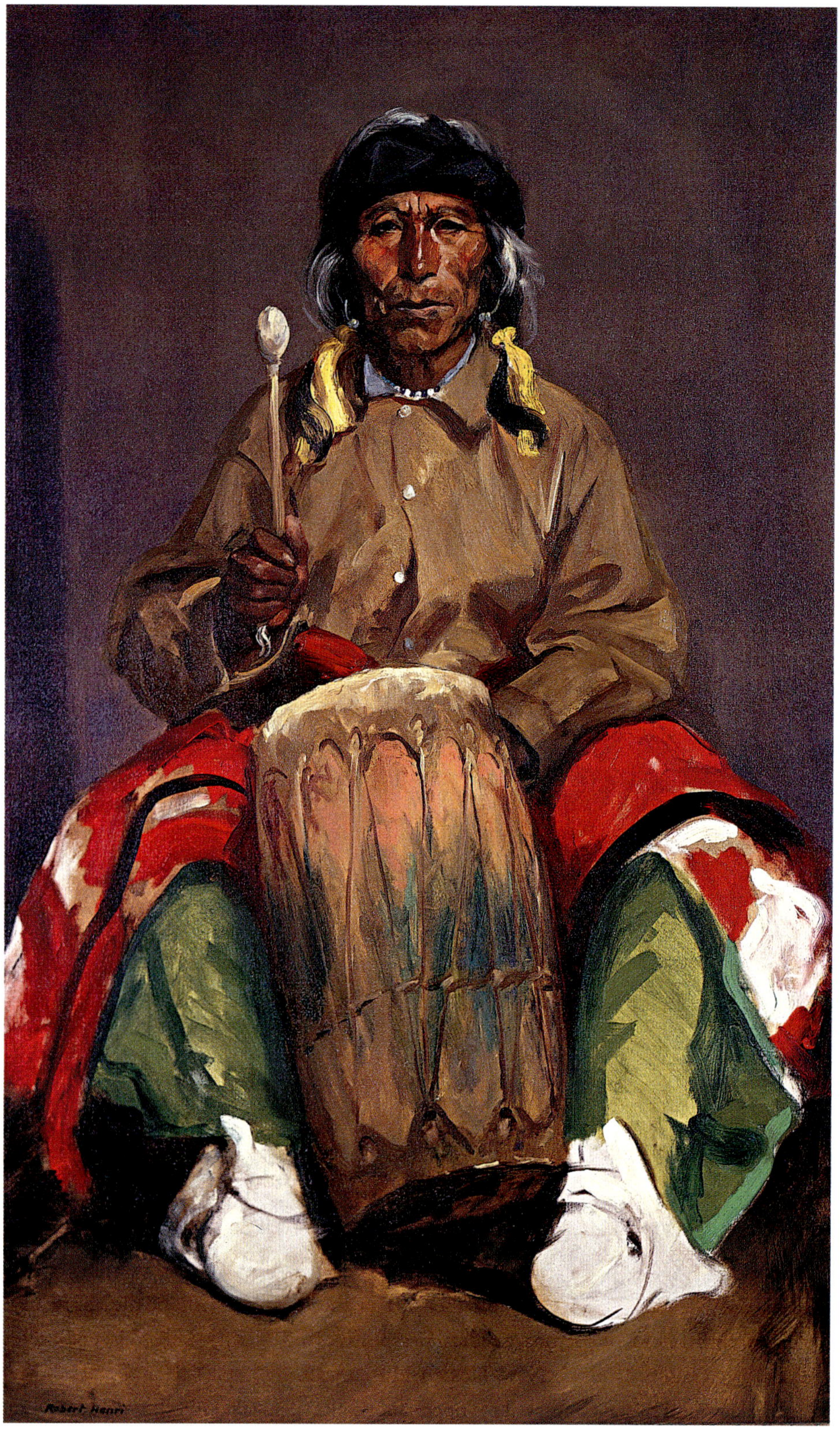

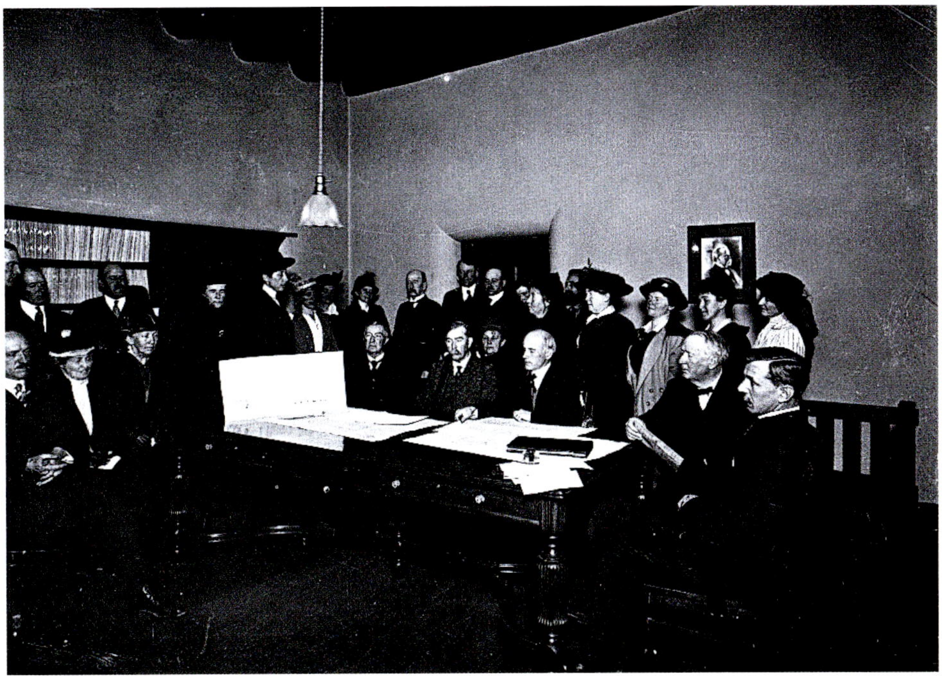

107
PHOTOGRAPHER UNKNOWN
COMMITTEE MEETING AT THE PALACE OF THE GOVERNORS CONSIDERING CHAPMAN'S RENDERING OF THE PROPOSED ART MUSEUM BUILDING, 1916
GELATIN SILVER PRINT, 8 X 10 IN. (20.3 X 25.4 CM)

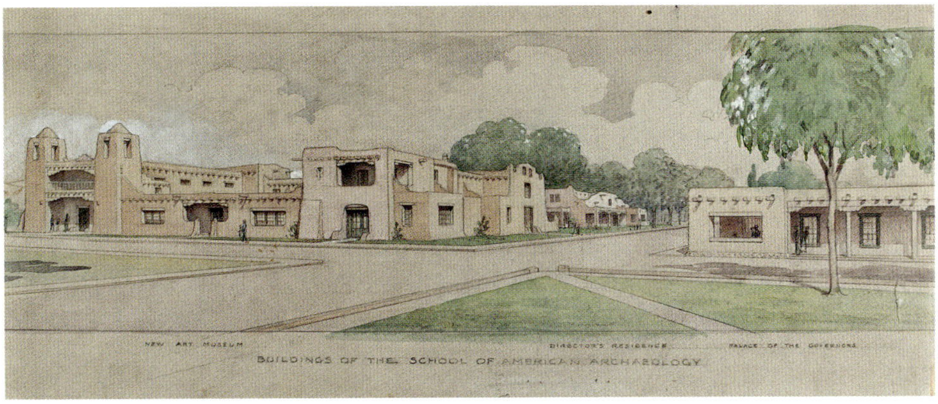

108
KENNETH CHAPMAN (1875–1986)
BUILDINGS OF THE SCHOOL OF AMERICAN ARCHAEOLOGY, CIRCA 1916
WATERCOLOR ON ILLUSTRATION BOARD, 8¾ X 20⅝ IN. (22.2 X 52.4 CM)

As they had in California, Rapp, Rapp, and Hendrickson based the new museum's design on the mission at Acoma Pueblo, but they also added an eclectic mix of elements from other Franciscan missions at Cochiti, Laguna, Pecos, San Felipe, and Santa Ana pueblos. Public meetings were held to discuss Chapman's renderings of Rapp, Rapp, and Hendrickson's design (fig. 107). One illustration showed the proposed art museum, the Palace of the Governors, and the School of American Research located together on the northwest corner of the Santa Fe Plaza as the cultural center of the Southwest (fig. 108).

Over one thousand people attended the museum's opening ceremony on November 27, 1917, and an interior photograph of the inaugural exhibition (fig. 109) shows Cassidy's *Cui Bono?* prominently installed. Hewett's efforts to promote New Mexico expanded after the museum's successful opening. In the fall of 1919, he resurrected the Santa Fe Fiesta, a commemoration of Don Diego de Vargas's reconquest of New Mexico that Santa Feans had held continuously from 1712 until the 1880s.

109
PHOTOGRAPHER UNKNOWN
EAST GALLERY NEW MEXICO MUSEUM OF ART—OPENING EXHIBITION, 1917
GLASS NEGATIVE, 8 x 10 IN. (20.3 x 25.4 CM)

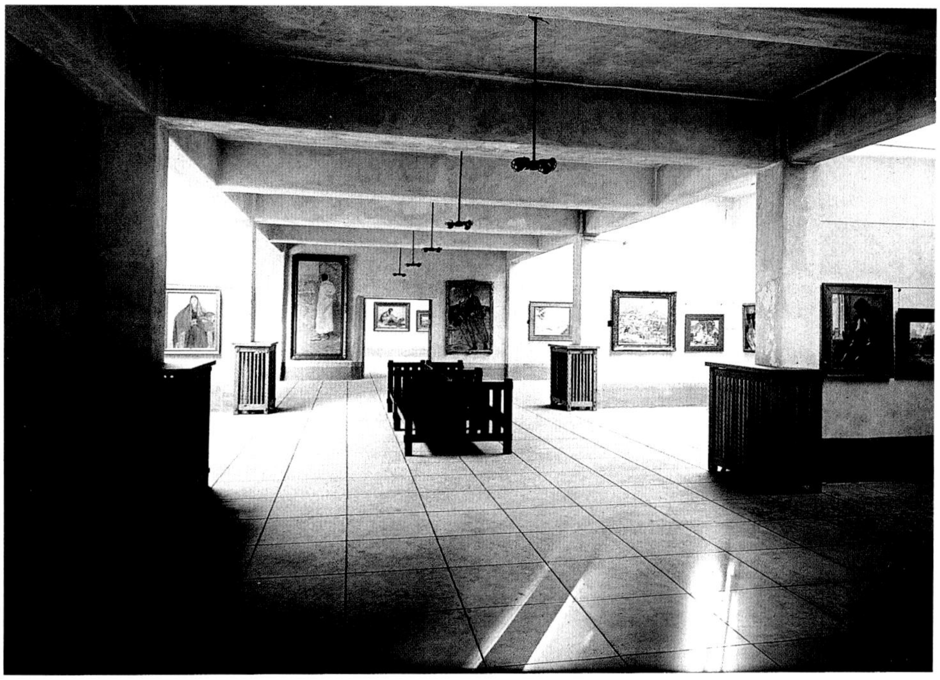

Hewett believed the fiesta was an opportunity to draw New Mexicans together for a three-day event. On the first day, the festivities began with Native American dances and activities, followed on the second day by a reenactment by Hispanos of De Vargas's entry into Santa Fe. On the third day, another reenactment depicted Kearny's U.S. troops marching into Santa Fe on August 18, 1846. More than anything the new version of the fiesta (fig. 110) demonstrated the potential for city fathers to invent an architectural style, utilize street theater, and promote art as a means of economic development.

110
WILLIAM H. ROBERTS (DATES UNKNOWN)
SANTA FE FIESTA, SANTA FE, NEW MEXICO, 1919
FILM NEGATIVE, 3½ x 6 IN. (8.9 x 15.2 CM)

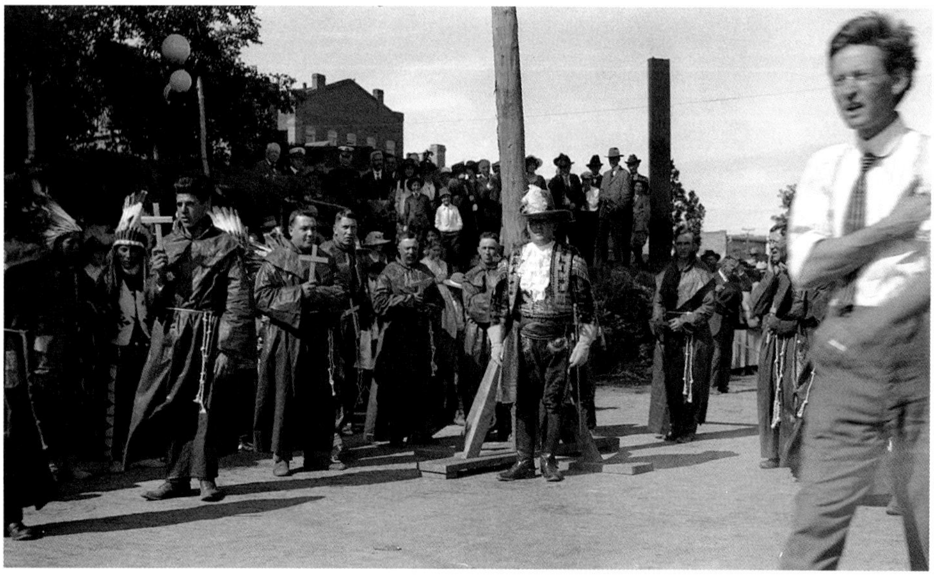

THE DEVELOPMENT OF ARTIST FRATERNITIES

In the December 1916 issue of *Art and Archaeology,* Paul A. F. Walter described the evolving "art colonies" in the region as "the Santa Fe–Taos art movement" (Walter 1916). While his concept offered some clarity, it did not include indigenous artists as part of the mix, underscoring the assumption that only European-Americans could be artists and work in art colonies. The idea of a New Mexico art movement whose scope included Native and Hispanic artists, as well as the newly arrived European-American painters, is more accurate and addresses the artistic interactions between ethnic groups across cultural divides.

Early in the twentieth century, artist fraternities developed as part of the New Mexico art movement, based on ethnicity, status, aesthetic views, and artistic accomplishments. Between the beginning of statehood in 1912 and the onset of the Great Depression, four art fraternities were established in northern New Mexico. The first was Hewett's Santa Fe Program. The project began around 1910 when anthropologists encouraged artists from San Ildefonso Pueblo to "improve" Native arts and create economic development but faded by the mid-1920s. The second fraternity, the Taos Society of Artists, was a formal, membership-only organization exclusive to accomplished academic painters active between 1915 and 1927. A third, less organized fraternity consisting of anti-academic painters existed from about 1915 through the beginning of the Great Depression. A fourth fraternity was comprised of cultural revivalists, including modern artists, philanthropists, and intellectuals, who decried the rise of cheap tourist trinkets in the 1920s and instead encouraged production of quality Pueblo pottery and Hispanic arts. Two fraternities developed after the start of the depression, the Georgia O'Keeffe Circle and the Transcendental Painting Group.

THE SANTA FE PROGRAM

Hewett considered the ancient pottery he was excavating in his archaeological work to be better made than contemporary Pueblo wares. He provided San Ildefonso potter Maria Martinez with a lump of unfired clay from an excavation and challenged her to do as well. Maria produced a narrow box circa 1909 that she decorated with images of an avanyu, a sacred feathered serpent copied from a petroglyph panel near her village (fig. 111). Other San Ildefonso potters, with encouragement from Hewett and Chapman, replicated the biscuit wares that the men were excavating nearby.

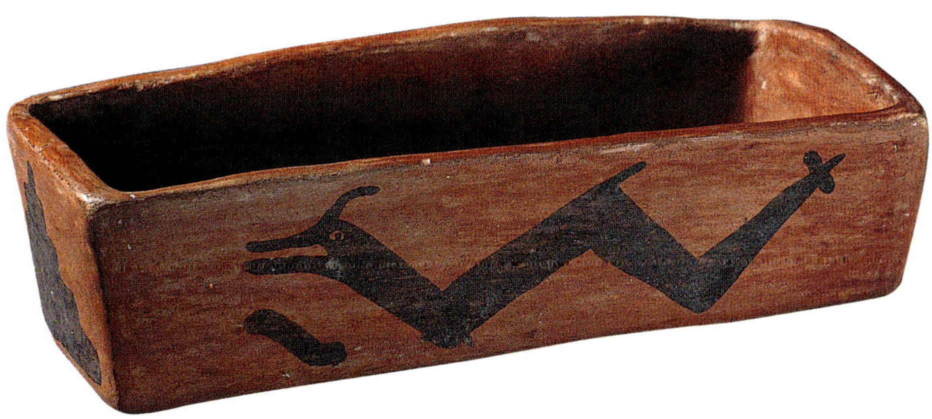

111
MARIA MARTINEZ (1887–1980)
REDWARE BOX, CIRCA 1909
CLAY AND PIGMENTS, 1 7/16 X 2 15/16 X 6 9/16 IN.
(4 X 7.5 X 16 CM)

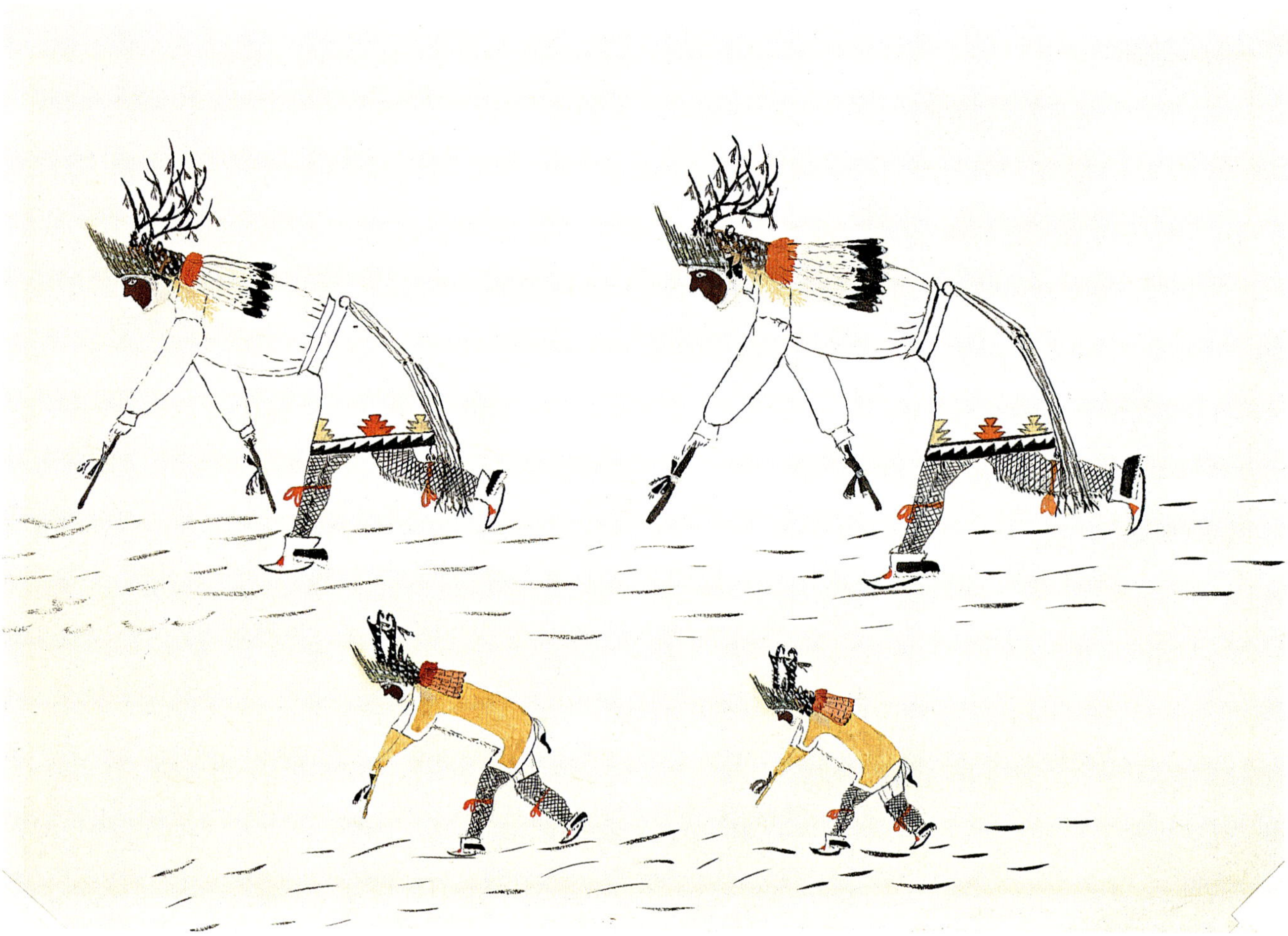

112
ALFREDO MONTOYA (WEN TSIREH)
(1892–1913)
DEER AND ANTELOPE DANCERS,
CIRCA 1911–1913
WATERCOLOR AND PENCIL ON
ILLUSTRATION BOARD, 14 x 19 IN.
(35.5 x 48.3 CM)

113
CRESCENCIO MARTINEZ (1879–1918)
CORN DANCER—WOMAN, 1918
WATERCOLOR ON PAPER, 14¼ x 11¼ IN.
(36.2 x 28.6 CM)

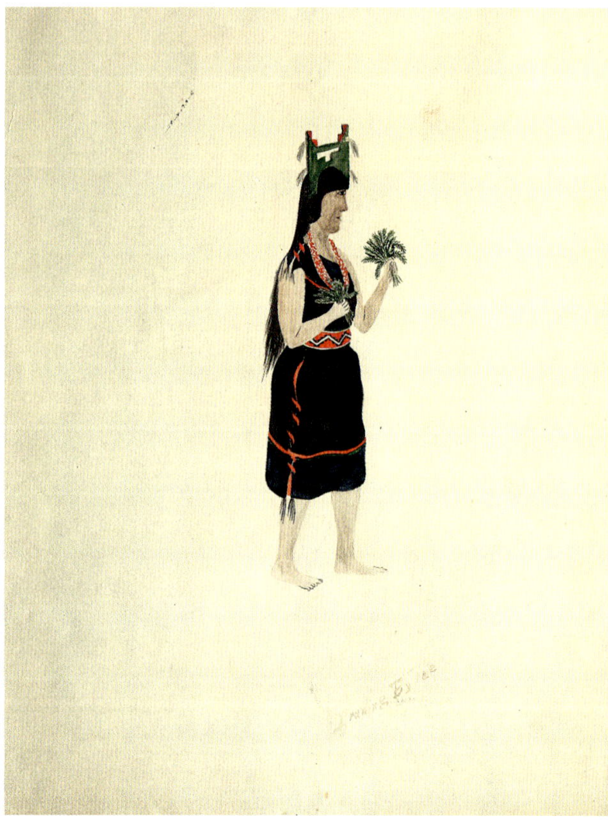

Hewett's work with potters at San Ildefonso Pueblo carried over to the Pueblo men he employed at his excavations. Around 1910, the workmen began selling pencil and watercolor images of Pueblo dancers. Hewett was fascinated by these images and asked the men to depict daily life and the ritual cycle at the pueblo in their work. Alfredo Montoya, for example, created and sold images such as *Deer and Antelope Dancers* (fig. 112). Montoya's painting demonstrates no knowledge of perspective or three-dimensional modeling, which pleased Hewett because he considered these paintings to be culturally pure and free from mainstream influences. Clearly Hewett was not interested in the aesthetic qualities of the images but instead considered these works to be visual anthropology produced by Pueblo insiders. Unfortunately, Montoya died in 1913, just at the point when a market was developing for his images of Pueblo life and ritual.

Hewett and Chapman continued working with painters and potters from San Ildefonso Pueblo throughout World War I. In 1917, Hewett commissioned Crescencio Martinez to paint twenty-three images depicting dancers from the ritual cycle at San Ildefonso Pueblo, including *Corn Dancer–Woman* (fig. 113). It appears that Hewett instructed Martinez to concentrate on individual dancers rather than lines of dancers. Martinez died in the 1918 influenza epidemic before finishing the project, leaving one image to be completed.

Martinez's nephew Alfonso Roybal (Awa Tsireh) also became a painter during this period, selling images to Hewett, writer and poet Alice Corbin Henderson, and other collectors. Roybal worked with Henderson's artist husband, William Penhallow Henderson, to develop more complex images, such as his circa 1922 *Basket Ceremony* (fig. 114). The painting depicts lines of male and female dancers, yet each figure shows individualistic facial features.

114
ALFONSO ROYBAL (AWA TSIREH) (1895–1955)
BASKET CEREMONY, CIRCA 1922
WATERCOLOR ON PAPER, 13 7/8 X 21 7/16 IN. (35.3 X 54.4 CM)

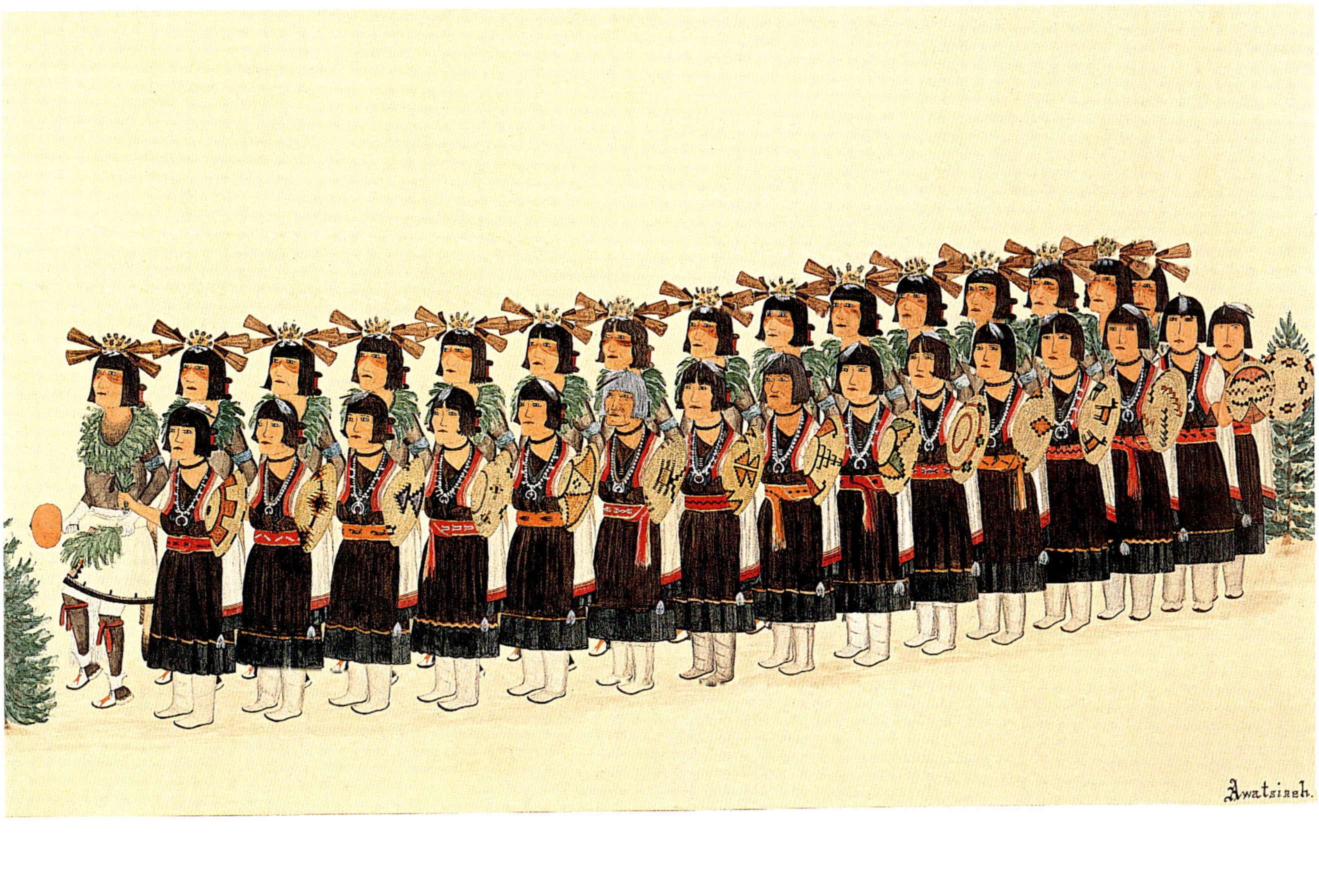

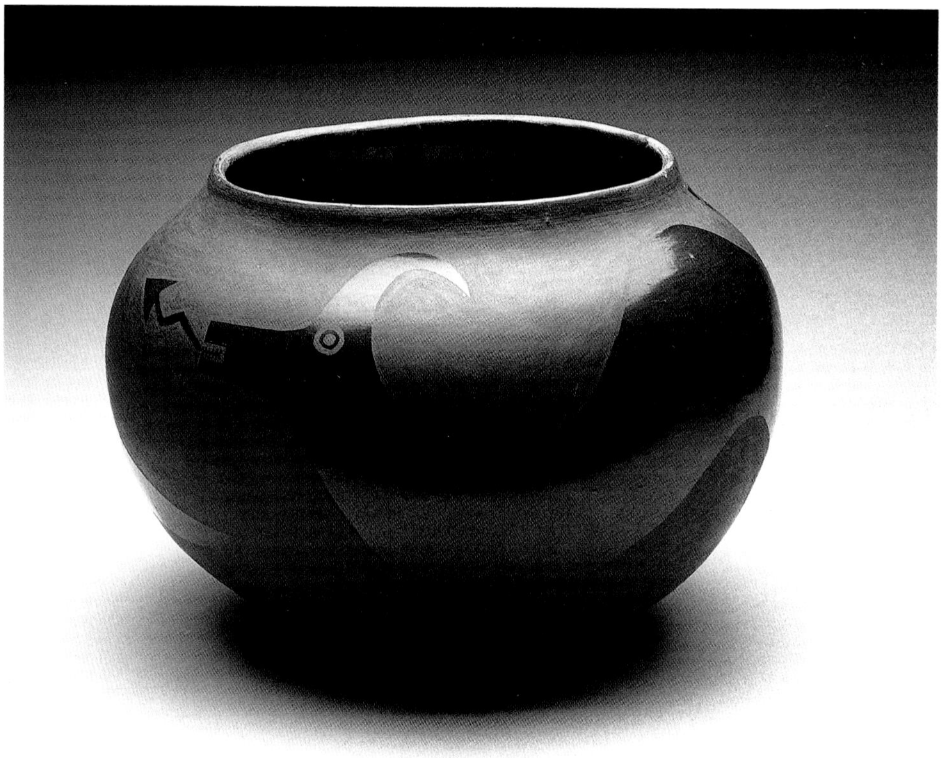

115
MARIA (1887–1980) AND JULIAN MARTINEZ (1885–1943)
BLACK-ON-MATTE JAR, CIRCA 1920
CLAY, 9⁵⁄₁₅ X 12⅜ IN. (23.7 X 31.5 CM)

In the spring of 1920, the New Mexico Museum of Art exhibited ceramics molded by Maria Martinez and painted by her husband Julian Martinez. Fourteen of the works were polychrome vessels, while three were the couple's new invention—polished black images on a matte black background (fig. 115). The nontraditional black-on-matte pieces were an instant success with the public even though they contradicted Hewett's directive that Native artists create works considered traditional for their respective tribal groups.

Two years later Kenneth Chapman organized the first Indian Fair exhibition in Santa Fe. The rules excluded nontraditional works as well as works by members of one tribe that looked like objects from another Pueblo group. Nonetheless, Maria Martinez entered both her San Ildefonso polychrome work and her invented black-on-matte pieces (fig. 116). She won best of show—a five dollar prize—for the large black ware jar at center in figure 116.

Public acceptance of Martinez's works forced Hewett to rethink his position at a time when he was abandoning economic development in Native communities. Hewett discussed his interactions with Pueblo artists in *Ancient Life in the American Southwest*, a memoir in which he egotistically lauds his efforts at social engineering, alleging that "the entire community has been restored to relative prosperity" because of the "revival of pottery making, painting, and other arts" (Hewett 1930, 80). Hewett's comments imply that San Ildefonso had all but disintegrated before he personally reinvigorated Pueblo life through the Santa Fe Program. This wasn't true, nor was his assertion that painting had been "a lost art" and that its revival "ranks as the most noteworthy achievement of the Santa Fe Pro-

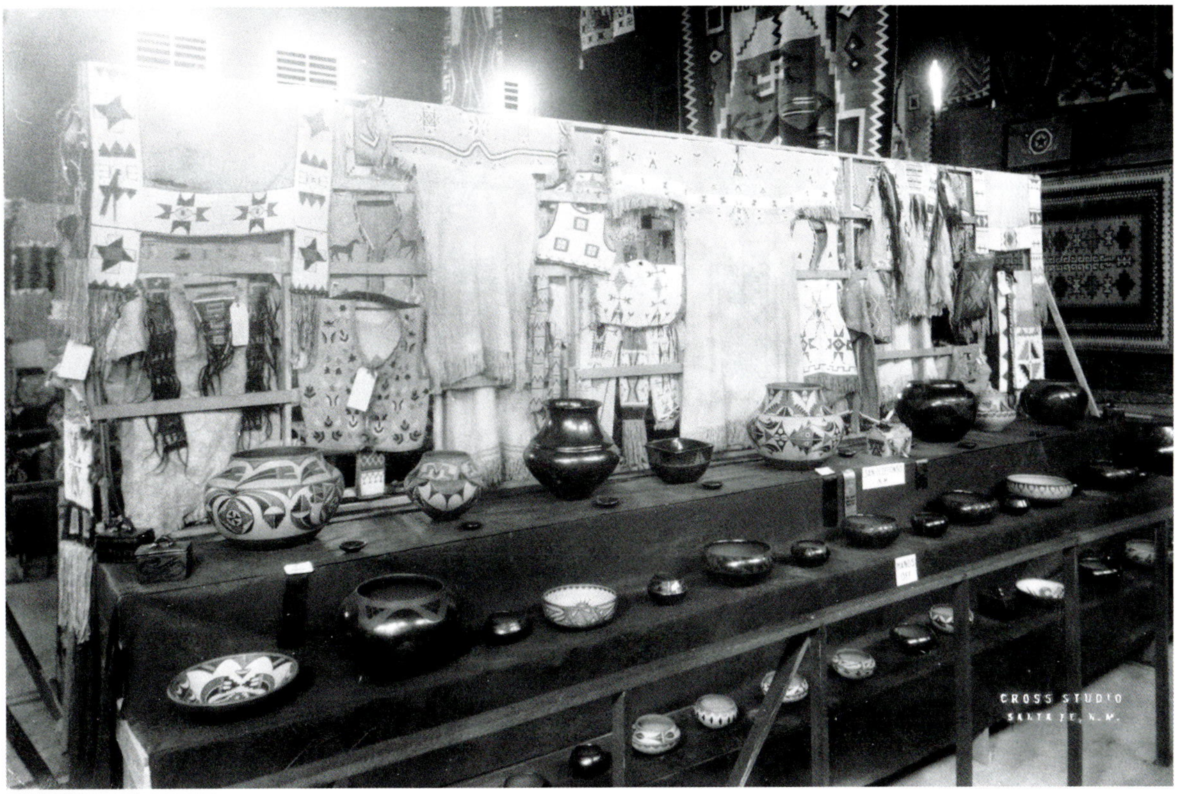

116
CROSS STUDIO (DATES UNKNOWN)
FIRST INDIAN FAIR, NATIONAL GUARD ARMORY, WASHINGTON AVENUE, SANTA FE, NEW MEXICO, 1922
GELATIN SILVER PRINT, 5 x 7 IN. (12.7 x 17.8 CM)

gram" (Hewett 1930, 148). The truth was that this first artist fraternity of Native artists and anthropologists was a purely colonial relationship dominated by the outsiders.

THE TAOS SOCIETY OF ARTISTS

E. Irving Couse's *Taos Pueblo–Moonlight* captures a romantic view of northern New Mexico that has attracted many to the region (fig. 117). Couse contrasted the glowing embers of a smoldering fire with the scene's deep evening hues, creating a powerfully affective image. The pyramidal form of the pueblo in the background is repeated in the crouching figures near the fire and the young mother with her four children. While viewers may consider this an ethnographically authentic view, the scene is a fantasy of what Pueblo life might have been like in a dimly lit past.

This idealized image of Pueblo life references two nineteenth-century ideals, manifest destiny and the noble savage. By the time Couse came to New Mexico, manifest destiny had been achieved with the connection between the Atlantic and Pacific. Contrary to nineteenth-century conventional wisdom, however, Native and Hispanic cultures did not disappear into the cultural melting pot. The concept of the noble savage promoted the belief that Native cultures lived in concert with nature before society was divided into hierarchies based on class and caste. This view contrasted strongly with the racist depictions of Native peoples as inherently warlike and uncivilized promoted during the High Plains Wars of the 1880s.

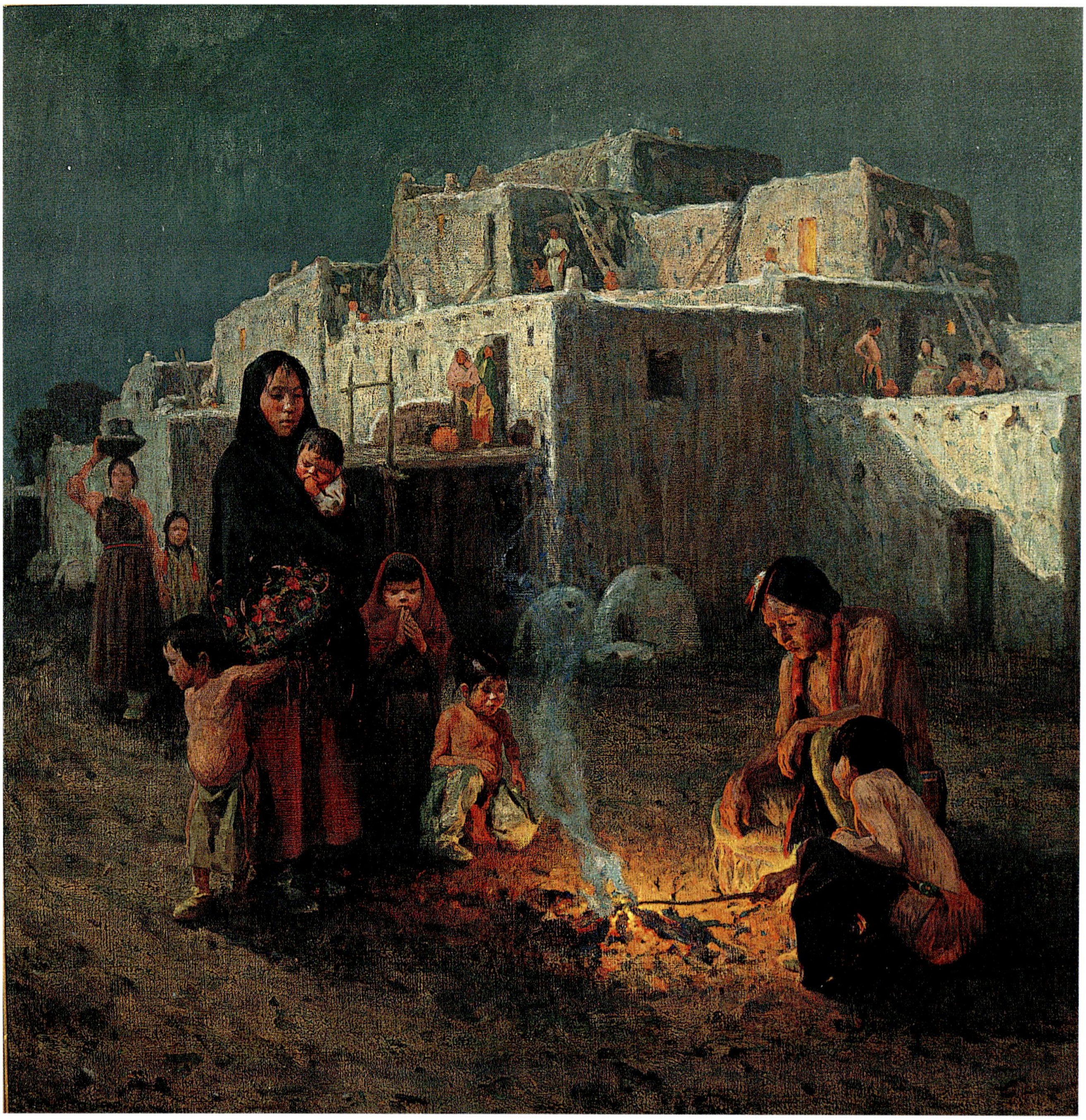

117
E. IRVING COUSE (1866–1936)
TAOS PUEBLO—MOONLIGHT, 1914
OIL ON CANVAS, 60 X 60 IN.
(152.4 X 152.4 CM)

On the cusp of World War I, Joseph Henry Sharp painted *The Stoic,* a scene depicting a Crow Indian warrior from Montana engaged in a painful ritual to prove his psychological strength (fig. 118). The warrior's son had died at an Indian school. To prove that he had the power to overcome this tragedy, the man killed four of his favorite ponies, lashed them to his back with thongs laced through his back muscles, with the intent of dragging the burden until he either collapsed or the thongs pulled through. *The Stoic* places a figure painted in an academic realist style in front of a post-impressionist landscape. By

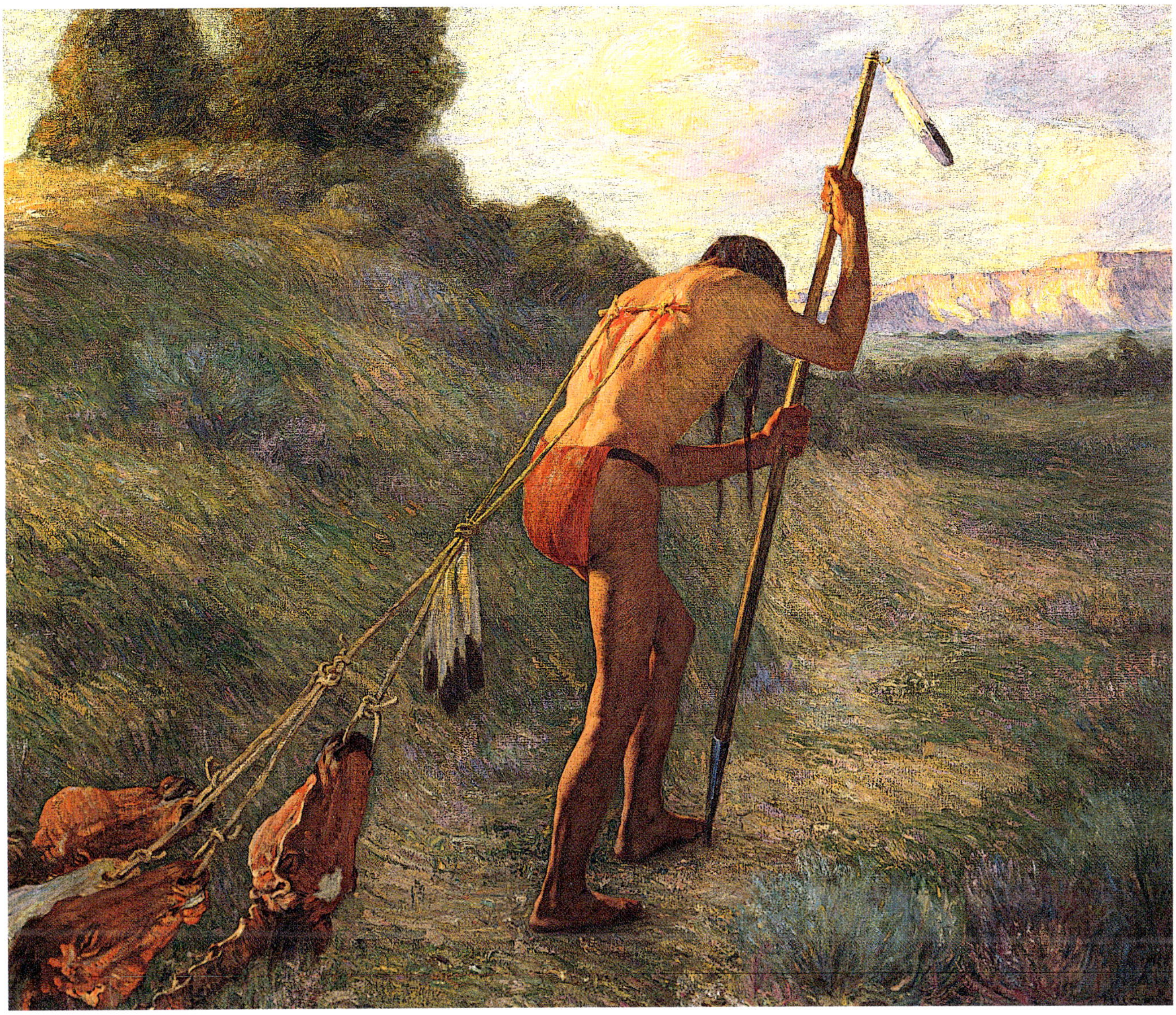

118
JOSEPH HENRY SHARP (1859–1953)
THE STOIC, 1914
OIL ON CANVAS, 52½ X 61½ IN. (133.4 X 156.2 CM)

portraying a Crow warrior in an impressionistic landscape, Sharp presents an idyllic view of Native people living in harmony with nature.

As western versions of East Coast history paintings, Couse's and Sharp's works challenge longstanding racist attitudes toward Native peoples. The allusions to history in these works lend credibility to the artists' not-so-subtle humanist messages opposing racist stereotyping of Native peoples.

Successful European-trained artists began summering in northern New Mexico at the end of the nineteenth century, using the tiny villages of northern New Mexico as places to do new work. These artists, including Couse and Sharp, sought new subjects that reflected America and American values. Oscar Berninghaus, Ernest L. Blumenschein, Herbert "Buck" Dunton, and Bert Geer Phillips also visited and were captivated by the spell of the Southwest. These six artists soon founded the Taos Society of Artists. Other

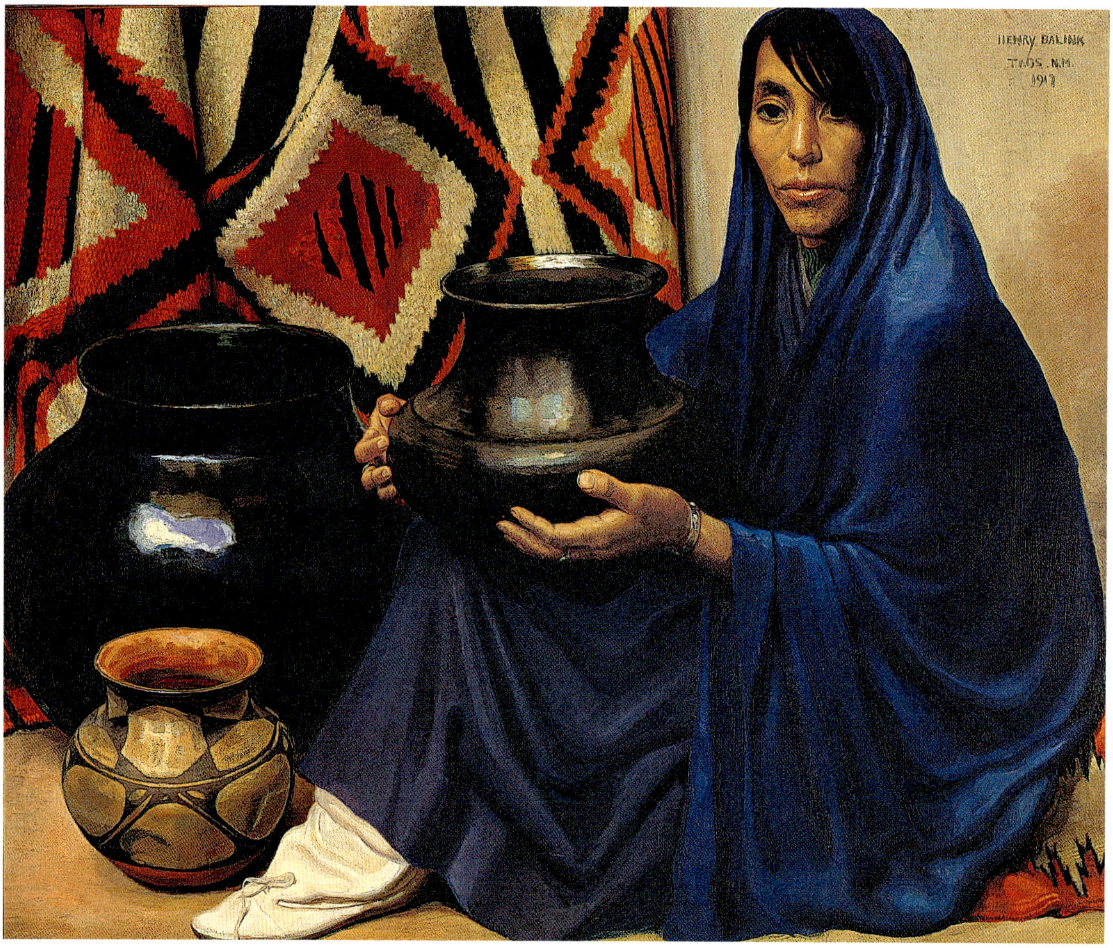

119
HENRY C. BALINK (1882–1963)
PUEBLO POTTERY, 1917
OIL ON CANVAS, 27 X 33 IN.
(68.6 X 83.8 CM)

artists voted into full membership in the Taos Society of Artists included Kenneth Adams, Catherine Critcher, E. Martin Hennings, Victor Higgins, Julius Rolshoven, and Walter Ufer, with associate memberships granted to Gustave Baumann, Randall Davey, Albert Groll, Robert Henri, B. J. O. Nordfeldt, John Sloan, and Birger Sandzen. Some of the associate members—including Baumann, Henri, and Sloan—who had opposed academic art in the past, retreated from that stance and accepted membership in the Taos Society.

During World War I, the society developed a decidedly xenophobic outlook and decided to bar any new members who were not native born. For example, Henry C. Balink was a popular academic painter of New Mexico scenes (fig. 119), yet he was barred from membership because he was an immigrant artist. The number of academic painters in northern New Mexico greatly exceeded the number of members of this elite society, though many people assumed that any painter working in northern New Mexico was a member.

Soon after the Taos Society of Artists was established, the group's aesthetic evolved in a modernist direction. The 1913 Armory Show, presented first in New York City and then in Chicago, acquainted American artists with post-impressionist developments in Europe. Despite the general conservatism of the society's academic painters, they began to incorporate visual aspects of works by European modernists. As the group members focused on works that incorporated elements of modernism, they abandoned the imposing narrative history painting and created smaller realist portraits of Native peoples.

This change in content can be seen in Bert Phillips's painting *Our Washerwoman's Family—New Mexico*, a portrait of three generations of Taos Hispanos (fig. 120). His abil-

120
BERT GEER PHILLIPS (1868–1956)
OUR WASHERWOMAN'S FAMILY—NEW MEXICO, CIRCA 1918
OIL ON CANVAS, 40½ X 41⅝ IN.
(102.9 X 105.7 CM)

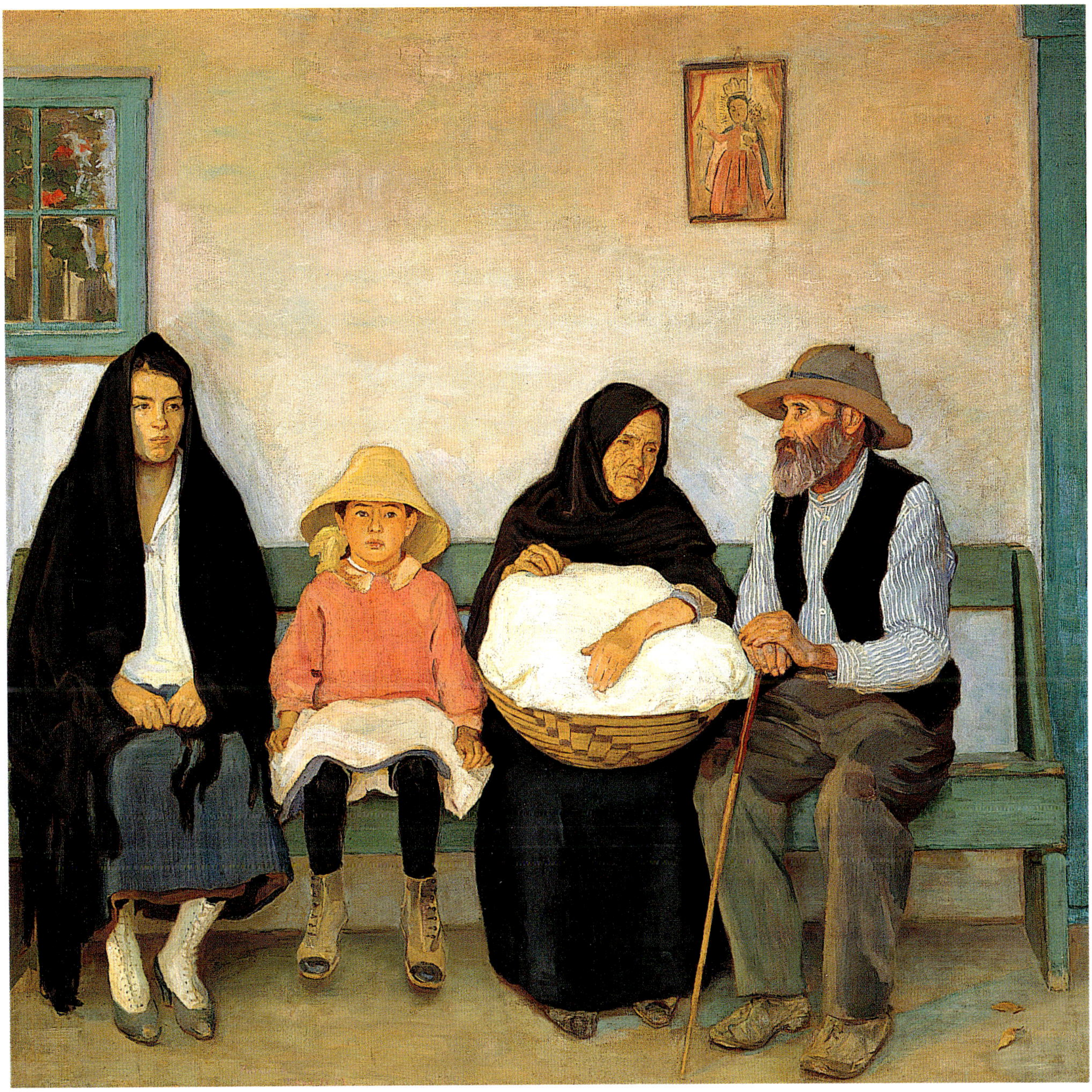

ity to capture the family's emotions in dabs of paint is truly captivating and draws viewers into the scene. Yet as viewers look closely at the subjects' faces, they can't miss their expressions of pain and discontent. Though the subjects were well known to Phillips, who was a resident of Taos, they were clearly unhappy about their status as subordinates to the elite, wealthy painter. Viewers are left with an insider's perspective on the social tensions between members of the art colony and the indigenous residents. Whether Phillips was being self-critical of his position in the community or simply was unaware of social realities in northern New Mexico is a question that remains unresolved.

121
WALTER UFER (1876–1936)
CHANCE ENCOUNTER, BEFORE 1936
OIL ON CANVAS, 20 X 25 IN.
(50.8 X 63.5 CM)

Walter Ufer's undated painting *Chance Encounter* portrays a quaint, sage-covered New Mexico landscape with two Native riders on horseback (fig. 121). Ufer's loose brush strokes create a wispy image in which the sage appears as fleeting as the white clouds behind the dark mountain. Ufer's impressionist style moves beyond the formality of society members' earlier works, verging on creating a repeatable genre with predictable

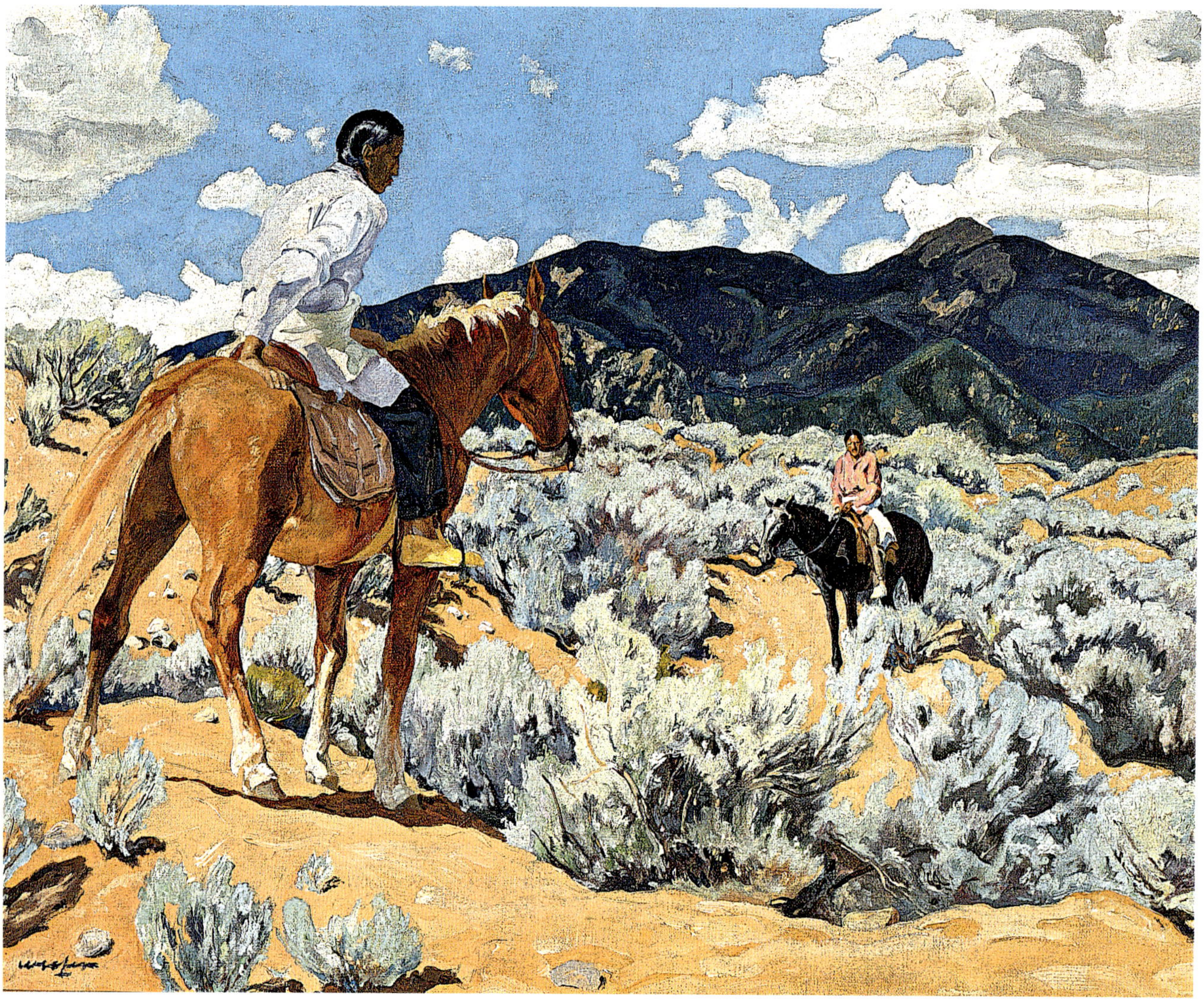

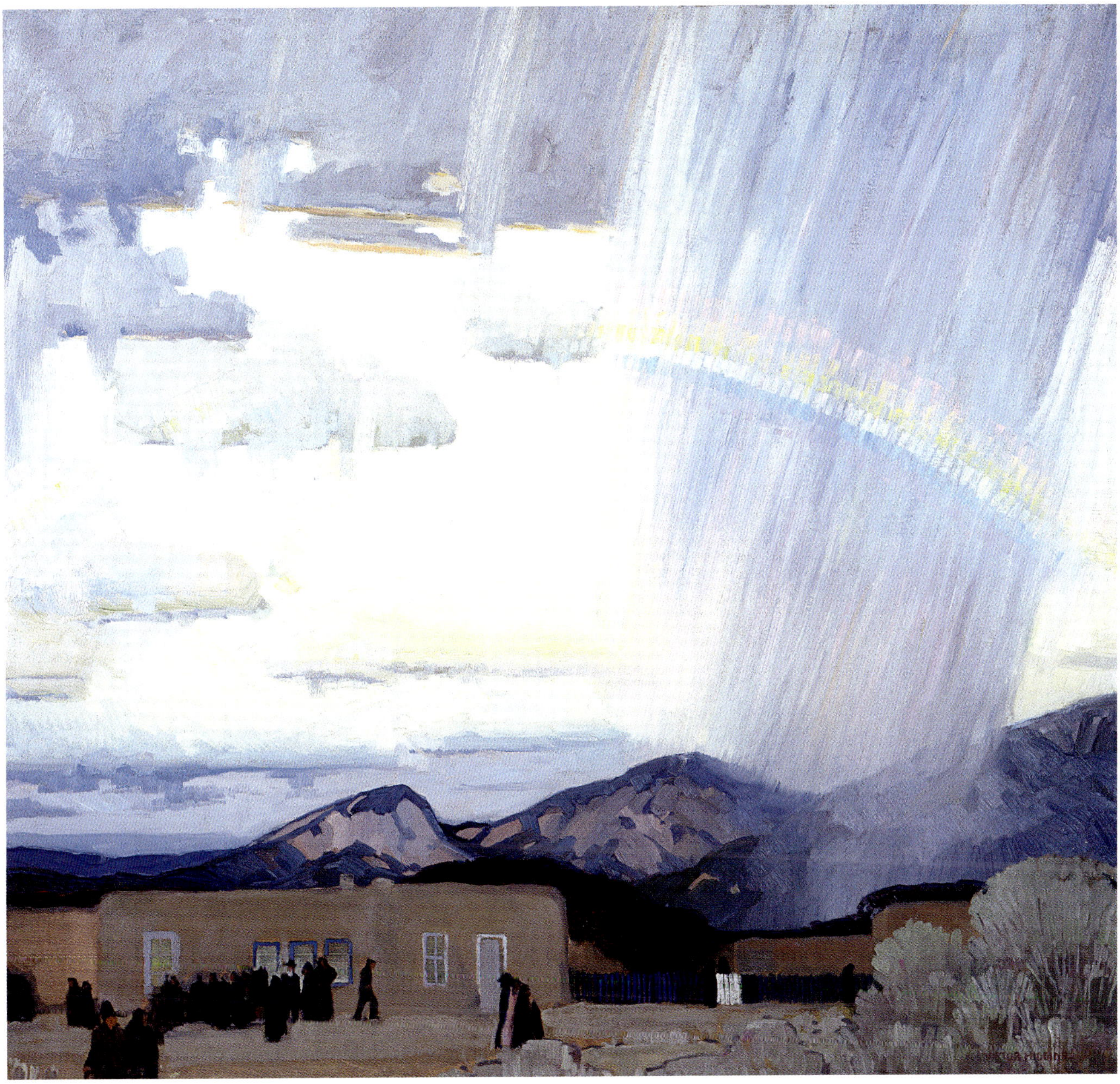

122
VICTOR HIGGINS (1884–1949)
WALKING RAIN (PABLITA PASSES),
CIRCA 1916–1917
OIL ON CANVAS, 39¾ X 42⅝ IN.
(101 X 108.3 CM)

elements, including Native Americans, horses, and sage against a backdrop of clouds. Meanwhile, Victor Higgins's paintings capture the New Mexico genre scene with a painterly approach in such works as his circa 1916–17 painting *Walking Rain (Pablita Passes)* (fig. 122).

The Taos Society of Artists accepted Catherine Carter Critcher as its last new member, and first woman member, just as the group was disbanding. Her circa 1927 academic

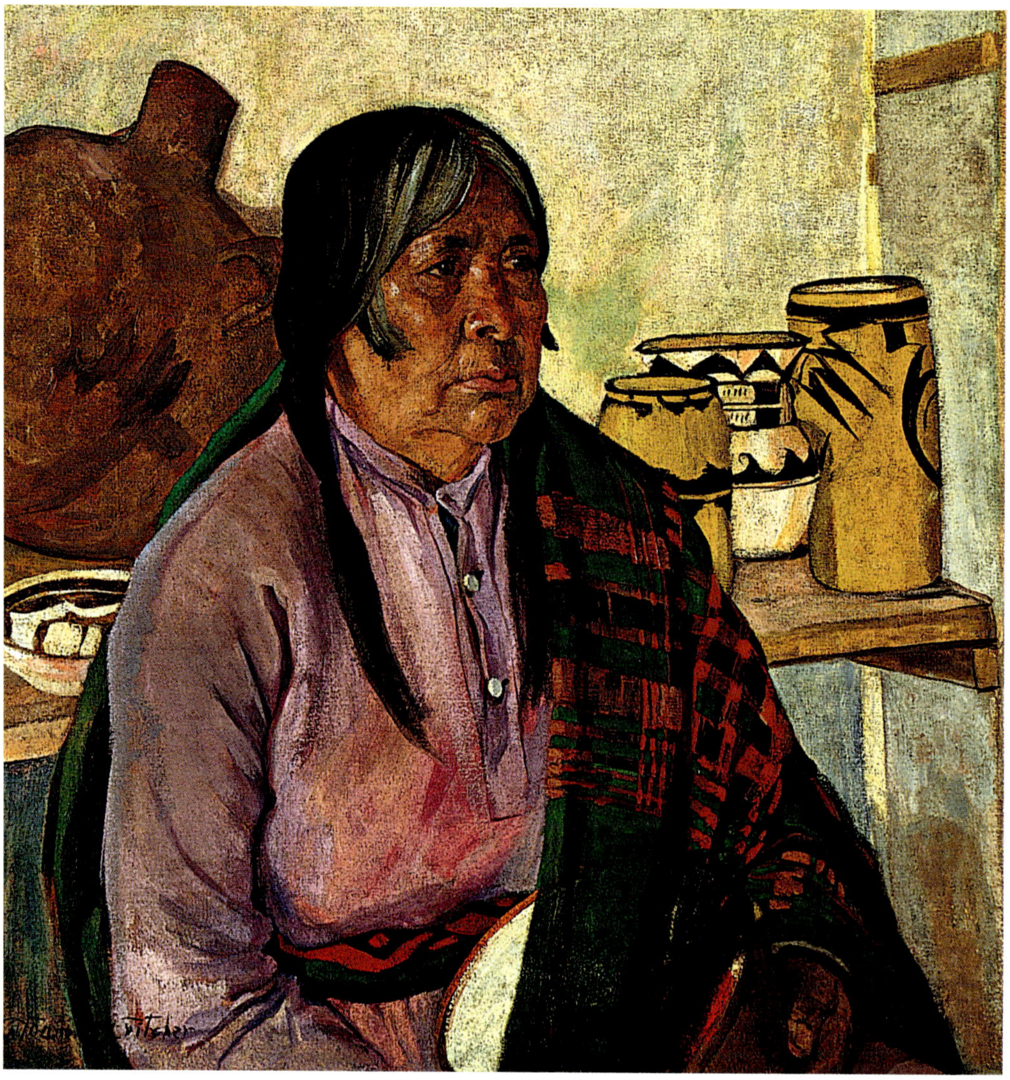

123
CATHERINE CARTER CRITCHER
(1868–1964)
HOPI POTTERY MAKER, CIRCA 1927
OIL ON CANVAS, 30 X 29 IN.
(76.2 X 73.7 CM)

portrait *Hopi Pottery Maker* (fig. 123) seems caught in a pre–World War I vision before the 1913 Armory Show brought aspects of European modernism to America.

On the other hand, W. Herbert "Buck" Dunton's painting *My Children* (fig. 124) is not an ethnic scene at all but a vision of his children at a time of great strife in his life. Dunton's bold, expressionist brush strokes and intense colors create a richness absent in many works by academic painters of the early twentieth century in New Mexico.

By the mid-1920s, the allure of realist paintings of Native Americans and Hispanos had faded. As automobile travel and magazine articles made the region accessible to millions, realist painters also moved on to experiment with modernism. The Taos Society of Artists disbanded in 1927. The elite attitudes that members had brought to New Mexico were now out of character with the Southwest. Younger academic painters, however, continued working as they had during the heyday of realist painting in twentieth-century New Mexico.

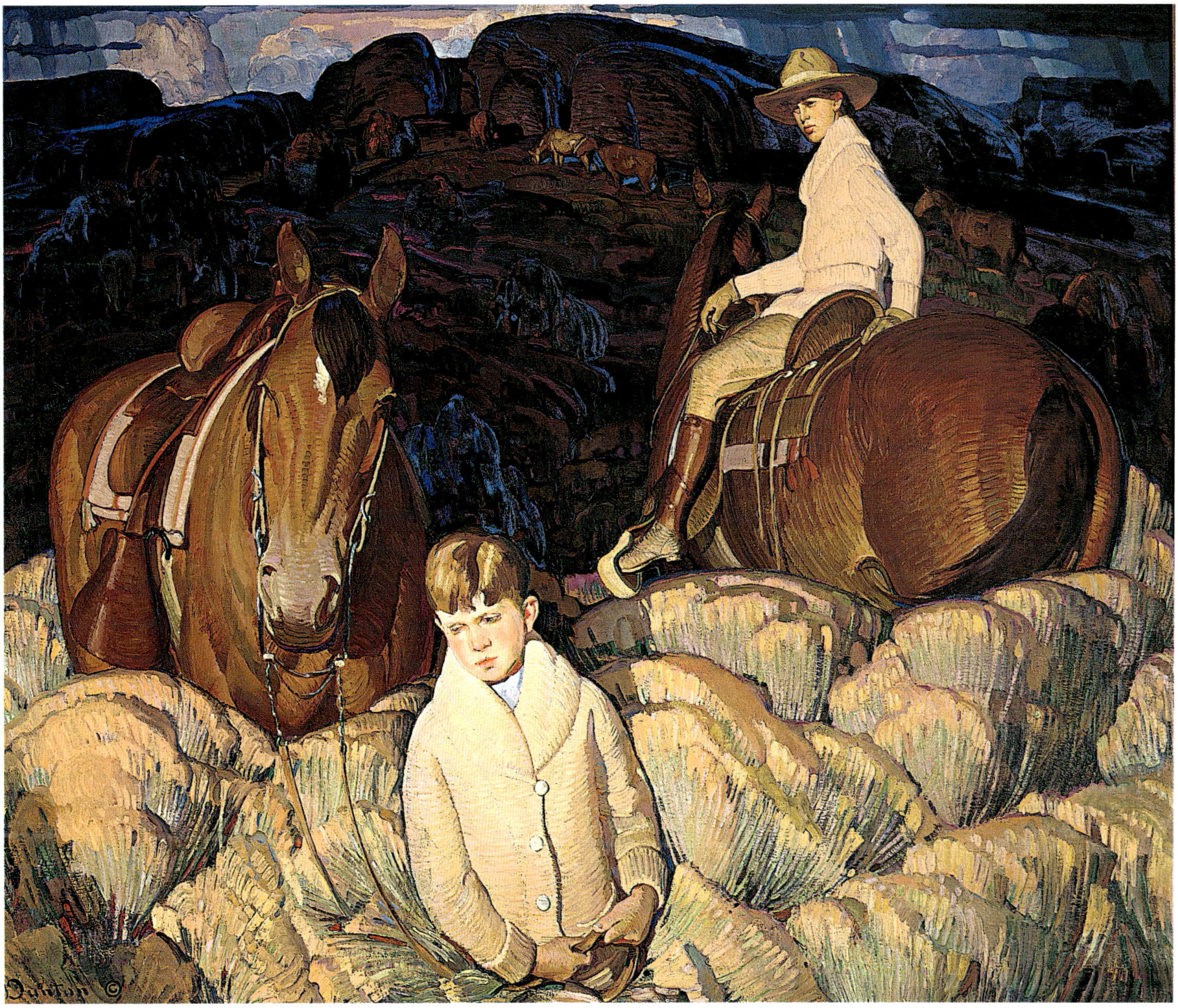

124
W. HERBERT DUNTON (1878–1936)
MY CHILDREN, 1920
OIL ON CANVAS, 50 X 60 IN.
(127 X 152.4 CM)

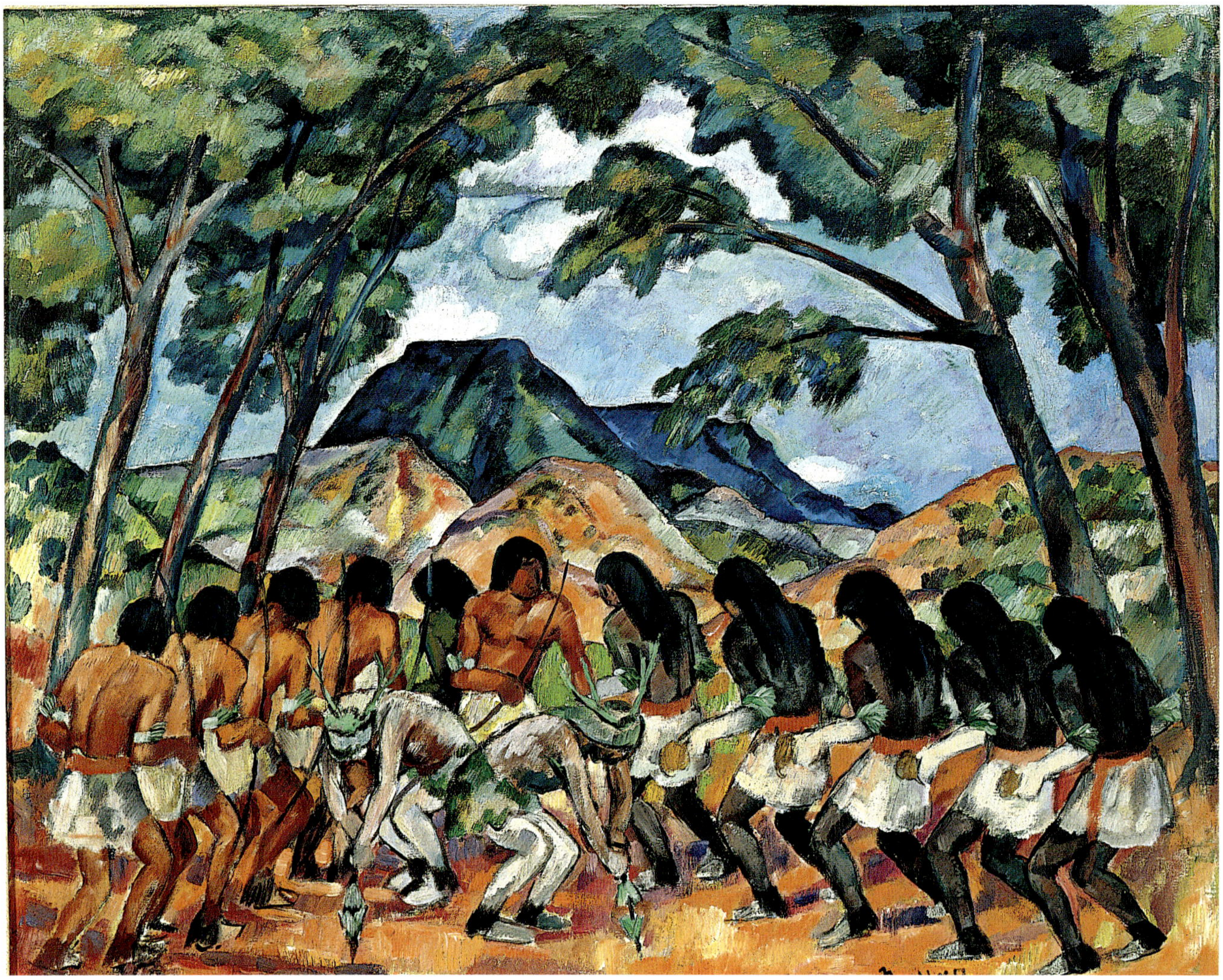

125
B. J. O. NORDFELDT (1878–1955)
ANTELOPE DANCE, 1919
OIL ON CANVAS, 33⅝ X 43 IN.
(85.4 X 109.2 CM)

THE ANTI-ACADEMICS

B. J. O. Nordfeldt moved to New Mexico with a stridently anti-academic outlook just after the armistice ended World War I. By 1919, Nordfeldt was creating powerful paintings of local subjects fractured into planes of flattened color influenced heavily by the French artist Paul Cézanne, such as *Antelope Dance* (fig. 125). Nordfeldt's works from the period pushed beyond the often tepid renderings of indigenous peoples that dominated exhibitions at the New Mexico Museum of Art during the teens and twenties.

Like Nordfeldt, William Penhallow Henderson experimented with Cézanne-esque works. His *Holy Week in New Mexico (Penitent Procession)* (fig. 126) presents a view of a Hispanic ritual, though the stylistic roots of this painting are less clear. While Henderson fragmented the scene, his planes of color are less flattened than Nordfeldt's. While both Henderson and Nordfeldt demonstrate the preoccupation with indigenous religious traditions at the beginning of the twentieth century, they do so in a manner that relies on the advanced painting styles of the period and offer a forceful alternative to academic work being created in Santa Fe at the time.

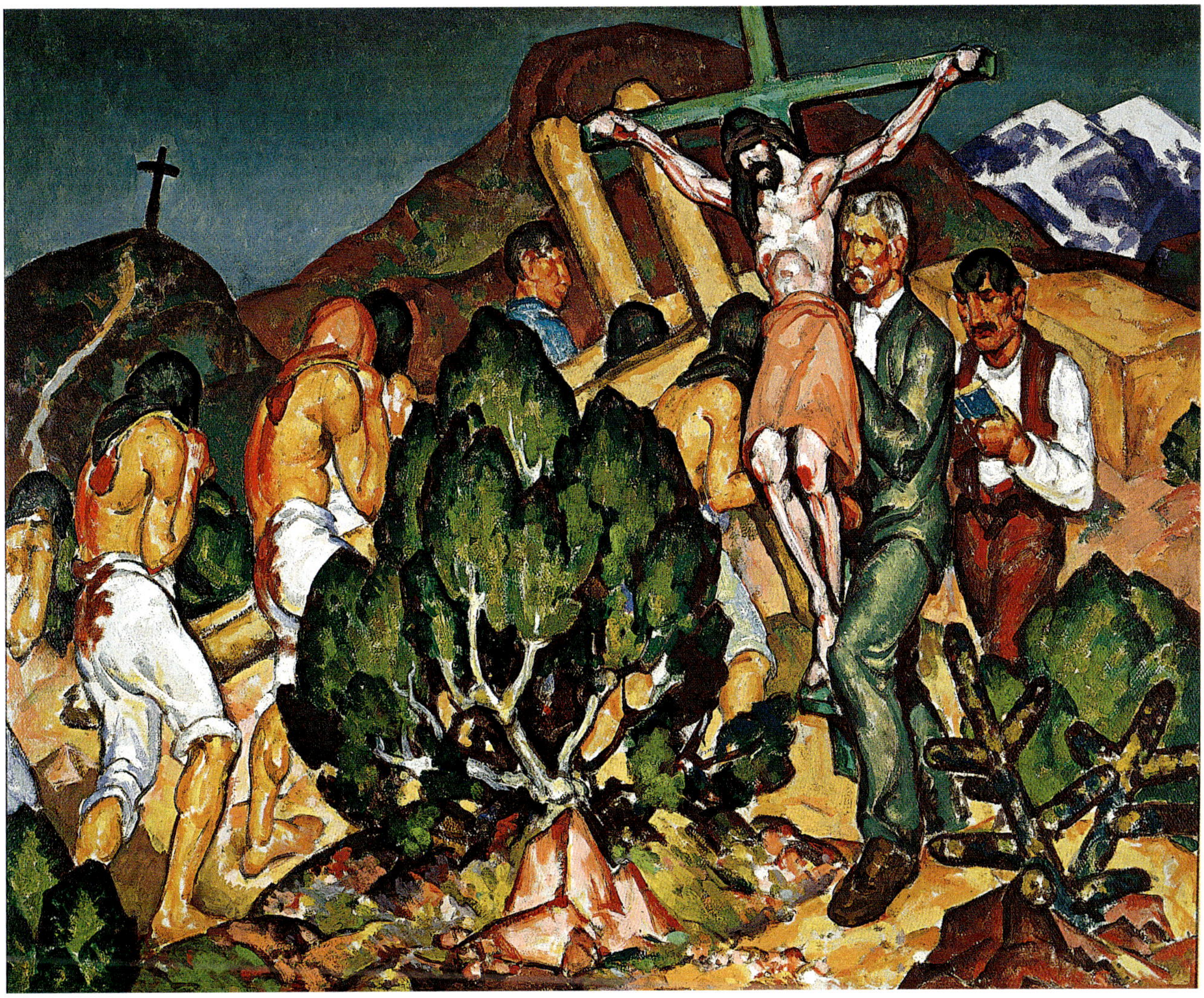

126
WILLIAM PENHALLOW HENDERSON
(1877–1943)
HOLY WEEK IN NEW MEXICO (PENITENT PROCESSION), 1919
OIL ON PANEL, 33 X 41 IN.
(83.8 X 104.1 CM)

John Sloan's 1919 painting *Under the Old Portal* (fig. 127) depicts a pair of young women parading under a portal along a street in Santa Fe. A well-dressed easterner leans against a post and leers at the women as they pass. The women appear to be flirting with the man and give the impression that they are a little tipsy in the late afternoon sun. At first, Sloan's painting might not register as an anti-academic work. But context is everything. Sloan painted this work after the ratification of Prohibition but before the law took effect, presenting the women as if they are on a last fling before Prohibition. The work is also a focused attack by Sloan on the prim and proper subjects that were integral to the academic ethos. Drunk women and lecherous men, though part of American popular culture, had not yet become appropriate subjects for art. Sloan, a member of the Ash Can School, gained fame as a cartoonist who poked fun at the foibles of urban life.

New York modernist Marsden Hartley played a critical role in the development of New Mexico art as both a painter and an essayist. In 1919, he painted *El Santo*, a still life of a Hispanic *retablo*, a Santa Clara jar, and a weaving (fig. 128). Viewers might assume that the objects in the painting are just cheap tourist curios, or anthropological artifacts of the

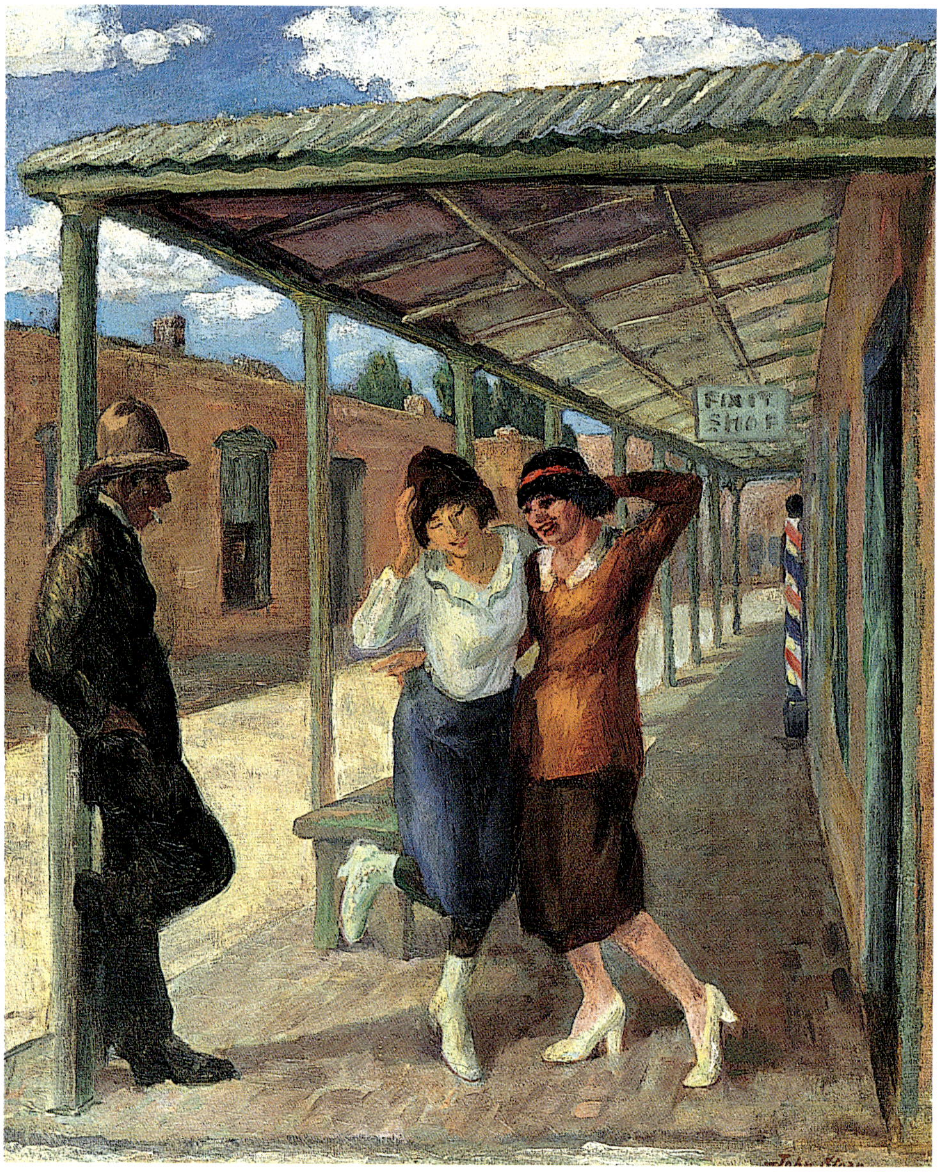

127
JOHN SLOAN (1871–1951)
UNDER THE OLD PORTAL (OLD PORTALE, SANTA FE), 1919 (REWORKED 1945)
OIL ON CANVAS, 24 x 20 IN. (61 x 50.8 CM)

past, but that assumption would misinterpret the work. Hartley presented the objects in *El Santo* not as studio props but as works of art from another culture.

Hartley had moved to New Mexico in 1918 in search of American subjects and an American style of painting. He stayed with Mabel Dodge Luhan in Taos but kept running into the conservative academic artists he knew from New York and found disagreeable. To escape their influence, Hartley moved to Santa Fe, where artists Paul Burlin and Natalie Curtis Burlin took him to Pueblo dances. He quickly decided that Pueblo ritual was the truly American art form that he sought.

Hartley was so excited about this revelation that he wrote a series of short essays explaining his views. Written to read like free verse, these essays set the stage for other modernist artists and anthropologists in Santa Fe to consider such Native art as Maria

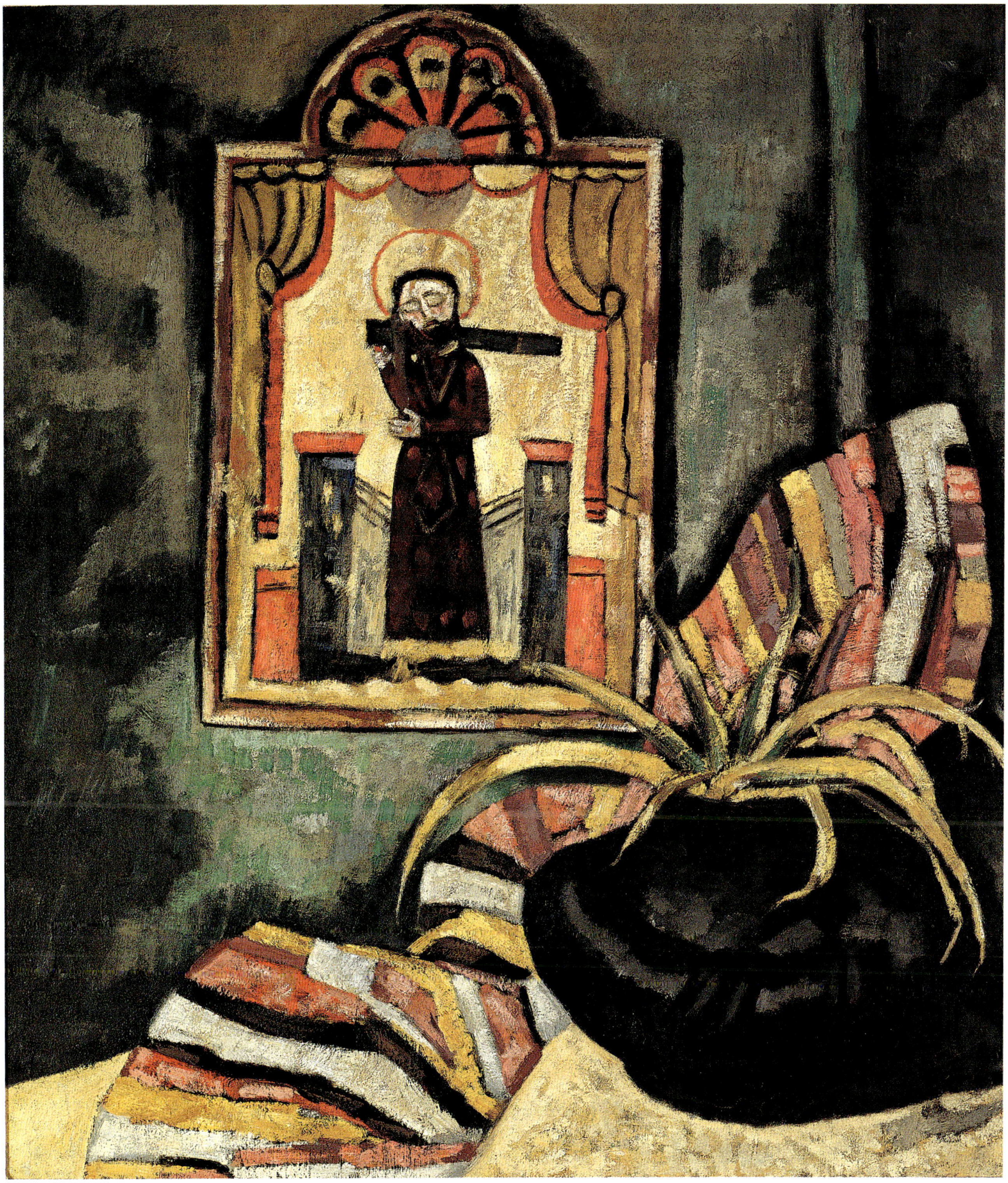

128
MARSDEN HARTLEY (1877–1943)
EL SANTO, 1919
OIL ON CANVAS, 36 x 32 IN.
(91.4 x 81.3 CM)

129
SHELDON PARSONS (1866–1943)
SANTA FE MOUNTAINS IN OCTOBER,
BEFORE 1919
OIL ON PLYWOOD PANEL, 36¼ X 23⅞ IN.
(92.1 X 60.6 CM)

and Julian Martinez's black-on-matte pottery (see fig. 115) not simply as anthropological constructs but in a broader context as art (Hartley 1918, 1919a, 1919b, 1920, 1922).

Today, Sheldon Parsons's painting *Santa Fe Mountains in October* (fig. 129) seems quaint and aesthetically tame. But at the end of the teens Parsons was the center of a major controversy over modernism in Santa Fe. Hewett had hired Parsons as the manager of the New Mexico Museum of Art. He was thus responsible for implementing the museum's open-door policy that allowed any New Mexico artist to exhibit their work without censorship.

In the fall of 1920, at the height of the presidential campaign, the *Santa Fe New Mexican* published an editorial describing the art being shown at the museum as "Bolshevik" (Udall 1984). The controversial description wasn't really about art but about the supposedly radical artists moving to northern New Mexico. And, apparently, Eugene V. Debs, who was running for president on the Socialist Party ticket, had much support among the painters of Santa Fe. Although Parsons had nothing to do with the selection of art on display at the museum, he became the fall guy, and Hewett fired him. Hewett then wrote a wishy-washy statement reaffirming support for the museum's open-door policy, and the controversy died. However, artists in Santa Fe had been put on notice that they needed to watch their behavior and their politics.

Anti-academic art in New Mexico hit a pinnacle in 1923 with the creation of powerful works by Ernest L. Blumenschein, Jozef Bakos, Gustave Baumann, Raymond Jonson, and Stuart Davis. Blumenschein was a founder of the Taos Society of Artists, but by 1923 his paintings were no longer academic canvases. *Dance at Taos* (fig. 130) combines a modernist style with ethnic subjects, avoiding the academic penchant for precise details to explore his personal response to a Pueblo dance as an abstraction of color, motion, rhythm, and sound.

During the 1920s, Gustave Baumann became well known for his woodblock prints of ethnic subjects in New Mexico. These images delighted locals and tourists alike with their elegant palette, handmade details, and simplified imagery. Most people never saw Baumann's gouache studies that translated southwestern scenes into flat planes of color. These studies allowed for the easy translation into wooden blocks from which the prints were printed.

Baumann's oil paintings, such as his 1923 *The Shalako* (fig. 131), offer an entirely different view of the region. This work is mysterious, graphic, and enchanting. It captures the experience of being at Zuni Pueblo early in December and staying up all night in the frigid air waiting for the appearance of larger-than-life mythic beings as part of an important ritual.

During the 1920s, the anti-academic artists concentrated on landscape images rather than the ethnic scenes popular with more traditional artists. Stuart Davis spent the summer of 1923 in New Mexico and found it difficult to adjust to the wide-open spaces and stylistic dominance of the Taos Society. Davis responded by abandoning color and working in grisaille, creating black-and-white paintings that he felt allowed him to transcend simply copying from nature. Davis's *New Mexican Peak* (fig. 132) is a good example of the type of images the artist painted at the end of his stay in the Southwest.

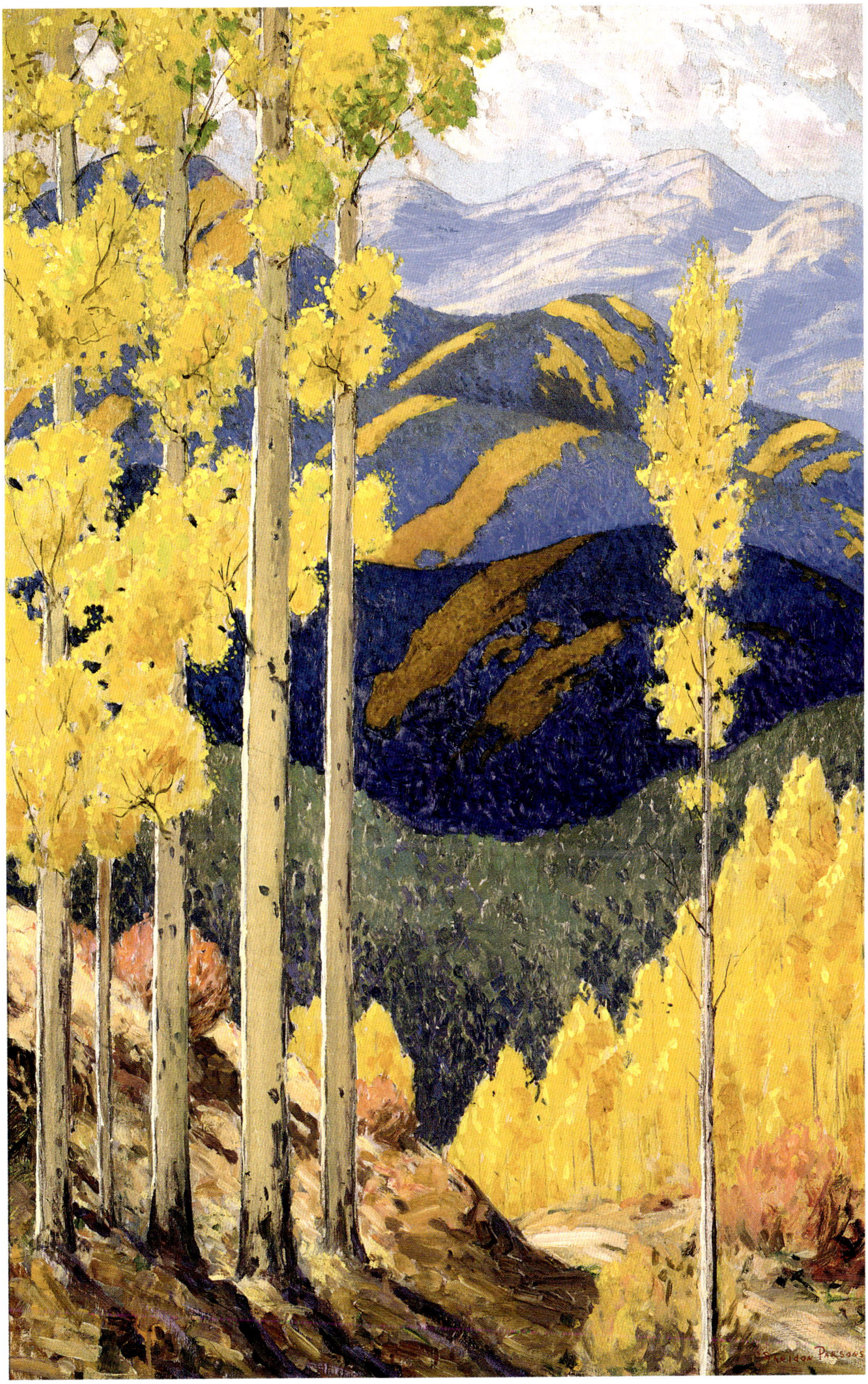
Sheldon Parsons

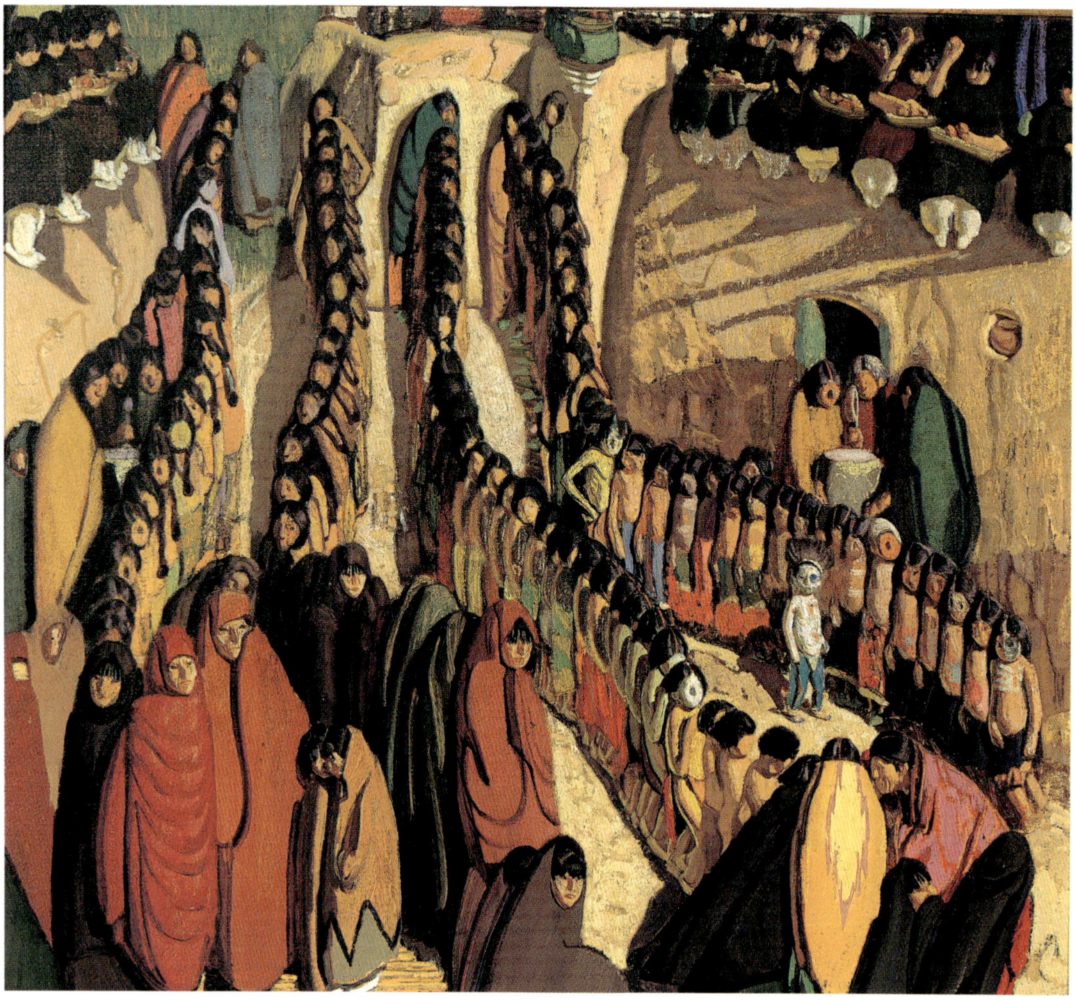

130
ERNEST L. BLUMENSCHEIN (1874–1960)
DANCE AT TAOS, 1923
OIL ON CANVAS, 23½ X 26½ IN.
(59.7 X 67.3 CM)

131
GUSTAVE BAUMANN (1881–1971)
THE SHALAKO, 1923
OIL ON BOARD WITH HAND-CARVED FRAME, 35½ X 60 IN. (90.2 X 152.4 CM)

132
STUART DAVIS (1894–1964)
NEW MEXICAN PEAK, 1923
OIL ON CANVAS, 21¼ X 31⅝ IN.
(54 X 80.3 CM)

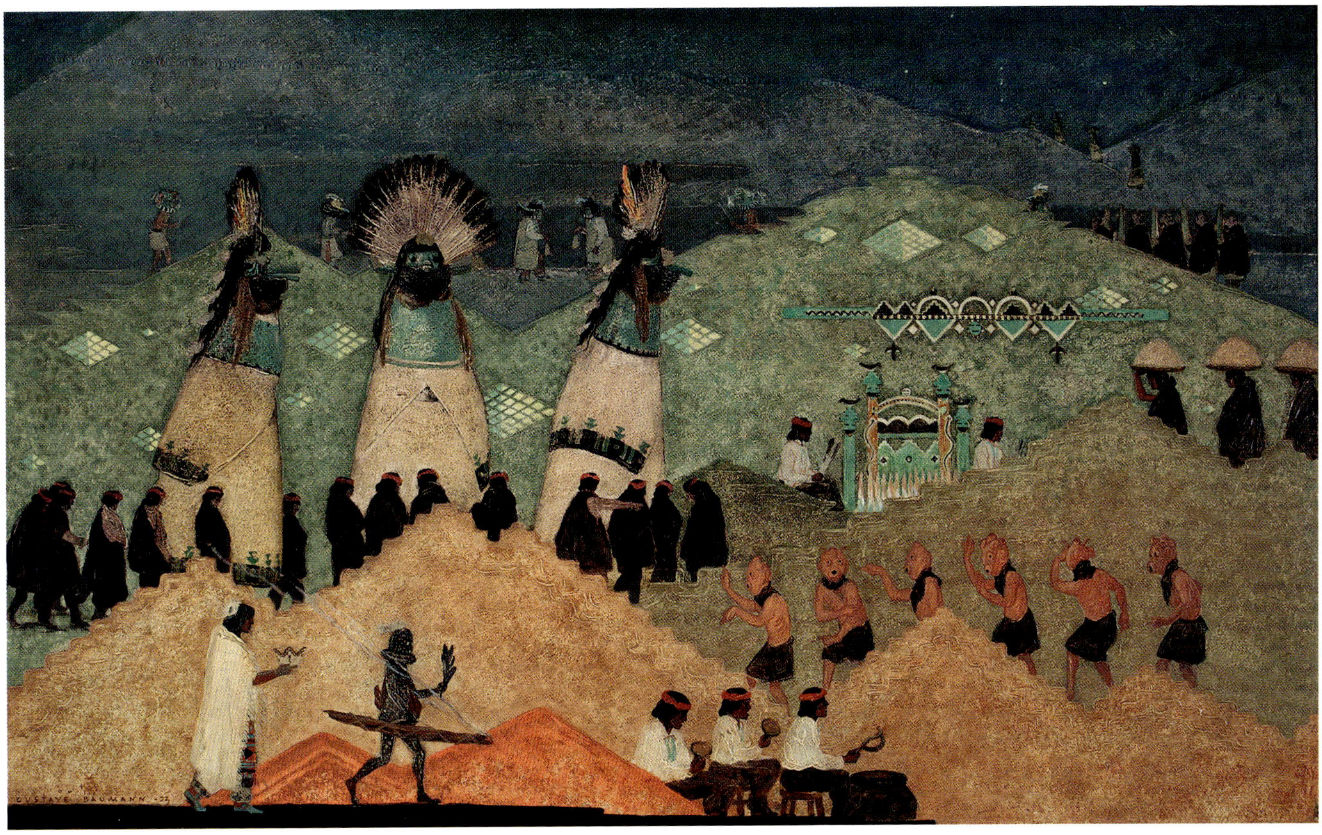

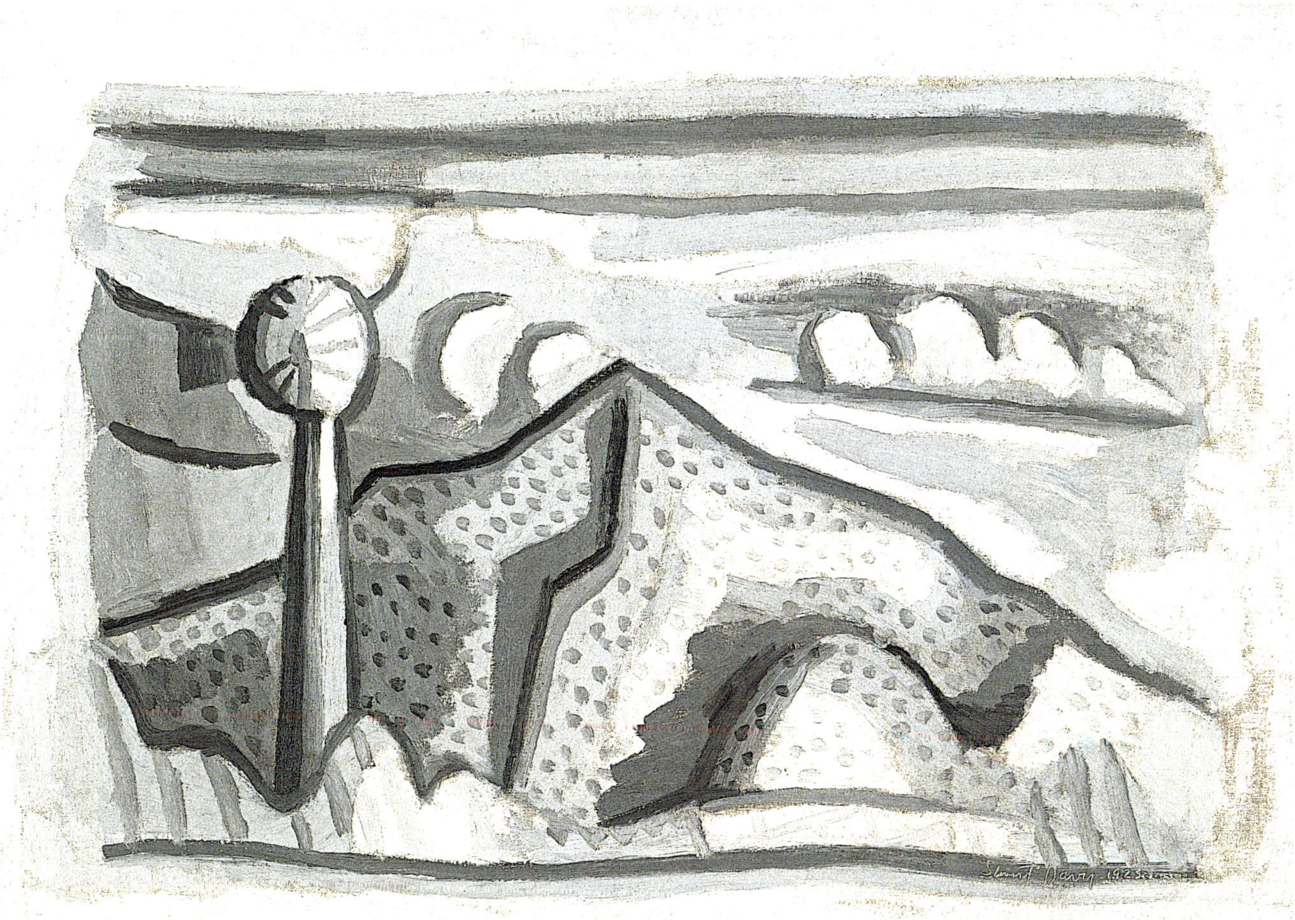

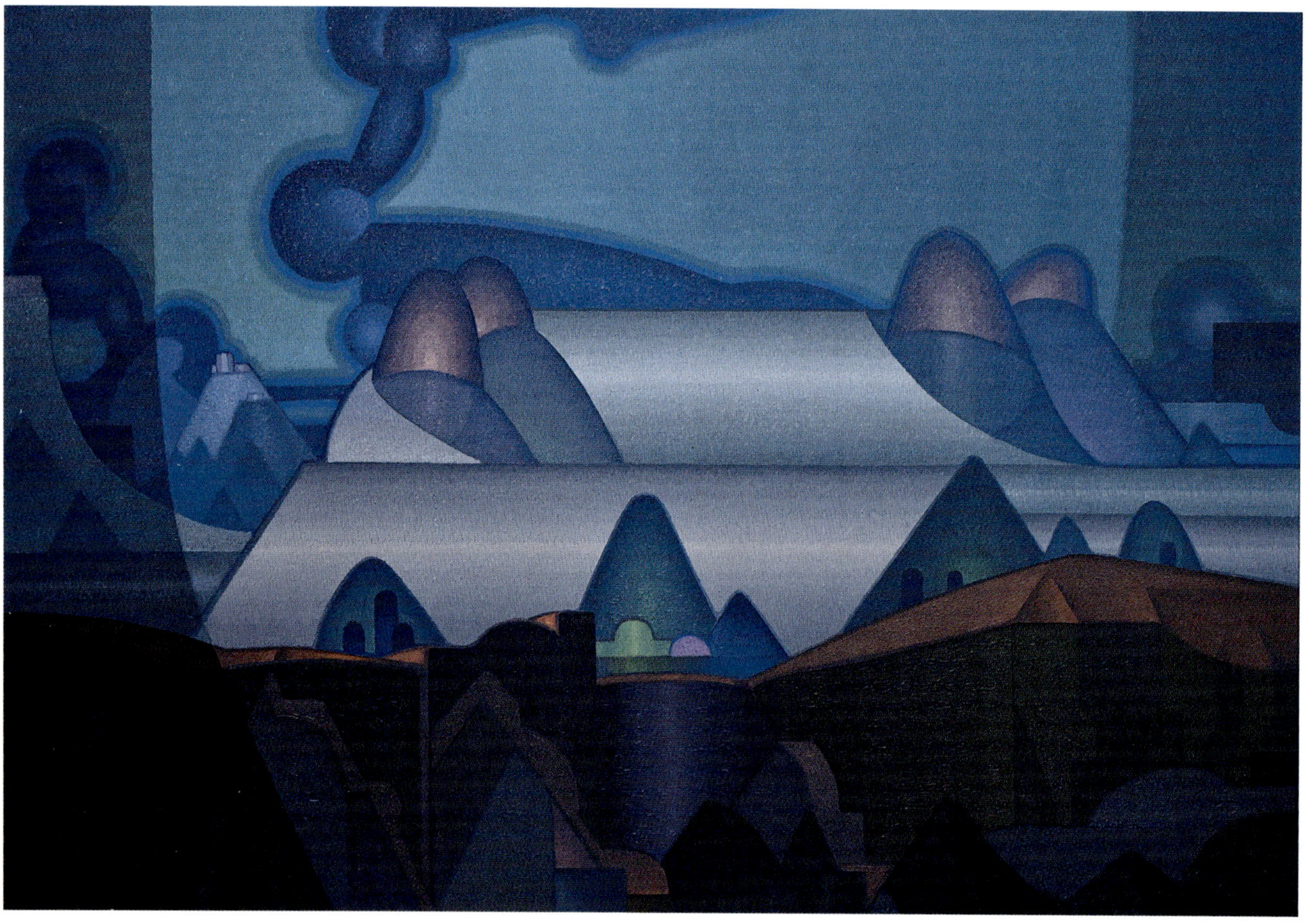

133
RAYMOND JONSON (1891–1982)
EARTH RHYTHMS NO. 2, 1923
OIL ON CANVAS, 27½ x 40⅝ IN.
(69.9 x 103.2 CM)

Raymond Jonson's *Earth Rhythms No. 2.* (fig. 133) was also painted in 1923. The painting, created by Jonson during a year in Chicago in which he prepared for a permanent move to New Mexico, anticipates his work to come. It is an abstraction of New Mexico land forms structured with dynamic symmetry, a design strategy based on the golden mean—a mathematical proportion alleged to infuse spiritual content into a work of art. As a young artist Jonson had been the lighting designer at the Chicago Little Theater. In this painting, New Mexico becomes a stage set complete with curtains, spotlights, and colored gels.

In November 1921, Jozef Bakos and four other young, newly arrived painters—Fremont Ellis, Walter Mruk, Willard Nash, and Will Shuster—had an exhibition at the Museum of Art. They were so pleased with the results that, in 1922, they named themselves Los Cinco Pintores (the Five Painters). The group, however, made a name for themselves more through their partying and bohemian outlook than the quality of their work.

Bakos's 1923 painting *The Springtime Rainbow* (fig. 134) incorporates the eclectic energy found in Nordfeldt's paintings but has a simpler composition. Bakos captures the explosive power of a winter storm in early spring in New Mexico. Although the group formally disbanded in 1926, Bakos, Ellis, Nash, and Shuster continued painting in town as the Los Cinco Pintores. While they had started out as a group of unconventional artists striving for a radical edge, they quickly realized those kinds of paintings had a limited market in the mid-1920s. Eventually, they retreated from experimental efforts and found a market in genre scenes of the region.

Andrew Dasburg, who visited Mabel Dodge Luhan shortly after she moved to Taos in 1918, aggressively challenged the academic paradigm in New Mexico by interpreting the landscape in a cubist manner. In works such as the 1928 *My Gate on the Camino* (fig. 135), Dasburg's sensitive brushstrokes produce flattened forms that the viewer's eyes translate into adobe forms, forests of trees, clouds, and distant mountains. While cubist imagery can sometimes feel forced and mechanical, Dasburg's landscapes mesmerize.

It is interesting to compare Dasburg's work with that of Agnes Pelton, another artist who first visited New Mexico in 1919 and stayed with Mabel Dodge Luhan shortly after

134
JOZEF G. BAKOS (1891–1977)
THE SPRINGTIME RAINBOW, 1923
OIL ON CANVAS, 29½ X 35½ IN.
(74.9 X 90.2 CM)

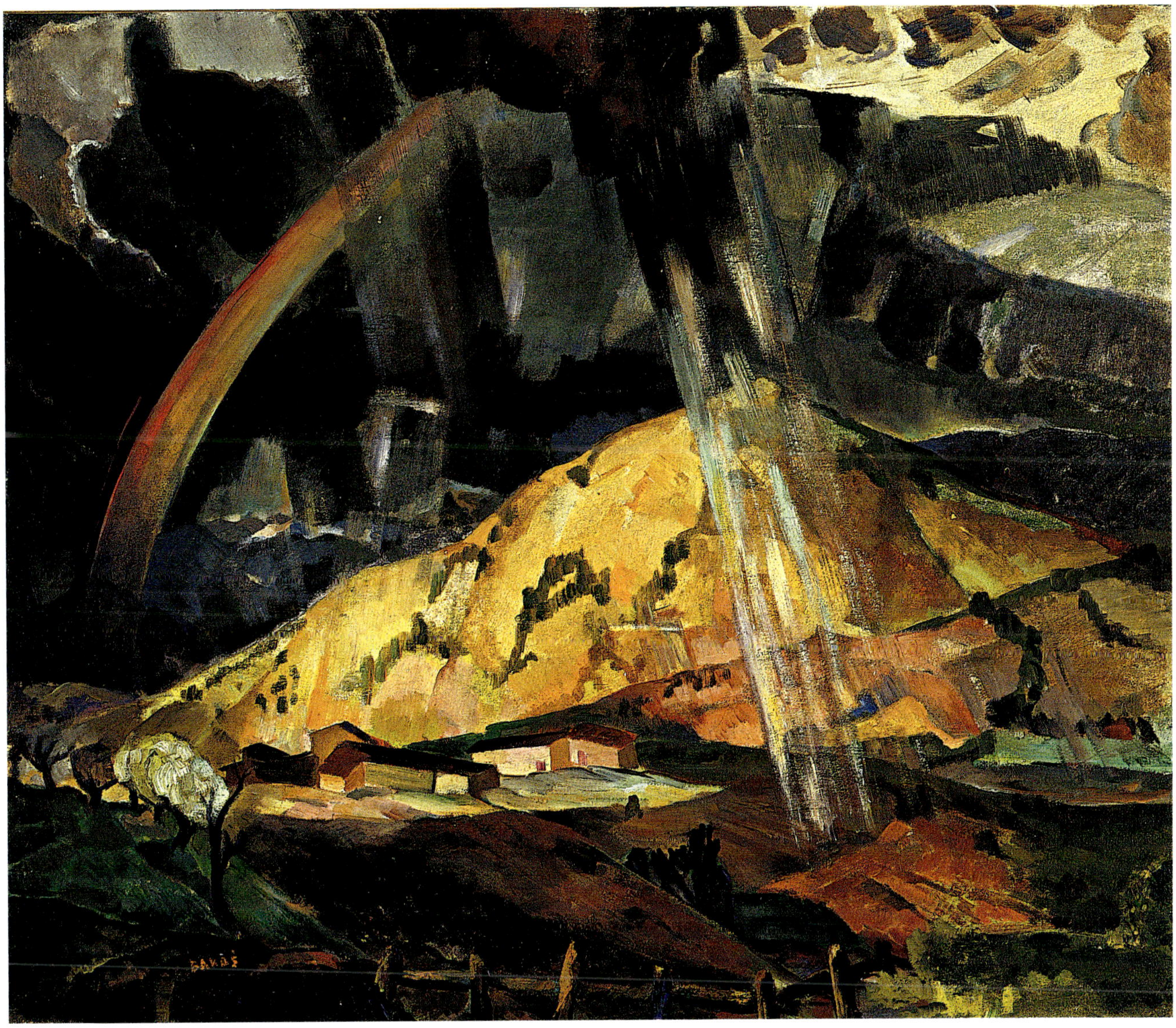

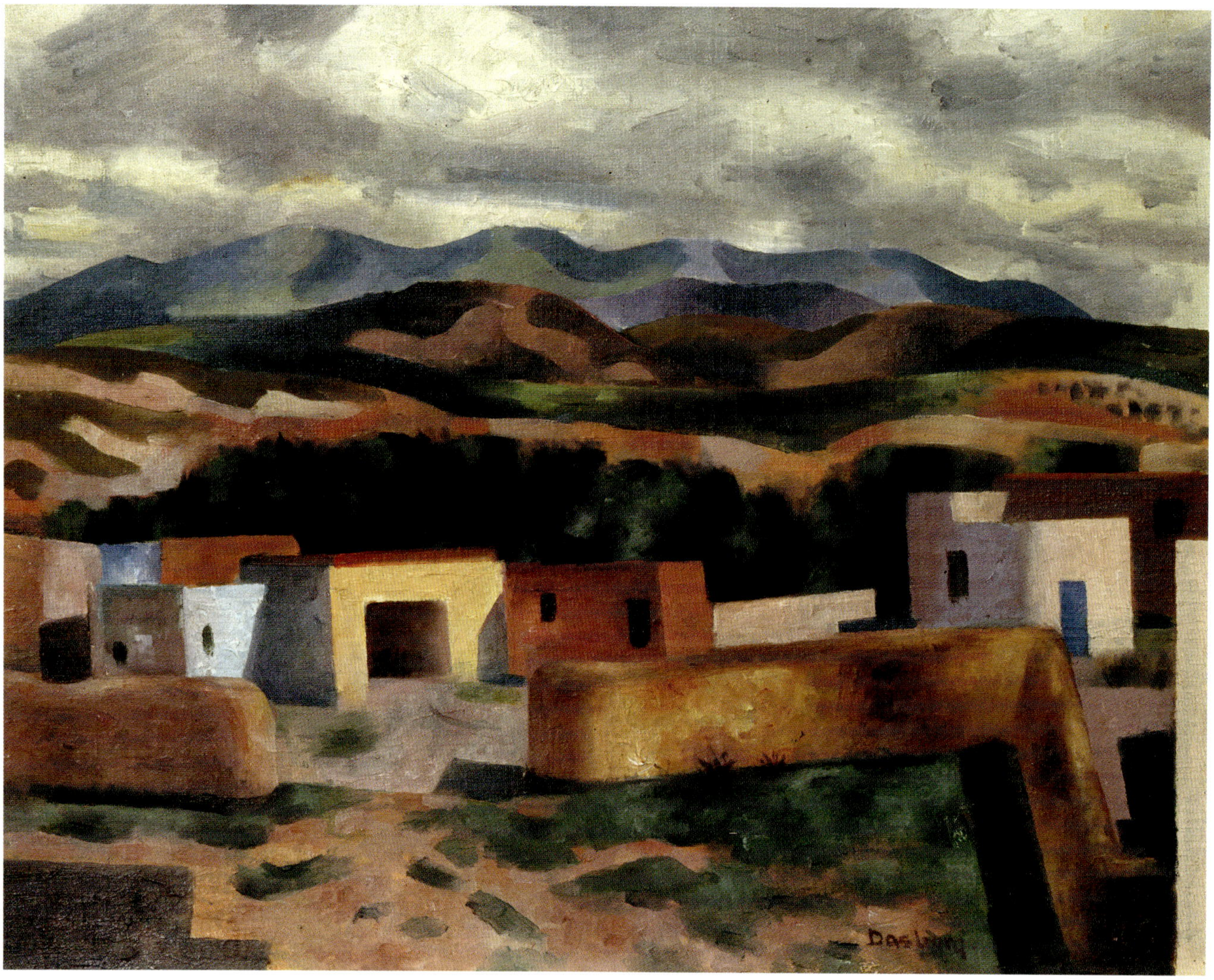

135
ANDREW DASBURG (1887–1979)
MY GATE ON THE CAMINO, 1928
OIL ON PANEL, 12¼ X 15½ IN.
(31.1 X 39.4 CM)

she moved to Taos. In 1928, Pelton established a permanent residence in Cathedral City, near Palm Springs in the California desert. There Pelton eked out a living painting desert landscapes that exude a painful feeling of loneliness and angst. In 1929, Pelton vacationed in Arizona and drew pastels of the Grand Canyon. As a work of art, *Untitled (Grand Canyon)* (fig. 136) moves harmoniously back and forth between a realist view looking into the canyon and a nonobjective abstraction. Like Dasburg, Pelton found ways to transform well-known landscapes into unique abstractions.

By the end of the 1920s, the artist fraternities that had capitalized on the ideas of economic development and cultural tourism in New Mexico had disintegrated. The stock market crash of October 1929 signaled the end of the post-statehood economic boom that had initially given rise to them. The next wave of artistic activity in New Mexico would more directly address the unintended negative consequences of tourism on Pueblo and Hispanic arts, as well as the revival of authentic indigenous art forms.

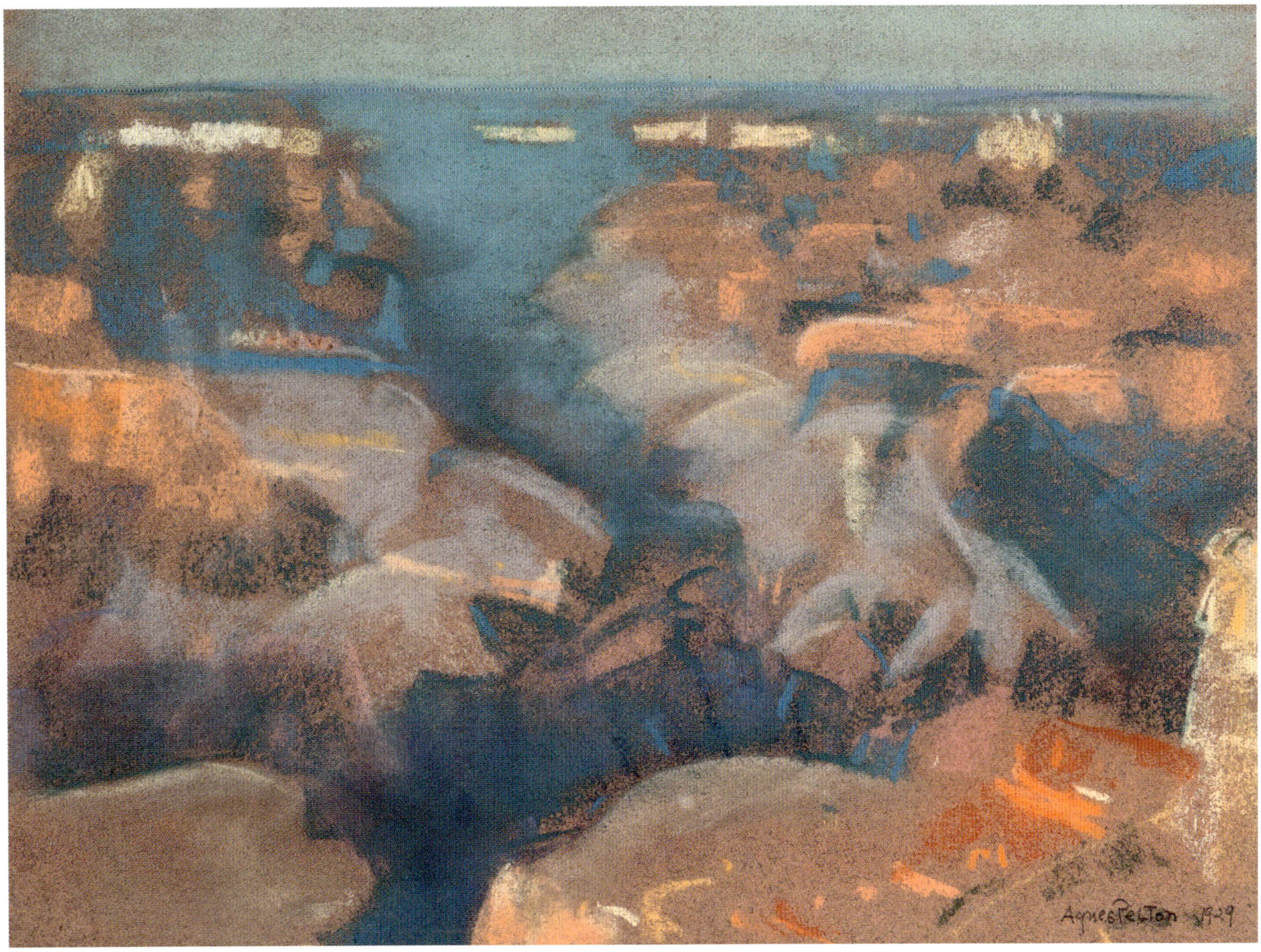

136
AGNES PELTON (1881–1961)
UNTITLED (GRAND CANYON), 1929
PASTEL ON PAPER, 10 x 13 IN. (25.4 x 33 CM)

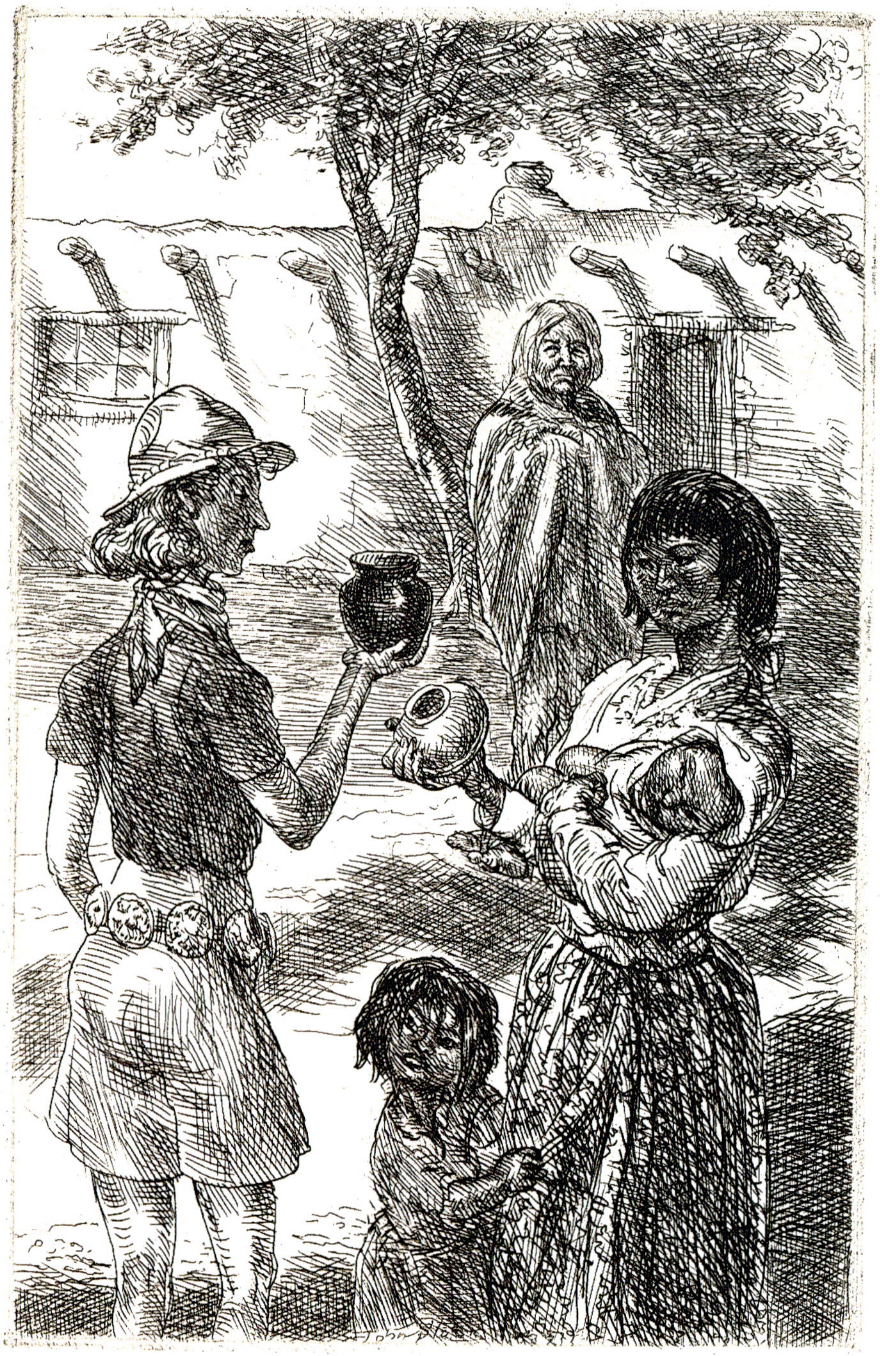

CHAPTER 6

Roaring Twenties to World War II

At the height of the Roaring Twenties, many artists and intellectuals in Santa Fe rejected Edgar Lee Hewett's dictatorial control over local art and cultural policies. Hewett served as director of both the Museum of New Mexico and the School of American Research (now the School for Advanced Research) and had close ties with state and city officials. He jumped from project to project, allowing older endeavors to flounder while opportunistically taking full credit for their early successes.

Undoubtedly, Hewett's inept handling of the 1920 "Bolshevik" art controversy played a key role in shattering the region's artistic unity. Newly arrived philanthropists, collectors, and artists also often found it difficult to work with Hewett and organized independent projects without his involvement. Community art activists lampooned indiscretions by tourists and sought to minimize the impact of tourism on indigenous arts. John Sloan led this effort through a series of etchings that focused on tourist behaviors offensive to locals. *The Black Pot* (fig. 137) highlights the class distinctions between a wealthy tourist and a Pueblo potter with a family to support. However, the etching implies that potters quit making well-crafted, functional vessels because they believed they could earn more money making inexpensive souvenirs.

Hewett's interest in the Santa Fe Program essentially ended in 1922 with the creation of the first Indian Fair, a project controlled by Hewett but organized by his longtime associate Kenneth Chapman. Fair organizers felt strongly that works associated with a specific Native group should be made only by members of that group. The public event also emphasized outsider opinions by anthropologists and collectors concerning the authenticity of the works of art. The fair evolved into Indian Market, an event still held each August in Santa Fe.

THE ARTISTIC REVIVALS

Sloan and others were dismayed by the unintended negative consequences of tourism on Pueblo and Hispanic arts, which led to efforts by concerned philanthropists and artists to revive the Pueblo and Hispanic arts that had been widely available at the end of the nineteenth century. A powerful motivation to improve local arts was the "salvage paradigm," the belief that contemporary goods were kitsch and that philanthropy could revive authentic indigenous objects and traditions that had existed in the past. Subsequently, philanthropists used their influence and resources to end commercialization and promote

137
JOHN SLOAN (1871–1951)
THE BLACK POT, 1925
ETCHING, 6 x 4 in. (15.2 x 10.2 cm)

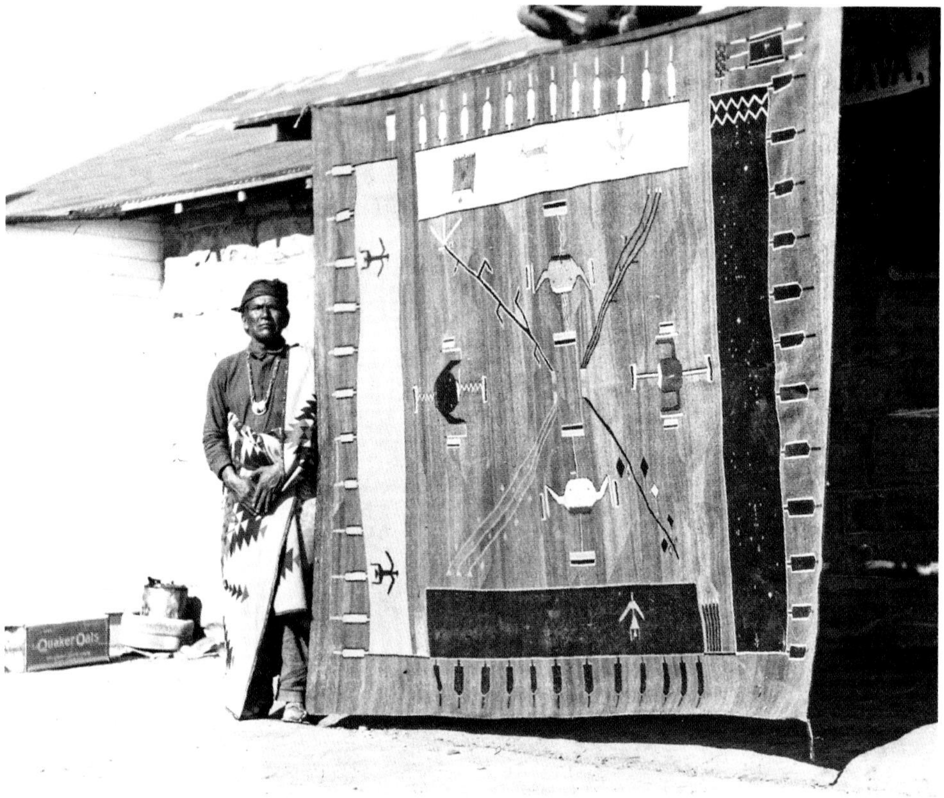

138
PROBABLY ARTHUR OR FRANCES NEWCOMB
HASTIIN KLAH WITH ONE OF HIS SANDPAINTING TAPESTRIES AT THE NEWCOMB TRADING POST, CIRCA 1927
GELATIN SILVER PRINT, 8 X 10 IN. (20.3 X 25.4 CM)

what they deemed to be high artistic standards. Unfortunately, this perspective again was based in part on the colonialist notion that outsiders know best.

In 1921, philanthropist Mary Cabot Wheelwright began collaborating with Diné weaver and ritual singer Hastiin Klah, who feared that Diné healing songs would be lost to mainstream influences (Newcomb 1981). Wheelwright encouraged Klah to incorporate into his weavings the ephemeral sand designs created as part of these healing rituals. Klah responded with a series of large weavings that depict the iconography of Diné healing chants (fig. 138). Wheelwright organized the Museum of Navajo Ceremonial Art (now the Wheelwright Museum of the American Indian) to preserve these images. Central to the museum is a gallery designed to look like a giant hogan to provide an appropriate context for viewing these works.

Traders and mail-order dealers began marketing Diné weavings at the end of the nineteenth century as floor coverings and suggesting designs that would look good in arts and crafts settings. Considering the multicolored weavings of the early twentieth century to be overly commercial and inauthentic, these European-American supporters of Native arts sought a return to weavings made with natural wools, or shades of gray made by carding together white and black wools.

The revivalists also encouraged Pueblo potters to stop production of popular forms—like candlesticks, ashtrays, and salt and pepper shakers—and revive serious forms that mimicked the functional pottery of the nineteenth century. While the best potters created large works, the downturn in tourism during the Great Depression worked against

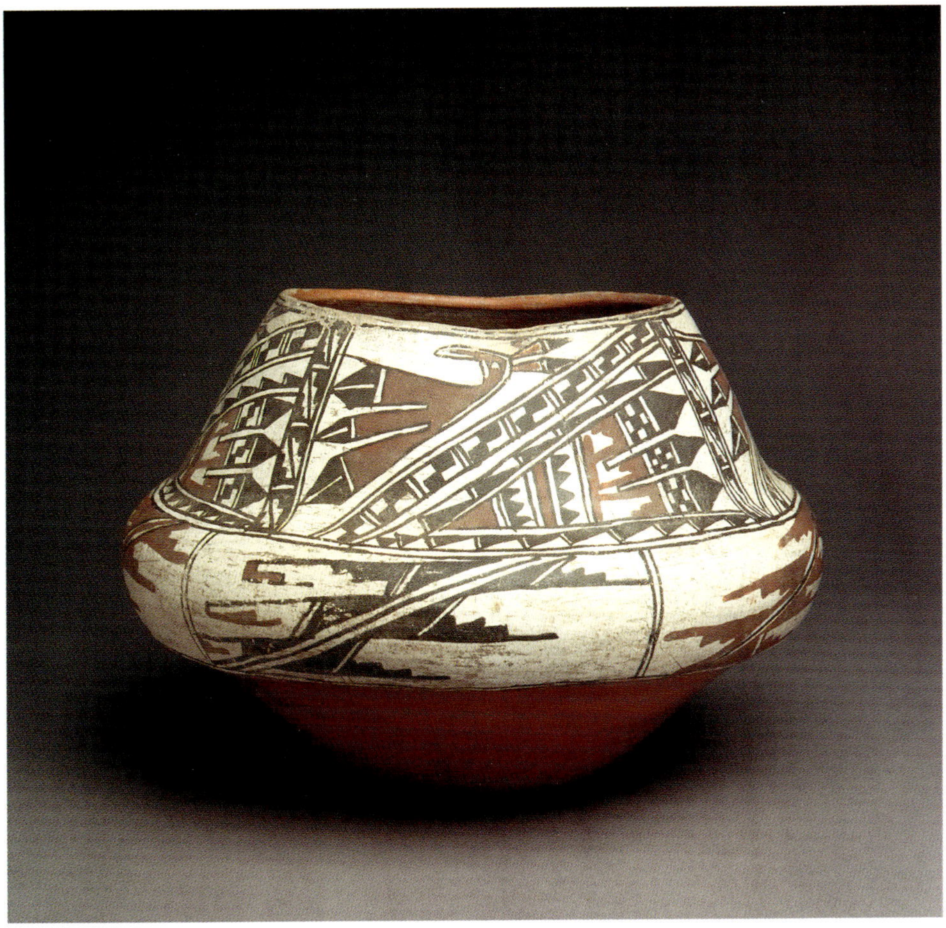

139
MAKER UNKNOWN
ZUNI PUEBLO ASHIWI POLYCHROME STORAGE JAR, CIRCA 1720
CLAY AND PIGMENTS, 9 x 13 IN.
(22.9 x 33 CM)

these efforts. With motor tourists only having spare change to purchase souvenirs, the trinkets sold well while the expensive, better-made works did not.

Dissatisfaction with Hewett's control of cultural policy in New Mexico grew into outright hostility in the 1920s. In 1922, individuals began discussing the problem that Pueblo potters no longer had access to the best examples of historic pottery because eastern museums and curio hunters were acquiring the best pieces for out-of-state collections. The discussions resulted in the creation of the Indian Arts Fund for building a private collection of historic Native arts that would be outside of Hewett's control. The diverse supporters of the Indian Arts Fund included philanthropists Mabel Dodge Luhan and Amelia White, as well as painters Frank Applegate, Andrew Dasburg, and B. J. O. Nordfeldt. The group's first acquisition was an Ashiwi Polychrome jar from Zuni, circa 1720 (fig. 139).

The private Laboratory of Anthropology was created at the end of the 1920s to house the Indian Arts Fund and to make the collection available to Native artists and others. Hewett believed that his former employees had conspired behind his back to create the lab. Financial difficulties plagued the new institution during the 1930s, but Hewett blocked any discussion of making it part of the state museum system. The state ultimately acquired the lab after Hewett's death, but the Indian Arts Fund maintained ownership of the collection.

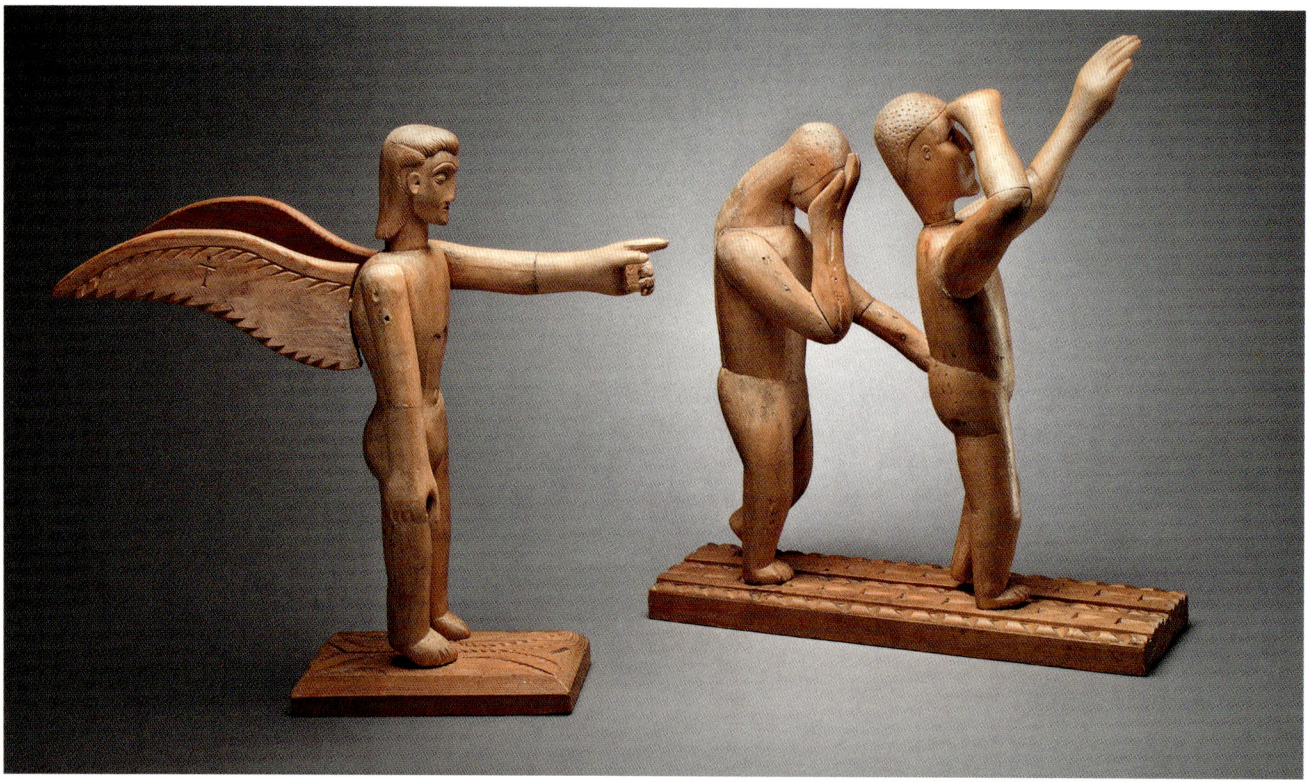

140
JOSÉ DOLORES LÓPEZ (1868–1937)
EXPULSION FROM THE GARDEN OF EDEN, CIRCA 1935
ASPEN, 12¾ X 14⅓ X 8 IN.
(32.4 X 36.8 X 20.3 CM)

At the beginning of the twentieth century, there was a decline in the production of Hispanic weavings and other traditional religious arts, followed by a revival of Hispanic arts in the 1920s that mirrored that of Native arts. Woodcarver José Dolores López started carving during World War I to overcome insomnia when his son was sent to fight in Europe. His first works were given to family and friends, but by the mid-1920s he had begun selling furniture and secular and religious sculptures, such as his circa 1930s *Expulsion from the Garden of Eden* (fig. 140).

Writer Loren Brown knew López and introducted him to Frank Applegate, who in turn introduced him to writer Mary Austin. Applegate and Austin's interest in López's carvings and other works by local artists led to the formation of the Spanish Colonial Arts Society in 1925. Members included philanthropists Leonora Curtin, Bronson M. Cutting, Mrs. Cyrus McCormick, and Mary C. Wheelwright; writers Ina Cassidy and Alice Corbin Henderson; and painters Gerald Cassidy, Kenneth Chapman, Andrew Dasburg, and Cady Wells. The group also promoted the revival of commercial weavings, such as the Chimayó blanket circa 1925 shown in figure 141. During the 1926 Fiesta de Santa Fe, the society organized a Spanish Market that paralleled the Indian Fair and that evolved into today's Spanish Market, held each July in Santa Fe.

These revivalist individuals and groups represent another fraternity within the New Mexico art movement, one composed of indigenous artists and their supporters that encouraged aesthetic self-reliance. While the primary audience for these artistic revivals was local, tourists also responded to the better-made traditional Native and Hispanic arts. Programs started by the revivalist societies are still active almost a century later.

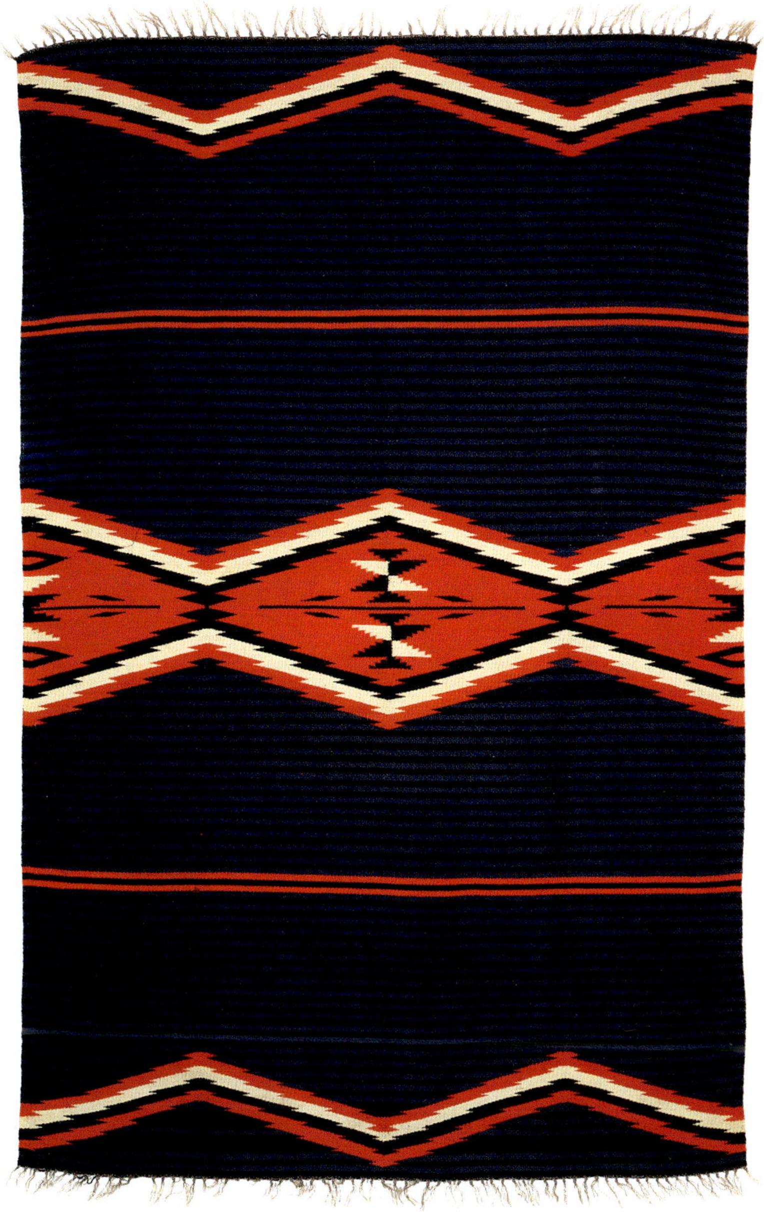

141
MAKER UNKNOWN
FRAZADA TIPO CHIMAYÓ / CHIMAYÓ BLANKET, CIRCA 1925
WOOL, COTTON, AND ANILINE DYES,
72 13/16 X 45 7/8 IN. (185 X 116.5 CM)

THE CIRCLE: O'KEEFFE, STIEGLITZ, AND MABEL DODGE LUHAN

The summer of 1929 marked the beginning of a decades-long relationship between the state of New Mexico and an elite group of artists associated with painter Georgia O'Keeffe, her husband Alfred Stieglitz, the photographer and gallerist, and modernist intellectual Mabel Dodge Luhan. Mabel, as she was known, was a wealthy New York City arts patron who moved to New Mexico in December 1917. She continued her patronage in New Mexico, attracting well-known writers, musicians, and artists to her compound in Taos. In time, she made a clean break with her New York past by marrying Tony Luhan, a Taos Pueblo man.

Andrew Dasburg and Marsden Hartley were the first artists in the circle to come to New Mexico after World War I. O'Keeffe and her close friend Rebecca Salsbury Strand accepted Mabel's invitation to visit her in Taos in May 1929. It was O'Keeffe's first trip to New Mexico, but Strand had visited in 1926. Later that summer, photographer Ansel Adams and painter John Marin also visited. Other artists who formed the core of the circle in New Mexico included John Candelario, Eliot Porter, Paul Strand, Cady Wells, and Edward Weston. Stieglitz, ironically, never visited New Mexico, but his artist friends, not to mention his wife, greatly influenced the development of southwestern art during the depression years.

Pedernal with Red Hills (fig. 142) exemplifies O'Keeffe's landscape paintings created during the 1930s in northern New Mexico. O'Keeffe responded directly to her environment and transformed the landscapes near the villages of Taos and Abiquiu into flattened, modernist forms. Pedernal is a tall, narrow butte whose top appears cocked to one side rather than being aligned with the horizon. Within O'Keeffe's work from the 1930s, Pedernal looms like a beacon showing the way to her favorite landscapes in the surrounding area.

Not all of O'Keeffe's landscape paintings from the 1930s are as clearly defined as her view of Pedernal and the colorful clay formations nearby. Her 1931 painting *Bear Lake* (fig. 143) can be interpreted from multiple perspectives. At first the image seems like an abstract painting of angular shapes and rich, earthy hues. But the image can also be flipped to appear as a representational view of a high mountain lake at sunset. When the painting was first exhibited at Stieglitz's gallery in 1932, the dark forms were on top so that the image looked more like a lake scene. However, the painting's original owners displayed its dark side at the bottom, thus emphasizing its alternative title, *Desert Abstraction.*

142
GEORGIA O'KEEFFE (1887–1986)
PEDERNAL WITH RED HILLS (RED HILLS WITH THE PEDERNAL), 1936
OIL ON LINEN, 19¾ X 29¾ IN.
(50.2 X 75.6 CM)

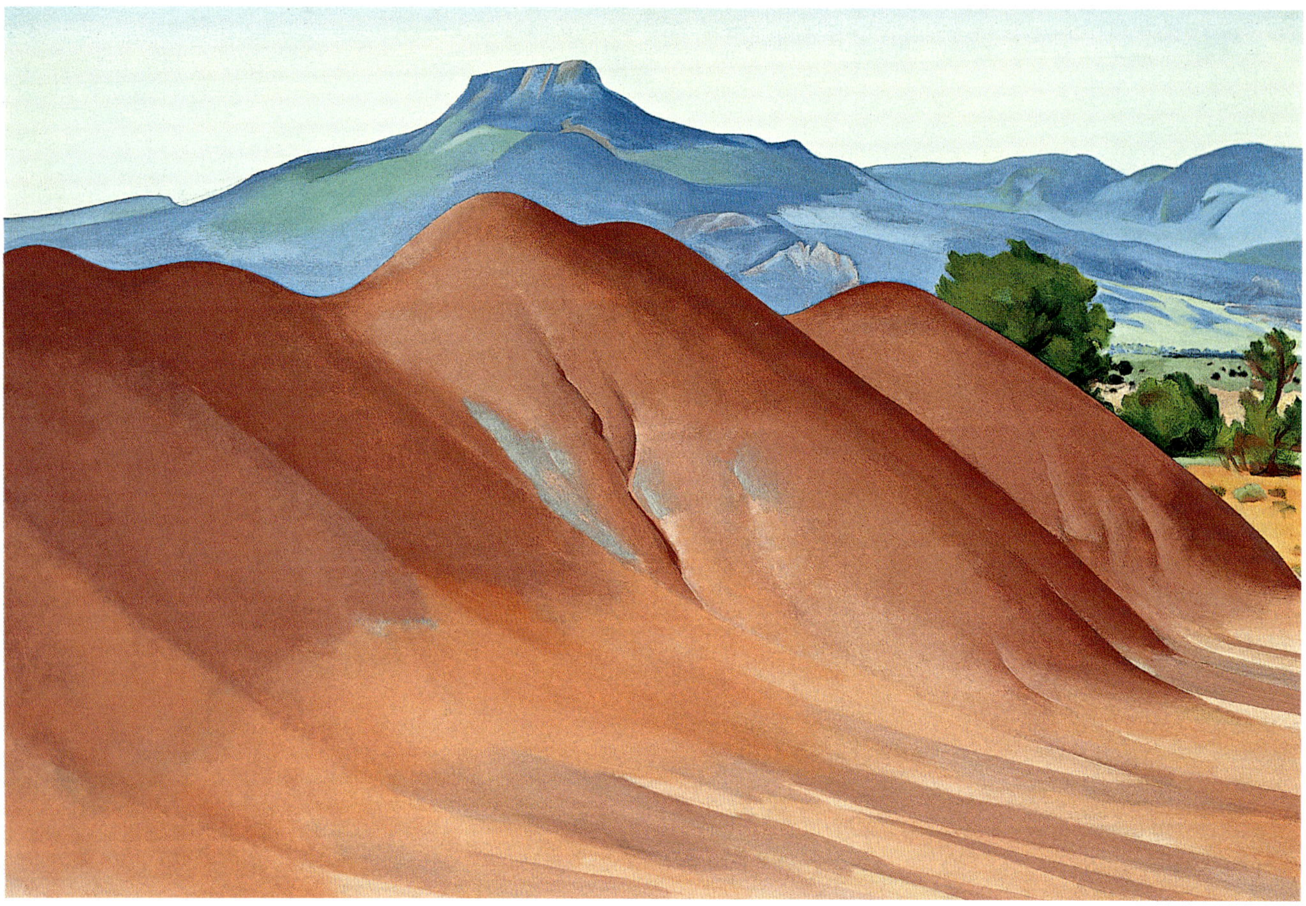

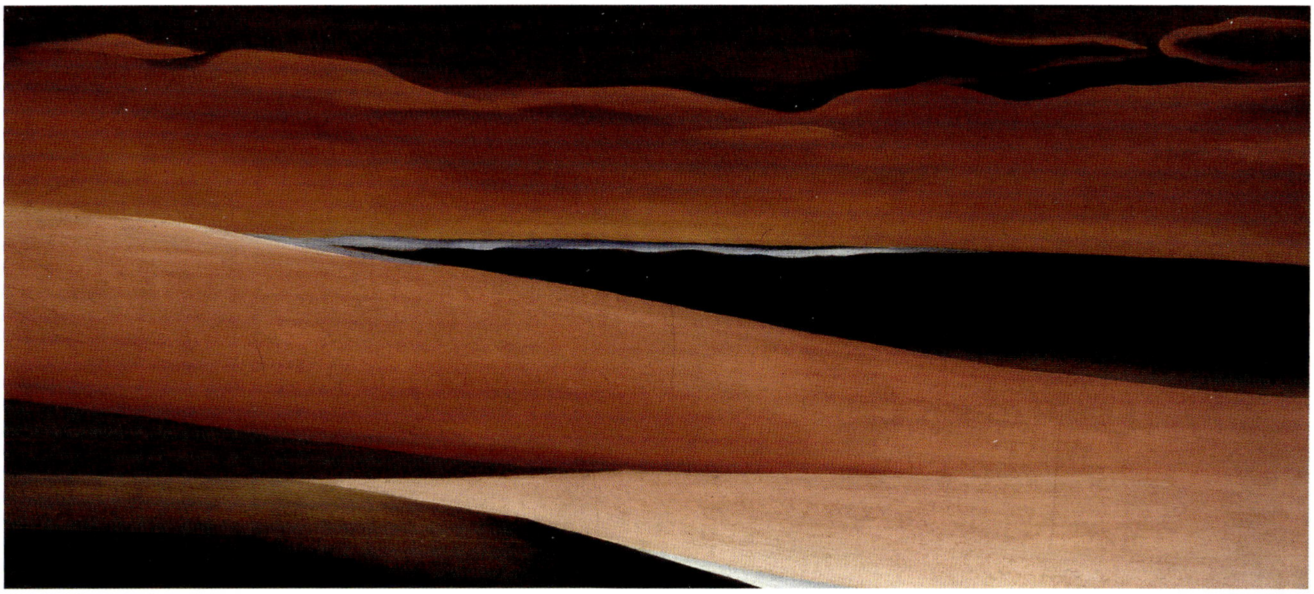

143
GEORGIA O'KEEFFE (1887–1986)
BEAR LAKE (DESERT ABSTRACTION), 1931
OIL ON CANVAS, 16½ X 36½ IN. (41.9 X 92.7 CM)

144
ALFRED STIEGLITZ (1864–1946)
EQUIVALENT, 1930
GELATIN SILVER PRINT, 3½ X 4½ IN. (8.9 X 11.4 CM)

In the 1920s and '30s, Stieglitz began experimenting with a series of abstract cloud photographs made without references to landscapes or horizons (fig. 144). These images emphasize purely visual forms and do not include representational aspects associated with most photographs. Stieglitz titled these works *Equivalent*s because he believed they served as abstract parallels to his emotional states. Both Stieglitz's *Equivalent* and O'Keeffe's *Bear Lake* are strongly abstract, and the artists were keenly aware of each other's intentions and conceptualizations.

Ansel Adams had visited New Mexico in 1927 and photographed at Taos Pueblo. He and writer Mary Austin, who was part of Mabel's circle of patrons and activists, collaborated on a book, *Taos Pueblo*, that combined his photographs with Austin's narrative. Adams's photographs brought together interesting modernist and pre-modernist ideas. Images of Native Americans at work had been a popular but predictable pre-modernist trope since the 1880s. However, Adams's use of close-value tones within the photographs transformed the pueblo into a modernist flattened, architectural form.

Modernist painter John Marin, like Adams, created images of New Mexico with flattened space and abstract forms that were both expressionistic and painterly. He spent the summers of 1929 and 1930 painting abstract watercolors known for their fresh brush strokes and simplification of forms that stunned the arts community of northern New Mexico. Marin's painting *Back of Ranchos Church* from 1930 (fig. 145) exemplifies the images he created over two summers of concentrated work. This painting expresses his response to an architectural icon while experimenting with geometric clouds. Marin's New Mexico watercolors influenced a generation of painters that included Margaret Fisher, Victor Higgins, Gina Knee, Ward Lockwood, William Lumpkins, Charles Mattox, and Cady Wells.

145
JOHN MARIN (1870–1953)
BACK OF RANCHOS CHURCH, 1930
WATERCOLOR ON PAPER, 15 x 20½ IN.
(38.1 x 52.1 CM)

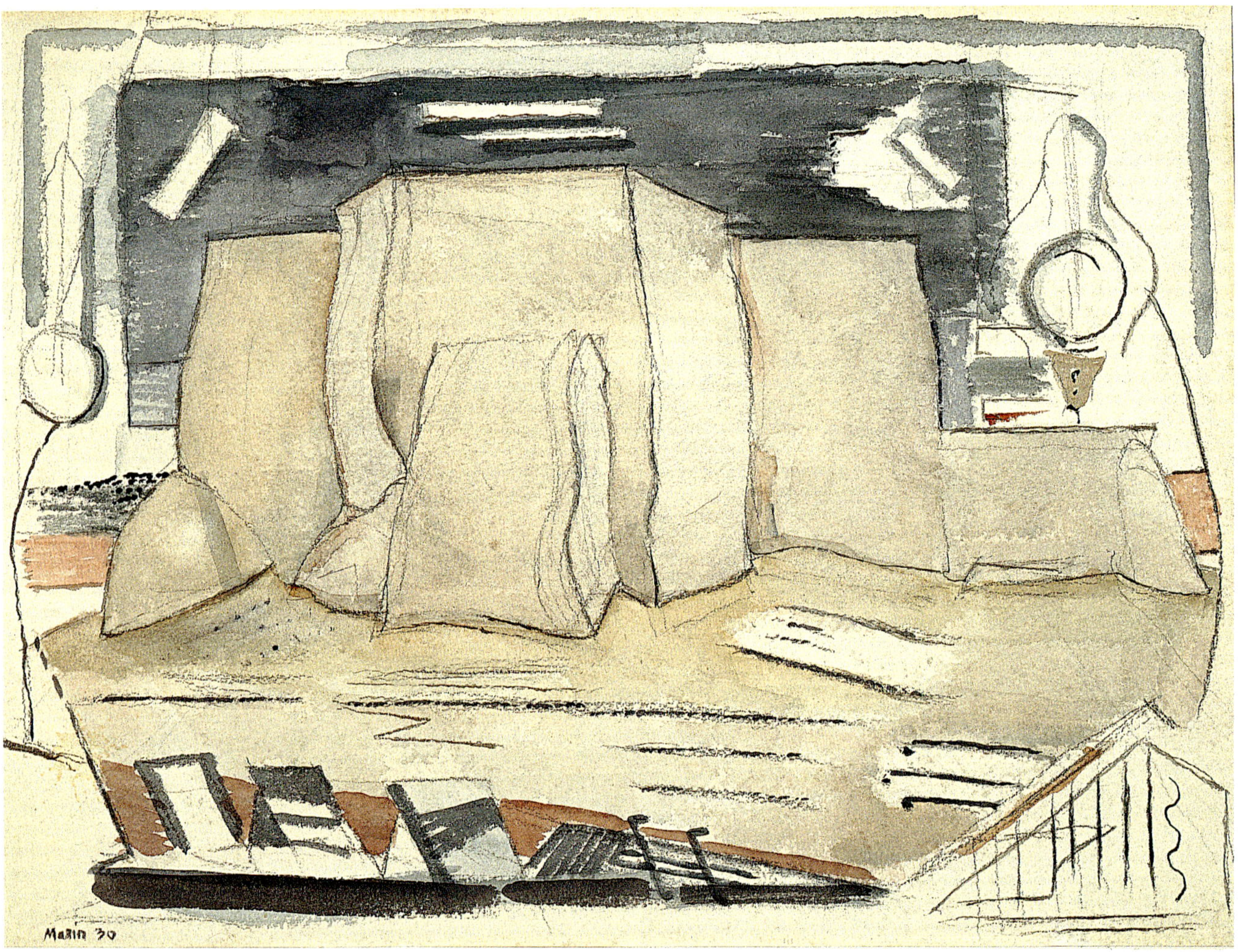

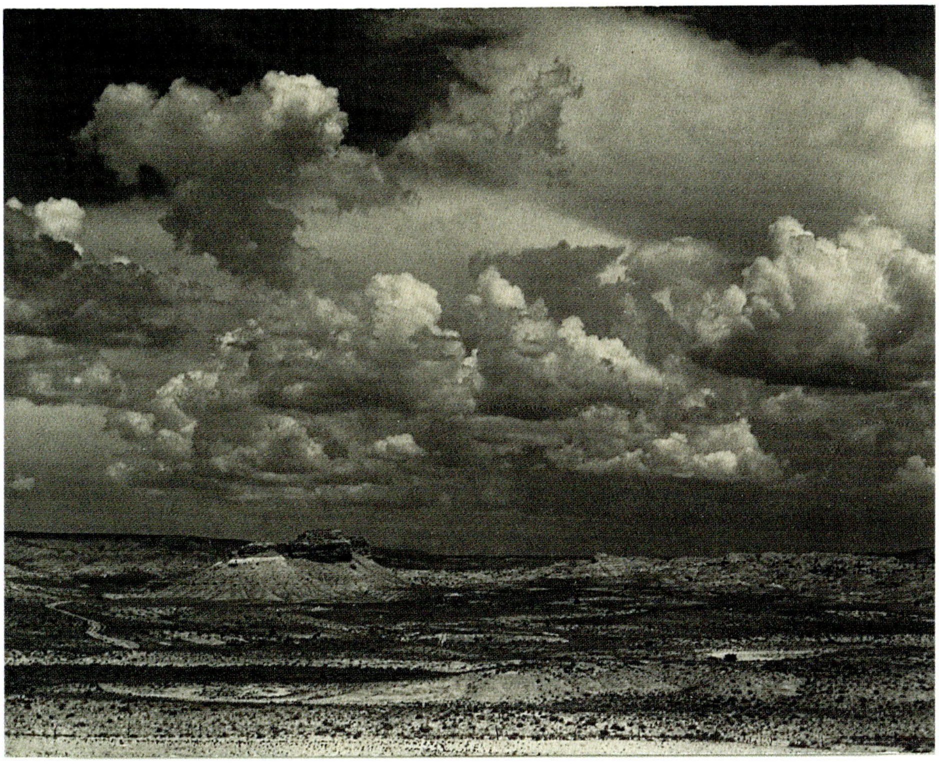

146
PAUL STRAND (1890–1976)
BADLANDS NEAR SANTA FE, NEW MEXICO, 1930
PLATINUM PRINT, 3⅝ X 4 11/16 IN. (9.2 X 11.9 CM)

Photographer Paul Strand, then Rebecca Strand's husband, also created iconic views of New Mexico but with the subtle details that can only be produced by platinum prints. Strand's 1930 photograph *Badlands Near Santa Fe, New Mexico* (fig. 146) captures the land forms in a manner that mimics the movement of the clouds above. The small contact print emphasizes the luminosity of the platinum process, which intensifies the billowing clouds glowing against the dense-blue New Mexico sky.

In the mid-1930s, O'Keeffe began mentoring the young photographer John S. Candelario, arranging for his work to be shown in Stieglitz's gallery in New York City. *Penitente Cross and Chapel, San Pedro* (fig. 147) addresses a subject that had become overworked by the 1930s. Candelario circumvents this problem by focusing on the cross as a graphic element that fractures the Penitente *morada* (meetinghouse) in the background, thus freeing himself to emphasize a modernist composition.

The O'Keeffe-Stieglitz-Mabel Dodge Luhan circle of artists chose to work in relative seclusion in northern New Mexico, had little to do with local artists eking out a living during the depression, and did not exhibit in the fiesta exhibitions at the Museum of Art.

PUBLIC ASSISTANCE AND THE ARTS

The Great Depression hit within six months of O'Keeffe's first visit to Taos, and the optimism that accompanied the Roaring Twenties quickly disappeared. But the hard times were already being felt in northern New Mexico by the time O'Keeffe returned in 1930.

147
JOHN S. CANDELARIO (1916–1993)
PENITENTE CROSS AND CHAPEL, SAN PEDRO, 1937
UNIQUE PLATINUM PRINT, 9 9/16 X 7 5/8 IN. (24.3 X 19.4 CM)

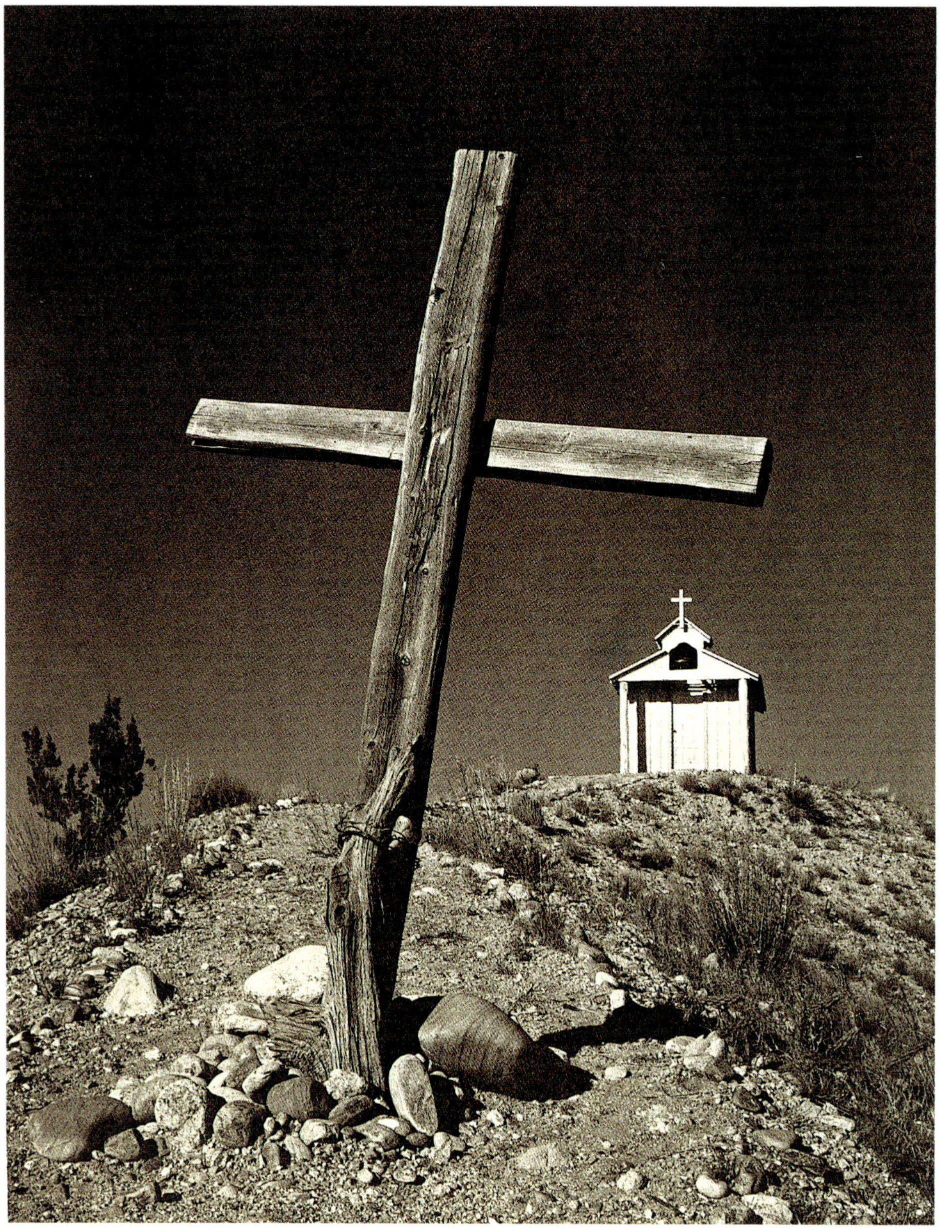

State and federal agencies tried to ameliorate the impact of the depression on the arts of the region. The state transformed a game-and-fish publication into *New Mexico Magazine* with the hope that articles lauding the cultural and natural sights would spur tourism.

The cover of the August 1933 issue of *New Mexico Magazine* featured *The Black Shawl* (fig. 148), a work by Esquípula Romero de Romero. The painting portrays the artist's daughter looking up at a cross seen only as a shadow cast on the rock face behind the figure. Romero de Romero accurately painted the masthead of the magazine into the background of the painting but later painted out the reference to the magazine. Nonetheless, faint traces can still be seen. Romero de Romero made his living painting signs and

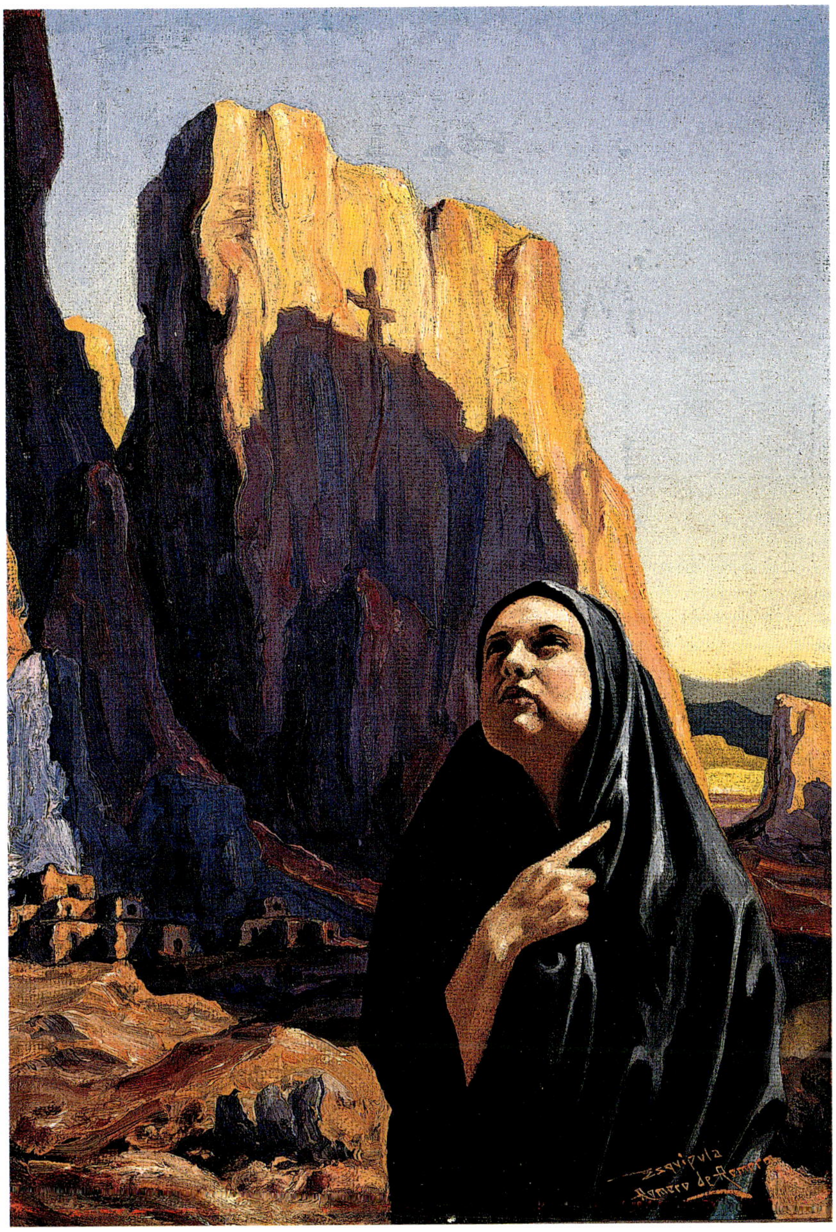

148
ESQUÍPULA ROMERO DE ROMERO
(1889–1975)
THE BLACK SHAWL, 1933
OIL ON MASONITE, 17 x 11½ IN.
(43.2 x 29.2 CM)

billboards in Albuquerque, although he had studied painting in Los Angeles, New York City, Philadelphia, and Mexico City. As interest in Hispanic arts increased during the 1930s, Romero de Romero became the best-known Hispanic painter in New Mexico.

In 1934, the federal government initiated the Public Works of Art Program, the first of many projects aimed at supporting artists and placing works of art in public buildings. As part of the program, Will Shuster produced eight frescos in the courtyard of the New Mexico Museum of Art that depict Pueblo lifeways and rituals (fig. 149). Raymond Jonson, who had attended the 1933–34 Century of Progress exposition in Chicago, painted *Cycles of Science,* a series of works addressing the importance of science and technology

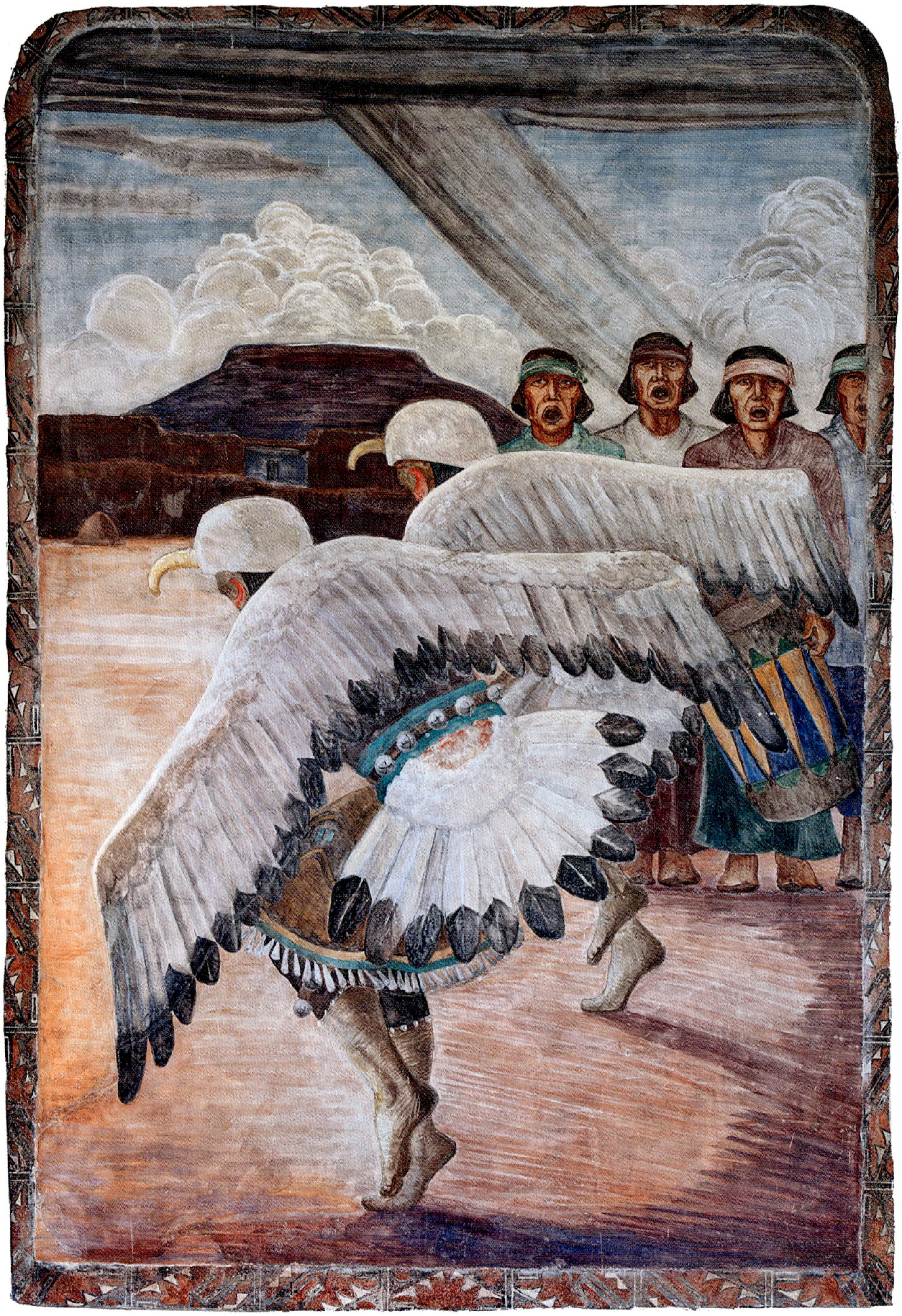

149
WILL SHUSTER (1893–1969)
THE VOICE OF THE SKY (THE EAGLE DANCE), 1934
FRESCO, 68¼ x 47¼ IN. (173.4 x 120 CM)

for the University of New Mexico and Eastern New Mexico University. Jonson's painting *Cycle of Science—Chemistry* (fig. 150) presents a theatrical abstraction of laboratory equipment.

Throughout the depression era, Robert Goddard was experimenting with liquid-fueled rockets in Roswell, New Mexico. Goddard became known as the father of modern rocketry, creating his experiments in a well-equipped machine shop that is now replicated in the Roswell Museum and Art Center. The rocket components that Goddard produced, such as his 1931–1932 *Combustion Chamber, Nozzle, and Jacket* (fig. 151), appear as sculptures reflecting the aspirations of an industrial society. Yet there is a striking formal similarity between the shapes in Jonson's painting and Goddard's rocket motor.

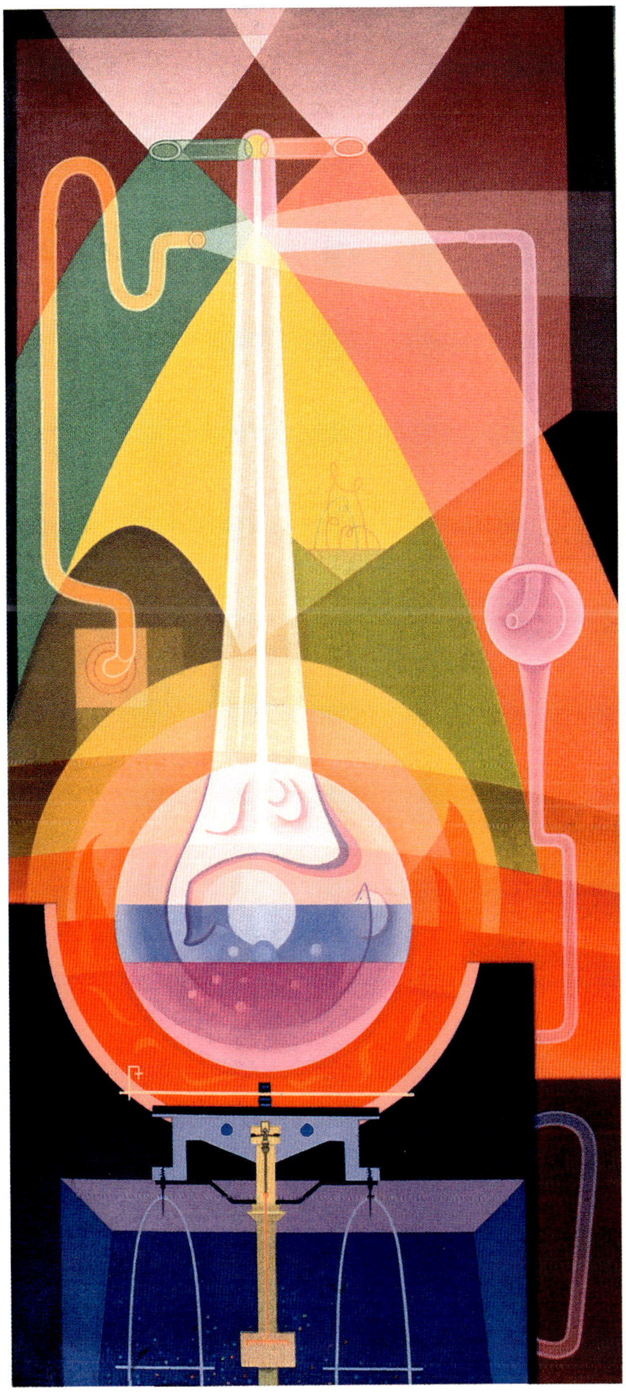

150
RAYMOND JONSON (1891–1982)
CYCLE OF SCIENCE—CHEMISTRY, 1934
OIL ON CANVAS, 80 X 37 IN. (203.2 X 94 CM)

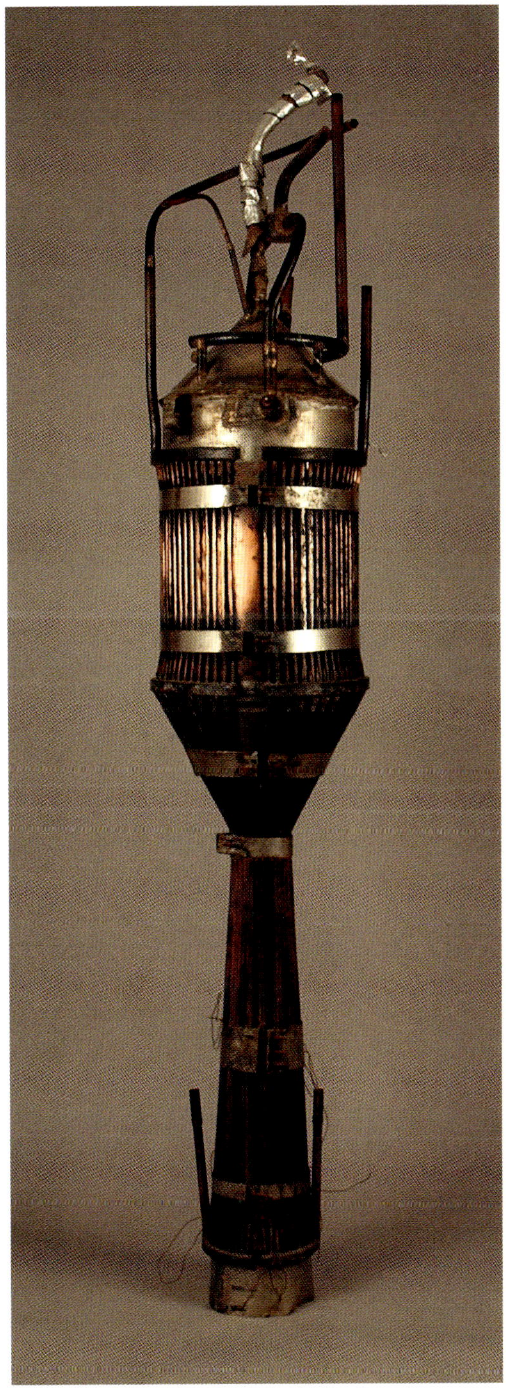

151
ROBERT GODDARD (1882–1945)
COMBUSTION CHAMBER, NOZZLE, AND JACKET, 1931–1932
ALUMINUM AND COPPER, 63.5 IN. (161.3 CM)

The Federal Art Project of the Works Progress Administration also supported artists, including James Stovall Morris, who synthesized a version of Midwest regional painting with a touch of surrealism. Morris's circa 1940 painting *Lightning* (fig. 152) depicts adobe buildings set in the vast spaces of New Mexico as a summer storm approaches. The figures in the foreground seem to be simultaneously trying to drive away the lightning while beckoning rains to water crops. Morris's surrealist twist transforms the painting into a mystical scene.

All together, depression-era federal arts programs supported more than 160 New Mexico artists. One of the most interesting aspects of the programs in New Mexico was the inclusion of Native American and Hispanic artists, who created pottery, *retablos*, furniture, weavings, tin frames and fixtures, and *colcha* embroidery made with hand-dyed wool threads. Among these artists was Juan Amadeo Sánchez, who became one of the pro-

152
JAMES STOVALL MORRIS (1898–1973)
LIGHTNING, CIRCA 1940
OIL ON CANVAS BOARD PANEL,
20 X 24 IN. (50.8 X 61 CM)

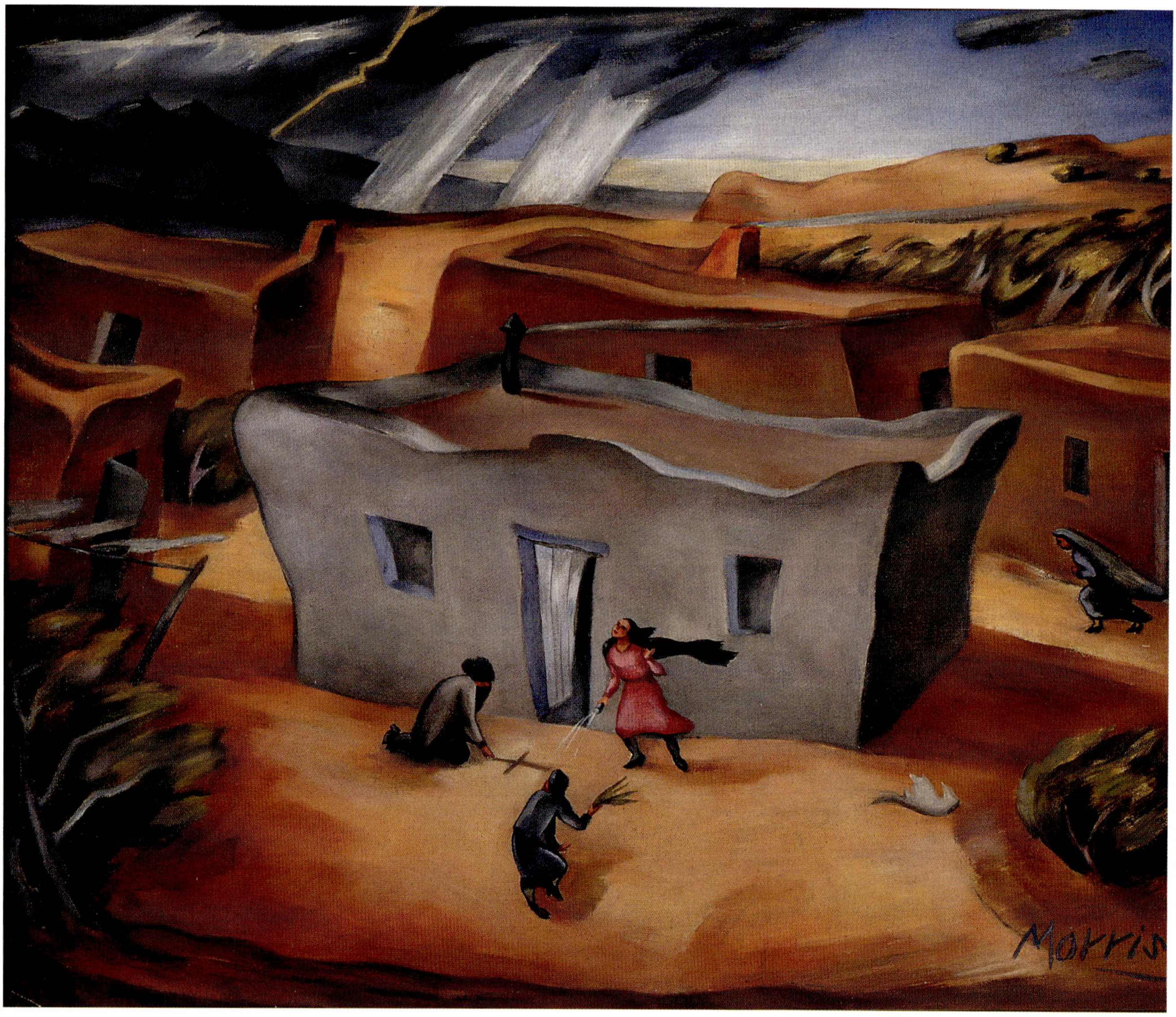

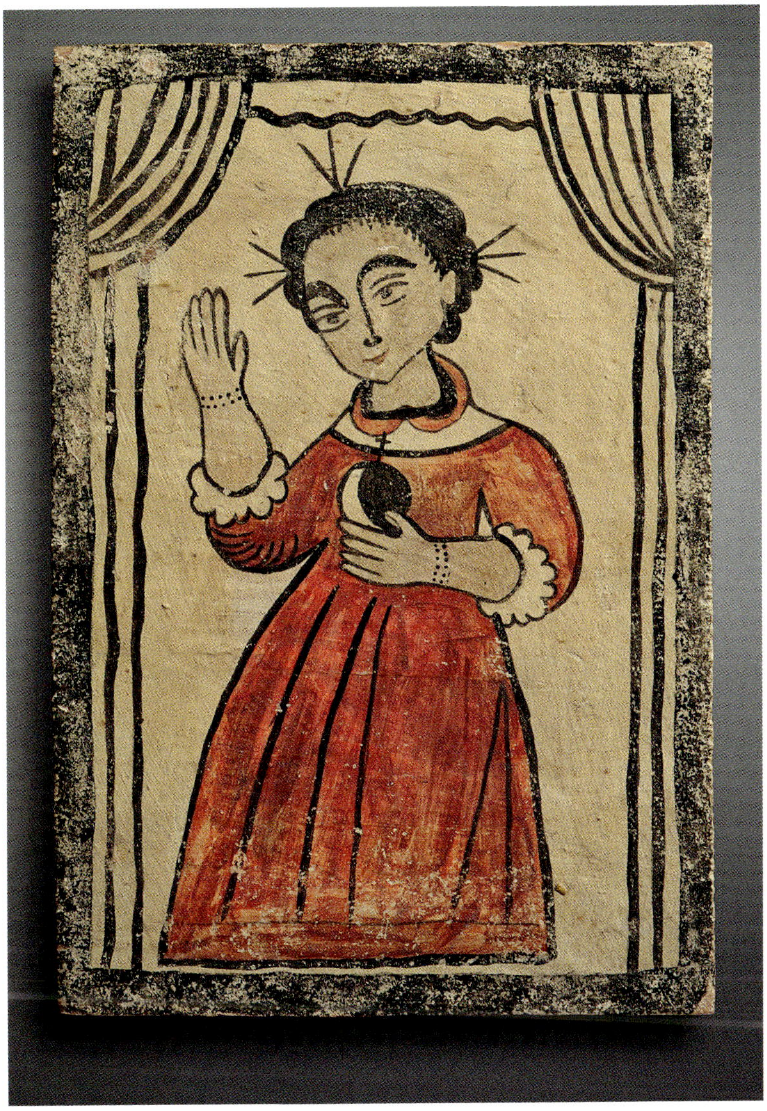

153
JUAN AMADEO SÁNCHEZ (1901–1969)
EL NIÑO JESÚS DE PRAGA / INFANT JESUS OF PRAGUE, 1936
GOUACHE ON WOOD, 9½ X 6½ IN.
(24.1 X 16.5 CM)

gram's successes. As a child, Sánchez had been abused by older youths and became partially handicapped. Nonetheless, he had learned to draw pictures. The Federal Art Project hired Sánchez to paint replicas of nineteenth-century *retablos*, such as *El Niño Jesús de Praga / Infant Jesus of Prague* (fig. 153). Sánchez's artistry quickly transcended the mere copying of works from the past, and his art was promoted by both Holger Cahill, national director of the Works Progress Administration–Federal Art Program, and Russell Vernon Hunter, director of the Works Progress Administration art program in New Mexico.

At the Santa Fe Indian School beginning in 1932, Dorothy Dunn offered boarding school students art instruction after their regular classes, allowing them, in violation of federal policy, to create images that related to their home lives, religions, and dress. Dunn also proposed that students produce a pan-Indian art style that incorporated pencil-drawn outlines filled in with flat planes of color (fig. 154).

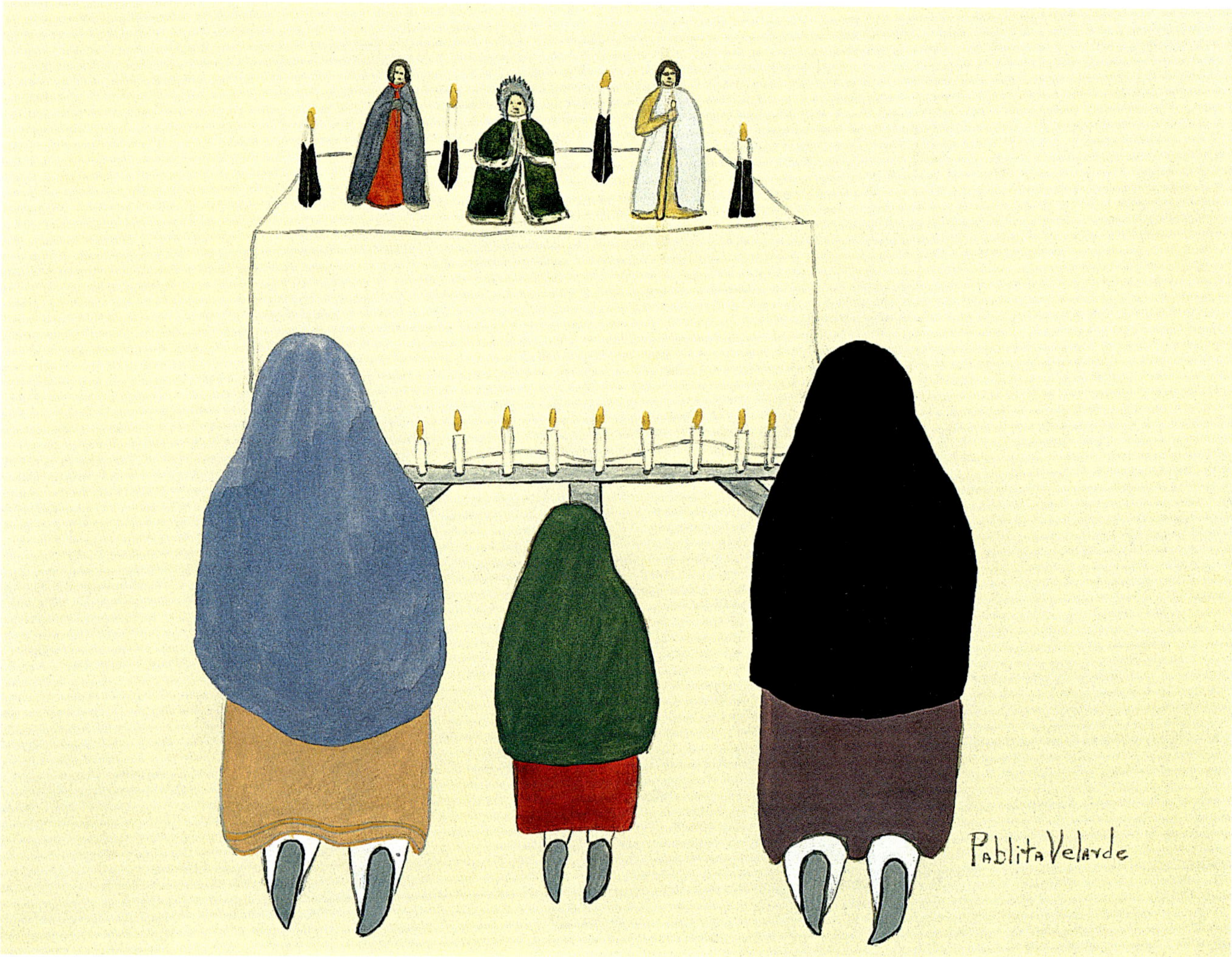

154
PABLITA VELARDE (TSE TSAN)
(1918–2006)
SANTA CLARA WOMEN BEFORE THE ALTAR, CIRCA 1933
WATERCOLOR ON ILLUSTRATION BOARD, 8 15/16 X 12 1/16 IN. (22.7 X 30.7 CM)

Dunn's students enjoyed this activity because it allowed them to think of Native rituals outside of the boarding school context while validating traditions that federal policy had tried to eliminate (fig. 155). The program was so popular that it was ultimately incorporated into the school's curriculum and was responsible for training a generation of Native artists. As students graduated and became practicing artists, the subject matter of their paintings expanded to include the relationship between Native peoples and the tourists who purchased their art. Gerald Nailor's untitled view of a Diné woman trying to sell a blanket to wealthy travelers is a classic example (fig. 156).

The Farm Security Administration hired writers and photographers to record the impact of the Great Depression on rural people beween 1935 and 1944. Photographers John Collier, Russell Lee, and Jack Delano worked in New Mexico recording industrial and rural scenes, from homesteads near Pie Town, New Mexico, to rodeos in northern New Mexico. Delano's 1943 photograph *Beatrice Davis, Clovis, N.M.* (see fig. 4) shows

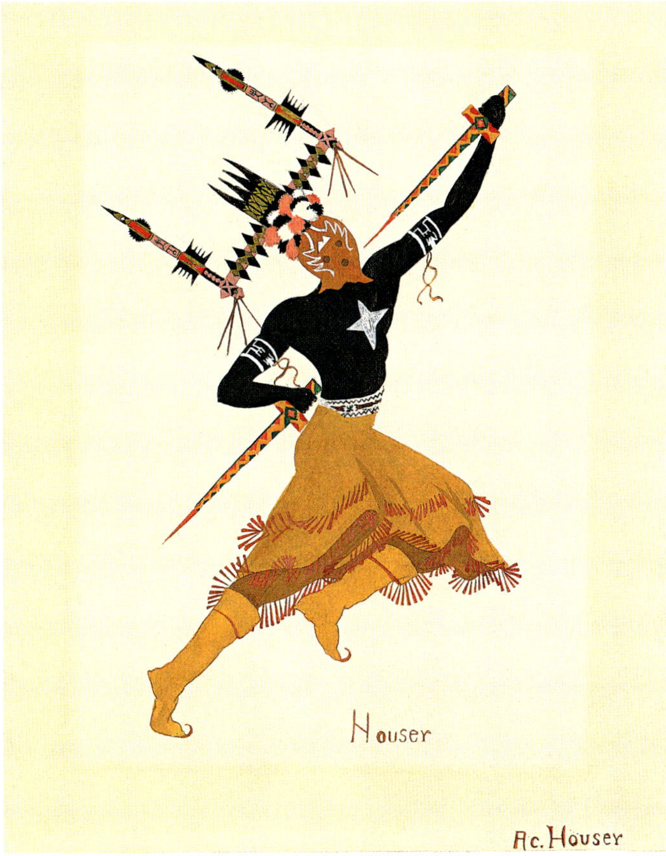

155
ALLAN HOUSER (1914–1994)
APACHE DEVIL DANCER, CIRCA 1943
GOUACHE ON ILLUSTRATION BOARD,
11$\frac{11}{16}$ X 9$\frac{5}{8}$ IN. (29.7 X 24.4 CM)

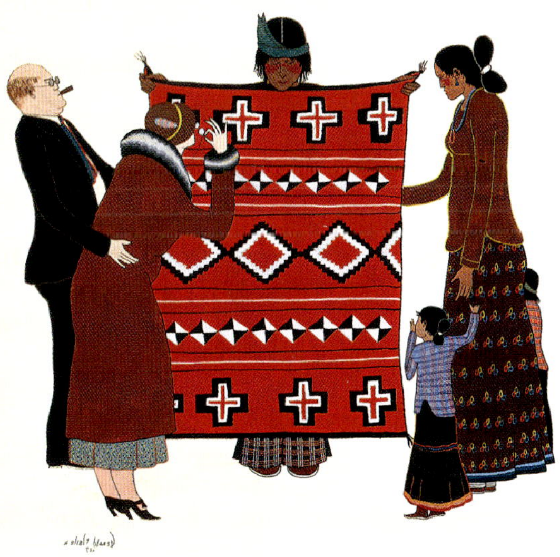

156
GERALD NAILOR (TOH YAH) (1917–1952)
UNTITLED (TOURISTS), CIRCA 1938
TEMPERA ON ILLUSTRATION BOARD,
14 X 12$\frac{5}{16}$ IN. (35.5 X 31.3 CM)

a woman who cleaned out boxcars for the Atchison, Topeka, and Santa Fe Railway. The image underscores the importance of rural workers for the World War II effort, as well as the nontraditional jobs done by women while men were serving in the military. FSA photographs introduced Americans to America in a powerful, affective manner.

TRANSCENDENTAL PAINTING GROUP

In 1938, as the Great Depression waned, Raymond Jonson and Emil Bisttram organized the Transcendental Painting Group, the last of the artist fraternities in New Mexico. These artists presented a manifesto proposing nonobjective art as a vehicle for spiritual transcendence. Like the Taos Society of Artists before them, the group organized exhibitions of their work but also served as a counterforce to Edgar Hewett's rejection of modernism.

The depression was a period of transition for Jonson, a time when he ceased creating abstractions of known objects and ventured into nonobjective art without references to the physical world. *Stream of Light* from 1933 is a tiny drawing that illuminated the way for himself (fig. 157). The dark charcoal image depicts a shaft of light that curves through the picture plane in a mysterious manner and is reflected in glowing elements toward the edge of the drawing.

To make up for dwindling sales of his paintings, Jonson took a teaching position at the University of New Mexico and sold art supplies out of his garage. The combination of Jonson's radical paintings from the period and his stock of art supplies made his Santa Fe garage a destination for adventuresome artists. Among them was William Lumpkins, who stopped by seeking Jonson's advice about his watercolors, which were heavily influenced by John Marin's work.

Lumpkins, who had grown up on ranches throughout the Southwest, was earning a living as an architect in the mid-1930s, but he was determined to find his own path as an artist painting abstractions. His 1935 work *This Was a Breakthru* (fig, 158) was the first nonobjective watercolor that Lumpkins felt was artistically successful.

Jonson supported younger artists experimenting with abstraction, including Stuart Walker, who had contracted rheumatic fever as a navy enlistee during World War I, resulting in permanent heart damage. Hoping to regain his health, Walker moved to Albuquerque after attending art school in Indianapolis. He made a living as a competent landscape painter, but after meeting Jonson in the mid-1930s he painted abstract watercolors and oils.

Walker's exquisitely crafted watercolor *No. 32,* circa 1937 (fig. 159) displays a delicate balance between forms. In 1939, Walker created another version of the painting in oils, *Composition No. 57* (fig. 160), and sent it to the art exhibition at the 1939 World's Fair in New York City. Walker considered *Composition No. 57* to be his best work and was crushed when it did not sell. The painting and the frame suffered minor damage at the fair, which he carefully repaired. Walker died from heart failure in 1940, shortly after giving the painting to a niece, who kept the work for almost seventy years.

Ed Garman became interested in abstraction while working on archaeological excavations and seeing the designs on pottery fragments. Garman became a close associate of

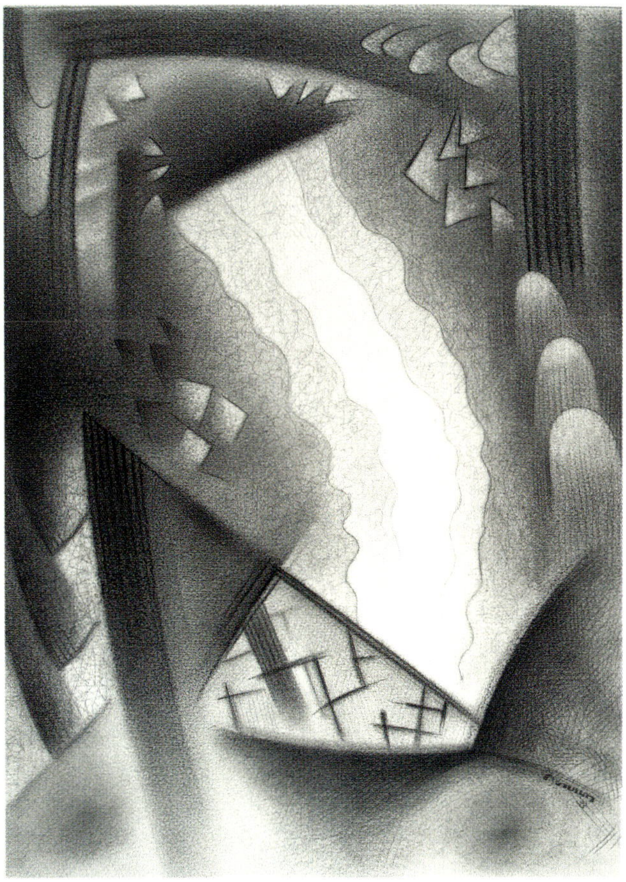

157
RAYMOND JONSON (1891–1982)
STREAM OF LIGHT, 1933
GRAPHITE ON PAPER, 15 x 11 IN.
(38.1 x 27.9 CM)

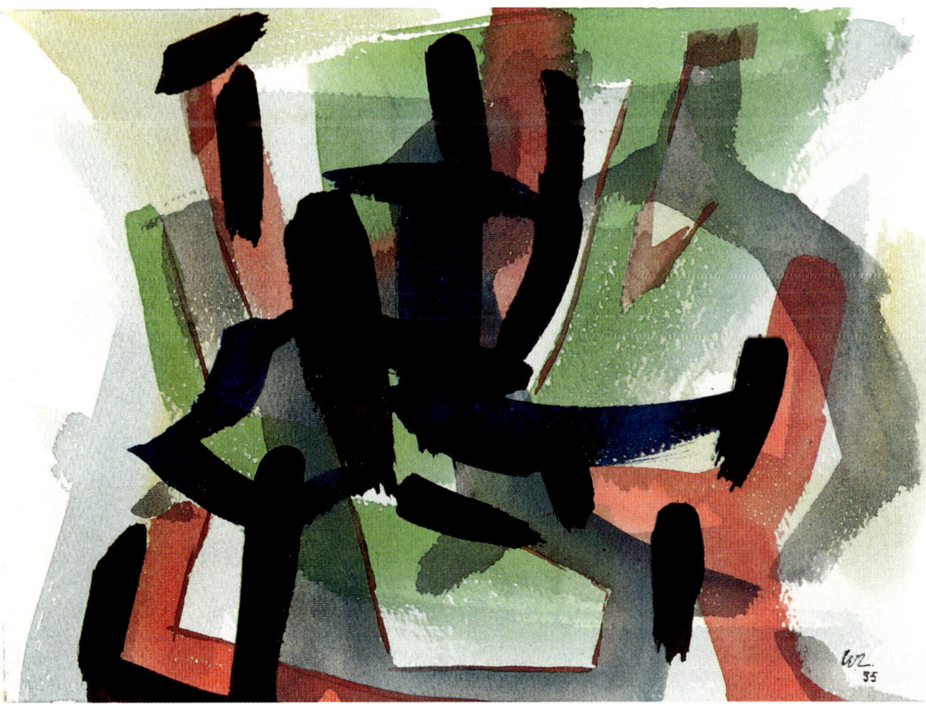

158
WILLIAM LUMPKINS (1909–2000)
THIS WAS A BREAKTHRU, 1935
WATERCOLOR ON PAPER, 7¾ x 10¾ IN.
(19.7 x 27.3 CM)

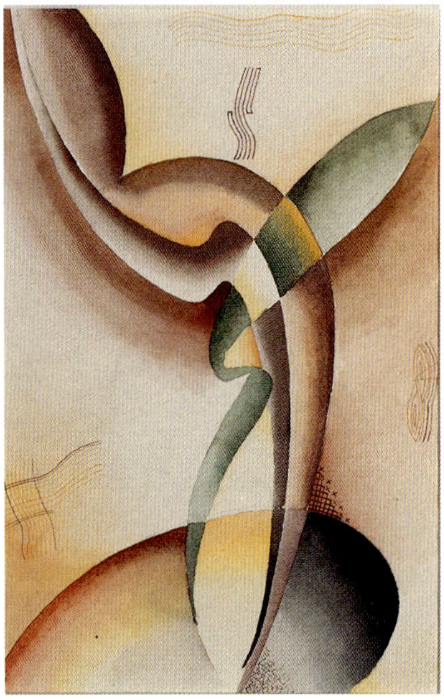

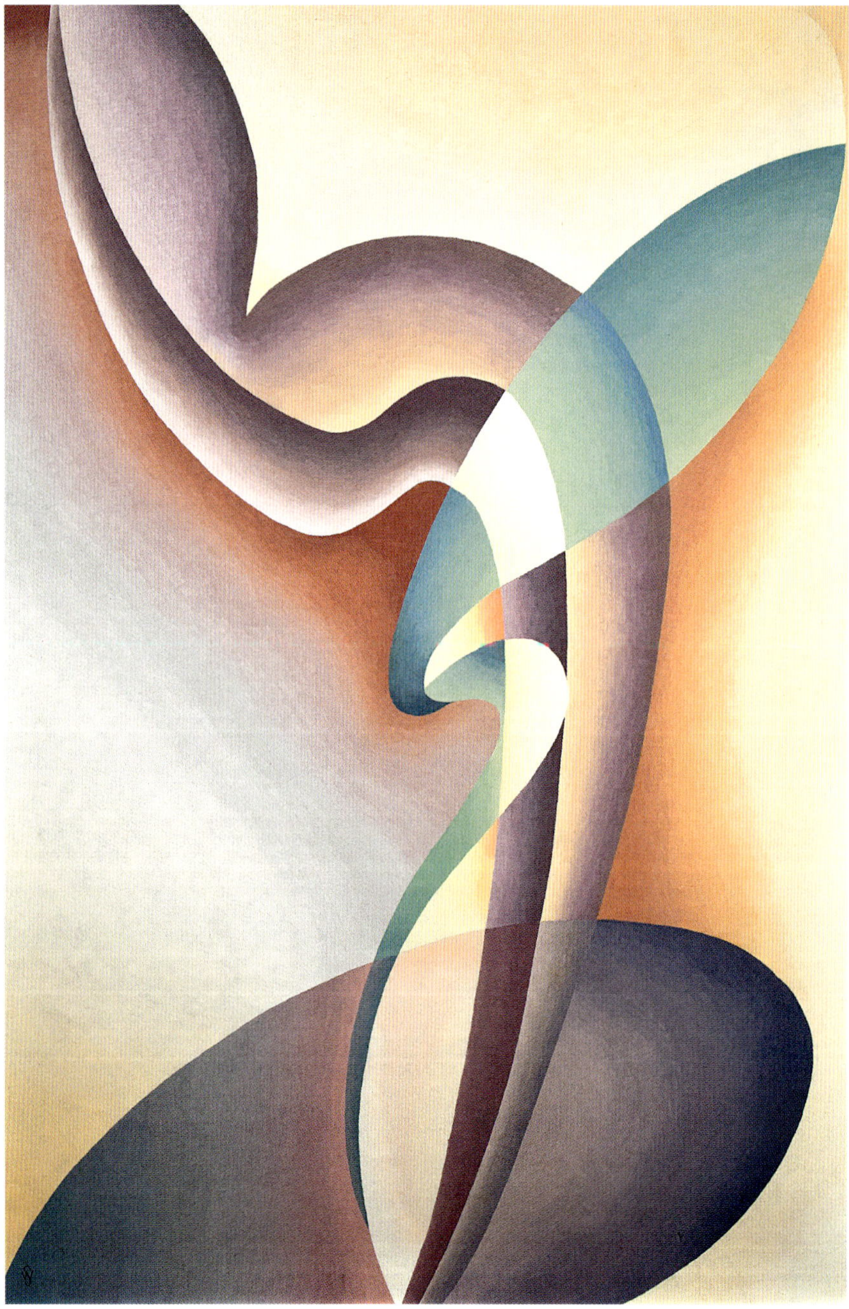

159
STUART WALKER (1904–1940)
NO. 32 (STUDY FOR COMPOSITION NO. 57), CIRCA 1937
WATERCOLOR ON PAPER, 9½ X 6½ IN.
(24.1 X 16.5 CM)

160
STUART WALKER (1904–1940)
COMPOSITION NO. 57, 1939
OIL ON CANVAS, 40¾ X 27¾ IN.
(103.5 X 70.5 CM)

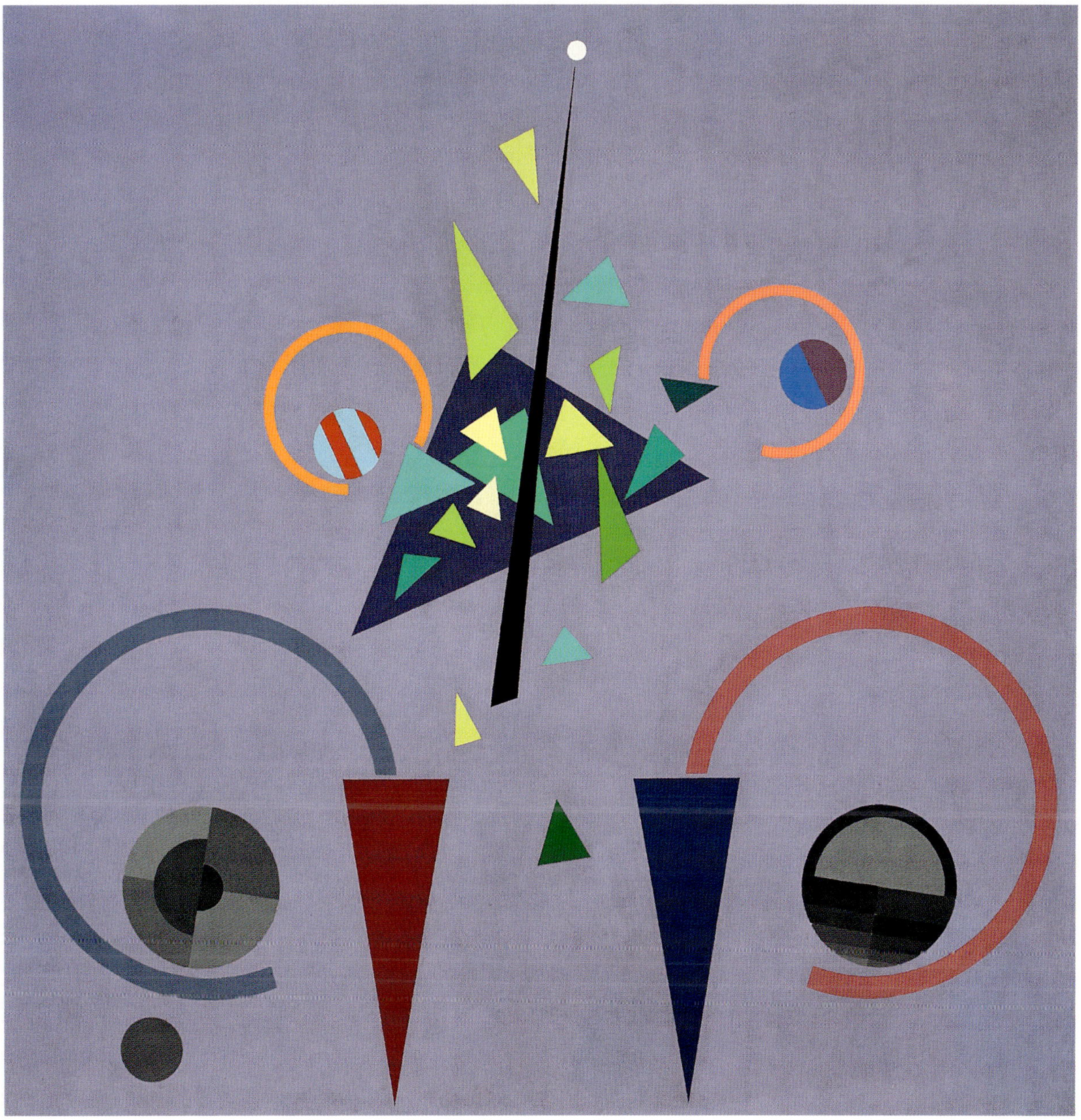

161
ED GARMAN (B. 1914)
NO. 283A, 1942
OIL ON BOARD, 23¾ X 23¾ IN.
(60.3 X 60.3 CM)

Jonson and created a large number of nonobjective works before joining the navy during World War II. Garman painted the small geometric work *No. 283A* (fig. 161), in which forms float in an enigmatic physical space drawn together by color harmonies, while the contrasting hues separate them and create a dynamic tension between elements.

Emil Bisttram made nonobjective paintings in Taos, but he was also fascinated by visualizations of atomic structures. Works such as his 1942 untitled drawing of what

162
EMIL BISTTRAM (1895–1976)
UNTITLED, 1942
COLOR PENCIL ON PAPER, 8¾ X 6¾ IN.
(22.2 X 17.1 CM)

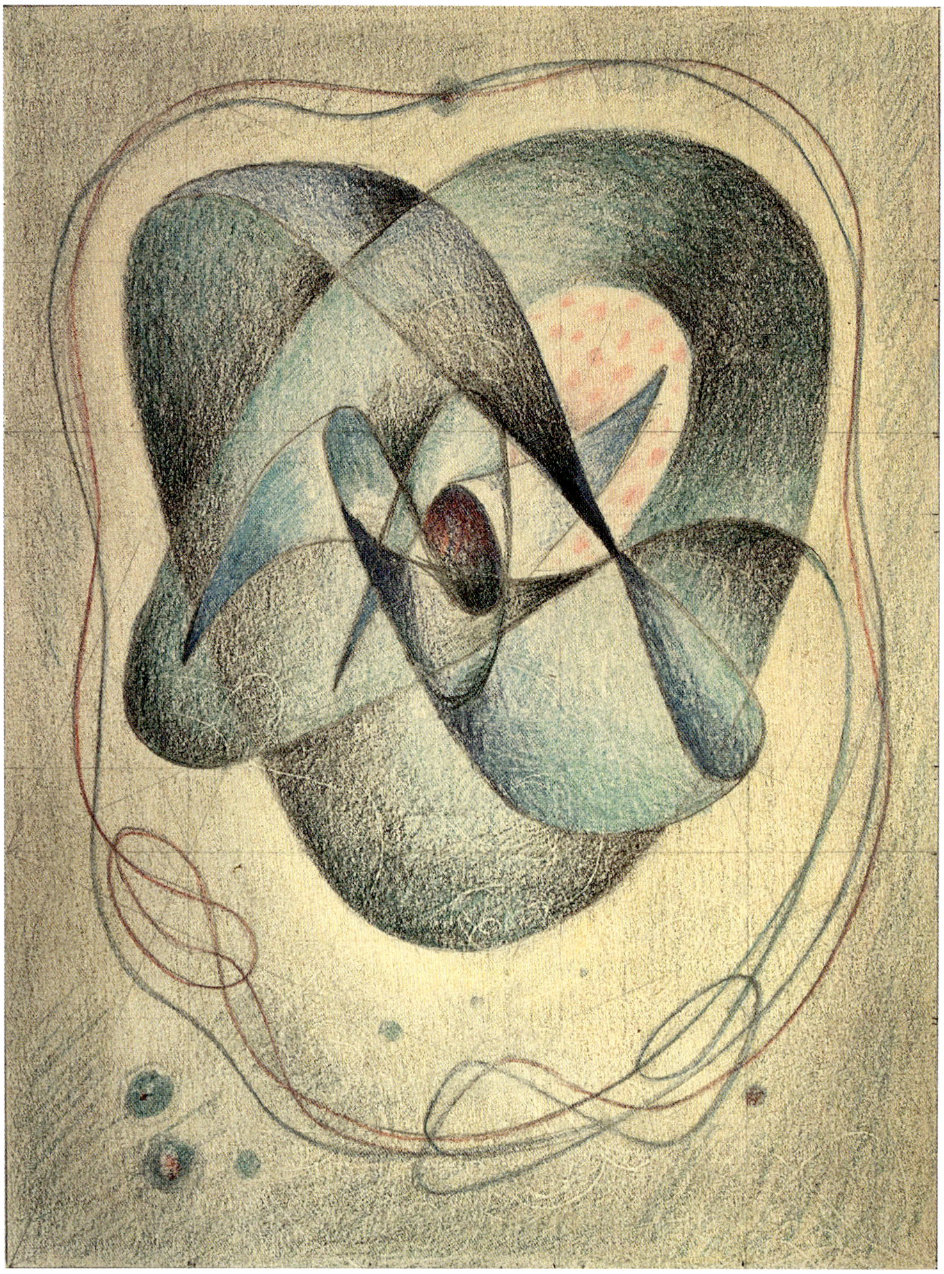

appears to be electron clouds around an atom (fig. 162) fuse abstract concepts of both art and science. The drawing challenges viewers to think about images derived from science but also about those that reflect the artist's subconscious memories.

Agnes Pelton, a founder of the Transcendental Painting Group, was perhaps its most fascinating member. Pelton corresponded with Raymond Jonson during the 1930s and shared with the group an interest in theosophy—a combination of elements taken from multiple Eastern religious traditions. However, ill health and poor finances prevented her from moving from California to New Mexico, where she could more actively collaborate with the other transcendental painters.

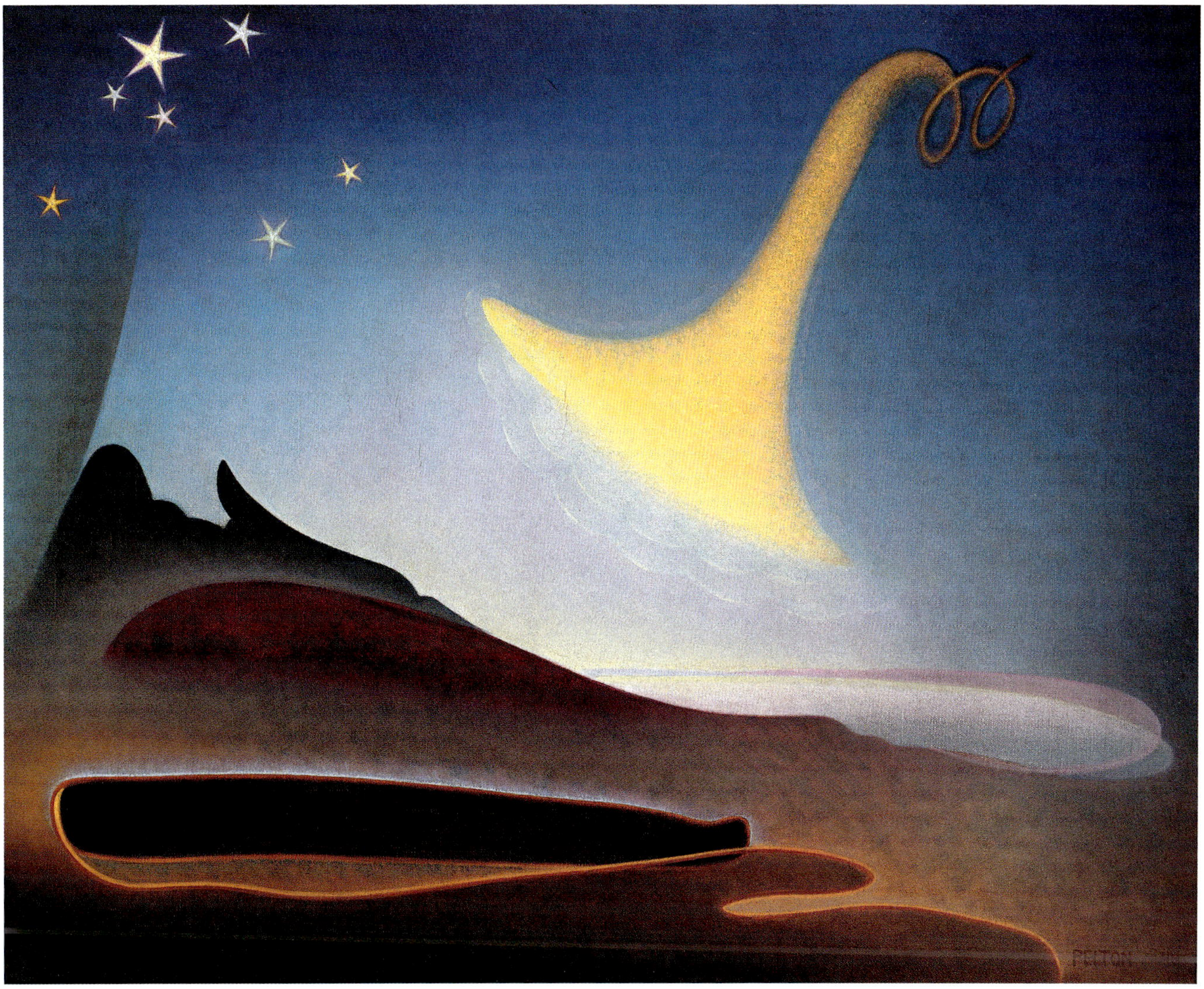

At first, her oil painting *Awakening (Memory of Father)* (fig. 163) seems to be a nonobjective landscape with a flower floating in the sky. But a closer look reveals incredible color shifts created through fine brush strokes and controlled stippling. As the title implies, this highly symbolic work alludes to multiple connotations associated with intellectual, mystical, physical, spiritual, and sexual awakenings. Indeed, Pelton's personal life is closely intertwined with this work. Her father deserted Pelton and her mother when she was a child and later died from an overdose of morphine. Pelton divulged in her notebooks that the painting's flowerlike form represents Gabriel's trumpet, and that as the trumpet sounds in the evening, the stars come out and her father rises from his grave. In this context, the distant mountains reveal themselves as a silhouette of her father.

163
AGNES PELTON (1881–1961)
AWAKENING (MEMORY OF FATHER),
1943
OIL ON CANVAS, 22 x 28 IN.
(55.9 x 71.1 CM)

World War II started just as the Transcendental Painting Group was clarifying their goals, and in 1942 they disbanded. Ed Garman joined the navy but painted small geometric works at sea. William Lumpkins joined the Army Air Corps and became a flight instruc-

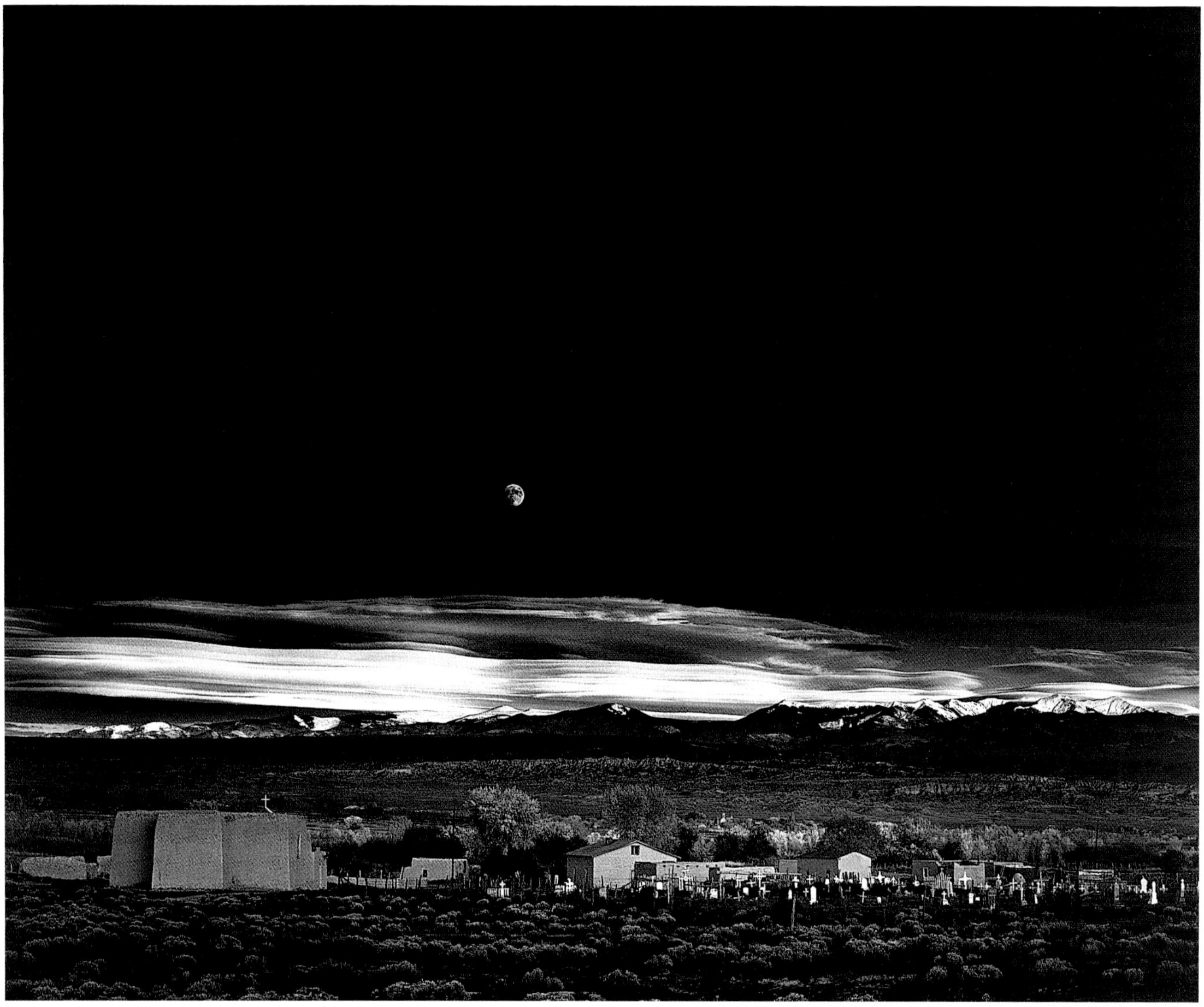

164
ANSEL ADAMS (1902–1984)
MOONRISE, HERNANDEZ, NEW MEXICO,
1941 (PRINTED 1980)
GELATIN SILVER PRINT, 15⅜ X 19⅛ IN.
(39.1 X 48.6 CM)

tor. Lauren Harris returned to Canada. Horace Towner Pierce was drafted, and his wife, Florence Miller Pierce, followed him to California.

Late on the afternoon of October 31, 1941, as Ansel Adams returned from a day of photography in northern New Mexico, he noticed the moon rising over the mountains as sunlight streaked through the clouds to illuminate the village of Hernandez. What appeared to be a spiritual light magically illuminated the church and the crosses in the adjacent cemetery. He pulled off the road, grabbed his eight-by-ten-inch view camera, and quickly prepared for a shot. Unfortunately, Adams's light meter was missing, leaving him to guess at the proper exposure. At 4:05 p.m., Adams tripped the shutter, only taking one exposure before the fast-changing light altered the scene.

Adams discussed the printing of *Moonrise, Hernandez, New Mexico* (fig. 164) in the book *Examples: The Making of 40 Photographs* (1983). He carefully developed the negative to control the tonal balance between the moon, the low clouds, and the Hispanic village, but the negative was underexposed. When Adams printed *Moonrise,* he was surprised that the work appeared as a nocturnal and not as a late-afternoon view. Today, this single image—with its eerie clouds, illuminated cemetery crosses, dense skies, and surreal landscape—has become an enduring symbol of the beauty and mystery of New Mexico.

Adams had no way of knowing that the United States would be at war with Japan within weeks of shooting *Moonrise* and that New Mexico would never be the same. *Moonrise* presents Hernandez as if the village and its traditional lifeways existed in a state of suspended animation in harmony with nature and religious traditions. The ideals implicit in this photograph continue to attract new generations to the moonlit nights of New Mexico. Indeed, in his one-second exposure Adams condensed three decades of New Mexico art into a single image.

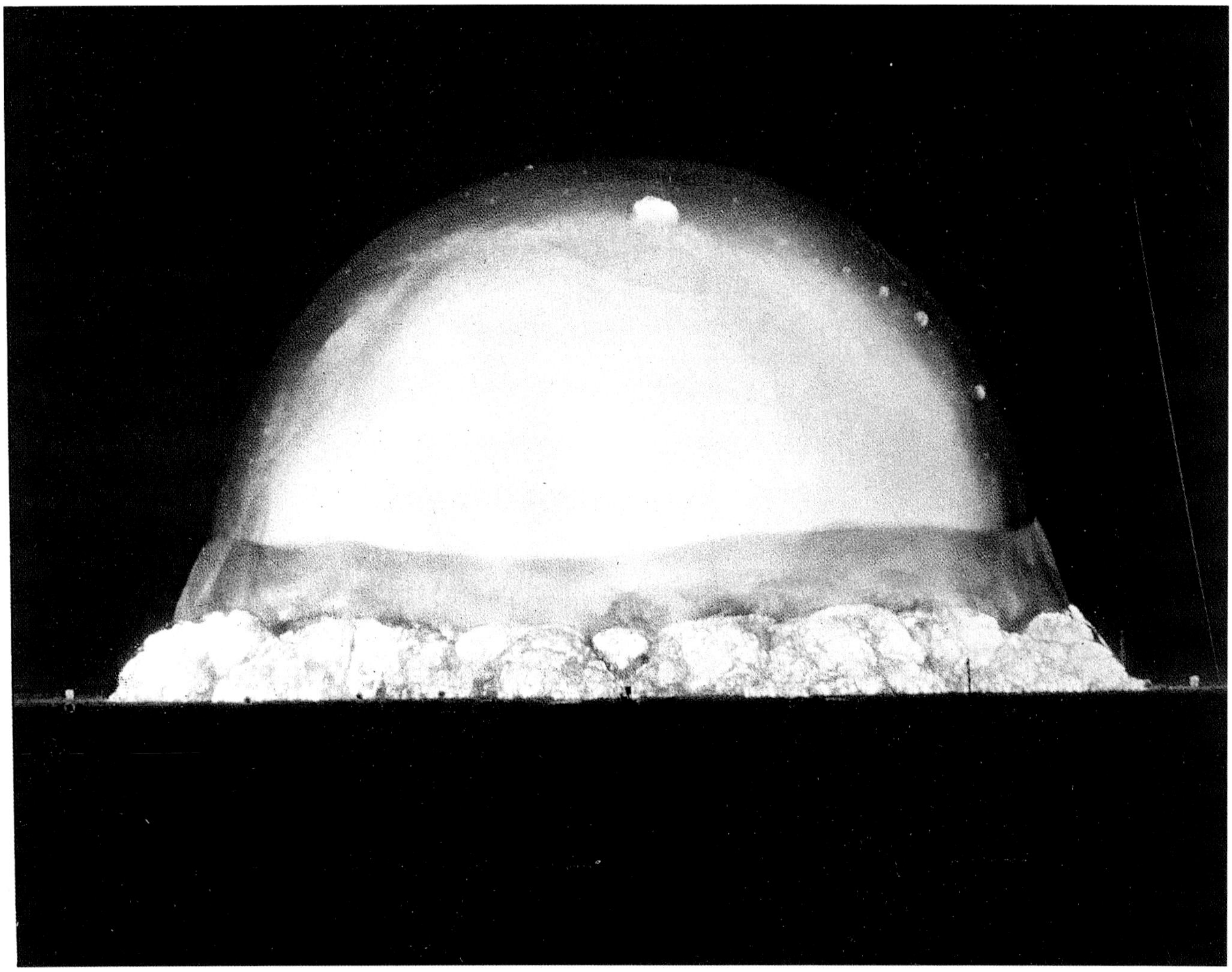

CHAPTER 7

Mainstreaming New Mexico Art

THE PHOTOGRAPH OF THE FIRST ATOMIC EXPLOSION at Trinity Site near Alamogordo, New Mexico, at dawn on July 19, 1945 (fig. 165), presents a hauntingly beautiful, deceptively simple, and frighteningly foreboding image that documents the most important single event in the 14,000 years of human activity in New Mexico, one that forever changed the world. Scientists and engineers working on the Manhattan Project at Los Alamos, New Mexico, didn't speak about creating an atomic bomb. Instead, they referred to their project using various names: The Gadget, The Device, The Thing, and The Beast. The project delivered Little Boy and Fat Man, operational versions of the bomb. On August 6, 1945, three weeks after the first detonation, Paul W. Tibbets Jr., piloting the B-29 Super Fortress *Enola Gay* over the Japanese industrial city of Hiroshima, dropped Little Boy, destroying the city, killing an estimated 150,000 people. Three days later, Frederick C. Bock dropped Fat Man on Nagasaki, killing another 30,000 to 40,000 people before the emperor of Japan finally surrendered, ending World War II.

As the war ended, Oscar Berninghaus painted *The Rabbit Hunter* (fig. 166), a depiction of men from Taos Pueblo hunting rabbits on horseback with bows and arrows, an anachronism in an age of high-altitude bombers and nuclear weapons in which Taos Pueblo hunters had shotguns and pickup trucks. Although the Taos Society of Artists had disbanded two decades earlier, Berninghaus continued to paint as if he were still a member. But much of the romance of the Southwest had ended with the war, as had the nostalgic genre paintings that had dominated New Mexico art for decades. Artists, and their audiences, had changed.

Shortly after the bombing of Pearl Harbor and the start of World War II, the U.S. government began moving people of Japanese ancestry from their homes to relocation camps located throughout the West. Federal rules also included Japanese-American citizens and Japanese aliens in the relocation. The camps were operated from February 1942 through September 1946. In New Mexico, an internment camp in Lordsburg held Japanese, and camps at Roswell and Fort Stanton held Germans as well as Japanese. A Santa Fe camp was operated by the Justice Department for individuals considered to be "dangerous enemy aliens," many of whom were teachers, journalists, ministers, or Buddhist leaders.

Jerry West's 2009 *Japanese Internment Camp* (fig. 167) was created from his memory of the Santa Fe camp, where his father, artist Hal West, and an uncle were employed,

165
BERLYN B. BRIXNER, OFFICIAL PHOTOGRAPHER, LOS ALAMOS PROJECT, OPTICS GROUP (G11) (1911–2009)
FIRST ATOMIC EXPLOSION AT A DISTANCE OF ABOUT FIVE MILES, TRINITY SITE, NEW MEXICO, JULY 16, 1945
GELATIN SILVER PRINT, 7¾ X 9¾ IN. (19.7 X 24.8 CM)

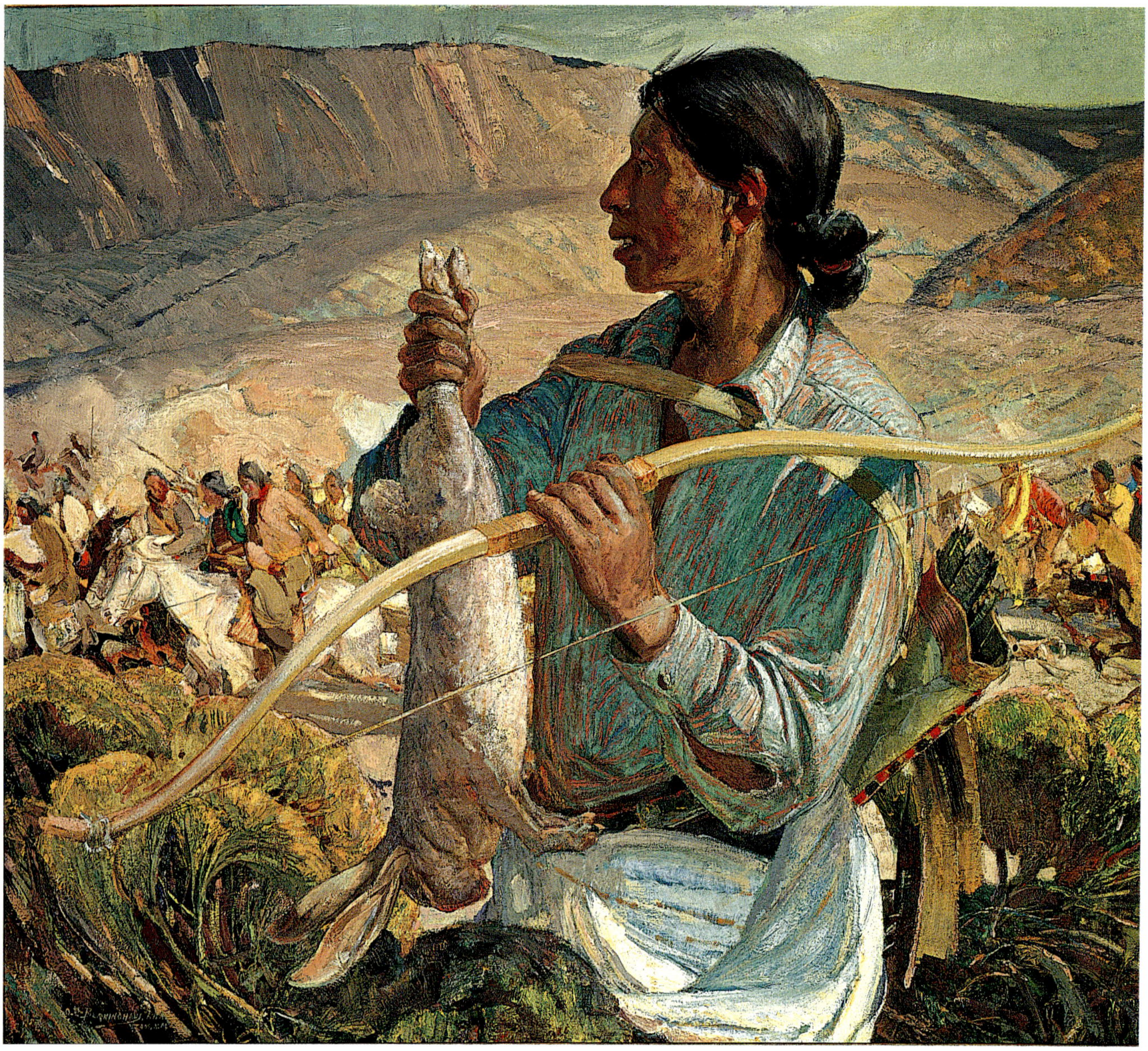

166
OSCAR BERNINGHAUS (1874–1952)
THE RABBIT HUNTER, CIRCA 1945
OIL ON CANVAS, 34½ X 39½ IN.
(87.6 X 100.3 CM)

as well as from sketches his father had drawn at the time. The prisonlike structure provides a stark contrast with the nostalgic New Mexican landscape.

Mineo Matoba and his family were sent to the Gila River Relocation Center on Arizona land leased from the Pima Tribe (Hirasuna 2005). He objected to camp, and authorities there considered him to be a troublemaker. They sent him to the detention center in Santa Fe but kept his family at the Gila River center. Matoba's separation from his family was unbearable, and because he wanted them to feel the family was still united in spite of the separation he hand carved, out of scrap wood, a small Butsudan, a Buddhist family shrine (fig. 168), sending it to them as a symbol of his love and their spiritual unity.

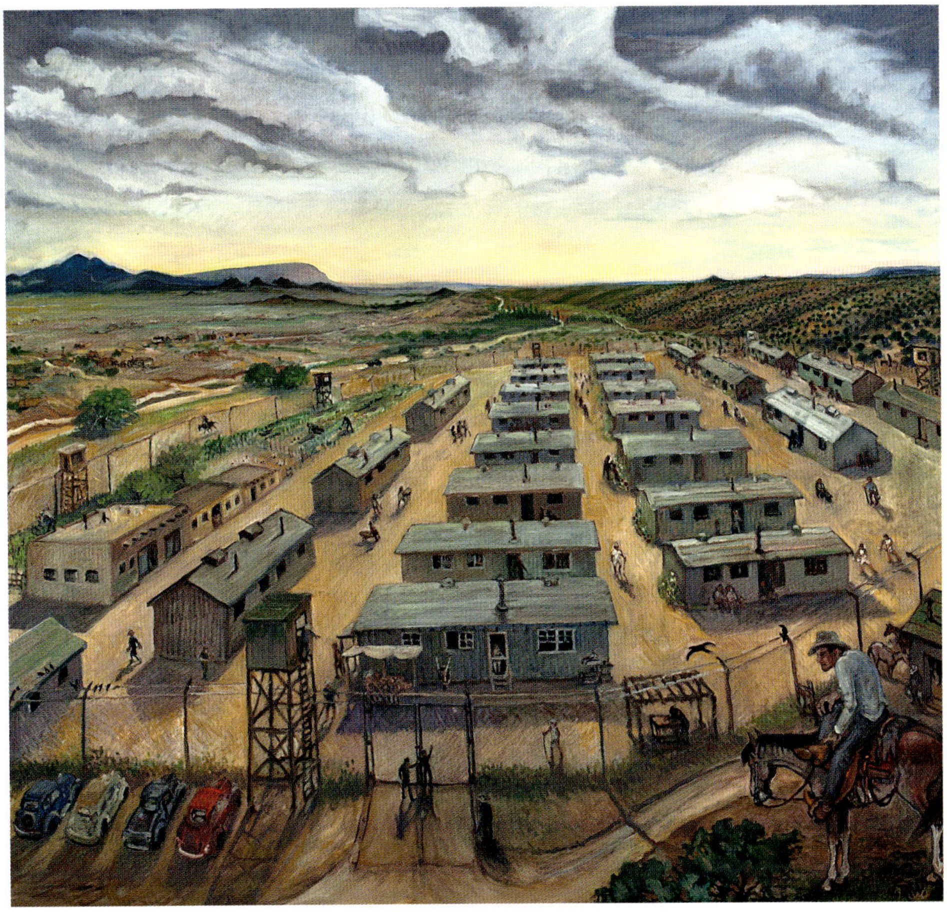

167
JERRY WEST (B. 1933)
JAPANESE INTERNMENT CAMP, 2009
OIL ON CANVAS, 56 x 54 IN. (142.2 x 137.2 CM)

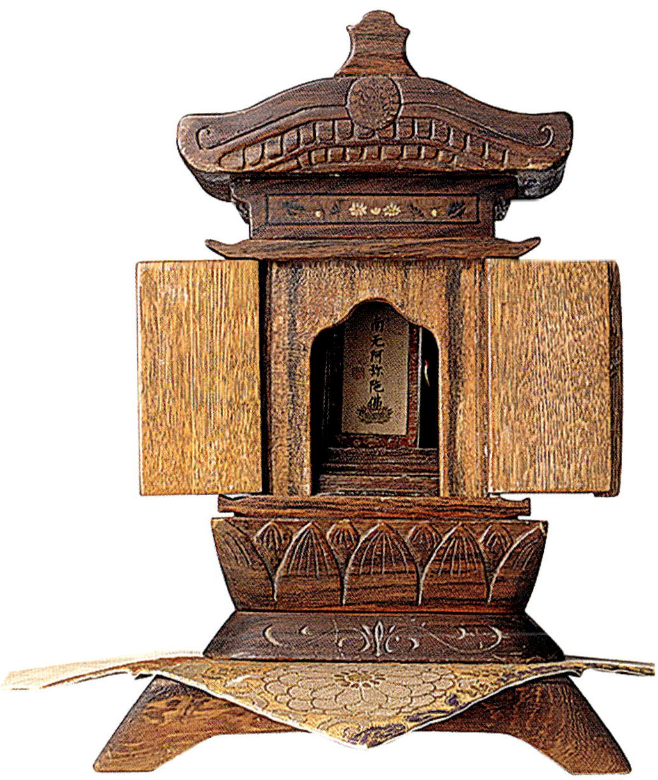

168
MINEO MATOBA (DATES UNKNOWN)
BUTSUDAN (MADE AT SANTA FE DETENTION CENTER, NEW MEXICO), 1942–1946
WOOD AND MIXED MEDIA, 12½ x 9 x 9 IN. (31.8 x 22.9 x 22.9 CM)

END OF AN ERA

Edgar Lee Hewett's dominance over southwestern art and culture had diminished steadily through the 1930s, but it ended with his death on December 31, 1946. Hewett's passing opened the way for the art of the region to respond to a rapidly changing world, a process that conflicted with the static view of New Mexico art that Hewett had developed after 1920.

The number of artists working in the Southwest increased year after year, as did the quantity of their work. In 1950, the work submitted for the fiesta exhibition exceeded the available space at the New Mexico Museum of Art. The only solution was to abandon the open-door policy that had been in effect since 1917. Consequently, the 1951 fiesta exhibition was juried and limited to a more manageable number of select works.

Artists who had worked in New Mexico since the opening of the museum reacted to the new policy with indignation, including John Sloan, who sent an angry telegram. Anti-academic artists like Sloan had long shown their work without having to submit to academic juries that generally rejected anti-academic images. But now the anti-academic artists were the established painters and did not want to submit their work to more contemporary juries. Once again, irony triumphed in New Mexico.

Fiesta exhibitions continued at the New Mexico Museum of Art while the museum also hosted a series of annual exhibitions focusing on paintings, sculptures, prints, or Native art. Roderick Mead had studied in Europe before returning to the United States and settling in Carlsbad. His woodcut print *Bird of Prey* (fig. 169) received a purchase award at the museum's Third Graphics Annual in 1949.

169
RODERICK MEAD (1900–1971)
BIRD OF PREY, 1949
WOODBLOCK PRINT, 8 x 9⅞ IN.
(20.3 x 25.1 CM)

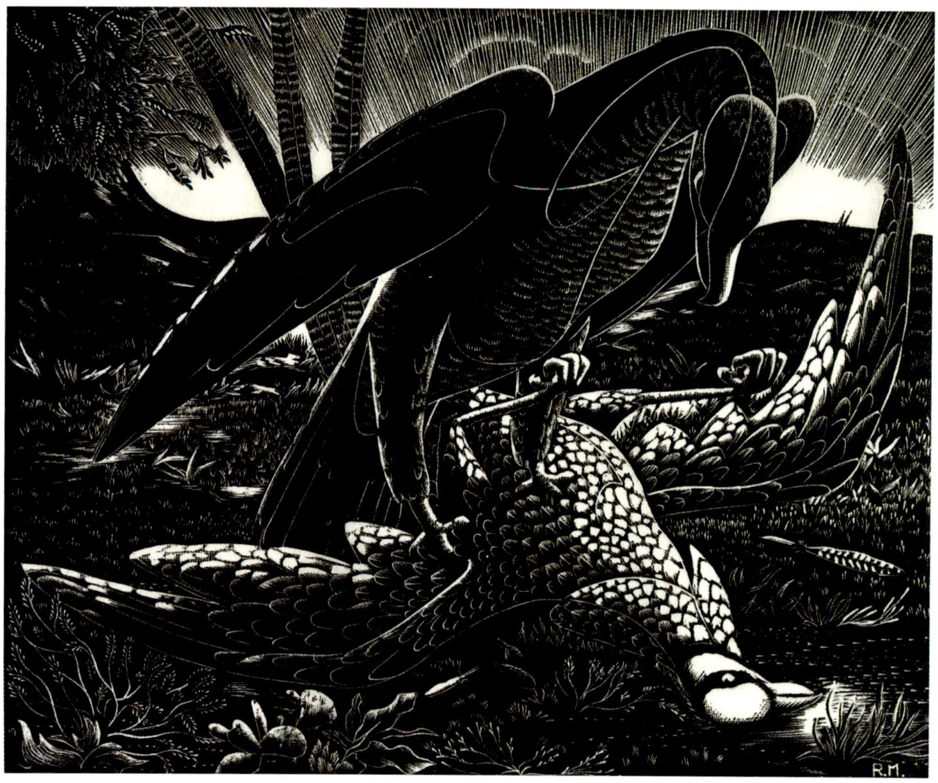

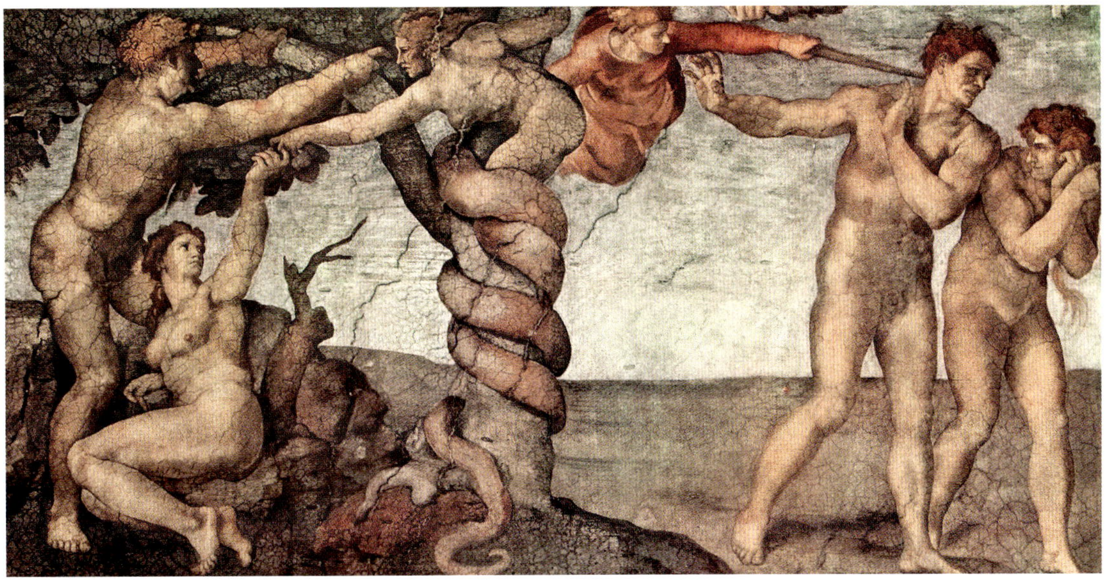

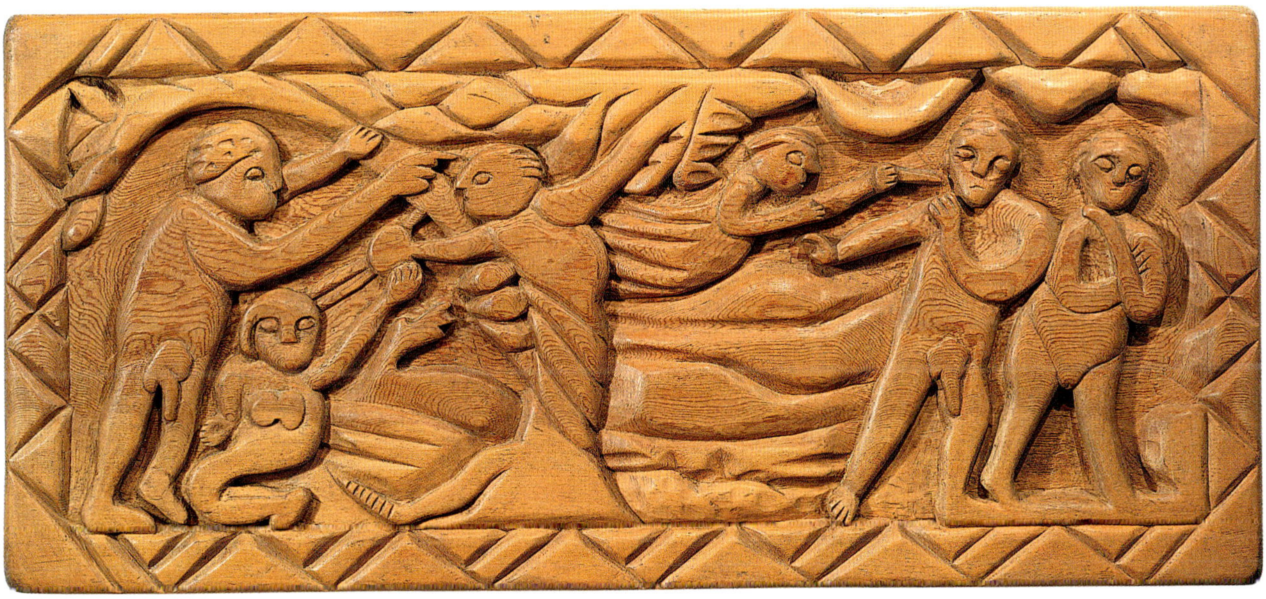

In Taos, Patrocinio Barela did odd jobs while making religious carvings that he sold or bartered. Barela was a troubled man and a self-taught artist who worked stylistically outside the more prescribed New Mexico Catholic *santero* tradition. Although Barela did not speak English, or read or write, he was moved by pictures of the Sistine Chapel that he saw in *Life* magazine (fig. 170) and decided to carve his own versions of the images. He acquired four planks of ponderosa pine just shy of four feet long and two inches thick and created *The Garden of Eden* (fig. 171), a powerful interpretation of a classic scene, along with three others.

170
MICHELANGELO (1475–1564)
SISTINE CHAPEL CEILING (GARDEN OF EDEN AND EXPULSION FROM THE GARDEN), 1508–1512
FRESCO

171
PATROCINIO BARELA (1908–1964)
THE GARDEN OF EDEN, CIRCA 1948
PINE, 21 X 48 X 2½ IN.
(53.3 X 121.9 X 6.4 CM)

172
REBECCA SALSBURY (STRAND) JAMES
(1891–1968)
ANGUS DEI, 1950
COLCHA EMBROIDERY, 7⅜ x 10½ IN.
(18.7 x 26.7 CM)

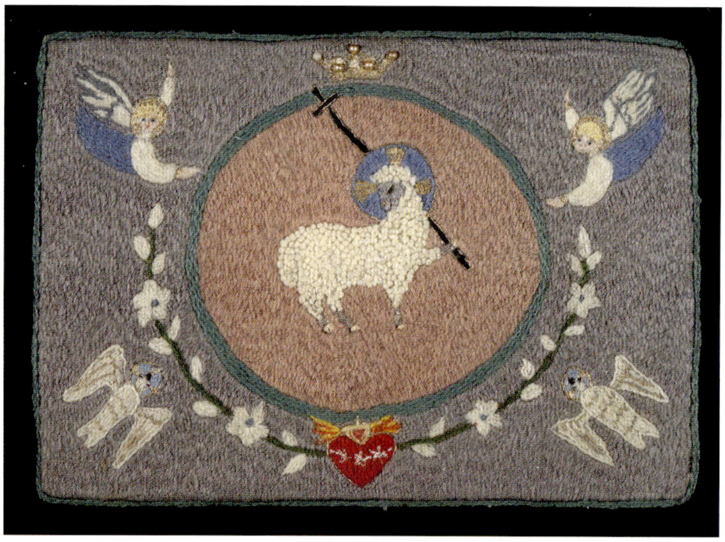

173
CADY WELLS (1904–1954)
REBECCA S. JAMES, DEC. 21, 1950
YARN ON LINEN, 15¾ x 14 IN.
(40 x 35.6 CM)

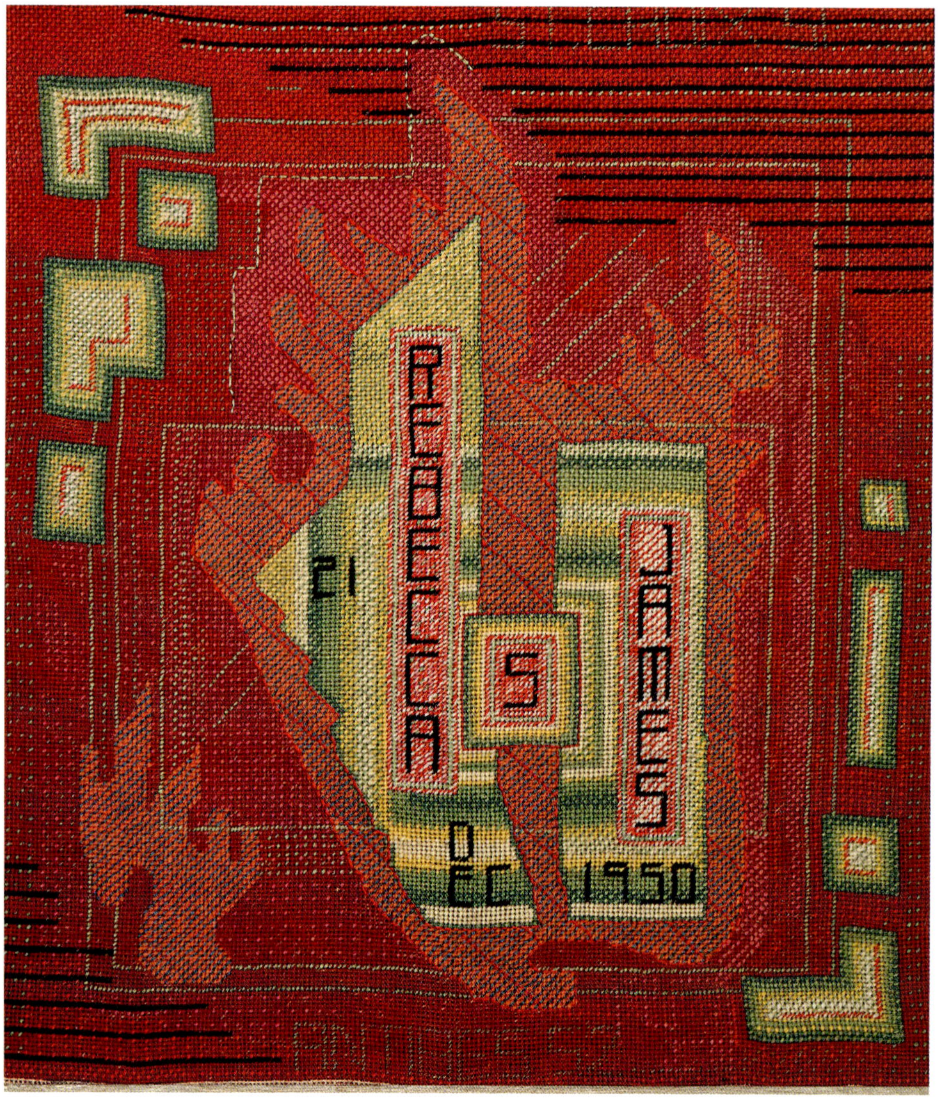

Northern New Mexico Catholic iconography, such as Barela's carving, captured the imagination of modern artists in the region. Rebecca Salsbury (Strand) James was interested in the folk technique of reverse painting on glass, and she also learned to dye wool yarns and sew them into complex embroideries. Her 1950 *Agnus Dei* (fig. 172) should not be considered folk art but rather a modernist image that appropriates local iconography.

Painter Cady Wells returned to New Mexico after World War II and continued painting expressionist watercolors, though they now had acquired a somber tone. He also renewed friendships, particularly with Rebecca James. At the end of 1950, Wells was staying in St. Croix and apparently missed his friend. He responded by creating a petit point abstraction, *Rebecca S. James, Dec. 21, 1950*, in red wool yarn (fig. 173), stitching James's name and the date. Wells's creation of a petit point referred to James's embroideries and was an interesting choice of media for a male artist at the time. Later, E. Boyd, the first curator of Spanish Colonial art at the Museum of International Folk Art and a close friend of Wells, acquired the work and donated it to the New Mexico Museum of Art. In addition to being an important New Mexico painter, Wells was a major collector of Spanish Colonial *retablos* and *bultos* and bequeathed works, including José Aragón's *Crucifixion with Mourning Figures* (fig. 76), to the Museum of International Folk Art. He also gave many items from his collection to the Spanish Colonial Arts Society.

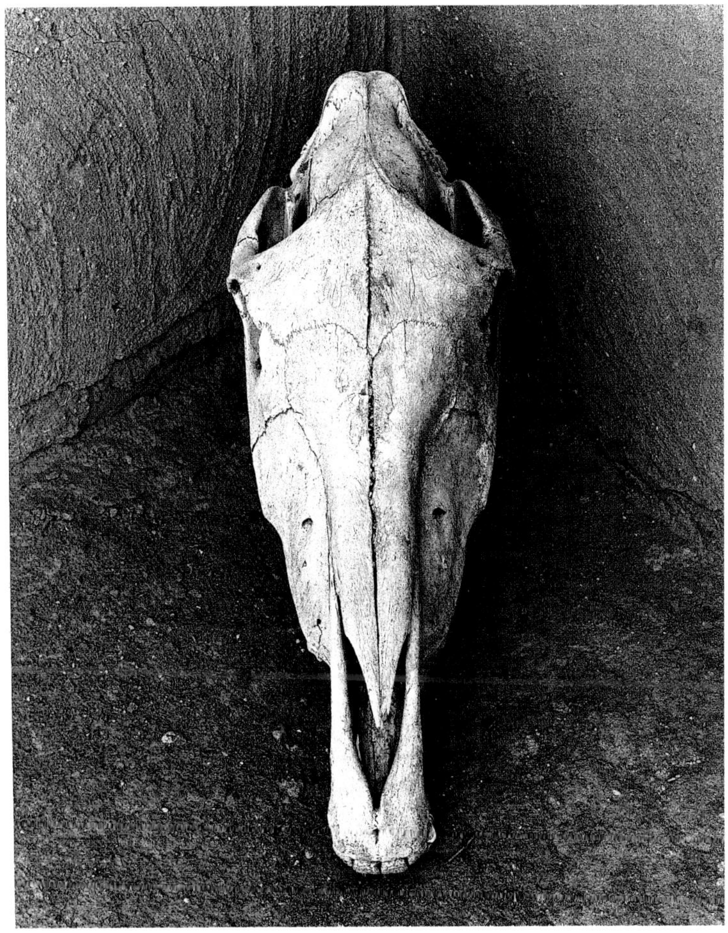

174
ELIOT PORTER (1901–1990)
HORSE SKULL, O'KEEFFE'S HOUSE, ABIQUIU, NEW MEXICO, AUGUST 5, 1952
GELATIN SILVER PRINT, 9⅜ X 7⅜ IN. (23.8 X 18.7 CM)

Like Wells, photographer Eliot Porter also maintained his ties to the O'Keeffe and Luhan circle of friends after the war. Porter's stark, ominous images from the 1950s, such as *Horse Skull, O'Keeffe's House, Abiquiu, New Mexico* (fig. 174), reflect his New Mexico experience and the emotional uncertainties of the Cold War.

During this period, painter Peter Hurd concentrated on figurative works. His subjects often included cowboys and scenes from the Hondo Valley in southeast New Mexico. His portrait of Gerald Maar (fig. 175) shows a young man exuding deep pride in his regional roots while contemplating his future—will he be drafted and sent to fight in the Korean War or saddle up and become a rancher?

Artistic change was in the air. Representational works of traditional subjects were losing their appeal in the uncertainties of the Cold War. Although artists like Will Shuster continued to paint regional scenes, his fellow painter Fremont Ellis acknowledged that the party had ended with his painting *Adios Amigo—Hasta La Vista* (fig. 176), depicting Shuster's funeral on a cold winter day in 1969 at the National Cemetery in Santa Fe.

175
PETER HURD (1904–1984)
PORTRAIT OF GERALD MAAR, 1952
EGG TEMPERA ON GESSO, 32½ x 38¼ IN.
(82.6 x 97.2 CM)

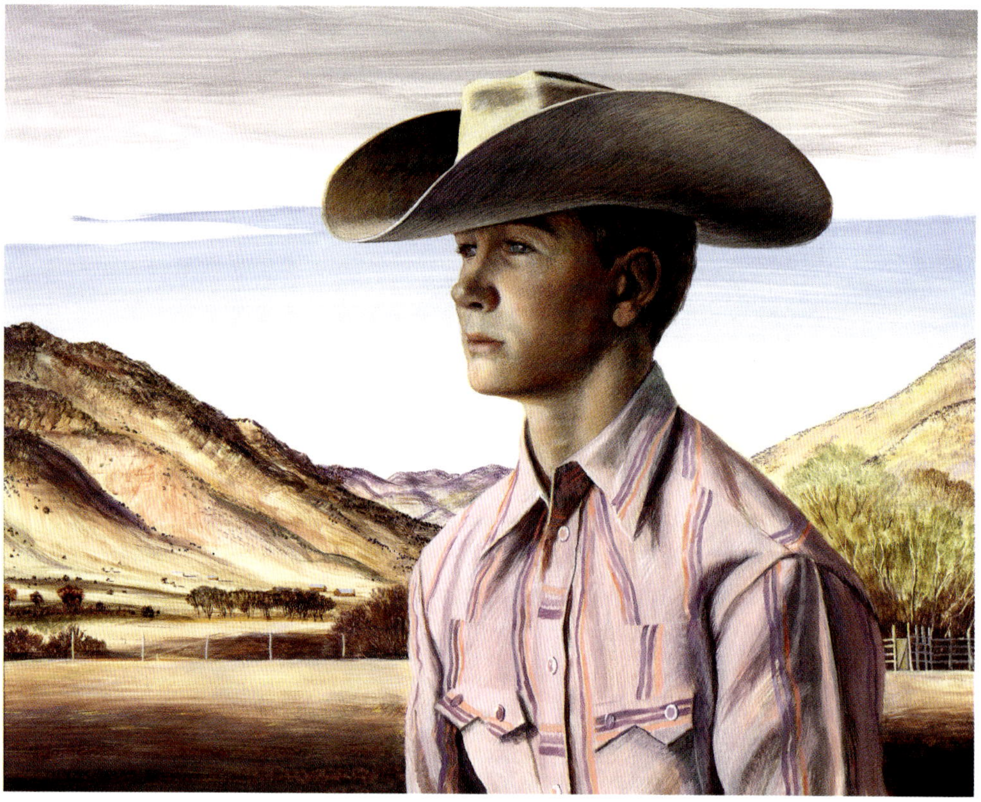

176
FREMONT F. ELLIS (1897–1985)
ADIOS AMIGO—HASTA LA VISTA, 1969
OIL ON CANVAS, 25 x 30 IN.
(63.5 x 76.2 CM)

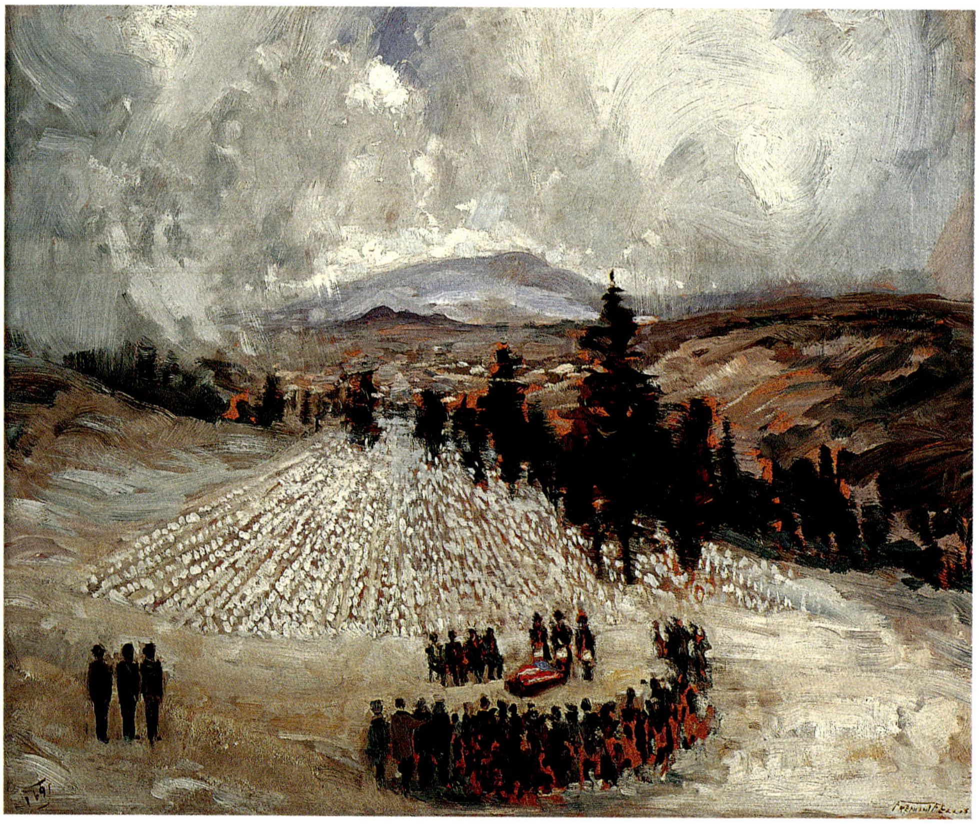

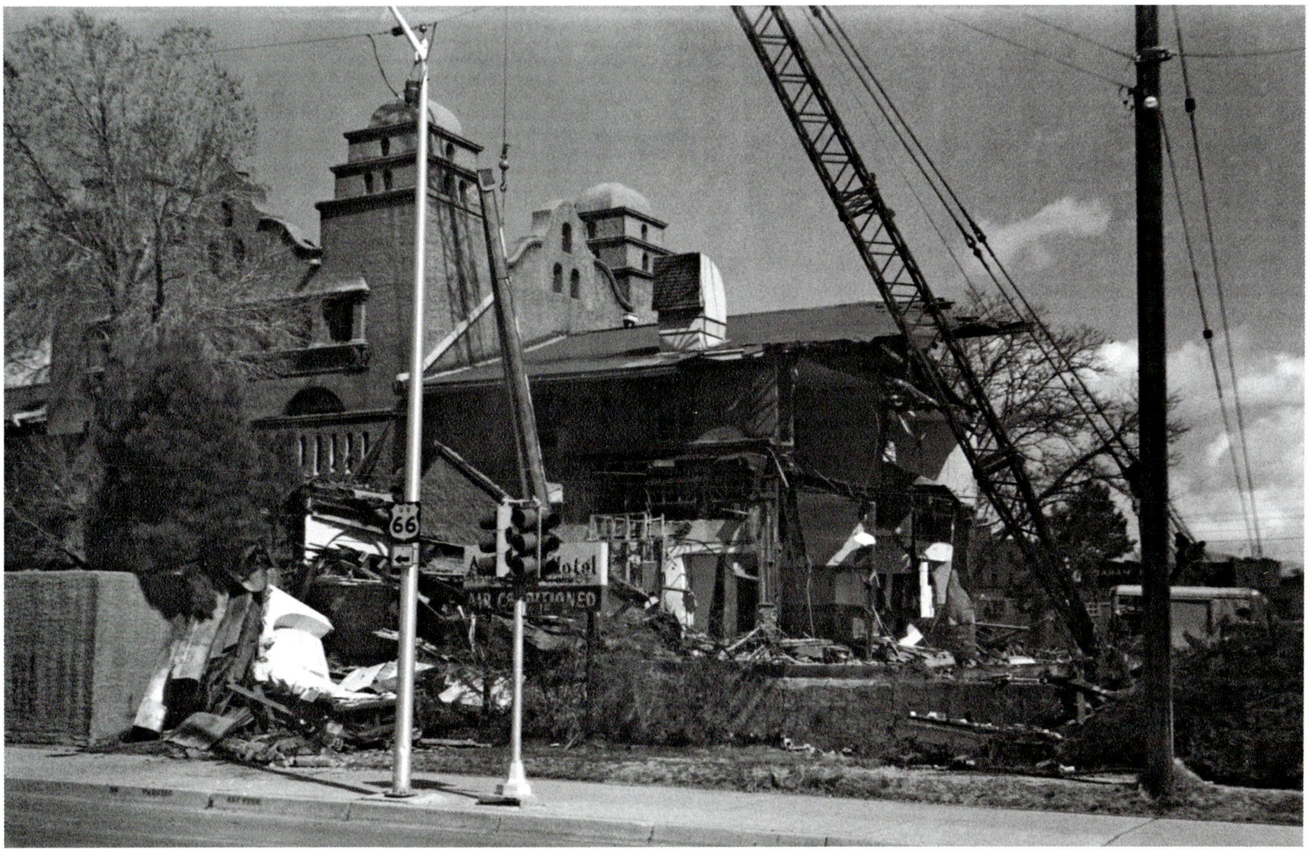

177
STEPHEN KEY MCLELLAN (DATES UNKNOWN)
DEMOLITION OF ALVARADO HOTEL, ALBUQUERQUE, NEW MEXICO, 1970
GELATIN SILVER PRINT, 8 X 10 IN. (20.3 X 25.4 CM)

World War II initiated irreversible change in New Mexico. Railway tourism had given way to automobiles and motels, and Albuquerque locals abandoned the decades-long habit of having Sunday dinner at the Fred Harvey restaurant in the Alvarado Hotel. The romance of prewar tourism finally came to an end in 1970 when the aging Alvarado Hotel was razed as part of the city's urban renewal project (fig. 177).

DEVELOPING CONTEMPORARY AESTHETIC IDEAS

New Mexico's population increased dramatically after World War II ended and troops returned home. Initially, the influx hinged on expanded military activities related to weapons research and training at local air force bases. Albuquerque, which grew the most rapidly, was transformed from a small town to a major city. With the influx of artists to Albuquerque in the early 1950s the center of modernist art in New Mexico shifted toward the University of New Mexico.

In 1950, Raymond Jonson, who was teaching full-time at the university, moved from Santa Fe to a Spanish–Pueblo Revival home designed by John Gaw Meem on the north side of campus. The basement of Jonson's residence became an exhibition space dedicated to abstract art known as the Jonson Gallery. It was the modernist hub of New Mexico and attracted contemporary aesthetic ideas to Albuquerque.

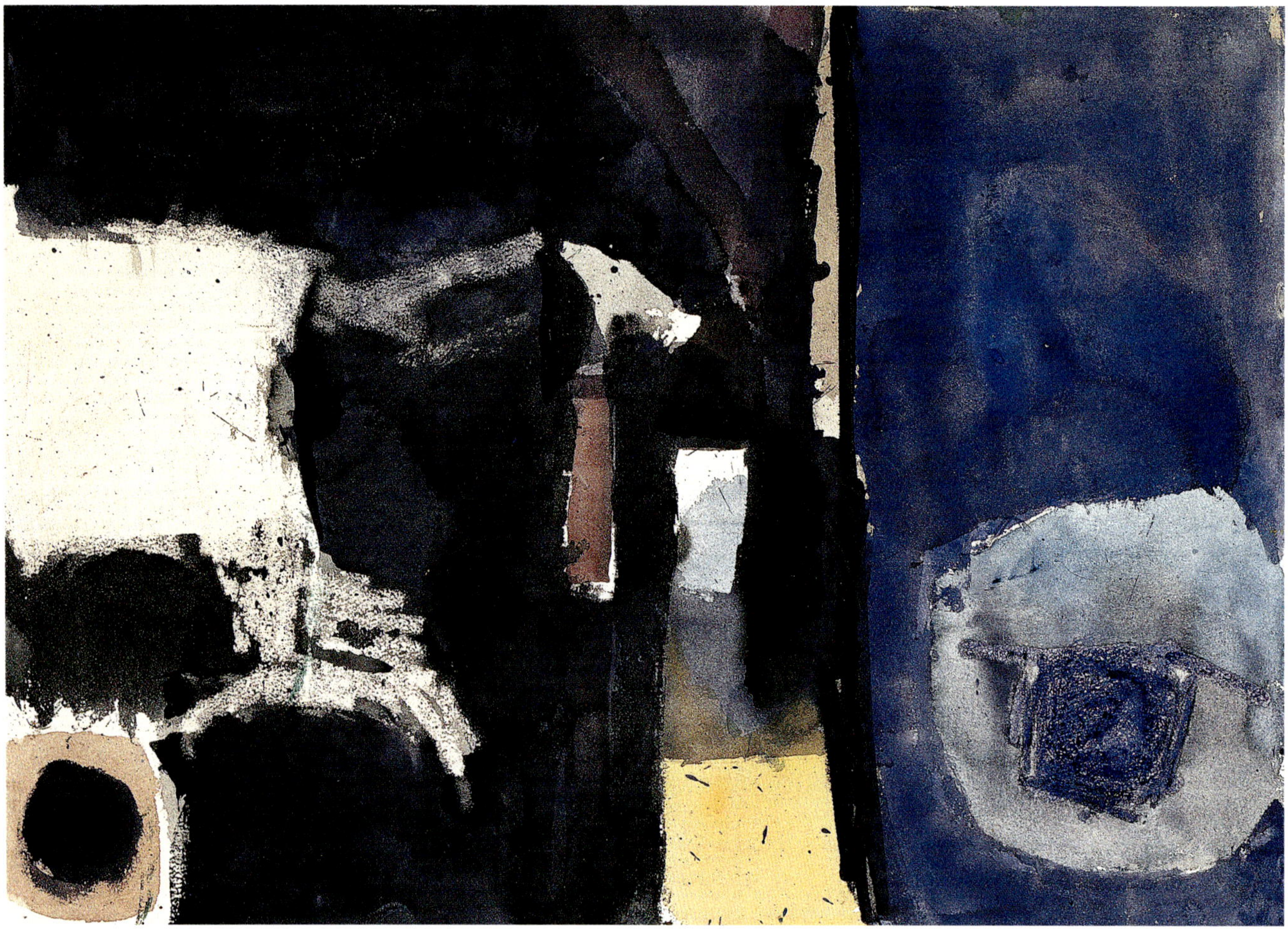

178
RICHARD DIEBENKORN (1922–1993)
UNTITLED (RD 2391), 1950–1951
GOUACHE ON PAPER, 14⅛ X 19⅞ IN.
(35.9 X 50.5 CM)

Richard Diebenkorn came to the University of New Mexico on the GI Bill and studied painting with Jonson (Boll et al. 1989). Diebenkorn was an experienced artist but expanded his interest in abstract and expressionist art during the two years he was at UNM. *Untitled (RD2391)* from 1950–51 (fig. 178) is an example of what he painted as a student at the university. But the art faculty balked at awarding Diebenkorn a master's degree when he hung a series of abstract expressionist works in his 1952 graduation exhibition. Most of the faculty still had a prewar artistic vision and felt that students should demonstrate academic painting skill.

Jonson threatened to resign over the incident, and ultimately the conservative faculty granted the degree. The episode underscored the aesthetic divisions that existed among the traditionalists, even within a university community that supported artistic freedom. Despite the faculty's lack of faith, Diebenkorn went on to become one of the best-known American painters of the late twentieth century.

Jonson continued mentoring students, including Joe H. Herrera, who had been a successful artist from Cochiti Pueblo before his service in World War II. His postwar studies with Jonson pushed him into abstraction, well beyond his successes with studio-style painting before the war (Bernstein and Rushing 1995). Herrera's 1953 painting

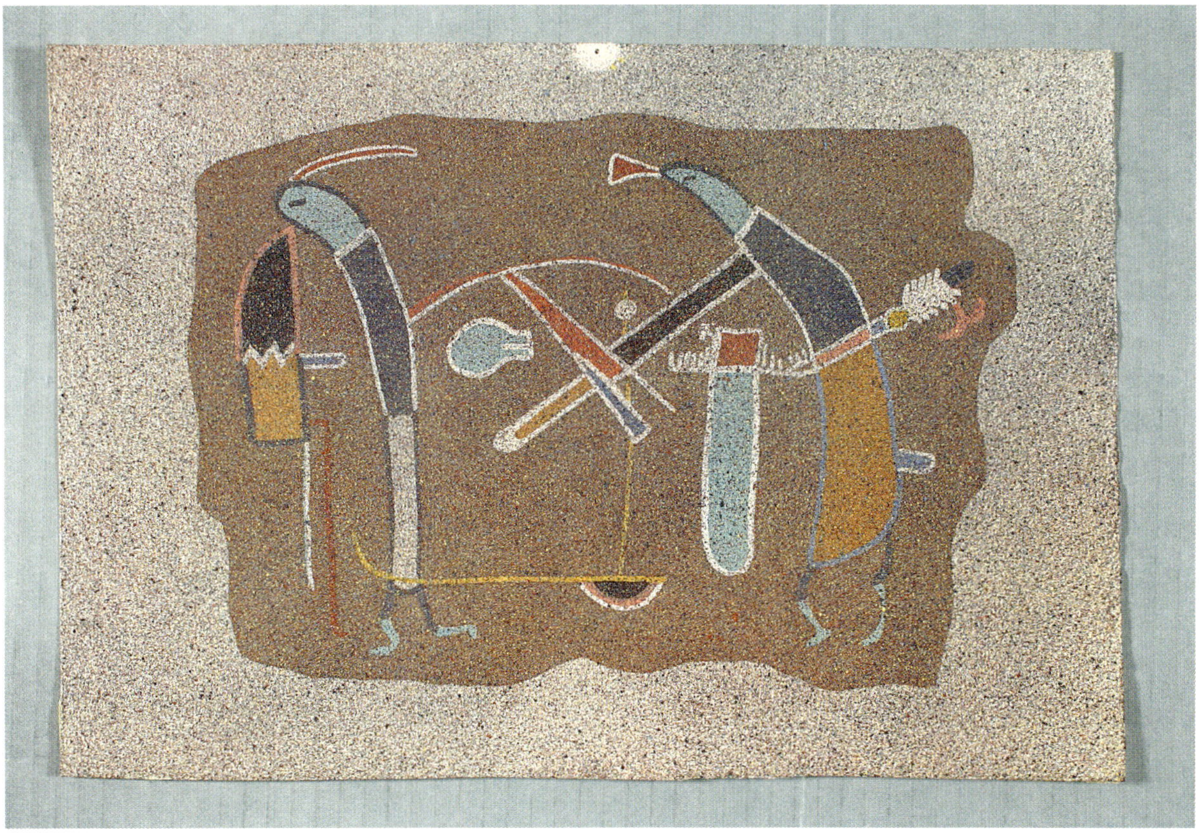

179
JOE H. HERRERA (SEE-RU) (1920–2001)
INDIAN MOTIF, 1953
CASEIN TEMPERA ON PAPER,
6½ X 9 IN. (27.9 X 33 CM)

Indian Motif (fig. 179) demonstrates his ability to combine aspects of mainstream abstraction with images based on Pueblo petroglyphs. After a successful alcove show at the New Mexico Museum of Art, Herrera showed paintings from this series at the Museum of Modern Art in New York City in 1952.

Aesthetic experimentation extended from the university and Jonson Gallery into the greater Albuquerque community. Adja Yunkers and Frederick O'Hara organized *Prints in the Desert*, a 1950 portfolio of modernist images that emphasized the works of young Albuquerque artists. Financially, this period was particularly difficult for abstractionists in Albuquerque; artists like Yunkers were forced to trade prints for food and medical services. Yunkers and O'Hara rented a vacant bean warehouse in the city's agricultural north valley, and in 1952 they converted it to the Albuquerque Modern Museum, a cooperative art center that organized exhibitions and classes but lasted only four years.

During the 1950s, the tensions between the abstract modernists and the supporters of traditional representation divided the artist communities of New Mexico. The combination of World War II, the Cold War, and the Korean War had made romantic views of New Mexico's mythic past seem out of touch with contemporary realities. This situation reflected a shift from the prewar period, when most artists were working with some form of ethnic subject matter, even those professing nonobjectivity.

In 1955, the Advisory Committee of the New Mexico Museum of Art granted Raymond Jonson a retrospective exhibition. Ernest Blumenschein served on the committee but had to leave the meeting before the vote and was furious when he learned the exhibition had been approved. The founding member of the long defunct Taos Society of Artists wrote a two-page typed letter to museum director Reginald Fisher that reflected the disagreements within the arts community:

> I was shocked beyond expression. Here is a mechanical artist, using mostly mechanical tools, doing work which has absolutely no connection or reflection of his life in New Mexico. Here is a man who has won no signal recognition, belongs to no highclass [*sic*] art group or society, and is not respected beyond a certain technical adroitness. . . .
>
> And when I think of Kenneth Adams, of Howard Cook and Benrimo. Also Dasburg, Peter Hurd, Randall Davey, Theordore Van Soelen and others of the top painters well known and with honors galore from outside—I am really ashamed of this action (NMMoA archives, Blumenschein file).

Blumenschein's letter reveals the depth of antagonism between abstraction and regional subject matter. Contemporary artists were just as hostile toward work they called "decorative" or "illustrative." These assessments would be repeated without resolution throughout the last decades of the twentieth century.

In 1961, printmaker and scholar Clinton Adams transformed the University of New Mexico Art Department into a program that promoted contemporary aesthetic ideas. Before coming to New Mexico, Adams and June Wayne had established the Tamarind Institute in Los Angeles to foster the revival of fine art lithography. Adams's color lithograph *Venus in Cibola V* (fig. 180) exemplifies the clarity and careful color sense of his images.

180
CLINTON ADAMS (1918–2002)
VENUS IN CIBOLA V, 1968
TWO-COLOR LITHOGRAPH, 6 x 7½ IN. (15.2 x 19.1 CM)

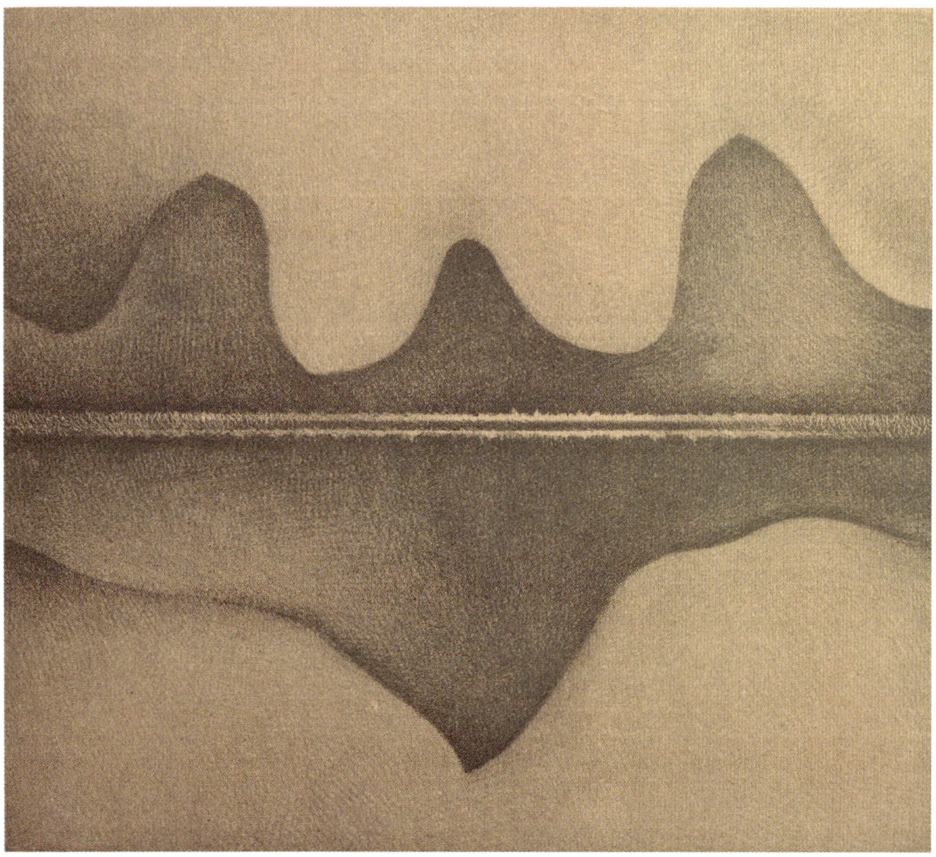

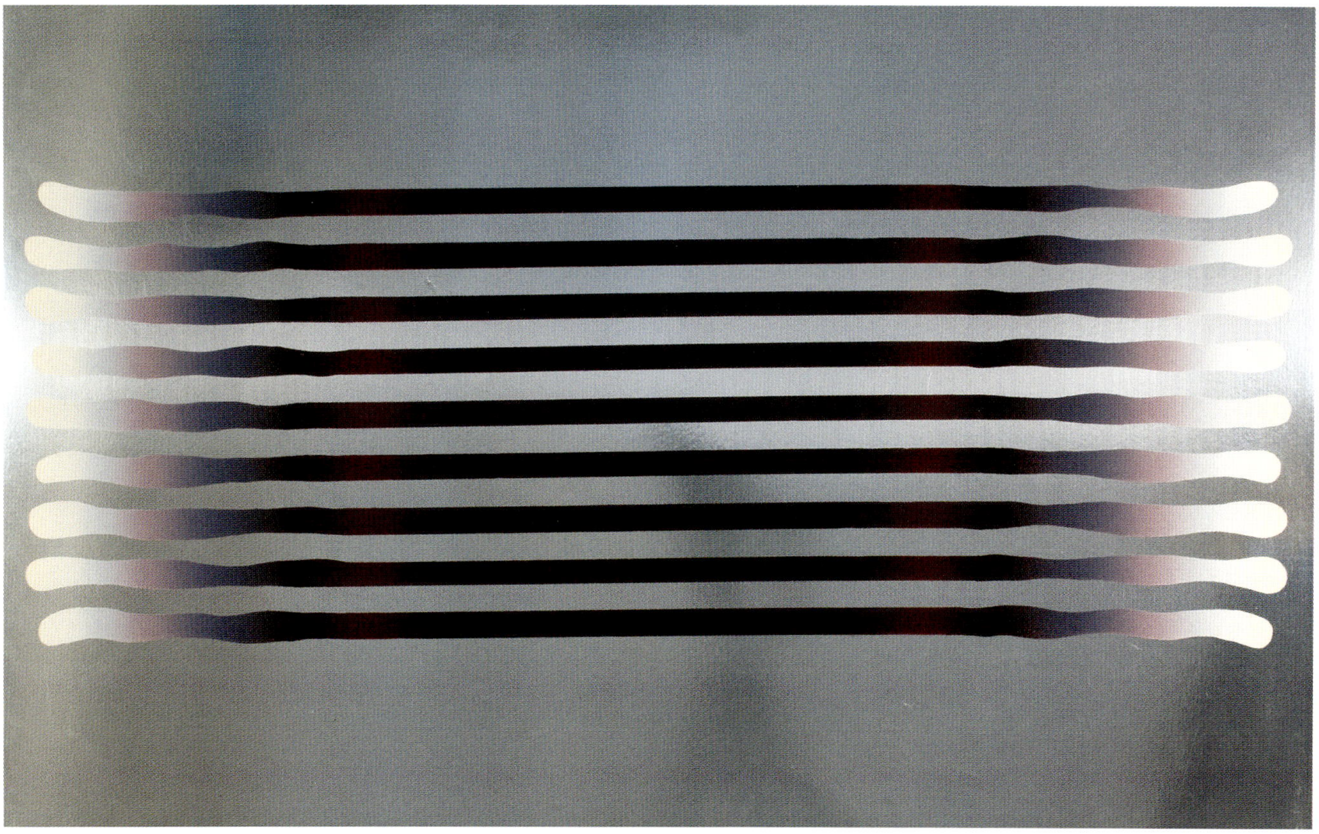

181
GARO Z. ANTREASIAN (B. 1922)
70-158, 1971
LITHOGRAPH, 40 X 24 IN. (101.6 X 61 CM)

Adams bolstered his approach by attracting Van Deren Coke to create a university art museum and teach photography and the history of photography, as well as his colleague Garo Z. Antreasian from the Tamarind Institute in Los Angeles to promote lithography. Antreasian's aesthetic emphasized abstract imagery and color lithography with works from this period, such as *70-158* (fig. 181), printed on metallic surfaces and unusual papers. In 1970, the Tamarind Institute itself relocated to the university with its internationally known program where students trained with well-known artists. Through these activities, Adams transformed Albuquerque into an important player in mainstream art at the end of the twentieth century.

Frederick Hammersley had been one of the geometric abstractionists who originated the concept of hard edge painting in Los Angeles before he moved to New Mexico in 1968. Hammersley created abstract works with flat planes of color, eschewing the type of expressionistic brush strokes dominant in abstract expressionist paintings of the 1950s. Instead, paintings such as *Biased, #9* (fig. 182) were based on permutations of tick-tack-toe squares. This work is particularly interesting because it displays Hammersley's use of isomeric design in repeating shapes both horizontally and vertically and color changes within the isomers that tend to hide the flip-flopping of repeated forms.

Hammersley and Charles Mattox also experimented with computer art at the University of New Mexico. Hammersley used characters of the alphabet as tones to create

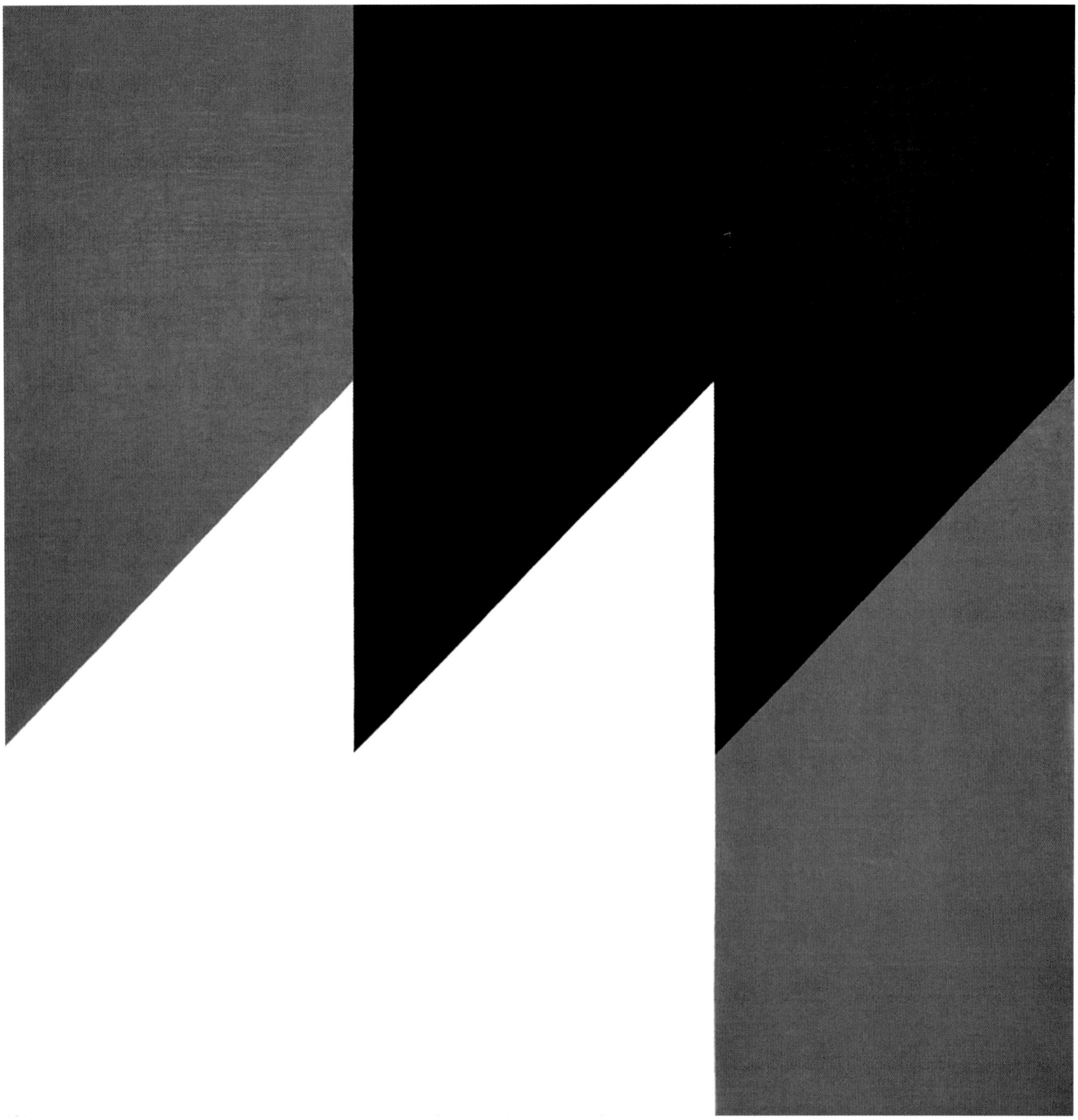

182
FREDERICK HAMMERSLEY (1919–2009)
BIASED, #9, 1978
OIL ON LINEN, 25 X 25 IN. (63.5 X 63.5 CM)

abstract black-and-white images. The inveterate punster titled his works with phrases that seem to indicate the actions of "figures" in the prints. *Tea Time* (fig. 183) plays on shapes that appear like overlapping capital *T*s right side up and upside down. Hammersley laboriously created seventy-two computer drawings, each requiring hundreds of hand-punched cards that directed the university's mainframe computer, work of many hours that would be accomplished in just minutes today.

183

FREDERICK HAMMERSLEY (1919–2009)

TEA TIME, 1969

COMPUTER PAPER, 8½ X 10½ IN. (21.6 X 26.7 CM)

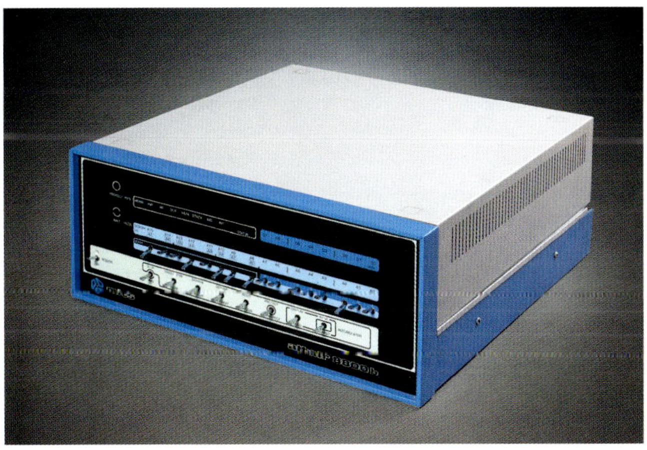

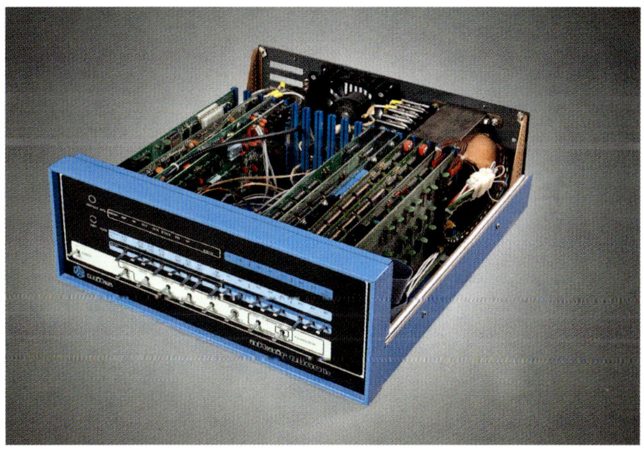

Computers represented an area of intense development in Albuquerque during the 1960s and 1970s. In the mid-1970s, Micro Instrumentation Telemetry Systems, Inc. (MITS) manufactured Altair computers and began selling them by mail order. Paul Allen and Bill Gates moved to Albuquerque to create software for the Altair (fig. 184). The two wrote a basic program for the computer, and MITS agreed to sell the software with their hardware. New Mexico nearly became an international computer center when Allen and Gates started Microsoft in Albuquerque, but the two ultimately moved to Seattle.

184

MICRO INSTRUMENTATION TELEMETRY SYSTEMS, INC. (MITS)

ALTAIR 8800B CENTRAL PROCESSING UNIT, 1977

MIXED MEDIA, 7 X 17 X 17 IN. (17.8 X 43.2 X 43.2 CM)

Words—and art made from language—are an important component of New Mexico art at the end of the twentieth century. Painter William Lumpkins, former member of the Transcendental Painting Group, created order from the chaotic and irrational through his Buddhist practice and abstract works. His interest in Buddhism began in the 1930s and continued after the war while he worked as an architect in California. His power as an artist, architect, and anchor of the arts community in Santa Fe resulted from the calm and focus he gained by his practice utilizing koans.

In Zen Buddhism, koans are questions, paradoxes, statements, or dialog intended to make an individual gain greater awareness through contemplation. Over many decades, Lumpkins collected koans related to his art and life, typing them on note cards and keeping them in five wooden recipe boxes (fig. 185). In the beginning of this work, Lumpkins describes his understanding of Zen practice and then offers hundreds of koans relating to art. For example:

> The brush and the paper must become one.
> Where there is evil, good will eventually emerge.
> The object as seen by twenty eyes is twenty different objects.

In this way Lumpkins transformed his non-Western practices into mainstream art in New Mexico.

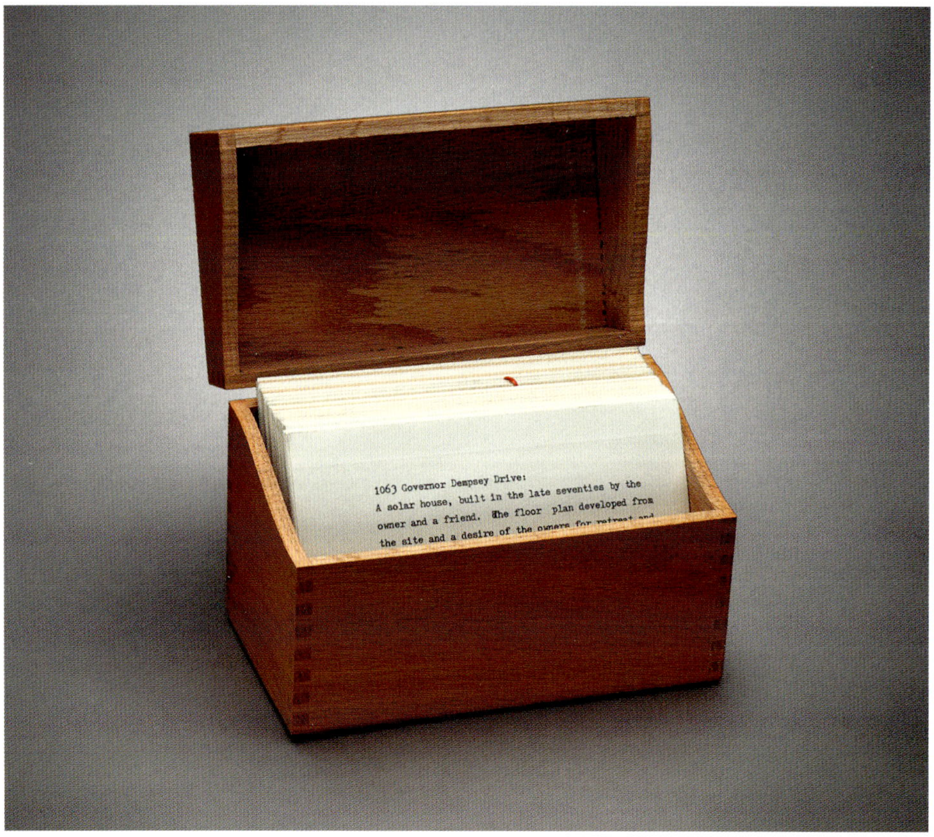

185
WILLIAM LUMPKINS (1909–2000)
KOANS, N.D.
TYPESCRIPT ON NOTE CARDS, 3 X 5 IN.
(7.6 X 12.7 CM)

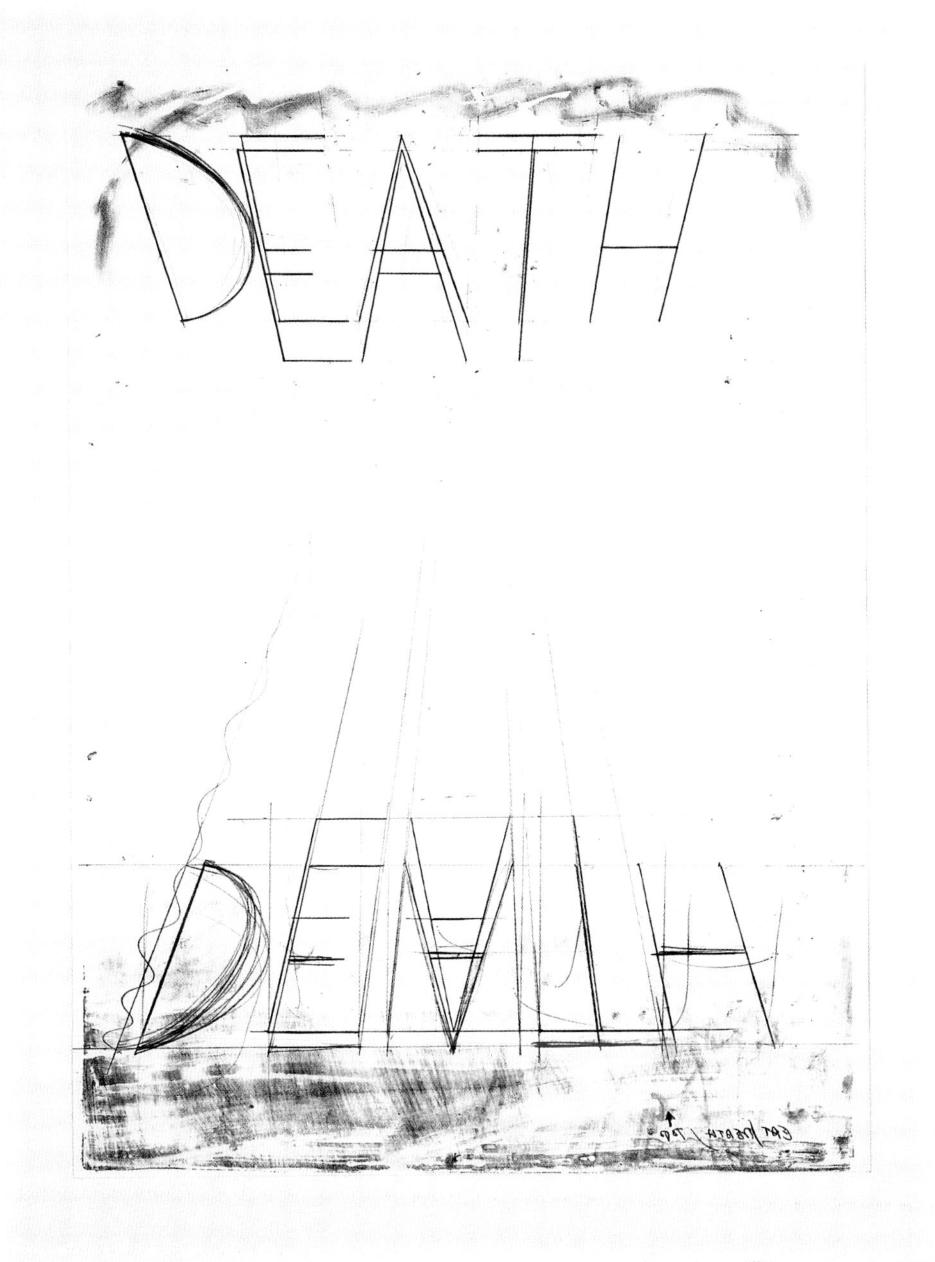

186
BRUCE NAUMAN (B. 1941)
EAT DEATH, 1976
LITHOGRAPH, 47 X 36 IN. (119.4 X 91.4 CM)

Bruce Nauman has repeatedly used words as a major aspect of his work since the 1960s. Nauman's word images, produced as lithographs or flashing neon works that become kinetic sculptures, have a broader function than simply expressing the artist's pointed views. *Eat Death* (fig. 186), for example, plays on the structure of the English language and the ambiguity of meaning that can result. Similarly, Nauman's *Live or Die* and *World Earth* raise ironic questions about the nature of contemporary life. Nauman's word works can be considered koans, not unlike Lumpkins's phrases.

Ironworker Tom Joyce began working as a blacksmith but quickly evolved from producing functional objects to creating conceptual works of art that address modern

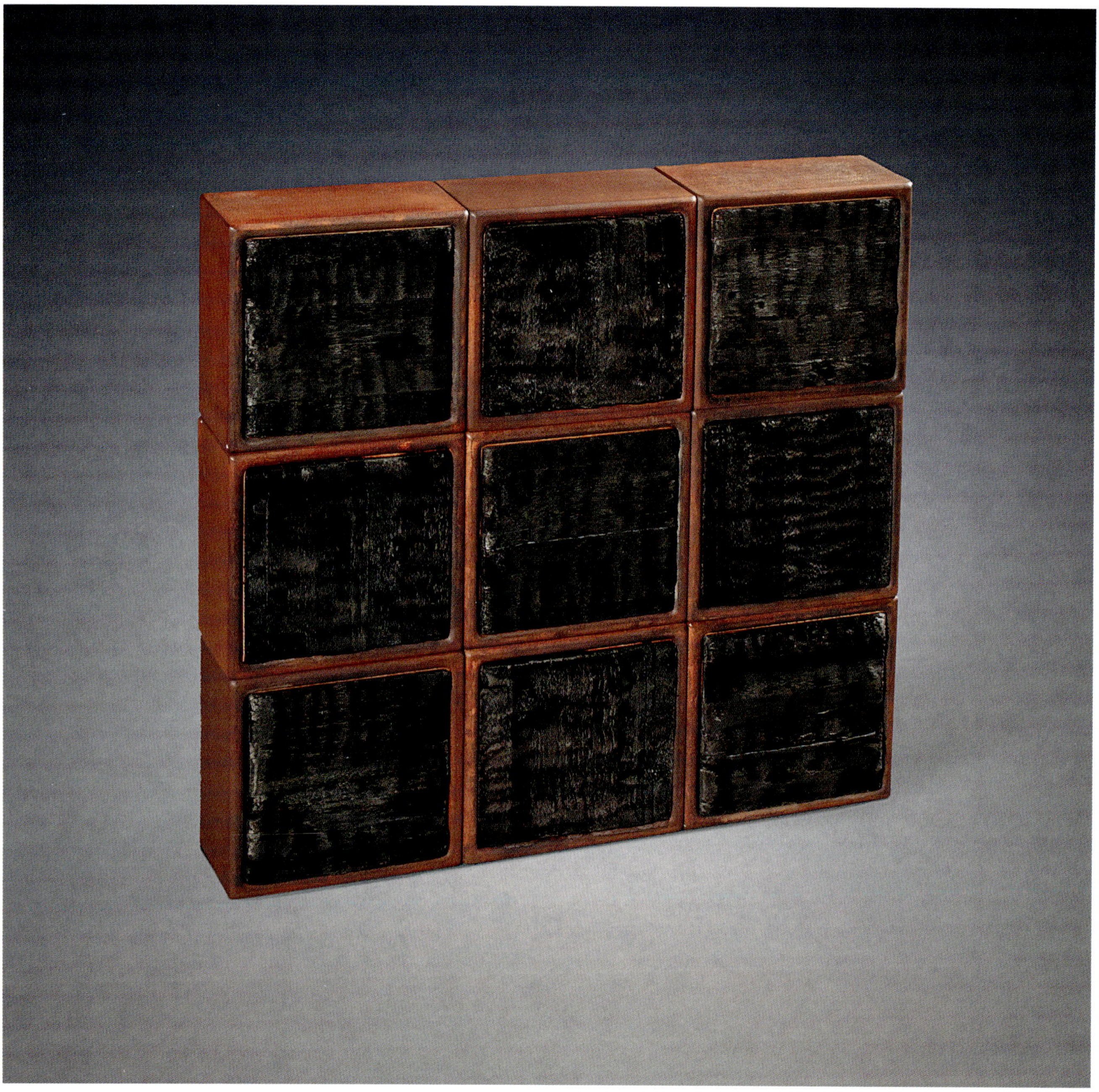

187
TOM JOYCE (B. 1956)
STACKS, 1994–1995
IRON AND FOUND BOOKS,
23¼ X 23½ X 4 IN. (59.1 X 59.7 X 10.2 CM)

life. *Stacks* (fig. 187) is composed of nine iron frames, each filled with books whose text is illegible because their spines have been stripped away and their pages have been burned. The sculpture engages the idea that book-burning represents ignorance and the defense of ideas with physical force rather than with persuasive argumentation.

Agnes Martin brought aesthetic calm to New Mexico with her simplified images that sought to reveal the inner peace she achieved through meditation practice (fig. 188). Her images can be seen as pages from a book in which the words describing her inner har-

188
AGNES MARTIN (1912–2004)
UNTITLED #6, 1980
ACRYLIC AND GRAPHITE ON GESSOED CANVAS, 72 x 72 IN. (182.9 x 182.9 CM)

189
RICHARD TUTTLE (B. 1941)
LOOSE LEAF NOTEBOOK DRAWING—BOX 10, GROUP 4, 1980–1982
WATERCOLOR ON PAPER, 10½ X 8 IN. (26.7 X 20.3 CM)

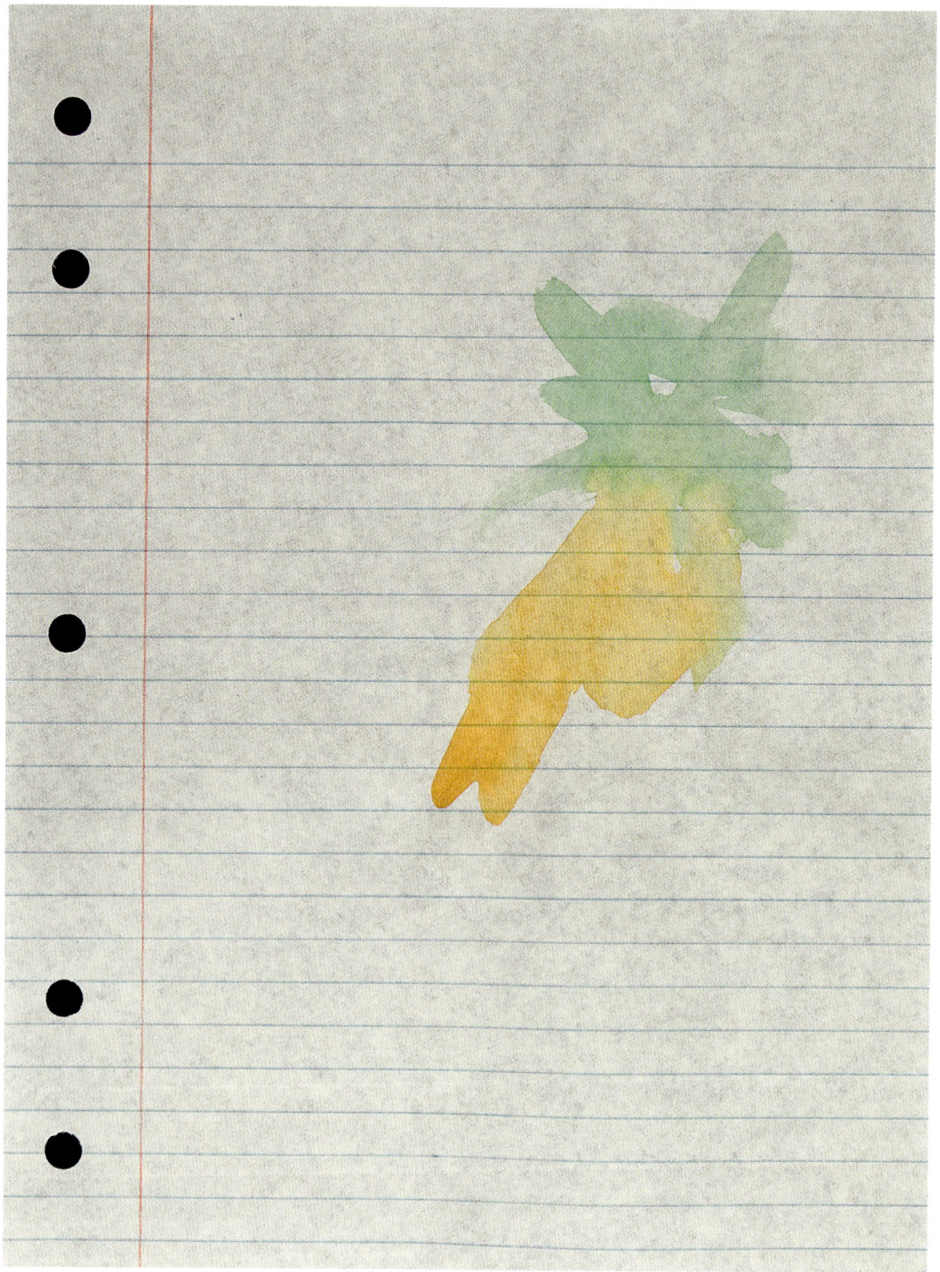

mony have been effaced. Canadian-born Martin first studied in New York before moving to New Mexico after World War II to continue. She then returned to Manhattan to experiment with grid-based imagery, developing her mature, nonobjective style before returning to the Southwest.

Martin meditated each night and envisioned her images, which she meticulously transferred to canvas when she awoke, as counterparts to her states of mind. Martin worked intuitively while using formalist structure through the use of horizontal grids.

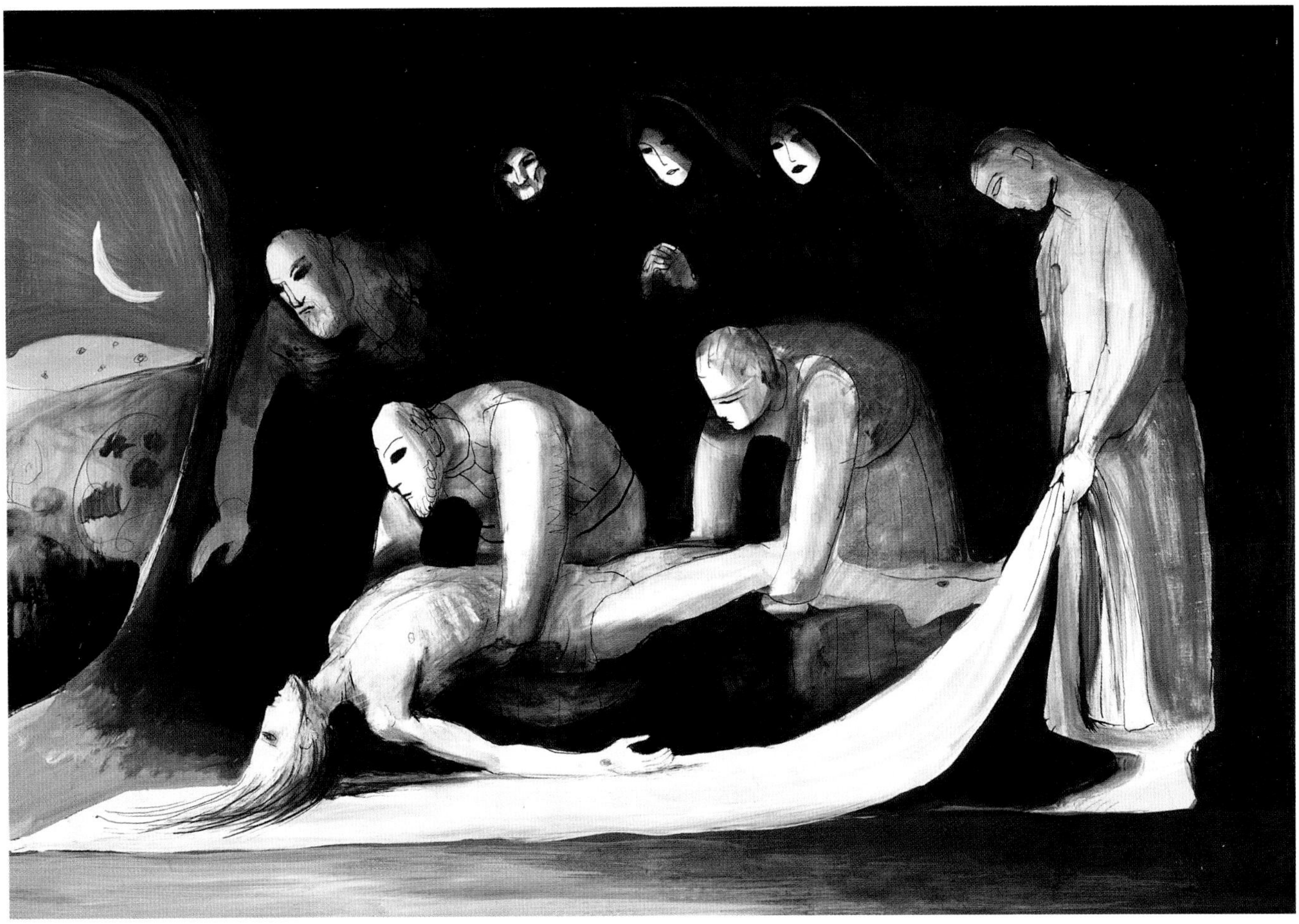

190
PETER W. ROGERS (B. 1933)
THE ENTOMBMENT, 1971
GOUACHE AND MIXED MEDIA,
20¼ X 29¾ IN. (51.4 X 75.6 CM)

Her paintings have haunting, indefinable qualities and thus remain open to multiple formalist and spiritual interpretations.

While in New York, Martin became close friends with Richard Tuttle, an artist who also creates highly sensitive, self-referential works such as *Loose Leaf Notebook Drawing–Box 10, Group 4* (fig. 189). The spiritualism expressed in Martin's and Tuttle's work is the antithesis of Peter W. Rogers's imagery based on Christian iconography. His works allude to Renaissance subjects and exude a mysterious, ghostly quality. *The Entombment* (fig. 190) presents a mystical view of disciples burying Christ. Rogers was born in England, worked in Spain, and brought a European illustrative style to Roswell, New Mexico.

Eugene Newmann also reconnects European religious painting to a New Mexico context in *Elevation and Entanglement in Ribera* (fig. 191). The work refers to both the artist's home in Ribera, New Mexico, and also to Peter Paul Rubens's 1610 *Elevation of the Cross*. Newmann's painting includes details from the earlier work but clearly references biblical events in a New Mexico context, as does Allan Graham's work *Chartres* (fig. 192). This painted sculpture appears as a Christ figure created in a simplified, angular manner, while the title alludes to a French cathedral and application of pages from a Diné Bible for regional cultural context.

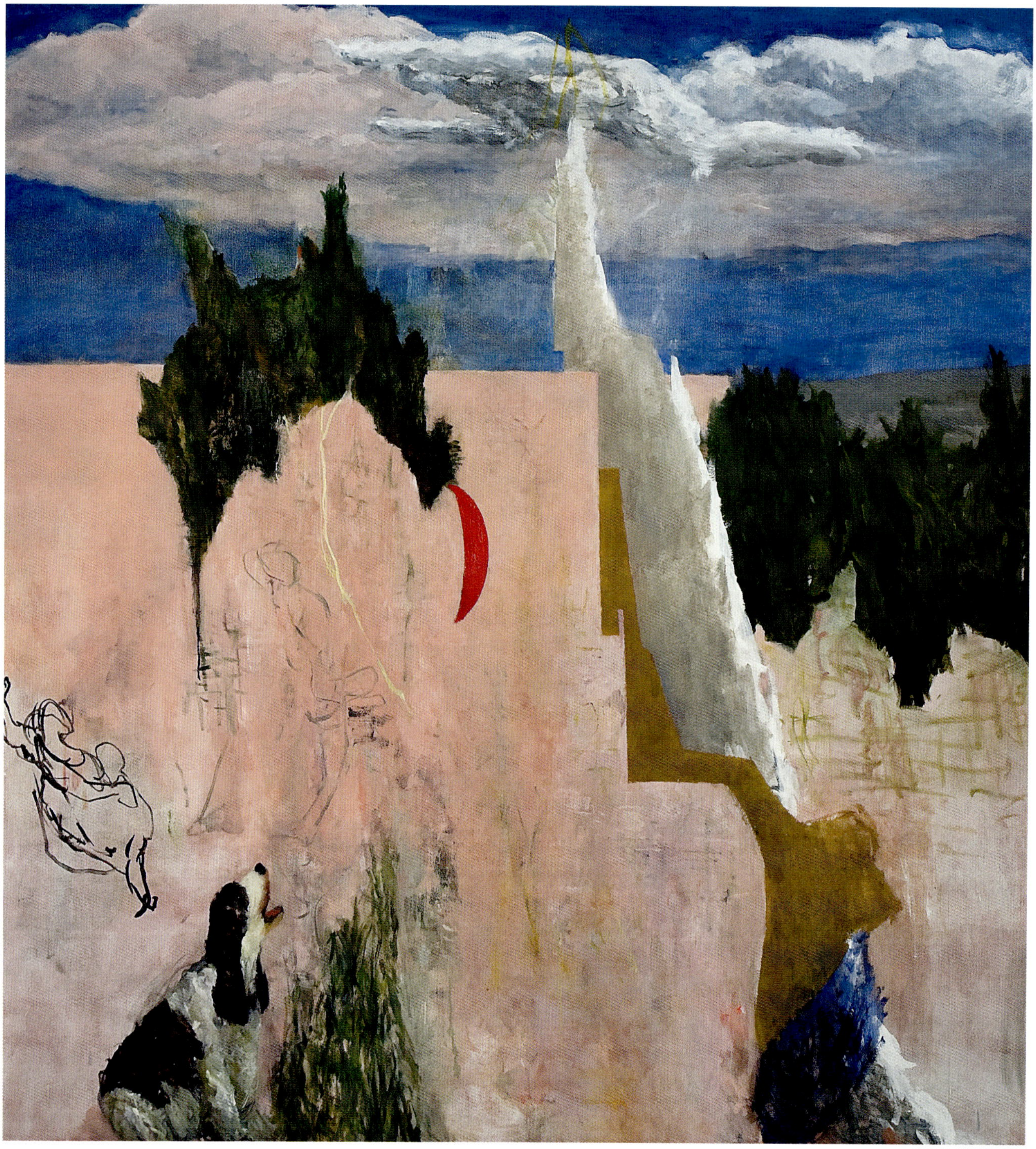

191
EUGENE NEWMANN (B. 1936)
ELEVATION AND ENTANGLEMENT IN RIBERA, 2009
OIL ON CANVAS, 66 X 62 IN.
(167.6 X 157.5 CM)

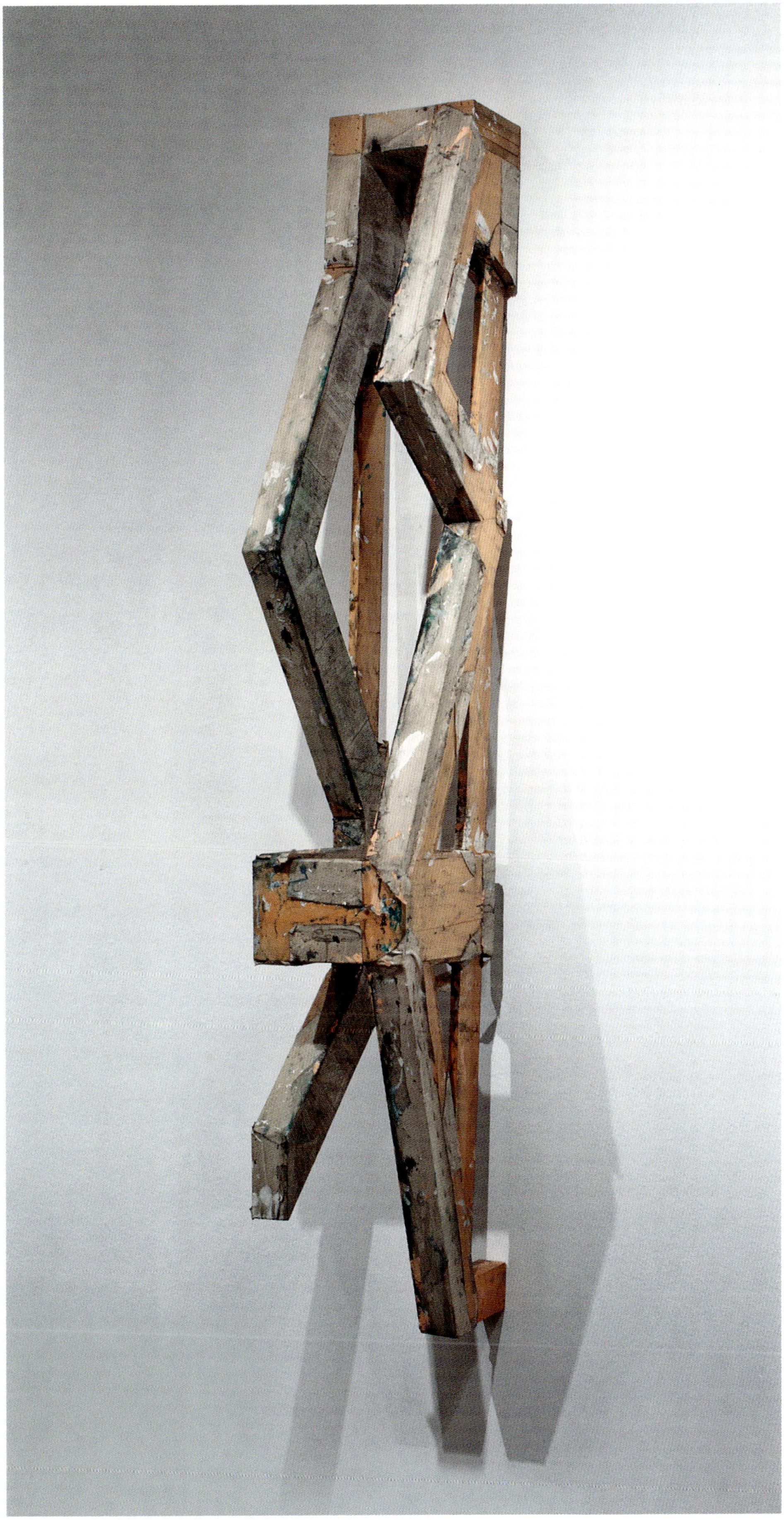

192

ALLAN GRAHAM (B. 1943)

CHARTRES, 1984

WOOD, CANVAS, PAGES FROM NAVAJO NEW TESTAMENT, AND WATER-BASED PIGMENT, 87 X 13 X 19 IN. (221 X 33 X 48.3 CM)

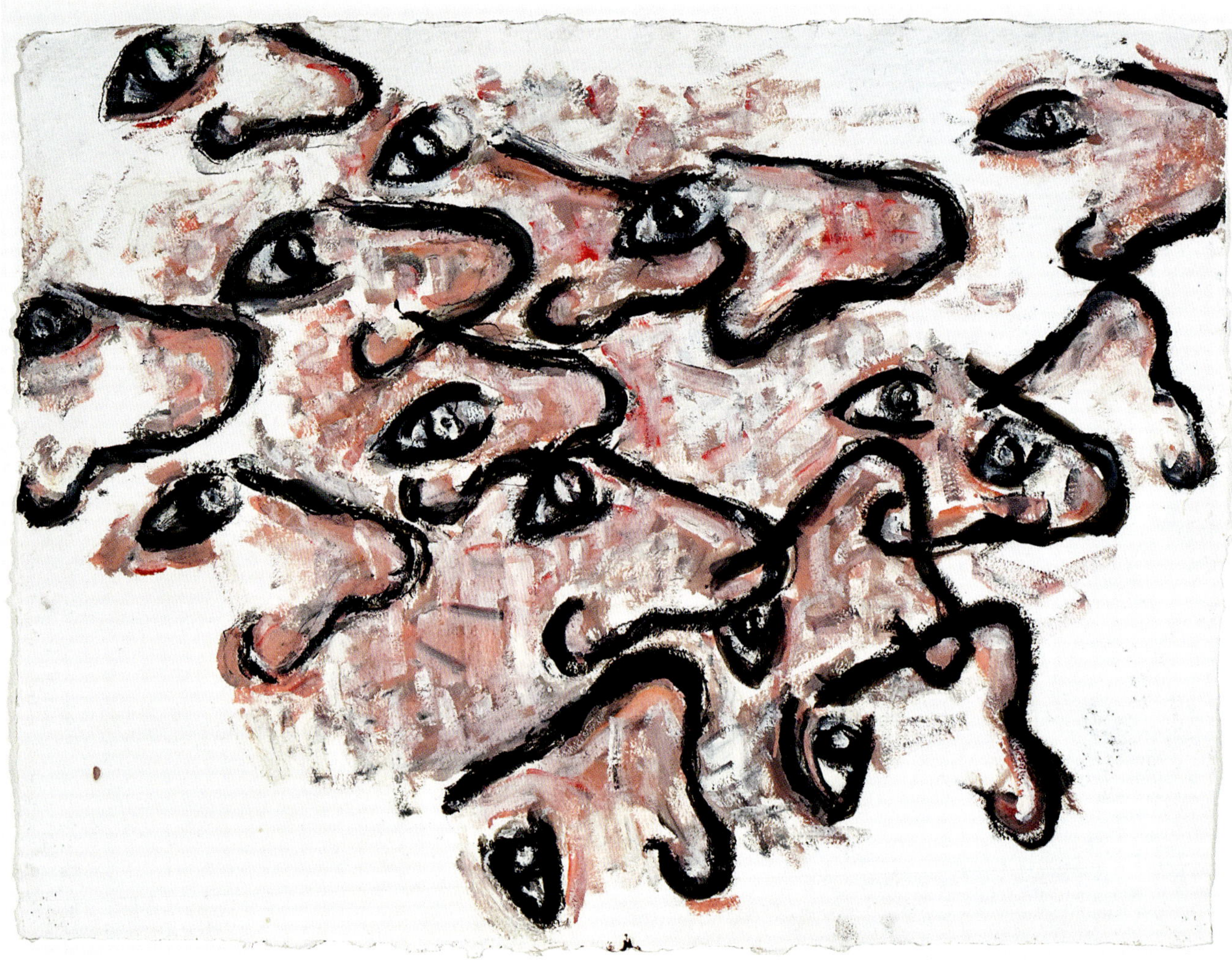

193
SUSAN ROTHENBERG (B. 1945)
NOSES AND EYES, 2006
OIL ON PAPER, 30 X 40 IN. (76.2 X 101.6 CM)

Susan Rothenberg's oil-on-paper painting *Noses and Eyes* (fig. 193) highlights tensions associated with crowds by compressing the experience of a public event into a crush of noses and eyes. The image is boldly painted with outlined figurative elements pressed together into a single form. Rothenberg's thick applications of oil paint, with hues that intermingle to create an expressive abstraction, give her works an iconic quality.

Paul Sarkisian addressed the paradoxical relationship between abstraction and realism while arguments simmered between supporters of the two perspectives. As a photo realist painter in California, his paintings of figurative images were three or four times larger than life size. In 1971–72, he created a twenty-one-foot-long *trompe l'oeile* painting of an El Paso bootmaker's storefront that had been transformed into a secondhand store (fig. 194). The painting addresses nostalgia for the Southwest of the past and the transformations that occur over time as objects acquire patina from use. Most viewers think of this work as exemplifying realism, but it actually is pure abstraction since a close look reveals a technique of using abstract spatter that melds into a representational image in the viewer's mind.

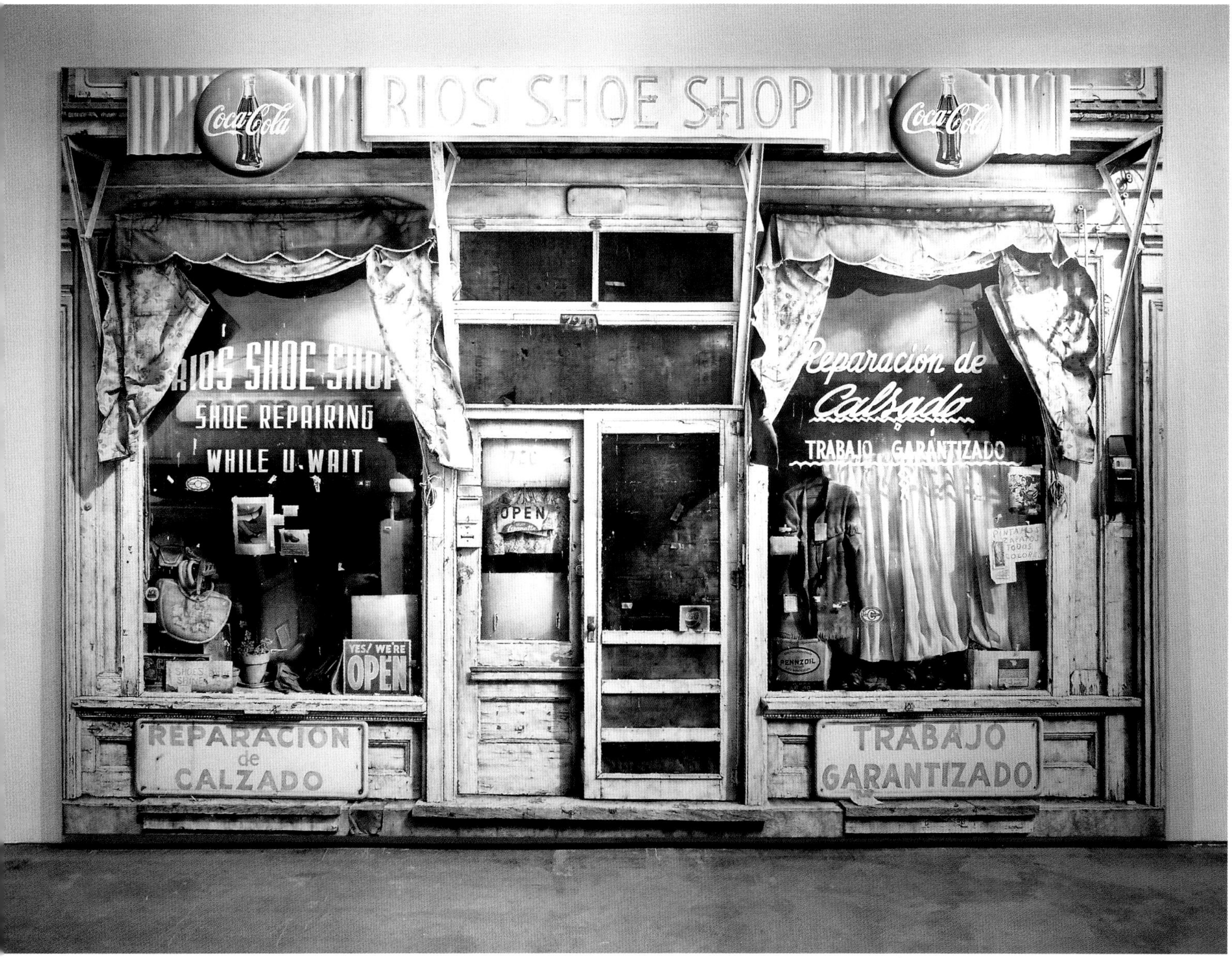

194
PAUL SARKISIAN (B. 1928)
EL PASO, 1971–1972
ACRYLIC ON CANVAS, 168 X 252 IN.
(426.7 X 640.1 CM)

Harry Nadler brought a rational form of abstraction to New Mexico during the late twentieth century through works like *Untitled (76B1)* (fig. 195). Nadler created an understructure for his drawings and paintings by first making a grid often based on the golden mean, a mathematical proportion related to the development of visually pleasing logarithmic spirals. Such foundations to his work imparted a spiritual quality that can be sensed but is difficult to clarify verbally.

At the same time that Nadler was creating his spiritualist drawings and paintings, feminist issues dominated much of the discussion in New Mexico art circles. Two decades before she moved to New Mexico Judy Chicago's work epitomized the feminist revolu-

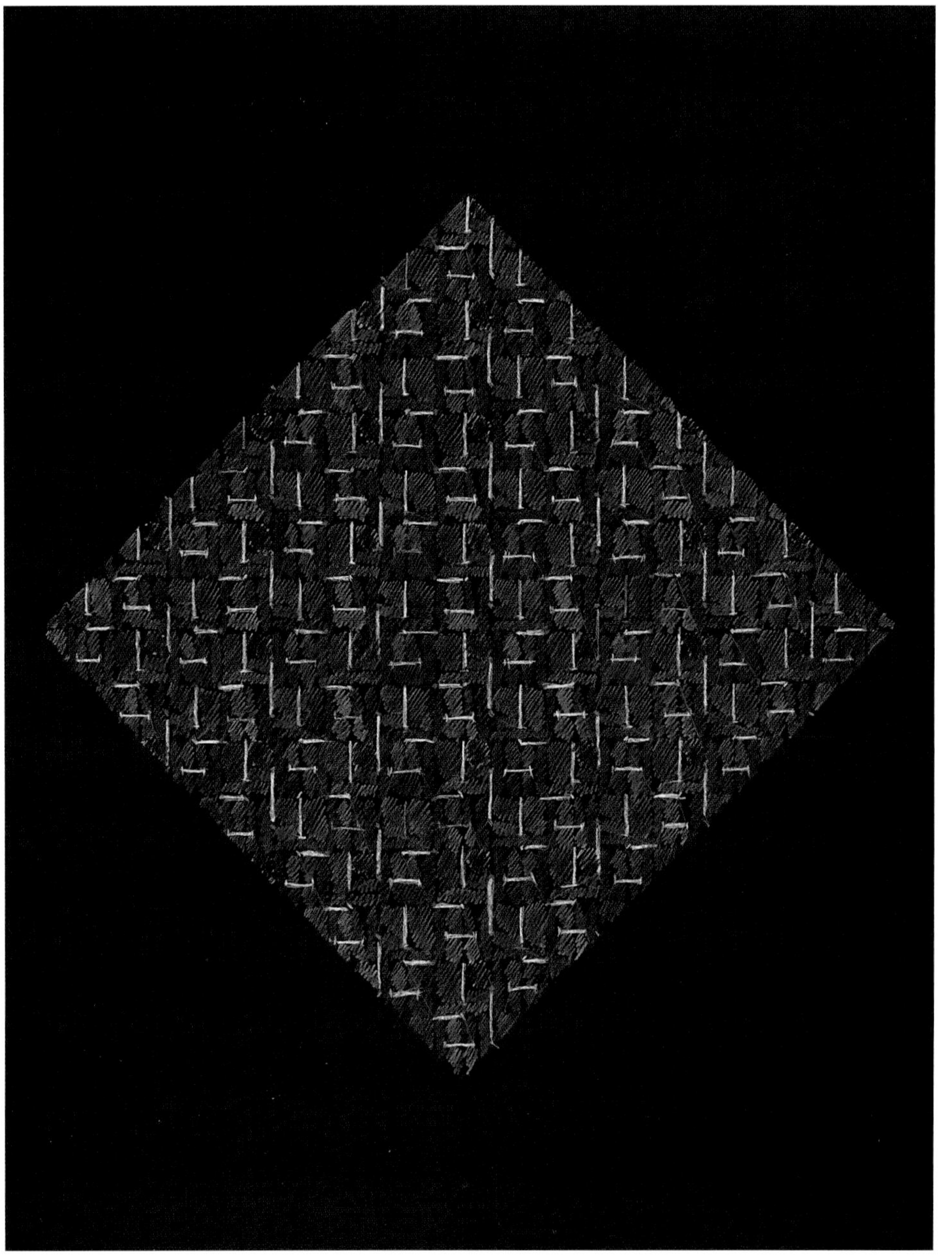

195
HARRY NADLER (1930–1990)
UNTITLED (76 B1), SEPTEMBER 21, 1976
ACRYLIC AND PENCIL ON PAPER, 26 x 20 IN. (66 x 50.8 CM)

tion that shook the art world in the 1970s. Through projects that range from honoring forgotten female artists to the Holocaust, Chicago often has focused on artists who have been left out of the art historical canon. *Peeling Back,* a tinted glass sculpture from 2000 (fig. 196), revisits Chicago's early metaphorical use of flower imagery as a complex reference to women and feminism, in this case in reference to the importance of feminist issues in the art history of New Mexico.

As feminism became an important theme in New Mexico art, artworks sometimes poked fun at a male-oriented society. Artist Anne Noggle's independent lifestyle dated to World War II, when she served as an aviator in the Woman's Air Corps, flying bombers

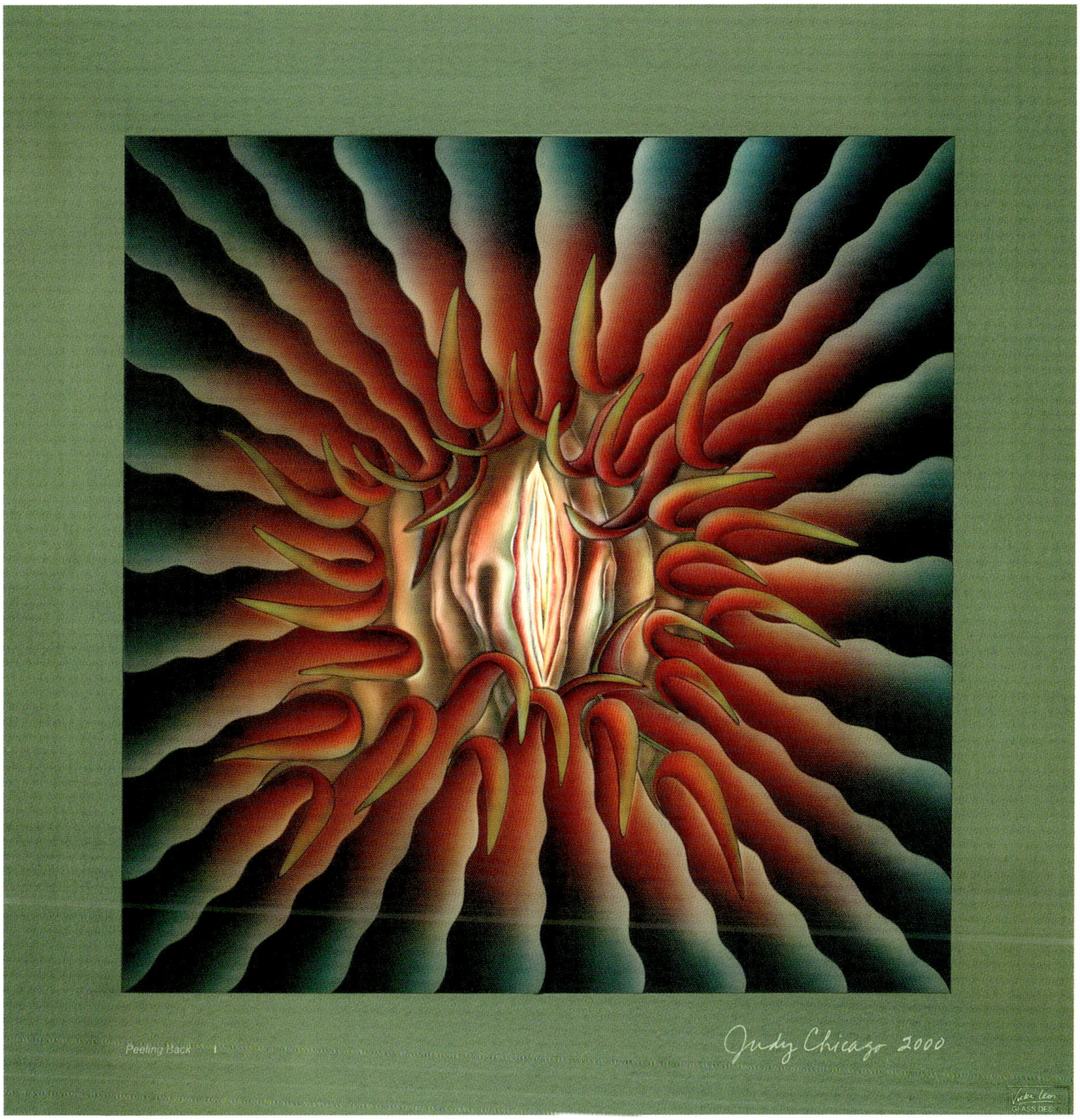

196
JUDY CHICAGO (B. 1939)
PEELING BACK, 2000
ETCHED LAMINATED AND MIRRORED GLASS WITH ACRYLIC, 29 X 29 X 4½ IN. (73.7 X 73.7 X 11.4 CM)

from the United States to Europe. Her photographs and self-portraits often relate to these experiences. Noggle's photograph *Vertical Stance* (fig. 197) shows her photographer friend Judith Golden at the old National Atomic Museum in Albuquerque with a guided missile in the background, a not-so-subtle allusion to the feminist joke that implements of war are merely substitutes for masculinity and power.

Feminist discussions in New Mexico about women's inclusion and exclusion, and women's imagery versus men's aesthetics, eventually led to similar discussions regarding Native and Hispanic imagery and calls for greater diversity in public collections and exhibitions. New Mexico artists responded to the national interest in civil rights, feminism,

197
ANNE NOGGLE (1922–2005)
VERTICAL STANCE (FROM THE SERIES EARTHBOUND—PLATE 26), 1979
CHROMOGENIC PRINT, 12⅞ X 9 IN. (32.7 X 22.9 CM)

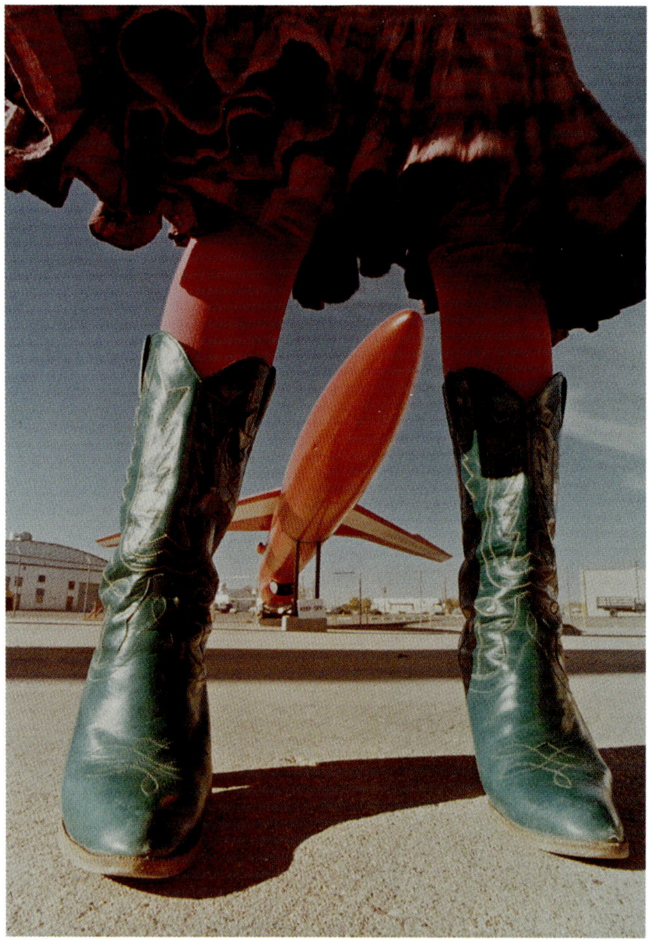

and social activism by raising conceptual questions about the nature of southwestern art, especially the longstanding hierarchy empowering mainstream concerns over indigenous aesthetic views. As a result, political narratives developed that addressed the complex social and artistic history of the region.

The mainstreaming of New Mexico art can be described as the movement from representational and abstract art to the production of nonobjective works. Constance DeJong's *Nitrate Painting XV* (fig. 198) is an example of how local artists have incorporated mainstream art into the Southwest. The work is a large copper panel that has been oxidized with washes of nitrates and acquired a deeply colored patina. Viewers are drawn by the simplicity of this work and by the rich colors of the oxides.

The mainstreaming of New Mexico art angered individuals who felt that abstract and nonobjective works were not New Mexican in character—implying that only representational landscapes and ethnic scenes fit the criteria. In reality, however, the New Mexico art associated with representational painters in Santa Fe and Taos was simply another version of the mainstreaming of western art that had occurred after the arrival of railroads in the 1880s. And, ironically, the Native art that had enthralled the realist, European-American artists was usually nonobjective.

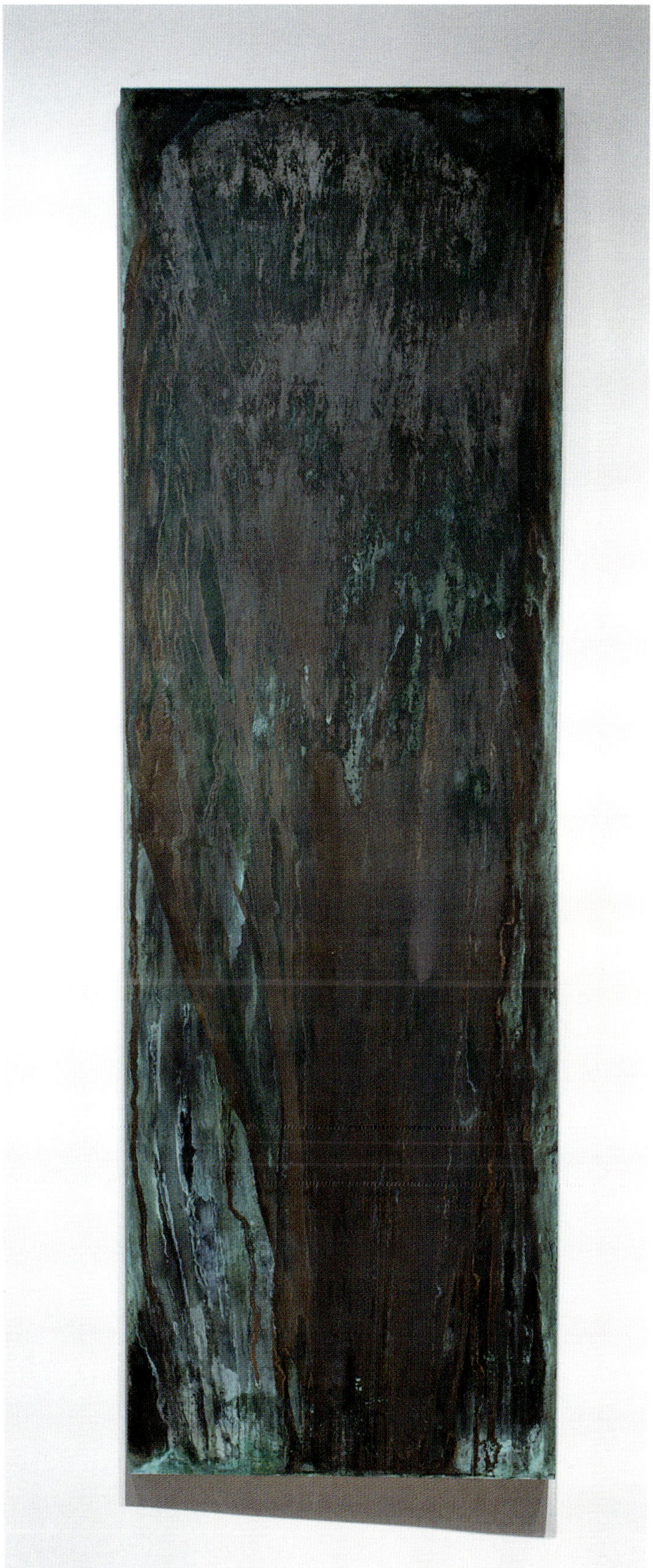

198

CONSTANCE DEJONG (B. 1950)

NITRATE PAINTING XV, 1996

CHEMICAL PATINATION ON COPPER, 96 X 32 X 4 IN. (243.8 X 81.3 X 10.2 CM)

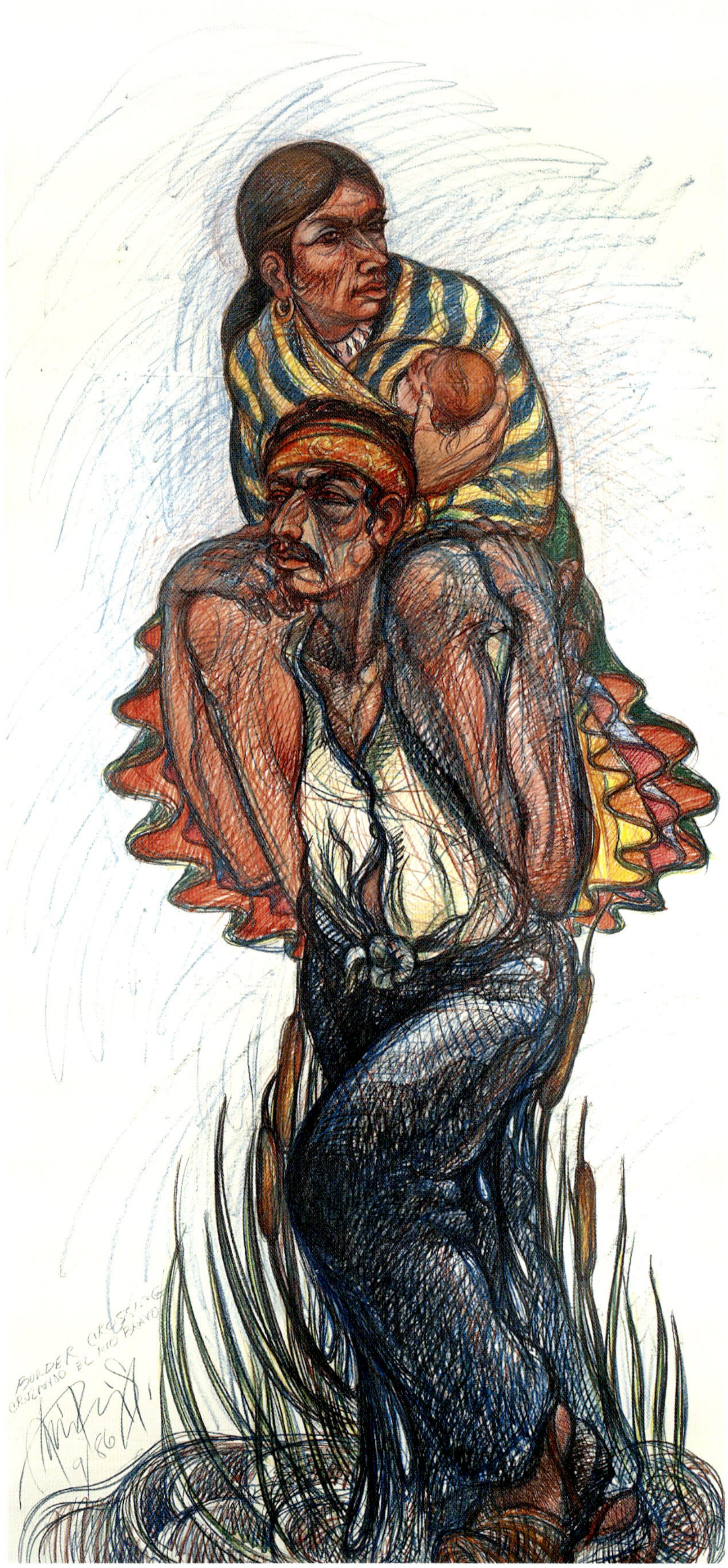
BORDER CROSSING
CRUZANDO EL RIO BRAVO
9/86

CHAPTER 8

The Changing Artistic Landscape

By the end of the twentieth century, the cultural landscape in New Mexico had changed so much that it barely resembled what had been before World War II. Culturally candid views replaced the mythic representations of Native and Hispanic peoples from the Southwest. Some artists responded to political movements in American society by directly addressing issues of gender, identity, and racism through their art. Others rejected political art altogether and emphasized spiritual issues beyond Judeo-Christian ones. A number of artists' works exemplify the changes that occurred in New Mexico art during this period and underscore the transformations that were taking place throughout the region and across cultural divides.

Luis A. Jiménez Jr.'s *Border Crossing (Cruzando el Rio Bravo)* (fig. 199) is a modern version of the *entrada*, though not based on a well-funded expedition moving north from Mexico with the expectation of instant wealth. The drawing is a preliminary study for the fiberglass sculpture of the same name that is displayed on the grounds of the New Mexico Museum of Art. Instead, this oil crayon drawing depicts Jiménez's father carrying him and his mother on his shoulders as they waded across the Rio Grande from Mexico to the United States. The image celebrates his father's physical and mental strength in coming to a new land with only the valuables he could carry on his back, and the larger-than-life scale of the drawing underscores the heroic nature of the crossing. Jiménez thus honors the efforts and sacrifices made by his parents that ultimately allowed him to become an artist. In the context of the history of New Mexico art, such a scene has been repeated many times—first by Native peoples, then by explorers, Hispanic colonists, and European Americans. Further, the work can be seen as a metaphor for the history of New Mexico and thus events that contributed to the evolution of New Mexico art.

Frederico M. Vigil also addresses the *entrada* in his fresco *Exodus: Influencias Positivas y Compadrazgo* (fig. 200), which commemorates the 400th anniversary of the founding of the Hispanic colony of New Mexico. Vigil's image emphasizes the cultural and personal interactions between Hispanics and Native Americans that nurtured the roots of modern New Mexico. The left side illustrates caravans of people, goods, and livestock moving north, while the right side depicts exchanges between southwestern peoples. The items around the border represent the crops and goods exchanged between communities. While Jiménez's work delves into the personal difficulties associated with creating a new life in a foreign land, Vigil's work highlights the positive cultural interactions that have occurred in New Mexico over time.

199
LUIS A. JIMÉNEZ JR. (1940–2006)
BORDER CROSSING (CRUZANDO EL RIO BRAVO), 1986
OIL CRAYON ON PAPER, 130 X 60 IN.
(330.2 X 152.4 CM)

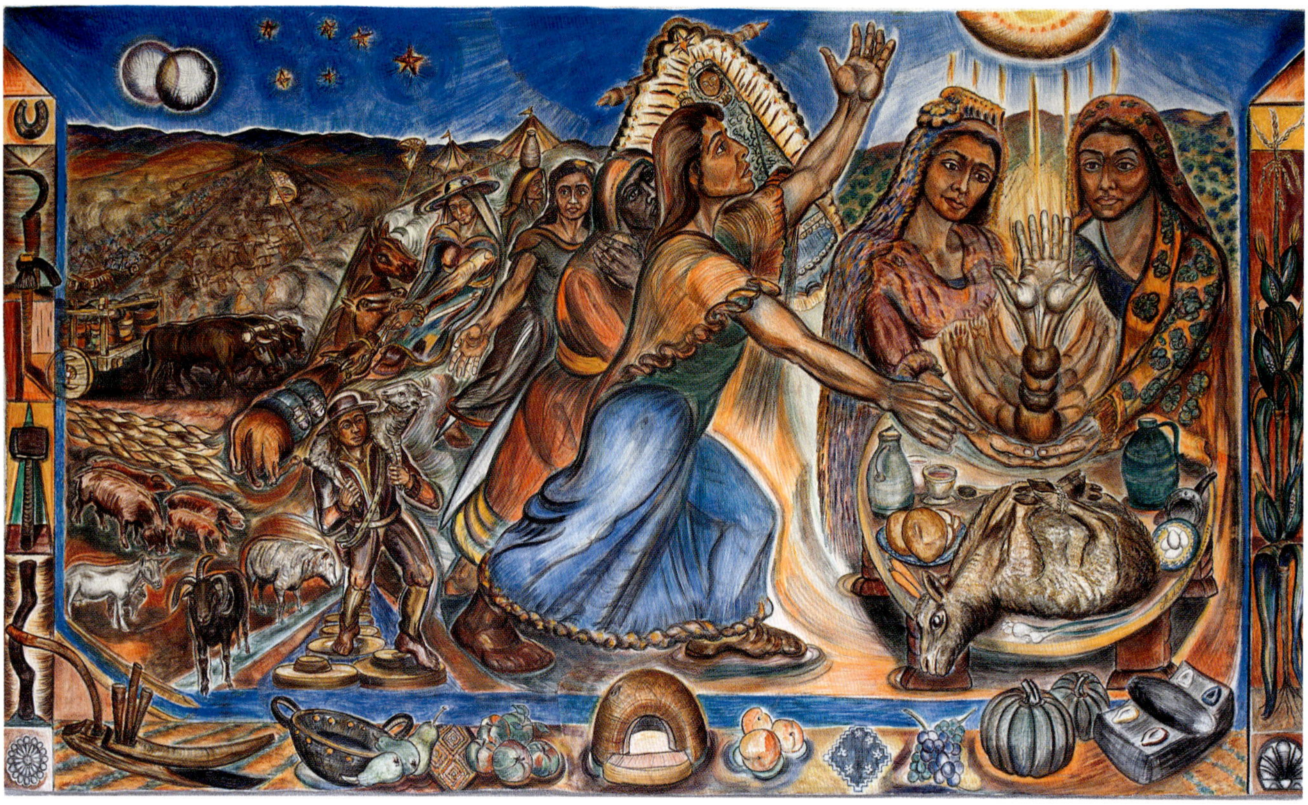

200
FREDERICO M. VIGIL (B. 1946)
EXODUS: INFLUENCIAS POSITIVAS Y COMPADRAZGO / EXODUS: POSITIVE INFLUENCES AND FRIENDSHIP, 1998
BUON FRESCO MURAL, 67 x 118½ IN. (170.2 x 301 CM)

201
DAVID TAYLOR (B. 1965)
BORDER MONUMENT NO. 210, 2009
ARCHIVAL INKJET PRINT, 24 x 31 IN. (61 x 78.7 CM)

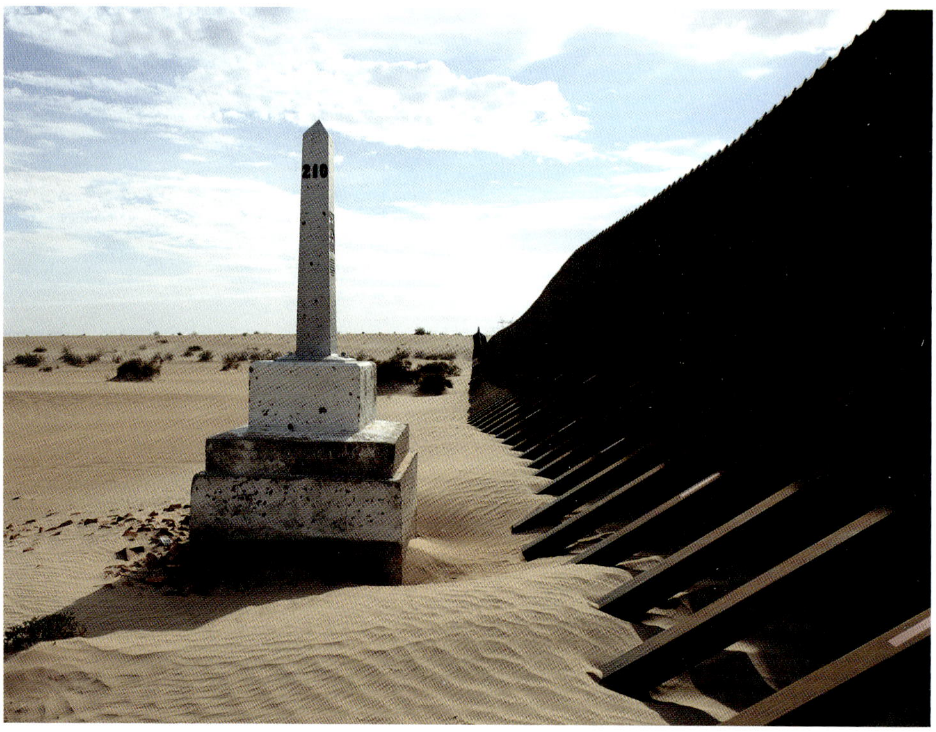

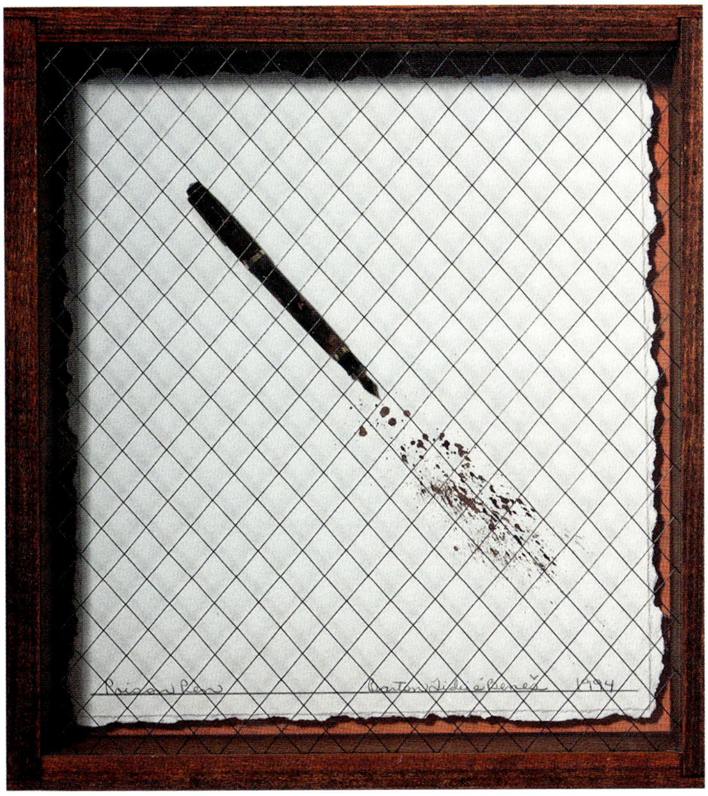

202
BARTON BENES (B. 1942)
POISON PEN, 1994
FOUNTAIN PEN AND HIV-INFECTED BLOOD, 16¼ X 15¼ X 3½ IN.
(41.3 X 38.7 X 8.9 CM)

David Taylor's work presents a third perspective on cultural interaction, this one based on the contemporary politics of immigration and the border. Taylor has photographed the U.S.-Mexico border with a dispassionate starkness. *Border Monument No. 210* (fig. 201) shows the relationship between one of the older border monuments placed at regular intervals and the unbroken steel fence that prevents undocumented travel between the two countries today. An interesting aspect of this image is the sand dunes created by the fence, which show faint ripples similar to the ripples on the Rio Grande that separates the countries, suggesting, ironically, that while immigrants like Jiménez's father could once ford the Rio Grande with its ripples, today no one can cross the sand, with its ripples, along the more secure border.

Barton Benes addresses the theme of segregation, the separation of one group from another based on stereotypes, from a very different point of view in his conceptual sculpture *Poison Pen* (fig. 202). The work shows an ink blot caused by spray from the artist's antique fountain pen. However, the liquid in the pen wasn't ink but Benes's AIDS-infected blood. The high-security glazing separates viewers from danger, real or imagined. The security glass in Benes's sculpture is not unlike the steel fence being constructed between Mexico and the United States. In this context, *Poison Pen* can also refer to xenophobic fear about undocumented workers in the United States.

Changing forms of transportation are important aspects of New Mexico's shifting cultural landscape. Photographer Alexander Eisenmann Harris has been drawn to scenes in northern New Mexico that reflect local cultural attitudes. *Black Mesa, Looking East*

203
ALEXANDER EISEMANN HARRIS
(B. 1949)
BLACK MESA, LOOKING EAST FROM FRED CATA'S 1957 CHEVROLET BELAIR,
1987 (PRINTED 1988)
CHROMOGENIC COLOR PRINT, 24 x 20½ IN. (61 x 52.1 CM)

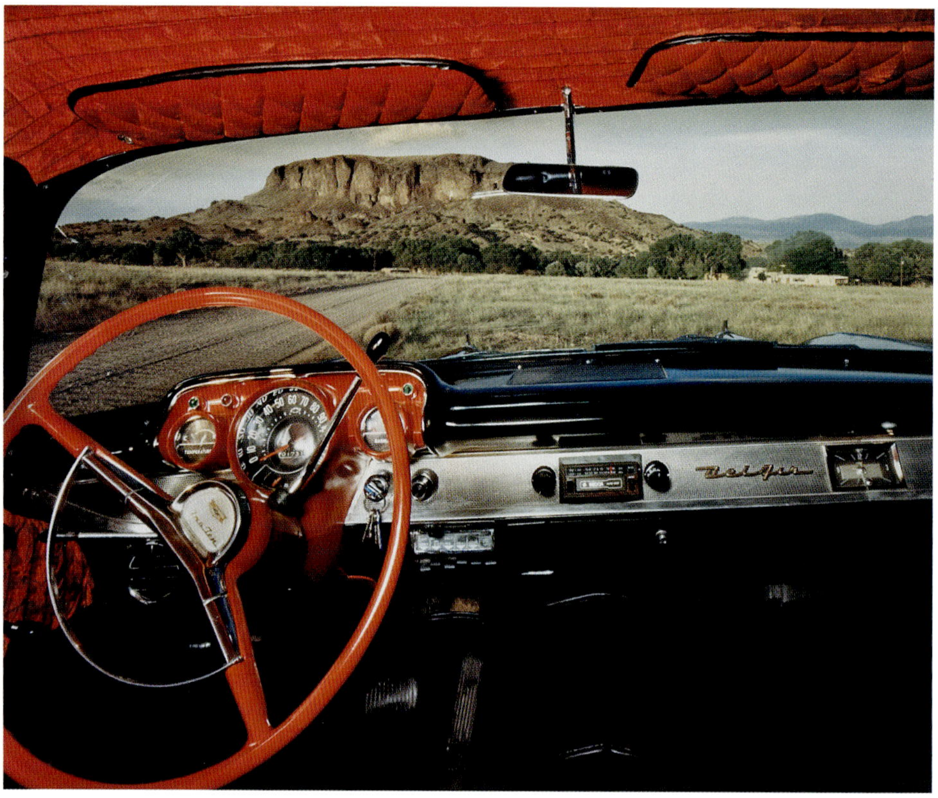

from Fred Cata's 1957 Chevrolet Belair (fig. 203) includes objects whose meanings are culturally specific to New Mexico. The automobile is not just a car—but a '57 Chevy whose fins, chrome details, textured aluminum trim, and optional V8 engine have captivated generations of car buffs since the mid-1950s. And Cata's Chevy isn't a stock car from the factory but is customized with a quilted headliner and matching visors, a style popular among Hispanic car buffs. The scene through the windshield is Black Mesa, a volcanic plug revered as sacred by Tewa Indians who live nearby. Taken together, Harris's photograph captures a sacred scene as observed from a customized, antique vehicle that has acquired a spiritual quality within the popular culture of northern New Mexico.

As with *Black Mesa,* knowledge of local customs is required to understand the symbolism and significance of Luis Tapia's polychromed wooden sculpture *Chima Altar, Bertram's Cruise* (fig. 204). Tapia began as a traditional *santero* making polychromed religious carvings and displaying his works at Spanish Market in Santa Fe. However, when he incorporated modern pigments in his works they were considered untraditional by the standards of the market. At the same time, Tapia investigated subjects related to the popular culture of northern New Mexico. *Chima Altar, Bertram's Cruise* re-creates the dashboard and bucket seats of an automobile in a way that is purely New Mexican.

Several culturally specific details are critical to understanding this work. First, the bucket seats are a reference to Spanish and Spanish–Pueblo Revival-style furniture. Second, the speedometer is stuck at an unsafe speed, a sign an accident is about to occur. Third,

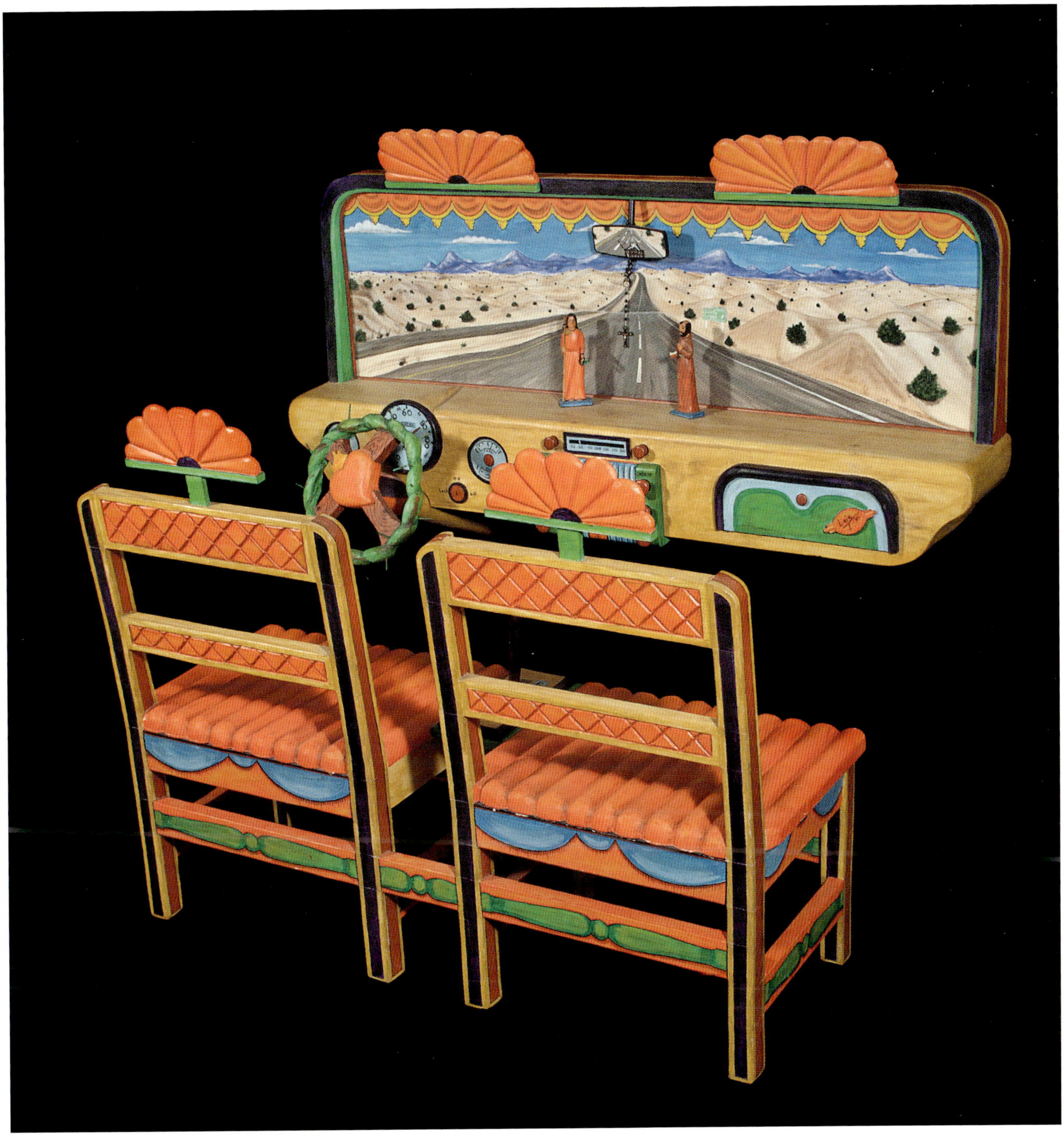

the scene taking place in the rearview mirror is a skeleton driving a local death cart. This northern New Mexico symbol of mortality sends the message that death is constantly chasing us and we need to live our lives in a manner that is cognizant of the dangers we face.

Charles M. Carrillo, a deeply religious man with a doctorate in archaeology, has not ventured into secular imagery and continues creating traditional *retablos* and *bultos* using

204
LUIS TAPIA (B. 1950)
CHIMA ALTAR, BERTRAM'S CRUISE,
1992
CARVED AND PAINTED WOOD, 34½ x 58 x 18¾ IN. (87.6 x 147.3 x 47.6 CM)

205
CHARLES M. CARRILLO (B. 1956)
SAN JERÓNIMO / ST. JEROME,
CIRCA 1990
GESSO AND WATER-BASED PIGMENTS
ON PINE, 17½ X 9 X 9 IN.
(44.5 X 22.9 X 22.9 CM)

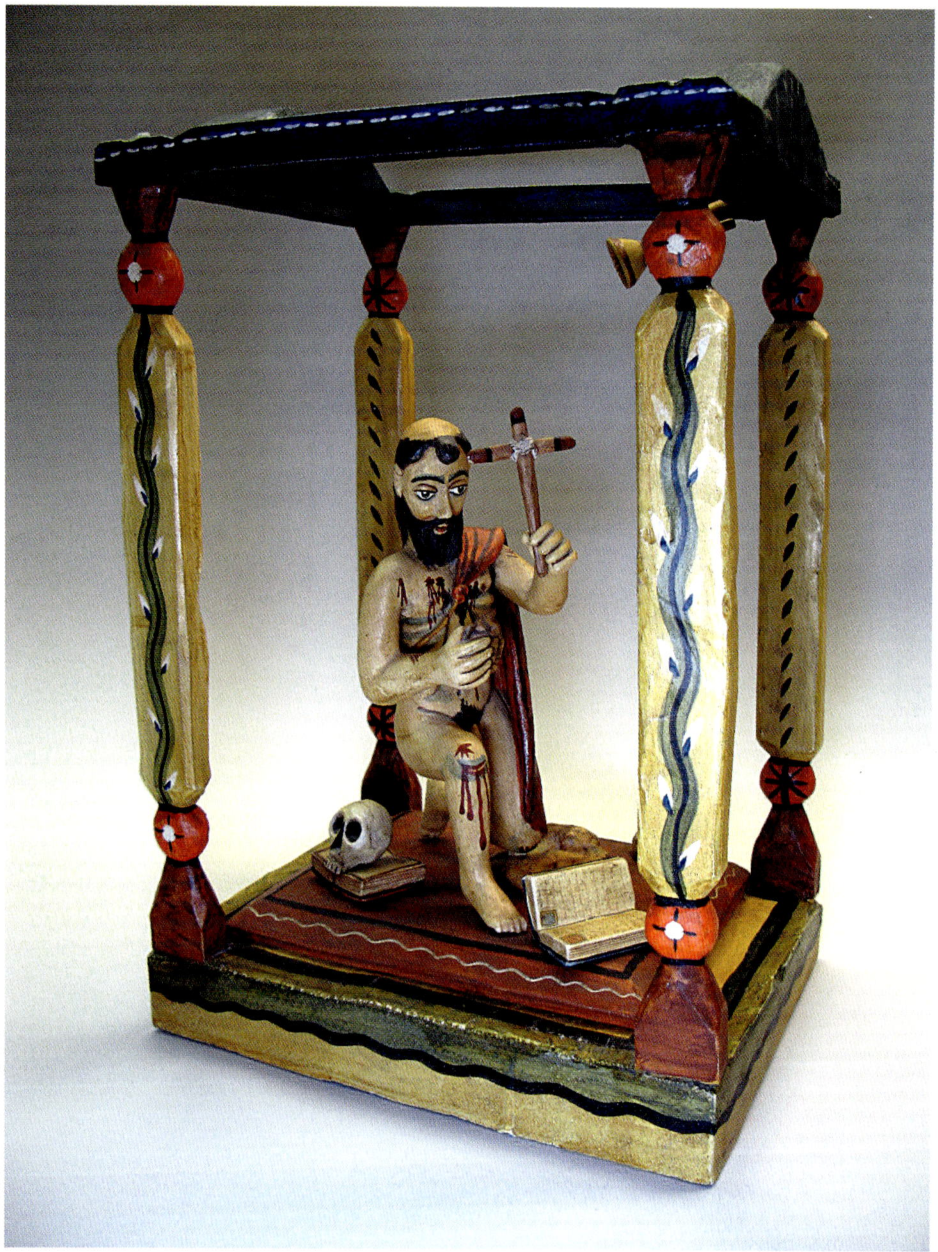

the iconography, materials, and processes developed in New Mexico in the eighteenth century. Sculptures such as *San Jerónimo / St. Jerome* (fig. 205) incorporate his own water-based pigments utilizing plant dyes, minerals, and clays found in New Mexico. Carrillo also creates his own gesso for priming his boards and carvings and seals his work with beeswax and varnishes made of piñon sap. Carrillo's religious works preserve both the spirituality and processes of the eighteenth- and nineteenth-century *santeros*.

Photographic depictions of contemporary Hispanic lifeways tend to avoid popular culture but not Miguel A. Gandert's images. *Reflexiones del Corazon*, his portfolio of lithographs printed at the Tamarind Institute in Albuquerque, often depict the street life of

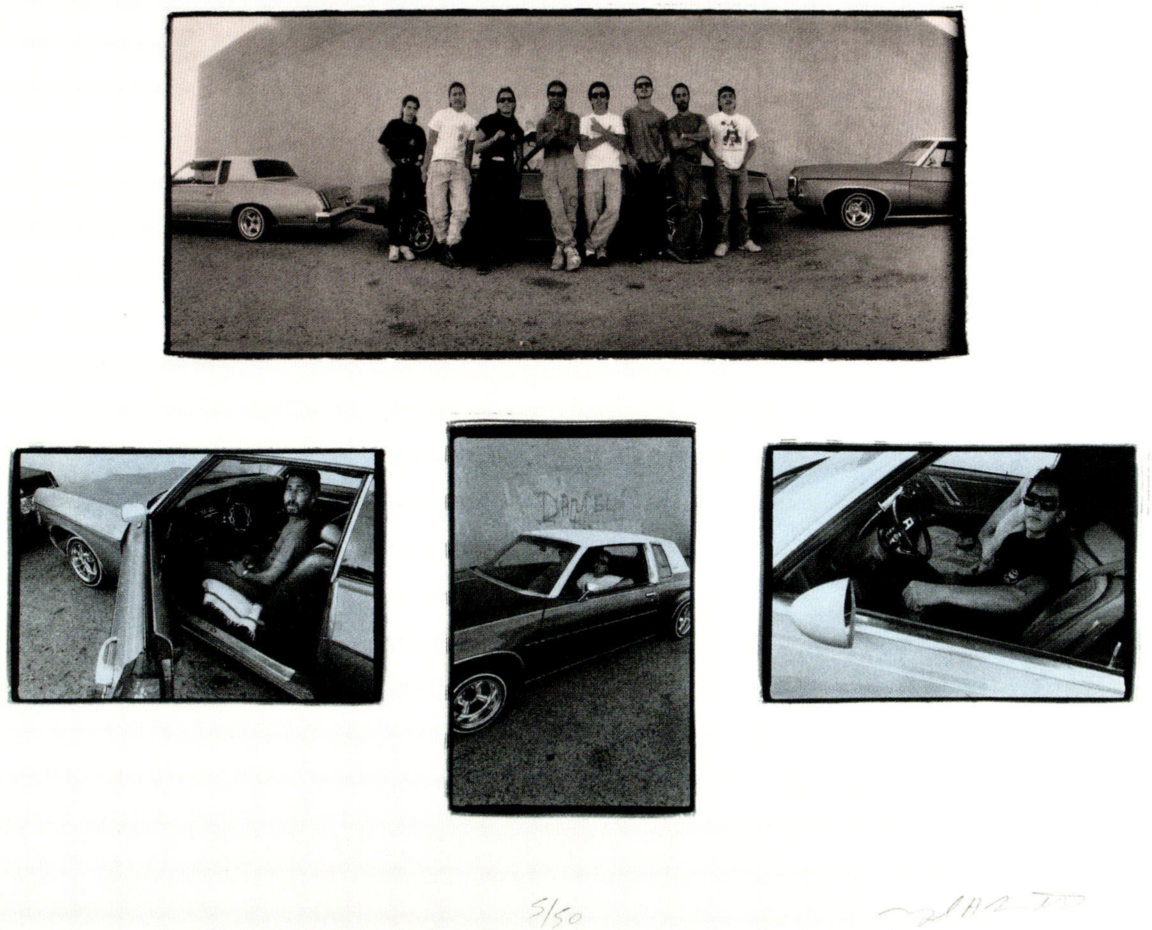

206
MIGUEL A. GANDERT (B. 1956)
LOWRIDERS (FROM THE REFLEXIONES DEL CORAZON PORTFOLIO), 1992
LITHOGRAPH, 11 x 15¼ IN. (27.9 x 38.7 CM)

the region. *Lowriders* (fig. 206) presents a series of small-scale images of cruisers posing in front of their custom automobiles. Their hairstyles, clothing, tattoos, and cars are symbols of their identities and express their cultural outlooks. However, Gandert's photographs are neither sensationalist nor photojournalistic in nature but instead aim for matter-of-fact, nonjudgmental observation.

As the speed and complexity of life in New Mexico increased exponentially during the twentieth century, some artists consciously tried to retard the process. Gloria Graham's drawing *Quartz 3 (#129)* (fig. 207) focuses on the meditative activity of hand drawing ink lines on a sheet of paper coated with kaolin, a pure clay that is both a medium and the message of Graham's piece—the search for clarity, integrity, morality, perfection, simplicity, and righteousness through meditation.

Tim Prythero also yearns for simplicity, but he discovers it in the recent past, which he perceives as a simpler time. In the process, the artist's compulsive interest in fine detail and exceptional skill as a sculptor come to the fore. In *Juanita's Taco Wagon* (fig. 208), a converted delivery truck is parked in front of a well-known furrier on Fourth Street in

207
GLORIA GRAHAM (B. 1940)
QUARTZ 3 (#129), 1997
INK ON KAOLIN, 14 X 14 IN.
(35.6 X 35.6 CM)

208
TIM PRYTHERO (B. 1962)
JUANITA'S TACO WAGON, 2005
MIXED MEDIA, 15½ X 22 X 11 IN.
(39.4 X 55.9 X 27.9 CM)

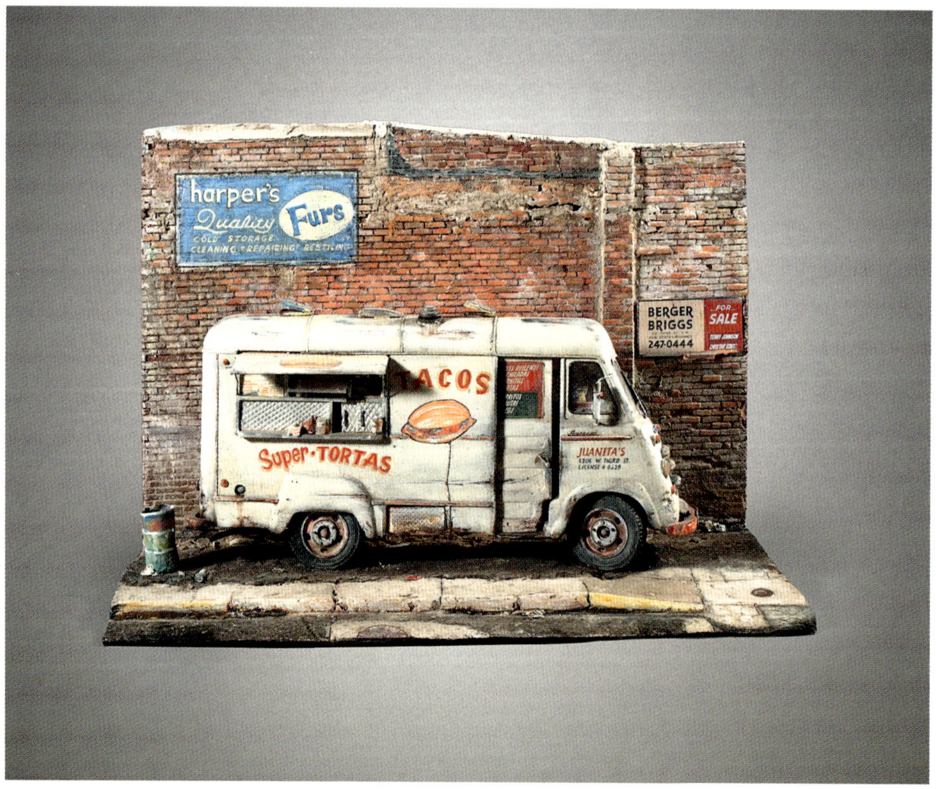

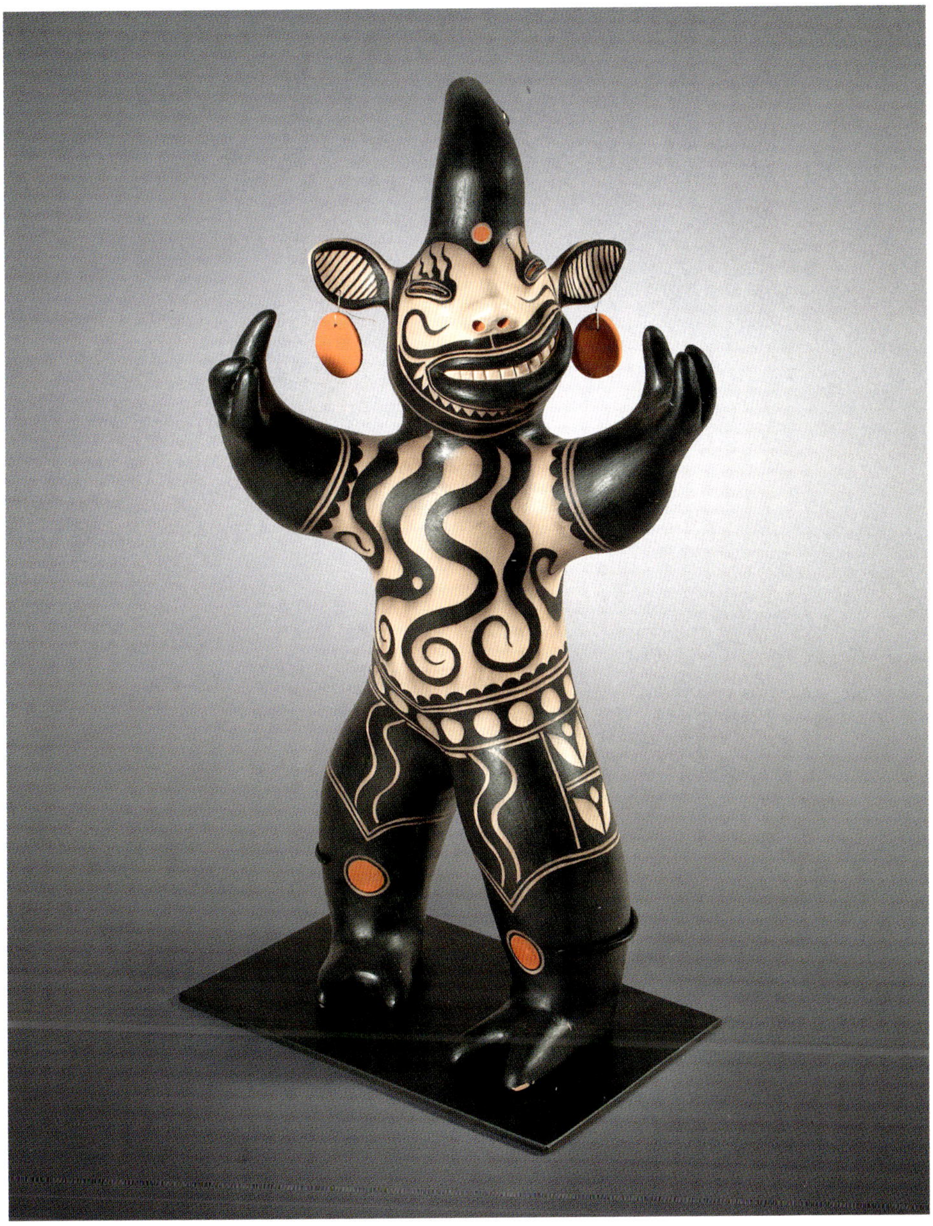

209
VIRGIL ORTIZ (B. 1969)
UNTITLED (OPERA SINGER), 2003
CLAY AND PIGMENTS, 24 X 15 IN.
(61 X 38.1 CM)

Albuquerque. The signage on the brick wall behind dates from a time when downtown was an elegant neighborhood, before the suburbanization of the city after World War II, although the wagon itself seems to have lost its allure.

This play between the modern and the historic is also found in the sculpture of an opera singer by Cochiti ceramist Virgil Ortiz (fig. 209). The creation of figurative sculptures dates to the nineteenth century (see fig. 95) when potters made works that often referred to circus performers with deformities. Ortiz has updated the genre to address modern traveling performers—the singers at the Santa Fe Opera. While the artist began by making ceramics, more recently he has ventured into high-fashion clothing design, where his quirky sense of humor often dominates his work.

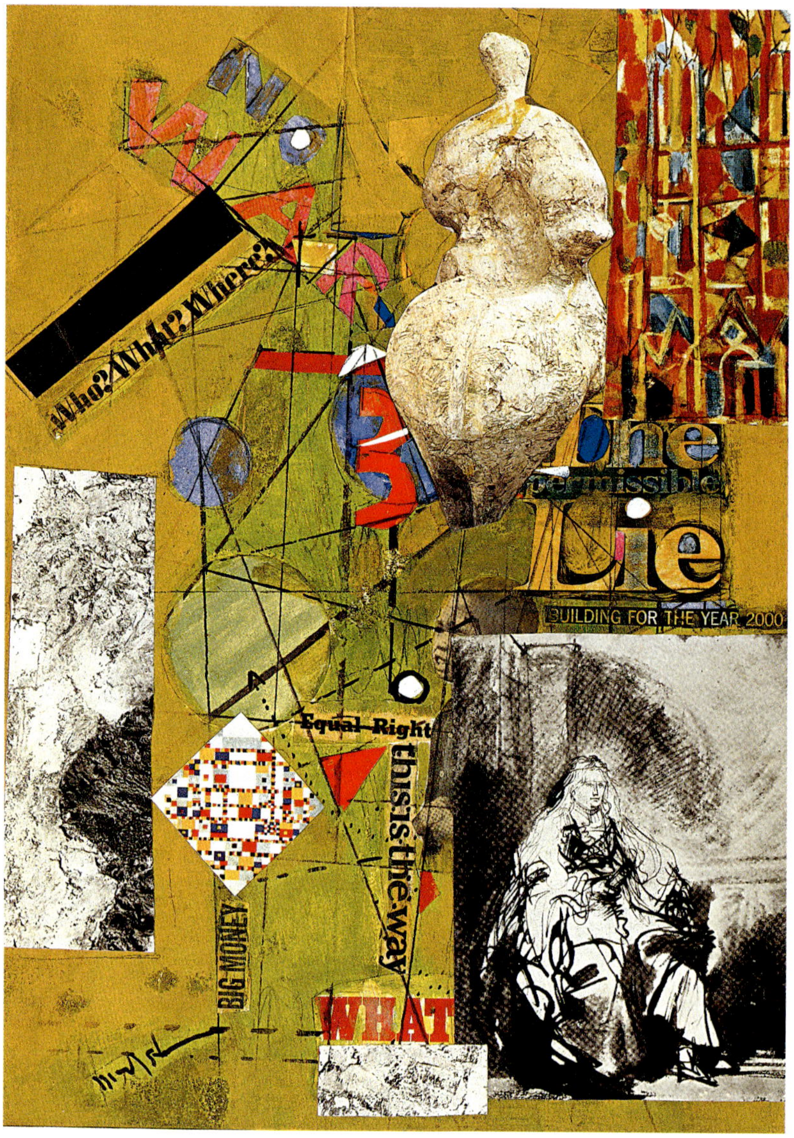

210
BEATRICE MANDELMAN (1912–1998)
NO WAR #1, CIRCA 1965
PHOTOGRAPHIC MATERIALS, COLLAGE, AND ACRYLIC ON BOARD, 21¼ X 15½ IN. (54 X 39.4 CM)

POLITICAL AND SOCIAL COMMENTARY IN ART

Other twentieth-century works engage subjects that have occurred in New Mexico art for almost a century, but in ways that reject the romantic depictions of earlier artists who looked at New Mexico from the outside.

Beatrice Mandelman's collage *No War #1* (fig. 210) expresses her objection to war in an unusual manner. The inclusion of words cut from magazines combined with written comments presents a vague point of view. Letters spelling "the Lie" only offer a vague criticism of governmental pronouncements about the war in Vietnam. Nonetheless, other artists followed Mandelman's efforts at political and social commentary in a more contemporary manner.

Documentary photography and photojournalism found new life after World War II as single-lens reflex cameras allowed for easier coverage of political events and social

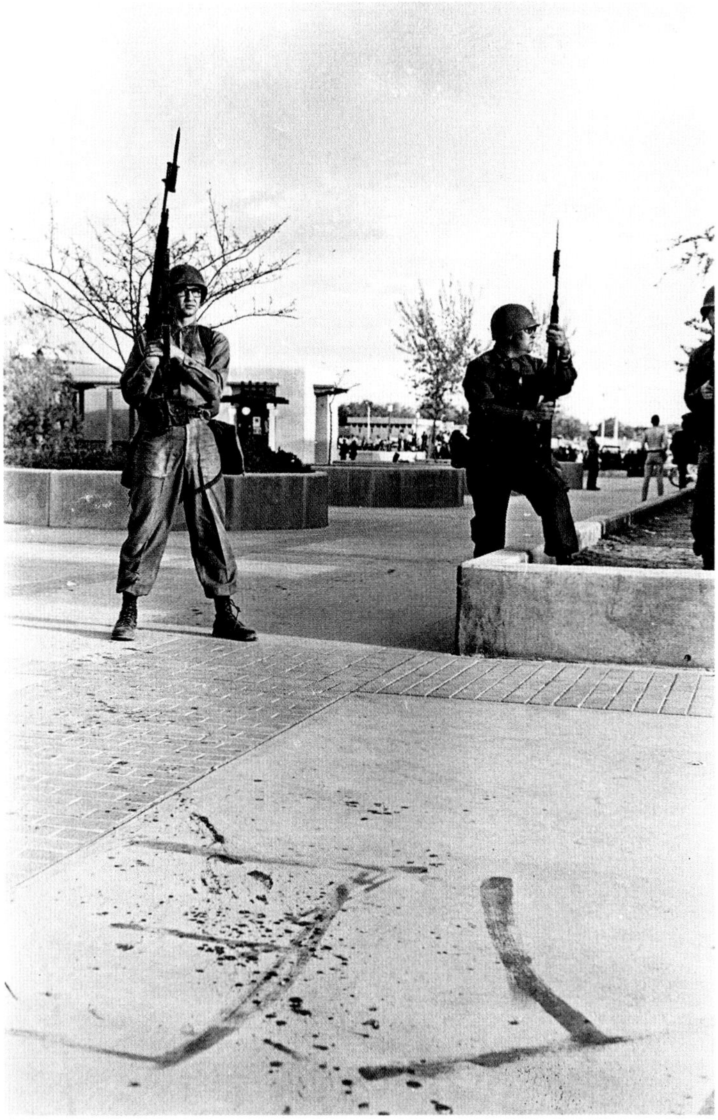

211
MAKER UNKNOWN
UNTITLED, 1970
GELATIN SILVER PRINT, 9½ X 6¼ IN.
(24.1 X 15.9 CM)

conditions. The photography program in the Art Department at the University of New Mexico was one of the best in the country, attracting talented students to study with Van Deren Coke. Subsequently, they played an important role in documenting political unrest on campus in May 1970 after President Richard Nixon invaded Cambodia, expanding the scope of the Vietnam War. That year faculty, staff, and students at UNM closed the campus after four students were shot and killed by National Guard troops at Kent State University. Tensions ran high as confrontations occurred between those supporting the war and those demanding "Out Now." Governor David Cargo called out the New Mexico National Guard to open the campus, and on May 8, 1970, troops carrying rifles and fixed bayonets stormed through the university, stabbing a dozen strikers. Art and journalism students photographed the strike, with the most dramatic photograph (fig. 211) showing two guardsmen standing ready behind a smear of blood from a bayoneted student.

During the late twentieth century, many New Mexico artists felt that the world was shattering politically and socially. Artists, including Rick Dillingham, James Drake, and Joel-Peter Witkin, responded by making fragmented imagery a component of their work.

Rick Dillingham was a ceramic artist and scholar specializing in Pueblo pottery. In 1972, he began making ceramic gas cans as commentary on the centrality of gasoline in modern lives, having concluded that gas cans were the modern equivalent to the water jars that had facilitated Pueblo lifeways for centuries. His ceramic gas cans emphasized the fragility of modern technology a year before the gas crisis of 1973.

Dillingham also created works that commented on the significance and use of Pueblo pottery. He noticed that when such pottery blew up during firing, the shards became discolored. When the broken vessels were glued back together, the discoloration accentuated the fracture lines. Dillingham incorporated these discoveries into his works by molding, painting, and firing his vessels, then breaking, repainting, refiring, and finally reconstructing the shards into finished works of art. His *Untitled (Globe)* (fig. 212) exemplifies the process, incorporating gold leaf as well as colored glazes that contrast with the vessel's elegant globular form. One way to think about these reconstructed objects is to consider them as sculptures about ceramic vessels, the process of their creation, and their breakage through use.

212
RICK DILLINGHAM (1952–1994)
UNTITLED (GLOBE) 1985–1986
CERAMIC, GOLD LEAF, ENAMEL, AND GLUE, 12 x 15 x 15 IN. (30.5 x 38.1 x 38.1 CM)

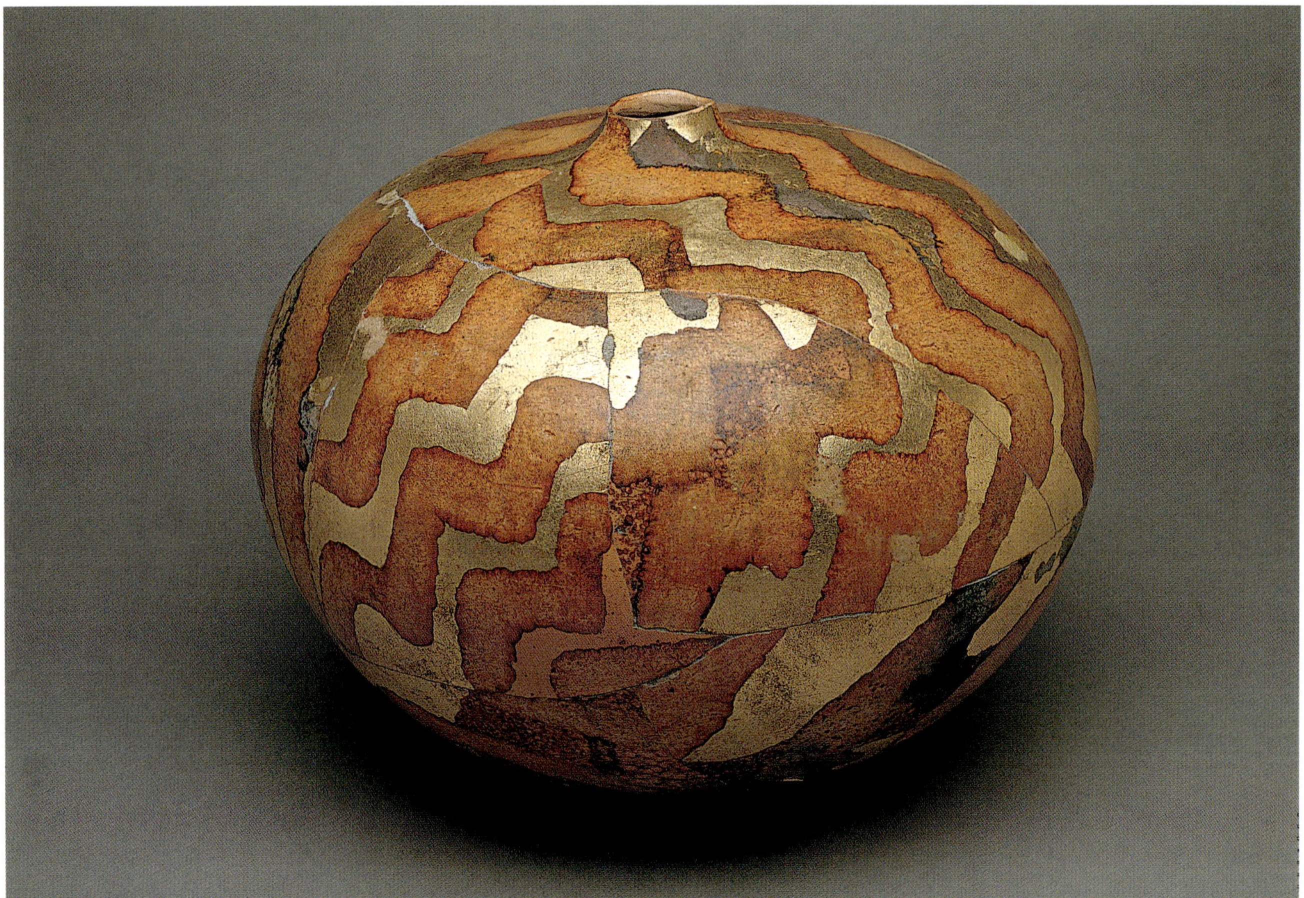

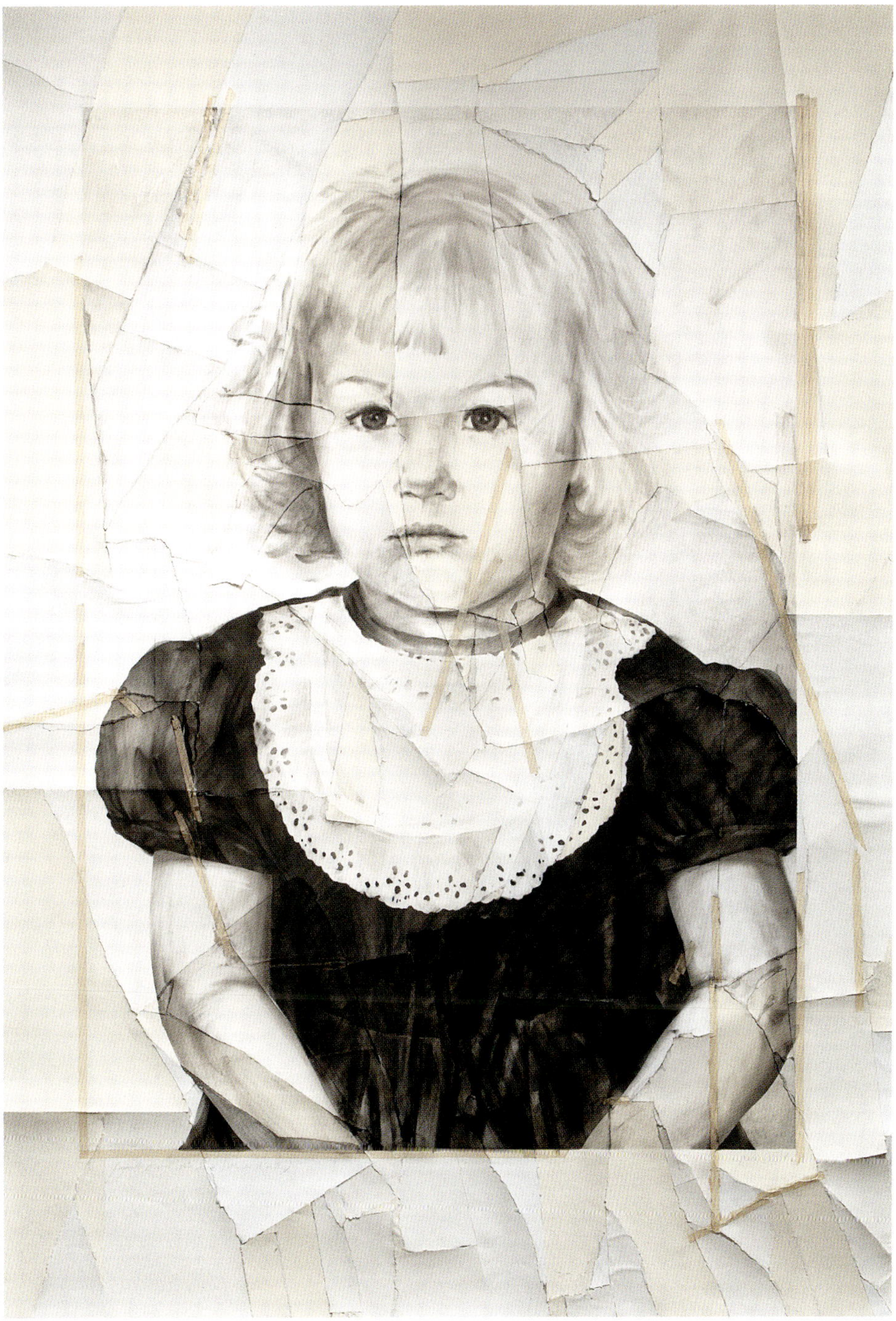

213
JAMES DRAKE (B. 1946)
JAYNELLE ACROSS THE SEA (WORLD WAR II), 2006
CHARCOAL AND TAPE ON PAPER MOUNTED ON CANVAS, 120 x 84 IN. (304.8 x 213.4 CM)

Issues of life and death radiate throughout James Drake's ten-foot drawing of his young cousin, Jaynelle, *Across the Sea (World War II)* (fig. 213). From a distance, the work could be mistaken for a three-inch grade-school photograph that has been torn to shreds and pasted back together. But up close the work reveals layers of drawn fragments superimposed on each other as Drake revised his work into a holistic vision.

214
JOEL-PETER WITKIN (B. 1939)
THE RESULT OF WAR: THE CORNUCOPIAN DOG, 1984
TONED GELATIN SILVER PRINT,
15 x 15 IN. (38.1 x 38.1 CM)

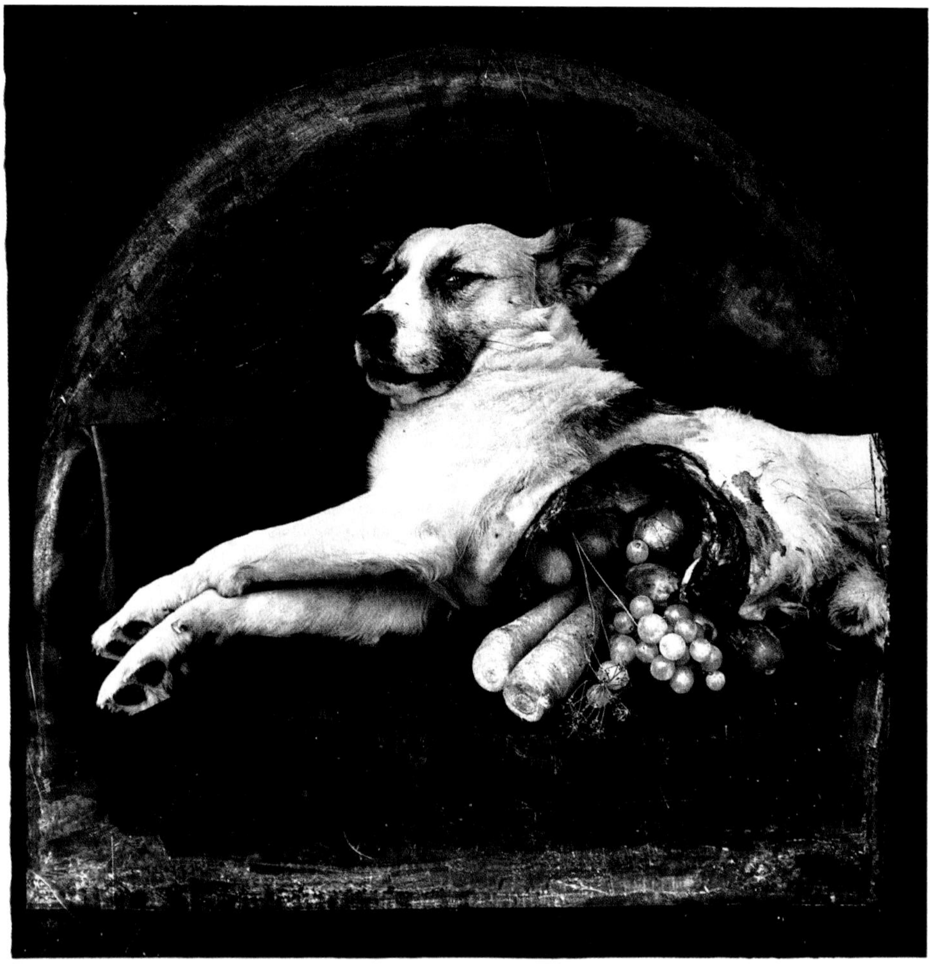

The startling story behind Drake's drawing causes viewers to think about nuclear weapons in a highly personal manner. Jaynelle's father was stationed in Japan after World War II, and he brought the family to Japan during his tour of duty. There Jaynelle was diagnosed with a malignant brain tumor. After Jaynelle died, the family blamed the tragedy on radiation from the nuclear explosions over Hiroshima and Nagasaki.

Joel-Peter Witkin pastiches visual fragments from multiple negatives so skillfully that they appear as a print from a single, unaltered negative. As a result, his images blur the distinction between fiction and truth, invention and documentation. This approach underpins his image *The Result of War: The Cornucopian Dog* (fig. 214). The photograph references Goya's series of etchings *The Disasters of War,* created to protest nineteenth-century wars between France and Spain.The cornucopia in this distasteful image, a symbol of abundancies, parodies the aphorism that the spoils of war go to the victor.

Meridel Rubenstein and Ellen Zweig investigate the development of the atomic bomb at Los Alamos, New Mexico, and its effect on the surrounding communities through their work *Portal to Archimedes Chamber* (fig. 215). This multimedia production includes video, still photography, spoken narratives, and sound effects that connect the invention

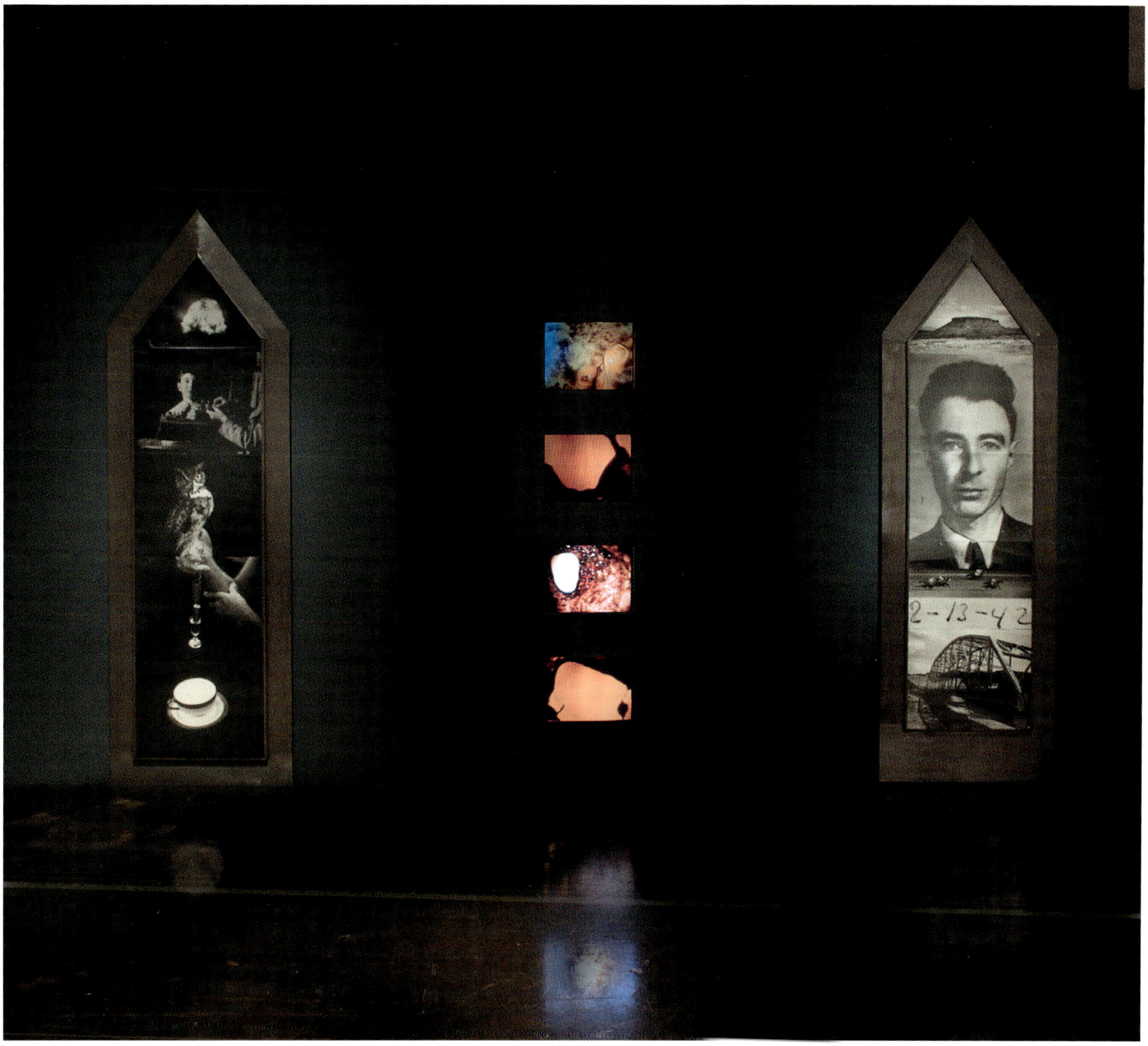

215
MERIDEL RUBENSTEIN (B. 1948) AND ELLEN ZWEIG (B. 1947)
PORTAL TO ARCHIMEDES' CHAMBER, 1990
PALLADIUM PRINTS, STEEL, LASER DISKS AND PLAYERS, AND VIDEO MONITORS, 111 x 236 x 50 IN. (281.9 x 599.4 x 127 CM)

of the atomic bomb with Archimedes, ancient Greek mathematician and military inventor who allegedly set Roman ships on fire with reflected sunlight, just as physicists invented a way to magically turn uranium into military weapons.

Ceramic sculptor Beverly Magennis sculpts representational forms, but she also works with designs created from commercial tiles that she fractures into abstract shapes. Over many years she tiled the exterior of her home in Albuquerque and landscaped the yard with ceramic figurines and plants. Magennis used the same process producing her chairs (fig. 216), which usually include ceramic cats or birds resting on their backs. Magennis combines seemingly naive subject matter with a sophisticated sense of design and quirky sense of humor.

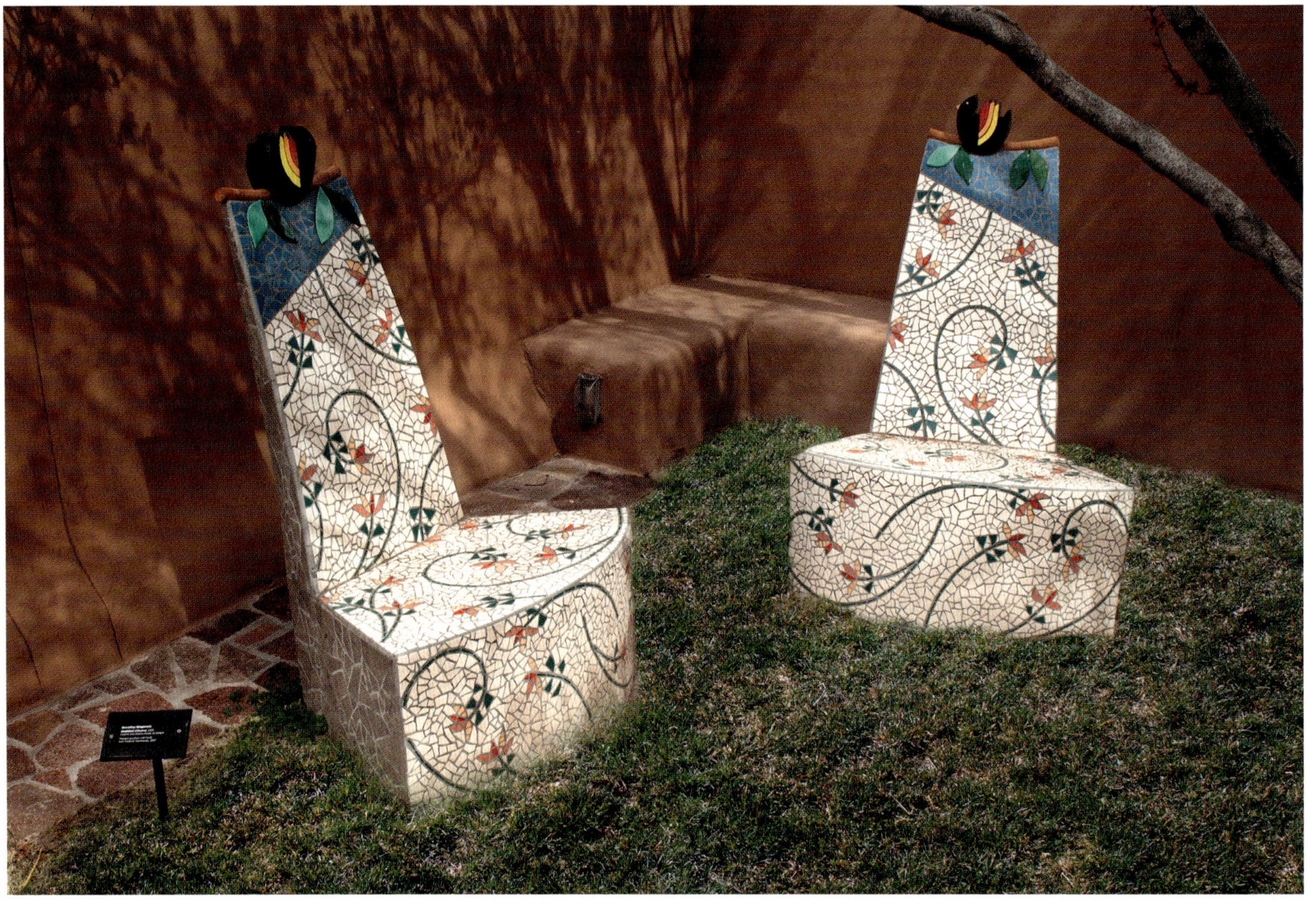

216
BEVERLY MAGENNIS (B. 1942)
UNTITLED (CHAIRS), 2000
CERAMIC AND CERAMIC MOSAIC ON CEMENT, 56½ X 38 IN. (143.5 X 96.5 CM)

T. C. Cannon's experiences living in communities fragmented by racism radicalized the young painter and convinced him that Native American history was an appropriate subject for contemporary art. He quickly developed a pop art style that attacked stereotypes of Native peoples and simultaneously reinterpreted the history of Native relations with non-Indians. *Washington Landscape with Peace Medal Indian* (fig. 217) exemplifies Cannon's work just before he died in an automobile wreck at age thirty-two.

During the nineteenth century, the federal government brought tribal leaders to Washington, DC, to sign treaties between Indian nations and the United States. Tribal leaders received top hats, peace medals on ribbons, and canes as part of the peace ceremonies and as symbols of their sovereign authority. But when pioneers, miners, homesteaders, and the federal government broke these treaties, all that remained were these empty symbols of a failed peace and posed photographs of Native delegations. Cannon combines these symbols into a sarcastic commentary on the past. The reds, blues, greens, and purples in Cannon's pop art-meets-Matisse style express the continuing clash between Native peoples and the federal government.

Cannon's angst-ridden self-portrait *Self with Star of David* (fig. 218) offers clues to his mental state during the 1970s. At the time he was impressed with his New York dealer, who was Jewish, and considered converting to Judaism. Cannon's interest in his Native

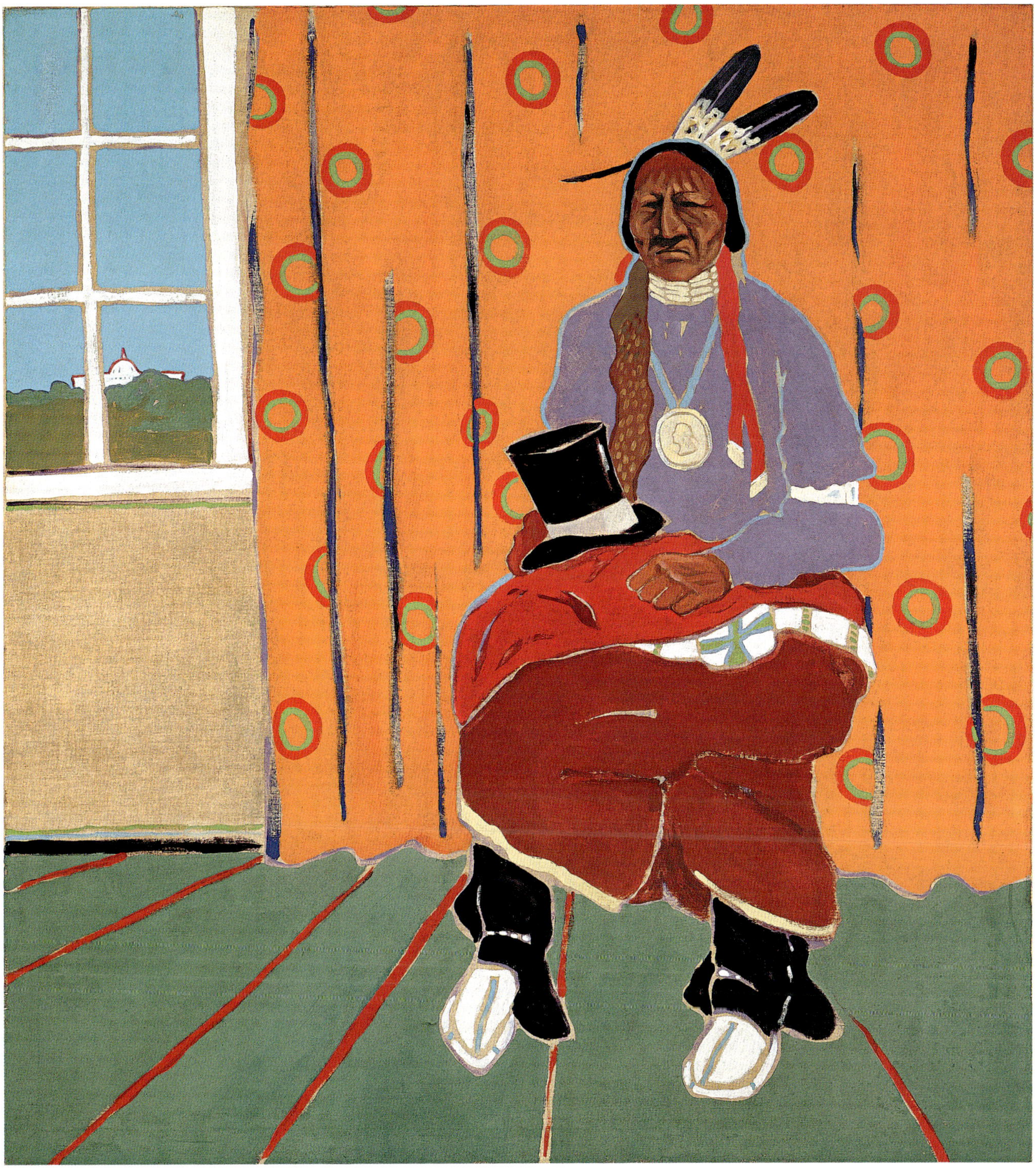

217
T. C. CANNON (1946–1978)
WASHINGTON LANDSCAPE WITH PEACE MEDAL INDIAN, 1976
ACRYLIC ON CANVAS, 50 X 45½ IN. (127 X 115.6 CM)

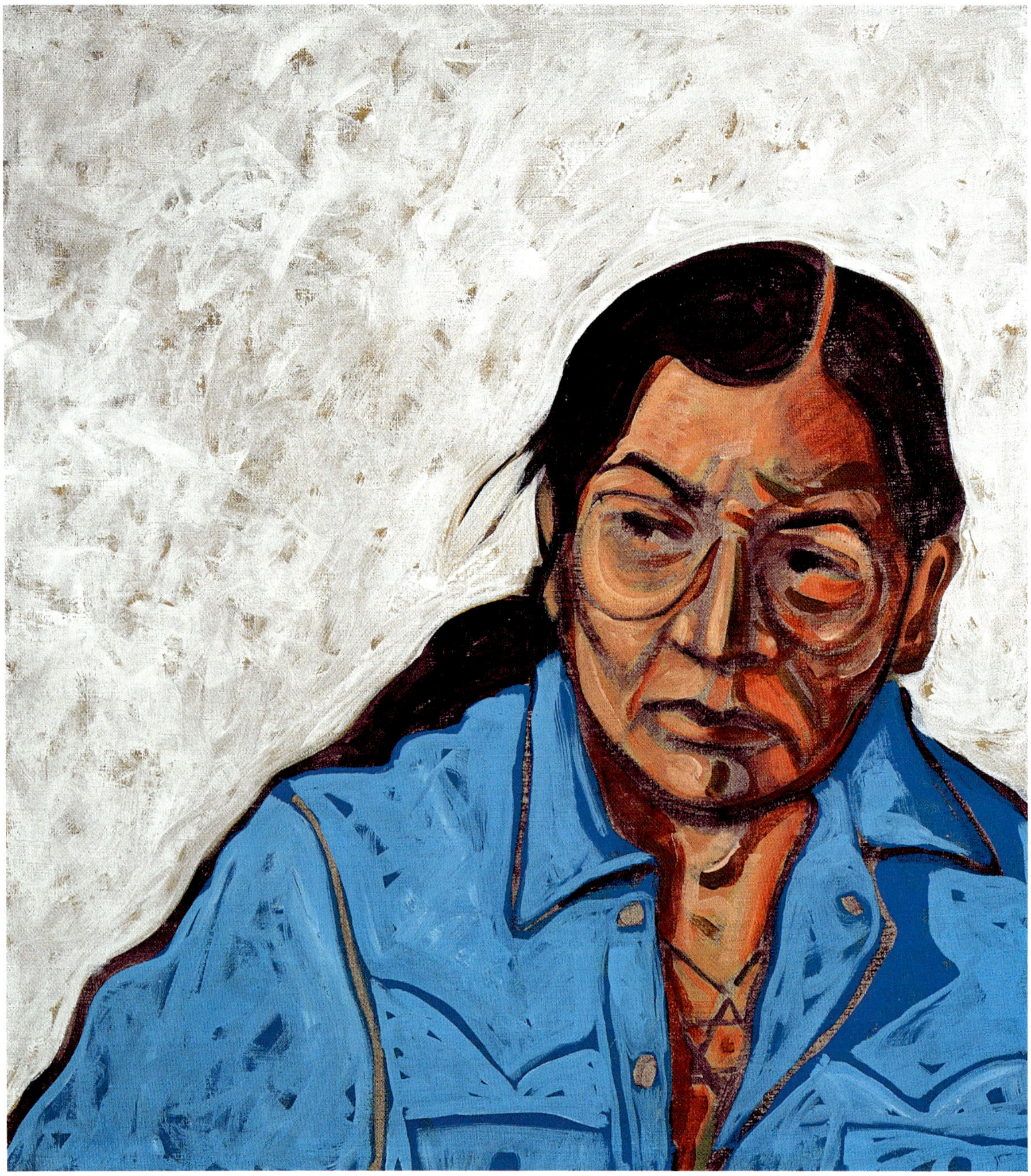

218
T. C. CANNON (1946–1978)
SELF WITH STAR OF DAVID, CIRCA 1975
OIL ON CANVAS, 22 X 20 IN.
(55.9 X 50.8 CM)

identity convinced his mentor Fritz Scholder that this was an important area of personal exploration. Scholder also fused a pop art approach to Native American subject matter with cutting humor, creating iconic images of life at the end of the twentieth century. In these works, the expressionistic brush work exudes the artist's self-confidence. Nonetheless, Scholder's 1971 self-portrait (fig. 219) provides insight into the angst the artist seems to have felt as he negotiated the political complexities of the mainstream art market.

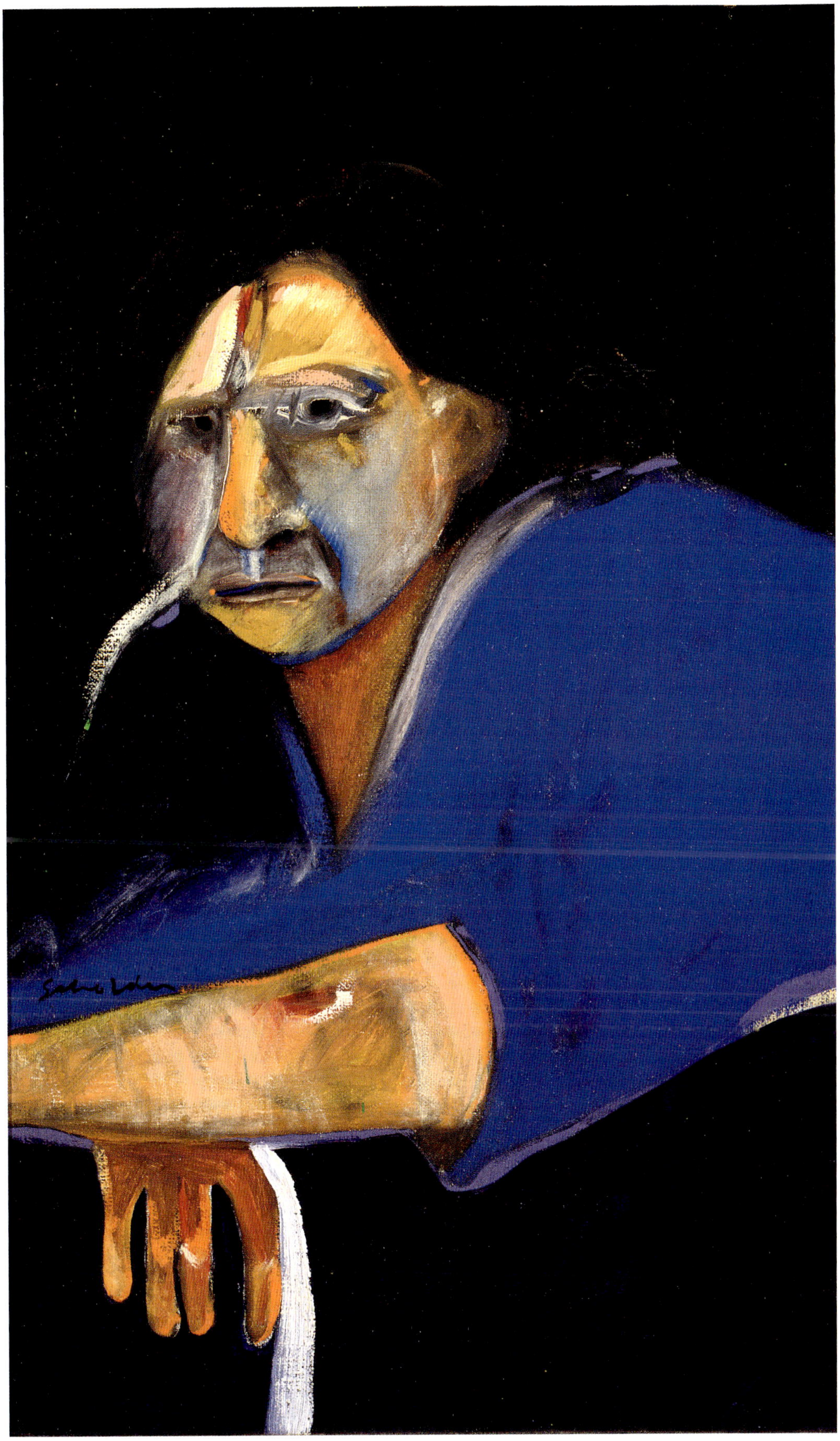

219
FRITZ SCHOLDER (1937–2005)
UNTITLED (SELF-PORTRAIT), 1971
OIL ON CANVAS, 30 3/16 X 18¼ IN.
(76.7 X 46.4 CM)

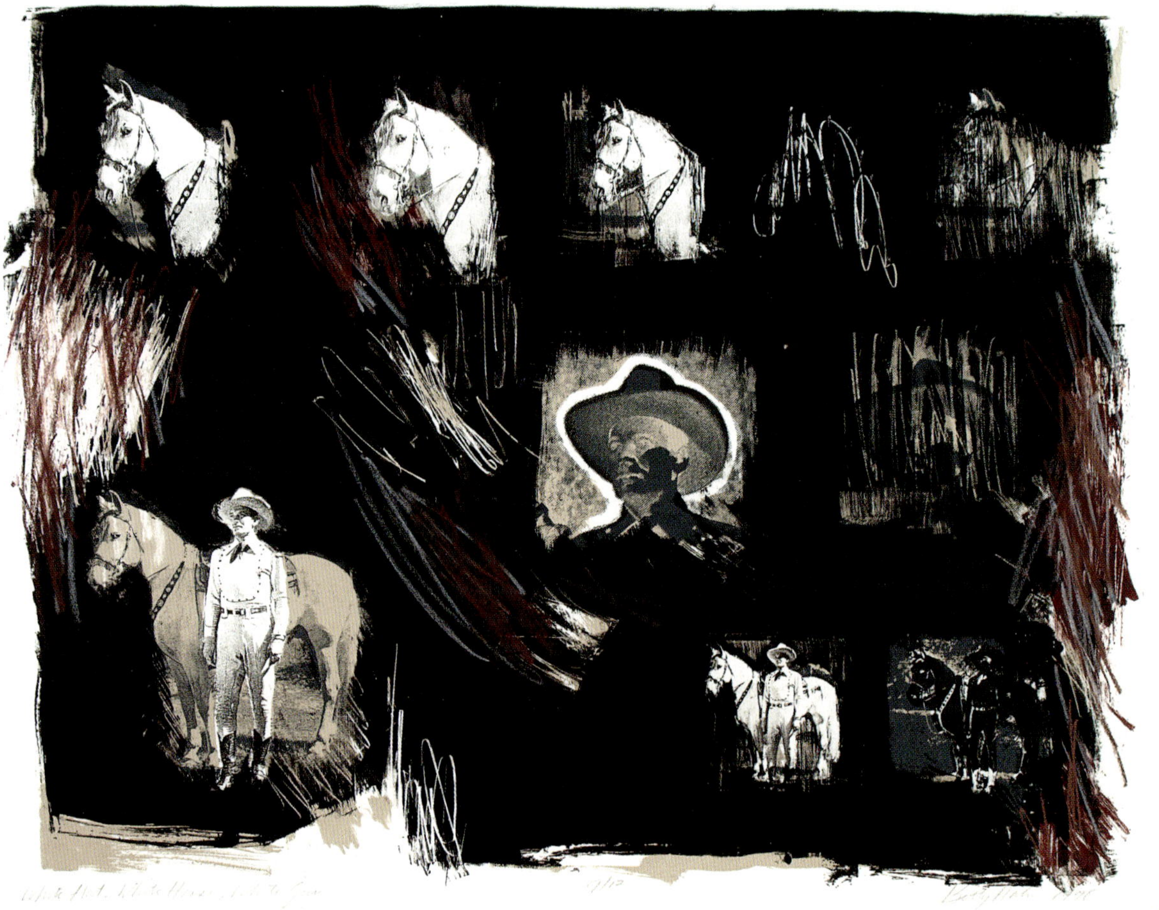

220
BETTY HAHN (B. 1940)
WHITE HAT, WHITE HORSE, WHITE GUY,
1998
FOUR-COLOR LITHOGRAPH WITH PHOTOGRAPHIC TRANSFER AND OIL PASTEL, 22⅛ X 30½ IN. (56.2 X 77.5 CM)

Betty Hahn's mixed media *White Hat, White Horse, White Guy* (fig. 220) seems perfectly in concert with Cannon's commentary on Native stereotypes. Hahn produced a series of images that criticize such stereotypes and rebuke the Hollywood version of western history. In this case, the white man is the Lone Ranger, and the dark print is a reflection of the cowboys-and-Indians myth of the West. In the Saturday morning *Lone Ranger* program of the 1950s, Tonto usually solves the problem with wisdom and insight, but the masked man happily takes credit for the good deed. The ultimate irony is that the Spanish word *tonto* means "fool," and clearly Tonto was no fool.

THE SPIRITUAL AND ART

The movement of young people to New Mexico as part of the counterculture revolution of the 1960s and 1970s, a movement that brought people back to the land but also back to the sky, renewed an interest in astrology and Eastern religions that had intrigued individuals associated with the Transcendental Painting Group three decades earlier. A

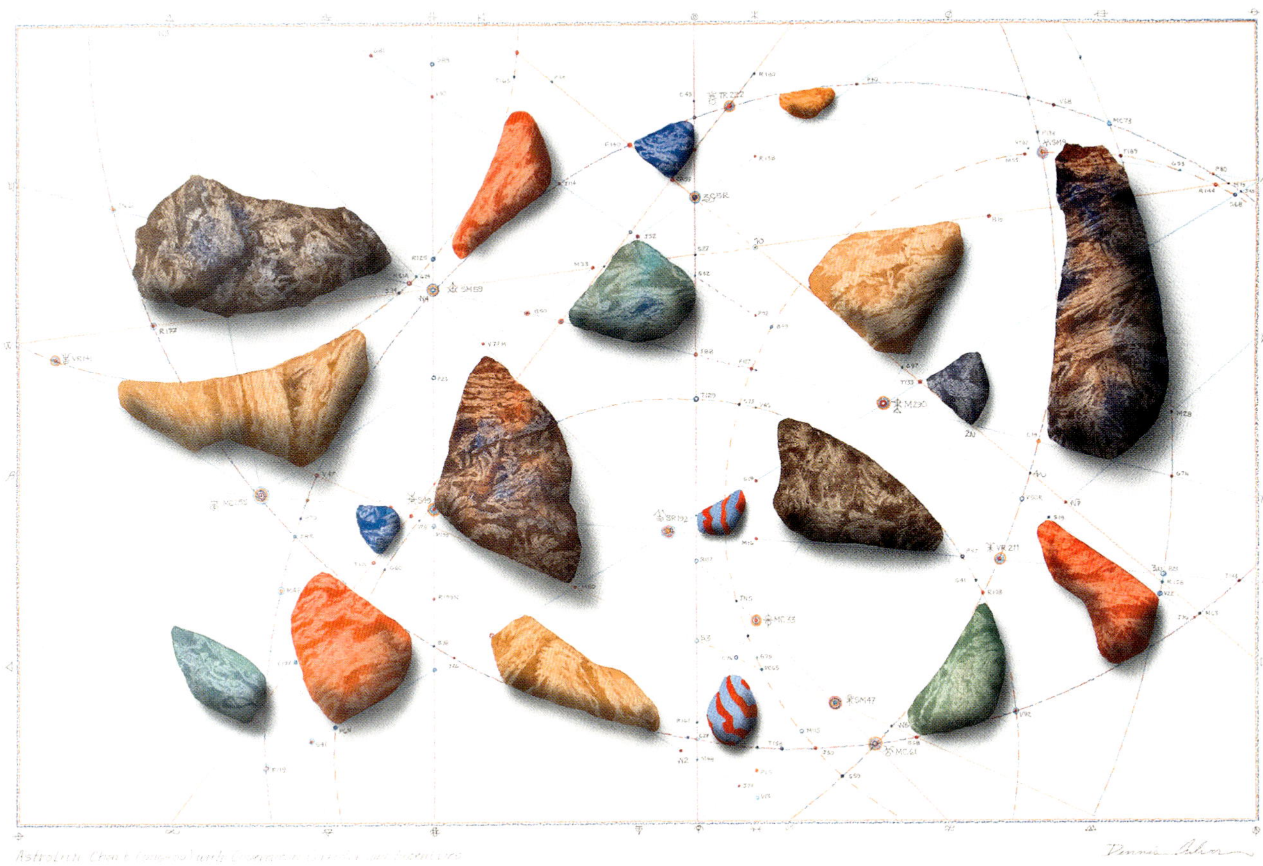

221
DENNIS CULVER (1945–2011)
ASTROLITH CHART (006-05) WITH COPERNICAN CORRIDOR AND ECCENTRICS, N.D.
COLOR PENCIL, WATERCOLOR ON PAPER, 22 X 30 IN. (55.9 X 76.2 CM)

deep distrust of science and a rejection of the conventional wisdom that was then taught at home and in school powered much of the 1960s youth culture. The agricultural traditions of New Mexico inspired in this generation the confidence that simple lifestyles could be empowering and spiritual.

Dennis Culver arrived in Santa Fe during the counterculture revolution. His watercolor and color-pencil painting *Astrolith Chart (006-05) with Copernican Corridor and Eccentrics* (fig. 221) is a tongue-in-cheek sky chart of astroliths, mythic constellations marked with strange rocks. This painting invokes an antiscientific approach to astrology, mysticism, and the occult but uses the appearance of scientific information to convince viewers of the veracity of the material.

The spiritual qualities associated with the order of the universe are the subject of the artistic explorations of sculptor Charles Ross. For three decades, Ross has been building *Star Axis*, an observatory pointing to the North Star that will allow visitors to understand Earth's predictable wobble as it travels through space on a 10,000-year-long cycle (fig. 222). This earthwork sculpture, which is cut into the side of a mesa near Las Vegas, New Mexico, is aligned with the sunrise and sunset on the summer and winter solstices.

Ross sees the order of the cosmos and the interconnectedness of its aspects as reflecting a spiritual dimension. Although physicists have not solved the unified field theory that explains the universe, it is clear that everything is interconnected, from tiny particles that last for a split second to enormous structures that are measured in light years. On a micro-

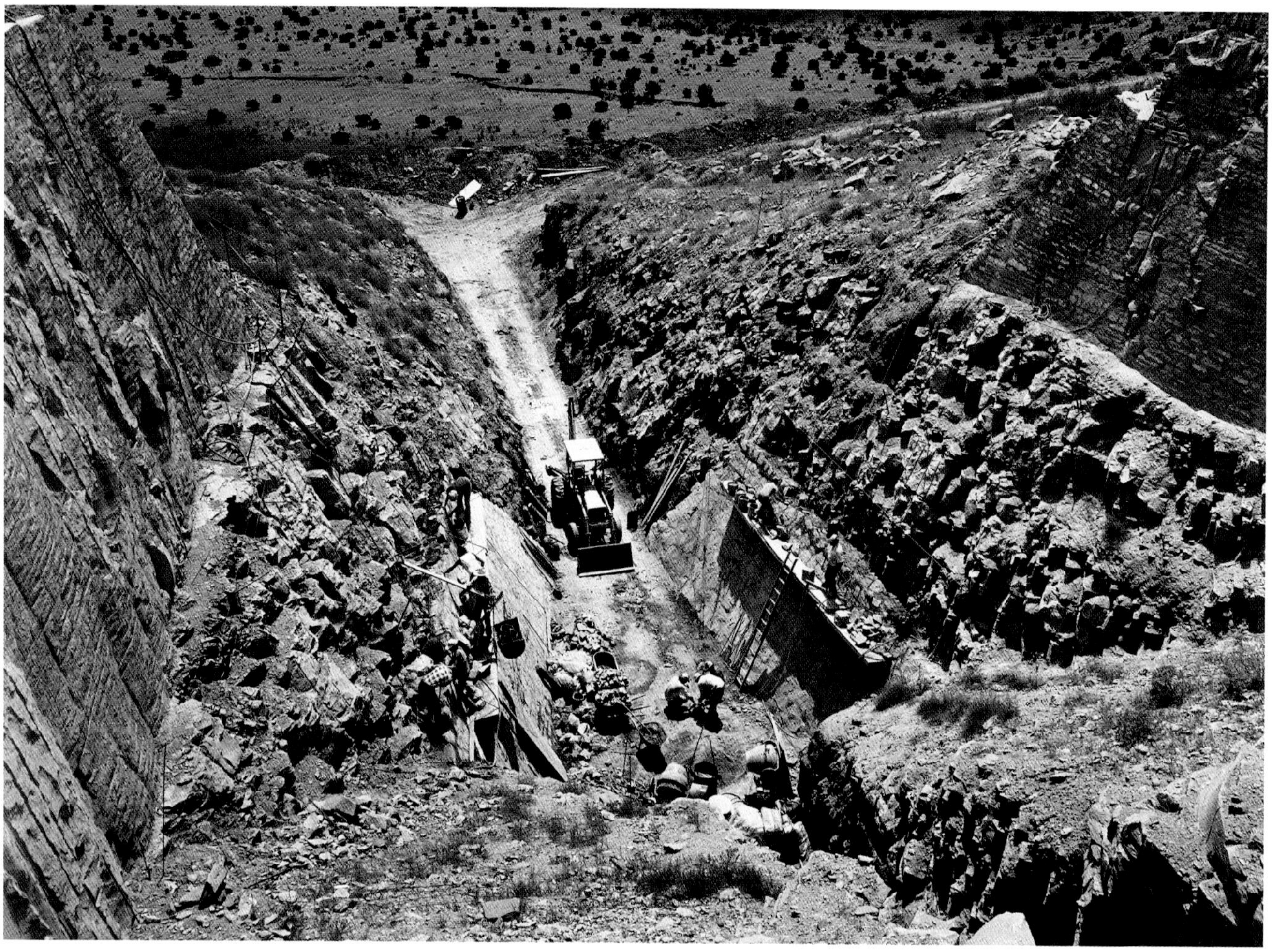

222
EDWARD RANNEY (B. 1942)
STAR AXIS, LOOKING SOUTH, 8/26/83,
1983
SELENIUM-TONED GELATIN SILVER PRINT, 10⅝ X 15 IN. (27 X 38.1 CM)

scopic scale, Ross investigates the breakdown of subatomic particles through works like *Cosmic Rain* (fig. 223). This large "drawing" was made by exploding blasting cord under piles of loose pigments on a piece of paper, distributing the colored pigments while tearing away part of the paper to create a series of white lines.

Most viewers have no idea how Jennifer Joseph created *#9.2* (fig. 224), a dazzling work that appears to float without supports. Constructed of acupuncture needles and wire, the work seems to change form as viewers move around the sculpture and the reflections dance within the room, but it is not a mobile that twists and turns. It gives the appearance of making order out of chaos, a spiritual experience out of a nebulae of nontraditional healing devices.

Florence Miller Pierce explores the cycles of life through resin sculptures that exude mystical qualities. Pierce, the youngest member of the Transcendental Painting Group, continued an interest in spirituality throughout her life. For the last twenty-five years of her life, she experimented with the visual qualities of light reflecting through veils of polyester resins.

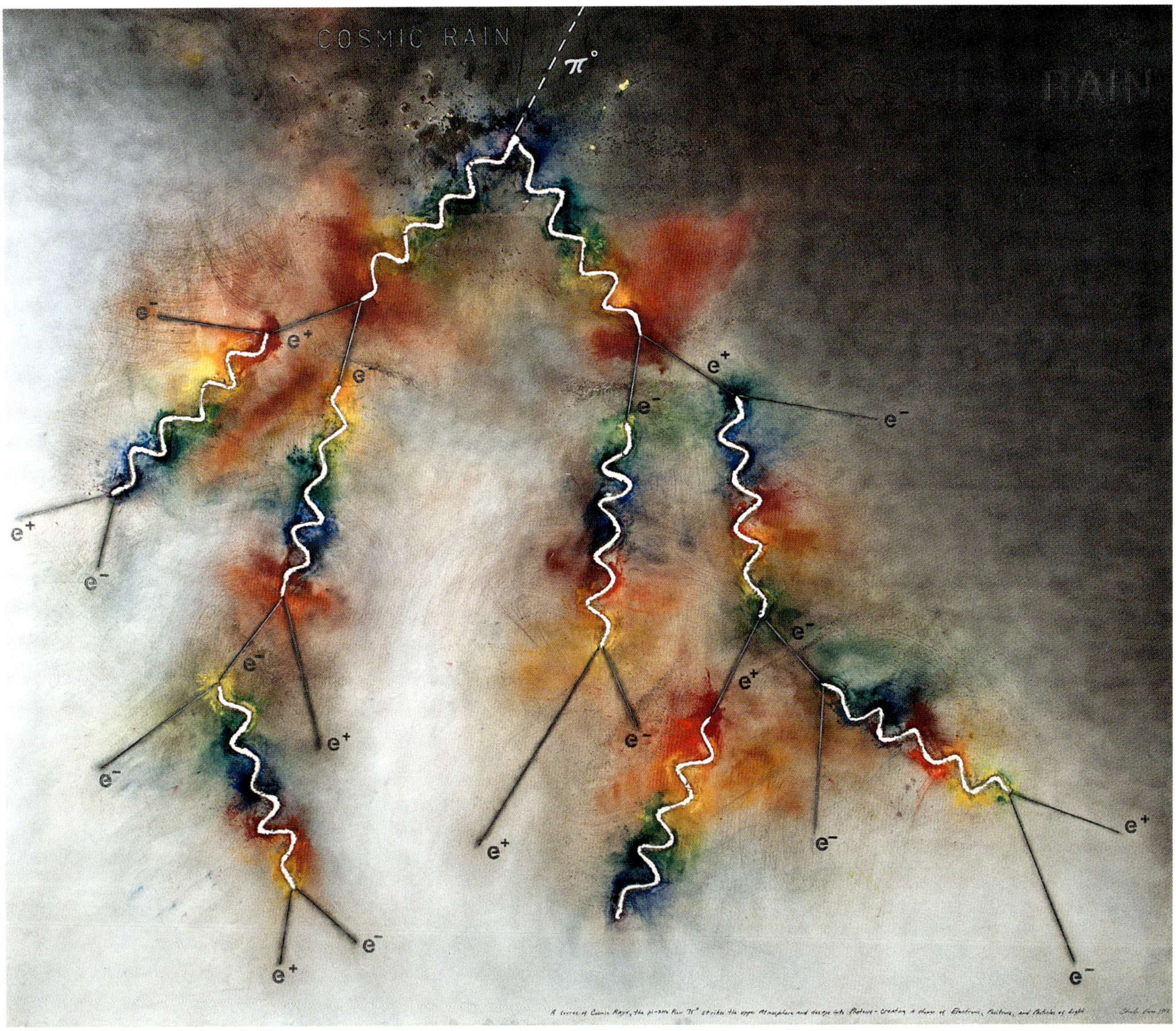

223
CHARLES ROSS (B. 1937)
COSMIC RAIN, 1993
POWDERED PIGMENT EXPLODED ONTO PAPER WITH GRAPHITE, 60½ X 71¾ IN. (153.7 X 182.2 CM)

Pierce's *Mons 2*, an allusion to the revelations one might find on a mountain peak (fig. 225), offers another experience. The work exudes a mystical light that changes with the cycle of the seasons and passing of hours of the day. Before sunrise the work is opaque and stark, but these qualities shift as light begins to stream in through a window and finally become tranquil as daylight recedes. Conceptually, this work reflects daily and seasonal physical and spiritual transformations in life. Rather than being visually static, it functions as a visual counterpart to human cycles: joy and pain, life and death, death and rebirth.

The light that bounces off Pierce's sculptures alludes to psychological and emotional qualities, for example, white light corresponding to purity, red light to passion, and blue to coldness. Such correspondences in Pierce's works invariably lead many to describe the light in her sculptures as spiritual. From a broader perspective, they are conceptual works

224
JENNIFER JOSEPH (B. 1966)
#9.2, 2006
ACUPUNCTURE NEEDLES AND WIRE, 38 x 15 x 15 IN. (96.5 x 38.1 x 38.1 CM)

OPPOSITE
225
FLORENCE MILLER PIERCE (1918–2007)
MONS 2, 1988
RESIN ON PLEXIGLAS, 88 x 14 x 2 IN. (223.5 x 35.6 x 5.1 CM)

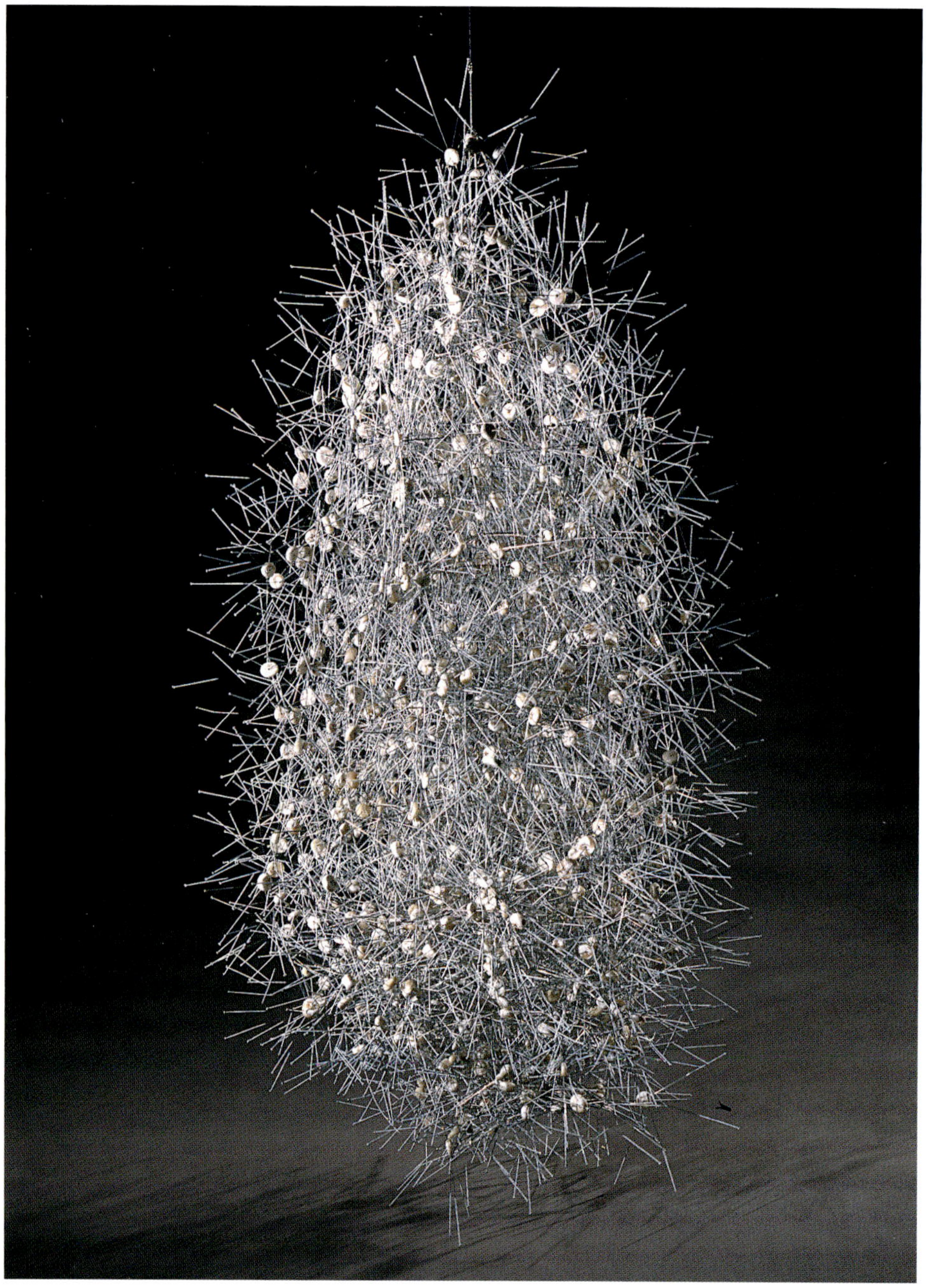

about time and the permanence of change in our daily lives. In many ways, Pierce's sculptures exemplify the quest for spirituality outside of organized religion at the end of the twentieth century.

By the end of the twentieth century, many New Mexico artists refocused on subjects that had been important earlier in the century but created highly personal expressions that transcended predictable genres and cultural stereotypes. This newfound freedom addressed political, social, and spiritual concerns in ways that had been unthinkable only a decade earlier, when much New Mexico art revolved around formalist concerns.

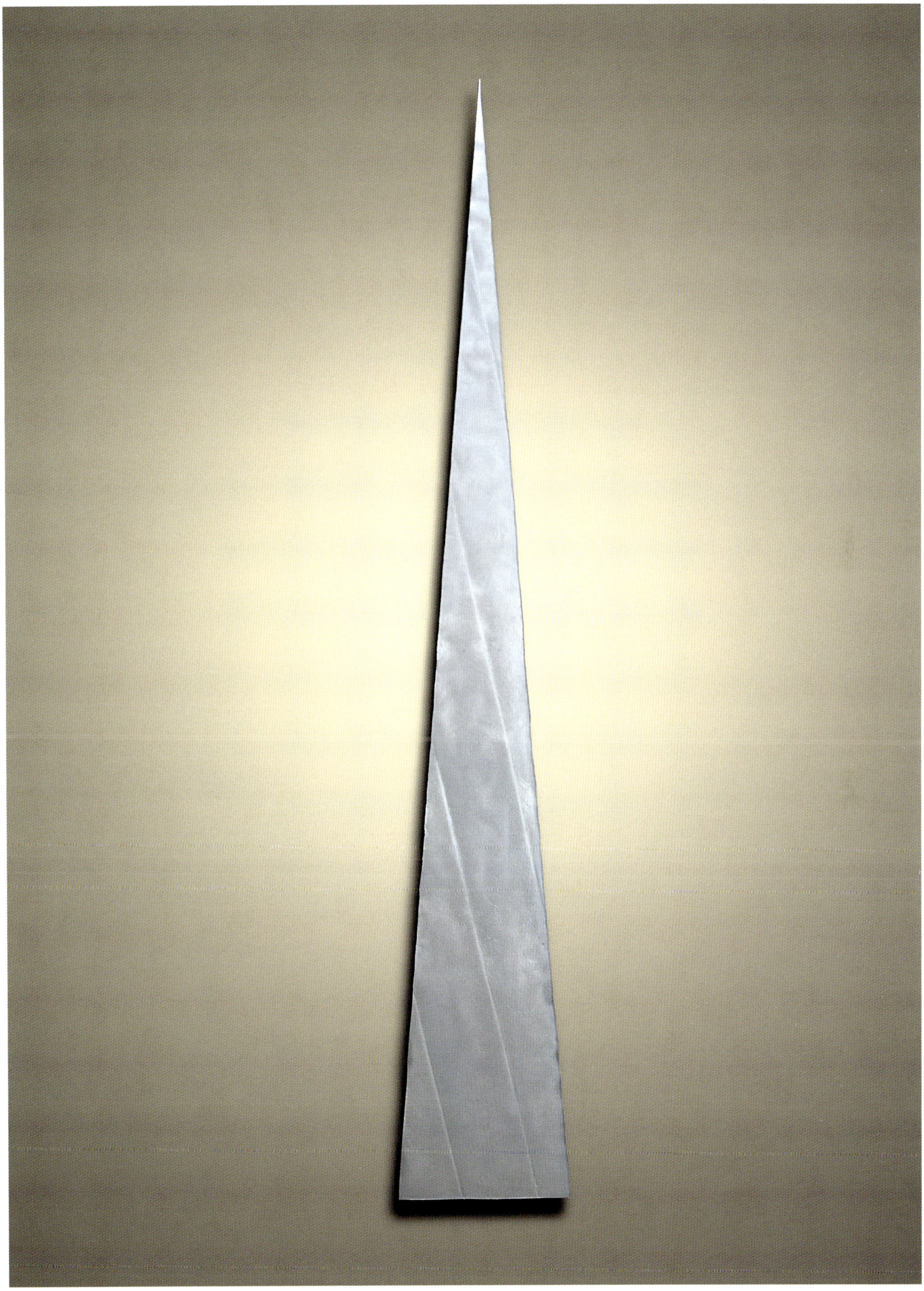

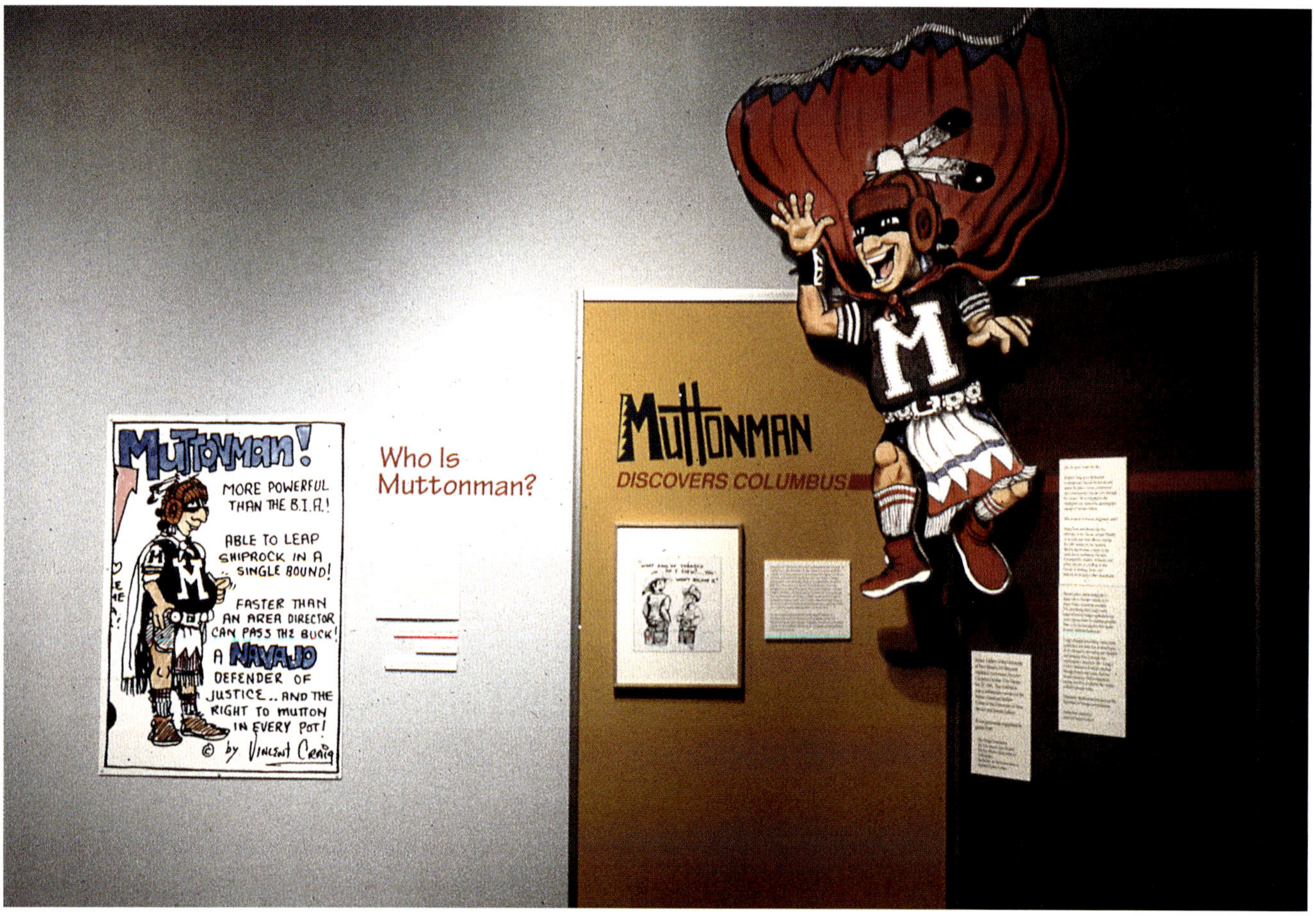

MUTTONMAN!
MORE POWERFUL THAN THE B.I.A.!
ABLE TO LEAP SHIPROCK IN A SINGLE BOUND!
FASTER THAN AN AREA DIRECTOR CAN PASS THE BUCK!
A NAVAJO DEFENDER OF JUSTICE.. AND THE RIGHT TO MUTTON IN EVERY POT!
© by Vincent Craig
Who Is Muttonman?
MUTTONMAN
DISCOVERS COLUMBUS

CHAPTER 9

Rethinking the Past—Envisioning the Future

In the two decades before the 1992 Columbus Quincentennial, images such as T. C. Cannon's *Washington Landscape with Peace Medal Indian* (see fig. 217) reverberated through New Mexico. Cannon's work initiated a late-twentieth-century movement that used art as a means of rethinking western history and the relationships between Native peoples and the federal government. In such art, humor and touches of irreverence underscore criticism but do not overwhelm either the subject or the audience.

Promotions around the Columbus Quincentennial motivated many Native artists to offer alternative perspectives. Diné performance artist and cartoonist Vincent Craig became a local hero when he lampooned the federal government's policy toward Native people in the *Navajo Times* newspaper. Craig invented the character Muttonman, a Diné shepherd who acquired superhuman powers after drinking uranium-contaminated water from the 1979 Church Rock uranium tailings pond spill and then challenged the Bureau of Indian Affairs and other agencies. For the Columbus Quincentennial, Craig created a series of cartoons that explained how Muttonman found Columbus when he was lost at sea and saved him from certain death (fig. 226). The cartoons were shown at the Experimental Gallery at the Smithsonian Institution in Washington, DC, the Navajo Tribal Museum in Window Rock, Arizona, and the Museum of Indian Arts and Culture in Santa Fe.

Jaune Quick-to-See Smith had been making prints and paintings that addressed stereotypes about Native peoples for more than a dozen years when she began focusing on the meaning of Columbus for Native peoples. *Paper Dolls for a Post-Columbian World* plays with ethnic, gender, and class issues as individuals put on and take off paper items of clothing. In *Flathead Headdress Collected by White's to Decorate Homes* (fig. 227), the artist notes that non-Indians acquired this object "after priests and U.S. Gov't. banned cultural ways such as speaking Salish and drumming, singing, or dancing." She further notes that the headdress was "sold at Sotheby's today for thousands of dollars to White Collectors seeking romance in their lives." In such works Quick-to-See Smith challenges the propriety of buying and selling ethnographic material across cultural boundaries.

Thomas Barrow explores the transformation of photography from a nineteenth-century reproductive medium into fine art during the twentieth century and how commercialization of photography and its popularity have impacted the medium. He considers to what extent photography has been devalued as photographic technology has made the medium easily available to many people. In the 1970s and 1980s, Barrow marked, marred, and collaged photographs into composite works of art.

226
VINCENT CRAIG (1950–2010)
MUTTONMAN DISCOVERS COLUMBUS AT THE SMITHSONIAN'S EXPERIMENTAL GALLERY, 1993
INSTALLATION

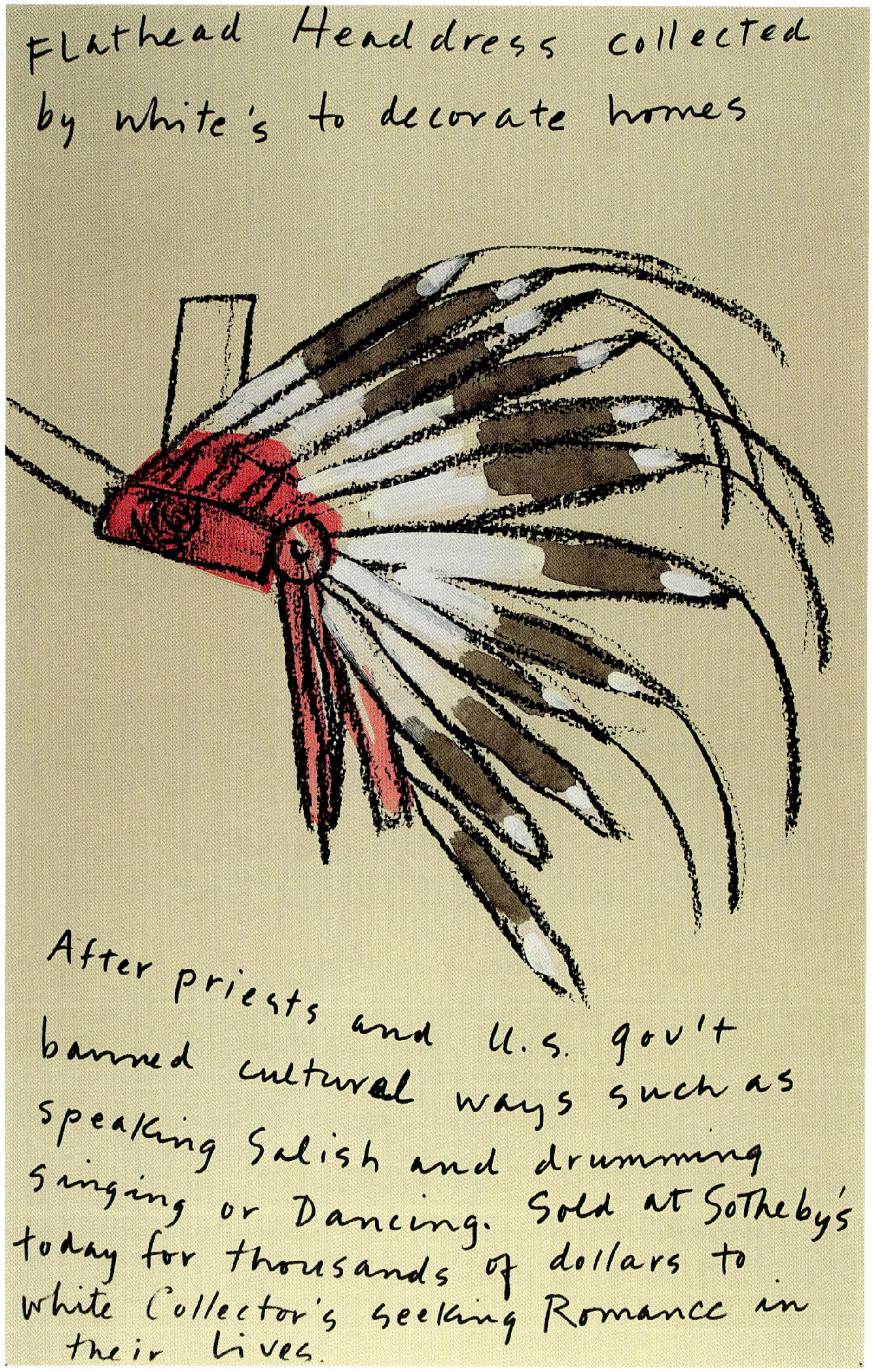

227
JAUNE QUICK-TO-SEE SMITH (B. 1940)
FLATHEAD HEADDRESS COLLECTED BY WHITE'S TO DECORATE HOMES (FROM THE SERIES PAPER DOLLS FOR A POST-COLUMBIAN WORLD), 1991
WATERCOLOR AND PENCIL OVER PHOTOCOPY PAPER, 17 X 11 IN.
(43.2 X 27.9 CM)

Barrow's mixed-media sculpture *The End of Photography* from 1993–94 (fig. 228) is an autobiographical work that references his changing attitudes toward the medium. The sculpture, a box of defaced photo-gaffes, looks like a box of trash from an artist's studio glued together with caulk. As a final irreverent gesture, Barrow elevated the box to a lofty position with four broken instant cameras that serve as feet. *End of Photography* challenges viewers to ponder the direction of photography as art, asking whether photographic images will be valued in the future.

Elizabeth Kay, who has been a painter of *retablos* since the 1980s, lives in the northern New Mexico village of Cundiyo, a few miles from Chimayó, where her husband runs a shop specializing in locally made *retablos* and *bultos*. Kay describes *Our Lady of Mount Pedernal* (fig. 229) in terms of her devotion to the arts and their unique role in the life and spirituality of New Mexico. She notes that individuals rely on the inspirational words of

228
THOMAS BARROW (B. 1938)
THE END OF PHOTOGRAPHY, 1993–1994
MIXED MEDIA WITH SX-70 PHOTOGRAPHS, 16 x 17 x 22 IN.
(40.6 x 43.2 x 55.9 CM)

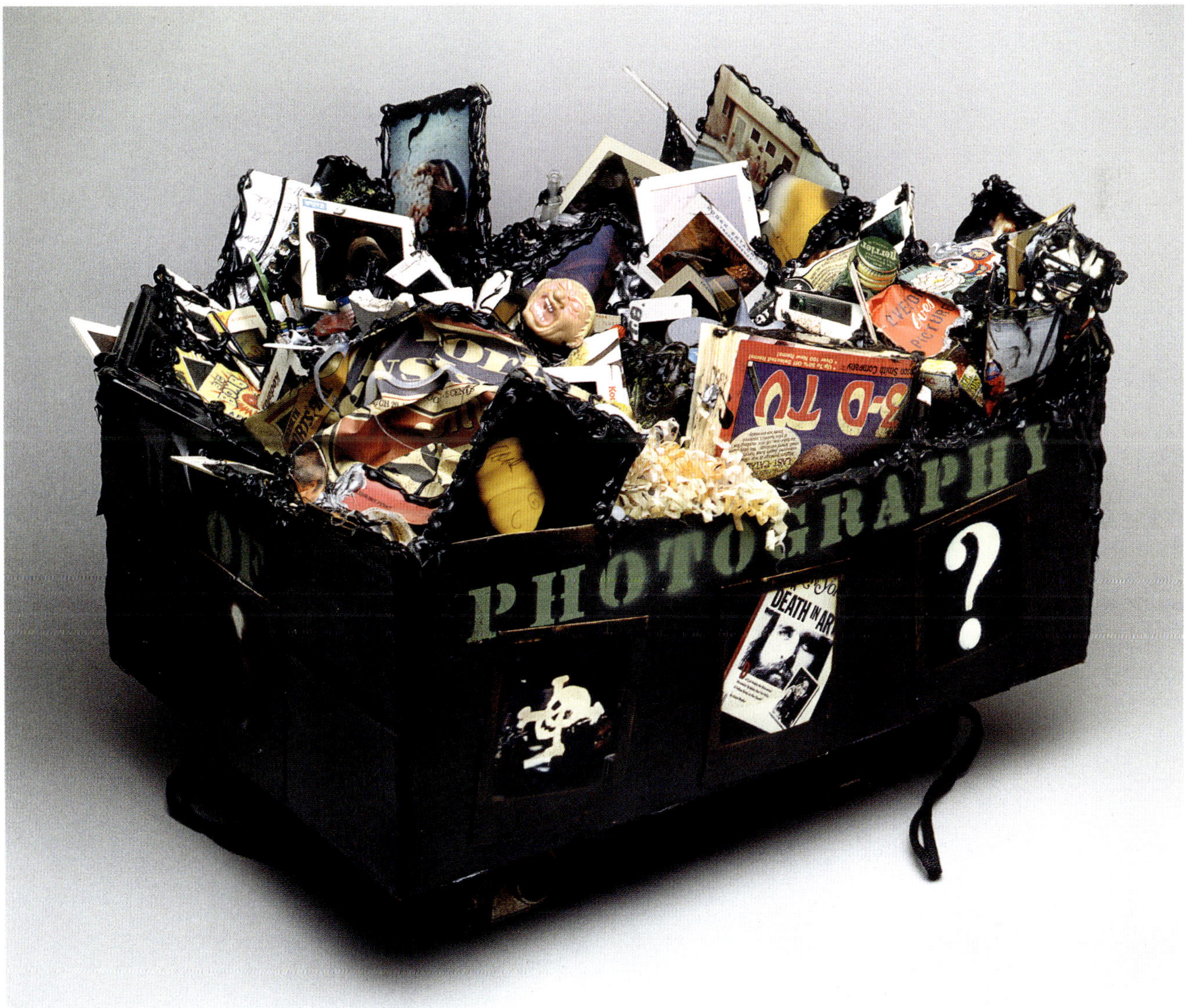

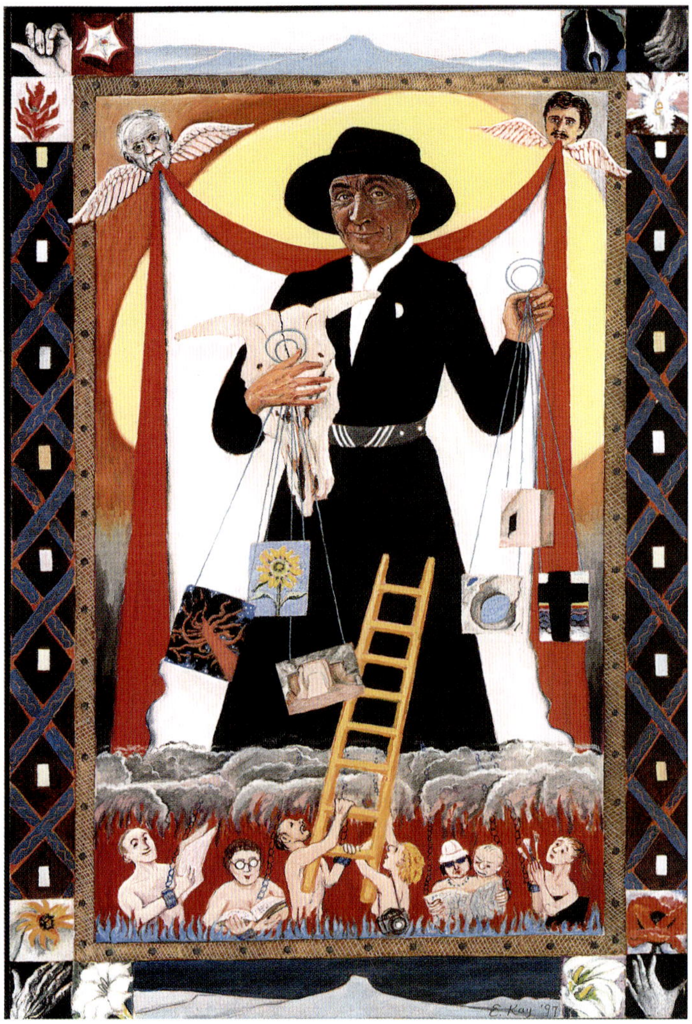

229
ELIZABETH KAY (B. 1953)
OUR LADY OF MOUNT PEDERNAL (TWENTIETH-CENTURY DEVOTION TO THE ARTS), 1997
OIL ON BOARD, 11⅝ X 7⅞ IN. (29.5 X 20 CM)

saints, as she did when she decided "to start anew—to strip away what I had been taught—to accept as true my own thinking."

Local wit has become an important survival strategy for New Mexico artists as economic booms have turned to busts. Donald Woodman's *Pedaling the Camino Real* (fig. 230) references the independent spirit of New Mexico. Woodman shot this portrait/self-portrait of himself and his wife, artist Judy Chicago, riding on the mesa overlooking Belen, New Mexico, with the sunlit Manzano Mountains in the background, an image that alludes to Marie Chabot's 1944 photograph of Georgia O'Keeffe on the buddy seat of Maurice Grosser's Harley-Davidson motorcycle.

Recent scholarship has discussed the diversity of Hispanic communities during the Spanish Colonial period. As a result, families are discovering information about ancestors that previously had been unknown. Richard Romero's *Guadalupana* (fig. 231) is a study in reclaiming a family's genealogy. Romero's version of Our Lady of Guadalupe includes a Star of David, an indication that he had discovered that some of his ancestors may have been *conversos*, or Jews who converted to Catholicism but continued to practice

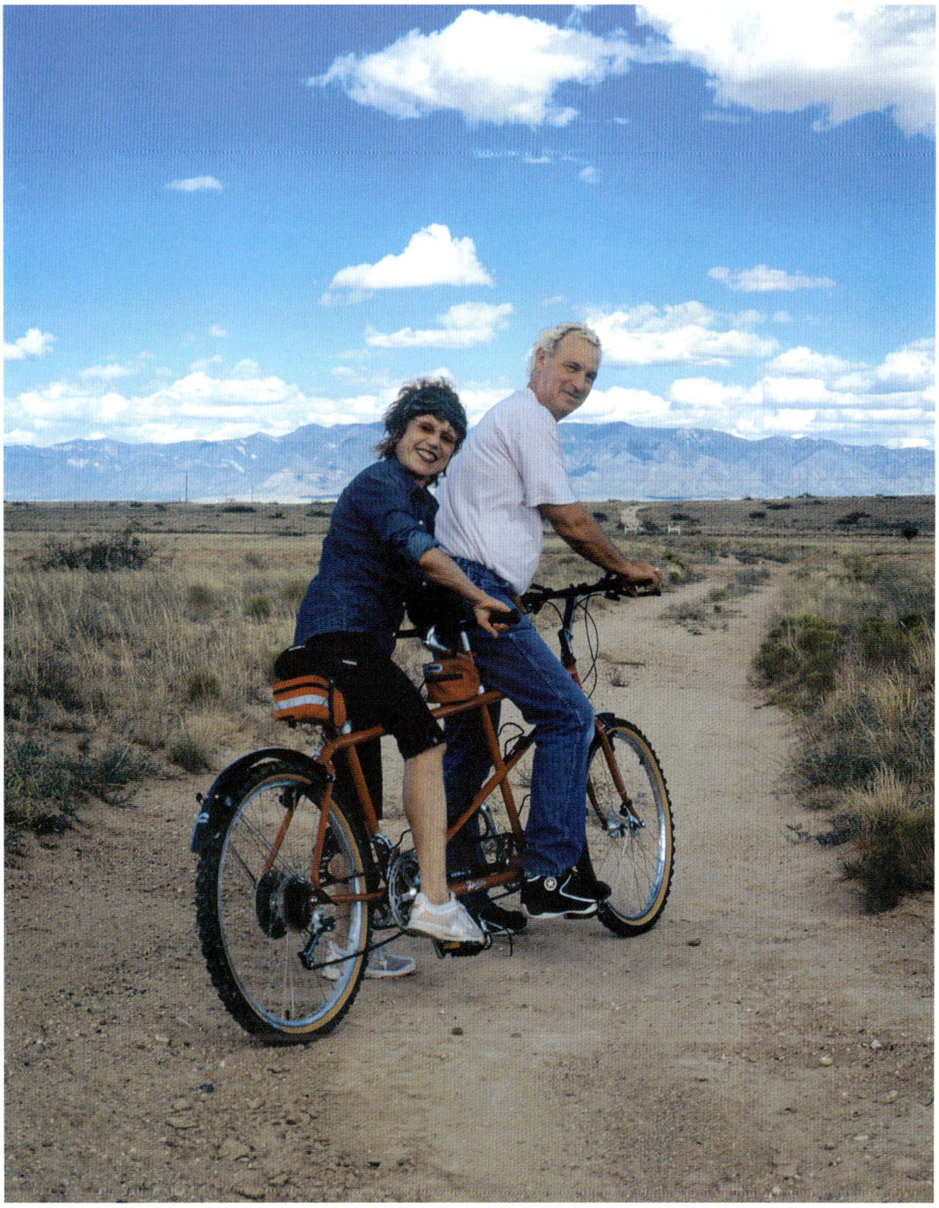

230
DONALD WOODMAN (B. 1945)
PEDALING THE CAMINO REAL, 2010
UNIQUE DIGITAL PRINT FROM TRANSPARENCY, 24 X 20 IN. (61 X 50.8 CM)

some Jewish rituals. During Spanish rule in New Mexico, the practice of Judaism was considered an offense against the Church, and individuals accused of doing so were sent to Mexico City to be tried by the Catholic Inquisition. Romero's carving is a powerful reminder of the diversity of family origins, as well as the diversity of beliefs that have coalesced in New Mexico.

Cartoonist Patrick Oliphant uses Billy the Kid, the legendary outlaw hero associated with the Lincoln County War, to satirize national politics. In his 1999 cartoon *Billy the Kid* (fig. 232), Oliphant transformed the nineteenth-century opponent of the Santa Fe Ring into a parody of President Bill Clinton. Oliphant based his character on a tintype of

231
RICHARD ROMERO (B. 1976)
GUADALUPANA, 1994
HAND-ADZED PINE AND WATER-BASED PAINTS, 48 X 27 X 1⅛ IN.
(121.9 X 68.6 X 2.9 CM)

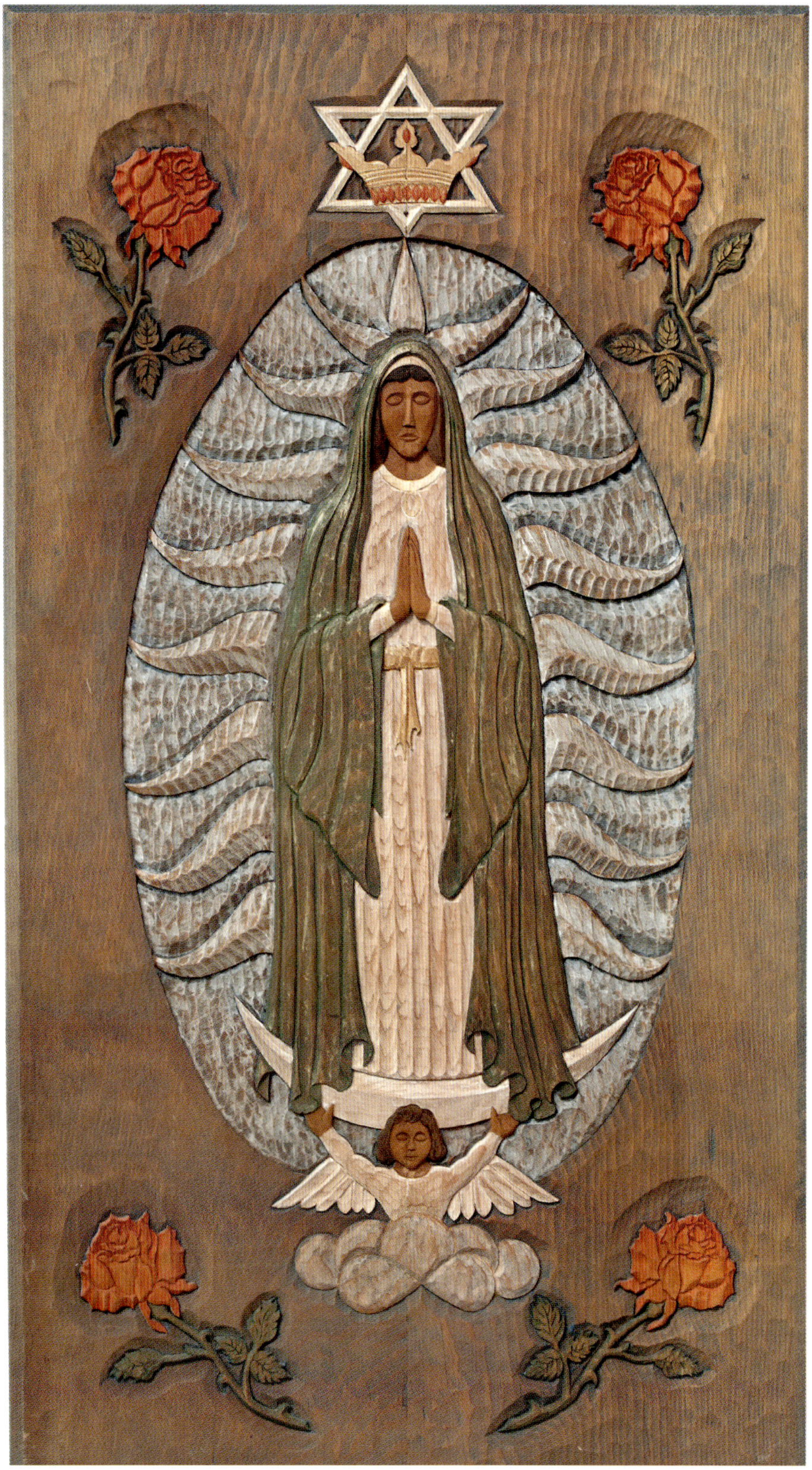

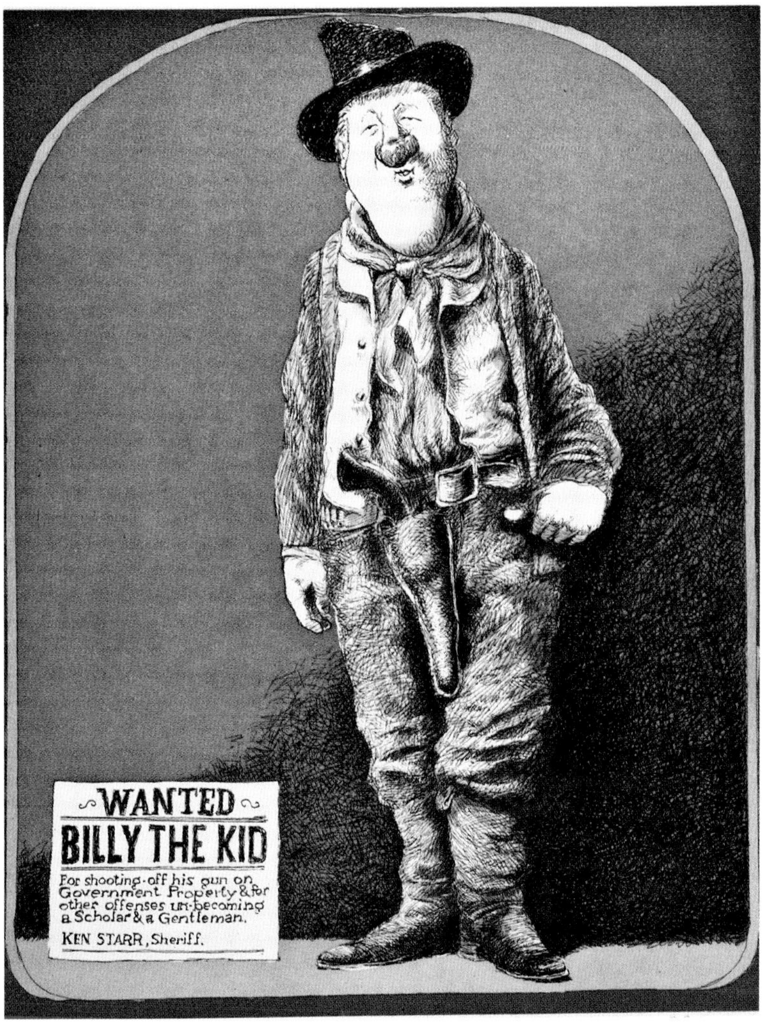

232
PATRICK OLIPHANT (B. 1935)
BILLY THE KID, 1999
ETCHING, 19 X 16 IN. (48.3 X 40.6 CM)

Billy the Kid but accentuated the features to make the image look more like Clinton. In this way, the artist pokes fun at the peculiarities of political life in a manner that is uniquely New Mexican.

Eddie Dominguez comments on the art of New Mexico in *Time of Reflection* (fig. 233), a ceramic work of 157 cups, plates, bowls, glasses, pitchers, vases, and candlesticks in a black cupboard. Each ceramic piece is finished in a shiny, highly reflective, black glaze. The set plays off the ironic visual situation where black objects that are extremely reflective appear white with dark shadows. The title of the work refers both to the surface characteristics of the pieces and to conceptual thinking about the art of the region. Clearly, the piece refers to Maria and Julian Martinez and the commercial development of their invention of matte-on-black pottery.

New Mexico art often seems contradictory or confusing to those unfamiliar with the region's multicultural mixing of languages and subjects. Ray Martín Abeyta addresses this quandary in *Indios* (fig. 234), a painting that challenges viewers to think about the terms used to describe New Mexico art. The composition appears as if it were an eighteenth-

233
EDDIE DOMINGUEZ (B. 1957)
TIME OF REFLECTION, 2001
GLAZED CERAMIC AND PAINTED WOOD,
85 X 43½ X 15½ IN. (215.9 X 110.5 X 39.4 CM)

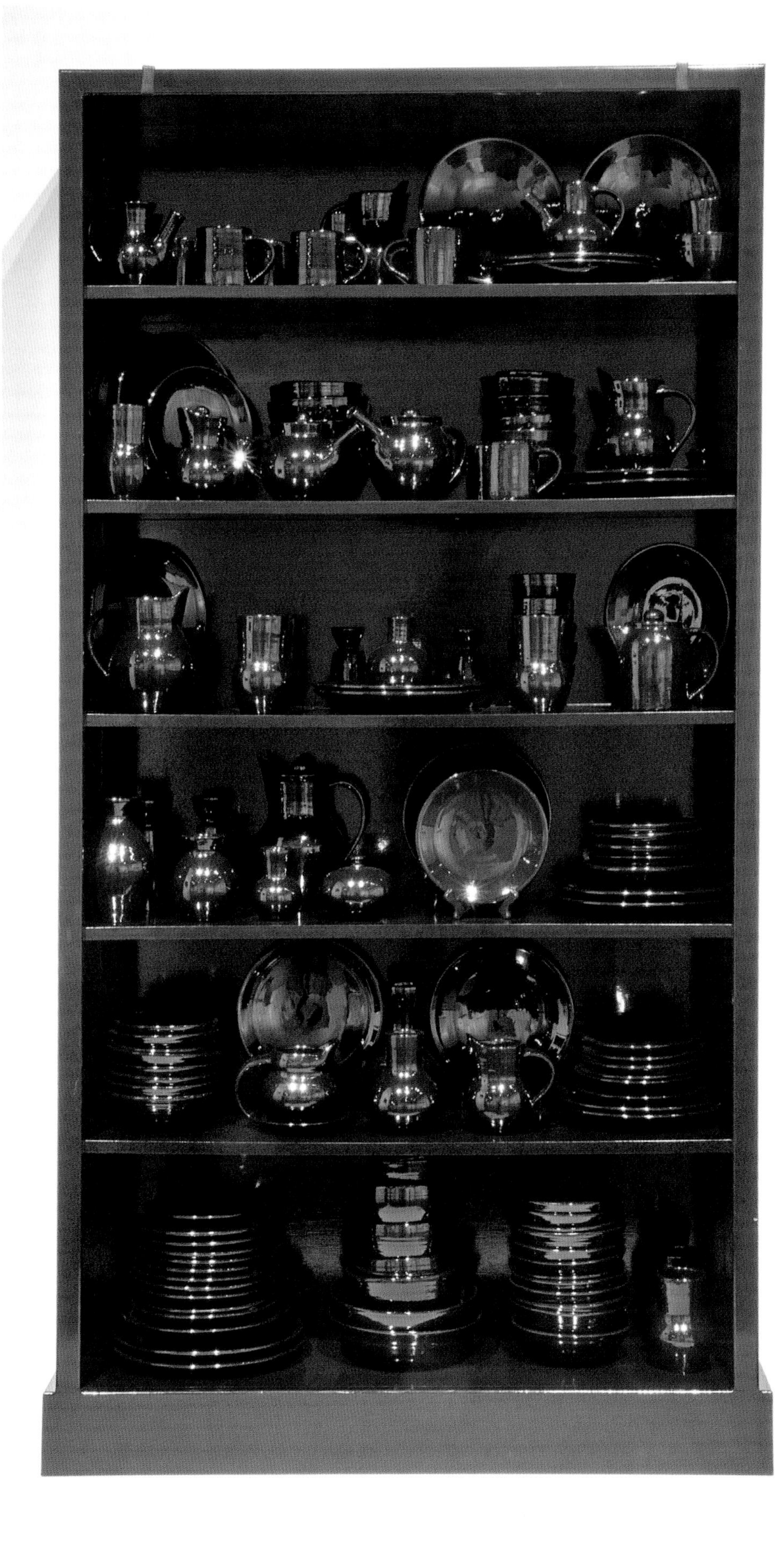

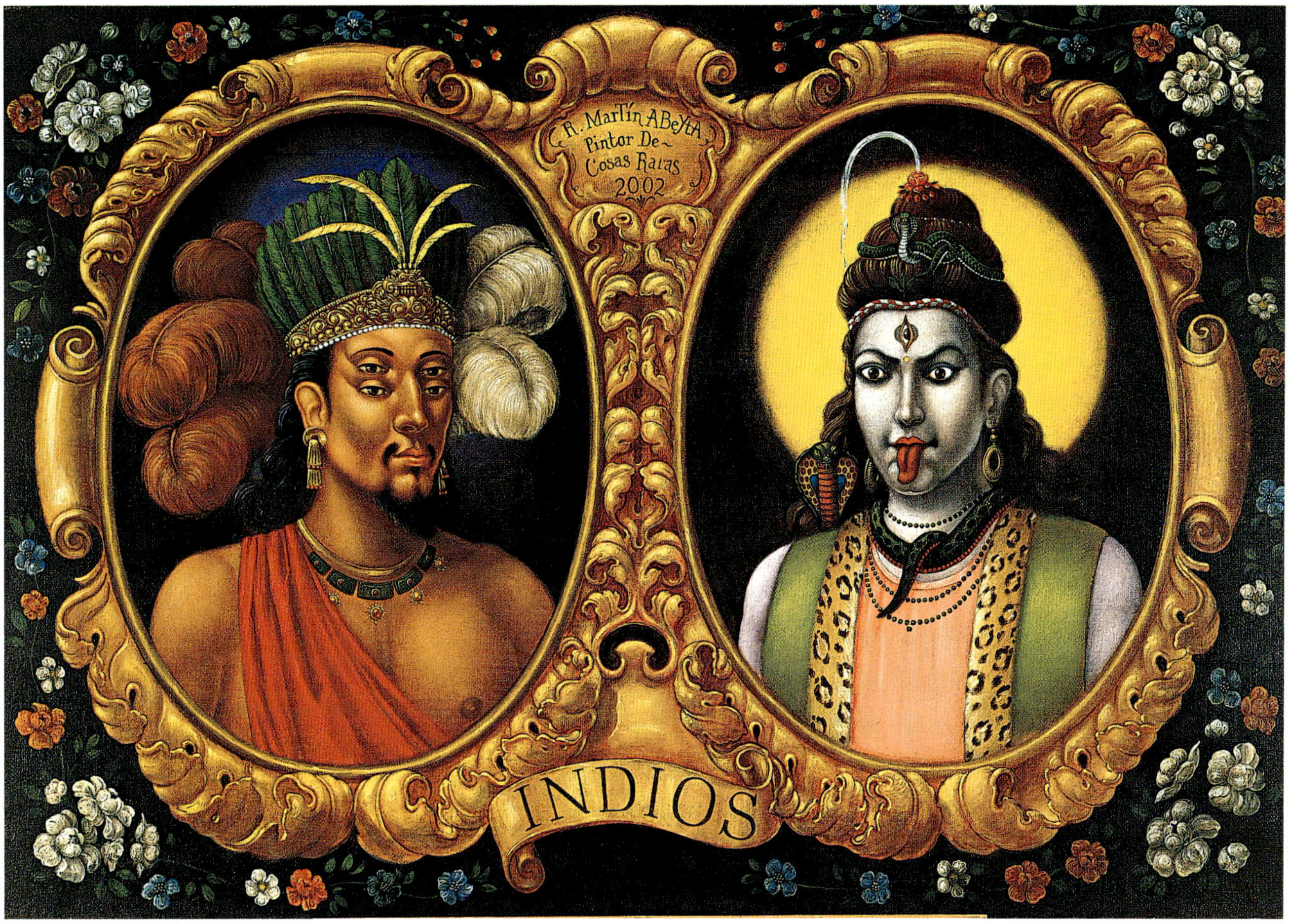

234
RAY MARTÍN ABEYTA (B. 1956)
INDIOS, 2002
OIL ON LINEN, 37 X 54 IN. (94 X 137.2 CM)

century religious painting from the highlands of Peru or Bolivia. The subject refers to Christopher Columbus's confusion about geography on encountering land in the Americas. He described the people he met as Indians, creating five centuries of terminological confusion.

The figures in the painting refer to the stereotyping of religious icons in ways that are elusive. Abeyta depicts the Hindu deity Shiva with his third eye representing enlightenment, while the serpents surrounding his body reference wisdom and eternity and the Ganges flows through his hair. The other deity depicted seems to be a fusion of the Meso-American god Quetzalcoatl and Shiva, but the portrayal is based on a misinterpretation of iconography. Hence Abeyta shows Quetzalcoatl appropriately wearing Quetzal feathers but also ostrich feathers, as if he were African. In short, Abeyta questions the accuracy of stereotypes and terminologies based on them, which are often misleading.

Marcus Amerman is known for representational images created with colored beads sewn into complex designs. In *Back to the Blanket* (fig. 235), he reinterprets Gerald Cassidy's painting *Cui Bono?*, wondering, along with Cassidy, who benefits from New Mexico art. Amerman's beadwork turns the image into a grid that closely approximates the color shifts and compositional attributes of Cassidy's painting. With *Back to the Blanket*, Amer-

235

MARCUS AMERMAN (B. 1959)

BACK TO THE BLANKET, 2008

SIZE 13 CUT BEADS ON FABRIC,

8 X 4½ IN. (20.3 X 11.4 CM)

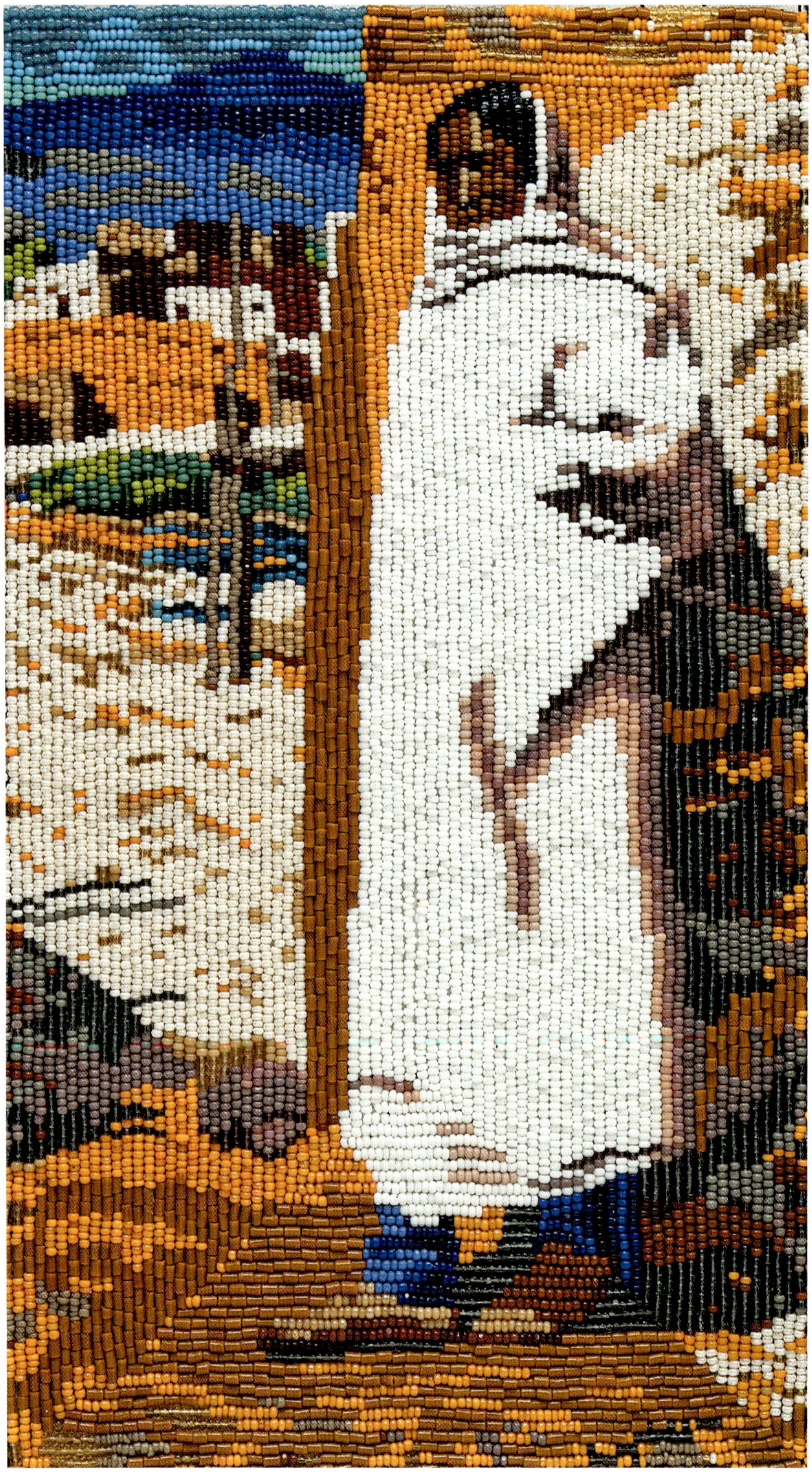

man reverses the actions of early twentieth-century academic painters and their images of Native peoples superimposed with colonial views. In this work, Amerman appropriates Cassidy's appropriations.

Diego Romero connects past, present, and future through ceramic vessels that allude to prehistoric Mimbres pottery (see fig. 52) and incorporates narrative scenes in the bottoms of bowls. Romero read comic books as a child and paints scenes inside his vessels in a cartoonlike style. *Siege of Santa Fe* (fig. 236) presents Romero's 2009 view of the 1680 Pueblo Revolt. The border is painted with an isomeric frieze that flips and flops around the rim of the vessel. Painted and unpainted areas of the frieze are equally balanced, making the design appear as a white design on a black background. However, when this visual illusion occurs on the narrative images of warriors, soldiers, and a mission in flames, it takes a few seconds to identify the subject as three pairs of Pueblo and Hispanic warriors posed in front of a burning mission with neither side apparently winning, implying a cultural standoff. *Siege* is graphically powerful and politically interesting, raising questions that encourage contemplation.

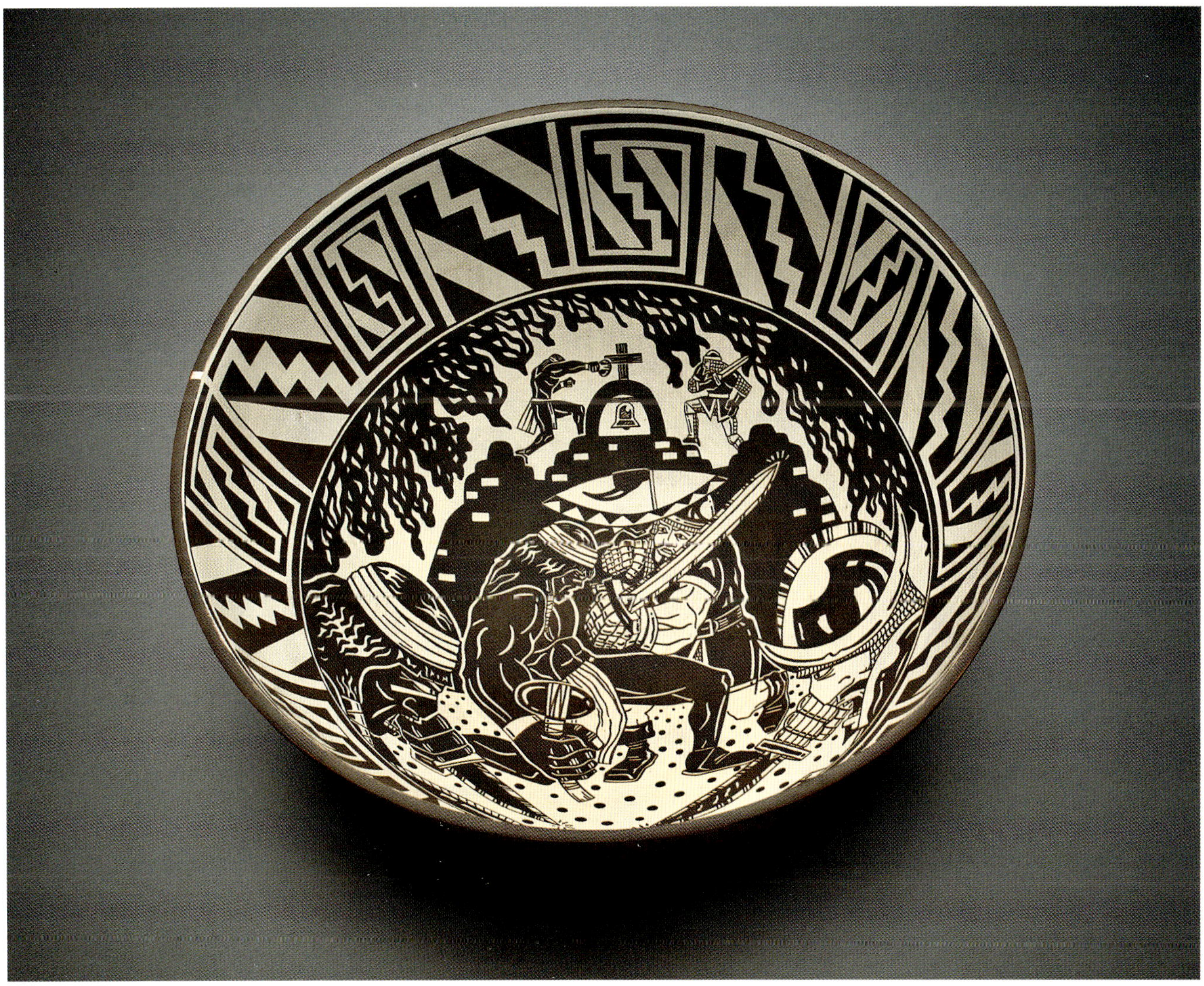

236
DIEGO ROMERO (B. 1964)
SIEGE OF SANTA FE, 2009
TERRACOTTA, 7¼ x 16 in. (18.4 x 40.6 cm)

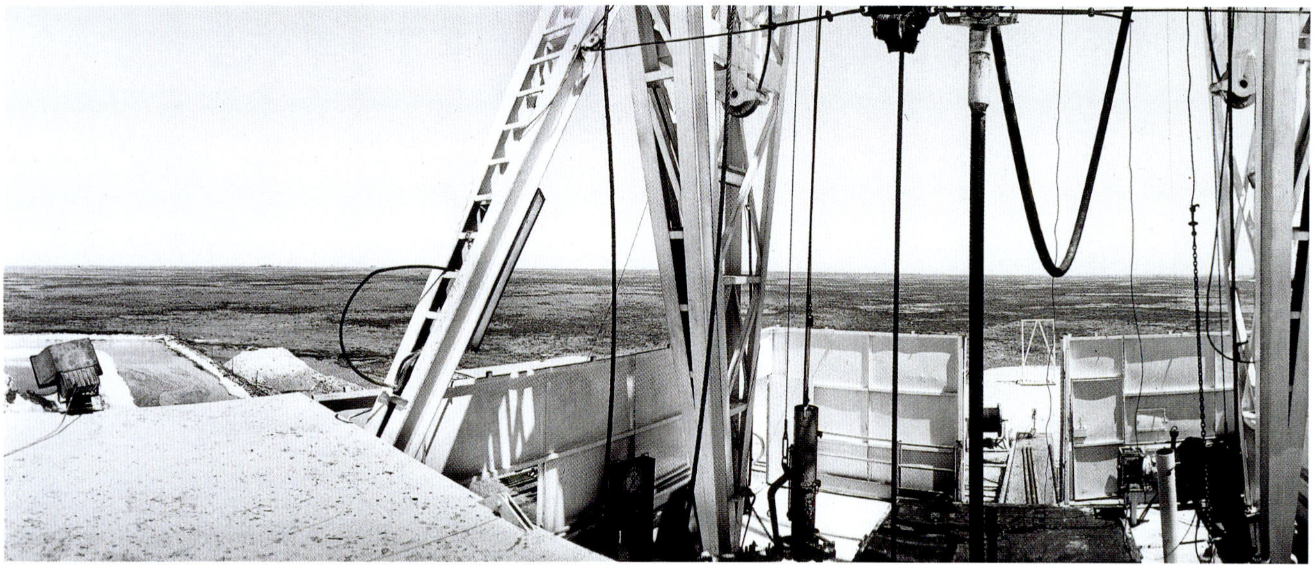

237
MARY E. PECK (B. 1952)
YATES PETROLEUM COMPANY, EXPLORATORY WELL, WEST OF LOVINGTON, NEW MEXICO, 1983
SELENIUM-TONED GELATIN SILVER PRINT, 7 X 16¾ IN. (17.8 X 42.5 CM)

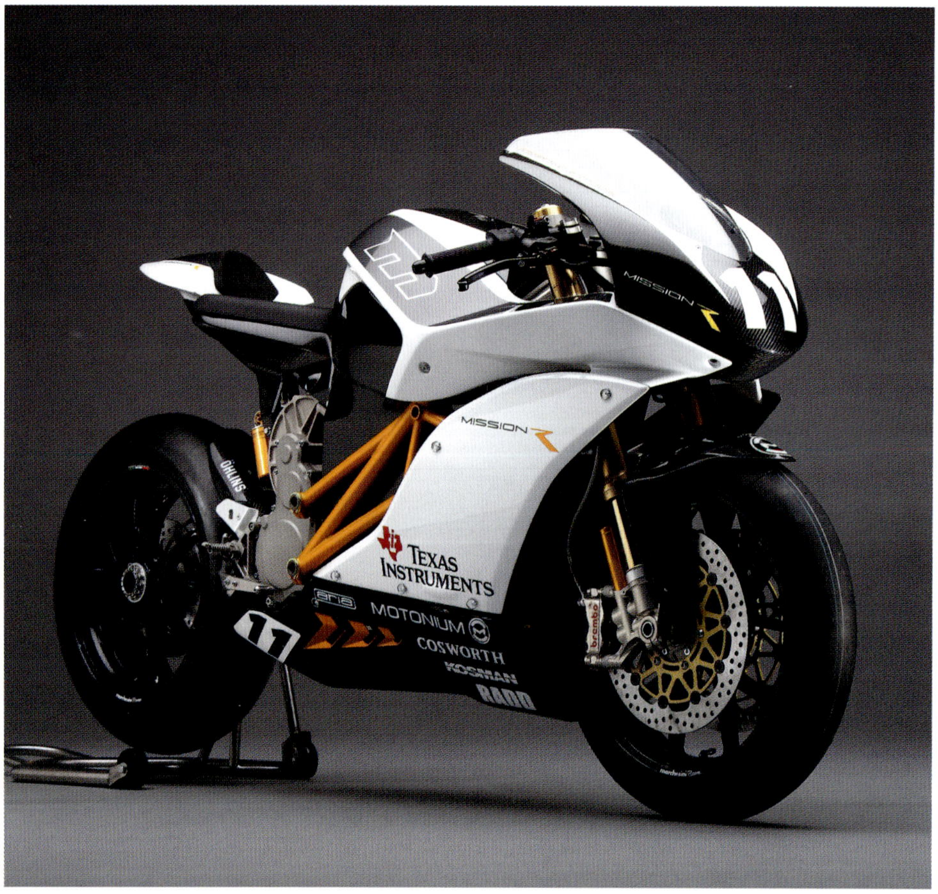

238
JAMES PARKER (B. 1946)
MISSION R ELECTRIC MOTORCYCLE, 2010
DIGITAL PHOTOGRAPH

At the end of the twentieth century, Mary E. Peck's photographs of the petroleum industry in New Mexico (fig. 237) underscore the state's important role in a gasoline-powered economy while revealing the hazards posed to the landscape. Other local artists are envisioning a carbon-neutral future. James Parker is an engineer who has been inventing and building experimental motorcycles for thirty years. Beginning in the 1980s he patented a series of motorcycle front ends that did not use bicycle-based twin forks. His most recent efforts involve designing the frame, engine housing, and transmission for Mission motors (fig. 238). Such artworks exemplify how artists have responded to recent social changes resulting from technological and economic transformations.

Artists making art about art became an important aspect of contemporary art in New Mexico at the end of the twentieth century. The most conceptually powerful works from the past continue to challenge artists to reposition those images and ideas in new cultural contexts. In the process, these works clarify the past and illuminate questions for the artistic culture.

AFTERTHOUGHTS

An underlying theme of this study is the dynamic between past and present, the historical and contemporary. As these works show, the past certainly influences the present, and it is difficult to consider the history of New Mexico art (figs. 239, 240) without superimposing contemporary attitudes.

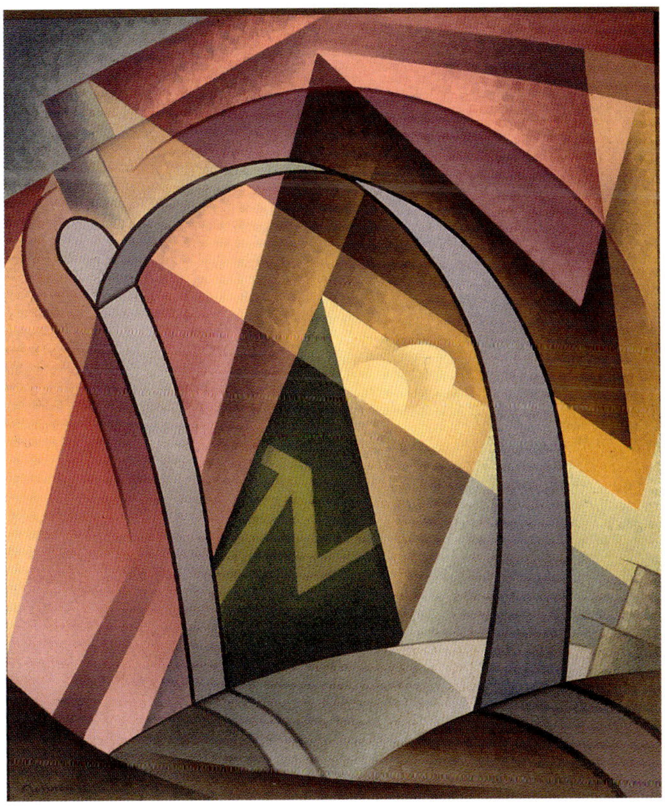

239
RAYMOND JONSON (1891–1982)
VARIATIONS ON RHYTHM N, 1932
OIL ON CANVAS, 37½ x 32½ IN.
(95.3 x 82.6 CM)

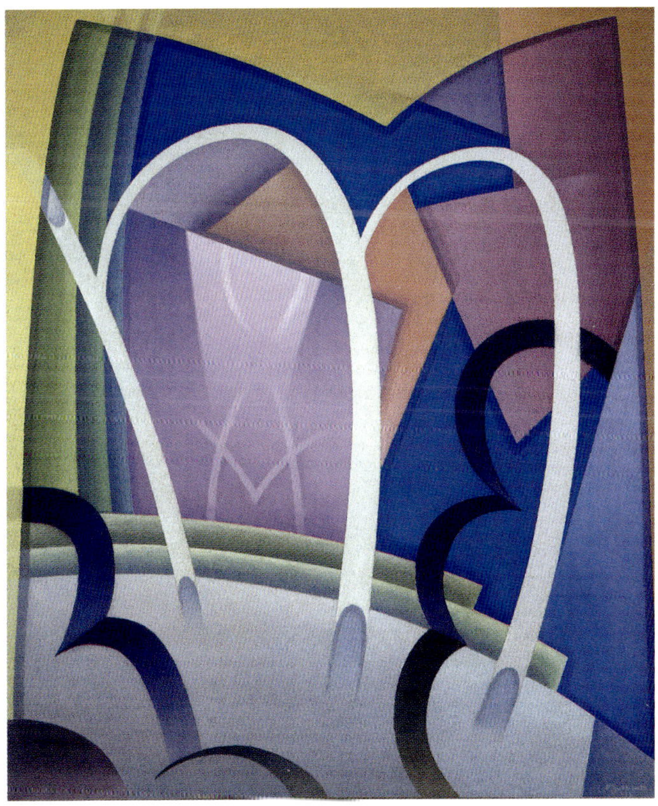

240
RAYMOND JONSON (1891–1982)
VARIATIONS ON RHYTHM M, 1932
OIL ON CANVAS, 38 x 33 IN.
(96.5 x 83.8 CM)

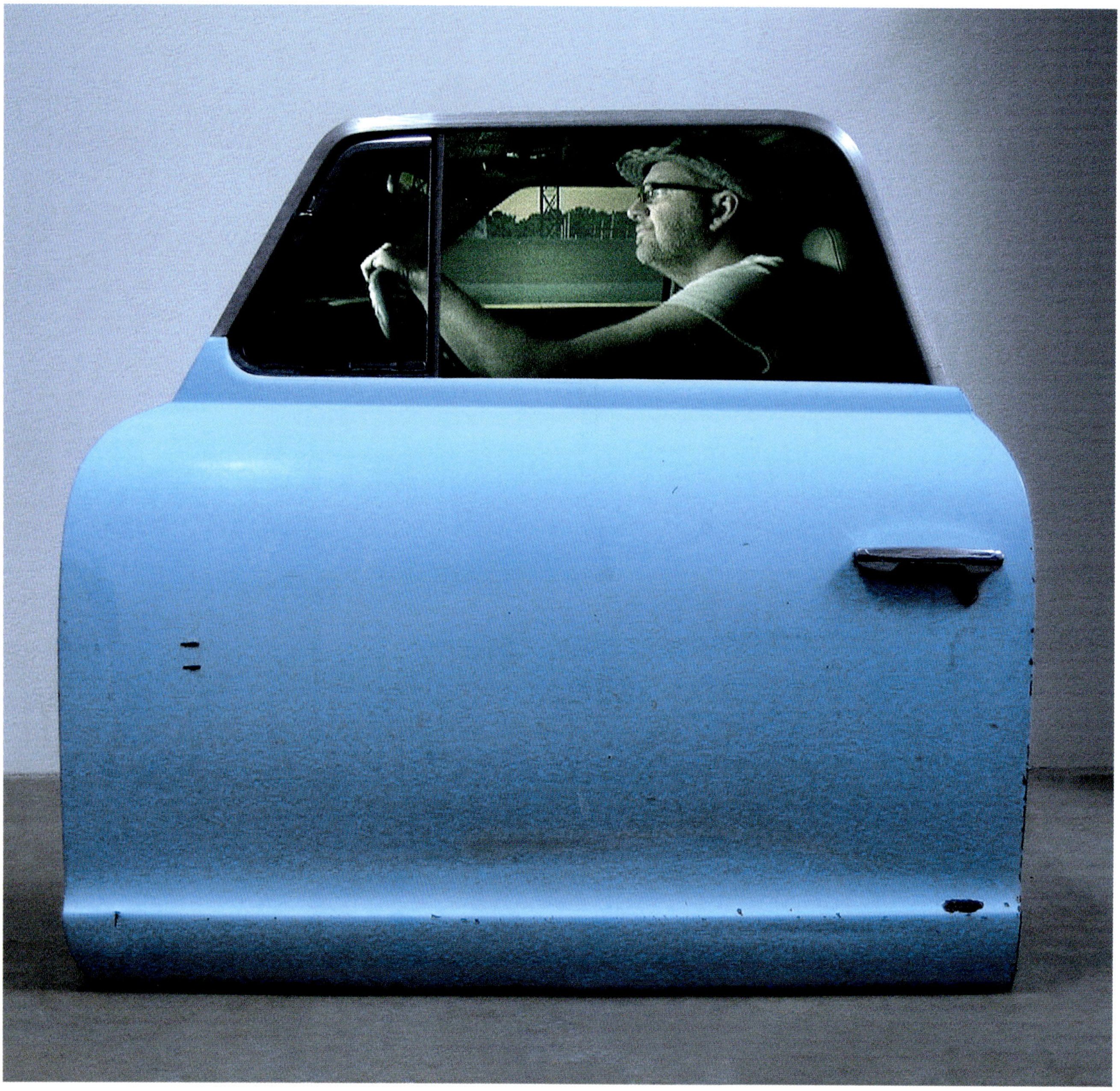

241
PETER SARKISIAN (B. 1965)
REGISTERED DRIVER: 58 RAMBLER, 2011
MIXED MEDIA AND VIDEO PROJECTION

Undoubtedly, future viewers will scoff at attitudes that seem acceptable today. Media artist Peter Sarkisian's *Registered Driver: 58 Rambler* (fig. 241) exemplifies this paradox as he projects a video image of himself as a modern driver on the window of a vintage automobile, conflating the present with history and casting history into the present.

This overview only begins to reveal the diversity of art that has been made in New Mexico. The chosen examples have focused on prime objects of change, those emphasizing artistic innovation, technological shifts, and changing worldviews. Presenting the history of New Mexico art as a single chronology helps to clarify cultural influence and fusions of aesthetic perspectives. In spite of interactions across cultural divides, ethnic traditions in the region have nevertheless retained their individuality.

It's about time to look at New Mexico art from this broader perspective and marvel at its dimensions.

Further Reading

THIS STUDY DEVELOPED FROM my early interest in Paleo-Indian stone tools as an undergraduate student working summers in Paul S. Martin's archaeological field school at Vernon, Arizona. One year, master knapper Don Crabtree demonstrated his skills, which I found mesmerizing. After experimenting with flint knapping, I quickly learned that it is not as simple as it looks. The experiences convinced me that such tools are also works of art that embody the social knowledge of Paleo-Indian bands.

New research on Paleo-Indians, which has increased interest in the earliest human activities in New Mexico, informs Chapter 1. David J. Meltzer's books are aimed at archaeological audiences but written in an accessible manner with interesting narratives that general readers can follow. His *First Peoples in a New World: Colonizing Ice Age America* and *Folsom: New Archaeological Investigations of a Classic Paleoindian Bison Kill* open up the lifeways of the first New Mexicans to a broad readership. *Clovis Revisited: New Perspectives on Paleoindian Adaptations from Blackwater Draw, New Mexico*, by Anthony T. Boldurian and John L. Cotter, describes the earliest discoveries of Clovis culture with extinct fauna, as well as experiments with Paleo-Indian materials. Many contemporary knappers rely on John Whittaker's *Flint Knapping: Making and Understanding Stone Tools* as a textbook for learning these skills, but the actual practice requires patience, experience, and a knowledge of suitable materials.

These volumes do not address Paleo-Indian materials in terms of the aesthetic qualities, which is my interest. The discussion of how contemporary interpretations consider knapping an artistic practice and stone tools as works of art presents my own ideas about the subject, which mesh with Jacques Maquet's distinction between works made to be art and those that become art by cultural transformation in *Introduction to Aesthetic Anthropology* (1979).

The background information presented in Chapter 2 summarizes general points about the discipline of archaeology made by Linda Cordell in her encyclopedic *Archaeology of the Southwest.* Stephen Lekson presents a provocative combination of the history of archaeology in the Southwest and a narrative of cultural life before European contact in *A History of the Ancient Southwest*. Stephen Plog, in *Ancient Peoples of the American Southwest*, gives a broad picture of Native American lifeways in Arizona, Colorado, New Mexico, and Utah.

While many people are familiar with the cultural traditions of the Ancestral Pueblo peoples of the greater Southwest, few are aware that these cultures marked astronomical events with petroglyphs carved into canyon walls. Anna Sofaer, the discoverer of the Sun Dagger (fig. 31), edited *Chaco Astronomy*, a volume that addresses sites where solar or lunar phenomena have been identified.

Stuart Peckham's *From This Earth: The Ancient Art of Pueblo Pottery* (1990) and Alfred E. Dittert Jr. and Fred Plog's *Generations in Clay: Pueblo Pottery of the American Southwest* (1980) offer surveys of Pueblo pottery from the earliest experiments to the historic period. These well-illustrated books are visually helpful, although both emphasize an anthropological approach. J. J. Brody's discussions of Ancestral Pueblo pottery in *Anasazi and Pueblo Painting* (1991) are accessible. *Mimbres Painted Pottery* (revised edition, 2004) includes mortuary images that are not included in this volume.

My discussion of Ancestral Pueblo design focuses on the use of positive and negative interlocking shapes as hallmarks of painted pottery and baskets. The term "isomers," used to describe these interlocking elements, is my own. Rather than being isolated phenomena, these positive and negative design motifs were created over vast areas of the Southwest and during more than five centuries of production.

Recent summaries provide new insights into the Spanish *entrada*, Pueblo Revolt, Hispanic reconquest, and the Mexican Republic. Thomas Chávez's *New Mexico: Past and Future* (2006) and John L. Kessell's *Pueblos, Spaniards, and the Kingdom of New Mexico* (2008) condense a complex history into lively narratives. Michael V. Wilcox, in *The Pueblo Revolt and the Mythology of Conquest* (2009), presents a history of Spanish and Pueblo relations from a Native view and clarifies the grievances that led to the Pueblo Revolt.

Against this backdrop, James F. Brooks investigates the class, caste, and social relationships during the Spanish Colonial period in *Captives and Cousins: Slavery, Kinship, and Community in the Southwest Borderlands* (2002). He explains the complexity within the Hispanic community, as well as the colonists' interactions with Comanche, Diné, and Pueblo groups, and describes how ethnic distinctions blurred as individuals married and economic relationships developed. Malcolm Ebright and Rick Hendricks reveal the complexities of life in northern New Mexico by concentrating on ethnic evolution and internal conflicts in *The Witches of Abiquiu* (2006). These works provide the cultural background for Chapter 3.

The breadth of these interactions is reflected in the art and material culture presented by William Wroth and Robin Farwell Gavin in *Converging Streams: Art of the Hispanic and Native American Southwest* (2010). In addition, there is a summary of Spanish Colonial art from the period in Gavin's *Traditional Arts of Spanish New Mexico*. In- depth discussions about *santero* production in New Mexico can be found in works by E. Boyd, such as *Popular Arts of Spanish New Mexico (1974),* and in more recent studies, such as Carmella Padilla and Donna Pierce's *Conexiones: Connections in Spanish Colonial Art* (2002). Because Hispanic art before 1680 was destroyed during the Pueblo Revolt, available imagery in this section emphasizes develpments in the *santero* tradition after 1780.

Discussions of Native pottery during the Spanish and American colonial periods include Francis H. Harlow's *Matte-Paint Pottery of the Tewa, Keres, and Zuni Pueblos*

(1973) and *Historic Pottery of the Pueblo Indians, 1680–1880* (1990), which Harlow wrote with Larry Frank.

The Territorial period initiated colonial relationships between the conquering Americans and the indigenous Native American and Hispanic communities. Marc Simmons's *New Mexico: An Interpretive History* (1988 reprint of 1977 edition) is particularly clear on this period. Because the imposition on Native and Hispanic communities of U.S. laws, economic relationships, religious rituals, and profiteering is reminiscent of Spain's dictates over the Pueblos during the *entrada,* I have described this as the American Colonial period in New Mexico.

The way art in the region changed rapidly after the arrival of railroads is expressed in collections of the New Mexico Museum of Art and in the literary magazines of the post-railroad era. Charles F. Lummis's writings in *Some Strange Corners of Our Country* and *The Spanish Pioneers* document his efforts to promote a colonial, southwesternist view and contain both racist descriptions of Hispanics and uncritical depictions of the Spanish colonists.

The first years after New Mexico achieved statehood were a time of rapid change. Chris Wilson examines this period in *The Myth of Santa Fe* (1997), a work that is both a cultural and architectural history. Dean A. Porter and Teresa Hays Eby's *Taos Artists and Their Patrons, 1898–1950* (1999) provides a beautifully illustrated view of academic painting during this period. Sharyn Rohlfsen Udall counters with *Modernist Painting in New Mexico, 1913–1935* (1984), a book that demonstrates the breadth of anti-academic art. A presentation of New Mexico art based on Edgar Lee Hewett's version of three cultures can be found in *Art in New Mexico, 1900–1945: Paths to Taos and Santa Fe,* by Charles C. Eldridge, Julie Schimmel, and William H. Truettner. Readers will find Kathryn Flynn's comprehensive *Treasures on New Mexico Trails* (1995) to be a tour guide to depression-era public art in the region. Native painting from The Studio at the Santa Fe Indian School is addressed by Bruce Bernstein and Jackson Rushing in *Modern by Tradition* (1995). These works are sources for the information in Chapters 5 and 6.

No single text summarizes the dramatic shifts in New Mexico art after World War II. Erika Doss catalogs the diversity of art that developed after the war in *Twentieth-Century American Art* (2002), which summarizes the movements that influenced New Mexico artists. The mainstreaming of the region's art is charted by Deborah Boll, Peter Walch, and MaLin Wilson in *Albuquerque '50s* (1989). The late-twentieth-century discussions emphasize monographs and collections of work by contemporary European-American, Hispanic, and Native American artists. Perhaps we are still too close to contemporary developments in New Mexico art to view these developments with dispassionate clarity.

The Art of New Mexico: How the West Is One (2007) reflects my interest in the social history of Southwest art and the dynamic that developed across ethnic and aesthetic divides. This work recognizes the artistic fusions that represent the oneness of New Mexico art, as well as the deep-rooted differences that maintain independence.

Readers will find that the bibliography only begins to address the diversity of information condensed into this volume.

Bibliography

Adams, Ansel

1983 *Examples: The Making of 40 Photographs.* Boston: Little Brown and Company.

Bartlett, Richard A.

1962 *Great Surveys of the American West.* Norman: University of Oklahoma Press.

Batkin, Jonathan

1999 *Clay People: Pueblo Indian Figurative Traditions*. Santa Fe: Wheelwright Museum of the American Indian.

1987 *Pottery of the Pueblos of New Mexico, 1700–1940.* Colorado Springs, CO: The Taylor Museum of the Colorado Springs Fine Arts Center.

Berlo, Janet, and Ruth B. Phillips

1998 *Native North American Art.* Oxford, England: Oxford University Press.

Bermingham, Peter

1980 *The New Deal in the Southwest, Arizona and New Mexico.* Tucson: University of Arizona Press.

Bernstein, Bruce

1994 "Potters and Patrons: The Creation of Pueblo Art Pottery." *American Indian Art* 20, no. 1 (Winter 1994): 70–79.

Bernstein, Bruce, and Jackson Rushing

1995 *Modern by Tradition*. Santa Fe: Museum of New Mexico Press.

Blumenschein, Ernest L.

1955 Letter to Reginald Fisher, June 1, 1955, NMMoA archives, Blumenschein file.

Boldurian, Anthony T., and John L. Cotter

1999 *Clovis Revisited: New Perspectives on Paleoindian Adaptations from Blackwater Draw, New Mexico*. Philadelphia: The University Museum and the University of Pennyslvania.

Boll, Deborah, Peter Walch, and MaLin Wilson

1989 *Albuquerque '50s.* Albuquerque: University of New Mexico Press.

Boyd, E.

1998 *Saints and Saint Makers of New Mexico*, revised edition. Santa Fe: Western Edge Press.

1974 *Popular Arts of Spanish New Mexico.* Santa Fe: Museum of New Mexico Press.

1972 *The New Mexico Santero.* Reprint. Santa Fe: Museum of New Mexico Press.

Briggs, Charles L.

1980 *The Wood Carvers of Cordova, New Mexico: Social Dimensions of an Artistic "Revival."* Knoxville: University of Tennessee Press.

Brody, J. J.
2004 *Mimbres Painted Pottery*, revised edition. Santa Fe: School of American Research Press.

1991 *Anasazi and Pueblo Painting*. Santa Fe: School of American Research Press.

1971 *Indian Painters and White Patrons*. Albuquerque: University of New Mexico Press.

Brooks, James F.
2002 *Captives and Cousins: Slavery, Kinship, and Community in the Southwest Borderlands.* Chapel Hill: University of North Carolina Press.

Carrillo, Charles M., and Thomas J. Steele
2008 *A Century of Retablos.* Phoenix and New York: Phoenix Art Museum and Hudson Hills Press.

Chávez, Thomas
2006 *New Mexico: Past and Future.* Albuquerque: University of New Mexico Press.

Coke, Van Deren
1979 *Photography in New Mexico: From the Daguerreotype to the Present.* Albuquerque: University of New Mexico Press.

1963 *Taos and Santa Fe: The Artist's Environment, 1882–1942.* Albuquerque: University of New Mexico Press.

Cordell, Linda
1997 *Archaeology of the Southwest. 2d ed.* San Diego, CA: Academic Press.

Coulter, Lane, and Maurice Dixon Jr.
1990 *New Mexico Tinwork, 1840–1940.* Albuquerque: University of New Mexico Press.

Cushing, Frank H.
1882–83 "My Adventures in Zuñi." (Part 1) *The Century* 25, no. 2 (December 1882–83): 191–207. (Part 2) *The Century* 25, no. 4 (February 1883): 502–11. (Part 3) *The Century* 25, no. 1 (May 1883): 28–47.

Dittert, Alfred E. Jr., and Fred Plog
1980 *Generations in Clay: Pueblo Pottery of the American Southwest.* Flagstaff, AZ: Northland Press.

Dixon, E. James
1999 *Bones, Boats and Bison: Archaeology and the First Colonization of Western North America*. Albuquerque: University of New Mexico Press.

Doss, Erika
2002 *Twentieth-Century American Art.* Oxford, England: Oxford University Press.

Douglas, Frederic H., and René d'Harnoncourt
1941 *Indian Art of the United States.* New York: Museum of Modern Art and Arno Press.

Dubin, Margaret
2001 *Native America Collected.* Albuquerque: University of New Mexico Press.

Dunbar-Ortiz, Roxanne
2007 *Roots of Resistance: A History of Land Tenure in New Mexico.* Norman: University of Oklahoma Press.

Dunn, Dorothy
1968 *American Indian Painting.* Albuquerque: University of New Mexico Press.

Ebright, Malcolm, and Rick Hendricks
2006 *The Witches of Abiquiu.* Albuquerque: University of New Mexico Press.

Eldridge, Charles C., Julie Schimmel, and William H. Truettner
1986 *Art in New Mexico,1900–1945: Paths to Taos and Santa Fe.* New York: Abbeville Press.

Fergusson, Erna
1985 *New Mexico: A Pageant of Three Peoples.* Reprint. Albuquerque: University of New Mexico Press.

"Fine Exhibit of Pottery." *El Palacio* 7, nos. 7–8 (July 1920): 217.
1920

Fleming, Paula Richardson, and Judith Lynn Luskey
1993 *Grand Endeavors of American Indian Photography.* Washington, DC: Smithsonian Institution Press.

Flynn, Kathryn, ed.
1995 *Treasures on New Mexico Trails.* Santa Fe: Sunstone Press.

Frank, Larry, and Francis H. Harlow
1990 *Historic Pottery of the Pueblo Indians, 1680–1880.* Atglen, PA: Schiffer Publishing, Ltd.

Gavin, Robin Farwell
1994 *Traditional Arts of Spanish New Mexico.* Santa Fe: Museum of New Mexico Press.

Graburn, Nelson H. H., ed.
1978 *Ethnic and Tourist Arts: Cultural Expressions from the Fourth World.* Berkeley: University of California Press.

Gutiérrez, Ramón A.
1991 *When Jesus Came the Corn Mothers Went Away: Marriage, Sexuality, and Power in New Mexico, 1500–1846.* Stanford, CA: Stanford University Press.

Halseth, Odd S.
1926 "The Revival of Pueblo Pottery Making." *El Palacio* 21 (15 September 1926): 135–54.

Hambridge, Jay
1967 *The Elements of Dynamic Symmetry.* Reprint. New York: Dover Publications.

Harlow, Francis H.
1973 *Matte-Paint Pottery of the Tewa, Keres, and Zuni Pueblos.* Santa Fe: Museum of New Mexico Press.

Hartley, Marsden
1922 "The Scientific Esthetic of the Redman." *Art and Archaeology* 13 (March 1922): 113–19.

1920 "Red Man Ceremonials: An American Plea for American Esthetics." *Art and Archaeology* 9 (January 1920): 7–14.

1919a "America As Landscape." *El Palacio* 6, no. 21(21 December 1919): 340–42.

1919b "Tribal Esthetics Dance Drama." *El Palacio* 6, no. 4 (8 February 1919): 53–55.

1918 "Aesthetic Sincerity." *El Palacio* 5, no. 20 (9 December 1918): 332–33.

Haynes, C. Vance Jr., and Bruce B. Huckell, eds.
2007 *Murray Springs: A Clovis Site with Multiple Activity Areas in the San Pedro Valley, Arizona.* Tucson: University of Arizona Press.

Hewett, Edgar Lee
1930 *Ancient Life in the American Southwest.* Indianapolis, IN: Bobbs-Merrill Company.

1918 "On the Opening of the Art Galleries." *Art and Archaeology* 7, nos. 1–2 (January–February 1918): 50–54.

Hirasuna, Delphine
2005 *The Art of Gaman: Arts and Crafts from the Japanese American Internment Camps 1942–1946.* Berkeley, CA: Ten Speed Press.

Howard, Kathleen L., and Diana F. Pardue
1996 *Inventing the Southwest: The Fred Harvey Company and Native American Art.* Flagstaff, AZ: Northland Publishing and the Heard Museum.

Hubbell, J. L.
1905 *Navajo Blankets and Indian Curios.* Ganado, AZ: J. L. Hubbell, Indian Trader.

Huckell, Bruce
1995 "Of Marshes and Maize: Preceramic Agricultural Settlements in the Cienega Valley, Southeastern Arizona." *Anthropological Papers*, no. 59. Tucson: University of Arizona Press.

Jackson, Helen Hunt
1880 *A Century of Dishonor.* Reprint. New York: Harper and Row.

Kaufman, Alice, and Christopher Selser
1985 *The Navajo Weaving Tradition: 1650 to the Present.* Tulsa, OK: Oak Council Books.

Kent, Kate Peck
1983 "Spanish , Navajo or Pueblo? A Guide to the Identification of Nineteenth-Century Southwestern Textiles." In Marta Weigle, *Hispanic Arts and Ethnohistory in the Southwest.* Santa Fe: Ancient City Press, 135–65.

Kessell, John L.
2008 *Pueblos, Spaniards, and the Kingdom of New Mexico.* Norman: University of Oklahoma Press.

Kilby, David
2008 *An Investigation of Clovis Caches: Content, Function, and Technological Organization.* Ph.D. diss. Department of Anthropology, University of New Mexico.

Kubler, George
1962 *The Shape of Time: Remarks on the History of Things.* New Haven, CT: Yale University Press.

Kuhn, Thomas S.
1962 *The Structure of Scientific Revolutions.* Chicago: University of Chicago Press.

Lamadrid, Enrique R.
2010 "Santiago y La Cruz Emplumada/St. James and the Plumed Cross." In William Wroth and Robin Farwell Gavin, *Converging Streams: Art of the Hispanic and Native American Southwest.* Santa Fe: Museum of Spanish Colonial Art, 147–155.

Lanmon, Dwight P., Lorraine Welling Lanmon, and Dominique Coulet du Gard
2007 *Josephine Foarde and the Glazed Pottery of Laguna Pueblo.* Albuquerque: University of New Mexico Press.

Lekson, Stephen H.
2008 *A History of the Ancient Southwest.* Santa Fe: School for Advanced Research Press.

LeBlanc, Stephen A.
2004 *Painted by a Distant Hand.* Cambridge, MA: Peabody Museum Press, Harvard University.

Lewis, Nancy Owen
2007 *A Peculiar Alchemy: A Centennial History of the School of American Research 1907–2007.* Santa Fe: School of American Research Press.

Lippard, Lucy R.
1998 *The Lure of the Local: Senses of Place in a Multicentered Society*. New York: New Press.

1990 *Mixed Blessings: New Art in a Multicultural America.* New York: Pantheon Books.

Lummis, Charles F.
1993 *The Spanish Pioneers*. Chicago: A. C. McClurg & Co.

1892 *Some Strange Corners of Our Country: The Wonderland of the Southwest.* New York: Century Company.

1889 "The Penitent Brothers." *The Cosmopolitan* 7, no.1 (May 1889): 41–51.

Lynes, Barbara Buhler, with Lesley Poling-Kempes and Frederick W. Turner
2004 *Georgia O'Keeffe and New Mexico: A Sense of Place.* Princeton, NJ: Princeton University Press and the Georgia O'Keeffe Museum.

MacCannell, Dean
1992 *Empty Meeting Grounds: The Tourist Papers*. London: Routledge.

1976 *The Tourist.* New York: Schocken Books.

Maquet, Jacques
1979 *Introduction to Aesthetic Anthropology*. Malibu, CA: Undena Publications.

Mather, Christine
1982 *Colonial Frontiers.* Santa Fe: Museum of International Folk Art.

Mather, Christine, and Jack Parsons
1993 *Santa Fe Style.* New York: Rizzoli.

Meltzer, David J.
2009 *First Peoples in a New World: Colonizing Ice Age America.* Berkeley: University of California Press.

2006 *Folsom: New Archaeological Investigations of a Classic Paleoindian Bison Kill.* Berkeley: University of California Press.

Nestor, Sarah
1978 *The Native Market of the Spanish New Mexican Craftsmen, Santa Fe, 1933–1940.* Santa Fe: Colonial New Mexico Historical Foundation.

Newcomb, Franc Johnson
1981 *Hosteen Klah*. Norman: University of Oklahoma Press.

Nunn, Tey Marianna
2001 *Sin Nombre: Hispana and Hispano Artists of the New Deal Era*. Albuquerque: University of New Mexico Press.

Padilla, Carmella, and Jack Parsons
2009 *Rancho de las Golondrinas: Living History in New Mexico's La Cienega Valley.* Santa Fe: Museum of New Mexico Press.

Padilla, Carmella, and Donna Pierce
2002 *Conexiones: Connections in Spanish Colonial Art.* Santa Fe: Museum of New Mexico Press.

Pearson, Ralph M.
1925 *How to See Modern Pictures*. New York: The Dial Press.

Peckham, Stuart
1990 *From This Earth: The Ancient Art of Pueblo Pottery*. Santa Fe: Museum of New Mexico Press.

Penney, David W.
2004 *North American Indian Art*. London and New York: Thames & Hudson.

Pierce, Donna, and Marta Weigle
1996 *Spanish New Mexico: The Spanish Colonial Arts Society Collection*. Santa Fe: Museum of New Mexico Press.

Plog, Stephen
1997 *Ancient Peoples of the American Southwest.* London: Thames & Hudson.

Porter, Dean A., and Teresa Hays Eby
1999 *Taos Artists and Their Patrons, 1898–1950.* South Bend, IN: Snite Museum of Art, University of Notre Dame.

Preucel, Robert W.
2002 *Archaeologies of the Pueblo Revolt: Identity, Meaning, and Renewal in the Pueblo World*. Albuquerque: University of New Mexico Press.

Reimer, P. J. et al.
"IntCal104 Terrestrial 14C Age Calibration,)-26 cal kyr BP." *Radiocarbon* 46, no. 3 (2004): 1029–1058.

Rudnick, Lois Palken, ed.
2009 *Cady Wells and Southwestern Modernism*. Santa Fe: Museum of New Mexico Press.

1984 *Mabel Dodge Luhan: New Woman, New Worlds.* Albuquerque: University of New Mexico Press.

Rushing, W. Jackson III
1999 *Native American Art in the Twentieth Century*. London: Routledge.

1995 *Native American Art and the New York Avant-Garde.* Austin: University of Texas Press.

Sanchez, George I.
1970 *Forgotten People: A Study of New Mexicans.* 2d ed. Albuquerque: Calvin Horn.

Saunders, Charles Francis
1910 "Ceramic Art of the Pueblo Indians." *The International Studio* 61, no. 163 (September 1910): 66–71.

Scholder, Fritz
1979 *Indian Kitsch: The Use and Misuse of Indian Images.* Flagstaff, AZ: Northland Publishing and Heard Museum, 1979.

Simmons, Marc
1988 *New Mexico: An Interpretive History.* Reprint. Albuquerque: University of New Mexico Press.

Snow, David H.
1983 "A Note on Encomienda Economics in Seventeenth-Century New Mexico." In Marta Weigle, *Hispanic Arts and Ethnohistory in the Southwest.* Santa Fe: Ancient City Press, 347–57.

Sofaer, Anna, ed.
2008 *Chaco Astronomy*. Santa Fe: Ocean Tree Books.

"The Southwest Indian Fair." *El Palacio* 13, no. 8 (16 October 1922): 93–97.
1922

Stone, Mary Van
1931 *Permanent Gallery Catalogue of the State Art Museum at Santa Fe, New Mexico.* Santa Fe: Museum of New Mexico and School of American Research.

Traugott, Joseph
2007 *The Art of New Mexico: How the West Is One.* Santa Fe: Museum of New Mexico Press.

Trenton, Patricia, and Patrick T. Houlihan
1989 *Native Americans: Five Centuries of Changing Images.* New York: Harry N. Abrams.

Truettner, William H., ed.
1991 *The West As America: Reinterpreting Images of the Frontier, 1820–1920.* Washington, DC: Smithsonian Institution Press.

Trujillo, Michael L.
2009 *Land of Disenchantment: Latina/o Identities and Transformations in Northern New Mexico.* Albuquerque: University of New Mexico Press.

Turner, David, ed.
1992 *Artists of 20th-Century New Mexico.* Santa Fe: Museum of New Mexico Press.

Udall, Sharyn Rohlfsen
1996 *Contested Terrain: Myth and Meanings in Southwest Art.* Albuquerque: University of New Mexico Press.

1987 *Santa Fe Art Colony, 1900–1942.* Santa Fe: Gerald Peters Gallery.

1984 *Modernist Painting in New Mexico, 1913–1935.* Albuquerque: University of New Mexico Press.

Walter, Paul A. F.
1916 "The Santa Fe Art Movement." *Art and Archaeology* 4, no. 6 (December): 330-38.

Washburn, Dorothy K.
2011 "Pattern Symmetries of the Chaco Phenomenon." *American Antiquity* 76, no. 2 (April).

Weigle, Marta
2007 *Brothers of Light, Brothers of Blood.* Reprint. Santa Fe: Sunstone Press.

1983 *Hispanic Arts and Ethnohistory in the Southwest.* Santa Fe: Ancient City Press.

Weigle, Marta, and Barbara A. Babcock, eds.
1996 *The Great Southwest of the Fred Harvey Company and the Santa Fe Railway.* Phoenix, AZ: Heard Museum.

Whittaker, John
1994 *Flint Knapping: Making and Understanding Stone Tools.* Austin: University of Texas Press.

Wilcox, Michael V.
2009 *The Pueblo Revolt and the Mythology of Conquest.* Berkeley: University of California Press.

Williamson, Ray A.
1984 *Living the Sky.* Norman: University of Oklahoma Press.

Wilson, Chris
1997 *The Myth of Santa Fe: Creating a Modern Regional Tradition.* Albuquerque: University of New Mexico Press.

Wroth, William, and Robin Farwell Gavin, eds.
2010 *Converging Streams: Art of the Hispanic and Native American Southwest.* Santa Fe: Museum of Spanish Colonial Art.

Young, Jane M.
1988 *Signs from the Ancestors.* Albuquerque: University of New Mexico Press.

Zakian, Michael
1995 *Agnes Pelton: Poet of Nature.* Palm Springs, CA: Palm Springs Desert Museum.

Acknowledgments

New Mexico Art Through Time has been made possible by the generous support of the New Mexico Humanities Council and by Newman's Own Foundation.

Craig Newbill and John Andrews, Santa Fe; Dwight Pithcathly, Las Cruces; and Terry Bumpass, of the Raton Museum, Raton, have been particularly supportive and helpful with this project.

New Mexico Art Through Time is an official project of the New Mexico State Centennial 1912–2012. Veronica N. Gonzales, Secretary, Department of Cultural Affairs, and Jodi Delaney, Executive Director of the New Mexico Centennial 1912–2012, have provided valuable support and organizational direction for this project. Patricia and Arthur Newman have been supportive of the educational outreach potential of this New Mexico Centennial Project.

As always, the staff at the Museum of New Mexico Press, Anna Gallegos, Director; Mary Wachs, Editorial Director; David Skolkin, Art Director; Renee Tambeau, Marketing Director, have done a superb job publishing this book.

Colleagues at the New Mexico Museum of Art have generously discussed the project and lent their support. Thank you to Director Mary Kershaw, Mary Jebsen, Laura Addison, Merry Scully, Katherine Ware, Daniel Goodman, Devon Skeele, and Ellen Zieselman. Special thanks to Michelle Gallagher Roberts for her organizational skills and efforts in securing images for this book.

Carmella Padilla offered valuable suggestions and insightful comments during the manuscript phase. Blair Clark, Museum Resources Division, Department of Cultural Affairs, has carefully photographed most of these objects for reproduction.

Linda Cordell, professor emeritus, University of New Mexico, generously offered suggestions for books to read and objects to consider. The project would not have been possible without her assistance.

My discussions with the following colleagues have made the research for this book a pleasure. Thanks to Daniel Kosharek, MaryAnne Redding, Thomas Jaehn, Thomas Leech, and Thomas Chavez.

Thanks to Tom Antreasian, Andrew Connors, Debby Slaney, and David S. Nacke, Albuquerque Museum; Matthew F. Schmader, Parks and Recreation Department, Albuquerque; Lorann Pendleton, David Hurst Thomas, and Barry Landua, Department of Anthropology, American Museum of Natural History, New York; Susan Charlas, Aperture Foundation, Paul Strand Archive, Millerton, New York; George Crawford, John Montgomery, and David Kilby, Blackwater Draw Site and Eastern New Mexico University, Portales; Carla K. Bradmon, Denver Museum of Nature and Science; Kathleen Shields and Viviette Hunt, Hammersley Foundation, Albuquerque; Mim Dixon, Albuquerque; Andrea Meditch, Sharyn Udall, Will Wroth, and Paige Pinnell; Alison Freese, Institute for Museum and Library Science, Washington, DC; Laurel Seth, International Folk Art Foundation, Santa Fe; Joseph Maes and Christine Mather, El Rancho de las Golondrinas, Santa Fe; Jim Harris, Lovington Museum, New Mexico; James Dixon, Bruce Huckell, and Catherine Baudoin, Maxwell Museum of Anthropology, University of New Mexico, Albuquerque; Tony Chavarria, David McNeece, Tony Thibodeau, Valerie Verzuh, Museum of Indian Arts and Culture/Laboratory of Anthropology, Santa Fe; Nicolasa Chavez, Ree Mobley, Paul Smutko, and Bobbie Sumberg, Museum of International Folk Art, Santa Fe; John Easley, Ann Scheflen, Kathryn Wroth, Museum of New Mexico Foundation, Santa Fe; Tey Marianna Nunn and David Gabel, National Hispanic Cultural Center, Albuquerque; Charles Haecker, National Park Service, Santa Fe; Estevan Rael-Gálvez, National Trust for Historic Preservation, Washington, DC; Claude Stephenson, New Mexico Arts Division, Santa Fe; Barbara Anderson and Mina Thompson, Museum Resources Division, Department of Cultural Affairs, Santa Fe; Louise Anne Haecker, New Mexico Historic Preservation Division, Santa Fe; Roy Campbell, North Carolina Museum of Natural Sciences, Raleigh; Eric Blinman, Robert Della Russo, Wolky Toll, and Dean Wilson, Office of Archaeological Studies, Santa Fe; Rick Hendricks and Dennis Trujillo, Office of the State Historian, Santa Fe; Andrew John Cecil and Stacie Petersen, Roswell Museum and Art Center; Linda Cordell, Laura Holt, Elisha Poons, and Jennifer Day, School of Advanced Research, Santa Fe; Anna Sofaer, Solstice Project, Santa Fe; Bruce Bernstein and John Torres Nez, Southwest Indian Arts Association, Santa Fe; Robin Farwell Gavin, Museum of Spanish Colonial Art, Santa Fe; Carol Christiansen, Random House, New York; Michelle Penhall, Robert Ware, and Bonnie Verardo, University of New Mexico Art Museum, Albuquerque; Lois Rudnick, professor emeritus, University of Massachusetts, Boston; J. J. Brody, professor emeritus, University of New Mexico, Albuquerque; Erika Doss, University of Notre Dame, Notre Dame; W. Jackson Rushing III, University of Oklahoma, Norman; Stephen Plog, University of Virginia, Charlottesville; Jonathan Batkin and Mary Katherine Logan, Wheelwright Museum of the American Indian, Santa Fe; Maureen Goldsmith, University of Pennsylvania Museum of Archaeology and Anthropology, Photo Archives, Philadelphia; and Charles Carrillo.

New Mexico Art Through Time has been germinating for decades. For more than twenty-five years these topics have been discussed regularly with my wife, Laurel Wallace, an artist and archaeologist. She offered insightful comments clarifying the text. It's about time we worked on more than this project.

Some artists who have been essential to the conceptualization of this book are no longer available for consultation. Conversations with Vincent Craig, Dennis Culver, Frederick Hammersley, Bill Lumpkins, Charles Mattox, and Florence Miller Pierce are truly missed.

Credits

All art courtesy of New Mexico Museum of Art, Santa Fe, unless otherwise noted.

These collections will be abbreviated as follows:
New Mexico Museum of Art: NMMA
Museum of Indian Arts & Culture/Laboratory of Anthropology: MIAC/LAB
Museum of International Folk Art: MOIFA

Fig. 1: Courtesy University of Pennsylvania Museum Photographic Archives, 141370. **Fig. 2:** Courtesy University of Pennsylvania Museum Photographic Archives, 36-19-3. Photo by Karen Mauch and John Chew. **Fig. 3:** Courtesy of the artist. **Fig. 4:** NMMA. New Mexico Farm Security Administration Collection, Museum purchase with funds from the Pinewood Foundation with additional support from Barbara Erdman, 1990. 1990.70.26a. **Fig. 5:** NMMA. Gift of anonymous donor, 1997 (1997.61.26), © Patrick Nagatani. **Fig. 6:** Courtesy, © Terry Bumpass. **Fig. 7:** Courtesy of the artist. **Fig. 8:** NMMA. Museum purchase, purchase prize Originals 2005 funded by New Mexico Committee National Museum of Women in the Arts, 2005 (2005.18.1ab) © Carol Sarkisian,. **Fig. 9:** NMMA. Gift of Herman C. and Bina L. Ilfeld, 1977 (2991.23P). **Fig. 11:** MIAC/LAB, 48178/11. **Fig. 12:** NMMA. Gift of an anonymous donor, 1984 (1984.46.1). © William Clift. **Fig. 13:** Courtesy University of Pennsylvania Museum Photoic Archives. Photo by Karen Mauch and John Chew 36-19-2. **Fig. 14:** Courtesy of the Blackwater Draw Collection, Eastern New Mexico University LA3324.24152. **Fig. 15:** Courtesy of the Maxwell Museum of Anthropology. Photo by Bernie Bernard 2011.14.1. **Fig. 16:** Courtesy of Image Archives, Denver Museum of Nature & Science. All rights reserved. E-51. **Fig. 17:** Courtesy of the Blackwater Draw Collection, Eastern New Mexico University, LA3324.25285. **Fig. 18:** Courtesy of the Blackwater Draw Collection, Eastern New Mexico University, LA3324.32095. **Fig. 19:** Courtesy of the Blackwater Draw Collection, Eastern New Mexico University. **Fig. 20:** Courtesy of the Blackwater Draw Collection, Eastern New Mexico University, LA3324.SIC274-1. **Fig. 21:** Courtesy of the Blackwater Draw Collection, Eastern New Mexico University, LA3324.24121. **Fig. 22:** Courtesy of the Blackwater Draw Collection, Eastern New Mexico University, LA3324.25313. **Fig. 23:** Courtesy of the Blackwater Draw Collection, Eastern New Mexico University, LA3324.25285. **Fig. 24:** Courtesy of the Blackwater Draw Collection, Eastern New Mexico University, LA3324.32864. **Fig. 25:** Courtesy of the Blackwater Draw Collection, Eastern New Mexico University, LA3324.25313. **Fig. 26:** Courtesy of the Blackwater Draw Collection, Eastern New Mexico University, LA3324.24123. **Fig. 27:** Courtesy of the Blackwater Draw Collection, Eastern New Mexico University, LA3324.25329. **Fig. 28:** Courtesy of the City of Albuquerque. Photo by Matt Schmader. **Fig. 29:** Courtesy of the Blackwater Draw Collection, Eastern New Mexico University. LA3324.5878. **Fig. 30:** MIAC/LAB, 51069/11. **Fig. 31:** Courtesy of the Solstice Project, © The Solstice Project, by Karl Kernberger. **Fig. 33:** MIAC/LAB, 08284/11. **Fig. 34:** MIAC/LAB, 51738/11. **Fig. 35:** MIAC/LAB, 21046/11. **Fig. 36:** MIAC/LAB, 08494/11. **Fig. 37:** MIAC/LAB, 08277/11. **Fig. 38:** MIAC/LAB, 43323/11. **Fig. 39:** MIAC/LAB, 43323/11. **Fig. 40:** Courtesy of the Division of Anthropology, American Museum of Natural History, H/3262. **Fig. 41:** MIAC/LAB, 18530/11. **Fig. 42:** Courtesy of the Division of Anthropology, American Museum of Natural History, H/3277. Photo Denis Finnin. **Fig. 43:** Saint Louis Art Museum, funds given by the Children's Art Festival, 175:1981. **Fig. 44:** MIAC/LAB, 08552/11. **Fig. 45:** Courtesy of the Division of Anthropology, American Museum of Natural History, H/3942. Photo Denis Finnin. **Fig. 46:** Courtesy Grants Chamber of Commerce. **Fig. 47:** Courtesy University of Pennsylvania Museum Photoic Archives, NA4925. **Fig. 48:** MIAC/LAB, 20175/11. **Fig. 49:** MIAC/LAB, 43321/11. **Fig. 50:** MIAC/LAB, 43080/11. **Fig. 51:** MIAC/LAB, 08872/11. **Fig. 52:** MIAC/LAB, 48178/11. **Fig. 53:** MIAC/LAB, 08332/11. **Fig. 54:** MIAC/LAB, 42939/11. **Fig. 55:** MIAC/LAB, 00790/11. **Fig. 56:** Courtesy of the U.S. Department of the Interior-Indian Affairs Museum Program. **Fig. 57:** MIAC/LAB, 50382/11. **Fig. 58:** Photo by Matt Schmader. Courtesy of the City of Albuquerque. **Fig. 59:** Courtesy Palace of the Governors Photo Archives (NMHM/DCA), 6197. **Fig. 60:** MIAC/LAB, 01955/11. **Fig. 61:** MIAC/LAB, 08551/11. **Fig. 62:** Photo Addison Doty, School for Advanced Research, IAF.2162. **Fig. 63:** MOIFA, IFAF Collection, FA.1962.15.1. **Fig. 64:** Courtesy Palace of the Governors Photo Archives (NMHM/DCA), 158345. **Fig. 65:** MIAC/LAB, 21864/11. **Fig. 66:** Photo Addison Doty, School for Advanced Research, IAF.999. **Fig. 67:** Photo by Addison Doty, Collection of Spanish Colonial Arts Society, Gift of Dr. Frank E. Mera, 1954.77. **Fig. 68:** Courtesy The Albuquerque Museum of Art and History, Museum purchase, 1979 General Obligation Bonds, PC.1982.4.1. **Fig. 69:** MOIFA, Bequest of Cady Wells, A9.1954.70R.**Fig. 70:**Courtesy Palace of the Governors Photo Archives (NMHM/DCA), 4870. **Fig. 71:** MIAC/LAB, 18704/11. **Fig. 72:** MOIFA,, IFAF Collection, FA.1968.20.4. **Fig. 73:** MOIFA, Gift of the Historical Society of New Mexico, A.1971.31.41. **Fig. 74:** MOIFA, IFAF Collection, FA.1989.40.23. **Fig. 75:** MOIFA, Gift of the Fred Harvey Collection, IFAF Collection,

FA.1979.64.100. **Fig. 76:** MOIFA, Bequest of Cady Wells, A9.1954.25R. **Fig. 77:** MOIFA, Gift of the Historical Society of New Mexico, A5.1952.8a-c. **Fig. 78:** MOIFA, Gift of the Historical Society of New Mexico, A5.1959.27. **Fig. 79:** MOIFA, Bequest of Cady Wells, A9.1954.11B. **Fig. 80:** MOIFA, Bequest of Cady Wells, A9.1954.112R. **Fig. 81:** MIAC/LAB, 45611/11. **Fig. 82:** Courtesy Palace of the Governors Photo Archives (NMHM/DCA), 9970. **Fig. 83:** Courtesy The Albuquerque Museum of Art and History, Museum purchase, 1995 General Obligation Bonds, PC1998.27.29. **Fig. 84:** MOIFA, IFAF Collection, FA.1975.28.1. **Fig. 85:** School for Advanced Research, Photo by Addison Doty, IAF.342. **Fig. 86:** MOIFA, Bequest of Cady Wells, A9.1954.55M. **Fig. 87:** MOIFA, Gift of the Flora W. Conrad Estate, IFAF Collection, FA.1970.27.7. **Fig. 88:** Dr. H.P. Mera Collection, gift of Mr. and Mrs. John Gaw Meem to the Spanish Colonial Arts Society, Museum of Spanish Colonial Art, Santa Fe, Photo by Jack Parsons, 1962.71. **Fig. 89:** MIAC/LAB, 09106/12. **Fig. 90:** Collection of Estevan Rael-Gálvez, Photo by Joseph Moure. **Fig. 91:** Purchased with funds from The Friends of Art, University of New Mexico Art Museum, Albuquerque, 85.16. **Fig. 92:** Collection of the Spanish Colonial Arts Society, Museum of Spanish Colonial Art, Santa Fe; Photo by Jack Parsons, 1975.3. **Fig. 93:** MOIFA, Gift of Steve and Dottie Diamant, A.2005.49.21. **Fig. 94:** MIAC/LAB, 09120/12. **Fig. 95:** MIAC/LAB, 54256/12. **Fig. 96:** MOIFA, L3.1951.5. **Fig. 97:** NMMA, Museum acquisition, 1965 (1879.23D). **Fig. 98:** NMMA, Gift of Mr. and Mrs. John A. Hill in memory of Maurice N. Mikesell, 1975 (3372.23P). **Fig. 99:** NMMA, Museum purchase, 1997 (1997.5.1). **Fig. 100:** From "The Penitent Brothers," by Charles F. Lummis, *Cosmopolitan Magazine*, May 1889, p.49. Author's Research Materials. **Fig. 101:** NMMA, Gift of John Wright Schaefer, 2007 (2007.31). **Fig. 102:** NMMA, Gift of Willis Adams Marean in memory of the artist, 1920 (132.23P). **Fig. 103:** NMMA. Archive Collection, Museum purchase, 2001. **Fig. 104:** NMMA. Gift of Gerald Cassidy, 1915 (282.23P). **Fig. 105:** NMMA. Gift of the Honorable Frank Springer, 1917 (2009.1.6). **Fig. 106:** NMMA, Gift of Robert Henri, 1916 (353.23P). **Fig. 107:** Courtesy Palace of the Governors Photo Archives (NMHM/DCA), 14235. **Fig. 108:** NMMA. Museum acquisition, before 1966 (1834.23D). **Fig. 109:** Courtesy Palace of the Governors Photo Archives (NMHM/DCA), 16781. **Fig. 110:** Courtesy Palace of the Governors Photo Archives (NMHM/DCA), 149978. **Fig. 111:** MIAC/LAB, 01769/12. **Fig. 112:** MIAC/LAB, 35467/13. **Fig. 113:** MIAC/LAB, 24161/13. **Fig. 114:** MIAC/LAB, 24358/13. **Fig. 115:** MIAC/LAB, 19494/12. **Fig. 116:** Courtesy Palace of the Governors Photo Archives (NMHM/DCA), 1500. **Fig. 117:** NMMA, Gift of Kibbey W. Couse, 1930 (352.23P). **Fig. 118:** NMMA, Gift of Joseph Henry Sharp, 1917 (395.23P). **Fig. 119:** NMMA, Gift of Herman C. and Bina L. Ilfeld, 1977 (2991.23P). **Fig. 120:** NMMA, Gift of Governor and Mrs. Arthur Seligman, 1918 (537.23P). **Fig. 121:** NMMA, Gift of the Museum of New Mexico Foundation in honor and memory of Mr. and Mrs. Lewis Barker, 1979 (4560.23P). **Fig. 122:** NMMA, Gift of Robert L. B. Tobin, 1992 (1992.6.1). **Fig. 123:** NMMA, Gift of Toy D. and Helen Savage, 1996 (1996.1.1). **Fig. 124:** NMMA, Gift of a friend, 1927 (351.23P). **Fig. 125:** NMMA, Museum purchase with funds from the Archaeological Society & Friends of Southwestern Art, 1920 (274.23P). **Fig. 126:** NMMA, Gift of Mrs. Edgar L. Rossin, 1952 (83.23P). **Fig. 127:** NMMA, Gift of Julius Gans, 1946 (22.23P). **Fig. 128:** NMMA, Anonymous gift from a friend of Southwest art, 1919 (523.23P). **Fig. 129:** NMMA, Museum acquisition, circa 1919 (59.23P). **Fig. 130 :** NMMA, Gift of Florence Dibbell Bartlett, 1947 (97.23P). **Fig. 131:** NMMA, Gift of Mrs. Jane H. Baumann, 1976 (3409.23P). © Ann Baumann. **Fig. 132:** NMMA, Museum purchase, 2005 (2005.15.1). **Fig. 133:** NMMA, Museum purchase, 2007 (2007.5). **Fig. 134:** NMMA, Gift of Jozef G. Bakos in honor of Teresa Bakos, 1974 (3098.23P). **Fig. 135:** NMMA, Gift of Mrs. R.J. Erickson, 1964 (1473.23P). **Fig. 136:** NMMA, Museum purchase, 1997 (1997.23.1). **Fig. 137:** NMMA, Gift of Mary Regensburg Feist, 2000 (2000.1.7). **Fig. 138:** Courtesy of the Wheelwright Museum of the American Indian, Santa Fe. **Fig. 139:** School for Advanced Research, Photo Addison Doty, IAF.1. **Fig. 140:** MOIFA, Gift of the Historical Society of New Mexico, A5.1998.1. **Fig. 141:** MOIFA, IFAF Collection, FA.1986.400.1. **Fig. 142:** NMMA, Bequest of Helen Miller Jones, 1986 (1986.137.18). © Georgia O'Keeffe Museum,. **Fig. 143:** On long term loan to NMMA from the Museum of New Mexico Foundation, (1984.336). © Georgia O'Keeffe Museum,. **Fig. 144:** NMMA, Bequest of the Rebecca Salsbury James Estate, 1968 (2280.23PH). © 2011 Georgia O'Keeffe Museum / Artists Rights Society (ARS), New York. **Fig. 145:** NMMA, Bequest of Helen Miller Jones, 1986 (1986.137.14.). © 2011 Estate of John Marin / Artists Rights Society (ARS), New York. **Fig. 146:** NMMA, Gift of Austin Lamont, 2002 (2003.13.1). © Aperture Foundation, Inc., Paul Strand Archive. **Fig. 147:** NMMA, Museum purchase from the John S. Candelario Estate, 1997 (1997.70.10). © Palace of the Governors Photo Archives. **Fig. 148:** NMMA, Museum purchase with funds from the Jordi M. Chilson Estate with additional support from the Friends of Contemporary Art, 1999 (1999.17.1). **Fig. 149:** NMMA, Funded through the Federal Emergency Relief Agency, 1934 (2006.29.5). **Fig. 150:** Jonson Reserve Retrospective Collection, University of New Mexico Art Museum, Albuquerque, © UNM Art Museum / Raymond Jonson Gallery, 82.221.1910. **Fig. 151:** Permanent Collection of the Roswell Museum and Art Center, Roswell, New Mexico (1958.028.0032). Photo by Michael Van Raes and Stacie Petersen. **Fig. 152:** On long term loan to the NMMA from the Fine Arts Program, Public Buildings Service, U.S. General Services Administration (1480.23P). **Fig. 153.** On long term loan to the (NMMA) from the Fine Arts Program, Public Buildings Service, U.S. General Services Administration (2009.17). **Fig. 154:** MIAC/LAB, 51455/13. **Fig. 155:** MIAC/LAB, © Chiinde LLC.51375/13. **Fig. 156:** MIAC/LAB, 51404/13. **Fig. 157:** NMMA, Gift of Arthur Johnson, 1975 (3217.23D). © UNM Art Museum / Raymond Jonson Gallery. **Fig. 158:** NMMA, Gift of the William and Norma L. Lumpkins Trust, 1989 (1989.180.1). **Fig. 159:** NMMA, Museum purchase with funds from Bob Nurock and Frederick Hammersley, 2009 (2009.27). **Fig. 160:** NMMA, Museum purchase with additional support from Frederick Hammersley and Robert Nurok, 2009 (2009.3). **Fig. 161:** NMMA, Museum purchase, 2007 (2007.38). © Ed Garman. **Fig. 162:** NMMA, Museum purchase, 1997 (1997.43.1). **Fig. 163:** NMMA, Museum purchase, 2005 (2005.27.1). **Fig. 164:** NMMA, Gift of the Museum of New Mexico Foundation, 1982 (1982.13.1). © 2011 The Ansel Adams Publishing Rights Trust. **Fig. 165:** Courtesy Palace of the Governors Photo Archives (NMHM/DCA), 29314. **Fig. 166:** NMMA, Gift of John A. and Margaret Hill in memory of Maurice N. Mikesell, 1975 (3369.23P). **Fig. 167:** NMMA, Gift of Meridel Rubenstein, 2011. © Jerry West. **Fig. 168:** Courtesy of Mineo Matoba. Collection of the National Japanese American Historical Society, Inc. From *The Art of Gaman: Arts and Crafts from the Japanese American Internment Camps 1942-1946*, by Delphine Hirasuna. Berkeley: Ten Speed Press, 2005. p.105. Photo by Terry Heffernan, 1996.024.1-7 **Fig. 169:** NMMA, Purchase Award with funds from Hill & Canyon School of the Arts, 3rd Graphics Annual, 1949 (79.23G). © Elaine Mead Murphy. **Fig. 170:** From "Michelangelo's Sistine Chapel," *Life Magazine*, December 26, 1949, pp. 35-36. Author's Research Materials. Photo by Frank Lerner / reproduction by Blair Clark. **Fig. 171:** NMMA, Gift of the Weatherhead Foundation, Cleveland and New York, 1970 (2585.23S). **Fig. 172:** NMMA, Museum purchase,

1998 (1998.35.1). **Fig. 173:** NMMA, Gift of E. Boyd Estate, 1975 (3308.23P). **Fig. 174:** NMMA, Gift of Gilbert Hitchcock in cooperation with the New Mexico Council on Photography, 1984 (1984.594.6). © 1990 Amon Carter Museum of American Art, Fort Worth, Texas. **Fig. 175:** NMMA, Gift of Thomas F. Ryan, 1993 (1993.38.1). © Hurd La Rinconada Gallery. **Fig. 176:** NMMA, Gift of Fremont F. Ellis, 1969 (2422.23P). **Fig. 177:** Courtesy Palace of the Governors Photo Archives (NMHM/DCA), 58707. **Fig. 178:** Collection of Dr. Lawrence Lazarus, © The Estate of Richard Diebenkorn. **Fig. 179:** Bequest of Raymond Jonson, University of New Mexico Art Museum, Albuquerque, 82.221.1362. **Fig. 180:** NMMA, Gift of Marjorie Devon, 2004 (2004.22.3). © Mary E. Adams / Estate of Clinton Adams. **Fig. 181:** NMMA, Gift of Hill's Galleries, 1975 (3357.23G). © Garo Z. Antreasian. **Fig. 182:** Courtesy of the Frederick Hammersley Foundation, © Frederick Hammersley Foundation, GPA0090.1978. **Fig. 183:** NMMA, Gift of Frederick Hammersley, 2002 (2002.22.67). © Frederick Hammersley Foundation. **Fig. 184:** Courtesy The Albuquerque Museum of Art and History, Gift of Steven J. Lambert, PC1986.3.1.a. **Fig. 185:** NMMA, Gift of the William Lumpkins Estate, 2007 (2007.29). © Lumpkins Trust. **Fig. 186:** NMMA, Gift of the Rick Dillingham Estate, 1994 (1994.67.64). © 2011 Bruce Nauman / Artists Rights Society (ARS), New York. **Fig. 187:** NMMA, Gift of the Adolf and Virginia Dehn Foundation, 2005 (2005.5.1a-i). © Tom Joyce. **Fig. 188:** NMMA, Gift of the American Art Foundation, 1982 (1982.14). © 2011 Agnes Martin / Artists Rights Society (ARS), New York. **Fig. 189:** NMMA, The Dorothy and Herbert Vogel Collection: Fifty Works for Fifty States, a joint initiative of the Trustees of the Dorothy and Herbert Vogel Collection and the National Gallery of Art, with generous support of the National Endowments for the Arts and the Institute of Museum and Library Services, 2009 (2009.36.49g). © Richard Tuttle. **Fig. 190:** NMMA, Gift of Agnes Sims, 1972 (2936.23P). © Peter W. Rogers. **Fig. 191:** NMMA, Gift of David and Gita Kronen, 2010 (2010.8). © Eugene Newmann. **Fig. 192:** NMMA, Gift of Gifford and Joann Phillips, 1987 (1987.399.1). © Allan Graham. **Fig. 193:** NMMA, Museum purchase with funds from the Museum of New Mexico Acquisition Fund, 2008 (2008.51). © 2011 Susan Rothenberg / Artists Rights Society (ARS), New York. **Fig. 194:** Courtesy of Sarkisian Trust, © Paul Sarkisian. **Fig. 195:** NMMA, Gift of Helen Sturges Nadler, 1994 (1994.27.1). © Helen Sturges Nadler. **Fig. 196:** NMMA, Museum purchase, 2007 (2007.4). © Judy Chicago. **Fig. 197:** NMMA, Gift of Patrick Nagatani, 2008 (2008.46). © Anne Noggle Foundatio.n **Fig. 198:** Courtesy of Dr. Jonathan Abrams and Fay Abrams, © Constance DeJong. **Fig. 199:** NMMA, Museum purchase with funds from the Los Trigos Fund, 1994 (1994.72.1). © 2011 Estate of Luis A. Jiménez Jr. / Artists Rights Society (ARS), New York. **Fig. 200:** NMMA, Commissioned by the Museum in commemoration of the Cuartocentenario with funds provided by the City of Santa Fe Cuartocentenario, Herbert Beenhouwer, Susan McGreely and the Museum of New Mexico Foundation, 1998 (1998.5.1). © Frederico M. Vigil. **Fig. 201:** Courtesy of James Kelly Contemporary, © 2009 David Taylor. **Fig. 202:** NMMA, Gift of Jonathan Abrams and Fay Abrams, 2008 (2008.39.2). © Barton Benes. **Fig. 203:** NMMA, Gift of Rosina Yue, 1999 (1999.21.1). © Alexander Harris. **Fig. 204:** NMMA, Museum purchase with funds donated by Lynn Steuer, 1992 (1993.2.1ab). © Luis Tapia. **Fig. 205:** Collection of the Spanish Colonial Arts Society, Gift of Nancy Clark Reynolds, © Charles M. Carrillo, 1999.37. **Fig. 206:** NMMA, Gift of Tamarind Institute, 1993 (1993.67.1g). © Miguel A. Gandert. **Fig. 207:** NMMA, Gift of Charlotte Grey Jackson, 2009 (2009.42.1). © Gloria Graham. **Fig. 208:** NMMA, Museum purchase with funds from Frederick Hammersley, 2007 (2007.28). © Tim Prythero. **Fig. 209:** NMMA, Museum purchase with funds from the Herzstein Family Acquisition Endowment Fund and Bob Nurock with additional support from Andrea Fisher, 2008 (2008.7). © Virgil Ortiz. **Fig. 210:** NMMA, Gift of the Beatrice Mandelman Ribak Estate, 2003 (2003.3.9). © Mandelman-Ribak Foundation. **Fig. 211:** Courtesy of Paige Pinnell. **Fig. 212:** NMMA, Gift of Mr. and Mrs. Mel Pfaelzer, Mr. Jack Satin, and Mr. and Mrs. John Metzenberg, 1987 (1987.66.1). © Rick Dillingham Estate. **Fig. 213:** NMMA, Museum purchase with funds from the Friends of Contemporary Art and an anonymous donor, 2008 (2008.14). © James Drake. **Fig. 214:** NMMA, Gift of Joel-Peter Witkin, 1987 (1987.316.2). © Joel-Peter Witkin. **Fig. 215:** NMMA, Museum purchase with funds from the Jordie M. Chilson Estate, 1997 (1997.53.1a-s). © Meridel Rubenstein and Ellen Zweig. **Fig. 216:** NMMA, Museum purchase with funds from Frederick Hammersley, 2007 (2007.39ab). © Beverly Magennis. **Fig. 217:** NMMA, Gift of Nancy and Richard Bloch, 2001 (2001.13.1). © Joyce Cannon Yi - Executor of T. C. Cannon Estate. **Fig. 218:** NMMA, Museum purchase with support from Bob Nurock and a gift from the Samuel and Ethel Ballen Estate, 2008 (2008.17). © Joyce Cannon Yi - Executor of T. C. Cannon Estate. **Fig. 219:** NMMA, Gift of Harvey Mudd, 1983 (1983.44). © Fritz Scholder Estate. **Fig. 220:** NMMA, Gift of Betty Hahn, 2010 (2010.24.2). © Betty Hahn. **Fig. 221:** NMMA, Museum purchase, 1983 (1983.31). © Dennis Culver. **Fig. 222:** NMMA, Gift of Edward Ranney from the New Mexico Photoic Survey Project, Museum of Fine Arts, 1981-1984, funded by a grant from the National Endowment for the Arts, 1985 (1985.117.10). © Edward Ranney. **Fig. 223:** NMMA, Gift of Sally and Wynn Kramarsky, New York, 2009 (2009.13.20). © Charles Ross. **Fig. 224:** NMMA, Museum purchase with funds from the Boeckman Acquisition Fund, 2006 (2006.38). © Jennifer Joseph. **Fig. 225:** NMMA, Gift of Jonathan Abrams and Fay Abrams, 2008 (2008.39.1). **Fig. 226:** Author's Research Materials. Photo by Joseph Traugott. **Fig. 227:** NMMA, Gift of Lucy R. Lippard, 1999 (1999.15.301.13). © Jaune Quick-To-See Smith. **Fig. 228:** NMMA, Museum purchase with funds from the Herzstein Family Acquisition Endowment, 2007 (2007.37). © Thomas Barrow. **Fig. 229:** NMMA, Gift of Ray and Judy Dewey, 2008 (2008.43). © Elizabeth Kay. **Fig. 230:** Courtesy of the artist, © Donald Woodman. **Fig. 231:** Gift of Kendall O. and Wilda I. Schlenker, courtesy National Hispanic Cultural Center Art Museum, 2002.19.36. **Fig. 232:** NMMA, Museum purchase with funds from Phyllis Sloane, 2008 (2008.34.2). © Patrick Oliphant, courtesy Susan Conway Gallery, Santa Fe, NM and Washington, DC. **Fig. 233:** NMMA, Museum purchase with funds from the Herzstein Family Acquisition Endowment Fund, 2001 (2001.28.1-.158). © Eddie Dominguez. **Fig. 234:** NMMA, Gift of Ray Graham and Ray Martin Abeyta, 2004 (2004.11). © Ray Martin Abeyta. **Fig. 235:** NMMA, Museum purchase with funds from Charmay B. Allred, Jeff and Darlene Anderson, the Clinton King Purchase Award and Jane and Bill Buchsbaum, 2008 (2008.50). © Marcus Amerman. **Fig. 236:** NMMA, Museum purchase with funds from the Boeckman Acquisition Fund and the Clinton King Purchase Award, 2010 (2010.21. © Diego Romero. **Fig. 237:** NMMA, Gift of Mary Peck from the New Mexico Photoic Survey Project, Museum of Fine Arts, 1981-1984, funded by a grant from the National Endowment for the Arts, 1985 (1985.115.16). © Mary E. Peck. **Fig. 238:** Courtesy of the artist, © Mission Motors. Photo Kevin Wing and Greg Alter. **Fig. 239:** NMMA, Gift of Raymond Jonson, 1936 (287.23P). © UNM Art Museum / Raymond Jonson Gallery. **Fig. 240:** NMMA, Gift of Raymond Jonson, 1936 (286.23P). © UNM Art Museum / Raymond Jonson Gallery. **Fig. 241:** Courtesy of the artist, © Peter Sarkisian.

Index

Page numbers in italics refer to illustrations